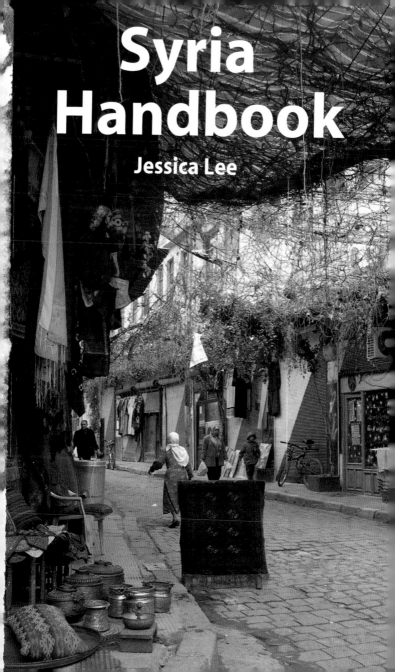

Syria
Handbook

Jessica Lee

Footprint story

Tread your own path

Footprint Handbooks ›

Footprint Surfing Europe ›

Footprint South American Handbook 2010

Updated Annually ›

It was 1921

Ireland had just been partitioned, the British miners were striking for more pay and the federation of British industry had an idea. Exports were booming in South America – how about a handbook for businessmen trading in that far away continent? The Anglo-South American Handbook was born that year, written by W Koebel, the most prolific writer on Latin America of his day.

1924

Two editions later the book was 'privatized' and in 1924, in the hands of Royal Mail, the steamship company for South America, it became The South American Handbook, subtitled 'South America in a nutshell'. This annual publication became the 'bible' for generations of travellers to South America and remains so to this day. In the early days travel was by sea and the Handbook gave all the details needed for the long voyage from Europe. What to wear for dinner; how to arrange a cricket match with the Cable & Wireless staff on the Cape Verde Islands and a full account of the journey from Liverpool up the Amazon to Manaus: 5898 miles without changing cabin!

1939

As the continent opened up, the South American Handbook reported the new Pan Am flying boat services, and the fortnightly airship service from Rio to Europe on the Graf Zeppelin. For reasons still unclear but with extraordinary determination, the annual editions continued through the Second World War.

1970s

Many more people discovered South America and the backpacking trail started to develop. All the while the Handbook was gathering fans, including literary vagabonds such as Paul Theroux and Graham Greene (who once sent some updates addressed to "The publishers of the best travel guide in the world, Bath, England").

1990s

During the 1990s the company set about developing a new travel guide series using this legendary title as the flagship. By 1997 there were over a dozen guides in the series and the Footprint imprint was launched.

2000s

The series grew quickly and there were soon Footprint travel guides covering more than 150 countries. In 2004, Footprint launched its first thematic guide: *Surfing Europe*, packed with colour photographs, maps and charts. This was followed by further thematic guides such as *Diving the World*, *Snowboarding the World*, *Body and Soul escapes*, *Travel with Kids* and *European City Breaks*.

2010

Today we continue the traditions of the last 89 years that have served legions of travellers so well. We believe that these help to make Footprint guides different. Our policy is to use authors who are genuine experts who write for independent travellers; people possessing a spirit of adventure, looking to get off the beaten track.

Title page: Street in old Damascus. **Above:** Hammam domes on Aleppo's citadel.

Syria has always been a crossroads. Kings, caliphs, crusaders and conquerors have all carved their way through here leaving crumbling reminders of past glories scattered across the countryside. Vast ruins spread out over desert sands, fairytale castles perch on hill tops; Syria groans under a weight of monuments that few other countries can match.

In the cities, thread your way deep enough into the belly of the souqs and it's as if the clocks had stopped a few centuries back. Spice scents the air as donkeys, laden with produce, plod their way down narrow alleys beneath buildings that slope precariously inwards, reducing the sky to a sliver of blue in between.

But this nation is so much more than a living museum. Syrians, quick to smile and welcome strangers, are the real star attraction. Invitations to talk and drink tea, to come home for dinner, are daily occurrences for travellers, who discover that the legendary Syrian hospitality is the real highlight of a journey here.

Houses hug the cliff side in the Christian village of Maaloula.

Contents

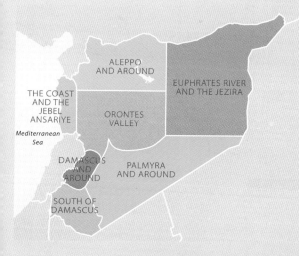

Syria highlights

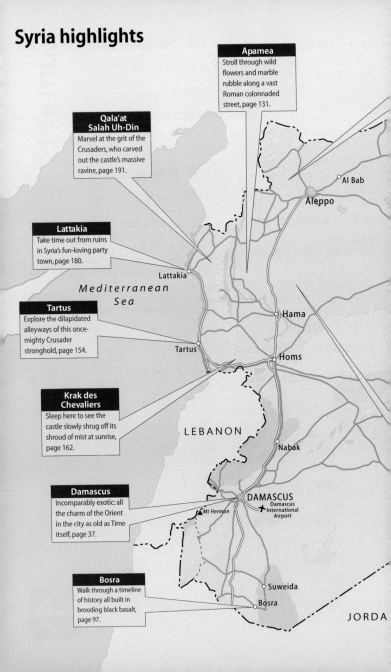

Apamea
Stroll through wild flowers and marble rubble along a vast Roman colonnaded street, page 131.

Qala'at Salah Uh-Din
Marvel at the grit of the Crusaders, who carved out the castle's massive ravine, page 191.

Lattakia
Take time out from ruins in Syria's fun-loving party town, page 180.

Tartus
Explore the dilapidated alleyways of this once-mighty Crusader stronghold, page 154.

Krak des Chevaliers
Sleep here to see the castle slowly shrug off its shroud of mist at sunrise, page 162.

Damascus
Incomparably exotic: all the charm of the Orient in the city as old as Time itself, page 37.

Bosra
Walk through a timeline of history all built in brooding black basalt, page 97.

Al Bab

Aleppo

Mediterranean Sea

Lattakia

Hama

Tartus

Homs

LEBANON

Nabak

DAMASCUS
Damascus International Airport

▲ Mt Hermon

Suweida

Bosra

JORDA

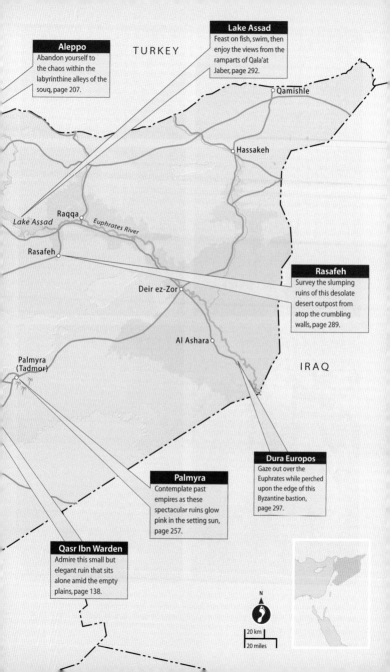

Aleppo
Abandon yourself to the chaos within the labyrinthine alleys of the souq, page 207.

Lake Assad
Feast on fish, swim, then enjoy the views from the ramparts of Qala'at Jaber, page 292.

TURKEY

Qamishle

Hassakeh

Raqqa
Lake Assad
Euphrates River

Rasafeh

Deir ez-Zor

Rasafeh
Survey the slumping ruins of this desolate desert outpost from atop the crumbling walls, page 289.

Al Ashara

Palmyra
(Tadmor)

IRAQ

Dura Europos
Gaze out over the Euphrates while perched upon the edge of this Byzantine bastion, page 297.

Palmyra
Contemplate past empires as these spectacular ruins glow pink in the setting sun, page 257.

Qasr Ibn Warden
Admire this small but elegant ruin that sits alone amid the empty plains, page 138.

N

20 km
20 miles

1: One of Hama's groaning *norias* (waterwheels). 2: The fascinating dilapidated backstreets of Tartus. 3: The long and lonely colonnaded street at Apamea. 4: In the city of Damascus, the hands of artisans are engaged in work. 5: Camel in the ancient caravan town of Palmyra. 6: The view over the lonely ruins of Qala'at Salah ud-Din.

Contents

Footprint features

Essentials

Planning your trip

Where to go

Syria groans under a weight of history that not many other countries can boast. The astonishing array of ruins and historical sites here can be mind-boggling to the visitor and those who try to fit too much into a short trip soon find themselves befuddled with ruin-fatigue. Although compact and relatively easy to travel around, you'll enjoy yourself more if you visit fewer sites and see them properly rather than rushing between ruins to try and cram them all in.

The ancient cities of **Damascus** and **Aleppo** both deserve as much time as you can afford them. You could simply spend days exploring the souqs and seeking out the multitude of architectural gems within, but outside the medieval walls of the old quarters these cities are also vibrant modern metropolises that buzz with the dynamism of contemporary Syrian life. Both cities are within easy reach of nearby sites. The black basalt remains of **Bosra**, with their massive Roman theatre, are a day trip from Damascus, while forays to the eerie and atmospheric ruins of the **Dead Cities** can be arranged in Aleppo.

Remnants of the Greek and Roman period are scattered liberally throughout the country but if you only have time for one big ruin, make it **Palmyra**. The spectacular remains of this caravan town rise majestically out of the vast expanse of the desert-steppe and are, undoubtedly, one of the most impressive sights in the Middle East.

The Syrian coast may not be a beach bum's paradise but this region more than makes up for its lack of sunbathing potential with its sheer beauty. Tucked into the verdant hills of the **Jebel Ansariye** is a line of atmospheric Crusader castles. **Krak des Chevaliers** is the most famous and best preserved but **Qala'at Salah ud-Din** and **Qala'at Marqab** are also worth visiting for their breathtakingly beautiful and lonely locations.

The area around **Hama** provides a wealth of sightseeing opportunities and the town itself is already a firm favourite with travellers who come to see the famous groaning *norias* (waterwheels). The impressive Roman ruin of **Apamea** and the elegant Byzantine architecture of **Qasr Ibn Warden** are two of the many highlights of this area.

If you have the time head east to the Euphrates and Jezira region where, on the edge of the desert, the crumbling walls of **Rasafeh** loom up, providing a dramatic prelude to this huge and awesome fortified city. Already a popular choice with Syrian holidaymakers, the astonishing vast expanse of **Lake Assad** is fast becoming a must-do for visitors to this region. If you're exploring this section of the country, camping beside the lake's sparkling blue waters is an excellent alternative to staying in the night in the nearby town of Raqqa. Right to the southeast, overlooking the mighty Euphrates River, is the dusty, lonely remains of **Dura Europos**. It's a long hot drive to get here but worth every minute for the stunning views out onto the expansive green plains below.

One week

Trying to cover too much ground in one week will leave you exhausted but even with this limited time you should be able to cover Damascus, Aleppo and the major sites of Palmyra and Krak des Chevaliers. The following circuit can be comfortably achieved by public transport as well as by private vehicle.

Most people begin their Syrian journey in **Damascus** (2 nights). Concentrate your time in the Old City where most of the sights are based, including the awe-inspiring Umayyad Mosque and the opulently decorated Azem Palace. In the New City don't miss visiting the National Museum, which contains extensive collections from sites all over Syria. From Damascus, head out into the desert to **Palmyra** (1 night). Get here for sunset over the ruins from Qala'at Ibn Maan and rise early the next morning to spend a few hours thoroughly exploring the site. In the early afternoon journey to **Krak des Chevaliers** (1 night) and spend the next morning delving into the nooks and crannies of this spectacular castle. (As an alternative to spending the night at Krak, you could stay in Hama or Homs and visit the castle from there.) After you've finished your sightseeing head to Syria's second city, **Aleppo** (2 nights), where the chaotic labyrinth of the souqs and the formidable citadel are the major highlights. From here you can either return to Damascus or, if you're overlanding, head to the nearby Turkish border.

Two weeks

If planned well two weeks allows you the flexibility to see some of the coast and maybe some of the sights to the east. Though it's not at all impossible to do the following itinerary with a combination of public transport and some ride-negotiation with locals, due to irregular services (or non-existent services) to sights in the east you'd be better to allow three weeks if you're not using private transport at all.

After discovering the delights of **Damascus** (3 nights) take a day trip to nearby Bosra for its impressive Roman theatre. Then head to **Hama** (2 nights), which makes a great base for visits to the Roman site of Apamea and some of the more southern Dead Cities. From here you can either do an excursion to the grand Crusader castle of **Krak des Chevaliers** (1 night) as well or choose to spend the night there to witness sunrise. Then travel on to fun-loving **Lattakia** (2 nights), which makes an excellent base for nearby Qala'at Salah ud-Din and the bronze-age site of Ugarit (if you get up early enough you can visit both sites in one very long day). Take the scenic train journey to **Aleppo** (2 nights), to see the lush countryside of the Jebel Ansariye. After you've finished all your bargaining in the city's souqs head east to **Lake Assad** (1 night) for some swimming and relaxation before heading to **Palmyra** (2 nights) via a long day's drive visiting the colossal desert ruins of Rasafeh and Qasr al-Heir al-Sharki. After you've finished admiring Palmyra's impressive monuments, head back to Damascus to finish.

One month

One month (or longer) gives you the time to really explore the country and get off the beaten path. You also have the flexibility to change your schedule and accept and enjoy any surprising opportunities that present themselves on your journey.

Damascus (7 nights) deserves as much time as you can allow and you can also visit a multitude of surrounding sights while here (Maaloula and Bosra should be on your list). Then travel on to **Palmyra** (1 night), before heading to **Deir ez-Zor** (2 nights) to see the

Byzantine city of Dura Europos. From here head to **Lake Assad** (2 nights) (or Raqqa) via the twin ruins of Halabiye and Zalabiye, and spend the next day exploring Rasafeh. Next, journey to **Aleppo** (4 nights) from where you can visit Qala'at Samaan and some of the Dead Cities as day trips. Take the train to the coast using **Lattakia** (3 nights) and **Tartus** (2 nights) as your bases to further delve into this region. Qala'at Marqab, Kassab and Arwad Island are just a few of the highlights here. Afterwards spend the night at **Krak des Chevaliers** (1 night) to truly appreciate the castle in the early morning light, before backtracking slightly to **Hama** (4 nights), which is a good place to station yourself for a few days to see sights such as Qasr Ibn Warden, Homs and Masyaf. If you can, try to spend a night at **Deir Mar Musa** (1 night) before heading back to Damascus to leave.

When to go

Syria is at its best during spring (late March to early June) and autumn (early September to early November). During both these seasons temperatures are pleasantly mild (15-20°C). Spring is when the country is at its greenest, the wild flowers are in full blossom and the showers and cooler air mean that the atmosphere is free from haze, so you get the best views. During the summer (early June to early September) it is generally very hot and dry, with temperatures averaging 30°C and sometimes reaching above 40°C, particularly from mid-July to mid-August. Sightseeing in such conditions can be very hard work. Winter (mid-November to mid-March) by contrast can be bitterly cold, temperatures often fall close to freezing and this is also when the majority of the rainfall comes.

Another element to factor into planning, is *Ramadan* (the Muslim month of fasting). During this month Muslims do not drink, eat or smoke from sunrise to sunset and although non-Muslims are not expected to join in, you should refrain from eating, drinking and smoking in public. Also, many smaller businesses will close during daylight hours and some will not open for the entire month, although shops and tourist sites are open as normal. Travelling in Syria at this time can be frustrating but if you do find yourself here during *Ramadan* you will probably be rewarded by constant invitations to share *Iftar* (the evening meal that breaks the daily fast) with the many Syrians that you meet, leaving you with an unforgettable insight into Islam and Arab culture. For the dates of *Ramadan*, see page 23.

Getting there

Air

Syria's two international airports are in Damascus and Aleppo. Damascus is the main hub with more connections to Europe. Both airports have flights to other Middle Eastern destinations. Direct flights to Syria are accessible and affordable from Europe but for cheap flights from Australasia and North America you will need to shop around a little. Flights from both destinations will involve at least one stopover en route. For the cheapest possible flights, consider flying to another Middle Eastern country and travelling overland, or booking an onward flight, from there. Recommended online booking agencies where you can compare airfares include **www.expedia.com**, **www.cheapflights.com** and **www.skyscanner.net**.

Flights from UK

The cheapest direct flights from London start at UK£300 with **BMI** (www.flybmi.com), who have daily flights to Damascus. **British Airways** (www.britishairways.com) and **Syrian Air** (www.syriaair.com) both also fly direct. Cheaper deals are available if you don't mind a lengthy stopover on the way. Good options include **Austrian Airlines** (www.aua.com), **Royal Jordanian** (www.rj.com), **Emirates** (www.emirates.com) and **Turkish Airlines** (www.thy.com).

An even cheaper option would be to fly from London to Istanbul and then travel overland to the border. Both **Easyjet** (www.easyjet.com) and **Pegasus Airlines** (www.pegasusairlines.com) have flights from London to Istanbul for as little as UK£39.

Flights from the rest of Europe

Syrian Air (www.syriaair.com) has direct flights from several European cities. Other airlines that provide direct flights include **Air France** (www.airfrance.com), **Austrian Airlines** (www.aua.com), **Alitalia** (www.alitalia.com), **Cyprus Airways** (cyprusairways.com) and **Czech Airlines** (czechairlines.com). Flights start from an average of EU£400.

Flights from North America

There are no direct flights to Syria from North America. To get the best deal you can either fly to London or another European city first, or via another city in the Middle East. Both **Emirates** (www.emirates.com), and **Etihad** (www.etihadairways.com), fly via the Gulf States and onward to Damascus. Flights to Damascus, via Dubai, from Los Angeles and New York start from US$700 one way or US$1100 return.

Flights from Australia and New Zealand

The quickest routes are offered by **Emirates** (www.emirates.com), **Qantas** (www.qantas.com.au), and **Etihad** (www.etihadairways.com). Flights from Australia via Dubai cost from AU$1400 one-way or AU$1800 return. From New Zealand prices tend to be higher, with one way tickets costing from NZ$2200 and returns from NZ$3000. It is usually cheaper looking into flights to other Middle Eastern destinations such as Istanbul, Dubai and Amman and booking separate onward flights or overland travel to Syria from there. It's worth noting that from Dubai the new airline **Flydubai** (www.flydubai.com) offers daily flights to Damascus and Aleppo from US$80.

For airport departure tax information, see page 33.

Border crossings into Syria

On entering Syria you will be given an entry/exit form to fill out, which you then hand to the immigration official for processing with your passport. When you have been stamped into Syria you will be given back this form. Don't lose it as you will have to supply it when exiting the country.

From Jordan
There are two land borders between Jordan and Syria. If you travel by bus or service taxi from Amman you will use the Jabir/Nasib border. The nearby Ramtha/Deraa border tends to be less hectic. Both borders are open 24 hours, and each has currency exchange facilities on both sides. There is a JOD5 departure tax from Jordan.

From Lebanon
There are four border crossings between Lebanon and Syria. The main one is Jdaide on the Beirut-Damascus highway. The second is at El Qaa, on the road between Baalbek and Homs. The third is at Aarida, on the road between Tripoli and Tartus. The fourth is Dabousiyeh, which links Tripoli with the motorway running between Homs and Tartus. Changing money is not a problem at any of the borders. Make sure you change up all your Lebanese Lira on the border as it's not accepted anywhere else in Syria. There is no departure tax from Lebanon.

From Turkey
There are several border posts between Turkey and Syria. The most important and frequently used crossing is the hectic Cilvegözü/Bab al-Hawa border between Antakya and Aleppo. There are currency exchange facilities on the Turkish side.

An interesting alternative is the Yayladgi/Kassab crossing, linking Antakya with Lattakia. This is a minor border post, though tourists seem to have no problems crossing here, and the road between the two cities is very beautiful.

For those with a sense of adventure, there is a series of minor border posts between the two countries along Syria's northern border. These border posts are little more than a shack that houses the customs and immigration facilities and you will have to walk between the border posts. The Akçakale/Tell Aybad border below Sanliurfa has a money exchange (behind customs on the Syrian side) and there are taxis that can take you to Aleppo. If you're way out east in Turkey you can catch a *dolmus* from Mardin to Nusaybin and then walk 500 m to the Nusaybin/Qamishle border post. It's then a 1 km walk into Qamishle where you can catch buses to destinations in the Jezira and to Damascus and Aleppo. There is no departure tax from Turkey.
See page 33 for land departure tax from Syria.

Road

You can cross into Syria from Jordan, Lebanon and Turkey. The land borders with Iraq and Israel remain out of the question for the time being.

From Amman in **Jordan**, JETT ① *Al-Malek al-Hussein St, Shmeisani, T962-656 64146, www.jet.com.jo*, operate buses to Damascus at 0700 and 0800 (4½ hours, JOD6). There are also plentiful share taxis leaving to Damascus from Amman's Abdali bus station (Al-Malek al-Hussein St, Jebel Amman). Taxis depart when full (3½ hours, JOD12).

From **Lebanon** frequent buses and service taxis ply the route between Beirut and Syria. Beirut's large **Charles Helou bus station** ① *Av Charles Helou, East Downtown*, has frequent departures to Damascus from Zone A and Aleppo from Zone B. **Saad bus company** (T961-701 42999) services both destinations (S£600). Service taxis leave for Damascus, Aleppo and Lattakia throughout the day and have similar prices.

If you're coming from **Turkey**, direct tickets from Istanbul to Aleppo always involve changing buses in Antakya, so it makes more sense to buy a ticket to Antakya and scout around for the bus soonest to depart from there. **Kent** (T9-0326 213 4722), and **Has** (T9-0326 444 0031), have daily departures from Antakya to Aleppo at 0930 (three hours, TYL10). You can also buy tickets to Damascus from Antakya but be aware that in most cases this involves a bus change in Aleppo.

Drivers no longer need a *carnet de passage en douane* to enter Syria by **car**. As long as the driver is permanently residing abroad and only entering Syria for a short stay, the border process only involves purchasing a car temporary entry card for US$40 and car insurance for US$30.

If you are driving from Jordan, the **Ramtha/Deraa** border is a good alternative to the extremely busy **Jabir/Nasib** border nearby. It's 180 km from Amman to Damascus. From Lebanon, the most popular point of entry is the **Jdaide** border on the Beirut–Damascus highway, though you should have no problems on the alternate routes between Baalbek and Homs and Tripoli and Tartus. There are several entry points between Turkey and Syria but the most important and frequently used crossing is **Cilvegözü/Bab al-Hawa** border which links Antakya and Aleppo (see Border crossings box, page 14).

Sea

There are currently no passenger ferry services between Limassol (Cyprus) and Lattakia, though this may change in the future. For up-to-date ferry information on travelling from Cyprus to Syria see the website www.varianostravel.com.

Train

From Jordan

The **Hejaz** railway between Amman and Damascus has been suspended for the foreseeable future as much-needed track repairs take place. This is the last remaining fragment of the Ottoman Hejaz Railway that once linked Damascus to Medina and was famously attacked by T E Lawrence and his Bedouin compatriots during the Arab Revolt in 1917. For up-to-date information on when/if the service will be up and running again, ring the **Hejaz Railway office** ① *Amman, T00962-6 48 95413*, or ask at Kadem Station in Damascus.

From Turkey

The **Toros Express** sleeper train between Istanbul and Aleppo has been temporarily suspended while construction of a new high-speed line in Turkey is completed. Services are set to resume at some stage in 2010. For information on the service resuming, ask at Haydarpasa Station in Istanbul and Baghdad Station in Aleppo, or visit the Turkish railway website (www.tcdd.gov.tr). There is also a twice-weekly service (seater-only) from Mersin and Adana to Aleppo (see page 231).

Getting around

Travel between the main centres in Syria is relatively easy and cheap. The bus network stretches nearly all over the country while the recently improved rail network is a good option in the west. If you are travelling by public transport, some of the more far-flung sights (particularly the **Dead Cities** and the **Euphrates** region) provide more of a challenge to visit. It's worthwhile hiring a car/driver to save time, but with careful planning, and a lot of patience, it's not impossible to visit most sights using a combination of public transport and negotiating rides with locals.

Air

As Syria is small enough to travel around by road, domestic flights are pretty unnecessary. For those with very limited time, **Syrian Air** (www.syriaair.com) operate reasonably priced flights from **Damascus** to **Aleppo**, **Lattakia**, **Deir ez-Zor** and **Qamishle** (see page 76).

Road

Bus
There are plenty of privately owned bus companies operating large air-conditioned coach services (known as **Pullman** buses) between the main centres in Syria. Due to competition prices tend to be cheap and services frequent and, in general, you don't have to pre-book tickets. Of the many companies, **Kadmous** and **Al-Ahliah** seem to operate the most extensive routes. All Pullman bus services are non-smoking except for the driver, so if you have problems with cigarette fumes be sure to ask for a seat towards the back of the bus. On many routes you will need to show your passport to purchase tickets.

As well as the Pullmans there are still some old mid-size buses (known as **Hob-hob** buses) plying routes between the smaller towns. Services tend to leave when the bus is full and are generally cheaper (and slower) then the Pullman buses.

Microbus Although cramped, uncomfortable and hot (in summer), **microbuses** provide transport to many of the smaller places that the big Pullman buses don't service. They are particularly useful for routes between smaller towns along the coast and the Orontes Valley, and getting to sights such as Apamea, The Dead Cities and Krak des Chevaliers. Microbuses leave from their own garages (usually a dusty parking lot) and there are no set departure times so you just need to turn up, ask around and wait for the next service to leave (usually when it's full).

Car
Hiring a car is an attractive option in Syria, particularly if you intend to visit remoter areas where public transport can be erratic or non-existent. The vast majority of car-hire firms are based in Damascus, though centres like Aleppo and Lattakia also have branches of the international car-hire firms. While the local companies are sometimes significantly cheaper than the international ones (some offer cars for as little as US$30 per day, as opposed to an average of around US$60 per day), it is very important to check the rental conditions and insurance cover carefully, as some smaller local companies don't offer any cover other than third party with their vehicles. In such cases, if you have an accident you

Road rules and driving conditions

Vehicles drive on the right in Syria. Make sure you always have all your documents with you, including your passport. Official speed limits do exist, although these are seldom enforced and certainly never adhered to. Note that the tow-away zones in big cities *are* enforced, and if you park in one of these you may well return to find that your car has been removed.

There is a great deal of variation in the quality of roads and you have to be prepared for some pretty erratic behaviour from other road users. The backbone of Syria's road network is the Damascus–Aleppo highway running north-south between the two cities. Although this is a good-quality motorway for most of its length, great care still needs to be taken when driving on it. As well as fast new cars hurtling up and down it at speeds well in excess of 150 kph, you have to watch out for tractors bumbling along at maybe 20 kph, buses stopping suddenly to pick up passengers, people doing U-turns across the central reservation and sometimes driving in the wrong direction down the hard shoulder.

From Damascus there are also good motorways heading south towards the Jordanian border and west towards the Lebanese border, while another motorway runs west from Homs and then north along the Mediterranean coast via Tartus to Lattakia. The highway along the Euphrates River between Aleppo and Deir ez-Zor and other important highways, such as those linking Damascus, Homs and Deir ez-Zor with Palmyra, are normal roads, in some places fairly wide and in others surprisingly narrow, though generally in good condition.

A huge amount of work has been carried out in recent years widening and resurfacing roads throughout the country. Nevertheless, there are still plenty of very narrow minor roads, often heavily pot-holed or poorly surfaced. Particular care needs to be taken in the coastal Jebel Ansariye mountains.

One of the great joys of driving in Syria is that as soon as you get out of the major cities (where heavy congestion and chaotic driving are the norm) the amount of traffic on the roads is minimal. One exception to this is the highway between Aleppo and Lattakia, which is always full of heavy lorry traffic along the whole of its length. If at all possible, driving at night anywhere in Syria (except in well-lit urban areas) should be avoided altogether; the twin hazards of some vehicles having faulty lights or no lights at all, and others leaving their main beams permanently on, makes for a potentially lethal combination.

will usually be liable for the full cost of the repairs. If you have an accident, make sure you obtain a police report; without one, even full insurance arrangements may be invalidated.

The minimum age for car hire varies between 21 and 25. Most companies require that you have held a full licence for at least one year. An international driving licence is not compulsory, although it is useful to have one in any case. Most companies have a minimum rental period of three days. There is usually a choice between limited mileage (usually up to 125 km) and unlimited mileage; unless you are sure that you are not going to be covering any great distances, it generally works out cheaper in the end to go for unlimited mileage. Most companies require either a credit card or a cash deposit, usually in the region of US$500-1000.

Budget (www.budget-sy.com) and **Europcar** (www.europcar-middleeast.com) are two of the main international car-rental firms in Syria. Both have offices in Damascus and Aleppo. With Budget, the minimum rental period is three days, with small car rental starting from US$55 per day with unlimited mileage. A medium-sized car starts from US$75. You have to pay a deposit (credit cards accepted) of US$600, which you get back when you return the car. Europcar's rates tend to be higher: with limited mileage and a three-day rental, small cars start from US$80 per day and medium-sized cars from US$90 per day, but if you are renting a car for more than one week the daily rate drops substantially. **Marmou Car Hire** (www.marmou.com) is a good local car-hire company with offices in Damascus. Their rates are as low as US$35 per day for the cheapest car, with their most expensive car US$80 per day. They have excellent weekly rental rates from US$220-500. Car hire has limited mileage of 120 km per day with an extra charge of 30 cents per kilometre if you go over this. All car rentals include full insurance.

Bicycle

For those considering cycling in Syria, be aware that the heat during summer is fierce, and head winds and cross-winds can be a real problem (good tail winds always seem to be remarkably elusive). Given the distances involved, it is worth considering putting your bike on a bus for the longer journeys (slogging across the Syrian desert to Palmyra, for example, is only really for those interested in testing their endurance to the limit). Pullman buses have enough room to stow bicycles in their luggage compartments, while older buses generally have a large rack on the roof.

If you bring your own hi-tech mountain or touring bike, bear in mind that spares will be difficult to find. It is perhaps worth considering buying a bike in Syria; although it will be heavier, slower and without the same range of gear ratios, you will at least be able to find spares for it. You will find workshops where you can get most repairs carried out in almost every town, but you should still carry your own basic tool kit and a supply of spares. Probably the most attractive areas to cyclists are the coastal Jebel Ansariye mountains and the so-called Dead City region around Aleppo; here traffic is minimal and the scenery very beautiful, even if the terrain is hilly.

Negotiating rides/hitchhiking

Some remote sites (particularly in the east and in the Dead City region) are unable to be reached without your own transport. If this isn't an option you'll need to depend on negotiating rides or hitchhiking. For many Syrians in rural areas this mode of transport is a common way of getting around. Be aware though, that hitchhiking anywhere has inherent risks and no one (especially females) should ever hitchhike alone.

Train

The Syrian train network has vastly improved in recent years making train travel a viable and inexpensive option for travellers, at least along the main route between Damascus and Aleppo and to the coast, from Aleppo to Lattakia. Both routes boast comfortable new air-conditioned trains.

First-class tickets are good value and are worthwhile. There are five services per day between Damascus and Aleppo but be aware that some departures are in the very early morning hours, or in the evening, denying passengers of any views en route. The journey between Aleppo and Lattakia is particularly beautiful. Always take your passport when buying train tickets.

For most of the rest of the country train travel is unfeasible due to lacklustre services, inconvenient departure times, old and uncomfortable carriages and inconveniently placed railway stations that are far out of towns.

Sleeping

Most of the main cities and tourism centres have a reasonable amount of accommodation for all budgets. Many smaller towns tend to have one or two hotels, usually in the mid-range or budget categories. In Damascus and Aleppo, a burgeoning number of old Ottoman houses and palaces have recently been converted into atmospheric and unusual top-end hotels, making a welcome addition to the luxury market, which had until now been dominated by the chain-hotels.

Be aware that hotel facilities, even in the top-end bracket, are usually not to the same standard as the West. Hot water can be erratic in all but the luxury end of the market. Many mid-range hotel rooms may boast TV and air-conditioning but that doesn't mean they work. It is always wise to ask to see the room and check that everything works before actually checking in. Making up for a shortfall with facilities, hotel staff are usually incredibly helpful and eager to please.

While the lower mid-range and budget hotels accept payment in S£s, practically all hotels from **B** category upwards prefer to be paid in US$. Just to confuse things, many mid-range and top-end hotels in Aleppo prefer to be paid in Euro. Most luxury and mid-range hotels now also accept major credit cards. Nearly all hotels above **C** category also charge an extra 10% government tax; be sure to check whether this is included in the price you are quoted. See box, page 20, for details of hotel price categories.

Hotels in some places, most notably Palmyra and to a lesser extent Hama, show marked variations in prices between the low and high seasons. In the case of Palmyra, the high season is March-April and August-December, while in Hama it is April-May and July-October. Elsewhere, prices generally stay stable throughout the year, although there are small variations in some categories in Damascus, where the high season is during the summer months (July-October).

Camping

There are very few official campsites in Syria. Beside the Damascus–Aleppo motorway just outside Damascus, the government-run **Harasta** campsite is a thoroughly unappealing place: noisy, with little natural shade and very basic toilet/shower facilities. By contrast, the privately run **Camping Kaddour** to the west of Aleppo is very pleasant and Palmyra has a lovely campground amidst the date palms.

Providing you have your own equipment, there are plenty of opportunities for 'unofficial' camping. The coastal Jebel Ansariye mountains are probably the most beautiful area, with plenty of attractive woodlands complete with streams and waterfalls offering idyllic sites. Camping at some of the more remote historic monuments and archaeological sites is also an option, although you should ask permission first. In more populated areas, camping will certainly generate a great deal of curiosity amongst local people, and in all likelihood you will be invited to stay in someone's house; trying to persuade them that you actually want to camp may be difficult.

Sleeping price codes

LL	Over US$200	**L**	US$151-200
AL	US$101-150	**A**	US$66-100
B	US$46-65	**C**	US$31-45
D	US$21-30	**E**	US$20 and under

Price codes refer to the cost of two people sharing a double room in the high season.

Top-end hotels (LL-AL)
As well as the multinational chain hotels that are present at all the main tourist centres, and come complete with all the mod-cons you'd expect at this price, there are now many beautifully restored 17th/18th-century palaces in Damascus and Aleppo that have opened up as independently run hotels. Although most won't offer the same amount of facilities as the multinationals, they more than make up for it with character and atmosphere. All hotel rooms in this category will have air-conditioning, satellite TV, and attached bath at the very least, and the hotels will offer a whole host of services for the visitor, usually an on-site restaurant and bar, and sometimes a swimming pool.

Mid-range hotels (A-C)
Hotels in this category are usually comfortable, though there can be a lot of variation in the quality of facilities. Most mid-range hotel rooms come with air-conditioning, satellite TV, and attached bath though in the lower end of the category you may only have a fan. Cleanliness standards can diverge hugely, as can room size and availability of hot water. It's always a good idea to check the room before confirming that you will take it.

Budget hotels (D-E)
At the higher end of the scale many budget hotel rooms can be as good as those in the mid-range category, just as comfortable and with the same facilities, and so are exceptional value. At the lower end are the very simplest of hotels which offer very basic rooms, usually just with a fan and shared toilet/shower facilities. Cleanliness and hygiene varies greatly. There are some real bargains (particularly in Hama and Damascus), clean, friendly and well run, but also some really squalid places. The better run places are very backpacker savvy and often offer dormitory accommodation and rooftop dorms as well during summer.

Eating price codes

🍴🍴🍴 over US$12   🍴🍴 US$6–12   🍴 under US$6

Prices refer to the average cost of a two-course meal for one person, not including drinks or service charge.

Eating and drinking → *For Arabic cuisine, see page 354.*

Food

Syria's cuisine is essentially classic Arabic fare. **Meat**, in the form of lamb or chicken, features fairly prominently in the Arab diet, along with staples such as chickpeas (in the form of falafels or hummus), rice, salads and mezze, and of course bread (*khubz*). Despite the prominence of meat in the diet, **vegetarians** can be sure of a nutritious and reasonably varied diet with the wide variety of predominantly vegetable-based mezze dishes on offer.

When Syrian food is done well, it is delicious, and in Damascus and Aleppo there are a host of excellent restaurants where the menu selections are varied and imaginative. Be aware that in many smaller towns though, you will find yourself confronted by a rather predictable choice of roast chicken, meat kebabs, hummus, salad and chips. Those on a tight budget will find the choice particularly monotonous with a diet made up of *shawarma* and falafel and the occasional half roast chicken.

International cuisine and **fast food** are available in the bigger towns and in the restaurants of the luxury hotels.

Drink

Tea and **coffee** compete as the national drinks. Both are served in the usual Arabic way and if you ask for milk it will be usually powdered or UHT. If you prefer instant coffee you need to ask for *Nescafe*. You can get excellent freshly squeezed **fruit juices** all over the country, and **fizzy drinks** and **mineral water** are widely available.

Although bars are not that common outside of Damascus, many visitors are surprised at how readily available **alcohol** is in what is a predominantly Muslim country. This reflects the diverse nature of society in Syria (Chrisitians account for around 10% of the population), and also its essentially tolerant nature. Wine, locally brewed and imported beers and *arak* (the Arabic liqueur) are available at many restaurants and liquer stores, while imported spirits are usually obtainable from the more top-end eateries and hotels.

Locally brewed beers include *Al-Chark*, from Aleppo and *Barada* from Damascus. Neither are particularly good and you have to watch out for out-of-date bottles, but when fresh and properly chilled, they are certainly drinkable. Look out for the excellent imported Lebanese lagers *Al-Maaza* and *Lazziza*, which are both excellent.

Festivals and events

For further details on festivals contact the Ministry of Tourism (www.syriatourism.org).

April/May
Palmyra Desert Festival This major event runs for 3 days and draws locals as well as foreign visitors. In the day there is a full programme of horse and camel racing, while the evenings host performances of folk dancing and traditional music in the restored Roman theatre in the midst of the ruins.

July/August
Jazz Lives In Syria Festival This annual festival brings international artists to Damascus and Aleppo for 1 week of concerts. For more information visit www.jazzlivesinsyria.com.

September
Bosra Festival This festival uses Bosra's huge Roman theatre as a venue for a lively programme of music, singing, dancing and drama, with many visiting acts from abroad. The festival dates change yearly, for further details visit www.bosrafestival.org.
Silk Road Festival Organized by the Ministry of Tourism, this annual event stages cultural performances celebrating the history of the trade routes. Concerts and events are held in Damascus, Aleppo and Palmyra.

Public holidays

The following dates are fixed public holidays; many of the major Muslim and Christian holidays are also public holidays, although their dates vary from year to year. Only those holidays marked * are celebrated nationally; the remainder are celebrated in a limited way, perhaps with a cultural event and certain government offices closing, or in the case of something like Marine's Day, with that section of the armed forces having a holiday.

1 Jan New Year's Day*
22 Feb Union Day
8 Mar Revolution Day*
22 Mar Arab League Day
17 Apr Independence Day*
1 May Workers' Day*
6 May Martyrs' Day*
29 May Marine's Day
6 Oct Veteran's Day
16 Oct Flight Day
16 Nov Correctionist Movement Day
14 Dec Peasants' Day
25 Dec Christmas Day*

Islamic holidays

Islamic holidays are calculated according to the lunar calendar and therefore fall on different dates each year (see box, page 23), for projected dates from 2010-2013.

Ras as-Sana (Islamic New Year) 1st Muharram. The first 10 days of the year are regarded as holy, especially the 10th.
Ashoura 9th and 10th Muharram. Anniversary of the killing of Hussein, commemorated by Shi'ite Muslims (Shi'ites are a small minority in Syria, so this event is not widely celebrated). Ashoura also celebrates the meeting of Adam and Eve after leaving Paradise, and the end of the Flood.
Moulid an-Nabi The Prophet Muhammad's birthday. 12th Rabi al-Awwal.
Leilat al-Meiraj Ascension of Muhammad from Haram al-Sharif (Temple Mount) in Jerusalem. 27th Rajab.
Ramadan The Islamic month of fasting. The most important event in the Islamic calender. 21st Ramadan is the *Shab-e-Qadr* or 'Night of Prayer'.
Eid al-Fitr Literally 'the small feast'. 3 days of celebration, beginning 1st Shawwal, to mark the end of Ramadan.

Islamic holidays (approximate dates)

Holiday	2010	2011	2012	2013
Islamic New Year	18 Dec 2009 (1431)	9 Dec 2010 (1432)	26 Nov 2011 (1433)	15 Nov 2012 (1434)
Moulid an-Nabi (Prophet's birthday)	26 Feb	15 Feb	4 Feb	24 Jan
Leilat al-Meiraj	8 Jul	28 Jun	16 Jun	5 Jun
Ramadan	11 Aug	1 Aug	20 Jul	9 Jul
Eid al-Fitr	10 Sep	30 Aug	19 Aug	8 Aug
Eid al-Adha	16 Nov	6 Nov	26 Oct	15 Oct

Eid al-Adha Literally 'the great feast'. Begins on 10th Zilhaj and lasts 4 days. Commemorates Ibrahim's (Abraham's) near sacrifice of his son Ismail (though in Christian and Judaic tradition it is Isaac who is nearly sacrificed), and coincides with the *Hajj*, or pilgrimage to Mecca. Marked by the sacrifice of a sheep, feasting and donations to the poor.

Christian holidays

In addition to the fixed-date Christian holidays listed above under Public holidays, Good Friday and Easter Sunday are both public as well as religious holidays; each are celebrated on different dates every year, in the case of both the Western (Latin) and Eastern (Orthodox) churches.

Shopping

Syria is something of a paradise for souvenir, handicraft and antique hunters. The most interesting and rewarding places to go exploring are the souqs of Damascus and Aleppo. Things to look out for include: wooden chess sets and backgammon boards; wooden boxes inlaid with mother-of-pearl; carpets and rugs; jewellery; gold and silverware; brassware; carpets; hand-painted tiles; Damascene swords; musical instruments; *narghiles*; fabrics and silk brocades (for which Damascus is famous); and all manner of antiques.

Bargaining is the name of the game in the souqs. If you want to get a rough idea of how much things cost, head to the specialist handicraft markets in Damascus (see page 74) and Aleppo (see page 228) before diving into the souqs.

Activities and tours

Arabic language courses
Many international students come to Syria to learn Arabic due to the quality and relative low cost of the courses available. The main centre of language teaching is Damascus, although there are some language schools in Aleppo as well. There's a variety of courses on offer for students of all levels and many locals also offer private tuition. See page 75, for further details.

Camel and 4WD safaris
Palmyra is the base for camel and 4WD safaris out into the desert though, despite the ample potential, this has yet to be properly developed as an activity. However, if you are interested in making a trip into the desert, many small tour operators (who mostly work out of the hotels rather than have their own shops) in Palmyra can arrange this for you. A typical trip usually involves an overnight stay at a Bedouin encampment but most tour operators can organize longer or shorter itineraries. (See page 281, for details of Palmyra tours.)

Hammams
The ultimate bathing experience, a hammam, or Turkish bath, is a communal bathing house that is very much part of the culture in Syria. Hammams are about more than getting clean, though you will definitely do that. Going to a hammam is a social occasion that can extend for hours as neighbours and friends gather in the marble confines of the bathhouse to gossip, exchange news and relax together.

Hammams are segregated in Syria, either being purely male or female or with separate times set aside for women and men. The typical hammam experience consists of a sauna, wash, exfoliation and then a massage, although you can pay for each service separately. Most hammams use the locally made olive oil soap for washing, but it is perfectly acceptable to bring your own shampoo and soap along if you prefer.

Damascus has the best selection of hammams, some of which are housed in beautifully restored buildings that have been running for 400 years.

Hiking
There are certainly plenty of opportunities for hiking, most notably in the coastal **Jebel Ansariye** mountains and the limestone hills **around Aleppo**, though this is not really

recognized as an activity in Syria. If you want to do it you will have to bring all your own equipment for camping, etc, and be prepared for the fact that there are no maps of a sufficiently small scale for hiking, nor any official guides.

Tours

There are many small local companies in both Damascus and Aleppo that can make up a Syrian itinerary for you and provide drivers and guides.

In Damascus **Beroia Travel and Tourism** specialize in unusual tours (cooking, architecture, trekking) that focus on specialist interests (see page 76).

Halabia Travel and Tourism in Aleppo organize country-wide itineraries of any length and have myriad services for visitors (see page 230).

Responsible tourism

Clothing

Syrians place a lot of importance on smartness and cleanliness and making the effort to be presentable in public will earn you greater respect. Singlets, low-cut tops, bare midriffs, above-the-knee shorts and skirts and other skimpy clothing are not acceptable dress in Syria and often cause offence. The key to remember is shoulders and knees (and everything in-between) should be covered at all times. This rule applies to men as well as women. See also 'Visiting mosques' below.

Conduct

Syrians are incredibly welcoming and open and will go out of their way to help foreigners. Return this gesture by being equally polite and friendly.

Making the effort to use a little of the language will be greatly appreciated. Syrians are always ecstatically happy and surprised when a foreigner speaks Arabic, even if it is only a few words. Except among more cosmopolitan people it is not usual for a man and woman to shake hands when meeting. Instead place your right hand across your heart; this can also be used as a sign of thank you as well. Open displays of affection between couples are not acceptable in public and can cause great offence. Conversely, it is completely normal for friends of the same sex (male and female) to hold hands and link arms in public.

While eating a shared meal like mezze, it's acceptable to use your left hand to tear bread but the right hand should be used to take from the communal bowls and also to pass things to people. Always tuck your feet in towards you when sitting down. Feet are considered unclean and it's very rude to point them at someone. Also, crossing your legs while seated is considered rude by some more conservative people.

Visiting mosques Non-Muslims are welcome in most mosques in Syria, although in some Shi'ite mosques they are only allowed into the courtyard and not the prayer hall itself. In any case, always seek permission before entering a mosque. Remember that shoes must be removed before entering the prayer hall, although socks can be left on. It is very important that both men and women dress modestly, covering arms and legs (shorts are not acceptable) and in the case of women, wearing a headscarf. At larger, more important mosques, such as the Umayyad Mosque in Damascus, women are required to hire a full-length black hooded robe at the entrance (and men also if they attempt to enter in shorts).

How big is your footprint?

BYO bag

The sad sight of hundreds of plastic bags littering the roadside for miles in some parts of the country is one of the more unpleasant sights to greet travellers in Syria. Do your bit for the environment and bring your own reusable bag for shopping instead of adding to the plastic waste mountain.

Don't litter

A lack of bins in public areas isn't a licence to litter. If you can't find somewhere to dump your rubbish then hang onto it until you can dispose of it properly. Smokers should never throw their cigarette butts onto the ground. There is an excellent range of portable travel ashtrays now available to store your butts until you find a bin.

Always ask before taking photos

Do not take photos of people without asking their permission first. Some people, especially women in more conservative rural areas, will not allow it. Most people will pose quite happily – especially if you show them the result afterwards – but it is polite to ask first.

Find out about the country you're travelling in

Learn about local etiquette and culture; consider local norms and behaviour and dress appropriately for local cultures and situations.

Spend your money wisely

Support locally owned hotels and transport and buy locally made crafts and souvenirs so that your money is supporting the communities you are travelling through. Use common sense when bargaining – the few dollars you save may be a week's salary to others.

Conserve water

Like the rest of the Middle East, Syria suffers from water restrictions, especially in the hot summer months. Keep showers as short as possible.

Learn the language

A little effort goes a long way in Syria. Just learning the traditional Arabic greeting a *salaam alaikum* (peace be upon you) and its reply *wa alaikum asalaam* (and upon you be peace) will win you a crowd of new friends and a lot of respect.

Essentials A-Z

Accident and emergency

In the event of an emergency contact the relevant service: (police T112, ambulance T110, traffic police T115, fire T113), and your embassy (see below). An official police/medical report is required for insurance claims.

Bargaining

Although there are plenty of exceptions, as a rule just about everything, including the price of hotel rooms, can be bargained over. When shopping, particularly in the souqs, it is the expected way of doing business. Successful bargaining is something of an art. Give yourself plenty of time and be prepared to sit around drinking cups of tea and exchanging small talk: it is all part of the process. At the end of the day, if you think the final price is too high, be prepared to walk away empty handed (as often as not you will be called back to hear one 'final, last, lowest possible' price, at which point you can begin bargaining all over again). Conversely, try to avoid relentlessly driving down the price just for the sake of it; if you stop to consider the amount you are offering and compare it with prices back home, you may realize that you are being downright mean.

Children

Children are positively doted on in Syria. 'Do you have children?', or, more commonly, 'How many children do you have?' is a standard question asked of foreigners. Unlike in Europe or North America, children are warmly welcomed in restaurants, and most hotels will go out of their way to accommodate them. If you are travelling with children, you will constantly find yourself receiving offers of help and hospitality. There are of course important

health considerations specific to children but facilities are reasonably good in all but the most out-of-the-way places within the country.

Customs and duty free

Everyone is allowed to bring in a duty free allowance of 570 ml of spirits and 200 cigarettes. Ammunition, firearms, and birds of any type (live, stuffed or frozen) are prohibited. Since the swine influenza outbreak in 2009 the importing of all pork products has been banned as well.

If you bring more than US$5000 into the country or take out more than US$2000, you are officially supposed to declare it. In practice this is very rarely enforced, but if you want to be absolutely sure of avoiding potential problems, stick to the rules.

Disabled travellers

Provisions for disabled travellers are largely non-existent in Syria and getting around the country can present huge problems. Urban areas generally have uneven, cracked and pot-holed pavements, with ridiculously high kerbs, while visiting historic sites often involves traversing rough, uneven ground unsuitable for wheelchairs. Careful planning will be required if you plan on travelling in Syria but, despite the considerable obstacles, you can be sure that people everywhere will be extremely accommodating and helpful.

Electricity

220 volts, 50 AC. European 2-pin sockets are the norm. Electricity supply is on the whole reliable, although power cuts do occur (particularly in Aleppo).

Embassies and consulates

Syrian embassies abroad

→ For embassies based in Damascus, see page 79.
For a complete list of Syrian embassies and
consulates abroad, see http://www.embassies
abroad.com/embassies-of/Syria.

Australia, 41 Culgoa Circuit, O'Malley,
Canberra, T02-6286 5235,
www.syrianembassy.org.au.
Canada, 151 Slater St, Suite 1000
Ottawa, Ontario, T613-569 5556,
www.syrianembassy.ca.
Egypt, 18 Abdel Rehim Sabry St, Dokki, Cairo,
T02-2335 8806, syrian-embassy@hotmail.com.
France, 20 rue Vaneau, Paris, T01-4062 6100,
www.amb-syr.fr.
Germany, Rauchstrasse 25, Berlin,
T030-501 770, www.syrianembassy.de.
Greece, Dimandidou 61, P. Psychico, Athens,
T210-672 5577, www.syrianembassy.gr.
Italy, Piazza del'Ara Coeli 1, Rome,
T066-749 801, Syria@email.it.
Japan, Homat-Jade, 6-19-45 Akasaka,
Minato-ku 107 Tokyo, T03-586 8977.
Jordan, Abdoun, Prince Hashem bin
Alhussein St, Amman, T06-592 0684,
www.syrianembassy.jo.
Spain, Plaza Platería Martínez 1, Madrid,
T91-420 1602.
Turkey, Abdullah Cevdet, Sokak No 7,
Cankaya, Ankara, T312-440 9657; Consulate:
Macka Cad no 59/3, Tesvikiye, Istanbul,
T212-232 6721.
UK, 8 Belgrave Sq, London, T0207-245 9012,
www.syrianembassy.co.uk.
USA, 2215 Wyoming Av, NW Washington DC,
T202-232 6313, www.syrianembassy.us.

Gay and lesbian travellers

Homosexuality is illegal in Syria, and
very much frowned on. Pre-marriage
homosexuality amongst men is probably far
more widespread than most Syrians would
admit, but it remains a taboo subject. The
idea of women engaging in lesbian
relationships is something which Syrian
men seem totally unable to come to terms
with, and most would deny that it occurs at
all. Gay and lesbian travellers are therefore
advised to be discreet about their sexuality.
Paradoxically, the carefully segregated nature
of society means that public behaviour
which would be seen as inappropriate
between members of the opposite sex
(eg holding hands, kissing on the cheek,
etc) is acceptable between members of
the same sex.

Health

See your GP or travel clinic at least 6 weeks
before departure for general advice on
travel risks and vaccinations. Try phoning a
specialist travel clinic if your own doctor is
unfamiliar with health conditions in Syria.
Make sure you have sufficient medical travel
insurance, get a dental check, know your
own blood group and if you suffer a long-
term condition such as diabetes or epilepsy,
obtain a Medic Alert bracelet/necklace
(www.medicalert.co.uk). If you wear
glasses, take a copy of your prescription.

Vaccinations
It is advisable to vaccinate against **polio**,
diphtheria, **tetanus**, **typhoid**, **hepatitis A**
and **hepatitis B**. If you're going to more
remote areas consider having the **rabies**
vaccination. You are not required to show a
yellow-fever vaccination certificate on arrival
unless you are arriving from a yellow-fever-
infected country. You may also be required t
o show a vaccination certificate if you have
visited a yellow-fever-infected country at
any stage during the last month and may be
turned away if you can't produce one. The
occurrence of malaria is rare in Syria though
there have been reported cases. It is sensible
to avoid being bitten as much as possible;
cover bare skin and use an insect repellent.
The most common and effective repellent is
diethyl metatoluamide (DEET). DEET liquid is

best for arms and face (take care around eyes and with spectacles; DEET dissolves plastic). Aerosol spray is good for clothes and ankles and liquid DEET can be dissolved in water and used to impregnate cotton clothes and mosquito nets. Impregnated wrist and ankle bands can also be useful. Contact your travel clinic before travel to find out up-to-date information on malaria-risk and discuss anti-malarial drugs.

Health risks

Stomach upsets are common among travellers to Syria. They're mainly caused by the change in diet (Syrian food is heavy on oil which can be hard to digest for people unused to this diet). The most common cause of prolonged travellers' **diarrhoea** is from eating contaminated food or drinking tap water. Diarrhoea may be also caused by viruses, bacteria (such as E-coli), protozoal (such as giardia), salmonella and cholera. It may be accompanied by vomiting or by severe abdominal pain. Any kind of diarrhoea responds well to the replacement of water and salts. Sachets of rehydration salts can be bought in most chemists and can be dissolved in water. If the symptoms persist, consult a doctor. To avoid diarrhoea, drink only bottled or boiled water, avoid having ice in drinks and peel fruit and vegetables before eating. Use your sense when choosing a restaurant; if it's a busy, popular place it's more likely to be safe to eat there and food is more likely to be fresh.

In the summer months **heat exhaustion** and **heatstroke** are common health risks in Syria. This is prevented by drinking enough fluids throughout the day (your urine will be pale if you are drinking enough). Symptoms of heat exhaustion and heatstroke are similar and include dizziness, tiredness and headache. Use lots of fluids or better, rehydration salts mixed with water, to replenish fluids and salts and find somewhere cool and shady to recover.

If you suspect heatstroke rather than heat exhaustion, you need to cool the body down quickly (cold showers are particularly effective) and may require hospital treatment for electrolyte replacement by intravenous drip.

If you get sick

Contact your embassy or consulate for a list of doctors and dentists who speak your language, or at least some English. Doctors and health facilities in major cities are also listed in the Directory sections of this book. Good-quality healthcare is available in the larger centres but it can be expensive, especially hospitalization. Make sure you have adequate insurance (see below).

Useful websites

www.btha.org, British Travel Health Association.
www.fco.gov.uk, British Foreign and Commonwealth Office travel site has useful information on each country, people, climate and a list of UK embassies/consulates.
www.fitfortravel.scot.nhs.uk, A-Z of vaccine/health advice for each country.
www.who.int, World Health Organization site with vaccine and health advice.

Insurance

Always take out comprehensive insurance before you travel, including full medical cover and extra cover for any activities (hiking, rafting, skiing, riding, etc) that you may undertake. Check exactly what's being offered, the maximum cover for each element and also the excess you will have to pay in the case of a claim. Keep details of your policy and the insurance company's telephone number with you at all times and get a police report for any lost or stolen items.

Internet

President Bashar Assad's only official position prior to becoming president was as head of the Syrian Computer Society, and he is said to have been directly responsible for introducing the internet in Syria. Since his coming to power the internet has flourished in Syria and you shouldn't have too many problems in finding somewhere to log on. Damascus has a decent number of internet cafés and many restaurants and hotels in the city now provide free Wi-Fi (though don't expect it to work all the time). Outside of the capital most medium-sized towns can boast at least one internet café.

Costs for internet use are about S£100 per hr and connections tend to be on the slow side. Remember to save your work frequently, as power cuts are common. Note that certain sites are currently banned in Syria, including www.facebook.com and www.couchsurfers.com. Savvy internet café staff can usually bypass the ban and hook you up if you ask them nicely. Some internet cafés need to register your passport before you can log on.

Language

Arabic is the national language in Syria but even in very remote areas, you will usually be able to find someone who speaks at least a little English, while in the major towns and cities and at important tourist sites, English is fairly widely spoken. Many older generation Syrians also speak a little French. See page 350, for a list of useful Arabic words and phrases.

Money

Currency
→ €1=S£68; £1=S£76; US$1=S£46 (Nov 2009)
The basic unit of currency is the Syrian pound (S£) or lira. Notes come in denominations of S£1000, S£500, S£100 and S£50. Coins come

in denominations of S£25, S£10, S£5, S£2 and S£1. The division of the S£ into 100 piastres is largely redundant.

Changing money
The influx of ATM machines over the past few years has made travelling in Syria much easier. The Commercial Bank of Syria (CBS) has ATMs in most medium-sized towns but their machines sometimes don't accept foreign cards (even if they display Maestro, Visa and Cirrus network signs). Cards linked to the maestro network tend to have the most problems. ATMs linked to branches of the Bank of Syria and Overseas are usually reliable for most foreign debit/credit cards. Damascus, Aleppo, Hama, Homs, Lattakia and Tartus all have reliable ATMs but in smaller towns you may run into problems and it is not sensible to depend solely on using ATMs.

It's still advisable to carry plenty of **cash** (in US$) for the times when an ATM won't accept your card and for the smaller towns. Cash can be changed at most banks (including branches of CBS), and exchange offices (which are open for longer hours than the banks). Most mid and top-range hotels also prefer to be paid in US$.

These days **traveller's cheques (TCs)** are more a hindrance than a help in Syria and you'd be better off using a mixture of ATM withdrawals and cash. Changing TCs is a lengthy and involved process that can take up an entire morning. Branches of CBS change TCs and charge a flat fee of S£25 per transaction.

Most major **credit cards** (Visa, MasterCard, American Express, Diners Club) are accepted at the more expensive hotels and restaurants, and at larger tourist souvenir and handicraft shops in the main cities. They can also be used to pay for airline tickets and car hire. Note that over-the-counter bank cash advances are officially not possible in Syria. That said, the situation is becoming much more relaxed and some of the luxury hotels, large shops and several private companies are willing to do so. If you need a cash advance ask at your hotel or anywhere displaying a Visa, MasterCard or American Express sign. Be aware that you will have to pay a hefty fee for the service.

Using the **black market** won't save you any money as the rates offered are the same as the banks. The black market is most active in the area around Martyrs Sq in Damascus and in the city souqs. If you need to change money outside of banking hours ask at your hotel reception. Staff are usually happy to exchange cash at the official bank rate.

Changing S£ back into hard currency is very difficult in Syria. If you are flying out, be aware that the airport bank won't change S£ into dollars either. It's really a case of trying not to end up with too many S£s left over. If you are leaving overland there is no problem in changing S£ at the Jordanian, Lebanese and Turkish border.

Cost of living and travelling
The cost of living and travelling in Syria is far cheaper than in Europe or North America and in comparison to neighbouring Lebanon, Jordan and Turkey, travel in Syria can be very economical. Be aware though that prices have risen dramatically over the past couple of years and how much you spend will depend not only on the degree of comfort you want to travel in, but also on how much you want to do in a given amount of time.

Accommodation will be your biggest expense in Syria, especially in Damascus and Aleppo where rooms are in high demand. In contrast, eating out is remarkably cheap, even in the fanciest restaurants. A 2-course meal in an expensive restaurant rarely works out at more than US$10-$15 per head and those on tight budgets will rarely pay over US$2 per meal by existing on a diet of mostly *shawarma* and *falafel*.

Travelling by public transport is inexpensive with tickets seldom costing over US$4. If you plan on hiring a car/driver budget approximately US$60-100 per day for travel costs. Entry fees to major museums and sites are cheap but if you plan on seeing

a lot they can add up. Entry costs S£75 for small sites and S£150 for larger ones but those with an international student card (ISIC) are given huge discounts.

Those on tight budgets can exist on about US$25 per day by living on a diet of *shawarma* and *falafel* and by staying in the cheapest of budget hotels and using dormitories where available. A budget of US$50-70 per day would be much more comfortable and would allow you to eat a more varied diet, stay in decent budget/ mid-range accommodation and hire a car/driver for the more out-of-the-way sights. Luxury travel (boutique hotels, the best restaurants and a private vehicle, perhaps with driver and guide), means moving into the equivalent price ranges as for luxury travel in Europe and North America; basically from US$150-200 per day upwards.

Opening hours

Banks, **post offices** and **government offices** are usually open Sat-Thu 0800-1400, though in the cities some banks and post offices open until 1700. Official **shop** opening hours are Sat-Thu 0800-1400 and 1600-1800, but many now open throughout the day especially in the larger towns. **Museums** and **sights** are normally open from 0900-1800 in summer (Apr-Sep) and from 0900-1600 in winter (Oct-Mar). Most close on Tue though there are exceptions to the rule.

Prohibitions

If you do find yourself in legal trouble in Syria be aware that your embassy cannot help you get out of trouble, but they are a useful source of advice for seeking translators and English-speaking lawyers. For a list of embassies in Damascus, see page 79.

Drugs

Possession of narcotics is illegal in Syria. Those caught in possession risk a long prison sentence and/or deportation. There is a marked intolerance to drug-taking in Syria and the drugs scene is distinctly seedy (not to mention paranoid) and best avoided.

Homosexuality

See Gay and lesbian travellers, above.

Photography

Avoid taking pictures of military installations, or anything that might be construed as 'sensitive'. In Syria, the definition of 'sensitive' can include bridges and very unimportant public buildings, which may have an armed guard at the entrance.

Post

Airmail **letters** (up to 20 g) cost S£50 to Europe and S£55 to North America or Australia/NZ. **Postcards** cost S£30 to Europe and S£35 to North America or Australia/NZ. Postal services tend to be slow when posted outside Damascus but generally reliable.

To send a **parcel**, you should take it unwrapped to the post office, where its contents will be inspected. Parcels to the UK/Europe cost S£525 per kg, and to North America or Australia/NZ S£625.

There is a **poste restante** counter at the central post office in Damascus (open Sat-Thu 0800-1700, closed Fri). To collect mail you must present your passport as ID and pay S£10 per item of mail. Mail sent here should have your surname in capital letters and underlined to avoid it being filed under your first name. It should be addressed to: c/o Poste Restante, Central Post Office, Said al-Jabri Ave, Damascus, Syria.

DHL have a branch in Damascus (see page 80).

Safety

Syria is probably the safest of all the Middle Eastern countries in which to travel. Theft and violent crime are virtually unheard of and you are safe wandering around the big cities at any time of the day or night (notwithstanding the inevitable offers of help if you are looking lost). Nevertheless, the usual precautions are advisable with regard to valuables: never leave them unattended in hotel rooms, and keep your money and important documents (passport, etc) on your person, preferably in a money-belt or something similar.

Lone women may encounter minor hassle, though it almost always consists of nothing more than constant offers of marriage and is usually easily ignored. If you do find yourself being harassed don't be afraid to call for assistance. Most Syrians are appalled by this behaviour and will quickly come to your aid.

Probably the biggest danger tourists face is on the roads. Syrian driving is erratic, to say the least, and you need to keep a close eye on traffic (not to mention pedestrians, donkeys and a whole host of other dangers) when using the roads. When crossing a busy road as a pedestrian, use your right hand, to make the hand signal for '*astena*' ('wait' in Arabic): bring the tip of your thumb to meet in the middle of the tips of your fingers and show this hand gesture to oncoming traffic. Surprisingly, this is actually extremely effective at stopping traffic. Syrian drivers like to speed. If you've hired a driver never be afraid to tell him to slow down or stop if you're not comfortable. The best advice if you're driving on Syrian roads is to practise defensive driving and always be aware of what might be coming up further along the road.

Student travellers

Anyone in full-time education is entitled to an **International Student Identity Card** (ISIC). These are issued by student travel offices and travel agencies across the world. In Syria an ISIC card is enormously valuable since it entitles you to massive discounts on entry fees to museums and historic sites. Due to the amount of fake ISIC cards now in distribution, at some sites your card will be very carefully scrutinized and you will not be issued a discounted entry rate unless you are also under 26.

Taxes

Airport departure tax
At the time of research, people departing the country by air are still being charged the hefty airport departure tax of S£1500 but there is talk of phasing this out in the near future. Check with your hotel for up-to-date information.

Land departure tax
Departure tax is S£500 if you are leaving via a land border into Jordan or Lebanon and S£550 via the Bab al-Hawa border into Turkey.

Other taxes
Most top-end hotels add a 10% government tax to the room rate. Expensive restaurants also usually add 10% service tax to your bill.

Telephone

To call Syria from overseas dial your international access code, followed by Syria's country code 963 and then the area/town code (dropping the 0). To call an international phone number from within Syria dial 00, followed by the country code.

Most travellers are able to use their mobile phones in Syria – ask your provider before you travel. Pay-as-you-go SIM cards are available from phone shops and mobile phone provider offices. **Syriatel** (www.syriatel.com) have offices in all main towns. Take your passport along to register a new SIM card. You can purchase a Syriatel SIM card with 400 units for S£365 (valid for

135 days) or one with 1200 units for S£835 (valid for 220 days).

The cheapest way of making international (and national) calls is by card-phone. There are currently 2 card-phone systems operating in Syria. Damascus, Aleppo and Hama use the Easycomm system. Cards come in denominations of S£200 (for national calls only), S£500 and S£1000 (national and international calls). Easycomm card-phone booths can be found dotted all over Damascus and Aleppo and less so in Hama. The cards themselves are sold at shops near the booths (often from late-opening juice bars and the like; just ask around), or else from the main telephone office.

The older card-phone system is operated by the Syrian Telephone Exchange and found throughout the rest of the country. The cards are made of very thin plastic (they are easily damaged, so handle them carefully). They come in values of S£250 (national), S£500 and S£1000, though often only the latter is available. STE card-phones are located at the main telephone offices only (either inside or just outside), where you can also buy the cards (either over the counter, or else from semi-official touts outside). Here you will also find some coin-operated phone booths, good for national calls only.

Time

Syria is 2 hrs ahead of GMT Oct-Apr, and 3 hrs ahead May-Sep.

Tipping

Tipping is very much a way of life in Syria. In restaurants 10% is acceptable though remember that the more expensive restaurants often add a service charge anyway. Any person who provides a service (driver, guide, hotel porter) will expect a tip

The entry/exit stamp game

Syria will not issue you with a visa, or allow you entry into the country, even with a visa, if there is any evidence of a visit to Israel in your passport. If you wish to visit Israel as well as Syria, the safest option is to leave Israel till last. If you are planning on visiting Israel from Egypt or Jordan before heading to Syria, it is important to know that, although the Israeli authorities are willing to stamp a separate piece of paper rather than your passport (provided you ask), your exit stamps from Egypt or Jordan (on your way into Israel) are evidence that you have entered the country. Thus, if you enter or leave Israel via the Rafah or Taba border crossings with Egypt, the Egyptian entry/exit stamp (complete with the name of the border in Arabic) will alert the Syrian authorities to the fact that you have been in Israel. Likewise for the Wadi Arabah/Arava and Jisr Sheikh Hussein/Jordan River border crossings between Israel and Jordan.

However, there are two other options. If you fly from Tel Aviv to Amman, your Jordanian entry stamp will simply be for Queen Alia International Airport and therefore will not provide any conclusive

evidence that you have been in Israel, allowing you to continue on to Syria. The second option is to visit Israel from Jordan via the King Hussein (Allenby) Bridge border crossing, and return the same way. At this border crossing (and only this one), the Jordanian authorities are sometimes willing to put your exit/entry stamps on a separate sheet of paper, so leaving no evidence of a visit to Israel in your passport. This option does completely depend on the whim of the Jordanian border officials on the day; if they decide that they will not use a separate sheet of paper for your exit stamp then you must be prepared to either turn back at the border and not enter Israel, or go ahead to Israel and not visit Syria. Note too that this option will only work if you do a round trip from Jordan to Israel and back again.

If you fly to Israel and then enter Jordan by the King Hussein (Allenby) Bridge border crossing and ask to have your Jordanian entry stamp on a separate piece of paper, when you try to enter Syria, the absence of a Jordanian entry stamp will be enough to alert the authorities.

and what you give them is really down to your own discretion.

Tourist information

Syria does not have any dedicated tourist offices abroad, although their embassies can provide you with a selection of the Ministry of Tourism's free maps/pamphlets. All main towns and tourist centres have a tourist information office which hand out the free Ministry of Tourism maps. Staff are always friendly and willing to help but usually don't have much information. The Ministry of

Tourism's website (see below) has some useful information and a handy calendar of events.

Useful websites

www.fco.gov.uk Homepage of the British Foreign and Commonwealth Office; gives current safety recommendations regarding travel in Syria.
www.newsfromsyria.com Excellent website with up-to-date news from the country.
www.syriatourism.org Official website of Syria's Ministry of Tourism.
www.whatsonsyria.com Web version of the free monthly magazine with events listings and lots of useful information for visitors.

Visas and immigration

Syrian visas

For detailed and up-to-date information on applying for a Syrian visa, contact your nearest Syrian embassy (see above for contact details of Syrian embassies abroad). All foreign nationals, except for nationals of Arab countries, require a visa to enter Syria. Your passport must be valid for at least 6 months beyond your intended stay. **Note** Anyone whose passport shows evidence of a trip to Israel is not allowed into the country (see box, opposite).

Single entry tourist visas are valid for 3 months from the date of issue and allow for a stay of up to 15 days. **Multiple entry** visas are valid for 6 months from the date of issue but again only allow for a stay of 15 days. Visa costs vary by nationality, check with the Syrian embassy for details.

In nearly all cases the tourist visa must be obtained before arriving in Syria. The only official exceptions to this rule are for nationalities that do not have a Syrian embassy in their country (eg New Zealanders and Dutch). These nationalities are entitled to a visa at the point of entry. In practice though, in the past couple of years, it has also been possible for Australians to be issued visas on arrival in Syria despite there being a Syrian embassy in Australia. This really all depends on the whims of the immigration officials at your time of entry and the best rule is for you to apply for your visa beforehand if you have a Syrian embassy in your home country.

Applying for a Syrian visa in a neighbouring country has become decidedly tricky in recent years. The Syrian embassy in Turkey is the only embassy that is still officially issuing visas to non-residents. Foreigners can apply at either the consulate in Istanbul or the embassy in Ankara. Visas take 1 working day to be processed and you will need to bring along a letter of recommendation from your country's embassy in Turkey, which you will most likely be charged a hefty fee for. Please be aware that some countries embassies refuse to supply letters of recommendation. Officially you can only apply for a Syrian visa in Jordan if you don't have a Syrian embassy in your home country, though in practice even if this is the case, you may be turned away and told to get your visa on the border. The Syrian embassy in Egypt has also stopped processing visas for foreigners, though there is always the odd exception to the rule that succeeds in getting one. As there is no Syrian embassy in Lebanon it is impossible to apply for a visa from there.

Visa extensions (of up to 2 months) are easily obtained once in Syria from any office of the Immigration and Passport Department, which have a branch in most main towns. Don't bother applying for an extension until your 14th day or you will most likely be told to come back again. Processing of extensions can usually be done on the same day and you will have to supply about 6 passport-sized photographs and a letter from your hotel. The cost of the extension varies from office to office but is always minimal. In general it is usually easier and faster to apply for an extension in any town other than Damascus (the offices in Tartus, Lattakia and Hama are particularly efficient).

Immigration

On arrival in Syria you have to fill out an **entry/exit card**. Keep this with you at all times throughout your trip in Syria as when you leave the country you will be asked to hand it in.

Weights and measures

The metric system is used in Syria.

Women travellers

Generally, women travelling alone in Syria experience no more harassment than is the norm in most European countries; the majority report it to be amongst the most relaxed country in the Middle East in this respect. While solo female travel can be demanding, there are also distinct advantages. In the vast majority of situations women are treated with great respect. Seasoned female travellers in Syria argue that they get the best of both worlds. As a foreigner they are generally accorded the status of 'honorary males' in public, while in private they have access to female society, from which men are excluded. When invited to a Muslim Syrian household, male guests are usually confined to the guest room while women are whisked away behind the scenes into the 'real' household, where they can meet wives, mothers, sisters and other members of the extended family.

Amongst Syria's Christians (and amongst wealthier Syrians of any background), social etiquette and codes of dress are much more relaxed. Nevertheless, women travellers should make an effort to dress modestly and will find they garner more respect and experience less hassle if they do. Wearing a wedding ring may help to classify you as 'respectably married', while photos of a husband and children (whether real or imaginary) will further raise your status.

Remember that most Syrian women do not travel alone, and in more remote areas are rarely seen in public. The widely held perception of Western women is based on the images in Western magazines, films and satellite TV, which portray them as having 'loose' sexual morals. This can lead to problems of sexual harassment. Cases of violent sexual assault are, however, extremely rare and a firm, unambiguous response will deal with most situations. In public, the best approach is to make a scene; someone is bound to come to your aid, while the perpetrator will quickly vanish in a cloud of shame. Predictably enough, many women travellers report receiving far more unwanted attention after dark in the red-light districts of Damascus (Martyrs' Square) and Aleppo (the area of cheap hotels bounded by Baron St, Al-Maari St, Al-Kouwatly St and Bab al-Faraj St).

Working and volunteering

Work and volunteer opportunities in Syria are few and far between. A useful website for volunteer opportunities is www.volunteer abroad.com/Syria. If you have a TEFL (Teaching English as a Foreign Language) qualification, you may be able to find work as a teacher. The British Council (Maysaloun St, Shaalan, Damascus, T011-331 0631, www.britishcouncil.org/syria, and Al-Sabeel Dabbagh Building, Franciscan St, Aleppo, T021-228 0302) recruits qualified English teachers from the UK for their language programs. Another option is Berlitz (Bramkeh, Damascus, T011-213 2256, and Aleppo, T021-263 2715, www.bertitz.sy), who have language centres teaching English, French, German and Spanish.

Contents

Footprint features

Damascus & around

Ancient and beautiful, Damascus doesn't fail to enchant. The Old City is a maze of creaky old buildings that slump over twisting, narrow alleyways and getting lost is a mandatory part of the experience. During the day the winding streets of this fascinating quarter are alive with the bustle of shoppers and sightseers bargaining over goods in the souqs, while in the evening, old men dust off their backgammon boards and set up camp outside on the pavement, engrossed in battle.

At the heart of it all is the Umayyad Mosque, its huge dome and minarets rising majestically above its surroundings. But the mosque's history, just like that of the city itself, stretches back far beyond Islamic times. This is the city where St Paul was baptized and began his preaching, where all the great trade routes of the world once converged in an ancient hub of commerce. Local legend even claims that this is the setting of the original Garden of Eden. It's no wonder that Damascus lays claim to the title of oldest continuously inhabited city in the world.

Look a little deeper behind this picturesque daydream of a city and you'll notice the vibrant modern progress as well. Tourism is booming here and behind nondescript doors in dusty alleys lie sumptuous palaces restored to their former glory as boutique hotels and restaurants. If you want to live out any Arabian Nights-style fairytale then this is the place to splash out and do it. Young, upwardly mobile Syrians flock to the pavement-terraces of European-style cafés that have brought cappuccino culture to the city. Outside the walls the sprawling metropolis of the new town may not be as pretty as the Old City but is host to the fabulous National Museum, a must-see for anyone interested in Syria's history.

If you can pull yourself away from exploring the Old City's nooks and crannies, there are several day trips that can be comfortably made from here, including the cliff-side village of Maaloula, where they still speak the language of Christ and the black basalt ruins of Bosra to the south, one of Syria's best preserved Roman era sights.

Damascus

Most of the city's sights are concentrated in the Old City and, if you have limited time, this is where you should focus your sightseeing. The various monuments are described below in as near as possible a logical order, but when exploring the Old City it is not really possible to conduct a detailed tour without a considerable amount of doubling back on yourself.
▶▶ *For listings, see pages 70-80.*

Ins and outs

Getting there and away

Damascus is Syria's major transport hub with frequent connections stretching to all major centres in the country by public transport. There are also bus services to Jordan, Lebanon and Turkey from here. Microbuses ply the routes between the city and the small surrounding towns (such as Maaloula), which the bigger buses don't service.

Damascus International Airport is roughly 30 km to the southeast of the city centre and handles the vast majority of international flights arriving in Syria as well as frequent domestic flights to Aleppo and Lattakia and a few per week to Qamishle and Deir ez-Zor. There is a taxi-stand inside the airport terminal. A taxi to the city centre will cost about S£700, but if you arrive late at night you may be charged more.

The city has two major bus stations. The Harasta Pullman Bus Station services all destinations to the north of Damascus including transport from Turkey, while the Al-Samariyeh Bus Station has connections to all the destinations to the south, including Jordan and Lebanon. Both terminals are out of the city centre. A taxi from either to the centre should cost around S£90.

All trains arrive into Kadem Station. There are good connections to Aleppo and daily services from Lattakia, Tartus, Deir-ez Zor, Hassakeh and Qameshli. There is a friendly and helpful information desk here. A taxi from the station into the city centre will cost about S£70.

Getting around

Damascus is a relatively compact city, and for the most part walking is the best way to get around (in the Old City it is really the only way). Taxis are plentiful and cheap (S£30-40 for trips within the city centre) and therefore a convenient way to get between districts, or to/from the bus and train stations. These days, most have working meters; but if not, agree on a fare before setting off. The microbuses ('*meecro*' or '*servees*'), which zip all over the city, are difficult to get to grips with unless you can read Arabic, though certain routes can be useful.

One of the main terminals for microbuses is under Assad Bridge. There are services from here to the Harasta Pullman bus station as well as to Abbaseen and Mezzeh. Journeys cost S£5-10. Bear in mind that they cannot really accommodate large items of luggage, although you can always try paying for two seats.

Orientation

Although modern-day Damascus spreads over a large area, its core is surprisingly compact. The Old City comprises a distinct area, enclosed within city walls which, for the most part, still survive. Immediately to the northwest of this is the main centre of the modern city. Here, Martyrs' Square (in Arabic 'al-Marjeh', but also known as Al-Shouhada Square) is the focus for many of the cheap hotels and restaurants (this is also Damascus' 'red-light' district).

Running west from the Citadel, which is situated at the northwest corner of the Old City, An Naser Street takes you past the Hejaz railway station, terminus for the famous Hejaz railway line, from where a major north-south axis runs along Said al-Jabri, Port Said and 29 May streets passing through the main commercial and business centre of the city. Intersecting this north-south axis is another major east-west axis, Shoukri al-Kouwatli Street.

Heading west, this takes you past the Tekkiyeh as-Suleimaniyeh complex and the National Museum, separated from the main road by a branch of the Barada River, before reaching Umawiyeen 'Square' (in fact a huge roundabout).

Just west of the National Museum the large Assad Bridge crosses Shoukri al-Kouwatli Street. Following it north and then northwest leads you up into the modern, fashionable Abu Roumaneh district where many of the foreign embassies are located. Further north still, the long ridge of Kassioun mountain dominates the skyline, with the ancient districts of Salihiye/Al-Charkasiye, once separated from the old city by countryside, strung out along its lower slopes.

1 Damascus overview

➡ Damascus maps
1 Damascus overview, page 40
2 Damascus centre, page 46
3 Damascus Old City, page 48
4 Umayyad Mosque, page 51

Extending southwest from Umawiyeen Square, meanwhile, is the modern district of Al-Mezzeh, strung out along the busy thoroughfare of Fayez Mansour Street. This newly affluent area of Damascus also houses a number of foreign embassies.

Tourist information

Main Tourist office ① *29 May St, T011-232 3953, www.syriantourism.org, Sat-Thu 0930-1900.* The staff on duty are friendly but the most information you'll get is a free map and some pamphlets. They have a habit of running out of English-language maps at this office but seem to have a huge stock of German- and French-language ones.

There's also a **Tourist Information Counter** ① *at the airport, open 24 hrs in theory but often unattended,* and a little **tourist office** ① *at the entrance to the Handicrafts Market, just off Omar Ben Abi Rabeea St, daily 0900-1900 (approx).* The staff here are ultra-friendly and seem to be more switched on with information.

Background

Earliest stages

The setting of Damascus is the key to its historical importance, and that a permanent settlement should develop here is no surprise. The Barada river, flowing down from the Anti-Lebanon mountains to the northeast, waters the *Ghouta* plain below and has created a large, fertile oasis on the edge of an otherwise harsh and inhospitable desert stretching south and east. Over the centuries, Damascus has continually found itself at an important strategic and commercial crossroads.

It is precisely because Damascus has been inhabited continuously throughout its long history that there is very little physical evidence of the earliest stages of its settlement. Each successive civilization has built over the foundations of the one which proceeded it. Excavations in the Old City and at Tel as-Salihiye to the east have nevertheless revealed evidence of settlement during the fourth and third millenniums BC respectively. Our knowledge of the early history of the city, however, comes primarily from fragmentary literary sources.

Amongst the large numbers of tablets discovered at Mari (see page 300), some, which date back to 2500 BC, make reference to Damascus (then known as *Dimashqa*), while slightly later tablets from Ebla (see page 143) make reference to *Dimaski*, although its exact relationship with these important city-states is far from clear.

Ancient empires

From around 2000 BC Damascus was settled by the **Amorites**, one of the many waves of Semitic peoples to migrate from the desert interior of the Arabian peninsula and settle in the fertile lands further north. Some 500 years later, the city came under **Egyptian** influence during the rule of Thutmosis III, as recorded in the Amarna tablets. In turn it then came under the control of the other great regional power of the time, the **Hittites**.

Sometime after 1200 BC the **Aramaeans** established themselves in the city, and from the 10th to eighth centuries BC *Aram Damascus* was the seat of an important Aramaean kingdom. It was during this period that the Temple of Haddad was built on the site of what is now the Umayyad Mosque. The Aramaeans clashed repeatedly with the biblical kingdoms of Israel and Judah, limiting their northward expansion, as chronicled at length in the Old Testament. At the same time, the Aramaeans came under repeated attack from the growing **Assyrian** Empire in northern Mesopotamia, and finally in 732 BC the city was devastated by the Assyrian king, Tiglath Pileser III. The **Babylonians** followed in 572 BC, led by King Nebuchadnezzar, and the **Achaemenid Persians** in 539 BC, under King Cyrus.

Greek and Roman eras

Following the defeat of the Persians by the **Greeks** at the battle of Issus, one of Alexander the Great's generals, Parmenion, captured Damascus in 332 BC and it was under subsequent Greek rule that a planned grid pattern of development was first applied to the city.

With the death of Alexander the Great in 323 BC, Damascus then found itself caught for two centuries between the competing ambitions of the **Seleucid** and **Ptolemid** Empires. However, decline in the influence of both left the door open to the **Nabateans** who, under Aretas III (84-56 BC), extended their empire to include Damascus.

The first **Roman** conquest of Syria came as early as 64 BC, but Damascus at that point remained of peripheral importance, with Nabatean control over what was effectively a semi-independent city-state continuing until as late as AD 54. Thus events such as the conversion of St Paul in the early years of Christianity took place before direct Roman control had been established. However, in the first century AD the Romans took direct control of Damascus and from that point onwards it grew in importance. In AD 117 the Emperor Hadrian declared it a metropolis, and in AD 222 Severus raised its status to that of a colony. Trade across what was now a relatively stable Roman Empire flourished, and Damascus reaped the rewards of being an important centre at the junction of major caravan routes.

There was a characteristically Roman flurry of building activity during this period. A *castrum* on the site of the citadel was established. The city walls were strengthened and gates were installed. The Temple of Haddad was expanded and embellished to become the Temple of Jupiter. The Via Recta (Straight Street) was widened and colonnaded to create the *decumanus maximus* and aqueducts were built; adding to the system of irrigation first developed by the Aramaeans to harness the waters of the Barada.

Byzantine Damascus

During the **Byzantine** era (from the fourth century AD) Christianity became firmly established in the city. The Temple of Jupiter was converted into a church dedicated to St John the Baptist and Damascus became the seat of a bishopric, second only to the patriarchate in Antioch. However, the Byzantine Empire found itself under constant threat from the **Sassanid Persians** and eventually in AD 612 Damascus was briefly occupied by them, before being regained by Heraclius in AD 628.

The Islamic empire's capital

This brief incursion by the Sassanids was the prelude to a far more permanent transition brought about by the expansion of the **Islamic** Empire of the nomadic tribes of the Arabian peninsula following the death of their Prophet Muhammad. Led by Khalid Ibn al-Walid, the Muslim army first took Damascus in AD 635, withdrawing to defeat Heraclius in the decisive battle of Yarmouk before occupying the city permanently in AD 636. Under this new regime, Damascus was at first a relatively unimportant outpost of an Islamic Empire whose political centre was Medina. However, in AD 661 the governor of Damascus, Mu'awiya, assumed the title of Caliph, initiating the **Umayyad** Dynasty and making Damascus the new capital of the Islamic Empire. For Syria, and particularly Damascus, this resulted in a great cultural flowering, most eloquently and enduringly expressed in the architecture of the Umayyad Mosque.

Umayyad rule lasted for nearly a hundred years until in AD 750 a new dynasty, that of the **Abbasids**, was established. Damascus was replaced by Baghdad as the capital of the Islamic Empire, and fell into decline. The unity of the now huge Islamic Empire began to give way to competing spheres of influence centred on Baghdad, Cairo, Mosul and Aleppo, with Damascus caught between them. From the ninth century it came under the control of the **Tulunids**, **Ikshidids** and **Fatimids** of Egypt, before passing in 1076 to the **Seljuk Turks** who had by then expanded from their capital at Isfahan to take control of both Aleppo and Mosul.

Seljuk rule was in an advanced state of decline by the time the **Crusaders** arrived in the 12th century. However, despite coming under attack three times in the first half of the century, Damascus was never taken by the Crusaders. Nur ud-Din, the **Zengid** ruler of Aleppo, assumed control of the city in 1154, and was followed by Salah ud-Din in 1174, who by that time had overthrown the Fatimids of Egypt to establish the **Ayyubid** Dynasty. Together, Nur ud-Din and Salah ud-Din led the Muslim resistance to the Crusaders and Damascus flourished once again as an important political centre.

The first **Mongol** invasion of 1260 brought devastation to Damascus and an abrupt end to Ayyubid rule. However the **Mamluk** Dynasty of Egypt quickly came to the rescue, defeating the Mongols and establishing their rule in Syria. Damascus flourished yet again, particularly under the rule of Baibars (1260-1277) and later under the governorship of Tengiz (1312-1339), becoming a second capital after Cairo and witnessing another burst of building activity. The Mongol threat continued, however, and after repelling an attack in 1299-1300, the city was largely destroyed by the Mongol leader Tamerlane in 1400. Although Mamluk rule was restored, the city never fully recovered under them.

Ottoman era

In 1516 the **Ottoman Turks**, led by Selim I, took Damascus and incorporated Syria into their huge empire. The Ottoman's control and protection of the *Hajj* (pilgrimage to Mecca) helped reinforce their claim to the Caliphate, and throughout their 400 years of rule Damascus was of central importance as the last great staging post on the annual pilgrimage. Inevitably for such a large empire, the city's governors enjoyed a large degree of independence. Indeed, the first Pasha of Damascus, **Al-Ghazali**, declared himself independent of Ottoman rule and the city suffered considerable damage when it was retaken by the armies of Suleiman I in 1521.

Later pashas exercised their independence more cautiously. Amongst the **Azem** family, who between themselves ruled for most of the 18th century, Darwish Pasha, Murad Pasha and most notably Assad Pasha were competent governors who did much to improve the city. However, corruption and stagnation began to set in and when Muhammad Ali, the Pasha of Cairo, rose against Ottoman rule in 1805, Damascus soon followed suit and control of the city passed to Muhammad Ali's son **Ibrahim** Pasha in 1832. His rule lasted until 1840 and saw a brief burst of civic improvements but the return to direct Ottoman rule also saw a return to stagnation. In 1860, clashes between Christian and Druze minorities in Lebanon spread to Damascus and culminated in a massacre of Christians living in the city, the Christians having maintained a minimal presence here since the Byzantine era. **Midhat** Pasha brought further civic improvements towards the end of the 19th century, and at the same time Damascus, with its large concentration of intellectuals, became a centre of Arab nationalism.

The French mandate and road to independence

When the Ottoman Turks allied with the Germans at the start of the First World War, Damascus became yet again an important strategic centre and its fall to the Allied forces in 1918 heralded the fall of the Ottoman Empire. The Arab nationalist dream of an independent Syria was briefly recognized under the leadership of **Feisal** (see page 327), who had been central to the Arab revolt upon which the Allies had relied so heavily. However, in the superpower carve-up that inevitably followed, this was replaced by French Mandate rule in 1920 and Damascus became for a while the capital of a mini-state. In 1925 an uprising against the French resulted in the bombing of Damascus which caused considerable damage, but it was not until 1945 that the city became the capital of an independent Syrian Arab Republic.

Modern Damascus

Today Damascus is a sprawling metropolis with all the trappings of a modern capital and Syria's major commercial and government hub. Like all large cities in the region it struggles with the problems of traffic, pollution and coping with an ever-expanding population caused by rural to urban drift in the last 50 years. This has been exacerbated recently by the huge number of Iraqi refugees who have flooded into Damascus since the Iraq war (see page 337).

Despite its problems, Damascus today is a vibrant, outward-looking city. Tourism is booming here and more and more derelict buildings in the Old City are being restored so that they can enjoy a new life as upmarket hotels and restaurants. There is a new push towards better urban planning to help ease the problems of over-population and an ambitious project for a Damascus metro line, helping to ease congestion on the city streets, is planned to be up and running by 2016. Damascenes are looking towards the future and the future, in this most ancient of cities, looks bright.

Sights

Citadel

① *Officially closed to the public and only opened up for concerts, but the north-side entrance is usually left open and nobody seems to mind if you wander in and have a look.*

The Citadel is an imposing structure standing at the northwest corner of the Old City, its massive western wall facing directly onto the modern thoroughfare of Ath Thawra Street. At the time of writing, it was undergoing extensive restoration – a painfully slow process which has been going on for more than 10 years – and closed to visitors. However you can view its walls from the outside and get some insight into the different stages of its tumultuous history. If you're in Damascus during one of the city's festivals (such as the Silk Road Festival) you may be lucky enough to gain access. The citadel is opened up and used to stage all of the city's major events.

Background

The site appears to have been utilized as a *castrum* or military camp during Roman times, probably during the reign of Diocletian, AD 284-305. Then, during the Byzantine and early Islamic periods, it was expanded to occupy roughly its present extent. After that there are no clear references to it until the Seljuk period (1058-1157) when a new fortress was constructed. After Salah ud-Din took control of Damascus in 1174 he strengthened it, adding a tower, and it became an important centre for his military operations. Most of what can be seen today, however, dates from the 13th century.

Under threat from both the Crusader attack and local Syrian intrigues, Al-Adil, brother of Salah ud-Din and successor to the Ayyubid leadership, set about building a new citadel in 1202. Work continued until well after his death, with new walls and towers being constructed along with a palace complex and mosque. In 1260 the great Mongol invasions from the east reached Damascus and the citadel was largely destroyed. It was subsequently rebuilt by the Mamluk Sultan Baibars, only to be attacked again by the Mongols in the 1300, and then destroyed by Tamerlane in 1400. During the Ottoman period the citadel was partially repaired but its importance declined and it gradually fell into disuse. Following Syrian independence, it was used once again as a barracks, and then later as a prison before work started on its restoration as a historic monument.

Tour of the citadel walls

Facing the western wall of the citadel from Ath Thawra Street, the whole of the southwest tower along with the curtain wall up to the small central gate is an obviously modern reconstruction. The new stonework is rather too neat and crisp perhaps, but it gives a good idea of the full proportions of the massive, solid southwest tower. This tower has carried the full brunt of sieges, fires and earthquakes over the centuries; since Al-Adil first built it in roughly its present form at the start of the 13th century, it has been destroyed and rebuilt no less than six times.

The remainder of the western wall has also been largely reconstructed, but this time using old stones from the Ayyubid and Mamluk periods. Various recycled architectural fragments bearing inscriptions and insignia can be seen in the upper parts of these walls. At eye level, just to the right of the central gate, there is one interesting block carved with a dragon and rosette (though unfortunately placed upside-down, making it a little difficult to identify as such). Note also the recently discovered and only partially reconstructed tower to the right of the main gate, thought to be one of two flanking it, which were built by Baibars but destroyed in an earthquake in 1759 and never rebuilt. The large metal statue of a mounted soldier in flowing gown that stands by the main gate is of Salah ud-Din.

The northwest tower shows evidence of various different stages of construction and reconstruction in its stonework, from the Ayyubid through to the Ottoman periods. When Baibars restored the citadel, he had a belvedere built on top of this tower, from where he would review his troops and hold audiences.

From the corner of the northwest tower, you can follow the small cobbled street that runs between the Barada River and the northern wall (this also makes a pleasant alternative to Hamidiyeh Souq as a way of reaching the Umayyad Mosque and surrounding areas). The stonework you see is entirely of Mamluk origin (with later reconstructions), Baibars having built a new wall some 10 m in front of Al-Adil's. You first pass a small squat tower with an inscription on the north face commemorating its reconstruction in 1508. The street then passes under an arch with an inscription above it. Once through the arch you are in fact inside the remains of another tower, rebuilt according to the inscription by Nawruz al-Haifizi in 1407. Further on is a rectangular tower with just a very small central entrance and three arrow slits in the walls. You come next to the northeast corner tower which shows evidence of repeated repair and reconstruction. Turning right, you can see in the east wall of the tower an Arabic inscription in an elaborate frame; the inscription names Al-Adil as the builder of the tower, although it was probably taken from another tower and re-used here during later repair and reconstruction work. From here you can visit the nearby gate to the Old City, Bab al-Faraj, and work your way along the northern section of the city walls, taking in also Bab al-Faradis, Bab as-Salaam and Bab Touma (see page 62).

② Damascus centre

➡ Damascus maps
1 Damascus overview, page 40
2 **Damascus centre, page 46**
3 Damascus Old City, page 48
4 Umayyad Mosque, page 51

200 metres
200 yards

Sleeping
Afamia 1 C3
Al-Haramain 2 C5

Al-Rabie 3 C5
Al-Saada 4 C5
French Palace 5 A5

Ghazal 6 C5
Orient Palace 7 C3
Salam 8 C2

Following the eastern wall southwards there are various fragments of inscriptions in it, followed by a long rectangular tower and then the large central gateway, today largely obscured by modern buildings. The remainder of the east wall, along with the whole of the south wall parallel with Hamidiyeh Souq, are likewise obscured.

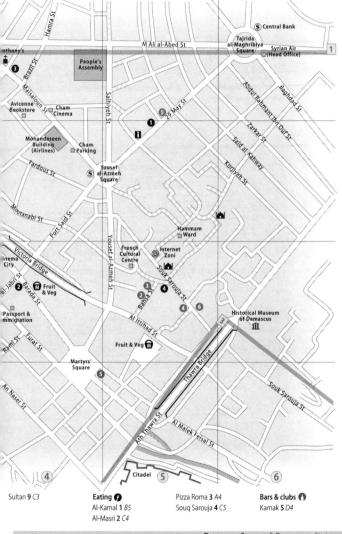

Sultan 9 C3

Eating
Al-Kamal 1 B5
Al-Masri 2 C4

Pizza Roma 3 A4
Souq Sarouja 4 C5

Bars & clubs
Karnak 5 D4

Old City

The Old City, retaining so much of its long and varied history, is certainly Damascus' greatest attraction. As soon as you step into it, you are drawn into a completely different, medieval world, only brought back to the present by the ringing horns of cars, trying to navigate the narrow lanes. From Saturday to Thursday you'll find yourself being swept along by the

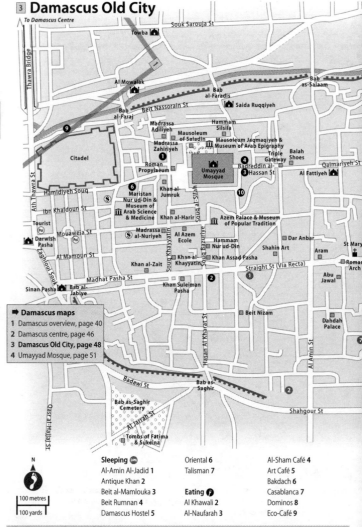

3 Damascus Old City

To Damascus Centre

Souk Sarouja St

Towba

Thawra Bridge

Bab as-Salaam

Al Mowalak

Bab al-Faradis

Beit Nassorain St

Bab al-Faraj

Saida Ruqqiyeh

Hammam Silsila

Madrassa Adiliyeh

Mausoleum of Saladin

Mausoleum Jaqmaqiyeh & Museum of Arab Epigraphy

Madrassa Zahiriyeh

Triple Gateway

Balah Shoes

Citadel

Roman Propylaeum

Umayyad Mosque

Badreddin al-Hassan St

Qaimariyeh St

Al Fattiyeh

Hamidiyeh Souq

Ath Thawra St

Maristan Nur ud-Din & Museum of Arab Science & Medicine

Khan al-Jumruk

Ibn Khaldoun St

Khan al-Harir

Azem Palace & Museum of Popular Tradition

Tourist

Darwish Pasha

Mouaweia St

Madrassa al-Nuriyeh

Al Azem Ecole

Dar Anbar

St Mary

Al Mamoun St

Khan al-Zait

Khan al-Khayyatin

Hammam Nur ud-Din

Shahin Art

Aram

Romar Arch

Souq al-Sitah

Souq Bazuriye

Khan Assad Pasha

Straight St (Via Recta)

Madhat Pasha St

Khan Suleiman Pasha

Abu Jawal

Sinan Pasha

Bab al-Jabiye

Beit Nizam

Dahdah Palace

Hasan Al Kharat St

Al Amin St

Badawi St

Bab as-Saghir

Qasr al-Hajaj St

Bab as-Saghir Cemetery

Al Jarrah St

Shahgour St

Tombs of Fatima & Sukeina

➡ Damascus maps
1 Damascus overview, page 40
2 Damascus centre, page 46
3 Damascus Old City, page 48
4 Umayyad Mosque, page 51

N

100 metres
100 yards

Sleeping
Al-Amin Al-Jadid 1
Antique Khan 2
Beit al-Mamlouka 3
Beit Rumnan 4
Damascus Hostel 5

Oriental 6
Talisman 7

Eating
Al Khawali 2
Al-Naufarah 3

Al-Sham Café 4
Art Café 5
Bakdach 6
Casablanca 7
Dominos 8
Eco-Café 9

crowds of shoppers scouring the ancient souqs for bargains or the shrouded groups of pilgrims threading their way through the streets to visit another sight. Visit on Friday morning and you'll find a different world, with most of the city silent and shut down.

Around practically every corner you will find another beautiful and atmospheric historic monument. Such immediate history might become overwhelming were it not for the fact that so many of these monuments are still in use, set firmly in the context of a living city.

Leilas **10**
Old Town **11**

Piano Bar **13**

Bars & clubs 🌓
Abu al-Azz **1**
Ninar Art Café **12**

Hamidiyeh Souq

This is the best way to enter the Old City for the first time, taking you through a colourful and lively souq directly to the Umayyad Mosque. This is a thoroughly Syrian market, and while travellers might hunt around for antique silver jewellery or Bedouin carpets, there are more people shopping for everyday items such as fabric, clothes, kitchen utensils, etc. In its present form the souq dates from the late 19th century, when the governor of Damascus, Rashid Nasha Pasha, modified the existing Souq al-Jadid by widening and straightening it, constructing two-storey shops along its length and erecting the corrugated-iron roofing. On completion, it was named after the Ottoman Sultan, Abdel Hamid II. History has taken its toll on the corrugated-iron roofing: the holes which pepper it were the result of the triumphant rifle shots of the Arab forces who rode into the city in the wake of the Ottoman and German retreat of 1917 and, later, the machine-gun fire rained down by French planes during the Druze rebellion of 1925.

As you approach the end of Hamadiyeh Souq, you get a glimpse of the towering, majestic southwest minaret of the Umayyad Mosque. At the same time, the remains of a **Roman Propylaeum** or monumental gateway (often mistakenly referred to as a triumphal arch) appear in front of you, marking the end of the souq. To the left are two huge free-standing columns and capitals, while to the right, three equally large columns and capitals support a segment of the original massive semi-circular arch, framed within a triangular pediment, which would once have extended across six columns. The *propylaeum* marks the outer gateway at the western end of the Temple of Jupiter which once stood on the present site of the Umayyad Mosque (see below). The Temple would originally have been approached from the east side, so that this *propylaeum* was in fact primarily an exit and the decoration is therefore on the inside. The best way to view the Roman remains is from the mosque side; from here you can see the true scale of the arch as well as the intricate decoration that adorns it.

Running at right angles to the *propylaeum* are the remains of an arcade, in fact a Byzantine shopping complex dating from around AD 330-340. Today, various Koran sellers can be found plying their trade along its length. Beyond this, you come out into an open square, cleared in recent years of the numerous shops and stalls that once filled the area. In front of you is the towering west wall of the Umayyad Mosque, 150 m in length and rising to over 100 m. Its stonework contains in it a record of the various historical phases, from the large-block lower courses of Roman origin, through the smaller stones of early Arab/Muslim times, to the occasional patches of modern restoration.

Umayyad Mosque

① *The ticket office is through a small gate to the left of the mosque's main entrance, signposted 'putting on special clothes room'. The usual tourist entrance is via the north gate (Bab al-Amara) which you access through the gardens, past the Mausoleum of Salah ud-Din. At the time of writing the gardens were a messy building site and tourists were being allowed to enter through the main gate in the west wall, Bab al-Barid, after buying their tickets. Open daily for tourists, except Fri 1230-1400 when it's closed for main prayers. Non-Muslims S£50 (includes entry to Mausoleum of Salah ud-Din). Women must wear the provided abeyyas and men not dressed modestly (knees showing) will have to wear a long skirt. Shoes must be taken off before entering the mosque and are carried with you (a small bag is handy for this).*

However many times you visit the Umayyad Mosque, the impact of this awe-inspiring building remains undiminished. If anything, it grows on you with every visit, and once you have paid due attention to the various architectural details, you are free to let the overall effect and atmosphere slowly soak in. And for all its grandeur and religious importance (it is one of the great holy sites of Islam after Mecca, Medina and the Dome of the Rock in Jerusalem), it is in no way a sombre place. Quite the contrary; gangs of young children run around the courtyard laughing and playing freely while families and groups of worshippers come and go; the scale and calm and beauty of the place easily absorbing and embracing the throng of human activity while never oppressing it. Here you can leave behind the crowds and congestion of Damascus and enter another world altogether, one which still manages to maintain a connection with the human and the ordinary, while at the same time somehow lifting it up into another level of significance.

Background

The Umayyad Mosque stands on a site of religious importance dating back to the second millennium BC. At this time a temple to Hadad, the **Aramaean** god of rain and fertility, and his consort Atargatis, existed here, although little is known about its exact form or extent. These gods came in time to be identified with the **Roman** gods Jupiter and Venus, and under Roman patronage the temple was expanded in the first century AD and then further embellished under the reign of Septimus Severus (AD 193-211), becoming known in the process as the Temple of Jupiter. The inner enclosure or *temenos* of the temple corresponded approximately with the walls of the present mosque and within this would have been the *cella* or central shrine. Surrounding the *temenos* was a much larger outer courtyard marked by a portico pierced by four gateways, traces of which still survive in the western *propylaeum* (see above) and also in the eastern triple-arched *propylaeum* and the column bases to the north of it (see below).

With the adoption of Christianity as the official religion of the Roman Empire (the point which also marks the start of the **Byzantine** era), the Temple of Jupiter was converted into a Christian church and dedicated to St John the Baptist, most probably during the reign of Emperor Theodosius (AD 379-395), who is thought to have ordered the destruction of the pagan shrine in the first year of his rule. In AD 636, following the defeat of the Byzantine forces of Heraclius at the Battle of Yarmouk, the Arab armies of Islam took Damascus. Initially, Christians continued to worship in the church, sharing the huge compound with Muslims who built a small *mihrab* in the south wall, which faced in the direction of Mecca.

However in AD 661, under the **Umayyad** Dynasty, Damascus became the capital of the Islamic Empire and with this shift, pressure increased for a purely Muslim place of worship. It was under the Umayyad Caliph Khalid Ibn al-Walid that the huge compound was finally appropriated and work started on an Islamic mosque on a grand scale in AD 708. The enterprise was an enormous one, which suffered various setbacks and entailed massive expenditure, but the end result was the greatest monument to Islam of that period.

Over the centuries the mosque has survived invasions, sackings, earthquakes and fires, although with each calamity it has undergone a transformation of one sort or another. The most devastating, and most recent calamity, came in 1893 when a fire largely destroyed the prayer hall. Restoration, involving the replacement of the interior columns

④ Umayyad Mosque

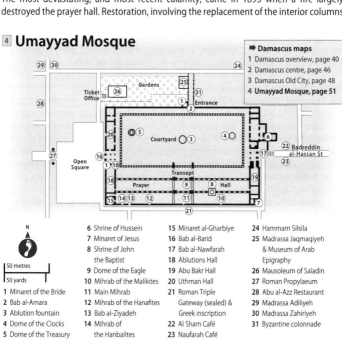

➡ **Damascus maps**
1 Damascus overview, page 40
2 Damascus centre, page 46
3 Damascus Old City, page 48
4 Umayyad Mosque, page 51

1 Minaret of the Bride
2 Bab al-Amara
3 Ablution fountain
4 Dome of the Clocks
5 Dome of the Treasury
6 Shrine of Hussein
7 Minaret of Jesus
8 Shrine of John the Baptist
9 Dome of the Eagle
10 Mihrab of the Malikites
11 Main Mihrab
12 Mihrab of the Hanafites
13 Bab al-Ziyadeh
14 Mihrab of the Hanbalites
15 Minaret al-Gharbiye
16 Bab al-Barid
17 Bab al-Nawfarah
18 Ablutions Hall
19 Abu Bakr Hall
20 Uthman Hall
21 Roman Triple Gateway (sealed) & Greek inscription
22 Al Sham Café
23 Naufarah Café
24 Hammam Silsila
25 Madrassa Jaqmaqiyeh & Museum of Arab Epigraphy
26 Mausoleum of Saladin
27 Roman Propylaeum
28 Abu al-Azz Restaurant
29 Madrassa Adiliyeh
30 Madrassa Zahiriyeh
31 Byzantine colonnade

Khalid Ibn al-Walid and the Umayyad Mosque

The Umayyad period brought with it a great flowering of architectural expression in Syria, drawing inspiration from the rich Byzantine, Persian, Mesopotamian and local influences which existed at the time. Khalid Ibn al-Walid, the sixth Umayyad Caliph, was famous in particular for his architectural enterprises. He was responsible for the building of the Al-Aqsa mosque in Jerusalem, and for the Great Mosque in Medina.

Al-Walid ordered work to start on the building of the Umayyad Mosque in Damascus in AD 708. The project lasted for seven years, reaching completion in AD 715, the same year as his death. Thousands of craftsmen were brought in from Constantinople and Egypt to work alongside the Syrian craftsmen. Originally, practically every surface was covered with mosaics, including the whole of the floor of the courtyard. Inside the prayer hall, 600 gold lanterns hung from the ceilings, while all the column capitals were plated with gold.

According to one account, it cost the state's entire revenue throughout this period. Another account relates how 400 chests each containing 14,000 dinars were needed to pay for the work, and that a total of 18 camels were needed to bring the receipts to Al-Walid, who had them burnt without even looking at them, saying: "We spent this for Allah and shall make no account of it."

and central dome, was undertaken by the Ottomans, although much of the original decoration and beauty were lost in the process. However, for all that, and perhaps because of the amalgam of different influences and modifications over the centuries, today the Umayyad Mosque stands out as an exceptionally beautiful monument.

Visiting the mosque

The courtyard The northern **Bab al-Amara** gate brings you into the courtyard of the mosque, with the prayer hall and its striking mosaic-covered central transept in front of you. The **courtyard**, measuring over 50 m by 120 m, is a huge open space paved with white marble slabs. These date from the late 19th-century restoration, which followed the great fire of 1893. Their effect is quite striking, particularly in bright sunlight, although one can only imagine what it must have been like when the whole area was covered with mosaics.

Surrounding the courtyard on three sides is an **arcade**. Along the east and west sides of the courtyard the arcade retains its original pattern of two circular columns interspaced by a square pillar, the latter being newly clad in marble, while along the north side, except for a few columns at either end, all have been replaced over the centuries by square pillars and recently clad. The inside walls of the arcades have likewise been decorated with marble as part of ongoing restoration work. All three arcades are topped by a smaller upper-storey arcade of delicate columns and arches, with fragments of mosaic surviving in places.

In the centre of the courtyard there is an **ablution fountain** of recent origin and on either side of it are small columns topped by newly added metal globes, meant to hold lanterns. Towards the west end of the courtyard, supported on eight columns topped by ornate Corinthian capitals, is a large, mosaic-covered octagonal structure with a domed top. This is known as the **Dome of the Treasury** (*Khubbet al-Khazneh* or *Beit al-Hal*). The structure, as the name suggests, was the mosque's treasury. It is thought to have been built in AD 788 by the Abbasid governor of Damascus, Fadil Ibn Salih, although the columns and capitals on which it rests are clearly recycled from Roman times. The fine mosaic work itself, consisting of plant motifs in green and gold, probably dates from 13th- or 14th-century restoration work. Towards the eastern end of the courtyard there is a smaller structure of identical design, though without the mosaic work and built much later (18th or 19th century), popularly known as the **Dome of the Clocks**. Predictably enough, it was used to house the mosque's clock collection.

In the northeast corner of the mosque, a doorway leads through into the **Shrine of Hussein**. According to legend, the head of this Shi'ite martyr, killed at the Battle of Karbala (see page 340), was brought here and placed in a niche by the Caliph Yazid as a way of humiliating the followers of Ali. Today the niche is fronted by a silver grille and has become an important place of pilgrimage for Shi'ites who come here in large numbers, although there are conflicting traditions as to the final resting place of his head.

Mosaics and minarets The most striking feature of the prayer hall from the outside is the façade of the central transept, which is covered in mosaics. It is by looking at these mosaics that you can best conjure up an idea of what the mosque originally looked like when almost every surface was likewise adorned. The mosaic work on the central transept consists largely of restoration carried out in the 1960s, with only the darker patches being original. The other area where sections of mosaic have been preserved and restored is along the western arcade. On the inside wall, towards the northern end, is a section known as the **Barada Panel**. The theory is that this is a depiction of the Barada River, lined with lush vegetation and enticing villas, as it was in ancient times, although it could equally represent a scene from Paradise. In the entrance hall, just inside **Bab al-Barid**, there are further elaborate mosaics which, like all the mosaics in the Umayyad Mosque, are notable for the complete absence of any human figures: such representations are considered blasphemous in Islamic tradition. The intricately painted wooden ceiling here (a restoration of the 15th-century original) is also particularly beautiful. Note also the huge bronze panelled wooden doors of the Bab al-Barid, which date from 1416. A good time to view the mosaics of the western arcade is in the evening when they are floodlit.

The mosque's three **minarets** can be viewed from different parts of the courtyard. Beside the Bab al-Amara in the centre of the northern wall is the **Minaret of the Bride**. The lower part dates from the ninth century, while the upper part was added in the late 12th century. According to a local story, its construction was originally financed by a merchant whose daughter was betrothed to the Caliph of the time, hence the name.

In the southwest corner is the **Minaret al-Gharbiye**, also known as the Minaret Qait Bey after the Mamluk Sultan who built it in 1488. It is particularly graceful and shows the strong Egyptian influence typical of the Mamluk period. In the southeast corner is the **Minaret of Jesus**, the tallest of the three. The main body is Ayyubid, dating from 1247 and replacing an Umayyad minaret, while the tip is Ottoman. According to Islamic belief, Jesus will descend from heaven to do battle with the Antichrist before the Day of Judgement, and according to local Damascene tradition, he will descend via this minaret. Both the southeast and southwest minarets are believed to have been built on the foundations of Roman towers, although some scholars have questioned this, pointing out that no other examples of Roman temples have towers at the corners.

The prayer hall The prayer hall occupies the whole of the southern length of the mosque, and basically follows a basilica plan, although the long, narrow, triple-aisled hall is broken by a central transept topped by a massive dome that serves to orientate worshippers towards the *mihrab* in the centre of the south wall. Some scholars suggest that the Muslim architects followed the plan of the existing Byzantine church, modifying it by adding the central transept, thus shifting the focus of the building away from the east wall where the altar would have been, to the *mihrab* in the centre of the south wall. However, there is no firm evidence to indicate the exact form or extent of the Byzantine church, and others argue that Al-Walid completely dismantled the church before starting work on the mosque. What you see today is largely the Ottoman reconstruction following the fire of 1893. Despite being in no way as elaborate as the original must have been, in its cavernous, cool, airy enormity it is still impressive. The floors are covered throughout with carpets, while numerous fans dangle from a huge height, wobbling as they spin.

In the central transept, the towering **Dome of the Eagle**, resting on four colossal pillars, is somewhat austere in its present form, though still awesome for its sheer size. Its name derives from the idea that the domed transept represents the head and body of an eagle, with the prayer hall extending to either side, representing the wings. As well as the main *mihrab* and *minbar* beside it, there are three other smaller *mihrabs* or niches, dedicated to the Hanbalites, Hanafites and Malikites, the three other schools of Sunni law besides the Shaffi school which was dominant in Damascus.

To the east of the central transept, encompassing two columns of the line nearest the south wall, is the **Shrine of John the Baptist**, consisting of an elaborate, dome-topped mausoleum made of marble. This dates from the Ottoman period, replacing an earlier wooden shrine which was destroyed in the fire of 1893. According to legend, during the building of the mosque, Al-Walid's workers discovered a casket buried underground containing the head of St John the Baptist, still with its hair and skin intact.

Mausoleum of Salah ud-Din

ⓘ *Access through small gate to the left of the mosque's main entrance, signposted 'putting on special clothes room'. Just through the gate is the ticket office, at the end of the path on the left is the dome-topped building of the mausoleum. Daily 1000-1700, non-Muslims S£50 (includes mosque entry), women must wear an abeyya (available in the ticket office) and men wearing shorts will be given a long skirt to wear. At the entry to the mausoleum remove your shoes, no photography allowed.*

For such a seminal figure in Arab history, the Mausoleum of Salah ud-Din is surprisingly small and unassuming. The dome-topped building dating from 1196, three years after the death of Salah ud-Din, originally stood within a larger *madrassa*, but nothing remains of this other than a solitary arch nearby. The mausoleum itself was in such an advanced state of disrepair by the end of the 19th century that when Kaiser Wilhelm II of Germany visited Damascus in 1898, he financed its restoration and donated a new tomb of white marble. Inside, the chamber is decorated with blue and white glazed tiles and bands of black, white and yellow stone. Alongside the white marble tomb donated by Wilhelm II is the original, a wooden one richly carved in black and gold and encased in glass.

Around the Umayyad Mosque

A little to the northwest of the Umayyad Mosque, facing each other across a narrow street, are the Madrassa Zahiriyeh and Madrassa Adiliyeh. Originally the **Madrassa Zahiriyeh** was the private house of Ayub, the father of Salah ud-Din. Following the death of the Mamluk Sultan Baibars in 1277, his son converted it into a religious school (*madrassa*), adding a mausoleum to house his father's body.

The recessed entrance, which dates from the building's conversion, is particularly imposing, consisting of contrasting black and yellow stonework, with three bands of marble above the level of the doorway carrying Arabic inscriptions and above these a finely executed semi-dome sculpted into intricate geometrical shapes. Today the building houses a library, but there is usually someone on hand to show you around and open up the mausoleum itself, which is kept locked.

Inside there is a small courtyard; the doorway immediately on the right leads into the mausoleum of Baibars, an ornately decorated, domed chamber which represents the main focus of interest. Opposite the entrance is a beautiful *mihrab* framed within strikingly patterned black and white marble. Each of the walls, themselves decorated with marble, contain two arched doorways, while running around the room is a wide band of lavish golden mosaic work in the same style as those of the Umayyad Mosque.

Construction work on the **Madrassa Adiliyeh** began towards the end of the 12th century, but it was left unfinished until the death of Sultan al-Adil Saif ud-Din (the brother of Salah ud-Din) in 1218, whereupon his son completed it to serve as the mausoleum of his father. The entrance, though impressive in its own right, is somewhat overshadowed by that of the Madrassa Zahiriyeh, while the mausoleum itself is a simple and unadorned domed chamber with broad arches in each wall. The remainder of the building, which consists of rooms arranged around a central courtyard, also houses a library.

Situated by the short colonnade leading to the northern Bab al-Amara gate of the Umayyad Mosque is **Madrassa Jaqmaqiyeh/Museum of Arab Epigraphy** ① *Wed-Mon 0900-1530, S£75, students S£5*, built by Jaqmaq al-Argunsawi, the Mamluk governor of Damascus from 1421-1422 and later king of Egypt from 1438-1452. This *madrassa* has an impressive entrance façade typical of the period, while the interior is also well preserved, housing a collection of Arab epigraphy, both in the form of carved inscriptions and some beautifully illuminated texts.

Continuing east from the entrance to the Madrassa Jaqmaqiyeh and then bearing right, you can weave your way through a series of narrow alleys to arrive on Badreddin al-Hassan Street, which runs east from the east gate of the Umayyad Mosque. But if instead you bear left and head north towards Bab al-Faradis, you pass on your right the **Saida Ruqqiyeh Mosque** ① *men and women have separate entrances, women will be given an abeyya to wear at entrance, men should not have knees or shoulders uncovered, shoes must be taken off before entering.* This Shi'ite mosque provides a complete contrast to anything else found in the Old City. For a start it was built in 1985. Its style, meanwhile, is entirely Iranian in inspiration (and indeed Iranian-built), as can be clearly seen from the distinctive onion-shaped dome. Inside, it is lavishly decorated with glazed tiles and copious amounts of marble, while the central dome is a dazzling mirror-mosaic. The overall effect is quite striking in its bright, fresh newness. It is also incredibly lively around evening prayers, thronging with families of Shi'ite pilgrims, mostly from Iran. The mosque stands on the site of a shrine to Lady Ruqqiyeh who died in AD 680 and was the daughter of Hussein, the great martyr of the Shi'ites. Hence its importance as a Shi'ite place of pilgrimage.

You can also skirt around the outside of the Umayyad Mosque by following its southern wall. You first pass Bab al-Ziada, which leads directly into the prayer hall. Further along, partially obscured by an electrical installation, there are the remains of a Roman triple gateway in the wall of the mosque. Originally, this served as the southern entrance into the inner temenos of the Roman temple. The Greek inscription on the central lintel (*"Thy Kingdom, O Christ, is an everlasting Kingdom, and Thy dominion endureth throughout all generations"*) clearly demonstrates that it remained in use during the Byzantine period, perhaps serving also as an entrance for both Christians and Muslims when they shared the temple compound during the early years of Islamic rule. However, with the construction of Al-Walid's mosque it was blocked up, since it interfered with the positioning of the central *mihrab* on the inside.

Bab al-Nawfarah and Badreddin al-Hassan Street

The eastern gate of the mosque, Bab al-Nawfarah ('Gate of the Fountain') was originally part of the main *propylaeum* or monumental entrance to the inner *temenos* of the Roman temple, the climax of an approach which began from the *agora* further to the east and culminated in a huge portico (no longer surviving) and triple gateway (the present Bab al-Nawfarah). A broad flight of stairs descends from this impressive gateway, down into Bareddin al-Hassan Street. At the bottom of the steps, on the right, is the *Al Naufarah* and opposite it the *Al Sham*, both lively places to stop for refreshments and watch the comings and goings along this street (see Cafés, page 73).

Continuing east along this street, after a little over 100 m you reach the remains of the **Triple Gateway**, which marked the eastern entrance to the outer compound of the Temple of Jupiter. The remains lie half buried in the ground, reducing their effect somewhat, though when you realize that the lintels which you can see just above ground level in fact crown the side portals, you get a sense of the original scale of the gateway. Like the monumental gateway at the end of Hamidiyeh Souq, the decoration is on the east-facing side.

If you follow the narrow street leading north immediately before the triple gateway (coming from the Umayyad Mosque), you can see on your left traces of the columns which formed the portico running around the outer courtyard of the Temple of Jupiter; in places just the column bases survive, elsewhere entire columns have been incorporated into the structures of buildings lining this street.

Continuing east from the triple gateway, the street becomes Qaimariyeh Street. Further along on the right is the **Al-Fatiyyeh Mosque**, built in 1742 as a *madrassa* by Fat'hy Effendi, a poet and Ottoman treasury official. This beautifully proportioned mosque is interesting for its combination of a typically Syrian/Mamluk style in the bands of black and white stone and the elegant decorative tiling, with a typically Ottoman plan in features such as the triple-domed porch that precedes the prayer hall. The overall effect, with a two-storey arcade around the quiet, shady central courtyard, is very pleasing.

Further east, Qaimariyeh Street gives way to a maze of narrow alleys extending northeast and southeast; following these alleys northeast gives access (with a little careful navigation) to the Christian quarter of Bab Touma.

Directly to the south of the Umayyad Mosque is the **Azem Palace**, which now also houses the Museum of Popular Tradition. To reach it, follow the narrow alley running south from the southwest corner of the mosque (this is **Souq al-Silah**, today largely given over to gold and jewellery, but previously the weapons market, or Souq Assagah), and turn left at what is effectively a T-junction.

Azem Palace and Museum of Popular Tradition

ⓘ *Wed-Mon 0900-1730 in summer, 0900-1530 in winter, closed Fri 1200-1430, S£150, students S£15.*

Built in 1749-1752 as a royal residence by the Ottoman governor of Damascus, Assad Pasha al-Azem, this palace is the largest, and amongst the most impressive, of the Ottoman period palaces to be found around Damascus. Entering it you are drawn immediately into another world of lavishly decorated rooms facing onto beautifully shady and tranquil courtyards with pools and fountains. The palace stands on the site of an earlier palace built by the Mamluk governor, Tengiz. It has been substantially restored, most notably after a fire in 1925, but the work was carried out carefully, preserving most of its original features. For a time it served to house the French Institute before being returned to the Azem family following independence. It was then sold to the Syrian government in 1951.

From the ticket booth, turn to the left and then right to enter the main *haremlek* or private family area. This, the largest courtyard, is particularly beautiful with its two pools and fountains, and its beds of tall, shady trees and shrubs. The rooms around the courtyard, luxuriously decorated with wood-panelled walls and ceilings, each contain displays along a different theme: musical instruments; a reception room with elaborate inlaid furniture; a marriage room containing beautiful glassware; a pilgrimage room complete with a richly embroidered *mahmal* (the camel-mounted palanquin used to carry dignitaries on the *Hajj* to Mecca); an armoury (daggers, swords, pistols and rifles); a 'grand' reception room; and the 'Salle de Djebel al-Arab', which houses various period costumes. There is also a private hammam complex and, in the south wall, a large, deep *iwan*.

A passage to the right of the ticket booth leads past carved wooden chests and panels and huge, richly decorated metal plates, through to the *salemlek* or visitors' area. There is another courtyard with a central pool which is surrounded by rooms, this time with displays more in line with a 'popular tradition' theme: domestic activities such as weaving and bread baking and handicrafts such as wood and metalwork, leatherwork, pottery, carpets, women's costumes and embroidered fabrics (some of them particularly delicate and beautiful).

Souq Bazuriye

The area extending west from the Azem Palace, between Hamidiyeh Souq and Mahdat Pasha Street, is well worth exploring for its souqs, khans and other historical monuments. Leaving the Azem Palace and turning left (south) into what is the main spice market, Souq Bazuriye, you pass on the left the **Hammam Nur ud-Din**, built by Nur ud-Din between 1154 and 1172 in order to raise funds for the building of the Madrassa al-Nuriyeh (see below). It is one of the oldest in Damascus and despite undergoing several restorations, and housing a soap factory for a time, it is today the best example of a fully functional Turkish bath complex in Damascus (see page 75). The large and elaborate domed reception chamber dates from the Ottoman period.

A little further along on the same side is the entrance to **Khan Assad Pasha** ⓘ *Sat-Thu 0900-1500, S£75, students S£5*, built by Assad Pasha al-Azem between 1751 and 1753.

An imposing gateway of black and white stone leads through into what is easily the most ambitious and spectacular of Damascus's khans. It follows an essentially Persian design, with the main courtyard covered. There are a total of eight domes arranged around a large circular opening in the ceiling which allows light to pour down onto a circular pool below. Four huge pillars connected by elegant arches support the ceiling. Around the sides of the courtyard are two storeys of rooms (those below being the store rooms while those above were sleeping quarters). Above them there is a gallery running all the way round the walls, framed in arches which connect also with the arches of the four central columns to form part of the support for the eight domes. The alternating grey and white stonework, together with the ingenious and beautifully proportioned design of the building, combine to create something of an architectural masterpiece. Stepping into this khan from the crowded souq outside, you are overwhelmed by the scale and sense of space.

Following the street running due west from the entrance to the Azem Palace, you pass on the left the **Al-Azem Ecole**. Originally this was the Madrassa Abdullah al-Azem Pasha, built in 1770 by the man of the same name who later went on to become the governor of Damascus and who represented the last of the Azem family, which governed Damascus between 1725 and 1809. Today the building houses an upmarket tourist souvenir/ antiques shop. Even if you are not interested in buying anything, the interior of the building is well worth a look, with its small courtyard and delicate columns and arches supporting a two-storey arcade around the sides. If you can get someone to take you up onto the roof, there are good views from here of the Umayyad Mosque.

Other madrassas and khans

Just past the Al-Azem Ecole there is a crossroads. Turning left into the narrow north-south street (**Souq Khayyatin**, the tailors' souq), immediately on the right is the entrance to the **Madrassa al-Nuriyeh**. Today the Mausoleum of Nur ud-Din is the only surviving part of this *madrassa*, which was built between 1167 and 1172 to house the tomb of one of the great Arab leaders of this period; two more modern mosques now stand on either side of the main courtyard. The mausoleum (which has itself undergone a certain amount of modification) is reached through a doorway on the left in the initial entrance hall. The mausoleum is kept locked but the caretaker is usually on hand to open it up. If not, you can peer in through the iron-grille window in the street, to the left of the main entrance. The simple chamber is topped by a tall honeycombed dome, with a band of Arabic inscription running around the walls and the marble tomb in the centre of the floor.

Continuing south along this street, on the right is the **Khan al-Khayyatin**, with a particularly beautiful arched entrance of alternating black and yellow stone with intricately carved decoration and Arabic inscriptions (though unfortunately partially obscured by small stalls on either side). Inside, the central dome has long ago collapsed although the arches which supported it still survive. The khan is occupied today by cotton embroidery and fabric shops.

Returning to the crossroads by the Al-Azem Ecole and Madrassa al-Nuriyeh, and heading north this time along the continuation of Souq Khayyatin, you pass first on the right the **Khan al-Harir**, the silk khan, the main entrance to which is via a narrow street on the right. The entrance doorway itself is the main feature of interest, being beautifully decorated. Continuing north, on the left is the entrance to the **Khan al-Jumruk** (the customs khan), a long L-shaped khan today occupied by brightly lit fabric shops, but still retaining its original domed roofing supported by arches.

If you head west from the crossroads by the Al-Azem Ecole and Madrassa al-Nuriyeh, following the main street, the second turning on the right (after about 200 m) brings you to the entrance of the **Maristan Nur ud-Din**. This can also be reached by taking a short detour from Souq Hamidiyeh (to do this, take the right turn at the point where there is a break in the corrugated-iron roofing of the Souq as you head east towards the Umayyad Mosque).

Maristan Nur ud-Din (or Bimaristan al-Nuri)

ⓘ *Sat-Thu 0900-1400, S£75, students S£5.*

Built by Nur ud-Din Zangai in 1154 as a hospital and medical school, this remarkable building was the most advanced medical institution of its time, and continued to function as a hospital until the 19th century. An archway with a honeycombed semi-dome frames the doorway, which utilizes a length of carved stone of clearly Roman/Classical origin as its lintel. The doors themselves, plated with metal and decorated with rivets arranged in patterns, are original. The entrance hall has an impressive central honeycombed dome and semi-domes to either side, decorated with a mixture of honeycombing and stalactites. A band of Arabic inscription runs around the room just below the level of the main dome.

Inside the main courtyard there is a large central pool and fountain. In each of the four walls there is a deep *iwan*, and on either side of each *iwan* is a door leading through to a room containing exhibits of the **Museum of Arab Science and Medicine**, which is housed here. Note the beautiful arches of carved stone lattice work above each door.

Displayed in the rooms is a varied collection of items from the world of Arab medicine; bottles of medicinal herbs, pharmaceutical accessories for measuring, grinding, distilling, etc, surgical instruments for dentistry and operations, talismans and other 'spiritual medicine' accessories and also various astronomical instruments.

Arab medicine was far more advanced than anything practised in Europe during this period, and Western medical knowledge only really began to progress with the translation of Arabic texts into Latin. The Arabs, for example, were the first to develop alcohol-based anaesthetics that could be inhaled. A sponge was soaked in a potent solution containing amongst other things hashish, opium and belladonna. It was then dried and stored; only needing to be soaked in alcohol prior to use. Unfortunately the explanation boards here are only in Arabic and French, but the displays are fascinating anyway.

Straight Street

Known at its western end by its Arabic name, Madhat Pasha Street, the famous Via Recta, or Straight Street, runs through the entire Old City, terminating at its eastern end with Bab Sharqi. Along its length, and as short diversions off it, there are several important historical monuments.

The Via Recta originates from Greek times when, following the conquests of Alexander the Great, a grid pattern was imposed on the Old City, which at that time was centred on a low mound just to the south of the street. During the first century AD, the Romans widened the street to make it into a major axis through the city (the *Decumanus maximus*), a function that it continues to fulfil today.

In Roman times the street was around 26 m wide and lined with a colonnade, but over the centuries shops and buildings gradually encroached from either side, and today it is only a fraction of its former width. In fact at its western end, the tiny narrow souqs which run parallel to it just to the south were originally part of the same street, only becoming separated from it when shops and stalls were erected in the middle of the wide thoroughfare. The gate at this important entrance to the Old City, the Arab period **Bab al-Jabiye** (Gate of the Water Trough), standing on the site of the Roman Gate of Jupiter, is also in amongst these narrow souqs, although you can't see much of it today.

The first section of Madhat Pasha Street is a lively, bustling souq boasting a wide variety of shops and traders. On the left after around 300 m (shortly before the left turning into Souq Khayyatin) are the entrances to three khans. The middle one, **Khan al-Zait** (the Olive Khan), is quiet and unassuming but its overall effect is very pretty with its pleasant, shaded courtyard and central pool surrounded by two galleries of arched arcading.

A little further along on the right, just past the turning for Souq Khayyatin, is **Khan Suleiman Pasha**, a rather vibrant but dilapidated place, full of the lively disorder of functioning workshops. It was built for the Ottoman governor of Damascus, Suleiman Pasha al-Azem in 1732. An unimposing entrance takes you into a vaulted passage which leads through into a large rectangular courtyard. This was once covered by two large domes, now collapsed, although parts of the arches that originally supported them still survive. An upstairs gallery which can be reached via a staircase from the entrance passage runs around the whole courtyard.

Continuing east, after the next crossroads (left into Souq Buzuriye, right down towards Bab as-Saghir) the very much local-orientated shops and stalls of Mahdat Pasha Street start to give way to more touristy shops selling brassware, swords and inlaid woodwork. If you take the second right turn after the crossroads, by a square black and white stone minaret (a small sign marks the turning), after 100 m you reach the entrance of **Beit Nizam** ① *Sat-Thu 0900-1400, no admission charge*, on the left. This beautiful 18th-century Ottoman house once served as the British consul's residence in Damascus. Today it is once again in the hands of the Nizam family, but it is open to the public. The decoration around the walls of the innermost courtyard is particularly beautiful. Although the rooms themselves are not usually opened up for tourists, their interior decoration is truly lavish and you can at least peer in through the windows.

Returning to Straight Street, the first left turn after the turning for Beit Nizem brings you to the entrance of **Dar Anbar** ① *Sat-Thu 0900-1400 in summer, 0900-1300 in winter, no admission charge*, on the right, another beautiful old house built for a wealthy Ottoman merchant in 1867. The building was used as a secondary school from 1920 and currently houses the offices of a team of architects charged with the restoration and preservation of Damascus' historical monuments. The inner courtyard (*haremlek*) has been completely restored, and the decoration around the walls of the courtyard is particularly beautiful and delicate.

Continuing east along Straight Street, the next feature of interest is the remains of a **Roman Arch**, today contained within a garden to the right of the modern road. The triple arch was discovered by builders during the period of French rule, buried underground by centuries' worth of debris, and re-erected on the surface. It is thought to have formed part of a *tetrapylon*, which would have stood at what was once an intersection of the east-west *decumanus maximus* (Straight Street) with a major north-south street or *cardo maximus*.

If you take the right turn immediately before the arch, and then turn right again at the crossroads just after a small dog-leg in the street, you arrive at **Dahdah Palace** ① *Mon-Sat 1000-1300 and 1630-1800, ring the bell for entry, no admission charge*, on the left. This little detour is fairly well signposted, which is a good thing because from the outside this beautiful 18th-century house is entirely unremarkable. Inside, however, you have a typically Syrian/Ottoman layout of rooms arranged around a large, shady courtyard. The large, beautifully decorated *iwan* is particularly impressive.

The Roman Arch also roughly marks the start of the **Christian quarter**, which extends to the northeast, reaching up to Bab Touma. Just beyond the arch, on the left, is the Greek Orthodox Patriarchate, **St Mary's Church** (Al-Mariam). Looking somewhat modern, having been clad in bright new stone, this church dates back to 1867. Its predecessor was

In the footsteps of St Paul

"As he neared Damascus on his journey, suddenly a light from heaven flashed around him. He fell to the ground and heard a voice say to him 'Saul, Saul, why do you persecute me?' 'Who are you, Lord?' Saul asked. 'I am Jesus, whom you are persecuting,' he replied. 'Now get up and go into the city, and you will be told what you must do.' " (Acts 9: 3). So began the Christian-hating Saul of Tarsus' conversion into St Paul.

There are three sites in the Christian quarter of Damascus traditionally associated with the story of St Paul in the Bible. Straight Street, where Saul of Tarsus stayed at the house of Judas after being blinded by a heavenly vision on the road to Damascus; St Ananias Chapel, commonly thought to be the site of the house of

Ananias, the early Christian convert who restored Saul's sight and baptised him Paul the Apostle; and St Paul's Chapel, identified popularly as the place where Saul was lowered by a basket from the walls in order to escape capture and murder by the Jews.

As for the place where St Paul received his divine vision while losing his physical sight, this was traditionally identified with the small village of Kokab, 15 km south-west of Damascus along the road to Quneitra, again without any firm evidence. However, in the 18th-century tradition found itself shifting the site somewhat closer to Damascus, to a point in the vicinity of the large Christian cemetery to the south of Bab Kisan. More recently, a small chapel has been built there to mark the spot.

burnt down during the great massacre of Christians and Druze in 1860. The site has been occupied by a church since Byzantine times.

Continuing east along Straight Street, you arrive eventually at **Bab Sharqi** (literally 'Eastern Gate'). This is the only gate to preserve its original Roman plan (in Roman times it was the Gate of the Sun), but it has undergone extensive restoration, and only the left-hand arch of the triple arch (as viewed from the inside) contains any original stonework. Two columns stand just inside the gate, remainders of the colonnade that would have lined the street on either side during Roman times.

Christian Quarter churches

If you follow the narrow street to the left immediately before Bab Sharqi, at the end of this street is **St Ananias Chapel** ① *daily 0900-1900, S£25*. A set of steps leads down to the cool, underground chapel reputedly standing on the site of the house of Ananias where Saul of Tarsus (later to become Paul the Apostle) was cured of his blindness. The chapel appears to have existed since Byzantine times, when it was known as the Church of the Holy Cross ('Musallabah' in Arabic).

Excavations first carried out on this spot in the 1920s revealed the apse of a small Byzantine chapel and, below it, the remains of a Roman temple. According to one line of reasoning, the house of Ananias was revered by early Christians. The Roman authorities, however, responded by building their own temple on the spot as a way of preventing Christians from coming here to worship. Only with the advent of the Byzantine era were the Christians able to build a church here.

St Paul's Chapel is popularly recognized as the site where Saul was lowered from the city walls to escape persecution by the Jews. It is reached by passing through Bab Sharqi and following the line of the city walls on the outside. The main road that you must walk along is particularly busy and unpleasant, but you have the chance to get a good look at this section of the Old City walls. The first stretch, as you walk from Bab Sharqi, consists mostly of recent restoration but as you approach Bab Kisan you can see the huge old Roman-period stone blocks in the lower courses, along with smaller stones from the Arab period higher up.

The chapel dedicated to St Paul is of 20th-century origin and, like the rest of the complex, belongs to the Greek Orthodox church. At the rear of the chapel you can see massive stone blocks, which are clearly of Roman origin. Originally the Roman gate of Saturn stood on this spot, but this was obliterated during the time of Nur ud-Din and the present gate into which St Paul's Chapel is built is a 14th-century Mamluk construction. The gate itself is best viewed from outside the walls. An arch frames the central door and above it is a single machicolation. On either side are towers with a band of carved decoration and medallions bearing the *Chi-Rho* symbol (adopted by Constantine as the symbol of the new Christian empire).

Northern gates and walls of the Old City
The city walls follow the same basic outline established in Hellenistic and Roman times, with a few minor variations. Various traces of the original Roman stonework can still be seen, although most of the surviving fabric of the walls is of Arab origin, dating from the 11th century onwards, when extensive repairs were carried out in order to strengthen the city's defences against the threat of Crusader and later Mongol attack. The gates of the Old City also generally correspond with the original Roman gates, although most have likewise been rebuilt in Arab times (Bab Sharqi, dealt with above, is an exception).

Bab al-Faraj (Gate of Deliverance), located in the northern city walls, close to the northeast corner of the Citadel, is one of the few gates which does not correspond with an earlier Roman gate. A gate was first built here by Nur ud-Din in the mid-12th century, although the existing double gateway is the result of later restoration. The inner doorway is a 13th-century Ayyubid reconstruction while the outer doorway is a 15th-century Mamluk reconstruction. In between the two, the covered passage between the two houses is a souq given over to blacksmiths and ironmongers.

Pass through the inner doorway and then, instead of turning left to go through the outer doorway, continue straight ahead (east) along Beit Nassorain Street, just inside the city walls. This picturesque, narrow lane is typical of the residential quarters of the Old City, with the ancient wood and plaster houses on either side leaning precariously and in one place actually touching, while elsewhere there are sections that are vaulted.

After around 250 m you reach a staggered crossroads. In front of you is the Saida Ruqqiyeh Mosque (see page 55), while turning left brings you to **Bab al-Faradis** (Gate of the Orchards, also known as Bab al-Amara and corresponding with the Roman Gate of Mercury). This gate is a 12th-century Ayyubid construction, and, like Bab al-Faraj, originally consisted of two parts, although today only the outer doorway along with a solitary arch of the inner doorway survives.

Continuing east from here, after another 250 m you reach **Bab as-Salaam** (Gate of Peace, corresponding with the Roman Gate of the Moon). This is the best preserved and most impressive of the Old City's gates. In its present form, the gate is once again a largely Ayyubid restoration dating from 1243, although an earlier reconstruction of the Roman original was carried out in 1172. The central arch contains within it a rectangular doorway topped by a massive lintel bearing an Arabic inscription, dedicated to the Ayyubid ruler Sultan al-Salih Ismael. On either side of the arch are large machicolations.

Pass through the gate to continue east (Bab as-Salaam is unusual in this respect in that it has an east-west alignment). For the first stretch the **Old City walls**, now to your right, are obscured by houses. But after a while the street crosses a stream (a branch of the Barada River) and runs between it and the city walls, giving you the chance to inspect them close-up. The large Roman stone blocks in the lower courses are clearly distinguishable from the smaller stones of the Arab and Turkish periods. In one place there is a column section which has been placed horizontally in the walls so that just its end is visible. The use of a Classical column to reinforce the structure of a wall in this way was a technique typical of the Crusaders, and was perhaps borrowed by the Arabs during 11th-12th century repairs to the walls.

At the end of the street you come out at **Bab Touma** (St Thomas' Gate, corresponding with the Roman Gate of Venus). Today this gate looks somewhat forlorn and dislocated, standing at the centre of a large, busy roundabout, the walls to either side having been dismantled to make way for the flow of traffic. The original Roman gate was reconstructed in 1227 during the Ayyubid period, with the Mamluk ruler Tengiz adding the machicolation in 1334. The gate takes its name from the son-in-law of the Byzantine Emperor Heraclius, Thomas, who led the resistance to the first Muslim assault on Damascus in AD 635. The gate gives its name to the Christian area that surrounds it, both inside and outside the walls of the Old City. The main thoroughfare running south from Bab Touma through this Christian part of the Old City intersects with Straight Street.

Around the Old City

There are a number of places of interest in the immediate vicinity of the Old City. People staying in the backpacker hotels of Souq Sarouja will be familiar with the picturesque old houses and narrow streets of **Sarouja district**. Less well known, however, is the extension of Souq Sarouja Street to the east of the modern Thawra Bridge.

Following this street east from Thawra Bridge, after about 500 m there is the **Towba Mosque** on the right (see Old City map). This large mosque was formerly a khan. According to local tradition, the khan gained a reputation as a brothel before being converted to a mosque – hence the name, which translates literally as Mosque of Repentance. The side entrance to the mosque (just off Souq Sarouja Street) is framed within a honeycombed arch, with a lintel bearing an Arabic inscription above the doorway. The courtyard, with its black and white stone paving, is reminiscent of that of the Umayyad Mosque, particularly in terms of the façade of the prayer hall. Inside the prayer hall, the *mihrab* is particularly beautifully decorated.

If you turn right at the junction by which this mosque is situated, and then right again immediately after, this narrow lane winds its way down to Al-Malek Feisal Street (if you go straight across the junction here you arrive at Bab al-Faraj). A short distance east along Al-Malek Feisal Street, on the right, is **Al-Mowalak Mosque**, also often referred to as the Bardabak Mosque after the prince, Bardabak al-Jaqni, who was responsible for its construction. The mosque has a beautifully decorated minaret in marble, along with an impressive honeycombed arch to the right of the main entrance.

Heading back west to Ath Thawra Street and then following it south, past the entrance to Souq Hamidiyeh, on the right after around 250 m is the **Darwish Pasha Mosque**. Built in 1574 by a governor of Damascus of the same name, the long façade of this mosque with its alternating bands of black and cream stonework is quite impressive, despite the pollution from the heavy traffic running past, which has left it in desperate need of cleaning. Inside, the pleasant courtyard with its central pool and fountain provides a peaceful respite from the frenetic activity outside. The panels of blue-glazed Damascene tiles on the façade of the prayer hall are particularly beautiful. Inside the prayer hall there is more tiling and an attractive *mihrab*, although a massive, intruding chandelier spoils the overall effect somewhat. The small octagonal building attached to the mosque by an arch contains the tomb of Darwish Pasha.

Continuing south, just past the entrance to Madhat Pasha/Straight Street, on the left this time, is the **Sinan Pasha Mosque**. The mosque dates from 1590, during the reign of an Ottoman governor of Damascus, Sinan Pasha (not to be confused with the great Ottoman architect of the same name who was responsible for the Tekkiyeh as-Suleimaniyeh mosque; see below). The façade is in the alternating black and cream bands of stone typical of Mamluk and Ottoman architecture, while the minaret is clad in distinctive green and turquoise glazed stone. Inside, there is once again a peaceful, shady courtyard and more panels of beautiful Damascene tiling in the arcades around the courtyard.

Just south of the Sinan Pasha Mosque, the road forks. Bearing right to head in a southerly direction, you are on Qasr al-Hajjaj Street, which becomes Midan Street a bit further south. Although now somewhat swamped by modern development, this axis represents the once distinct **Midan Quarter**, which extended south for several kilometres. Its significance lay in the fact that this was the route taken by pilgrims as they set off from the Old City on the *Hajj*, or pilgrimage to Mecca. As such, it developed over the centuries into an important thoroughfare lined by numerous mosques, mausoleums, religious schools, baths and other amenities catering for the pilgrims. The monuments strung out along this route are today in a somewhat dilapidated condition, and only for the really dedicated sightseer.

Bearing left at the junction just south of the Sinan Pasha Mosque to follow the line of the Old City walls, you pass through **Souq Sinaniye** with its stores selling sheepskins. Bearing left at the next fork, you are in Badawi Street, which heads east, passing on the left the **Bab as-Saghir** gate to the Old City (literally 'Little Gate', corresponding with the Roman Gate of Mars). The large stone blocks of the Roman foundations can still be seen, though the rest of the gate is a combination of Nur ud-Din's 12th-century reconstruction and later Ayyubid work.

To the southeast is the Muslim **Bab as-Saghir Cemetery**, an important place of pilgrimage for Shi'ites who come to visit two of the tombs there. One is the **Tomb of Fatima**, daughter of the Prophet and wife of Ali. The other is the **Tomb of Sukeina**, the daughter of Hussein and great-granddaughter of the Prophet. Most scholars agree that these are unlikely to be the genuine tombs of these two figures, but the tradition persists, attracting large numbers of Shi'ites from Iran. To enter, follow Al-Jarrah Street, which branches southwest off Badawi Street and runs through the centre of the cemetery; a gate on the left gives access to the southern half of the cemetery containing the two tombs.

Modern Damascus

In many ways, modern Damascus is just like any other large capital city the world over, with it congestion, pollution and faceless concrete high-rise developments. At the same time, however, it does manage to retain a certain Syrian feel to it in places. This is particularly true of the area round Martyrs' Square, where the hawkers, market stalls and hole-in-the-wall restaurants, selling roasted half-chickens and *falafel* or *shawarma* sandwiches, leave you in no doubt that this is an Arab capital. Heading for the commercial districts around Yousef al-Azmeh Square, the bland uniformity of airline offices, expensive hotels and shops selling fancy designer goods starts to assert itself more strongly. By the time you get out to the districts such as Abou Roumaneh, where the foreign embassies have made their home amidst affluent, fashionable residential areas, there is little to remind you that this is not Europe or America.

There is no doubt that the Old City and its environs are the main focus of historical interest in Damascus, but the modern city has its important monuments and places of interest too. The most notable of these are the Tekkiyeh as-Suleimaniyeh complex and the National Museum, next to each other on the south bank of the Barada River, just to the south of the busy east-west thoroughfare of Shoukri al-Kouwatli Street.

Tekkiyeh as-Suleimaniyeh Complex

① *The mosque itself is fenced off and closed to the public for important restructuring and restoration work at the moment, but you can see its beautiful façade and peaceful grounds from the alleyway.*

This large complex includes a mosque (currently closed to the public) and a *madrassa* (religious school), which now houses a handicrafts market. The mosque was built by Sinan Pasha, the great Ottoman architect (most famous for the Suleimaniye Mosque in Istanbul), in honour of the Sultan Suleiman I (Suleiman the Magnificent, 1520-1566). Its purpose was to provide an alternative starting point for the annual pilgrimage to Mecca, the organization of which was traditionally the responsibility of the governor of Damascus.

From the arched entrance off Omar Ben Abi Rabeea Street, a pedestrian lane lined with jewellery and antique shops leads to the main mosque. Halfway down on the left is the entrance to the old **Madrassa as-Selimiyeh**. This was actually a later addition, built during the reign of Suleiman's successor, Sultan Selim II (1566-1574) by another architect. The courtyard, with its subsided and uneven floor of black and white stone slabs and central fountain and pool, is rather atmospheric, with a slightly dilapidated charm about it. The surrounding arcade of arches and small domed rooms would once have housed religious students but is now given over to various handicrafts: inlaid woodwork, brass, copper and silverware, embroidered fabrics, paintings, carpets, musical instruments, etc.

The **Tekkiyeh as-Suleimaniyeh Mosque**, although not particularly grand in terms of its size, is a wonderful gem of Ottoman architecture. The mosque itself is clearly Turkish in inspiration, with its domed prayer hall and pointed, rocket-like minarets rising up on either side. The doorway of the prayer hall is decorated with honeycombing and delicately carved stalactites, while inside there is beautiful glazed blue and white tiling in the arches above the windows and doors. The courtyard in front of the mosque is more typically Syrian in design, with its black and white stone slabs and large central pool and fountain. Surrounding it on three sides are rooms originally meant to house the pilgrims preparing for the *Hajj*.

National Museum

① *Shoukri al-Kouwatli St, Wed-Mon 0900-1800 in summer, 0900-1600 in winter, S£150, students S£10, café and toilets are located within the museum grounds, no photography allowed.*

The National Museum of Damascus is the largest in Syria and boasts a wealth of artefacts covering some 11 millennia of Syria's rich history. Many of the great historical and archaeological sites in Syria, despite their importance and often spectacular settings, are stripped of their most important artefacts, and it is here that you have the opportunity actually to see them. Your appreciation of the vast majestic site of Dura Europos, for example, will be greatly enhanced if you can remember the fabulously preserved murals of the Jewish synagogue, or the Valley of the Tombs in Palmyra by the reconstruction of the Yarhai Hypogeum, both housed here. Likewise, it is the artefacts of sites such as Mari and Ebla that actually hold the key to appreciating their significance. Indeed, given the size of the collection, it is perhaps worth making two visits in order to appreciate this museum fully, ideally at the beginning and end of your trip.

The gardens of the museum contain numerous architectural fragments and items of statuary, often overlooked by visitors but well worth wandering round. The massive entrance to the museum consists of a reconstruction of the façade of the Umayyad Palace of Qasr al-Heir al-Gharbi in the Syrian desert to the west of Palmyra (see page 277), which was dismantled and transported here piece by piece.

To your right as you enter is the long west wing of the museum, containing the **pre-Classical** and **Arab-Islamic** collections, grouped for the most part according to the site (eg Ugarit, Ebla, Mari, etc). In the two upper floors of this wing there is a permanent exhibition of **contemporary art** (mostly paintings and some sculpture) as well as a rather desultory **prehistoric** section. To your left as you enter is the east wing, containing **Classical** and **Byzantine** collections. (So, if you want to view the exhibits chronologically, you have to go back and forth between the two wings.)

For those with a specialist interest, the excellent though outdated *Concise Guide* (which is anything but concise) is usually on sale at the ticket office (though it periodically sells out and the process of ordering another print run is painfully slow). Alternatively, if there is an organized group receiving a guided tour it is worth tagging along. Otherwise it is really a case of exploring and discovering as best you can for yourself.

The labelling throughout the museum has got a lot better in the last few years and detailed plaques are popping up all over the museum. There is also a massive futuristic overhaul of the museum planned for some time in the near future. It is not possible to give a detailed commentary on such a formidable a collection here, but there are certain collections/reconstructions that do deserve a special mention.

Probably the most famous aspect of the museum is the reconstruction of the mid-third century AD **Dura Europos Synagogue** at the far end of the east wing, across a small courtyard. Discovered at the site of Dura Europos (see page 297) in the 1930s, the synagogue is unique in that its walls were decorated with frescoes depicting scenes from the Old Testament, including human representations – something which goes against all Talmudic traditions. Equally remarkable is the fact that these frescoes should be so well preserved (because they were buried under sand). The walls of the synagogue consist of the original frescoes, much faded by time but still extremely impressive. The ceiling is a reconstruction of the original, with its painted wooden beams. It is unlit and receives little natural light (in order to protect the frescoes) so it takes a while for your eyes to adjust to the gloom.

Immediately before the courtyard leading to the synagogue, a flight of stairs leads down to the early second-century **Hypogeum of Yarhai** from the Valley of the Tombs in Palmyra. The hypogeum (underground burial chamber) is reconstructed from the original, giving an excellent insight into what these underground tombs would have originally looked like, with the compartment-shelves for sarcophagi built into the walls and sealed by funerary busts, while at the end of the main chamber to the right is the *triclinium*, where a funeral banquet would have been held.

Returning to ground level, stairs also lead up from here to the first floor and the **Salle de Hommes**. This contains an impressive collection of jewellery and coins, including iron and gold funerary masks discovered near Homs and dating from the first century AD.

Hejaz railway station

Completed in 1917, the Hejaz railway station marks the terminus of the famous railway line that ran from Damascus to Medina. The brain-child of the Ottoman Sultan Abdul Hamid II (1876-1909), the main purpose of the railway was to facilitate the passage of pilgrims undertaking the *Hajj* to Mecca. However, with the outbreak of the First World War, it became a vital transport and communications link for the Ottoman and German forces, leading to concerted attempts by the Allies to blow it up.

The interior of the building is worth inspecting, with its beautifully decorated wooden ceiling and balcony running around the main hall, and its large silver chandelier. Outside there is a steam engine on display, dating from 1908. No train services leave from the Hejaz station anymore.

Historical Museum of Damascus

① *The entrance to the musuem is set back from Ath Thawra Street just to the north of Thawra Bridge, via an arched gateway in the parking area of a government building Sat-Thu 0800-1400, S£75, students S£5.*

Little visited by tourists, this museum occupies the large **Beit Khalid al-Azem** (the palace of a former prime minister, Khalid al-Azem). The extensive complex is divided into a northern section which houses the museum, and a southern section which houses an important archive of historical documents not officially open to the public. From the entrance on the north side of the palace, a small initial courtyard leads through to the main courtyard, dotted with trees and shrubs, and with a fountain and pool on one side. This was the private family area of the palace (the *haramlek*). A large *iwan* occupies part of one wall, while the various rooms around the courtyard contain the museum's exhibits.

The quality of the decoration in the rooms is superb, easily matching that of the more famous Azem Palace in the Old City. Lavishly carved marble-work and intricately decorated wood panelling adorn the walls and ceilings and there are numerous items of inlaid wood furniture. One room contains an intriguing fountain, fashioned from stone into something that resembles a water-maze, which was used for games. Another room contains large scale models of the Old City, Salihiye district and various buildings and complexes around Damascus, as well as an interesting collection of old photographs.

A doorway at the end of the passage to the left of the *iwan* leads through to the southern half of the complex. This represents the public visitors' areas (the *salemlek*) and consists of a series of three courtyards. This is where the archive is housed and, although it is not officially open to the public, it is often possible to wander through and admire the impressive exterior decoration of the courtyards and rooms. If you do make it through to here, you can exit via the south door which leads out onto the eastern extension of Souq Sarouja Street.

Salihiye/Al Charkasiye district

Most of the monuments in this district are concentrated along Madares Assad ud-Din Lane. Generally closed to the public, you can admire their façades from outside. The lane is lively and atmospheric; full of vegetable stalls by day and shops serving *fuul* and hummus at outside tables by night. The approach to this district, northwest of the city centre, is through areas dominated by modern development. However, as you reach the lower, gentle slopes of Mount Kassioun, the streets begin to get narrower and the layout less regular.

This area was first settled during the mid-12th century when Hanbalite refugees, fleeing in the wake of the Crusader occupation of Jerusalem, were housed here by Nur ud-Din, who was keen to keep them separate from the rival Shaffi school that was predominant within the walled city. It then began to absorb the overspill from the walled city and with time became a well regarded district in its own right, inspiring many members of the ruling class to build mausoleums, mosques and *madrassas* in the area.

Mohi ud-Din Mosque

Roughly halfway along Mardares Assad ud-Din Lane, this mosque is open to the public and has a particularly beautiful Mamluk-style octagonal minaret. The mosque dates from the early 16th century and was built over the 13th century burial chamber of the famous Sufi mystic, Mohi ud-Din Ibn al-Arabi. It remains an important pilgrimage site for Sufis. Inside, to your left as you face the prayer hall, a flight of steps leads down to a domed chamber decorated with glazed blue and white tiles which houses the tomb of Al-Arabi. His tomb is the largest, contained within a silver grill surrounded by glass. The four other tombs in the chamber are of two of his sons (the double-tomb); Sheikh Muhammad Kharbutli, a devoted follower of Al-Arabi; Mahmoud Pasha Sirri al-Khunaji, a son-in-law of an Egyptian Khedive; and Abd al-Kader al-Jazairi, a famous Algerian patriot who resisted the French occupation of his country before finally being exiled to Damascus.

Hanbala Mosque

To the east of Mohi ud-Din Mosque, in a side street north off Madares Assad ud-Din Lane, this mosque dates from the early 13th century and was founded by Sheikh Omar Muhammad al-Maqdisi, the leader of the Hanbalite refugees from Jerusalem. Enclosed within unassuming (and easily missed) walls, the mosque interestingly has six classical columns in its courtyard.

Mount Kassioun

① *There is no public transport to the summit; unless you have your own transport, you must take a taxi, in which case you are advised to negotiate a return trip since there is little traffic along this road.*

Rising steeply to the northwest of Damascus is Mount Kassioun (1200 m), a bare, dry ridge of mountain which dominates the city on this side and provides a useful point of orientation. The mountain has a number of legends attached to it. A mosque built over a cave on the eastern slopes of the mountain, near the town of Barzeh (on the road to Saidnaya) is believed to mark the birthplace of Abraham. Most famously, it was from the summit of Mount Kassioun that Muhammad is said to have looked down on Damascus, not daring to enter this oasis of gardens and streams lest its earthly delights distracted him from his quest for heavenly paradise.

There are several good vantage points on its lower slopes that can be reached via the narrow lanes leading off to the north from Madares Assad ud-Din Street in Salihiye district. But the best views out over Damascus are from the top, reached via a road which hairpins its way up the mountain. In summer there are various cafés and stalls close to the summit where tourists and Damascenes alike come to enjoy the cooler air and take in the panorama of the city spread out below: today a sprawling urban mass which is a far cry from the paradise of greenery said to have so impressed Muhammad, but nevertheless an impressive sight. The best times to come up here are late afternoon for sunset over the city, and at night when it is lit up in all its glory.

Saida Zeinab Mosque

① A taxi to the mosque will cost around S£200-300 one way, depending on your bargaining powers. To get there by microbus (servees), take one from Fakhri al-Baroudi St to 'Garagat al-Sitt' (in the southern suburbs of Damascus), and change there for Saida Zeinab Mosque (Jamiaat Saida Zeinab). Non-Muslims are not allowed inside the prayer hall but you can get a good view from the courtyard outside. Women must wear the provided abeyya, men should not wear shorts or short-sleeves.

This fascinating mosque 10 km to the south of central Damascus, like the Saida Ruqqiyeh Mosque in the Old City, is an important place of pilgrimage for Shi'ite Muslims. It is also similar to its counterpart in the Old City in that it is relatively modern, Iranian-built and equally bright and colourful in its decoration. The huge square courtyard features towering circular minarets in two corners and a large gold-domed prayer hall in the centre. Practically every wall surface, including the entire height of the minarets, is decorated with boldly coloured glazed tiles bearing riotous floral patterns or elegant Qur'anic calligraphy. The overall effect is very striking. Inside the prayer hall, the decoration is even more exuberant, with patterned mirror-work complementing the coloured glazed tile-work. In the centre of the prayer hall is the **tomb of Saida Zeinab**, the granddaughter of Muhammad (there is another mosque of the same name in Cairo which also lays claim to being the burial place of Saida Zeinab). The tomb is protected by a silver grille and is almost invariably surrounded by crowds of pilgrims seeking her blessings or intervention.

Hotel and guesthouse prices
LL over US$200 **L** US$151-200 **AL** US$101-150
A US$66-100 **B** US$46-65 **C** US$31-45
D US$21-30 **E** US$20 and under
Restaurant prices
ŤŤŤ over US$12 ŤŤ US$6-12 Ť under US$6
See pages 19-21 for further information.

⓪ Sleeping

Damascus *p39, maps p40, p46 and p48*
Damascus has a distinct lack of decently priced
mid-range and budget accommodation. In
part, this is due to many hotels in these
categories catering solely for the busy Iranian
pilgrim market, which books up entire hotels
years in advance. Most of the hotels below
cater mainly to the foreign tourist market so
you'll only be battling other tourists over a bed
rather than a busload of Iranians. Especially in
summer, it's best to book ahead (at least for
your 1st night) in Damascus. Conversely, those
after luxury accommodation are now spoilt for
choice in the city. In recent years a whole host
of new boutique hotels, set in fabulously
restored old palaces, have opened up in the
Old City. If you want to treat yourself, then this
is the city to do it.

Most of the mid-range and budget
accommodation is based in the New City
with the budget hotels strung out around the
leafy alleyways of Souq Sarouja and in
neighbouring Martyr's Sq. Be aware that
Martyr's Sq is the red-light district of Damascus
and many of the budget hotels (not the ones
listed below) in this area double as brothels.
LL Talisman, Tal el-Hajara St, Old City,
T011-541 5379, www.talismanhotels.com.
Despite the dramatic red internal walls that
are a touch more Moroccan *riad* than
Damascene house, this old Jewish palace is
a heavenly dream. The whole place oozes
film-star glamour with rooms (a/c, satellite TV,
Wi-Fi) lavishly furnished with antique in-laid
furniture and chandeliers, and a small
swimming pool on-site.

LL-AL Beit al-Mamlouka, opposite
Hammam Bakri, just off Bakri St, near
Bab Touma, Old City, T011-543 0445,
www.almamlouka.com. An exceedingly
special boutique hotel festooned with lamps,
traditional textiles and antiques. Attention to
detail is key here and not a penny has been
spared in preserving the building's character;
from the gorgeous floor tiling and gloriously
restored original hand-painted ceilings to
some of the rooms to the fact that all the
mod-cons (a/c, satellite TV) are not on show.
A wonderfully atmospheric place to stay.
L Beit Rumman, Bab Touma, Old City,
T011-545 1092, www.beitrumman.com.
It's the super-friendly service here that sets
this little hotel apart. In a wonderful
300-year-old house with opulent tile-floors
and old stonework, the staff here work hard
to provide the personal touch. Rooms are
all individually decorated and come with a/c,
satellite TV and Wi-Fi. There's shady seating
areas in the internal courtyard, a basement
bar exclusively for guests' use and a rooftop
terrace with views over the city.
Recommended.
L Oriental, Abbara St, near Bab Sharqi,
Old City, T011-543 5336, www.orientalhotel-
sy.com. The subtle, yet elegant rooms here
have lovely old carpets and antique brass and
silverware on display. All surround a peaceful,
plant-filled shady courtyard that's the perfect
respite after a day sightseeing. Rooms have all
the usual mod-cons (a/c, satellite TV and
Wi-Fi), and the utterly charming staff are
happy to help fulfil your every wish.
AL Antique Khan, off Ameen St, Old City,
T011-541 9450, www.antiquekhan-hotel.com.
Tucked away down a tiny alleyway, the
Antique Khan has unusual rooms (some on
2 levels) all with a/c and satellite TV. There's a
shady leafy courtyard, lots of local artwork on
display and cheerful staff.
B Afamia, Furat St, T011-222 8963,
www.afamiahotel.com. Beloved by tour
groups, the Afamia is a solid choice in a

central location, with exceptionally friendly and helpful staff. Some of the older rooms are a little kooky (ask to see a few before deciding) but they're all spotlessly clean and come with a/c, satellite TV and Wi-Fi.

B Orient Palace, Hejaz Sq, T011-222 0502, www.orientpalacehotel.net. This grand old relic has seen better days, but if you can get past the obvious need for an interior update you can focus on its bygone era charm. Rooms (a/c, satellite TV, fridge) are sparsely furnished but beds are made with crisp white linen and the front rooms have balconies with excellent views over Hejaz Sq.

B Salam, Ibn Sina St, T011-221 6674, salamhotel@mail2world.com. Hidden away down a quiet alley behind the Hejaz Railway Station, this hotel has clean, decent-sized rooms (a/c and satellite TV) that are comfortably furnished if a little bland.

B Sultan, Al-Baroudi St, T011-222 5768, sultan.hotel@mail.sy. This long-standing travellers' haunt has helpful management and a cheerful communal lounge. Unfortunately the bright, clean rooms here (a/c and fan), are much too basic for the price. See if you can bargain them down.

C French Palace, 29 May St, T011-231 4015. Popular with local tourists, the grandma-style rooms here are all chintz and frills and come with a/c and satellite TV. It's a clean, well-maintained hotel and although there isn't much English spoken, the staff are welcoming.

D Al-Haramain, Bahsa St, Souq Sarouja, T011-231 9489, alharamain_hotel@yahoo.com. You can't go wrong with this Damascus backpacker institution that has spick-and-span clean rooms (fan only) with incredibly high old-style beds that all share clean bathrooms. It's in an atmospheric 800-year-old building with lovely old tiling on the floors and a small leafy courtyard to hang in. The staff here are friendly souls and can help with any query. Recommended.

D Al-Rabie, Bahsa St, Souq Sarouja, T011-231 8374, alrabiehotel@hotmail.com. Just up the road from the Al-Haramain, the Al-Rabie has

a wide variety of simple clean rooms (fan and fridge, some with a/c, shared bath), and a couple with attached bath. There's a huge courtyard always abuzz with fellow travellers, a roof-top dormitory for the budget-conscious, and management are helpful and efficient.

D Al-Saada, Souq Sarouja St, T011-231 1722. This quiet little hotel has basic rooms (fan only, a couple have attached baths) surrounding a shady courtyard that is covered in vines.

D Ghazal, Souq Sarouja St, T011-231 3736, www.ghazalhotel.com. The friendly Ghazal is a funky little place run by brothers: Muhammad, Ahmed and Said. There's a wide variety of clean, simple rooms (with fan, some with attached bath), a kitchen guests can use, and a large communal area decked out with traditional touches.

E Al-Amin Al-Jadid, Straight St, Old City, T011-542 0297, alaminhotel@yahoo.com. The friendly Al-Amin Al-Jadid is a welcome addition to the cheap hotel scene and the only budget accommodation option in the Old City. The rooms (fan only) are as basic as they get but the owner is a kind-hearted soul, there's free tea on offer at any time of the day, and the shared baths are kept clean. Recommended.

Long-stay accommodation

If you're planning on studying Arabic for a few months in Damascus (or staying in the city a long time for other reasons) it's more economic to rent a room than stay at the budget hotels. The shops along Bab Touma in the Old City usually display flyers in their windows advertising rooms for rent around the city and the 2 places below specialize in renting rooms to students of Arabic.

Damascus Hostel, Alkeshleh al-Abbara St, Old City, T011-541 4115, www.damascus hostel.com. This ramshackle, cheerful place has very simple rooms (fan only) that share baths, a kitchen, and groovy communal areas. There's free tea, coffee and water and a really friendly, homely, atmosphere. You can also stay here for shorter terms (though it's quite expensive if you're not staying for a whole month).

House of Damascus, behind Azem Palace, Old City, T0944-318 068, www.houseof damascus.com. Just like staying in your own share-house. This peaceful old house in the middle of the Old City has rooms with satellite TV and fan that share 2 baths. There's a small courtyard and shady terrace and 2 well-equipped little kitchens to use, making it perfect for long-stayers. Booking is essential.

● Eating

Damascus p39, maps p40, p46 and p48
Damascus is the place to splash out and treat yourself in a swanky restaurant. Many of the best restaurants are based in the Old City and are set in beautifully restored old houses that ooze atmosphere. Even better, a meal in these restaurants won't break the bank. There's generally a 10% government tax added to your bill at all the fancier places.

For cheap eats, the city is awash with little fast-food places. In the New City, Martyr's Sq has loads of *shawarma* and juice stands, all along 29 May St there are bakeries churning out Syrian pizza and on Hejaz Sq there's a bustling fast-food joint that serves good burgers, *shawarma*, chips and all manner of greasy goodness to late at night.

In the Old City there are 2 cheap and cheerful *shawarma* and *falafel* stalls basically opposite each other on Badreddin al-Hassan St. Both have seating on the pavement and the one on the left (walking towards the Umayyad Mosque) does a decent Syrian-style burger as well. There are bakeries and juice stands galore dotted around the Old City.

♥♥♥ **Old Town**, near Roman arch, just off Straight St, Old City, T011-542 8088. Daily 1300-1700 and 1930-late. This long-established place has a lovely courtyard (covered in winter) as well as indoor seating. The rather posh clientele come for the Italian and French dishes (including fresh pasta) but Arabic specialities are served as well. There's a pianist most evenings and alcohol is served.

♥♥ **Al-Kamal**, 29 May St, 1100-late. This old-timer restaurant in the New City has been around for years and still has a loyal following for its French-inspired dishes and friendly service.

♥♥ **Al-Khawali**, Straight St, Old City, T011-222 5808. Daily 1200-0200. Once you've had a meal here you'll soon see why so many famous faces (President Bashar al-Assad and King Carlos of Spain among them) come to Al-Khawali when in Damascus. Set in a wonderful old Damascene house, with tables in the huge courtyard or upstairs, this place has superb service, and an extensive menu with its own original takes on Syrian specialities as well as French-inspired dishes. Don't forget to order the *Al-Khawali hummus*; it's to die for.

♥♥ **Casablanca**, Hanania St, Old City, T011-541 7598. Daily 1230-0100. An upmarket, elegant place set in a beautifully restored old building. The food is primarily French with Arabic touches and there's live music in the evenings.

♥♥ **Leila's**, Umayyad mosque east-side, Old City. Daily 1100-late. Come here to eat on the rooftop terrace, with its gorgeous views over to the Umayyad mosque. The menu is a good mix of Arabic and continental and the salads are particularly good. The service can be a little sloppy and check your bill when paying as they've a habit of overcharging. Alcohol available sometimes.

♥ **Al-Masri**, Said al-Jabri St (sign in Arabic only). Closed in the evening. More closely resembling a narrow corridor than a restaurant, this clean, simple and unpretentious place is popular with locals for lunch and often busy. They serve a wide selection of Egyptian food (the restaurant's name is 'The Egyptian') at very reasonable prices and have a menu in English. The *fatteh* dishes are extremely generous and filling, Also a good place for *fuul* lovers to come for breakfast.

♥ **Art Café**, Tal el-Hajara St, Old City. Daily 1200-late. This cosy stone-walled restaurant does pasta, pizza and *falafel* plates all at reasonable prices. The staff are friendly and you can come here just for a coffee or beer.

Bakdach, Souq Hamidiyeh, Old City. Daily 0900-late. Join the huge queue at this Damascene institution, all waiting for their serving of delicious local-style ice cream. It's the perfect antidote to a hot day in the city and each cone comes covered in a generous helping of crushed pistachios.

Pizza Roma, just off Maisaloun St. Daily 1000-late. A small, clean diner-style place offering good-value pizzas, spaghetti and lasagne.

Cafés

Al-Naufarah, Badreddin al-Hassan St, Old City. Damascus' most famous café is at the bottom of the steps leading down from the east wall of the Umayyad Mosque. It's an extremely popular place to come and hang out for both Damascenes and visitors, and a great place to watch the general comings and goings or just rest after your sightseeing extravaganzas. In the evenings the café is host to the famous storytelling show of Abu Shadi (about 2000 daily) which, although in Arabic, is a captivating performance and the last of an ancient oral-storytelling tradition.

Al-Sham, Badredding al-Hassan St, Old City, Across the alley from the Al-Naufarah, the Al-Sham is another popular traditional café with pavement seating.

Dominos, Bab Touma, Old City. Daily 0930-late. This Parisian-style café and restaurant, dishes up great salads, crêpes and sandwiches, as well as making the best cappuccino in the city. The pavement terrace is always full of hip young things checking each other out and it's a great refuel stop after a few hours of walking around the city.

Eco-Café, north-side of the citadel. This peaceful little place is set within a colourful riot of blooming flowers and greenery that is the bio-diversity and ecological gardens of Damascus. It's a wonderful idea and a great place to escape the city.

Souq Sarouja, Crnr Souq Sarouja St and Bahsa St. A popular, simple little place with tables that spill out across the roadside. In the evenings, pretty fairy lights twinkle and groups of friends come to puff on *narghile* and play backgammon.

⊙ Entertainment

Damascus *p39, maps p40, p46 and p48*
Bars
There are plenty of little pubs in the Christian Quarter of the Old City, particularly by Bab Sharqi and along Bab Touma St. Of the restaurants and cafés above, you can just go for a drink at Art Café and Dominos.

Karnak, Martyr's Sq. Open 1100-late. For something a little different; this smoky little bolt-hole is up the stairs inside a liqueur store and has cheap big cans of local and imported beer, friendly service and brilliant views of the Martyr's Sq traffic chaos below. It's frequented mostly by solitary male drinkers who sit for hours puffing on *narghile* and drinking whiskey, but they're used to tourists dropping in.

Ninar Art Café, off Bab Sharqi, Old City. Daily 1000-late. This stone-walled place on 2 levels is a popular choice with locals and tourists alike. It's got a slightly bohemian vibe and there's decent pizza if you're feeling peckish. There's a decently stocked bar and big bottles of beer are served in blissfully chilled glasses.

Piano Bar, off Bab Sharqi (towards St Ananias Chapel), Old City. Daily 1200-late. If you love bad singing then karaoke at the Piano Bar makes for a highly entertaining night out. If you don't, it's best to stay away. Food is served as well.

Cinema

Cham Cinema, inside Cham Palace Hotel, Maisaloun St. There's a mixed-bag of Hollywood blockbusters, local movies and European art-house films on show at this small theatre.

Cinema City, inside Cattan Hotel building, Barada St. This modern cinema shows the latest Hollywood blockbusters as well as Middle Eastern movies.

Traditional shows

Abu al-Azz, just off Souq Hamadiyeh, signposted 'al-Azz Al Shamieh hall'. Daily 0900-late. The narrow passageway entrance, where delicious savoury pastries are served, conceals a spacious restaurant upstairs on 2 floors, elaborately decorated with marble mosaic walls and painted wood ceilings. All day long there's live Arabic music to listen to while you eat and at about 2200 every evening diners here are entertained by a Whirling Dervish performance.

⊛ Festivals and events

Damascus *p39, maps p40, p46 and p48*
Jul/Aug Jazz Lives In Syria Festival, 1 week of international jazz performances held at Damascus citadel.
Sep Silk Road Festival, a program of cultural events celebrating this ancient trade route with events held in Damascus, Aleppo and Palmyra.
Nov Damascus Film Festival, a celebration of independent film-making, showcasing many new pan-Arab productions at venues across the city.

O Shopping

Damascus *p39, maps p40, p46 and p48*
Damascus is a shopper's paradise with myriad selection of souvenirs to choose from. There are antiques, brassware, ceramics, woodwork, textiles and jewellery galore as well as cheap spices for the foodies, original paintings for the art hunter, all manner of swords for the military buffs and not forgetting the brocades and silks that Damascus is so justly famous for. The Old City is the obvious place to start looking and a rough guide to the shopping districts contained within it is below. The New City has a large handicrafts market set in the grounds of the Madrassa as-Selimiyeh (see page 65), where many artisans display their products. At nearly all places it's the norm to bargain.
Abu Jawal, just off Straight St, Abu Jawal's tiny shop is full of beautiful hand-painted blue and white tiles and ceramics that he makes himself. He's a friendly soul and you can watch him work as you browse.

Anat, Bab Sharqi. A beautifully presented store that sells high-quality, gorgeous textiles; made by women in the Palestinian refugee camp and women's cooperatives all over Syria. The women all share in any sales profits. There are lovely bags, bedcovers, shawls and cushion covers in dozens of colours and designs. It's a wonderful project and well worth your support.
Aram, Straight St, just before the Roman Arch. This place has a huge range of colourful etched and hand-painted glass from dainty tea-glasses to wine goblets and everything in between. There's a fascinating array of colours and designs from traditional Arabic to verging on the contemporary.
Balah Shoes, Qaimariyeh St. Hundreds of different styles of traditional leather sandals and moccasin-style shoes. If you can't find the style/size you want, Mr Balah (who is deaf but lip-reads in English) can custom-make a pair especially for you.
Shahin Art, just off Straight St, www.mshahinart.com. Writer and artist Mahmoud Shahin has built up quite a cult-following among travellers to Syria. He started painting seriously 15 years ago as a way of expressing his thoughts on religion and philosophy, after his novels were banned from being published. Since then he's held exhibitions in Europe as well as Syria. His tiny art gallery is filled to the brim with his modern and quirky original pieces.
Tekkiyeh as-Suleimaniyeh Handicrafts Market, Madrassa as-Selimiyeh, off Omar Ben Abi Rabeea. Along a pleasant shady alley strung with vines, 1 block over from the National Museum, a whole host of jewellers and craft stalls have been set up. Half-way down the alleyway is the entrance to the Madrassa as-Selimiyeh, which was once a school of religion but now houses artisan's workshops. There's original artwork, textiles and hand-painted furniture as well as leatherwork, ceramics and in-laid woodwork on offer. It's a good place to get an idea of what's available and an easy hassle-free place to browse and shop.

Old City shopping guide

Souq Hamidiyeh is the most famous shopping street in the Old City and a great place to stroll along, although much of what's on offer is aimed at local shoppers. There's brilliant browsing potential with meringue wedding dresses and lots of rather raunchy underwear on show. There are also lots of traditional clothing stalls, brocade, leatherwork, *narghile* stores and a few antique places here.

Around the **Umayyad Mosque** are numerous tourist-orientated shops. Around the plaza at the western entrance (as you come out of Souq Hamidiyeh) there are some high-quality stores selling jewellery, lamps, ceramics and inlaid wooden boxes. Following the walls of the mosque around to the southern and eastern sides is a whole host of tiny stalls selling a wide range of gifts (a lot of it cheap and cheerful tat).

Souq al-Silah running off the southern side of the Umayyad Mosque is all glittering with gold. Follow the road straight along until it turns into **Souq Bazuriye** (just after Azem Palace) and the gold is replaced with spice, natural remedies, perfumes and natural oils, and sweets.

Straight Street (Madhat Pasha St) has a kaleidoscope of shopping opportunities. At the Bab al-Jabiye end it's devoted to clothing with lots of *galabeyya* and *kuffiyeh* (the traditional chequered head-dress) shops. Then the spice and nut stalls begin to dominate, but the further up the road you walk (towards Bab Sharqi) the more antique shops begin to appear. You can hunt through brassware, silverware, brocade, woodwork and textiles, as well as glassware, ceramics and furniture.

Badreddin al-Hassan and Qamariyeh St runs off the eastern end of the Umayyad Mosque and there's original artwork, antiques, jewellery, clothing, textiles and woodwork to browse through.

Bookshops

There are a number of ad-hoc news-stands where you can find foreign newspapers, and a good news-stand on Straight St between the Roman Arch and Bab Touma St, though it only seems to be open in the mornings. Titles on offer include the *Herald Tribune*, the *Guardian*, the *Daily Telegraph* and the *Times*, as well as magazines such as *Newsweek*.
Avicenne, Al-Tuhami St. On a little street running parallel to Maisaloun St, this bookshop has a good selection of English- and French-language books on Syrian, Arab and Muslim history, art and architecture as well as some second-hand novels.

▲▲ Activities and tours

Damascus *p39, maps p40, p46 and p48*
Arabic language classes
Damascus is a centre for Arabic language studies, and institutes offer courses on all levels of study from beginner to advanced. There are also many private tutors offering lessons (usually from S£300-1000 per hr).
Arabic Language Centre, Damascus University, Mezzeh Highway, T011-212 9494, www.arabicindamascus.edu.sy. The ALC has an excellent reputation and is a popular choice among foreign students of the language. They run 12-week courses throughout the year for all levels of study. Classes generally run from 0900-1300, 5 days per week and cost approximately US$300 per course plus an initial placement test fee of S£500.
Arabic Language Institute, Mezzeh, Villat Sharkiyya, T011-613 2646, arabicinstitute@ mail.sy. There are 6 different levels of Arabic available with 14-week long courses starting on 1 Feb, 1 Jun and 1 Oct. Course fees are approximately US$200 per course, with an initial placement test fee of S£200. Classes run 5 days per week from 0900-1230.

Hammams
Hammam Bakri, Bakri St, T011-542 6606. Sat-Thu, women 1000-1700, men 1700-2400. Popular with tourists, this well-run place offers sauna, massage and scrub for about S£400.

Hammam Nur ud-Din, Souq Bazuriye, T011-222 9513, men only. Daily 0900-2400. This beautiful old building is the most famous hammam in the city as well as one of the oldest. The full works here is about S£600.

Hammam Silsila, north side of Umayyad Mosque, T011-222 0279. Men only, daily 0900-2300. More basic than the Nur ud-Din, you can opt just for a sauna here or for the full scrub treatment.

Hammam Ward, off Souq Sarouja St. Women Tue-Wed 1200-1700, men daily 0700-2400 (except Tue-Wed women's hours). For a total local experience head to this dilapidated building that's over 800 years old. They hardly ever see tourists and you'll get a hearty welcome. There are definately no frills and no English is spoken but you'll be scrubbed raw and squeaky clean at the end. Sauna and scrub costs approx S£400.

Tour operators

Most of the mid-range hotels and all of the luxury hotel can arrange guides, and cars with driver, and the Tourist Information Centres should be able to provide a list of qualified city guides for you. Some of the budget hotels can arrange day trips to places like Krak des Chevaliers. There are dozens of tour companies in the city all churning out the same-style tours.

Beroia Travel and Tourism, Bab Sharqi, Old City, T0933-221138, www.beroiatravel.com. Run by the dynamic May Mamarbachi, this excellent travel company specialize in doing off-beat, specialist-interest tours that cover Damascus, Syria and neighbouring countries. There are cooking tours, architectural tours, trekking and camping trips and day tours of old Damascene houses and little known Damascus art galleries. They focus on the personal touch here and certainly deliver. May can help you tailor-make a program to suit your needs and wants. 3 times a year (in May, Sep and Oct) they run fabulous cooking tours (that take in the historical sites as well) with chef, Anissa Helou. Recommended.

Eco-tourism Syria, www.ecotourismsyria.com. A young travel company that focus on nature projects as well as historical sites, going to places off the main tourist trail such as Al-Jabbul wetlands and Al-Talila nature reserve. The company aim to support bio-diversity projects and conservation within Syria.

⊖ Transport

Damascus *p39, maps p40, p46 and p48*
Air
Damascus International Airport, T011-453 0201 (flight enquiries T167), is 25 km to the southeast of the city centre and is Syria's main hub for international flights. A taxi from the city centre costs approximately S£700 but be prepared to pay more than this late at night. The airport bus unfortunately only runs from Mezzeh, not into the centre of town, so isn't practical for getting there. The airport has a branch of CBS bank for foreign exchange and ATM, car rental firm offices, a hotel reservations desk, a tourist information office, and an extremely cheap duty-free shop.

Most of the airline offices are based on Said al-Jabri St, around Hejaz Sq, including **Syrian Air**, T011-168 (for central reservations) and T011-169 (airport), or opposite the Cham Palace on Maisaloun St.

Domestic Distances between towns in Syria are generally small enough that you don't need to fly. If you do decide to take a domestic flight, **Syrian Air** has 2-3 flights daily to **Aleppo** (1 hr, S£1742); 2-3 flights daily (except on Tue) to **Lattakia** (1 hr, S£1242); 5 flights per week to **Qamishle** (1½ hrs, S£2242); and 2 per week to **Deir ez-Zor** (1½ hrs, S£1992).

International Syrian Air operate direct international flights to **Amsterdam**, **Athens**, **Cairo**, **Dubai**, **Istanbul**, **London**, **Madrid**, **Munich**, **Rome** and **Vienna**, among others. Other carriers that fly out of Damascus include BMI (T011-223 9800), **Emirates**

(T011-231 3452), **Egypt Air** (T011-223 3093), **Gulf Air** (T011-221 1267), **Royal Jordanian** (T011-221 1267), and **Turkish Airlines** (T011-222 7266). International airport departure tax is S£1500 but this is currently being phased out (and added into the cost of your flight). Ask your hotel for up-to-date information.

Bus

Damascus has 2 main bus stations: Harasta Pullman Station for all destinations north of the city and Al-Samarieh Station for the south. Both stations are out of town. A taxi to either from the centre costs about S£90 and takes about 25 mins (except in peak traffic, from about 1600-1800, when you should give yourself 1 hr to get there). Services are generally frequent enough that you can just turn up at the station and be on your way within an hour. You have to show your passport when buying bus tickets.

Harasta Pullman Station (Garaget Harasta Pullman): There are at least 30 companies here providing transport to all destinations to the north of Damascus, mostly on a/c buses. Kadmous and Al-Ahliah are 2 of the most reliable companies to use. Kadmous has several departures daily to **Aleppo** (4½ hrs, S£200), via **Hama** (3 hrs, S£115) at 0700, 1010, 1230, 1400, 1600 and 1900; **Raqqa** (6 hrs, S£225), via **Homs** (2½ hrs, S£115), at 0730, 0915, 1200, 1315, 1430, 1600, 1730 and 2300; **Deir ez-Zor** (7 hrs, S£300), via **Palmyra** (3½ hrs, S£175) at 0615, 0930, 1130, 1330, 1430, 1600, 1730, 1930 and 2230; and **Qamishle** (9 hrs, S£350) via **Hassakeh** (8 hrs, S£325) at 1230 and 2300. They also have buses to **Tartus** (3 hrs, S£200), every hour from 0530 and **Lattakia** (4 hrs, S£225), every 2 hrs from 0530.

International International services from the Harasta Pullman station: there are also a couple of companies offering transport to **Istanbul** but you'll always have to change buses in Antakya (just over the border).

It's always cheaper to go to **Antakya** direct from Aleppo.

Al-Samariyeh Bus Station (Garaget Al-Samariyeh): The huge, dusty Al-Samariyeh Bus Station can be slightly disconcerting at first glance but it's actually easy to navigate. It consists of 3 different car parks. The first (where some lazy taxi drivers drop you off) is full of microbuses. Walk to the back-left exit of this car park and you reach the Pullman Bus Station. Beyond this car park is the International Service Taxi car park. In the Pullman Station, there are about 6 companies that head to towns south of Damascus, as well as international services to **Amman** (Jordan) and **Beirut** (Lebanon). The companies also have a habit of swapping routes between each other but if you turn up to one ticket booth and they are no longer plying that route, they will point you in the right direction for the company that is.

At the time of writing Al-Rashed were the only company with services to **Bosra** (1½ hrs, S£100). Buses start at 0800 and leave every 2 hrs until 2000. **Damas Tour** run buses to **Suweida** (1½ hrs, S£70), and **Shahba** (1½ hrs, S£70). Buses start at 0600 and run every hr until 1900. **Al-Muhib** have services to **Deraa** which leave every 30 mins from 0800 (1½ hrs, S£80),

International services from the Al-Samariyeh bus station: There are a couple of different companies offering international services but **Challenge** seem to have the best buses. They have 2 normal services to **Amman** in Jordan, at 0830 and 1430 (5 hrs, S£500) and 1 VIP service at 1730 (S£700). To **Beirut** they have 1 bus per day which leaves at 1500 (4 hrs, S£400).

In the car park behind the Pullman station here are **international service taxis**. They tend to be a quicker (and more comfortable) option than the bus because you don't have to wait for an entire bus-load to fill out border procedures. Taxis leave at all times of the day, when full. A seat to either **Amman** or **Beirut** costs S£700.

Car hire

Budget (www.budget-sy.com) have 3 offices in Damascus: Argentina St (T011-224 4403) 29 May St (T011-231 8116) and at Damascus International Airport (T011-540 0070). **Europcar** (www.europcar-middleeast.com) have several offices throughout the city. The most central being inside the Meridian Hotel on Shoukri al-Kouwatli St (T0988-777 664). **Marmou Car Hire** (www.marmou.com) is a good local car-hire company and have an office at Damascus International Airport (T011-333 5959).

Microbus

Microbuses are useful for getting to the smaller towns in the surrounding area that aren't serviced by the Pullman buses. There are 2 microbus garages that travellers will find useful. **Maaloula Garage**, to the south of Abbasseen Sq, has frequent microbuses leaving for **Maaloula** (1 hr, S£40), and **Saidnaya** (1 hr, S£30). From **Abbasseen Garage**, just to the east of Abbasseen Sq, you can get a microbus to **Nabak** (for **Deir Mar Musa**) (1 hr, S£30).

Train

Kadem Station handles all incoming and outgoing train services. It's outside the city centre; a taxi here costs about S£70. The fast trains to Aleppo are particularly good, and are well worth considering as an alternative option to the bus.

There are 3 express services to **Aleppo** (4¼ hrs, 1st class S£240, 2nd class S£200), via **Homs** (2¼ hrs, 1st class S£135, 2nd class S£110), and **Hama** (3 hrs, 1st class S£165, 2nd class S£165), at 0700, 1615 and 2015. There's also a slow train at 1500.

There's an old slow train daily to **Lattakia** (5 hrs, S£155) via **Tartus** (4 hrs, S£115), at 1515 and a train at 1815 every day to **Deir ez-Zor** (7 hrs, 1st class S£200, 2nd class S£135), via **Raqqa** (5 hrs, 1st class S£165, 2nd class S£110).

Services on the old diesel-fired steam train that used to ply the scenic route from Damascus to the Barada Gorge unfortunately no longer begin from Damascus. This may change in the future so enquire at the station for up-to-date information. If you're a train journey enthusiast and want to ride on this train, you now have to journey out to Al-Hamie Station (about S£300 in a taxi) where you can pick up the service which runs daily (during summer months) at 1025 to Ain Fijeh. The return service to Al-Hamie leaves Ain Fijeh at 1700. See page 86.

International The Hejaz rail service between Damascus and Amman is currently suspended. If services do resume (and track maintenance along this line has been going on an awfully long time now so there's no guarantee they will), please be aware that this train journey can be a painfully slow, dusty and uncomfortable process (taking an average 9 hrs); though there's no denying the atmospheric experience of travelling along this route. Before services were suspended, trains left Damascus (Kadem Station) on Sun at 0730 arriving in Amman at 1700 (S£200). Tickets could only be bought on the day of travel.

❶ Directory

Damascus *p39, maps p40, p46 and p48*
Banks

Banks generally stay open later than the rest of the country in Damascus. Main branches (such as the **Commercial Bank of Syria – CBS** branches stated below) are generally open Sat-Thu 0830-2000 and Fri 0830-1400. Most banks in the city now have ATMs that are linked to the international networks. Be aware that cards on the maestro network don't work in some ATMs. In the New City, banks are clustered around Hejaz Sq and Yousef-al-Azmeh Sq, including branches of CBS which deal with foreign exchange and have ATMs. If your maestro card doesn't work in the CBS ATM, try the **Bank of Trade** and Industry ATM on Hejaz Sq. They generally work in this one. In the Old City there is a **Bank of Syria and Overseas** on Mouawela St that has an ATM that takes all foreign cards and an ATM opposite the **Maristan Nur ud-Din Museum** that is linked to the foreign networks.

Cultural centres

Take your passport with you if you want to be admitted to any of the centres. The **American Cultural Centre**, 87 Ata al-Ayoubi St, http://damascus.usembassy.gov/resources.html, is closed to the public until further notice (check the website for up-to-date details on this). **British Council**, off Maisaloun St, T011-331 0631, www.britishcouncil.org/ syria, Sat-Thu 0900-2000, is geared mostly to providing English-language courses, though they organize the odd event. The library here has a limited collection of books, mostly focusing on Britain. Upstairs on the 3rd floor there is a cafeteria with a selection of British newspapers on offer. **Centre Culturel Français**, Bahsa, T011-231 6181, www.ccf-damas.org, Mon-Sat 0900-2100, by far the most active of the cultural centres in Damascus, is housed in a large modern building complete with its own theatre/cinema and exhibition hall. A programme of events, published every 3 months, is available from the centre listing the varied programme of films, theatre, music, exhibitions, etc they organize. **Goethe Institute**, 8 Adnan Malki St, T011-371 9435, www.goethe.de/INS/sy/dam/deindex.html, has a programme of events, published bi-monthly (in German), which lists films, lectures, music, exhibitions, etc.

Embassies and consulates

In an emergency citizens of New Zealand and Ireland should use the UK embassy and Australian citizens should use the Canadian embassy.

If your passport is lost or stolen, your embassy should be able to help you obtain a replacement. However, except in the case of extreme emergencies, most foreign embassies are very reluctant to do anything else for their nationals.

Belgium, Al-Salaam St, No 10 (2nd and 3rd floor), Mezzeh east, T011-612 2189, www.diplomatie.be/damascus. **Canada**, Lot 12, Mezzeh Highway, T011-611 6692, www.syria.gc.ca. **Egypt**, El-Galaa St, Abu Roumaneh, T011-333 2932. **France**, Ata al-Ayoubi St, Al-Afif BP 769, T011-339 0200, consulat@ambafrance-sy.org. **Germany**, Abdul Manen Al-Riad St, T011-332 3800, www.deutschebotschaft-damaskus.org. **Italy**, al-Ayoubi St, BP 2216, T011-333 2621, www.ambdamasco.esteri.it. **Japan**, 18 Al-Mihdi Bin Baraka St, Abu Roumaneh, T011-333 8273. **Jordan**, Mezze Eastern Villas, Western Tarablus St, Building 27, T011-613 6260. **Netherlands**, Al-Jalaa St, Im Tello, Abu Roumaneh, T011-333 6871. **Spain**, Shafi St, Mezzeh East, T011-613 2900. **Turkey**, 58 Ziad Bin Abi Sufian St, Abu Roumaneh, T011-333 1411. **UK**, Kotob Building, 11 Muhammad Kurd Ali St, Malki, T011-373 9241, www.britishembassy.gov.uk/syria. **USA**, 2 Al-Mansour St, Abu Roumaneh, T011-339 1444, www.usembassy.state.gov.

Internet

There are dozens of internet cafés dotted around the city. Some ask to see your passport to register and some don't. **Damascus Internet** is located inside the main post office on Said al-Jabri St. **Internet Zone** is just of Souq Sarouja St, conveniently placed for people staying in the budget hotels. In the Old City **Mission Net** has friendly service, super-fast connections and new computers and is on Straight St, while **Dot Net** is on Bab Touma St.

Medical services

You won't have any problems finding a pharmacy in Damascus, they're everywhere. There are some excellently stocked large pharmacies in the new town along Port Said St. Damascus has several good private hospitals with high standards of medical care. **Shami Hospital** Ibrahim Hanano St, by junction with Jawaher Lal Nahro St, T011-373 5094 has English-speaking doctors and also includes a dental clinic.

Post
The **Main Post Office** is on Said al-Jabri St, Sat-Thu 0800-1900, Fri 0900-1400. The **EMS (Express Mail Service) office** is around the corner. It's better to send parcels by EMS rather than by regular mail. **DHL** has a branch nearby, just off Omar Ben Abi Rabeea St, Sat-Thu 0800-2000, Fri 0900-1400.

Telephone
There are numerous **Easycomm** card-phones dotted all over Damascus, with phonecards on sale from nearby shops, kiosks, juice bars and the like; just ask around. Finding a card-phone may be no problem, but the challenge is to find one which is not right next to a hopelessly busy/noisy junction or main road.

Visa extensions and travel permits
For **visa extensions** head to the **Passport and Immigration Office** on Furat St, between Martyr's Sq and Said al-Jabri St, Thu-Sat 0800-1400. You need 3 passport photos, a letter from your hotel, and must return to collect your passport the next day. This is one of the busiest places to extend your visa, and as well as having to come back the next day, expect to have to wait around quite a bit. Moreover, according to many travellers, the staff here are none too friendly or helpful. If you can time it right, it is far better to get this done elsewhere in Syria. The office at Aleppo is fairly efficient (same-day service), or go for a smaller town such as Tartus, Hama or Lattakia. You should be able to get a 2-month visa extension here. For **Quneitra Permits** you have to go to the **Ministry of the Interior** just to the north of Adnan Malki Sq, in Salihiye, Sun-Thu 0800-1400. You will need your passport, details of your car registration number and (if you've hired a driver), his name and ID number. Permits are free and valid for same day or the next day but if you've hired a driver it's best to go on the same day so that you can show his ID number.

Around Damascus

Damascus is a convenient base from which to explore the surrounding countryside. The places covered here are all easy day trips (or less) from the capital. Bear in mind that the major sites to the south of Damascus (Bosra, Suweidha, Qanawat and Shahba), which are dealt with separately in the South of Damascus chapter (see page 91), can also be visited as longer day trips. In addition Dumeir (on the route from Damascus to Palmyra, see page 277) and Deir Mar Musa (a detour from the Damascus–Aleppo motorway, see page 117) are also feasible as day trips, although if possible it is well worth staying overnight at the latter. ▸▸ For listings, see pages 89-90.

Damascus to Maaloula

From the Citadel, head north along Ath Thawra Street, over the flyover and under the underpass, following the signs for 'Barzeh'. Follow the road round to the right at *Ibn Nafis Hospital* (around 4 km from the centre of Damascus) and then go straight, ignoring the fork to the right soon after signposted for Aleppo and Lattakia. Just under 2 km beyond the *Ibn Nafis Hospital*, turn left at a crossroads. After this turning, there are frequent signs for Saidnaya and Maaloula. The road winds its way through rocky hills, passing first through the village of **Barzeh**, behind which, on the eastern slopes of Mount Kassioun, is a shrine said to mark the birthplace of Abraham. Around 4 km after the crossroads, bear right where the road forks (signposted), and then bear left soon after (not signposted). The road by now has emerged onto a wide flat plain. Around 27 km from Damascus you reach a large modern roundabout; go left here to ascend to the town of **Saidnaya.**

If you continue straight on past this roundabout, a little under 2 km further on there is a second roundabout with a newly built hospital beside it and a left turn signposted for Saidnaya. Around 600 m beyond this there is another left turn for Saidnaya, followed immediately after by a left turn leading up to **Cherubim Convent** (see page 85). Continuing straight along the main road, after around 15 km you pass through the large village of **Al Tawani**, before arriving at a T-junction (just under 24 km from the turning for Cherubim Convent). Turn left here (you pass soon after through a pair of concrete arches, complete with towers and crenulations, which mark the start of **Maaloula** village), and it is another 4 km into the centre (turning right takes you down to the main Damascus–Homs motorway). Arriving in the village, bear right at a roundabout, follow the road round to the right and then sharply left through an S-bend to climb up to Deir Mar Takla. Note that if you are heading for Saidnaya from Maaloula, the small right turn after you pass through the concrete arches is signposted only as an alternative route back to Damascus.

Maaloula → *For listings, see pages 89-90.*

Famous mostly for being one of the few places in Syria where Aramaic, the language of Christ, is still spoken, Maaloula is an important centre of Christianity. The town's butter-yellow and pale-blue houses are stacked higgledy-piggledy on top of another, huddled strikingly against the sheer cliffs that mark the edge of the Qallamoun mountains.

Some of the caves around Maaloula suggest that it was a centre for prehistoric settlement, while others appear to have been dug during Greek and Roman times and subsequently used by the early Christians as refuges from persecution. The occurrence of Aramaic in the region, together with the inscriptions found in some of the caves, confirm

Aramaic

Aramaic, much trumpeted as the language spoken by Jesus, first emerged in ancient Syria and Palestine far earlier, during the seventh to sixth centuries BC, when it began to replace Hebrew, with which it shares its roots as a Semitic language. It continued to be widely spoken throughout the region until the Arab conquest during the seventh century AD. Its importance to Christianity is undisputed and parts of the Bible, notably the Gospel of St Matthew, were originally written in Aramaic.

Sometimes referred to as West Syriac, Aramaic continues to be spoken in Maaloula, and in the nearby villages of Bakhaa and Jabadin, although in recent times it has been for the most part replaced by Arabic. This dialect also survives in the extreme northeast of Syria, amongst communities which have only recently returned to the area, preserving the language during centuries of exile in present-day northern Iraq and eastern Turkey.

Maaloula as one of the earliest centres of Christianity in the world. Later, during the Byzantine period, Christianity flourished in the area.

Ins and outs
Getting there and away There are microbuses from Damascus and from Saidnaya to here. Most microbuses will drop you off at the top of the hill at the Convent of St Takla car park saving you a walk up hill. When leaving, they pick up down the hill at the main intersection.

Deir Mar Takla (Convent of St Takla)
According to legend, this convent grew up around the shrine of St Takla (or St Thecla), daughter of one of the Selucid princes and a pupil of St Paul. The legend relates how Takla was being pursued by soldiers sent by her father to execute her for her Christian faith. Finding herself trapped against the sheer cliffs of Qallamoun, she prayed to God for help. Her prayer was answered when a narrow cleft was opened in the rock face, allowing her to escape to a small cave high up in the cliffs. St Takla is recognized locally as the first Christian martyr, although quite how this is so, when according to the legend she escaped her pursuers and lived in the cave until her peaceful death, is not entirely clear.

Most of the buildings of the current convent are of recent origin, and none show any evidence of surviving Byzantine work. The main chapel has a number of icons inside, while the shrine of St Takla is above, in the side of the rock face.

The defile
From the parking area to the left of the convent, a path leads up through a narrow defile, the rock on either side pressing in, almost to form a tunnel in places. This is the cleft in the cliffs referred to in the legend of St Takla, and there are numerous shrines and caves which have been dug into the rock along its length. It is also to this defile that Maaloula owes its name, the word meaning literally 'entrance' in Aramaic. The defile brings you out eventually at the top of the cliffs. Close to where it emerges, there is a restaurant with a pleasant garden terrace set amongst poplar trees. Bear left and follow the road up past the *Safir Maaloula* hotel to reach the monastery of Mar Sarkis. If you do not wish to walk, you can get to the monastery by car – bear left at the roundabout in the village.

Deir Mar Sarkis

ⓘ *Daily 0800-sunset, no admission charge but donation appreciated, shoulders and knees to be covered on entering the church, no photography allowed.*

The monastery of St Sarkis (or St Serge, from Sergius) is believed to have been founded in the early fourth century AD, on the site of an earlier Greek/Roman temple dedicated to Apollo. St Sarkis, along with St Bacchus, to whom the monastery is dedicated, were soldiers in the Roman army based at Rasafeh (see page 289). Having converted to Christianity, they refused to make sacrifices to the god Jupiter and were put to death. Their remains are believed to have been housed in the large basilica there, and during the Byzantine period Rasafeh was known as 'Sergiopolis' in honour of St Sarkis.

The entrance to Deir Mar Sarkis is through a low, awkward doorway, presumably a defensive feature. This leads through to a small, recently restored courtyard. On your left is a room labelled 'Museum and Souvenirs'. There is an excellent series of postcards of the monastery's icons on sale here, along with various items of religious kitsch. The square pit hewn out of the stone floor in this room was for pressing grapes.

At the far end of the courtyard, on the right, a passage leads through to the monastery's church. The main altar of the church, in the central apse, is of particular interest, consisting of a semi-circular slab of marble with a 7-cm rim around it. The fact that the altar is semi-circular is taken as evidence that it dates from before AD 325, the date of the First Council of Nicea, when it was decreed that all altars had to be flat and rectangular. The rim around the edge of the altar is thought to be a feature surviving from pagan times, when altars were used for animal sacrifices in which the blood had to be collected. As the monks of the monastery are quick to point out, however, the rim appears to have been simply a stylistic feature, as in this case there is no drainage point from which to collect the blood, nor is the rim engraved with the animals which were suitable for sacrifice, as was the norm on pagan altars. Below the altar is a small crypt. In the side-apse to the left is another altar, this one also with a rim, though rectangular in shape. Note the fresco in the dome above the altar, depicting the heavens with the Virgin Mary and Jesus surrounded by the saints Mathew, Mark, Luke and John.

The iconostasis of the church includes a number of particularly beautiful icons painted by St Michael of Crete in the early 19th century. The one above the entrance to the central apse is of St Sarkis and St Bacchus. On the pillar to the right of the entrance to the central apse is something you don't see often: Christ's crucifixion and the Last Supper portrayed in a single icon. It is also unusual in that Jesus is seated to the right of the table rather than in the centre. Also of interest is the icon of St John the Baptist, here smiling and relaxed, with his legs crossed (in contrast to the usual serious/formal depictions), having baptized Jesus and therefore completed his mission. Some of the icons in the church are thought to date back as far as the 13th century.

There is clear evidence in the church of its ancient origins. The lower part of the iconostasis consists of stone slabs taken from the earlier Greek/Roman temple, while some of the capitals appear to have originated from the same source. Above the arches separating the nave from the side aisles, wooden beams can be seen incorporated into the stonework. These are thought to have served to reinforce the church against earthquakes. Samples taken from them have indicated that they are Lebanese cedar, and around 2000 years old, suggesting that they too were recycled from the original temple. Outside the church, around the side, there is an even smaller arched entrance, now protected by a porch and sealed behind a metal door. In the immediate vicinity of the monastery there are several substantial rock-cut caves.

Maaloula to Yabroud

The road leading from the centre of Maaloula up to Deir Mar Sarkis is also the road to Yabroud. Some 4 km from the roundabout in Maaloula, turn right at a T-junction and then keep going straight, passing through two villages before descending steadily to reach the town of Yabroud, 19 km from Maaloula. En route, the Qallamoun mountains present a very different aspect, sloping up gently to the west, and revealing themselves as part of the plain itself, tilted up and sheared off to create the sheer cliffs that characterize the setting of Maaloula as seen from the east. Shortly before arriving in Yabroud, you pass on the right more rock-cut tombs dating from Roman times. Bear left as you enter the town to reach the centre; right takes you directly on to the Damascus–Homs motorway.

Yabroud

There is evidence of settlement in the area of Yabroud going back at least to the Mesolithic period (10,000-7500 BC), while in Roman times the town appears to have formed part of the territory placed under the control of Agrippa II. Its importance can be surmised from the discovery in Rome of an altar dedicated to *Malekiabrudis* or Jupiter Malek of Yabroud, the local form of Jupiter. Today Yabroud is a sizeable, prosperous and rapidly growing town, thriving on the narrow strip of fertile agricultural land in which it is set. In the centre there is the large Greek Catholic **Cathedral of Constantine and Helen**. This is thought to stand on the site of an earlier Temple of Jupiter, with stones from the temple having been incorporated into the fabric of the cathedral. Inside, the cathedral consists mostly of modern restoration, although there are some beautiful icons and traces of Roman architectural fragments in the apses. On the edges of the town the remains of another ancient church are being incorporated into a new church of modernistic design. Following the main road northeast out of Yabroud, after 8 km it joins the Damascus–Homs motorway just south of the town of Nabak. This route also offers a more interesting alternative for part of the otherwise motorway-bound journey between Damascus and Homs.

Saidnaya

Saidnaya's origins go back to ancient times, with evidence suggesting that it was inhabited at least from the sixth century BC, when it was known by the Aramaic name of 'Danaba'. Evidence of occupation can be found right the way through Greek and Roman times, and it emerged as an important centre of Christianity well before this became the official religion of the Roman Empire. By the time of the Crusades, Saidnaya was second only to Jerusalem as a centre of pilgrimage for Christians. Despite the town's impressive array of convents, monasteries, churches, chapels and shrines, today Saidnaya has a modern, nondescript air in places due to the plethora of new construction in the town.

Ins and outs

Getting there and away There are microbuses from Damascus, Maaloula and Nabak to here. Microbuses from Maaloula tend not to be as frequent.

Sights

In the centre, perched on a rocky hillock overlooking the town is the Greek Orthodox **Convent of Our Lady of Saidnaya**. From a distance it looks for all the world like a fortress and some people argue that this was the function it originally served. The convent is an important pilgrimage site for Christians and Muslims alike, the object of veneration being an icon of the Virgin Mary supposedly painted by St Luke. According to legend, the convent was founded by the Byzantine Emperor Justinian during the sixth century. Much damaged by earthquakes and the passage of time, today the convent is a jumbled mixture of old features and new restoration, much of the latter undertaken in recent years. Flights of stairs zigzag up from the parking area below the convent to the small low doorway leading inside. (Alternatively the tower to the left houses a lift.)

The main chapel has numerous painted gold icons and a wooden *iconostasis* in front of the altar. The pilgrimage shrine, known as *Shaghoura* ('the famous') is a small dark room around the right-hand side of the chapel on the outside. The icon attributed to St Luke is kept hidden in an ornate silver-doored niche, while either side of this there are a number of later icons. Numerous beaten silver crosses and other religious symbols left by pilgrims are pinned to the walls. The large room off the courtyard to the right of the shrine houses a small museum, containing mostly painted gold icons. You will need to track down someone with the key if it is not open.

The hillock on which the convent is perched was certainly the site of earlier shrines, including possibly a sun temple dating from Greek and Roman times. As you ascend by the road up to the car park below the convent, a **cave tomb** is visible cut into the side of the rock, sealed by a metal door. Above it are three carved niches each containing a pair of figures (today very worn and headless) and a conch shell semi-dome in the arch of the niches. Greek inscriptions date these tombs to AD 178, although in all probability they were first inhabited far earlier. Around Saidnaya there are a number of caves which have shown evidence of settlement since the early Stone Age, the most important of these being in the low rocky mound by the roundabout as you approach Saidnaya.

Amongst the houses that cluster around the convent there are numerous other small churches, monasteries and shrines dedicated to various saints. Some are very old, although the majority of these have undergone extensive restoration. The **Church of St Peter**, situated by the roundabout below the Convent of Our Lady of Saidnaya, on the southeast side, is a remarkably intact Roman building that has remained almost completely unmodified since its conversion to a church.

Just over 2 km to the northwest of Saidnaya, and accessible only by foot, is the **Monastery of Mar Thomas**, also originally a Roman Temple which was later converted into a monastery. The route is not obvious, so walk in the general direction and then ask – you should be pointed along the correct track with a bit of luck. The main building is a squat structure set in a courtyard. It has been partially restored, with a new cross of white stone now standing on the top. The building is locked and the keys kept at the main convent.

Around 8 km to the northeast of Saidnaya, strategically situated on the highest point of the local Qallamoun mountain range, is the **Cherubim Convent**. From the turning off the main Saidnaya–Maaloula road (see above), the narrow road winds its way steeply up to the convent, offering some excellent views along the way. The church itself is a small building, restored in 1982 when a new roof was added, but incorporating three classical columns and some huge stone blocks which attest to its origins sometime during the third century AD.

Today the church is dwarfed by a large and somewhat ungainly new school/orphanage. The keys to the church are held by the resident caretaker. Dotted around the grounds are various architectural fragments from Greek and Roman times. Adjacent to the church is a rocky outcrop topped by two crosses, from where there are panoramic views out over the town of Saidnaya and the surrounding countryside.

The Barada Gorge to Zabadani and Bloudan

From Damascus you can follow the narrow Barada river up through low hills which mark the southwest extremities of the Anti-Lebanon range, eventually arriving on the wide fertile plain of Zabadani. The town of Zabadani is the largest of several hill resorts in the area and popular amongst Syrians as a weekend retreat from the stifling summer heat of Damascus. The scenic route via the 'old' Zabadani road runs up through the green and well-wooded Barada gorge and is well worth the trip if you have your own car. This is also the route taken by the old narrow-gauge railway which, at the time of research, was still running from Al-Hamie to Ain Fijeh (before Zabadani) during the summer months. Services along this line are by an ancient Swiss-built diesel-fired steam train which hauls equally antiquated wooden carriages. It's an excruciatingly slow trip and the main reason for taking it is for the scenery and the novelty value (see page 78).

Damascus to Zabadani via the old road

From Umawiyeen Square head west along the continuation of Shoukri al-Kouwatli Street, keeping the Sheraton hotel on your left (signposted 'Dumar'). Continue straight through the busy town of Dumar (or 'Douma'). Around 10 km from Umawiyeen Square, shortly after passing the Barada Beer brewery on the left, there is a fork in the road with a petrol station in the wedge of the fork. Bear right here and just under 1 km further on you arrive at a T-junction with a large dual-carriageway. Go left here and right immediately after to rejoin the old Zabadani road.

The road first descends into a valley, the floor of which is surprisingly green and well-wooded, before starting to climb steadily, passing through several villages.

There are various summer restaurants along the road as it winds its way through the Barada gorge. Although their setting amongst shady trees is pleasant enough, the river itself – generally little more than a stream – is unfortunately very polluted, particularly in summer when most people visit and flow is at its minimum.

At **Ain Fijeh** (just under 20 km from the Umawiyeen Square, off to the right below the main road) there are a few restaurants close to the railway station. The village owes its name (and its existence) to the spring which emerges here and once used to add to the waters of the Barada river, though it is now piped directly to Damascus to supply the city's drinking water.

The small village of **Souq Wadi Barada** (28 km) stands on the site of the ancient Hellenistic town of **Abila**, which grew into an important centre on the route between Baalbek and Damascus. According to legend, it was on the mountain of Nebi Habil to the west of here that Cain buried Abel after killing him; hence the town's name. The only remains of the Hellenistic town, however, are in the occasional recycled architectural fragments to be found built into some of the houses.

Less than 2 km beyond the village, a series of rectangular doorways can be seen cut into the rock face on the opposite side of the now much narrowed gorge, marking a set of **Roman tombs**. The neatly hewn vaults each contain several compartments to house sarcophagi. To the left of the tombs (facing them from the road) a section of **irrigation channel** is visible, also of Roman origin or perhaps earlier, cut into the side of the rock face. Beyond this and above the level of the irrigation channel, there is a short stretch of **Roman road**, well preserved as it passes through a cutting. This is the road that connected Baalbek and Damascus. There are two inscriptions in the side of the cutting, both in Latin, which record how the road was restored following a landslide by the Legate Julius Verus, during the joint reign of Marcus Aurelius and Lucius Verus (AD 161-180). Reaching the tombs, irrigation channel or Roman road is rather tricky, and only for the sure-footed.

It is possible to **cross the gorge** from a point just past the Roman tombs, by walking across the rubbish-strewn bank from which the stream appears to emerge (if this is indeed one of the sources of the Barada, it can only be said that it starts as it means to go on), and then traversing a short though rather precarious section of concrete aqueduct to reach a path leading up to the tombs. Another option is to continue some 500 m along the modern road, around the corner to a point where a track leads off to the right. From here, double back along a track leading towards a small electricity pylon on a shoulder of the hillside. Just around the corner from this is the section of Roman road where it passes through a cutting. A little further on, it is possible to descend to the irrigation channel and follow it through a very deep and narrow cutting, followed by a short stretch of tunnel (not for the claustrophobic), and then past a couple of tricky sections where the outside wall has fallen away, to arrive at the tombs.

Continuing along the main road, after just under 3 km you reach what is in effect a T-junction. Bear right here (left to reach the Damascus–Beirut motorway) and follow the road for a further 12 km to reach Zabadani. This last stretch is across a broad, fertile plain boasting rich orchards of apples, apricots, walnuts, plums and cherries.

Zabadani

This popular hill resort has an affluent and, in summer at least, lively feel to it with plenty of well stocked shops along the main high street and a good selection of restaurants and cafés to choose from. Up on the hillside above the main town is a rapidly growing area of holiday homes owned by richer Syrians. The main high street, which crosses the railway line just by the station, is the focus for the modern town, with most of the shops, restaurants and cafés. Downhill from the station is 'old' Zabadani, quieter and more picturesque with an interesting old mosque in the centre and, close by, a Catholic church.

Getting there and away Regular microbuses run from the Al-Samariyeh bus station in Damascus (one hour, S£40) via the modern Beirut motorway. In Zabadani, microbuses cruise through the village picking people up for the return journey. If you have your own car, you can travel the far more picturesque route via the 'old' Zabadani road through the green and well-wooded Barada gorge (see above).

Bloudan

The town of Bloudan is situated 7 km to the east of Zabadani, at the slightly higher altitude of 1400 m. It is a smaller and somewhat more exclusive version of Zabadani, consisting mostly of modern concrete construction that has largely swamped the original Greek Orthodox and Catholic village out of which it grew. The main square is actually in the lower part of the town, and from here you can continue up the mountainside, passing ever more exclusive and fancy residences and restaurants along the way. Fridays are the best day to visit (this is true of Zabadani also), when the town is at its liveliest with day-trippers from Damascus, as well as visitors from Lebanon and Gulf-State holidaymakers.

Getting there and away As with Zabadani, microbuses from Damascus leave from Al-Samariyeh station but the services are not as frequent (one hour, S£40). If you want to visit both towns in the same day, note that there's no direct transport between the two and you'll have to hire a taxi from Zabadani.

If driving from Zabadani, the road hairpins its way up the mountainside, offering great views out over the valley below, before arriving in the town's main square.

Quneitra and the Golan Heights

Just 60 km to the southeast of Damascus are the Golan Heights, an area of high plateau between Mount Hermon and the northeastern shores of the Sea of Galilee, effectively marking the southern limits of the Anti-Lebanon mountains. Known in antiquity as the 'Gaulanitis' and then later as 'Jaulan', historically this area forms part of the wider Hauran region. Today it has become emblazoned in most people's minds as a potent symbol of the Arab-Israeli conflict.

Quneitra is a monument to the wanton destruction carried out by Israeli troops when they were forced to withdraw. It's a sad and depressing reminder of the continuing struggles of this region and how far there is still to go before they can be resolved.

Ins and outs
Getting there and away All visitors to Quneitra must obtain a **permit** in advance from the Ministry of the Interior in Damascus. Permits are free and are generally issued within around half an hour. However, they are only valid for 48 hours and you will need to have your own transport to be issued one (see page 80).

To drive from Damascus, head out of the city on the Mezzeh road (from Umawiyeen Square head southwest, keeping the Sheraton hotel on your right). Keep going straight to pass under the Beirut motorway (Quneitra is prominantly signposted straight ahead) and keep to this road all the way. After a while the looming outline of Mount Hermon comes clearly into view off to the right, often still streaked with snow as late as June. At the first check-post you come to, around 30 km from Damascus by a right turn signposted for Beit Saber, your permit and passport details are recorded in a book. A little further on, there are the remains of a large fortress on the right as you enter the town of Sa'asaa. Beyond Sa'asaa the countryside gives way to the distinctive rocky black basalt terrain of the Hauran. At Khan Arnabeh (61 km from Damascus) your permit and passport details will be recorded once again and a guide is assigned to show you around. It is a further 9 km on to Quneitra itself.

Background
Originally part of Syria, the Golan Heights were lost to Israel during the 1967 war. In 1973 Egypt and Syria launched simultaneous attacks on the Israeli-occupied Sinai and Golan Heights. Despite initial gains by Egypt and Syria, they were both subsequently pushed back and it was only in the negotiations following a ceasefire that Syria was able to regain some 450 sq km lost in the fighting. A UN-supervised demilitarized zone was established to separate the two sides, with Syria now administering this area under continued UN supervision.

The town of Quneitra today stands at the very edge of this demilitarized zone, with Israeli-occupied territory immediately beyond the barbed wire fences on its western outskirts. When the Israelis withdrew in 1973, they completely, and senselessly, demolished the town, leaving only the smashed, empty shells of buildings in their wake, and the Syrians have responded by leaving almost everything exactly as they found it, as a propaganda showcase against Israel.

Sights

You will be accompanied around the town by an official guide who is a Syrian army officer and is there for your safety (there are minefields in the area) only. You should tip your guide at the end of the 'tour'.

This battered ghost town has a sad, eerie atmosphere. Here, frozen in time, is an illustration of one of the great unresolved disputes of the Arab-Israeli conflict, a tangible episode of the modern history of the Middle East preserved in twisted metal and concrete. The UN military posts, the copious barbed wire and the Golan Heights themselves off to the west, all stand testimony to the continuing intractability of the dispute.

At the **hospital** you can inspect the heavily ruined shell of the building, while from the roof you can get good views over the town and the Golan Heights. Other prominent ruins include those of a **church** and a **mosque**. The **Liberated Quneitra Museum** is one of the few buildings to have been brought back into use. Housed in what was originally an Ottoman khan (of some interest in itself), the museum brings together a small collection of prehistoric, Roman and Byzantine artefacts; pottery, coins, architectural fragments, etc.

Following the main street to the very western extremity of the town, barbed wire marks the start of a stretch of **no man's land**, beyond which is effectively Israel. From the viewpoint you can see the two mountains to the east beyond the wide strip of cultivated land, the one to the left, bristling with the paraphernalia of Israel's observation and early warning systems, is Abou Nader, while the one to the right is Araam.

⦿ Around Damascus listings

For Sleeping and Eating price codes and other relevant information, see Essentials pages 19-21.

⬤ Sleeping

Maaloula *p81*

As well as Maaloula's 1 hotel, you can also stay the night in the spartan rooms of the Convent of St Takla. For cheap snacks, there are a couple of restaurants in the car park beside Deir Mar Takla.

AL Safir Maaloula, just before Deir Mar Sarkis, T011-777 0250, www.safirhotels.com. It doesn't look like much from the outside, but the bright rooms here are comfortable and nicely furnished, and come with a/c and satellite TV. Some of the rooms have great views over the valley. There's a swimming pool, restaurant, bar and coffee-shop, and the staff are ultra-friendly.

Saidnaya *p84*

Apart from the 1 hotel, you can also ask at the convent if it's possible to stay.

B Saidnaya, on the western outskirts of town (heading up into town from the 1st roundabout as you arrive from Damascus, a sign on the right points the way down a steep narrow street to the hotel), T011-595 3739. Simple but comfortable rooms, some with balcony. There's a restaurant and small swimming pool.

⦿ Eating

Maaloula *p81*

⫟ **Al-Barakeh**, on the road to Deir Mar Sarkis. This friendly little restaurant has a shaded courtyard and does the usual mix of mezze and grills.

⫠ **La Grotta**, entrance to Deir Mar Sarkis. A modern little café with that's good for a refreshment stop after visiting the church. They do great sandwiches and they've got a nice outside terrace to relax in.

Saidnaya *p84*

For snacks and sandwich places head to the main street just below the Convent of Our Lady of Saidnaya.

♥♥ **Al-Massaya**, main street below convent. Small but clean and pleasant restaurant serving reasonable food.

❀ Festivals and events

Maaloula *p81*

14 Sep Exhaltation of the Holy Cross, Maaloula's most important feast day, when fires are lit on top of the cliffs and there is dancing and fireworks. Feast of St Takla (24 Sep).

7 Oct Feast of St Sergius.

Saidnaya *p84*

7-8 Sep Feast of Our Lady of Saidnaya, Vast numbers of pilgrims, both Christian and Muslim, flock here every year for this event from all over the Middle East. People start arriving here a couple of days before, with the main celebrations taking place on the night of 7 Sep, and being repeated again on a smaller scale on the following night. Around this time practically every available inch of floor space within the Convent of Our Lady of Saidnaya is taken up with pilgrims

sleeping, praying, eating picnics, etc. Rooms at the town's only hotel, meanwhile, double in price and are soon all full.

⊖ Transport

Maaloula *p81*

Microbuses leave from the main intersection down the hill from Deir Mar Takla. To **Damascus** (1 hr, S£40) they leave frequently but start to peter out by early evening. To **Saidnaya** services aren't quite as regular but if you start off early enough from Damascus to Maaloula you can still quite easily do both Maaloula and Saidnaya in 1 day. If you want to go to **Deir Mar Musa** from Maaloula, catch the microbus to Saidnaya and change there for Nabak.

Saidnaya *p84*

Fairly frequent microbuses run from the main road in Saidnaya back to the the Maaloula Garage in **Damascus**, departing when full (1 hr, S£40). Public transport between Saidnaya and **Maaloula** is less frequent. Your best bet is to wait down on the main road and hitch; any traffic heading in that direction is sure to give you a lift. You can also get microbuses to **Nabak** (for Deir Mar Musa) from here.

Contents

Footprint features

Border crossings

South of Damascus: The Hauran

The Hauran, with its stark landscape of flat plateau and black basalt stone, is the southern gateway into Syria. If you're arriving from Jordan, the nondescript plains rolling onward for miles beside the highway will be your first impression of this region, but away from the main road artery the Hauran has its own, if rather austere, beauty. The Leja, in the centre of the region, is a broodingly dramatic landscape created by an immense sheet of lava, while between Bosra and Deraa is the particularly fertile Nuqra plain with its fields golden with wheat and barley in spring.

Historically a border region, marking the edge of Rome's eastern empire, the Hauran has played an important role throughout history. Bosra, with its ruins that stretch back to Nabatean times and its massive Roman theatre, is an obvious highlight, but among the other small towns there are more historical gems to be found. Shahba (ancient Philippopolis) was the birthplace of Philip the Arab, the local boy who rose to Roman emperor. Suweida has a small but stunning mosaic museum and Ezraa's church lays claim to be the resting place of St George. Most of the Hauran is within easy reach of Damascus, making exploring the sights here perfect for day trips from the city.

Ins and outs

Getting there and away

There are regular direct bus services from Damascus to each of the major places of interest. If you've crossed the bord er from Jordan by local public transport and want to visit Bosra on the way to Damascus, you need to be dropped in Deraa and catch a microbus from there. If you've caught a bus or service taxi direct from Amman they will use the Nasib/Jabir border crossing that bypasses Deraa and you won't be able to do this. ▸▸ *For further details, see page 97.*

Unfortunately public transport services between the towns in the Hauran are less reliable than connections to Damascus. The main problem is with the trip between Bosra and Suweida. For some reason there is no public transport along this route, making it very difficult to visit all the sites in one loop from Damascus. Instead it is more practical to make two separate day trips: one to Bosra (and perhaps Ezraa) and another to Shahba, Qanawat and Suweida.

With your own transport you are free to visit the sites in any order, although covering them all in one day would involve a pretty hectic schedule.

Background

The Hauran was for a time colonized by the **Greeks** under Alexander the Great, before the conflicts of the rival Seleucid and Ptolomid Empires opened the region to competing Nabatean and Jewish claims. Thus in 23 BC Augustus, ruler of the newly expanding Roman Empire, granted control over it to Herod the Great, the king of Judaea. Then in AD 34 it was briefly made part of the Roman Empire before being handed over to Herod Agrippa I by Caligula. In AD 70 the **Nabateans** made Bosra the new capital of their empire, although they never succeeded in extending their control over the whole region.

In AD 106 the **Romans**, who until then had exercised for the most part only nominal control over much of Syria, established the province of *Arabia*, with Bosra as its capital. Subsequently the Hauran flourished under the new stability brought by the *Pax Romana*. Agriculture was developed, making this one of the great granaries of the empire, while the important trade routes which passed through Bosra brought further prosperity. The rise to power of **Philip the Arab** as emperor in the mid-third century AD ensured that the Hauran maintained its importance, with Shahba being developed into a prosperous imperial city alongside Bosra.

During the **Byzantine** period the Hauran continued to prosper as an important centre of Christianity. However, following the **Muslim Arab invasions** of the seventh century the region fell into relative decline, becoming an unstable zone of conflict, first between the rival Fatimid and Abbasid dynasties and later the Muslims and Crusaders.

In the 18th and 19th centuries large numbers of Druze migrated into the area, first from Mount Lebanon and later from Damascus and surrounding areas. Thus the mountainous massif in the southeast became known as the Jebel Druze, and today this region remains something of a Druze enclave.

Damascus to Deraa and Bosra

The easiest and best (although by no means the most direct) route to Deraa is via the motorway running due south from Damascus. To join the motorway, head southwest from Umawiyeen Square along the Mezzeh Autostrade (keeping the Sheraton hotel on your right), and then, after just under 5 km, join the motorway ring-road around Damascus heading anticlockwise. The first exit you come to, after a further 5 km, is the motorway for Deraa, Bosra and the Jordanian border (clearly signposted). Around 77 km after joining the motorway, there is an exit clearly signposted for **Ezraa**, 3 km to the east (see below). From here it is just over 14 km to the exit for **Deraa** (clearly signposted). The exit for **Bosra** is just over 10 km further on, or you could continue on to cross into Jordan via the Nasib/Jabir border crossing. Taking the Deraa exit, after just over 9 km you arrive at a T-junction. Turn left here to join the old Deraa road. It is a further 6 km into the centre of Deraa, passing the huge new Assad's Athletic City sports complex on the way and entering the town along Damascus Street.

An **alternative route** is to take the old Deraa road, which runs roughly parallel to the motorway for the entire journey. From the Hejaz railway station, head south along Halbouni Street, eventually joining Khaled Ibn Walid Street and following it past Kadam railway station. Around 5 km south of Kadam station, continue straight past a right turn signposted for Deraa and Jordan (this turning takes you onto the motorway), and keep going straight. The old Deraa road is slightly more direct (105 km as opposed to 115 km), but also considerably slower and without any particular attractions along its route.

Ezraa

The town of Ezraa, identified with the ancient *Zorava*, was an important centre of Christianity during the Byzantine period, its bishop being invited to attend the Council of Chalcedon in AD 451. It is famous for the ancient and well preserved Greek Orthodox St George's Church (Mar Georgis).

Ins and outs
Getting there and away The easiest way to reach Ezraa by public transport is from Deraa (main bus station). If there is no bus going direct, catch one to Ash Sheikh Miskeen, and change there for Ezraa. Services along this route are reasonably frequent.

From Ezraa, there is a good road running southeast which traverses the lava-strewn Leja region to arrive at Suweida, 37 km away. Ask directions in the centre of Ezraa to pick up the correct road.

Sights
St George's Church ① *no fixed opening times or entrance fee, if the church is locked, ask around and someone will send for the caretaker; donation towards the upkeep of the church and perhaps a small tip for the caretaker is expected*, is 3 km to the north of the town centre. To get there from the motorway, bear right at the grain processing factory and continue until you come to the roundabout at the centre of town (marked by a mosque with a distinctive black and white banded minaret). Bear left here (signposted 'Archaeological Area') and keep following the road until you see the church. An inscription on the lintel of the central portal of the west entrance (around to the left from the current entrance), reads *"What was once a lodging place for demons has become a house of God; where once*

idols were sacrificed, there are now choirs of angels; where God was provoked to wrath, now He is propitiated." The inscription dates from AD 515, making this amongst the oldest functioning churches in Syria along with those of Saidnaya and Maaloula.

As the inscription suggests, the church stands on the site of an earlier pagan temple. Its design is of particular interest, representing one of the earliest examples of a basilica constructed on an octagonal plan and surmounted by a cupola. Inside, eight columns arranged in an octagon and connected by arches support the central cupola, a more recent metal and wood reconstruction of the original. This is enclosed within a basic square plan, with small chapels in each corner creating an octagonal effect. Note the corbelled ceiling of basalt slabs, one of which is carved with three medallions. On the east side, behind a simple wooden iconostasis, is an apse and two side-chambers which extend beyond the basic square plan to give a rectangular shape from the outside. In the central apse, behind the altar, is a tomb which, according to local tradition, is that of St George himself.

Just before you reach the church, on the right, are the **ruins of an Ayyubid mosque**. All that survives of it is the prayer hall, which is still largely intact, with two arcades of arches supported on a variety of pillars, columns and a double column. The corbelled ceiling is still in place, as is the black and white banded *mihrab*.

Nearby, down a small side-street, is the Greek Catholic **Church of St Elias**. Although this is also very old, dating from AD 542, it has undergone extensive reconstruction and restoration in recent years. Architecturally it is also interesting, the east-west orientated cruciform plan being unusual for Syria. Inside, a central square of pillars and arches supports the cupola, which is a modern affair. The internal walls are now all plastered, but on the outside you can still see much of the original stonework, complete with various inscriptions and carvings.

Deraa → *For listings, see pages 112-114.*

Today, there is not a great deal of interest in Deraa, but the town has been identified with the ancient Edrei, mentioned in the Bible as one of the residences of Og, king of Bashan. During the Byzantine period it was known as Adraa. During the early 20th century Deraa prospered when it became a station on the Hejaz railway line, which ran between Damascus and Medina. These days the town is useful mostly as a base for visiting Bosra, Tell Shahab and Ezraa. It is also the place to go from if you wish to cross the border into Jordan by local transport.

Ins and outs
Getting there and away The main bus station is inconveniently located around 3 km to the east of the town centre, on the road to Bosra. There are regular microbus services connecting Deraa with Bosra and Pullman buses to Damascus, as well as less regular microbus services running between Deraa and Suweida.

Orientation Deraa's hotels and restaurants are along Ibrahim Hanano St, just to the south of the railway station, while the main sights are a couple of kilometres to the south, across the river in the older part of the town.

Tourist information There is a small **tourist information office** ① *Sat-Thu 0800-1430, on the old road to Damascus, just north of where it crosses the railway tracks.*

Sights

In the southern part of the town is the **Omari Mosque**. Built in 1253 by the Ayyubid Emir, Nasser ud-Din Osman Ibn Ali, it follows the same basic plan as the Umayyad Mosque in Damascus. In one corner is a distinctive square tower-minaret. Inside you find yourself in a large courtyard with the prayer hall to the right as you enter. Around the three remaining sides is an arcade supported by two parallel rows of columns and arches. The columns (almost certainly taken from the Roman theatre next door) are unusually short and topped by an odd assortment of capitals, with the stonework of the arches making up the remaining height. The prayer hall has three parallel rows of arches, also supported on squat columns, with a central transept marking the *mihrab*.

Across the road from the mosque there is an area of excavations including, at the far end of the site, the scant remains of a **Roman theatre**, parts of which have been rather insensitively restored. In the excavated pits closer to the mosque you can see sections of columns and various capitals just like those found in the mosque.

For those with a fascination for the bygone days of steam, the **railway station**, in the centre of the modern (northern) half of the town, is perhaps worth a visit. When the Hejaz railway between Damascus and Jordan is up and running again (currently suspended for track maintenance), the train stops here. Looking at the general state of dilapidation all around (various decaying steam engines can be seen standing in the sidings around the station), it's not hard to see why trains are currently not running on this line.

On Ibrahim Hanano Street there is the **Syndicate of Fine Arts** ① *Thu-Sat 0900-1400, free*, which contains a small but interesting collection of paintings (and some sculpture) by artists from southern Syria.

Around Deraa

Tell Shahab

Head west out of Deraa at the roundabout at the end of Ash Shouhada Street and after 8 km take the road branching off to the left. Follow this road, passing a staggered crossroads before taking a small left turn after 8 km. Bear right after 1500 m to arrive at Tell Shahab, where there are the ruins of a castle at a point where the remains of the old branch line from Deraa to Haifa passes through a deep cutting. A short distance further on the road peters out in an open area of ground overlooking a deep gorge which drains into the Yarmouk River. On the opposite side a waterfall feeds two pools at different levels. The ruins of ancient irrigation channels and watermills can be seen on either side. This picturesque spot is ideal for a picnic, and in summer there are usually a couple of snack stalls open. It is possible to scramble down to the foot of the valley, and then up to the pools if you fancy a swim.

Ain al-Zezoun

Returning to the point where you took the small left turn (16 km from Deraa) and continuing along this road for a further 4 km, you arrive at the town of Ain al-Zezoun. Follow the road right through the town and bear off to the left at the roundabout at the far end of town. This brings you to a large, permanent spring feeding a waterfall, and a restaurant overlooking the deep valley of the Yarmouk River, which here forms the border with Jordan. The views out over the Yarmouk River Valley from the terrace of the restaurant are spectacular, although the food and drinks here are expensive. Traces of the old Deraa-Haifa railway line can be seen down in the valley.

Border crossing: Syria–Jordan

All the international coaches and the majority of the service taxis heading for Amman from Damascus now go via the **Nasib/Jabir border** crossing to the southeast of Deraa for the simple reason that it is on the motorway route between the two capitals, making it the quickest way to go. If you are travelling with your own vehicle, the **Deraa/Ramtha** border, 4 km to the south of Deraa, is preferable in that it is much quieter.

If you wish to cross via the Deraa/Ramtha border using local public transport (if, for example you want to visit Bosra before heading into Jordan), there are service taxis in Deraa which shuttle across the border to Ramtha. Regular buses and minibuses run from Ramtha to other towns in northern Jordan; if you cannot find a direct connection for Amman, take one to Irbid or Zarqa and change again there.

Crossing the border into Jordan

From the Deraa/Ramtha border it is 92 km to the centre of Amman, the most direct route being via Jerash. Although this route is marked on most maps as simply a major road, it has in fact been upgraded to a motorway for most of its length. From the Nasib/Jabir border it is 96 km to Amman on a fast motorway all the way.

Whichever border you cross at, exit formalities are quite straightforward. You have to pay S£500 departure tax on the Syrian side. One-month single-entry Jordanian visas can be obtained on the spot (these now cost JD10 – around US$15 – irrespective of nationality). The banks at the border offer much the same rates as are found in Amman.

Mzerieb

If you continue straight on at the first junction 8 km west of Deraa, you arrive after 5 km at the town of Mzerieb. Taking a left turn in the centre brings you to a small lake, with a pleasant lakeside restaurant complete with pedalos and rowboats for hire.

Deraa to Bosra

From Deraa a good road heads east (out past the bus station), passing over the Damascus motorway (9 km) before arriving in Bosra (40 km). This road takes you through the fertile countryside of the **Nuqra plain**, which supports rich crops of wheat, barley, chickpeas, sesame and watermelons. During the Roman period this part of the Hauran region represented one of the major grain producing regions of the empire (the name Nuqra translates literally as 'granary'), although it is only in recent years that it has begun to recover from long centuries of decline and neglect.

Bosra (Busra ash-Sham) → *For listings, see pages 112-114.*

Ancient Bosra has been a prize conquest for conquerors throughout history, who have adorned this early capital with their grand building projects. From Nabataean and Roman remains to Byzantine and Islamic monuments; Bosra's sombre black basalt buildings are a visual timeline of Syria's history. Hidden until the 1950s under the fortifications of a medieval citadel, the Roman theatre here is one of the largest and best preserved in the world. The rest of the old town is an interesting synthesis of various architectural styles; a colonnaded street leads to an early-Islamic era mosque, a Byzantine basilica sits near a Nabataean arch. And intermingling through all this architectural history are the modern dwellings of Bosra's residents, whose squat houses lean up against ruins, fusing the past and present together.

Less than two hours' journey from Damascus, Bosra makes for an excellent day trip from the capital.

Ins and outs

Getting there and away Coaches run directly between Bosra and Damascus throughout the day, and there are regular microbuses to Deraa, but no services to Suweida. Buses from Damascus drop you off at the main plaza, right next door to the citadel. If you are arriving by bus from Damascus it's best to buy your return ticket back to Damascus as soon as you get to town. The town itself is compact and easily explored on foot.

Tourist information The small tourist information office is located just to the south of the theatre/citadel. They seem to keep their own hours and when open can do little more than offer you the usual Ministry of Tourism free pamphlets/maps. You'd be better off talking to the friendly folk at *Caracalla Restaurant* (see listings, below) or taking a look at the fabulous website they've set up all about Bosra, www.bosracity.com.

Background

Earliest history and Roman rule The earliest references to Bosra, then known as *Busrana*, can be found in the records of the Egyptian pharaoh Tuthmosis III (15th century BC). It was occupied by the Greeks following Alexander the Great's conquest of the region, and controlled by the **Seleucids** for a time after his death and the subsequent division of his

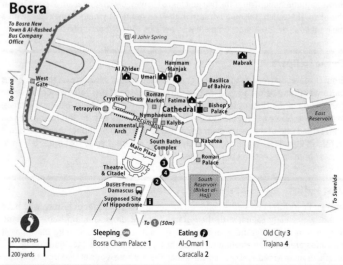

Bosra

Sleeping 🛏️
Bosra Cham Palace **1**

Eating 🍴
Al-Omari **1**
Caracalla **2**

Old City **3**
Trajana **4**

A prophet foretold

According to Muslim tradition, long before he became a prophet, Muhammad would often accompany his uncle, Abu Talib, on the long journeys between Mecca and Damascus with the trading caravans. It was during one of these journeys as a child that the caravan stopped in Bosra, and all the Meccan merchants were invited to a feast by a local Nestorian monk called Bahira. During the meal Bahira noticed that the child Muhammad had the mark of a future prophet (versions differ on how he perceived this), and

found the prediction of his coming in the gospels which he possessed.

According to some, Muhammad and Bahira engaged in many theological discussions that were directly responsible for incorporating aspects of Christianity into the Qur'an, but this particular interpretation has no place in Muslim tradition as, according to Muslim belief, the Qur'an is the direct word of God, and Muhammad was merely the medium through which the message was transmitted.

empire. It was then seized by Judas Maccabeus in 163 BC after his campaign against the Ammonites, and during the first century BC came under the control of the **Nabateans**. Later, during the first century AD, they briefly made it the capital of their empire.

The most significant period in the city's history began with Trajan's conquest of the region and the imposition of direct **Roman rule** in AD 106. The new Roman province of *Arabia* was established and Bosra chosen as its capital. A Roman legion was stationed in the city, which was renamed *Nova Traiana Bostra* and major building works instigated, as befitted an important provincial capital. At the same time, the building of Trajan's road network linking Damascus, Bosra, Amman and Aqaba (the *Via Nova Traiana*) meant that Bosra found itself at the intersection of this north-south route and the east-west route between the Mediterranean and Mesopotamia, bringing great prosperity to the city. Alexander Severus (AD 222-235) raised its status to a colony, and under the rule of Philip the Arab (AD 244-249) it was made a metropolis. Throughout this period the Romans also developed the agricultural potential of the surrounding Nuqra plain, building irrigation systems and introducing new crops.

Byzantine and Islamic era During the **Byzantine** period Bosra continued to flourish as an important centre of Christianity, becoming the seat of a bishopric and later an archbishopric. During the sixth century AD one of the largest cathedrals in the region was built here, the remains of which can still be seen today. According to legend, Muhammad passed through the city around this time and was received by the monk Bahira (see box, above).

Out on the edges of the desert, Bosra was amongst the first cities of Syria to fall to the Muslim invaders in AD 632. The **Islamic** era brought with it relative decline for Bosra, which soon found itself in a somewhat precarious position, caught in the ninth century AD between the competing ambitions of Fatimid Cairo and Abbasid Damascus. In the 12th century it was twice attacked by the Crusaders, though both times unsuccessfully. However, its location at the junction of important trade routes, as well as its new function as a halting place on the *Hajj*, or pilgrimage to Mecca, ensured it a continuing place in Muslim history, as demonstrated by the town's various Islamic monuments. The Ayyubids, responding to the threat posed by the Crusaders, completed the fortifications of the citadel which encloses the Roman theatre and these were substantially repaired by Baibars in 1261 following the first Mongol invasion.

Ultimately, however, the overall state of insecurity prompted the Mecca pilgrimage to shift westwards to the relatively safe route passing through Deraa, forcing Bosra into obscurity. By the 19th century the city was all but deserted, the citadel and theatre filled with sand and most of the other Roman, Byzantine and Muslim monuments either buried or abandoned. But the city had another renaissance after 1860 when significant numbers of Druze settled here and Bosra once again came to the attention of the outside world.

Theatre and citadel
ⓘ *Entrance on main plaza, daily 0900-1900 in summer, 0900-1600 in winter, S£150, students S£10.*
This is certainly the most remarkable of Bosra's monuments and the town's main attraction. What you see from the outside is the **Arab citadel**, an imposing structure consisting of eight strongly fortified towers with connecting curtain walls built in a semi-circle to fit like a jacket around the theatre inside. These outer walls and towers of the citadel are of Ayyubid origin, built after 1200 by the Sultan of Damascus, Al-Adil, and by his son As Salih, in response to the Crusader threat. Prior to this, the theatre had been less comprehensively guarded by two towers flanking the *scaenae frons* (stage façade), built in 1088 by the recently installed Seljuk rulers of Damascus. A third tower was added in the southwest, backing onto the *cavea* (auditorium seating) of the theatre, in 1147-1148. Following Al-Adil's construction of the Ayyubid outer fortifications, various other structures were built within the theatre itself, including a mosque and palace complex, although these were dismantled during the restoration work carried out from 1947-1970.

Visiting the theatre Entry to the citadel and theatre is from the east side, by a bridge across the moat. This brings you to a large entrance hall where the ticket office is located. Turning right, a vaulted passage slopes down, leading behind the *scaenae frons* of the theatre. Halfway down, a stairway on the right (and a smaller one on the left) leads to the upper terrace of this part of the citadel, which serves as an **open-air museum** where various statues and architectural fragments collected from around Bosra are displayed. The southwest tower of the outer fortifications houses a small **'Folk Traditions' museum**. Here you can view some depictions of everyday life and a collection of old jewellery and costumes. It's worth a quick look, if only for a glimpse of the inside of the tower; if it is locked, ask at the ticket office to gain entry.

Bearing left from the entrance hall, after a short distance you come to a staircase leading to an upper terrace which runs around the space between the citadel and the theatre, taking you past the 'Folk Traditions' museum and round to the open-air museum. Staying at ground level, you enter the system of vaulted tunnels running under the *cavea* of the theatre, and by ascending through any of the wonderfully named *vomitoria*, you can gain access to the **Roman theatre** itself. After the warren-like enclosure of the vaulted tunnels, the sheer scale of this is breathtaking. Built early in the second century AD, probably during the reign of Trajan, it was one of the many grand public buildings erected during this period, when Bosra flourished as the capital of the newly established *Provincia Arabia*. Although well preserved by the enclosing Ayyubid fortifications, and by the fact that it filled up with sand over the centuries, substantial restoration work was nevertheless necessary, both to the *cavea* and the *scaenae frons*.

The *cavea* consists of a total of 37 tiers of seating that would have accommodated an audience of up to 9000. Running around the top of are a series of columns which probably served to support a sunshade. The majority of the Corinthian columns behind the stage area are copies, but they give an idea of the decoration that once adorned the entire height of the *scenae frons*. Today the upper parts of this, stripped of their decoration, are somewhat severe.

Old City

To the north of the theatre and citadel is the old Roman city of Bosra, its streets laid out in traditional grid pattern with an approximate north-south and east-west alignment. Until recently this was for the most part hidden under the buildings of the contemporary town, and it is only in the last few years that these have started to be cleared away to reveal the full extent of the Roman settlement, although much undoubtedly still remains buried, particularly in the area further to the north.

The south baths and nymphaeum From the northwest corner of the citadel an excavated street lined with column bases runs north to a **monumental arch** consisting of a central arch flanked by two smaller side-arches. An inscription dates it to the early third century AD and reveals that it was built in honour of the III Cyrenaica Legion. The monumental arch marks the intersection with the main east-west street, or *decumanus* of the old Roman town, which has been excavated along most of its length to show the column bases of the colonnade which once lined it. In places, complete columns along with their Ionic capitals have been re-erected, although the majority of these appear to have been removed and reused in later buildings.

Turning to the right are the ruins of the extensive **south baths** complex. Dating from the late second to the early third century AD, these baths (one of three in the town) were built on a grand scale, although they are now in an advanced state of ruin. The main entrance was from the *decumanus*, with an eight-columned portico (of which almost nothing remains) leading through to the *apodyterium* or changing room; a large octagonal hall, the domed ceiling of which has collapsed. Beyond this was the *frigidarium* (cold room), followed by the *tepidarium* (warm room), with a *calidarium* (hot room) on either side. The *calidarium* on the east side still has its ceiling largely intact (at the time of writing it was supported by a mass of wooden scaffolding to prevent its collapse), while the one on the west side is for the most part in ruins. Adjacent to the baths on the east side are the remains of what was perhaps an *agora* or public meeting place, a rectangular area lined with recently re-erected columns.

Almost opposite the baths, on the north side of the street, are four enormous Corinthian columns towering to a height of 13 m and placed at a 45° angle to the *decumanus*, spanning the corner with a major north-south street which leads off it at this point. These once formed part of what must have been a truly spectacular **nymphaeum**, or public water fountain. On the opposite corner there is a tall column and fragment of wall supporting a richly decorated section of entablature, along with a slender column to the north; this is the remains of a **kalybe**, a type of shrine used to display statuary.

The Roman market, Umari Mosque and Hammam Manjak Heading north along the street leading off from the *decumanus*, on your left are the remains of a long rectangular **Roman market**. Part of the open plaza of this market has been repaved in recent years, while the long rectangular building with its arched doorways and niches (a later Muslim addition) has been consolidated.

Further north, also on the left, is the large **Umari Mosque** ① *if the main entrance from the north-south street is closed, try walking around to the west side where there is another entrance, shoes should be left at the entrance, knees and shoulders covered and women* *should wear a headscarf*, which is popularly attributed to the second Caliph, Umar Ibn al-Khattab (AD 634-644), under whose leadership Syria was conquered in AD 636. If true, this would make it one of the earliest surviving mosques in Syria. Others argue that it was built during the reign of the Umayyad Caliph, Yazid II (AD 720-724). However, in its present form, the mosque dates mostly from the 12th-13th centuries, when the Ayyubids extensively rebuilt and enlarged it. The distinctive square tower-minaret is most obviously Umayyad in style, although the upper parts of it show Ayyubid influences. The excavation of the main north-south street revealed a series of bricked-up Roman arches in the lower courses of this east wall (still visible today), thought to be the remains of a Roman temple on which the mosque was built. In the north wall of the mosque, meanwhile, sections of recycled basalt columns laid horizontally in the stonework as reinforcement can be seen, this pattern of construction dating from the 13th century enlargement of the mosque. Inside, the main courtyard (now covered by a tin roof) is surrounded on three sides by a double arcade, with a single arcade on the fourth side. Most of the columns of the arcades are clearly of classical origin, with a mixture of different capitals surmounting them. Having been abandoned and left derelict at some point, the mosque was restored in three phases from the 1930s onwards and today serves as Bosra's main mosque, as well as a *madrassa* (religious school) for children.

Opposite the Umari Mosque is the restored (though no longer functioning) **Hammam Manjak** ① *if the baths are locked ask at the Umari Mosque for the caretaker to open them up*, a Mamluk period bath house dating from 1372. These baths were built to service the pilgrims stopping in Bosra en route to Mecca. They represent the last phase of building work undertaken during the Muslim period before the Mecca pilgrimage route shifted to the west, precipitating the final decline in Bosra's importance. The entrance leads first into the main reception hall, a square room with a large pool in the centre and raised stone benches around the sides. Four arches forming a square once supported a central dome. A doorway in the north side of the room leads through to the bathing chambers, of which there are fewer than 11.

Northeast of the citadel Retracing your steps to the main east-west *decumanus* and following it east, you pass on the right an area of excavations that has revealed part of a Nabatean building of uncertain function. The street ends with a **Nabatean arch**, which was probably the entrance to a Nabatean temple compound or palace. The whole area to the east of the arch is thought to have been the site of the Nabatean settlement that grew up here when Bosra became the new capital of their empire, although nothing has been excavated. During the Roman period the arch appears to have been used to mark the eastern extremities of the planned Roman city.

To the south of the Nabatean arch are the ruins of a substantial **Roman palace** (perhaps the residence of the governor of *Provincia Arabia*), although little remains to be appreciated today. A little further to the south is the huge **south reservoir**. Of Roman construction and measuring over 120 m by 150 m in size, it represents one of the largest man-made water storages found in the region. One reason for Bosra's enduring importance was the existence of a reliable, year-round water supply, a resource which the Romans made full use of by building the reservoir, and something that was of equal importance during the Muslim period (the reservoir's Arabic name, *Birkat al-Hajj*, translates literally as 'pool of the pilgrimage').

Heading north from the Nabatean arch, you arrive first at the remains of a Byzantine **cathedral** on the right. Today the fenced-off site is in an advanced state of ruin, strewn with various architectural fragments and with only its basic outline and the semi-circular apse area clearly discernible, along with a couple of standing columns. The cathedral dates from AD 512 and was dedicated by Julianus, the archbishop of Bosra, to the Syrian saints Sergius, Bacchus and Leontius (Sergius and Bacchus were both from Rasafeh, see page 289). Although the size of the cathedral can only be appreciated today from the outline of the foundations, its present state of ruin is comparatively recent. Mid-19th-century descriptions of the cathedral reveal that it was a complex and innovative structure for its period, consisting of a circle within a square, topped by a large central dome. On the east side is a choir surrounded by small side rooms extended beyond the basic plan. Just to the east of the cathedral are the indistinct remains of what was the **Bishop's palace**.

Just to the north of the cathedral, between two branches of the street, is the **Mosque of Fatima**. This small mosque consists of a simple square building with a distinctive square tower-minaret which actually stands separate from the main building. The mosque was built by the Fatimid rulers of Egypt during the 11th century and is named after the Prophet's daughter, Fatima, who was the wife of Ali, to whom the Shi'ite Fatimids traced their origins. The minaret, similar in style to that of the Umari Mosque, is an early 14th-century addition.

A little further to the north again, on the right, are the ruins of the **Basilica of Bahira**. Originally a civic building of some sort, probably dating from the third century, it was converted into a church some time during the Byzantine period. The basic structure of the building, rectangular in shape with a semicircular apse at the east end, survives up to the level of the roof. The church is associated with the legend of the monk Bahira.

Continuing north, you arrive after around 200 m at a newly cobbled street; turn right here to reach the **Mabrak Mosque** with its distinctive egg-shaped dome and half-ruined square minaret. According to legend, this mosque marks the spot where the camel carrying the first copy of the Qur'an to arrive in Syria knelt down to rest (the name translates literally as the 'kneeling mosque'). In another version of the legend, the mosque is said to mark the spot where Muhammad's own camel knelt when he stopped here to pray. Entry to the mosque is through a low doorway from the cobbled street running east-west along the northern edges of the town. Note also the small doorways on either side, still with their original solid stone doors (of Roman origin) in place. The room directly in front of the central entrance and courtyard currently serves as the prayer hall of the mosque. To the right is the oldest part of the mosque, dating in its present form to 1136. The *mihrab*, with its conch shell semi-dome (clearly of Roman origin) is slightly offset from the alignment of the wall in order to face exactly to Mecca. By the *mihrab* is a large stone slab with an indentation that is said to be the spot where the camel knelt. To the left of the central courtyard a set of steps and tiny doorway (actually originally a window) leads through to a large cruciform wing, built in the 12th-13th centuries as a *madrassa*, the earliest example of a religious school in Syria. The complex and somewhat awkward internal layout of the whole building is indicative of the numerous modifications made to it over time.

Northwest of the citadel Returning to the main east-west *decumanus* of the Roman city and following it west, beyond the monumental arch on the left, you pass on the right a series of rectangular ventilation shafts at street level. These mark a long, narrow **underground chamber** probably dating from the first half of the second century AD and used for the storage of food and other products. Steps at its western end lead down, giving access to the vault, known technically as a *cryptoporticus*. Just to the west of this, past a turning leading to the north, the street can be seen to widen considerably to form an open circular area. Along with a large square platform on one side, this is all that remains of a **tetrapylon** that once marked the intersection with another north-south street. Continuing west, you arrive eventually at the **west gate** of the Roman city, known locally as the 'Bab al-Hawa' or 'Gate of the Wind'. Dating from the second century AD, it is a plain and imposing, if somewhat severe, structure consisting of a massive single arch topped by a barrel vault. To the north and south of the gate are the remains of the **Roman walls** of the old city, in places restored but for the most part in a poor state of repair, much of their stones having been removed during the building of the Arab citadel.

Bosra to Suweida

To continue on to Suweida from Bosra, with your own transport, head east out of the town past the bus stop. After 9 km, turn left at a crossroads and continue north for 24 km, passing through the villages of Qraya and Rassas, to arrive in Suweida. Going by this route, you also have the option of making a detour to **Salkhad** (see page 111).

Damascus to Suweida

To join the Suweida road from Damascus, the easiest (though by no means the most direct) route is to go via the motorway ring road that encircles the southern half of the capital. Head southwest from Umawiyeen Square along the Mezzeh autostrade (keeping the Sheraton hotel on your right). After just under 5 km, join the motorway ring road around Damascus heading anticlockwise. After another 9 km (having passed the exit for the motorway to Deraa, Bosra and the Jordanian border), the exit for the Suweida road is signposted, immediately before the airport road exit.

The Suweida road heads southeast from Damascus, taking you past the colourful Saida Zainab Mosque, see page 69. Once clear of the capital, the road first traverses a somewhat dreary plain before passing across the rather more atmospheric **Hauran plateau** with its landscape of dark, volcanic soils strewn with the ubiquitous black basalt rock typical of the region. Approaching the town of **Shahba**, the ridges of the **Jebel al-Arab** range come into view off to the left. The main road in fact bypasses Shahba; to reach the town, take the signposted fork off to the left, some 73 km after the Saida Zeinab Mosque (the fork is more or less opposite the distinctive cone of an extinct volcano to the right of the road). From the fork it is a further 2 km into the centre of town, see page 105.

Suweilim

Continuing along the main road past the fork for Shahba, you come next to the village of Suweilim (signposted 'Sleim' and marked 'Selim' or 'Salim' on most maps). Entering the village, the corner fragment of a **temple** is visible off to the right of the road in the northwest corner of the village. Clearly of Roman origin and thought to date from the late second-early third century AD, the decoration on this surviving fragment is impressive, although today nothing more remains of what would appear to have been a temple of considerable size. A little further along the main road, in the centre of the village, there is a left turn signposted to Qanawat (see below).

Atil

Continuing south along the main road, 3 km beyond the left turn for Qanawat, there is another left turn leading into the centre of the village of Atil (marked 'Atheel' on some maps). Taking this turning, you can visit two small **Roman temples**. The first, down a side street on the left, is the best preserved, with the remains of a beautifully decorated door-frame and niches on either side. On the left, a stone bears a Greek inscription which dates the temple to AD 151, during the reign of Antoninus Pius. Inside, there is a double arch structure which would have supported the roof. Continue along the same street and then turn right to reach the second temple. There is less to see here, the remains being partially obscured by surrounding buildings, though the roof is still largely intact. Note also the interesting course of carved stonework in one wall.

Atil to Suweida

Returning to the main road and continuing south, after 4 km you arrive in Suweida, passing first a roundabout boasting a huge portrait of Assad, followed by a second roundabout with an equally large bronze relief of his son Basel on horseback clutching a trophy, in an adaptation of the ubiquitous photograph of him.

Suweida → *For listings, see pages 112-114.*

Today, Suweida serves as the capital of the Hauran region, a modern and rapidly expanding town with a mixed population of Druze and Greek Orthodox Christians, and a certain air of affluence about it.The northeastern area of the town in the vicinity of the new museum in particular boasts a number of luxurious houses (and some extravagant architecture). Other than a few scant remains from the Nabatean and Roman periods dotted around the town, it is the museum that is the main attraction and reason for visiting Suweida nowadays. The town can be easily visited as a day trip from Damascus, which is a good thing as the accommodation situation here is pretty dismal.

Ins and outs

Getting there and away Pullman buses run regularly from Damascus to Suweida. You can also get microbuses to/from Shahba. The main bus station is at the northern edge of town, by the roundabout with the bronze relief of Basel on horseback.

Orientation The main road from Damascus runs north-south through the centre of Suweida. The main bus station is beside this road (on the right as you head south). Suweida Museum is 2 km to the northeast of the town centre, on the road to Qanawat. If you are arriving in Suweida with your own transport from the north, or if you find yourself deposited at the new bus station by the roundabout with the bronze relief of Basel on horseback, head east from this roundabout up the hill to reach the museum; turn left at the second crossroads and the museum is a few metres along on the right.

Tourist information The tourist information office is just to the north of this roundabout, on the same side, although it appears to be closed more often than not and is of little use in any case.

Background

During the first century BC Suweida was occupied by the Nabateans. Early in the second century AD it was conquered by the Romans and later named *Dionysias*. By the fifth century it had become an important centre of Christianity and the seat of a Bishopric, a position it still holds. Unfortunately, the town's most important ancient monuments were plundered prior to the First World War by Ottoman troops in search of building materials for their barracks. During the French Mandate period, the town was further remodelled. Those monuments which did survive suffered yet more damage with the building of the modern road which runs north-south through the town, although in recent years efforts have been made to salvage some of the town's heritage.

Suweida Museum

① *2 km to the northeast of the town centre, on the road to Qanawat, Wed-Mon 0900-1800 in summer, 0900-1600 in winter, S£150, students S£10.*

This small museum is a delight to visit. On the ground floor are various architectural fragments, statues and items of pottery, mostly from Shahba. The statues and architectural fragments dating from the Roman period are particularly delicately executed and all the more impressive for having been fashioned from the hard, unyielding basalt of the Hauran. The highlight of the museum, however, is the collection of mosaics, also from Shahba, displayed in the central domed hall. Going round the hall in an anticlockwise direction from the entrance, they depict Artemis surprised while bathing; Venus doing her make-up; Thetis (or Tethys) surrounded by sea monsters; four panels with scenes of lions chasing gazelle, and cocks and hens picking at flowers; Bacchus, Ariadne and Pluto, with personifications of the four seasons in each corner of the border; and Thetis and Peleus. The first three are the most impressive, and the expressiveness of the faces a testament to the remarkable skill of the craftsmen. The last two, however, are badly damaged. There are also a few interesting pieces of sculpture displayed in the central hall. Upstairs is a small 'popular tradition' display.

Archaeological remnants

Heading south through Suweida along the main road, in the southern part of the town you come to a roundabout with a large arch in the centre, while to the left of the road is a series of five columns. A little further on, to the left of the road below ground level is a rather intriguing section of richly decorated entablature supported on columns. Further on, on the same side, are the remains of a large church which has been modified and had contemporary houses built onto it. Another smaller church has also been identified nearby, believed to be one of the oldest churches in the world, though there is little for the casual observer to see and in any case it is hidden away inside a walled compound. Back on the main road, a little further along on the right, are the remains of a small, partially restored theatre.

Qanawat

On the slopes of the Jebel al-Arab massif, the village of Qanawat has some impressive ruins. Qanawat is set amongst a relatively verdant landscape of trees, vineyards and grassy terraces, which provides a pleasant relief from the often arid, brooding black basalt landscape of the rest of the Hauran. The Wadi al-Ghar is the source of Qanawat's fertility and the importance of harnessing its waters can be deduced from the village's name; it translates as 'canal'.

Ins and outs

Getting there and away Qanawat is 7 km to the northeast of Suweida. If driving from Suweida head northeast on Kanawat Street, past the museum on the right, and keep going straight. Microbuses from Suweida to here can be quite erratic, particularly in winter. Microbuses will drop you off in Qanawat, in the square by the Seraya. Be sure to check when the last bus makes the return trip so you don't get stuck.

Orientation Entering Qanawat, you arrive at a roundabout with a statue of a lion in the centre (5 km from Suweida museum). If you turn right here, this road takes you directly up to the Seraya, Qanawat's most impressive monument, passing a number of minor remains before arriving at the Seraya itself.

Background

Although its origins certainly go back much further, the first detailed information about Qanawat dates from the time of Herod Agrippa I (AD 37-44). Herod Agrippa went on to suffer a major defeat at the hands of the various tribes of the region which the Nabatean and Jewish kingdoms struggled to control. During the **Roman** period it became one of the cities of the *Decapolis*, a loose confederation of cities in southern Syria and northern Jordan. Early in the second century AD it became part of the new Roman province of *Arabia*, and many of the major monuments which survive today date from the reign of Trajan (AD 98-117). By the end of the second century it had been renamed *Septimia Kanatha* by the emperor Septimius Severus. Christianity flourished here, as elsewhere in the Hauran during the fourth and fifth centuries, and it became the seat of a bishopric, with various Roman monuments being converted to churches. After the arrival of Islam, however, it appears to have fallen into decline, remaining all but abandoned until the Druze settlement in the region in the 19th century. If you wander through the village today, in addition to the surviving monuments, you can see evidence of Qanawat's ancient origins in the numerous architectural fragments taken from various ruins and reused in contemporary buildings.

Ruins on the road to the Seraya

Arriving from Suweida at the roundabout with the lion statue and going straight across, after around 500 m you pass the remains of the **Helios temple** off to the left, marked by seven standing columns, each still topped by delicately carved capitals. Along with the platform on which these stand, this is all that remains of the temple. There are excellent views from this vantage point out across the Hauran plateau. Further along, at the second small crossroads (just past a government building on the right which incorporates some columns of Roman origin), turn right to climb up the hillside, keeping the gorge of the Wadi al-Ghar to your left. Just on the opposite side of the stream, the ruins of a small **theatre** and **nymphaeum** can be made out from the road.

The Seraya

① *Daily 0900-sunset, S£75, students S£5. If the gate is closed, ask in the surrounding shops for the caretaker who will come and open it. One of the shops across the road from the entrance serves tea, coffee, soft drinks and alcohol.*

At the top of the hill, you arrive at an open square containing the ruins of the **Seraya**, now set within a fenced-off area. The Seraya, or Serai (from the Turkish for palace), consists of two adjoining Roman structures, which were later modified into Christian churches during the Byzantine period. The entrance is in the western side of the complex, through a small doorway just to the right of the central, elaborately decorated door. This western part of the complex is thought to have originally been a Roman *praetorium* or governor's palace, entered from the north via a columned portico. At the south end of the building are three semicircular niches probably originally used to display statuary, but used as a *martyrium* (a small shrine for holy relics) when the building was converted to a church. To judge from the candles which can be found placed in the niches, the shrine is still venerated by local Christians.

In accordance with Christian tradition, the altar was built against the eastern wall, thus giving the building an east-west orientation, although nothing remains of this today. Passing through one of the openings in the eastern wall, you come to what appears to have been the Roman *atrium*, or courtyard, with two rows of columns still standing. The south wall of the atrium is pierced by a large monumental doorway which is particularly beautifully decorated.

Passing through this, you come to the remains of a rectangular building, possibly a temple during the Roman period. Like the first building, its north-south orientation was rotated through 90° during the Christian period by building an altar on the east side; the semicircular chancel on which the altar stood can still be seen. Today, a large circular stone basin occupies the chancel. According to one theory, the atrium and building to the south once formed a single rectangular courtyard surrounded by a colonnade, with the dividing wall and monumental entrance being added during the fourth or fifth centuries.

Qanawat to Shahba via Mushanef

If you have your own transport, you can drive from Qanawat to the village of Mushanef, with its interesting temple ruins, and on to Shahba. This pleasant, if somewhat lengthy, detour (43 km in all) takes you through the beautiful rolling hills of the **Jebel al-Arab**. From the Seraya in Qanawat, ask directions to pick up the road towards Mushanef. After passing through the village of Muf'Allah (3 km) the narrow road winds its way through fields and past apple orchards. In the village of **Taibeh** (13 km from Qanawat), bear right. The road descends into a valley and crosses a small bridge. Just after the bridge, bear right where the road forks and keep on following this road to arrive in Mushanef, 20 km from Qanawat.

Mushanef

In the centre of the small and otherwise uninteresting village of Mushanef are the remains of a **Roman temple**. The temple is set within a large open courtyard and stands on a podium, with steps leading up to it. On the basis of an inscription found here, it is thought to date to AD 171, during the reign of Marcus Aurelius, though another inscription referring to Herod Agrippa I (AD 37-44) indicates that it already existed in some form at that time. A peculiar hotch-potch of architectural fragments has been incorporated into the fabric of the temple, reflecting reconstruction work at some point in its history. One of the walls is leaning at a precarious angle, while another part of the temple has been modified into a dwelling which is still lived in today. While not a particularly notable monument, the overall effect is somehow quite striking.

Mushanef to Shahba

Ask directions again to pick up the main road to Shahba. Keep following this road, which passes through a number of villages along the way, to arrive eventually in Shahba, 23 km from Mushanef (arriving by this route you enter Shahba through the east gate of the old Roman city).

Shahba, the ancient city of Philippopolis, was unique in that it was an entirely Roman project, rather than a modification or extension of a pre-existing city (as was the case with Bosra and most other cities developed by the Romans in the Middle East). Something of a white elephant of a monumental town to the Emperor Philip the Arab, it was only during the last century that Shahba became a centre of Druze settlement. Today the place is a small, bustling market town with an almost entirely Druze population and it makes an easy day trip from Damascus.

Ins and outs

Getting there and away There are regular services by luxury Pullman buses from Damascus (Al-Samariyeh Station) to here and frequent connections by microbus to Suweida. If you want to visit Shahba and Suweida both on the same day from Damascus, it makes more sense to visit Suweida first, and then catch a microbus to Shahba.

Buses and microbuses arrive and depart from the roundabout in the centre of town. Check what time the last bus leaves as this varies according to the season and demand.

Background

Perhaps seeking to build a lasting monument to his own glory, and to re-create something of the imperial grandeur of Rome in the land of his birth, Philip the Arab planned this new Roman city on a grand scale. At an altitude of 1050 m on the outlying ridges of the Jebel al-Arab massif, he built a city enclosed within a rectangle of walls (of which only the outline now survives), with four gates corresponding to the cardinal points of the compass. The town was laid out according to the traditional Roman grid pattern of streets and endowed with a number of large civic buildings meant to reflect its importance alongside Bosra, the existing provincial capital. Construction work started soon after Philip became Emperor in AD 244, but the project appears to have been prematurely abandoned following his sudden death five years later, with less than half the town's area actually having been built upon. Although it continued to be inhabited well into the fourth century, Philippopolis failed to secure any lasting role for itself in the region and was eventually abandoned altogether.

Sights

Entering the town from the north, you pass through the partially reconstructed remains of the northern gate of the Roman city, consisting of a large central arch flanked by two smaller ones. This main north-south street corresponds with the *cardo maximus* of the Roman city. The roundabout in the centre of the town likewise marks the junction with the east-west *decumanus*. The cobbled street running west from this central roundabout leads to the main cluster of Roman remains. A short distance up on the right there is a series of columns which mark the remains of a **portico** to a temple. Originally there would have been four columns, but the second from the right is missing and has been replaced by a stone block featuring a carved relief of a man with an inscription below. A little further on, to the left of the street, is a large open square, once the **forum** of the Roman town.

Dominating the far (western) end of the square is the imposing **palace façade**, consisting of a series of large niches arranged in a semicircle. The broad flight of stairs leading up to the façade is a modern reconstruction. The purpose of the structure, though

Syria's man in Rome

The millennium celebrations of the founding of Rome were a glittering affair, as the Imperial city pulled out all the stops to commemorate the Roman Empire's birth. Presiding over this lavish party was the Roman Emperor, Marcus Julius Philippus, better known to history as Philip the Arab.

This ambitious local Hauran boy, who rose to the Empire's highest title, joined the Praetorian guard and quickly rose to the position of Praetorian prefect. When the Emperor Gordian III was killed during battle against the Persians,

Philip was hailed as the new Emperor by his legions, a position which the Senate in Rome confirmed in AD 244. Despite becoming the most powerful man of the most powerful empire of that era, his attachment to the land of his birth remained strong and it was at his birthplace, Shahba, that he founded a new city to be called Philippopolis. His vision of a grand new Roman city was never to be finished; in AD 249, after five years in the job, Philip was murdered in a military mutiny near present-day Verona.

not entirely clear, is thought to have been to display statues of Philip the Arab and his family. The cobbled street continues via an arched tunnel under which are the further remains of the palace complex, although these are somewhat obscured by later buildings.

On the south side of the square, there are the remains of a small **temple**, thought to have been dedicated to Philip's father Julius Marinus. A Greek inscription can be seen over the doorway, while inside, the three remaining walls each contain a large arched niche flanked by smaller ones on each side. The stone benches arranged in a horseshoe shape around the inside suggest that the building perhaps also served as a meeting place of some sort. The small holes which can be seen in the stonework indicate that the interior was originally clad in marble. In the left-hand corner of the south wall, a set of stairs leads up to the roof, from where you can get a good overview of the palace façade and the theatre.

Just to the south of the temple is the **theatre**. Although small in size and in no way comparable with the theatre at Bosra, this is the best preserved and perhaps most impressive remnant of Philippopolis. In recent years the *cavea* and *scenae frons* have been restored.

Returning to the roundabout in the centre of town and following the main street south, the first turning on the left leads past the baths and museum. Although the **baths complex** is now for the most part in a fairly advanced state of ruin, the towering walls and arched doorways of the main reception hall are still standing, giving an idea of their monumental scale and elaborate layout. Again, the numerous small holes in the stonework indicate that the interior was marble-clad. At the east end of the complex, a walkway with a sign above it reading 'Especial Entrance' leads to a small Muslim shrine.

On the opposite side of the street, a little further on, is the **mosaics museum** ① *daily 0900-1800 in summer, 0900-1600 in winter, S£75, students S£5, if the museum is closed within opening hours, ask at the museum shop opposite and they will telephone the caretaker*, which stands on the site of a private house dating from the second quarter of the fourth century and contains an impressive collection of beautifully preserved mosaics, all but one of which are displayed in situ. The mosaics depict a number of scenes from classical mythology: Bacchus, the god of wine; Tethys, goddess of the sea; the wedding feast of Dionysus and Ariadne; Orpheus, the Greek musician and poet; Aphrodite and Ares in a love scene (taken from Book Eight of *Odyssey*, lines 266-270); and the Three Graces.

Leaving Shahba, if you head south along the main street, this road passes through the **southern gate** of the Roman city (identical in plan to the northern gate, though better preserved) and after 7 km rejoins the main Damascus–Suweida highway.

Suweida to Bosra via Salkhad

If you are en route between Suweida and Bosra with your own transport, you can make a short detour to the town of Salkhad, dominated by the ruins of a hilltop castle. It is easy to see why this hill would once have been of major strategic significance, providing as it does such a commanding vantage point from which to control the surrounding countryside and, overall, it is these panoramic views that are the town's main attraction.

Head south out of Suweida along the main road and keep following this road for 24 km, passing through the villages of Rassas and Qraya along the way, until you arrive at a crossroads. Turn left here (right for Bosra) and follow this road for a further 14 km to arrive at Salkhad. The town is built around the distinctive cone of an extinct volcano, with the castle dominating its summit and visible from miles around.

Salkhad Castle

Salkhad has been identified with the biblical town of *Salecah*, which was within the territory captured by Moses from Og, the king of Bashan (Deuteronomy 3:10; Joshua 12:5 and 13:11). Its importance continued into the Islamic period, with the present castle dating from the period of Ayyubid rule, when together with Bosra it served as a forward defence for the Damascus-based Caliphate against attacks from the south. You have to walk the last bit up to the castle, which is now in a fairly advanced state of ruin. Its continued strategic significance in the recent past can be seen from the various concrete structures of the Syrian army in amongst the older ruins, including a rather forlorn-looking hexagonal watchtower on the highest point of the castle. These days, however, the army appears to have all but abandoned it.

For Sleeping and Eating price codes and other relevant information, see Essentials pages 19-21.

⊜ Sleeping

Deraa *p95*
You'd be much better off visiting Deraa as a day trips from Damascus than staying here the night but if you've arrived too late to cross the border into Jordan and do get stuck here, the below places are fine for a night.
C Orient Palace (Al-Chark), Ibrahim Hanano St, T015-238 304. This is the best available accommodation in Deraa, though it's pricey. The clean rooms here are technically 'suites' with separate sitting areas, fan and TV. Decent restaurant.
D Al-Hadood, 3 km to the south of Deraa, just short of the Jordanian border, T015-237 703. This basic but friendly place has clean rooms, some with attached baths.

Bosra *p97, map p98*
There are only 2 options: the luxury 5-star hotel belonging to the Cham chain, or the Bedouin tent at Caracalla Restaurant. During the Bosra festival, accommodation here (and in Deraa) will be booked up well in advance.
L Bosra Cham Palace, Mayloun St, T015-790 488, www.chamhotels.com/bosra. Reasonably comfortable rooms with a/c, satellite TV and balcony. There's all the facilities you'd expect at this price: restaurant, bar, swimming pool, shops, etc. The hotel is eerily quiet, unless a tour group stops by or during the Bosra Festival.
E Caracalla, Main Plaza, T0944-550 410, www.bosracity.com. A godsend if you find yourself stuck without a bus ticket back to Damascus or you're coming from/to Jordan and want to overnight at Bosra on the way. Caracalla's owner has rigged up a Bedouin-style tent in the shady garden of his restaurant (see Eating, below), where travellers can crash for the night. It's cheap, there are clean toilets, they provide blankets,

and you're only a couple of steps away from cold beer and good food.

⊙ Eating

Deraa *p95*
As well as the restaurant in the **Orient Palace**, there are a number of simple restaurants along Ibrahim Hanano St where you can get the usual selection of *falafels, shawarmas,* kebabs, roast chicken, etc. The open square to the south of Ibrahim Hanano St has a pleasant café for tea, coffee and *narghiles.*

Bosra *p97, map p98*
♥ Caracalla, Main Plaza. Owned by the beret-wearing, chilled-out Mechal al-Adawi (who speaks fluent English, French and Italian), Caracalla has a shady vine-covered courtyard seating area and serves up large portions of simple but wholesome food. There's no menu, it's just whatever they decide to cook on the day, but it's always tasty. Alcohol served.
♥ Old City, Main Plaza, right beside the Citadel entrance. Either sit inside amid the basalt arches and corbelling, or outside, in the vine-shaded area. Interesting selection of local dishes from the Hauran region and Syrian specialities you don't find on the average menu.
♥ Trajana, Main Plaza. Another restaurant here with great outside seating. Dishes up a tasty array of Arabic cuisine from mezze to kebabs and grills.

Cafés
Al-Omari, opposite Umari Mosque. Owned by the friendly Suleiman Al-Shahma, who also works for the city's antiquities department and has written a book on Bosra, this cute little café is a good place to stop for a drink during sightseeing. There's a shady courtyard out back where Suleiman will brew up some tea and show you his fascinating collection of old black and white photos of

Bosra before the archaeologists started excavating in the 1950s.

Suweida *p105*

There's no shortage of simple but reasonable snack places in the town centre. There's some little places serving up *shawarma* on the main road running north-south through town, or alternatively, try exploring the maze of streets to the south and west of Sultan al-Atrush Sq, where there are numerous other snack places and basic restaurants.

Shahba *p109*

There are various simple takeaway places along the main north-south street serving *falafel* sandwiches and the like, while by the roundabout in the centre of town you can get more substantial snacks of roast chicken, etc.

⊛ Festivals and events

Bosra *p97, map p98*

Aug/Sep Bosra Festival. The superb Roman theatre at Bosra is impressive at any time, but once a year it comes alive with a festival of music, dancing, singing and drama, giving a contemporary insight into the atmosphere that must have prevailed during its heyday. The festival is held every year (usually in Sep but sometimes earlier) and runs for 9 days.

⊖ Transport

Deraa *p95*
Bus

The bus station is 3 km to the east of the town centre. A taxi from the centre costs about S£25. Al-Muhib, bus company has regular services to **Damascus** (Al-Samariyeh station) every 30 mins 0700-2100 (1½ hrs, S£80), Their ticket office/bus stop is located at the east end of Ash Shouhada St, which saves you the trouble of going out to the main bus station.

Microbus

Frequent microbuses to **Bosra** (S£30) leave from the main bus station. On Fri and Sat microbus services tend to be less regular.

Service taxi

International service taxis run throughout the day to **Ramtha** (the 1st town on the Jordanian side of the border), and charge S£150 per seat. You have to wait for the other seats to fill up before they will leave. You can catch a service taxi at the main bus station or you can sometimes pick them up from the taxi stand at the western end of Ibrahim Hanano St.

Bosra *p97, map p98*
Bus

There's a bit of bus-mafia action going on between Damascus and Bosra and now only **Al-Rashed** ply Pullman buses between these 2 destinations (having paid off their competition). They have buses to **Damascus** every 2 hrs from 0600 to 2000 (1½ hrs, S£100). It's strongly advised to buy your bus ticket as soon as you get to Bosra as the buses can fill up fast, particularly on Fri and Sat when locals journey into the city. The Al-Rashed ticket office is, annoyingly, in Bosra new town but **Caracalla Restaurant** also helpfully sell tickets (no extra charge). They can also get the bus to pick you up from the main plaza (where it dropped you off) if there are enough people.

Microbus and taxi

There are regular microbuses to **Deraa** (S£30) from here. You need to flag them down on the main road. Pullman bus services from Deraa to Damascus are more frequent so it's a good option to catch a microbus to here if you get stuck without a return bus ticket from Bosra. Microbus services tend to be almost non-existent on Fri.

A taxi from Bosra to **Suweida** shouldn't cost anymore than S£500. A private taxi to **Jordan** from here should be about S£2500.

Suweida *p105*

The main bus station is on the main road to Damascus, beside the Basel Assad statue roundabout. **Damas Tours** operate Pullman buses to **Damascus** (Al-Samariyeh Station) from here, leaving every hr from 0600 to 1900 (1½ hrs, S£70). There are also regular microbuses to **Shahba**, **Deraa** and **Ezra**. Microbuses to **Qanawat** leave from 16 Tishreen St near the centre of town and are somewhat erratic. A taxi from Suweida to **Bosra** shouldn't cost anymore than S£500.

Shahba *p109*

All buses and microbuses leave from the main roundabout in the centre of town. **Damas Tour** run buses to **Damascus**

(Al-Samariyeh Station) every hr from 0600-1900 though in winter the last bus is likely to be at 1700 (1½ hrs, S£70). There are regular microbuses to **Suweida** running throughout the day, when full.

⊙ Directory

Bosra *p97, map p98*
Banks There is a CBS exchange booth near the main plaza (beside the tourist information office) which changes cash. Quite a lot of the time it's closed. If you get stuck for cash, head to the **Bosra Cham Palace Hotel** where there's a foreign exchange desk open 24 hrs.

Contents

Footprint features

Orontes Valley

Heading north from Damascus, the central plains of the Orontes Valley are sandwiched between the coastal mountains to the west and the desert to the east. It was here that a string of powerful city-states grew up; some flourishing to this day while others rose and fell with the fortunes of different civilizations, leaving only vestiges of their history behind for archaeologists to mull over.

Travellers tend to gravitate towards easy-going Hama, with its groaning waterwheels. Long a favourite stop on Syria's tourist circuit, the town's mix of excellent facilities, clued-up hotel staff and central location make it a perfect launching pad for forays into the region. Ask a Syrian what their favourite city is though, and the answer is likely to be Homs. Usually bypassed by travellers because of its ugly industrial outskirts, at its heart Homs has a friendly, vibrant souq that is still well off the beaten trail.

Out of the cities, after travelling through fields loaded with wheat, cotton and sugar beet, you'll encounter the ruins that are testament to this region's vital importance throughout history: Apamea with its gloriously long colonnaded street, lonely Qasr Ibn Warden, on the edge of the desert, and the Ismaili castle of Masyaf, once an Assassin's stronghold.

Ins and outs

Getting there and away

The two main centres of Homs and Hama are well connected to each other and the rest of the country by public transport. Bus services are regular and efficient and both towns are on the train route that plies between Damascus and Aleppo.

Getting around

Most of the smaller towns are accessible by microbus from either Homs or Hama. Homs is the town you need to head to if you want to travel to Krak des Chevaliers by local transport. There are regular microbuses from Homs' microbus station to Al-Hosn town (below the castle). Other major sites such as Apamea and Masyaf have microbus services from Hama but if you are short on time you'd probably be better off hiring a car/driver to for the day from Hama; that way you'll be able to visit a few sights in one day.

Damascus to Homs and Hama → *For listings, see pages 145-150.*

The most direct route north from Damascus to Homs is on the Damascus–Aleppo highway, a fast though not altogether inspiring motorway. If you have your own transport, there is an interesting and scenic diversion for part of this journey, through the towns of Saidnaya, Maaloula and Yabroud. You rejoin the motorway close to Nabak. For details, see page 81.

Deir Mar Musa

Perched in a ravine in the hills 14 km to the northeast of Nabak is the tiny monastery of Deir Mar Musa. With stunning views out over the Syrian desert to the east, as well as some remarkable frescoes in its church, it is an almost magical place and well worth the effort involved in reaching it. The monastery can feasibly be visited as a day trips from Damascus or as a detour en route to Homs, but staying overnight gives you the opportunity to really appreciate the sense of space, the tranquillity and the overwhelming beauty of sunset and sunrise.

Ins and outs From the roundabout and large mosque at the centre of Nabak ask directions to pick up the rough track leading up to the monastery. The track winds its way up into the hills, terminating abruptly at the entrance to a ravine. From here a footpath descends, gently at first but then more steeply with some scrambling involved, to reach the monastery (around a 15- to 20-minute walk).

Background An Ethiopian monk, Mar Musa (St Moses), is believed to have retreated here sometime in the sixth century, having founded several monasteries in the area. Already there was a Roman watchtower on the site, guarding the caravan route to Palmyra; the arched doorway to the kitchen of the present monastery is thought to represent part of the original tower. A parchment document now held in the British Museum confirms that a small community existed here by the end of the sixth century, though nothing else is known about this early phase of settlement. By the 11th century, the church had been built and for the next four centuries the monastery flourished, before falling into decline after the 15th century and eventually being abandoned in 1831. Then, in 1984, restoration work began, initiated by an Italian former Jesuit, Paulo Dell' Oglio, with help from the Syrian

Catholic community and donations from Italy. In 1991 the monastery and its community, an eclectic group of monks and nuns from Europe and the Middle East, was officially re-founded under the aegis of the Syrian Catholic Church.

Sights Aside from the stunning views out over the desert from the terrace of the monastery, the highlight is the **church** itself, in which a series of remarkable **frescoes** have been preserved, some dating as far back as the 11th century, when the church was first built. Those on the rear wall have been cleaned and are particularly impressive. The overall effect inside the church, with the frescoes gradually emerging as your eyes become accustomed to the gloom, is one of ancient, solemn religiosity, particularly if you stay for the evening service with its chanting and music. There is also a small museum housing a collection of pottery, coins and other archaeological finds from the area. Around the monastery there are numerous caves, some of which are used as sleeping quarters by the monks.

North to Homs

Returning to the motorway and continuing north, the road begins to descend from the area of plateau around Nabak. Further north from here, the mountains of the Anti-Lebanon range to the west, which have until now run parallel to the motorway, begin to trail away, giving way to a corridor of flat plain stretching to the sea, bounded by the Anti-Lebanon to the south and the Jebel Ansariye to the north. This corridor is known as the **Homs Gap**. It represents the only unobstructed route from the sea, inland into the heart of Syria and as such has been a route of major strategic importance throughout history. Approaching Homs along the motorway, you can tell when you are parallel with the Homs Gap: the trees that line the road all lean precariously in the same direction, forced into this position by the winds that are funnelled through here between the mountains.

Immediately before a railway bridge crosses the road, 148 km from Damascus, there is a left turn signposted for Qusayr, amongst other places, 20 km to the southwest. Just under 3 km to the north of the village of Qusayr on the opposite bank of the Orontes River (here just a stream) is **Tell Nebi Mend**, site of the Bronze Age fortress-city of Kadesh. This was also the scene of a great battle between the Egyptian king Ramses II and the Hittite king Muwatallis in the 13th century BC. However, despite the historical and archaeological importance of the site, there is little for the casual visitor to see.

Homs → *For listings, see pages 145-150.*

They say you should never judge a book by its cover and travellers would do well to remember this advice as they drive through the dull industrial outskirts of Homs. Beneath that concrete-block factory exterior is Syria's best kept secret; a relaxed, easygoing city that boasts the country's friendliest people. Seldom visited by tourists, Homs' souqs are a delight; a maze of colourful, lively and twisting alleyways where you're as likely to spend your time drinking tea with the vendors as bargaining for goods. Both the souqs and the Christian quarter are dotted with numerous ancient buildings, many of them dilapidated old relics but nevertheless providing intriguing glimpses of Mamluk architecture.

Ins and outs

Getting there and away Homs is a major road transport hub and has good bus connections with the rest of the country, as well as numerous microbuses serving surrounding areas. It is also on the railway line running between Damascus and Aleppo, and any train running between the two cities stops here. The main Pullman bus station and microbus station are next door to each other, just under 3 km from the city centre. A taxi to the centre from here costs approximately S£30. If you've come into town from Palmyra on an old-style bus, you'll probably be dropped at the old 'Hob-hob' bus station which is a good 6 km from the centre.

Homs is the most obvious (or at least closest) place from which to visit the Crusader castle of Krak des Chevaliers, and there are regular services from the microbus station. However, given the better accommodation to be found in Hama, many people elect to stay there instead. For details of Krak des Chevaliers and the various routes by which it can be reached, see page 162.

Getting around You really need a taxi (or a local microbus) to get to and from the bus/microbus stations and the railway station, but once you are in the centre, the city is easily explored on foot. There are plenty of taxis hanging around if you need them and a journey within town shouldn't cost more than S£25.

Tourist information The **tourist information office** ⓘ *Sat-Thu 0830-1400 and 1600-2100*, is in a small building in the centre of the strip of gardens on the south side of Shoukri al-Kouwatli Street. The afternoon shift sees just a token presence here. The staff can supply you with the Ministry of Tourism pamphlet/map of Homs.

Background
Although there is evidence of settlement as early as the first millennium BC, Homs only rose to prominence during the Roman period under the Latin name *Emesa*, when it emerged as an important regional centre. It owed much of its wealth to its close trading

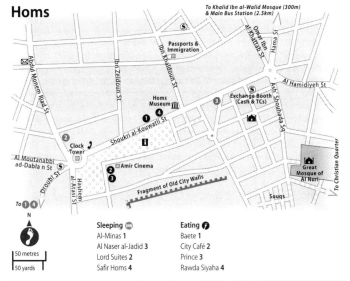

Homs

To Khalid Ibn al-Walid Mosque (300m) & Main Bus Station (2.5km)

Passports & Immigration

Homs Museum 🏛

Exchange-Booth (Cash & TCs)

Al Hamidiyeh St

Shoukri al-Kouwatli St

Clock Tower ♪

Amir Cinema

Al Moutanabbi ad-Dabla n St

Fragment of Old City Walls

Great Mosque of Al Nuri

To Christian Quarter

Souqs

To

N

50 metres
50 yards

Sleeping 🛏
Al-Minas **1**
Al Naser al-Jadid **3**
Lord Suites **2**
Safir Homs **4**

Eating 🍴
Baete **1**
City Café **2**
Prince **3**
Rawda Siyaha **4**

ties with Palmyra to the east, a fact attested to by the numerous references to *Emesa* in Palmyrene documents.

More importantly, it also found itself close to the centre of **Roman** political life following the marriage of the future Emperor of Rome, Septimius Severus, to **Julia Domna**, a daughter of the High Priest of *Emesa* in AD 187. Julia Domna played a central role during the reign of her husband (AD 193-211) and following his death she managed to ensure that her sons, Caracalla and Geta, jointly inherited the position of Emperor. Continued Syrian ascendency in Rome was ensured, but this period was marked also by a rapid decline into degeneracy. In AD 212 Caracalla murdered his brother Geta and took the title of Emperor for himself, embarking on a reign of terror which saw tens of thousands murdered. Following Caracalla's own murder in AD 217, **Elagabalus**, the grandson of Julia Domna's sister, Julia Maesa, rose to power. Although still only a boy of 14, Elagabalus was also the High Priest of *Emesa*. He brought with him to Rome the sun god Baal, represented in Homs by a black stone, and raised the worship of the god to the status of an official religion. His reign was an orgy of debauchery bordering on madness and after four years he was murdered by members of the Praetorian Guard. The black stone was sent back to Homs, where it continued to be venerated locally. Fifty years later it once again rose to prominence throughout the empire when the Emperor Aurelian came to Homs to make offerings to Baal prior to his defeat of Queen Zenobia. Aurelian attributed his success to the sun god's intervention and went on to build a temple to *Sol Invictus* (the 'Invincible Sun') in Rome, raising Baal once again to the status of official religion. In the meantime, Elagabalus was succeeded by his cousin Alexander Severus who, although also only a boy of 13, proved himself more worthy of the title of Emperor, bringing about a number of important reforms and checking the worst excesses of the imperial court. He was murdered in AD 235 following a revolt within the army, bringing to an end this Syrian Dynasty in Rome.

During the **Byzantine** period, Homs became an important centre of Christianity, and remains so today. There is a significant Christian population and various churches in the eastern part of the city. In AD 540 it suffered serious damage at the hands of the Persians, before falling in AD 635 to the Muslim invaders, led by the Arab general Khalid Ibn al-Walid, whose tomb is in the city's main mosque. The **Islamic period** saw it develop as a centre for the more puritanical elements of the Muslim faith, who opposed the relative liberalism of the Umayyad court in Damascus. Despite its proximity to the Crusader stronghold of Krak des Chevaliers, it resisted coming under their control, falling instead under the orbit of the new Zengid rulers of Aleppo in 1130. From this time onwards, although it continued to be an important commercial centre, in political terms it fell into relative obscurity, eclipsed by the larger and more influential city-states of Damascus and Aleppo. It was only during the 20th century that it developed as an important industrial centre, with oil and sugar refineries as well as phosphate treatment centres largely overshadowing the traditional spinning and weaving industries.

Museum

① *Shoukri al-Kouwatli St, Sat-Thu 0900-1600, S£150, students S£10.*

This small museum contains a selection of artefacts found in the region of Homs and covers the prehistoric through to the Islamic periods. There are some interesting pieces, but unfortunately nothing is labelled in English. Upstairs there is a collection of paintings by the local artist J Traboulsi.

Old City Walls

To the south of Shoukri al-Kouwatli Street there is a short section of the Old City walls still standing (just). Most of what you can see here dates from the Ottoman period, though the tumbled remains of a much more ancient wall, built of huge stone blocks, is visible in places. At the western end of the wall there is a circular corner tower which has been converted into the minaret of a mosque, its lower courses built of large stone blocks and a couple of horizontally laid column drums. The remains are today somewhat dwarfed by a rather striking and impressive new complex of government offices. More fragments of the Old City walls can also be seen at the eastern edges of the Christian quarter, running south from Bab Tadmor. For the most part these walls have been lost to recent buildings, but in places you can still see traces of large, ancient stone blocks forming the foundations of contemporary buildings, or else later Mamluk/Ottoman stonework incorporated into walls, and at one point a semi-circular bastion tower.

Khalid Ibn al-Walid Mosque

ⓘ *Off Hama St, there are separate entrances for men and women. Modest dress is essential and women should wear a headscarf and will be given an abeyya to wear. Shoes to be removed at entrance.*

Although of recent construction (early 1900s), the Khalid Ibn al-Walid Mosque is an impressive example of Turkish architecture, with its large courtyard and walls strikingly decorated in alternating bands of black and white stone. Inside the large prayer hall, four massive columns support a central dome, while in one corner is a large, ornate domed mausoleum containing the tomb of the Arab General Khalid Ibn al-Walid. Walid is celebrated in Islamic history for leading the Muslim conquest of Syria, decisively beating the Byzantine army of Heraclius at the Battle of Yarmouk before taking Damascus. In addition to his military acumen, he showed great foresight in guaranteeing the security of the people, thus ensuring that the new invaders came to be accepted by the local population. However, once the Muslims had established themselves in Syria, the need for military expertise was replaced by a need for administrators, and Walid found himself excluded from the court of the Caliph Umar, living out the remainder of his life in obscurity in Homs. That this city was where he died is well documented, although whether the present mausoleum actually contains his remains is open to question.

Great Mosque of Al-Nuri

ⓘ *Ash'Shouhada Sq, women and men should dress modestly and women should wear a headscarf. Shoes to be removed at entrance.*

The Great Mosque of Al Nuri is believed to stand on the site of a pagan sun temple (perhaps the temple of Baal), and was later the site of a Christian church dedicated to St John. As the name suggests, the mosque is attributed to the 12th century Zengid ruler Nur ud-Din, although it has undergone extensive modifications over the centuries. The main arched entrance, with its black and white stone decoration and carved Arabic inscriptions on either side, is impressive. Inside, the large rectangular courtyard is unusual in that it includes a raised terrace area along one wall, perhaps representing a part of the podium on which the *cella* of the pagan temple would have stood. Note the ornate Corinthian capital decorating one side of the raised terrace area, opposite the main entrance (this terrace is used as an additional prayer area, so don't walk on it with your shoes). There are a couple of other architectural fragments dotted around the courtyard, including a rectangular basalt basin, perhaps a sarcophagus, with heavily worn decorations on it. The *mihrab* of the prayer hall has remnants of mosaics inside its arch, although this is spoilt somewhat by the amplifier bolted into it. A couple of the columns used in the mosque's construction are clearly of Roman origin.

The souqs
A complex maze of narrow streets and covered souqs extend south and east from the Great Mosque of Al-Nuri towards the ancient citadel. They are every bit as lively and colourful as those of Aleppo or Damascus, and perhaps more authentic, at least for the absence of antique/handicraft shops geared exclusively towards tourists. Mondays, when the fruit and vegetable markets are freshly stocked, are particularly busy, and you can watch a huge variety of town and country folk going about their business. There are also a number of good clothes shops where you can pick up a lurid silk shirt (or perhaps even something a little more staid) for next to nothing. In any case, you can wander around at will and absorb something of the atmosphere, safe in the knowledge that you won't be dragged into someone's shop 'just for looking'.

The Christian Quarter
To the east of the main town centre is the Christian quarter, one of the few remaining areas of the town alongside the souqs that still retains many of its old buildings and gives some idea of what the city must have been like before its recent industrial expansion. In contrast to the essentially conservative Muslim areas of the town, the Christian quarter provides a strikingly different atmosphere, particularly early in the evening when groups of women stroll around sporting the latest fashions and hairdos.

Al-Zunnar Church ① *Al-Warsheh St, if the church is locked, knock on the door of the diocese office and the friendly people there will summon someone to open it up for you.* In its present form, the Al-Zunnar Church (Church of the Virgin's Girdle), dates from 1852, with further renovations carried out in 1966. However, it stands on the site of a much earlier church, probably dating back as far as the fourth century, and perhaps as early as AD 59. In 1953 an old manuscript belonging to the church was found, detailing the existence of a sacred relic, the girdle of the Virgin Mary, which had been concealed in the altar of the church during its reconstruction a century earlier. The altar was subsequently dismantled and the relic duly revealed. Today the girdle, which consists of a small and not exactly awe-inspiring piece of decaying fabric, is rolled up inside a reliquary and displayed in a small shrine along with the original casket in which it was found. Beside the shrine is the hollowed-out stone block and cover from the altar in which it was hidden.

Mar Elian Church ① *off Al-Warsheh St, ring the bell if the gate is locked.* This church looks every bit as unassuming from the outside as the Al-Zunnar church. However, inside it contains **frescoes** dating back at least to the 12th century. The church takes its name from St Elian, who according to legend was the son of an important Roman official from Homs. He refused to renounce his Christian beliefs and was put to death as a result towards the end of the third century. A church was built in his memory in the fourth century and his remains interred in the crypt. It was only in 1969 when renovations were being carried out on the church that the plaster which covered the walls was removed, revealing some beautiful frescoes in the crypt area. Today these are complemented by bright new frescoes painted in the main nave and side-aisles of the church by two Romanian iconographers, depicting various scenes from the life of St Elian. As well as being striking pieces of art in their own right, they provide an interesting reminder of how the older frescoes would have appeared when first painted. The small chapel to the right of the main crypt contains the tomb of St Elian, along with the oldest of the frescoes, believed by some to date back as far as the sixth century. The beautiful wooden iconostasis that separates the crypt from the rest of the church has some interesting old icons in its upper register. The feast of St Elian is celebrated each year on 6 February, attracting large numbers of pilgrims. St Elian was a physician by trade and various miracles of healing are attributed to him.

Azze Hrawe ① *3rd intersection on the right on Afram Basoum St, Sat-Thu 0900-1400.* This recently restored Mamluk residence was built by one Ali Ibn Abi al-Fadl al-Azzhari during the period of Baibars' rule (1260-1277), and now hosts a National Folklore Museum. Inside is a courtyard with a fountain in the centre. A large terraced iwan occupies one side of the courtyard, with an impressive conch shell semi-dome. In the wall opposite, note the two carved lions, popular symbols from the Mamluk era. You can explore the various rooms around the courtyard on the ground and first floors, and also get up onto the roof.

Homs to Hama

It is a further 47 km on to Hama from Homs. To pick up the motorway, head north out of town along Hama Street, passing the bus/microbus station, and keep going straight. Once out of town, the road crosses a large open plain. After around 21 km a high bridge carries you over the Orontes River. To the west a dam has been built creating a large lake, while below the dam to the east the river is reduced to a small trickle. Most striking, however, is the sense you get here of the depth to which the Orontes River has cut into the surrounding countryside to create a deep gorge. The remainder of the route into Hama offers nothing of special interest.

Hama → *For listings, see pages 145-150.*

Hama's attractive setting along the Orontes river has long made it a favoured stop on any Syrian journey. Famed for its huge *norias* (or waterwheels), whose groans and creaks are the backdrop to time spent here, Hama's relaxed, traveller-friendly outlook make it a good place to linger. The town's tranquil atmosphere belies the tragedy of its past. In 1982 this town became the setting for one of the most brutal incidents of Hafaz al-Assad's rule when an uprising was harshly crushed by government troops, killing thousands and destroying much of the old town.

Rebuilt since then, Hama today has excellent accommodation options and is a good base for exploring the surrounding region. While the cooler months of April and September are the best times to visit in terms of the climate, it is during the summer months that you can see the otherwise idle *norias* in action.

Ins and outs
Getting there and away Well connected with the rest of the country, Hama's well-ordered Pullman bus station is on Al-Murabet Street, 2.5 km southwest of the centre. From here into town it's about a 20-minute walk, straight up Al-Murabet Street until the turn-off into Kouwatli Street (about S£30 in a taxi).

The train station is on the eastern edge of town and all services between Damascus and Aleppo stop here en route. Microbuses provide connections to places of interest in the surrounding countryside and depart from two different garages in town.

Getting around For the most part Hama is small enough to explore on foot, but taxis are easily found if you don't fancy the hike to the bus/train stations. Taxi drivers are quite good about using their meter in Hama, but if yours isn't, a journey within town shouldn't cost anymore than S£25.

Tourist information The **tourist information office** ① *Sat-Thu 0830-1730*, has the usual town map but not much else in information. You'd be better off talking to the staff at either the Cairo or Riad hotels.

Background
Although nothing remains to be seen of Hama's ancient history apart from artefacts preserved in the museum, evidence of settlement going back as far as the **Neolithic** period has been uncovered in the course of extensive excavations of the large mound on which the town's citadel stood. This was also the site of a fortress during the late second to early first millennium BC when the town, then known as 'Hamath', was the capital of the Syro-Hittite kingdom of the Aramaeans. In 720 BC it was completely destroyed by the Assyrian armies of Sargon, and only regained some measure of prosperity under the Seleucids, when it became known as 'Epiphania' after the Seleucid king Antiochus IV Epiphanes (175-164 BC).

Under the **Romans** and **Byzantines** it continued to prosper in relative obscurity until it fell in the Muslim conquest in the seventh century AD. It continued as a town of little importance during the Muslim period, caught between the competing city-states of Aleppo and Damascus. The **Ayyubid** period, however, brought with it relative prosperity. Given by Salah ud-Din to one of his nephews, the town subsequently managed to retain a certain degree of independence as a sovereign principality well into the Mamluk period. It was during this time that the first of the town's *norias* were constructed. During the **Ottoman** period Hama was incorporated into the *sanjak* of Tripoli, although within this it also enjoyed the position of chief town of a *pashalik*.

Perhaps due to its relative isolation, during the rule of Hafaz al-Assad Hama developed as a fiercely conservative centre of Sunni orthodoxy and became the focus for opposition to Assad's regime, which led to the tragic **Hama Uprising**. The opposition was led by the extremist Islamic movement, the Muslim Brotherhood, which was intent on replacing the secular, modernist ideology of Assad's Baathist government with strict Islamic rule. The Brotherhood had been waging a bloody campaign of terrorism targeted at members of Assad's Alawi sect and at the foundations of the state for several years, carrying out numerous bombings and assassinations, including the murder of at least 32 Alawi officer cadets in a bomb attack on the Aleppo Artillery School in 1979. Assad responded to this threat to his authority with increasing brutality and to many it seemed that the country was on the brink of civil war.

The showdown finally came in February 1982, when an army unit was ambushed while patrolling the narrow souqs of Hama's Old City. The Brotherhood quickly put out a call for a general uprising in the city. The government's response, led by Assad's brother Rifa'at, was swift, although the scale of that response shocked even those who understood the full implications of the showdown. An all-out battle ensued which was to last for three weeks and devastate the city, leaving much of it flattened and thousands of its inhabitants dead (the site of the **Apamee Cham Palace** hotel, for example, was once a densely populated area of narrow streets and souqs). According to an Amnesty International report of November 1983, the estimates of the numbers killed ranged from 10,000-25,000.

Following the events of 1982, Assad ensured that a huge amount of investment was poured in, building new roads, public buildings and housing estates, in an attempt to create a 'new start' for the town. Today it is these modern aspects of Hama, with its wide streets and large new housing developments, which first make an impression.

Norias

Set in a natural depression surrounded by low hills, Hama faces a peculiar problem in that although the Orontes flows through it, all the surrounding land is at a higher level, making it difficult to irrigate. Previous attempts to tackle this problem were made as early as the Byzantine period, but the Ayyubids were the first to do so on a grand scale in the 13th century, and it is to them that Hama owes the earliest of its unusual wooden waterwheels, or *norias*. These lifted the water from river level, depositing it in raised aqueducts which then carried it to nearby fields. Today there are a total of 17 of these enormous contraptions at various points along the river as it flows through the town. For much of the year they stand idle, the waters of the Orontes largely diverted to modern irrigation schemes, reducing the river to an insubstantial and heavily polluted trickle insufficient to power them. During the summer, however, the river is returned to its full flow and the restored *norias* turn as they did in the past.

About 1 km upstream (east) of the town centre, there is a group of two pairs of *norias* known as the **Four Norias of Bechiriyat**, with the **4 Norias** restaurant opposite. Heading west from the centre of town, the largest waterwheel, with a diameter of 20 m, is the **Al Muhammediyeh**, by a small stone footbridge to the west of the citadel mound. This was built by the Mamluks in the 14th century (an inscription on the adjoining aqueduct gives the date as 1361) to supply the Great Mosque with water.

Old town

The best preserved remnants of Hama as it was before 1982 are along the west bank of the Orontes River where it swings north in the centre of town. Just past the **Al Rowdah** restaurant a small alleyway leads off to the right, immediately before one of the town's original aqueducts crosses the main road. If you follow this alleyway and bear right where it forks, you come first to the **Alatoman Hammam** on the left, see page 147.

Just past the hammam, on the same side, is the **Ateliers des Peintures** ① *daily 0900-2200*. This traditional building, its rooms arranged in typical Arabic style around a central courtyard, has been converted into artists' studios. The works on display here are also for sale, but even if you aren't interested in buying, it is well worth checking out the contemporary Syrian art scene.

Continuing north along the alleyway, past the Azem Palace, and bearing right where it forks, you pass two large *norias* on the right before going through a vaulted passage that meets the main road and bridge from where you get an excellent view of the **Al-Nuri Mosque** to your left and the two *norias*.

Azem Palace (or Beit al-Azem)

① *Old town, Wed-Mon 0900-1800, S£75, students S£10.*

This 18th-century building was the palace of the governor of Hama, Assad Pasha al-Azem, who went on to become the governor of Damascus, where he built a larger version according to the same basic plan (see page 57). Extensively damaged during the 1982 uprising, it has now been largely restored. Though not as grand as the Damascus Azem Palace, it nevertheless has a great deal of charm, evoking the atmosphere of such Ottoman buildings beautifully, with its shady courtyards, fountains and richly decorated rooms.

Various architectural fragments and pieces of sculpture are dotted around the main courtyard, which served as the *salemlek*, or visitors' area. Stairs lead up to the upper courtyard, where there is a particularly striking grand reception room; an arched portico protects the ornate façade, while inside every surface is lavishly decorated with painted woodwork, banded stonework and patterned marble. The central section of the room is topped by a large dome. The other rooms opening onto this upper courtyard contain 'popular traditions' displays, with costumed mannequins depicting scenes from everyday life, though it is the decoration in the rooms themselves that is most impressive. From the entrance area, you can also see the palace's private hammam, and from here you can go through to a smaller courtyard that served as the *haremlek*, or family and women's quarters.

Hama

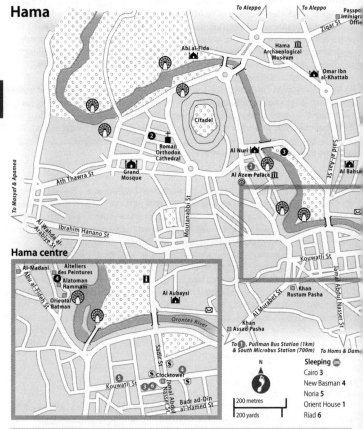

Al-Nuri Mosque

ⓘ The mosque is only open around prayer times. If the local imam shows you round, he will expect a small payment for his troubles. Women and men should be modestly dressed to enter, and women should wear a headscarf.

Construction of the Al-Nuri Mosque began in 1172 during the reign of Nur ud-Din, as detailed in the lengthy Arabic inscription on the outside wall, by the entrance opposite the prayer hall. The square tower-minaret of the mosque is original and features alternating bands of black and white stone, giving way in places to interwoven and chequered patterns. Inside, there is an arched and vaulted arcade around three sides of the courtyard, with the prayer hall occupying the fourth, and a pool for ablutions in the centre. Note the delicate classical column topped by a Corinthian capital incorporated into the arcade at one point.

Sarah **2**   Le Jardan **3**

Eating ⑦
Aspasia **4**
4 Norias **1**
Family Club **2**

Noria (Water wheel) 🚲

Citadel

Practically nothing remains to be seen today on the archaeologically important citadel mound, which was subject to extensive excavations by the Dutch. In the archaeological museum (see below) you can see photos of these excavations. The summit of the mound is now occupied by a landscaped garden which is a popular picnic site amongst the residents of Hama, particularly on Fridays. This is also a good place to come for a bird's-eye view over Hama.

Roman Orthodox Cathedral

Following the main street leading west from the roundabout to the south of the citadel mound, you pass first on your right the Roman Orthodox Cathedral, while further along on the left is the Grand Mosque. The huge modern Roman Orthodox Cathedral replaces an earlier one that was destroyed in 1982. Beside the cathedral there is a small chapel, also newly rebuilt. Known as the 'Church of the Entrance of Theotokus to the Temple', it is thought to originally date from the fourth century and to have stood on the site of an earlier pagan temple. In places the original, much larger, Roman-period stones have been used in the reconstruction. Beside the cathedral and chapel, overlooked by the large, modern residence of the Roman Orthodox Bishop, is an area of deep excavations. The foundations of another

Byzantine church, complete with a fourth century mosaic (currently hidden under a layer of gravel for protection) have been discovered here.

Grand Mosque

① *Officially there are special times for tourists (0930-1230 and 1600-1900 in summer; 0900-1130 and 1400-1600 in winter), though in practice you can visit at any time. Be sure to dress modestly; women should wear a headscarf.*

Almost completely destroyed in the 1982 Hama uprising, the Grand Mosque has now been fully restored. Although it has the feel of a modern replica, the reconstruction is faithful to the original in practically every detail and has been skilfully carried out. The original was built by the Umayyads, and like the Umayyad Mosque in Damascus, stood on the site of a Christian church which was itself built on top of the remains of an earlier pagan temple. The mosque has two minarets. One is a square tower adjacent to the prayer hall (visually the more striking of the two), which can be dated by an inscription to 1124, though some argue that its base in fact dates from the Umayyad period. The other is octagonal in shape, dating from 1427 and representing an excellent example of Mamluk architecture. In the courtyard there is a 'treasury' consisting of a domed structure supported on eight columns carved with Kufic inscriptions and topped by Corinthian capitals (clearly of Roman origin). It is identical to the treasury of the Umayyad Mosque in Damascus, except for the absence of mosaic decoration. The side entrance to the prayer hall, by the square tower-minaret, has a lintel of Roman or Byzantine origin which is richly decorated with floral designs; much of this wall of the prayer hall consists of large old stone blocks and contains several other architectural fragments from the Roman and Byzantine eras. A doorway in the side of the main courtyard (beside the treasury) leads through into a small square courtyard giving access to a domed mausoleum containing two tombs, said to be those of two 13th-century Ayyubid kings.

Khans

Two Ottoman period khans can be found along Al-Murabet Street as it runs southwest towards the bus station. The first of these, **Khan Rustum Pasha**, dates from 1556 and has recently been restored. Although it is officially only open for exhibitions you are allowed to enter to have a look around. The second, **Khan Assad Pasha**, dating from 1738, has a larger and more impressive doorway, and is used as an orphanage so is not open to visitors.

Souqs

Before reaching Khan Assad Pasha, extending north from Al-Murabet Street is a maze of narrow streets housing the main concentration of Hama's crowded and colourful souqs. On the north side of the river, meanwhile, running parallel to the main Hama road on the right, there are some remnants of much older souqs which were largely destroyed in 1982. Turn right into a new street just before the tourist information office on the opposite side of the road, then immediately left to wander along a narrow alley and then into a covered stretch of these souqs, which primarily serve the Bedouin from the surrounding countryside (mornings are the best time to come).

If you continue straight along the new street leading east, you will see after a short distance a small area of old buildings off to the right (practically all that remains of what was previously a dense area of souqs; today this area is a rather bleak mixture of ruined buildings and half-completed modern housing blocks). At the end of a vaulted passage on the right is the 11th-century **Al Aubaysi Mosque**, still looked after by descendents of

Sheikh Muhammad Aubaysi, who immigrated to Syria after the fall of Andalusia, and whose tomb is inside the mosque. Attached to the mosque was a small palace and baths complex, though today this is completely in ruins.

Hama Archaeological Museum

ⓘ *Said al-Aas St, Wed-Mon 0900-1800 in summer, 0900-1600 in winter, S£150, students S£10.*
On the north side of the river, just past the huge new Omar Ibn al-Khattab Mosque, Hama's prestigious, purpose-built museum is excellently presented and well worth a visit. Dotted around the museum's gardens are numerous capitals, columns, carved basalt doors and various other architectural fragments. Of particular note are the artefacts housed under protective wooden structures: a series of mosaic floors, a couple of life-size statues, a set of huge amphorae and a richly carved sarcophagus. The museum itself is built around a central courtyard with a fountain and pool in the centre. You work your way around anticlockwise, with each hall being colour-coded according to the epoch it covers.

The first hall covers the **palaeolithic/neolithic** and **chalcolithic/Bronze Age**. It takes you from the earliest Stone Age, through the first settlements and beginnings of agriculture, to the development of urban centres with clear, well written interpretation boards and interesting displays.

The **Iron Age** hall includes some very beautiful artefacts, including an eighth-century BC human figurine made of bronze and covered in gold leaf, and a ninth-century BC ivory cup with its handle carved into the shape of an ibex. Dominating the hall is a massive carved basalt lion (largely a reconstruction, but impressive nevertheless) found on Hama's citadel mound. This would have originally stood guard at the gates of the Royal Palace, which occupied the citadel mound during the ninth century BC. Typically neo-Hittite in style, the similarity with the lions and figures at the entrance to Aleppo Museum, and the lion at Ain Dara, is quite striking. There is also a scale model of the Royal Palace and, on the wall behind, a series of photos of the excavations carried out on the citadel mound (all the work here was destroyed during the 1982 uprising).

Two halls are dedicated to the **Hellenistic/Roman/Byzantine** periods. The first contains various sarcophagi (including one of terracotta and lead, and a reconstruction of an unusual wooden one), as well as gold burial ornaments, pottery, glassware, funerary stele, etc. Particularly striking is a statue of a female figure, possibly a deity, found in a Roman tomb dating from the second century AD, while the fresco on a fragment of stucco depicting Narcissus at a spring, found in a second to third century AD Roman tomb, is still remarkably clear. The highlight of the second hall is a really stunning Roman mosaic discovered at the village of Miriamin, to the southwest of Hama. This large, exceptionally well preserved third-century AD mosaic is made of unusually small *tesserae*, providing excellent detail. It depicts a group of women playing music and dancing, and provides insight into the musical instruments of this period. Around the border is a broad band of lavish decoration with hunting scenes, cupids amidst swirling acanthus leaves and vine scrolls, and personifications of the four seasons.

The last hall, devoted to the **Islamic** period, contains some nice pottery and a very beautiful wooden *minbar* from the Al-Nuri Mosque. Of great interest, though chronologically out of place, is a fragment of mosaic dating from AD 469 found at Apamea. This depicts part of a *noria*, confirming that this method of extracting water from the Orontes was already in use during the Byzantine era.

Around Hama

Hama makes an ideal base from which to visit a number of sites in the surrounding countryside. Most obviously, these include Apamea (arguably the most impressive site in the area), Masyaf, Qala'at Shmemis and Qasr Ibn Warden. Further afield, Krak des Chevaliers can reasonably be visited as a day trip from Hama (see page 162), a popular alternative to using Homs as a base. The town of Maarat al-Numan (see page 141) with its beautiful mosaics museum and the nearby Dead City sites centred around Bara (see page 247) are also within reasonably easy reach, both in fact closer to Hama than to Aleppo.

Ins and outs

Getting there and away Both the *Cairo* and *Riad* hotels run regular guided tours to the various places of interest around Hama. If you are pressed for time, these offer an excellent chance to see a great deal more than is possible in a short time by public transport. However, if you have plenty of time but a limited budget it is possible to get to the majority of the places by microbus (see under Transport page 149). Not so easy by public transport is a trip out to **Qasr Ibn Warden**. Taking a tour (or hiring a car) here is a good option.

Hama to Apamea

The route from Hama to Apamea takes you past the castle of **Qala'at Sheizar**, a convenient place to break the journey. If you are travelling by public transport, it makes more sense to leave this for the return journey, if you still have enough time.

From the centre of Hama, head west along Ibrabim Hanano Street, going straight across the double roundabouts near the railway station to continue northwest. Bear left at the next roundabout you come to (you have no option here) and then just after crossing the railway line (7 km from the centre of Hama), bear right (signposted for Mahardeh; left signposted for Masyaf). After a further 20 km, entering the Christian town of Mahardeh, turn left at a roundabout and then right at the next roundabout (both signposted for 'Afamia' and 'Sheizar'). Following this road, you soon pass on the right the ruins of Qala'at Sheizar, strung out along a ridge above a village of the same name.

Continuing past the ruins and across the Orontes River, after around 15 km the road begins to climb up onto a low plateau giving good views of the surrounding countryside. Arriving in the centre of the town of As Qeilebiyeh (49 km from Hama), go straight across two roundabouts and follow the main road around to the right as it descends again from the plateau. Continue straight on this road to arrive in the modern village of Qala'at Mudiq, 56 km from Hama.

Qala'at Sheizar According to legend this is the site of the **Roman** city of Cesara, thought to have first been settled by the forces of Alexander the Great. However, the most important period of its history dates from the 10th to the 12th centuries AD, when its great strategic value, guarding an important crossing point over the Orontes, ensured it a central role in the power struggles of the period. By the 10th century the Fatimids had built a castle and established themselves here, only to be driven out by Byzantine forces in AD 999. They in turn were eventually driven out by a local clan, the **Banu Munquid**, in 1081. In the following years Sheizar became a base for attacks against the Crusaders, who had established themselves in Apamea. Repeated attempts in the early part of the 12th century by the Crusaders to overrun it failed, resulting in an uneasy treaty between them and the

Banu Munqid in 1110. The **Byzantines** similarly attempted unsuccessfully to take it on two occasions and it was only due to an earthquake in 1157 that the castle was eventually destroyed. The Zengid ruler Nur ud-Din subsequently repaired it and based a garrison here, but an earthquake again struck in 1170, and further repairs were not carried out until 1233, under the Ayyubids. In 1260 it was overrun by the Mongol invaders, and following their defeat in 1281, Baibars restored it and established a **Mamluk** garrison here. However, it was abandoned as a military base soon after and quickly fell into ruin, becoming instead a source of building materials for the village below.

The ruins are best entered from the north end; head for the old, 11-arched bridge (known as *Jisr Ibn Munqid* after the Munqid family) off to the right of the modern road where it crosses the Orontes and climb up from there. This brings you to the northern gate complex, a largely Mamluk construction with evidence of recycled Greek/Roman columns. At the southern end of the ridge you can see the remains of an Ayyubid tower. Overall, the ruins are more impressive when seen looking up from the road, although there are good views from the top.

Apamea (Afamia or Qala'at Madiq) → *For listings, see pages 145-150.*

Reminiscent of Palmyra to the east, the majestic colonnaded street of Apamea is a grand road to nowhere, stretching for nearly 2 km along the hilltop. The setting here is beautiful, backed by mountains and the ruins themselves wallowing amid wild-flowers and weeds. In spring it is particularly pretty as toppled columns are bordered by bright blooms and the whole site is surrounded by a sea of wheat.

Ins and outs

Getting there and away If you are arriving in Qala'at Mudiq by public transport, ask to be dropped off at the museum (*mat-haf* in Arabic), by the main road, on the right as you drive in from the south. Having visited the museum, you can then walk to the main ruins (a 15- to 20-minute stroll). Turn right out of the museum entrance and left at the top of this short street, then bear off to the right to follow a rough track as it climbs up through the dusty village, with the citadel off to the left. Continue straight past the theatre ruins on your right, then bear off to the left slightly to join the modern road, which takes you directly to the ticket office and café at the southern end of the site. To drive right up to the site, continue straight on past the museum and take the sharp right turn at the northern edge of the village. This takes you past the old citadel of Qala'at Mudiq, perched up on top of a steep hillock, and then down to the ruins.

Background

Following the death of Alexander the Great and the subsequent break-up of his empire, Seleucus I Nicator rose to power in northern Syria, establishing the **Seleucid Empire** early in the third century BC. Previously known as *Pharnake* and renamed *Pella* by Alexander the Great, Apamea (named after Seleucus's Persian wife) was one of a number of settlements that he greatly expanded, making it into an important military base and provincial centre. Others in the area which received a similar treatment included Antioch (present day Antakya in Turkey), which became the capital, its seaport Seleucia, and Laodicea (present-day Lattakia), which served as Apamea's port.

During the Seleucid period, Apamea flourished in its new role. At its height it is estimated to have comprised a population of some 120,000. Strabo records that a stud was established here with no less than 30,000 mares and 3000 stallions. Similarly, up to 500 elephants were kept here and trained for use in warfare.

The fortunes of the Seleucids fluctuated dramatically, their empire expanding and contracting repeatedly, but by the first century BC it was in terminal decline, and finally in 64 BC Apamea fell to the armies of Pompey. Under the **Romans** it continued to be an important military centre. A severe earthquake in AD 115 caused serious damage, but also resulted in a new burst of building activity, particularly during the reigns of Trajan (AD 98-117) and Marcus Aurelius (AD 161-180); thus almost all the archaeological remains to be seen at the site today date from the second century. By this time, Apamea was a flourishing city, with a population of perhaps half a million, and an important cultural centre. It was here, for example, that the philosophical school of thought known as Neo-Platonism was developed, combining Platonism with oriental elements, so continuing a process of synthesis between Hellenistic/Roman and oriental concepts that had begun under the Seleucids.

Its prosperity continued into the **Byzantine** period, when it became the seat of a bishopric and the capital of *Syria Secunda* province. However, in AD 540 the Persian armies of Chosroes I invaded Syria, sacking Aleppo and Antioch before descending on Apamea. Byzantine rule was restored for a while, albeit under tribute, but in AD 611 the Persians attacked Syria once again, taking Apamea in AD 612. Their occupation lasted until AD 628, when the Byzantines briefly regained it before finally losing it to the Muslim invaders in AD 636.

During the **Islamic** period Apamea declined in importance. In 1106 it was occupied by the Crusaders, led by the Norman, Tancred. They were eventually ousted by Nur ud-Din in 1149, but soon after, in 1157, it was all but destroyed in a severe earthquake. The Mamluks still made use of the acropolis, building the present citadel there, while during the Ottoman period it retained a certain importance as a halting place on the pilgrimage to Mecca.

Museum

① *Wed-Mon 0900-1800, S£75, students S£5.*

Set in a restored 16th-century Ottoman khan, this simple but highly effective museum displays some of the mosaics found at Apamea, along with numerous funerary *stelae* and various architectural fragments. In the centre of the large open courtyard are steps leading down to what was once a reservoir. Running around the courtyard are long vaulted chambers which once served as stables and now house a selection of the beautiful mosaics along with sarcophagi, inscribed stone tablets, statues, etc. Spacious and deliciously cool in summer, the lighting inside is, however, a little dim.

Theatre

In a depression to the right of the path coming from the museum, shortly before it joins the modern approach road to the main ruins, is the theatre. This was originally a massive structure, nearly 140 m in diameter, making it even larger than the theatre at Bosra. However, now in an advanced state of ruin, it is difficult to make out its plan from close up. A partially reconstructed doorway which would have led through to the *scenae frons* and stage area still stands, along with a stretch of passageway, but the *cavea* of the theatre has almost completely disappeared. A much better overview can be had by looking down onto it from the citadel.

Citadel

Perched on top of a steep hillock is the citadel and old village of Qala'at Mudiq, quite an imposing sight from a distance. This strategic position has no doubt been utilized at least since Seleucid times, although all that remains today are sections of the 13th-century Mamluk walls, made up of a mixture of recycled masonry from earlier fortifications. Inside, the village is a maze of narrow, cobbled streets and a jumble of new and old buildings. There are excellent views out over the Orontes Valley and Jebel Ansariye (as well as of the main ruins and theatre) from the main gate. If you are willing to let someone show you around, even better views can be had from various points along the walls and from the roofs of some houses. Be prepared, however, for very persistent attempts to sell you 'antique' artefacts – a thriving cottage industry in the village and something you are unlikely to escape in any case.

Main ruins

ⓘ *There are no opening times as such for the main ruins since the site is not fenced in, but there is an official fee of S£150, students S£10, at Apamea and there's a ticket booth at the Antioch Gate entry to the site. There is little shade so take adequate sun protection, the site toilets are inside the cafeteria, which has a selection of hot and cold drinks.*

The north-south **Colonnaded Street** or *cardo maximus*, forms the main backbone of the ruins and the prime attraction of the site. Stretching for nearly 2 km, it is longer even than Palmyra's. Little today remains of the porticoes that once lined the street on either side, but the original paving still survives in places, complete with the ruts worn in it by the passing of chariots. The re-erected columns are what really give it its grandeur, with their Corinthian capitals and connecting entablature which varies between Doric, Ionic and Corinthian in style. The modern approach road, which intersects it near its southern end, in fact follows the line of the ancient east-west *decumanus*. At the intersection is the **Apamee Cham Cafeteria** and a ticket booth.

Following the colonnaded street north, immediately on the right are the ruined remains of a **nymphaeum**. A little further up on the left you can see the outline of a small church, followed soon after by the **agora**. Consisting of a long rectangular area, little remains to be seen today other than two rows of column bases at its southern end (part of a short transverse street by which the agora was approached), and to the north a large pile of stones which once formed a second, monumental entrance. Further off to the west, hidden by a rise, a low mound is all that remains to be seen of the **Temple of Zeus**, the result of an order by the Bishop Marcellus in AD 384 that it be dismantled. Back on the main colonnaded street, opposite the pile of stones which mark the monumental entrance to the agora, the columns are deeply fluted in a corkscrew pattern with striking effect, a decorative device unique to Apamea.

Continuing north, you pass along a section with rather obviously re-erected columns, their plainness emphasizing the elaborate floral decoration of the capitals. Immediately after these columns end there is the excavated base of a large, star-shaped votive column in the centre of the street. This marks an intersection (no longer visible), beyond which there is an open stretch with some more fluted columns on the right, followed by the foundations and low walls of buildings, also on the right. At the north end of these, three large stone slabs can be seen, two of which are carved with reliefs depicting scenes from the legends of Bacchus; one shows Lycurgus entangled by Bacchus in the branches of a vine, while the other shows Pan holding his pipes and tending to a flock of goats. A little further on, the remaining length of the colonnaded street has been the most extensively restored, and highly effectively, to give a good idea of its original glory. This last section is also the oldest, dating almost entirely from first phase of reconstruction carried out by Trajan following the earthquake of AD 115. You come first to a recently restored and beautifully proportioned **portico** on the right, its taller columns set forward from the line of the colonnade and crowned by a triangular pediment. Further up there is a large re-erected votive column in the centre of the street (again marking an intersection), followed soon after on the right by the remains of a **baths complex**. This was built on a grand scale, although little remains to be seen of it now. Just beyond it the walls of buildings on either side of the street behind the colonnade have been reconstructed to show two storeys of windows.

Finally, at the north end of the colonnaded street you reach the **Antioch gate**. Extending off to the left here is a well preserved section of the city walls. On a clear day there are good views from here across the Al-Ghab, with the Jebel Ansariye beyond. The so-called Antioch gate appears to have been modified and extended at some stage to form a fortified keep. At the far end is a precarious looking arch surrounded by tumbled rubble. Parts of the keep have been excavated in recent years to reveal terracotta pipes that were laid at a later stage, above the level of the original paving.

Returning to the **Apamee Cham Cafeteria** at the intersection of the *cardo maximus* and *decumanus*, and following the latter east, on the left after around 400 m there are the remains of a **Roman villa complex**. It has an impressive entrance complete with decorated lintel and porch on the west side, albeit extensively reinforced with concrete. Inside is a large courtyard surrounded by 26 re-erected columns, and a smaller courtyard surrounded by rooms. On the opposite side of the road is an extensive area of ruins which has been identified as the **cathedral**. Now just a jumble of column bases, low walls and foundations, this was the most important of the Byzantine places of worship and underwent several stages of enlargement. Many of the mosaics displayed in Apamea's museum were uncovered here (the cathedral having been built over an earlier Roman structure), while according to legend the cathedral itself housed one of the relics of the True Cross, making it a major centre of pilgrimage.

Heading south from the cafeteria and intersection, on the right are the remains of a **church**, dating from the sixth century during the reign of Justinian. Only the foundations remain, but these clearly indicate its basic circular plan, with a semicircular apse extending from the eastern side. Further south, on the left-hand side of the street, are the remains of the **Church of St Cosmas and St Damien**, again only consisting of the foundations and parts of the lower walls. This church, also of the sixth century, was an enlargement of an earlier fifth-century church which in turn stood on the site of a fourth-century synagogue. The southern limit of the colonnaded street is marked by the **Emesa (Homs) gate**, of which little remains.

North from Apamea

From Apamea you can continue due north through the Al Ghab to join, after around 35 km, the road between Aleppo and Lattakia, 7 km to the east of the town of **Jisr al-Shuhgur** (for details of this town and the route between Aleppo and Lattakia, see page 252). Following this route you also have the option of diverting off it to climb up into the Jebel Ansariye to the hill resort of **Slunfeh**.

To do the latter, take a small left turn 4 km to the north of Apamea and follow this road west. After a further 6 km, go straight over a crossroads at the village of Al Karim, to arrive at a T-junction 7 km further on (17 km from Apamea). Turn right here to head north. After just under 6 km you pass a right turn in the village of Mardash signposted for 'Afamea' and 'Al Rasief'. Just over 12 km further on, turn left (signposted in Arabic only). This road climbs steeply in a long series of switchbacks up into the mountains and then follows the line of a ridge, with various viewpoints providing spectacular views out over the Al Ghab and beyond (providing that it is not too hazy). You pass some radio transmitters on the left and soon after begin to descend to the town of Slunfeh (see page 191).

If you continue north past the left turn climbing up into the mountains, after approximately 4 km, a little way beyond a small artificial lake on the left, the ruins of **Qala'at Burzey** come into view, up on the mountainside to your left. This 12th-century Crusader castle finally fell to Salah ud-Din during the remarkable campaign he conducted in the summer of 1188 in which the Crusader presence in Syria was greatly weakened. The site appears to have been occupied more or less continuously since the Seleucid era, although today even the Crusader remains are fairly minimal. It is a steep scramble up to the ruins, and although they are not that impressive in themselves, there are excellent views out onto the Al Ghab. You can continue north on this road to join the Aleppo–Lattakia road just west of Jisr al-Shuhgur.

Masyaf → *For listings, see pages 145-150.*

Masyaf is famous for its strikingly located and well preserved Ismaili castle. The old part of the town is also quite attractive, with its interesting medieval mosque, a lively market and a couple of khans, and is worth wandering round if you have the time.

Ins and outs
Getting there and away From Hama, follow directions as for Qala'at Sheizar and Apamea, and then bear left instead of right at the signposted junction just after crossing the railway line (7 km from the centre of Hama). Continue straight on this road, heading west through fertile, open farmland to arrive in Masyaf, 42 km from Hama. Approaching Masyaf, the Ismaili castle looms up impressively above the plains, framed by the backdrop of the Jebel Ansariye. Both the castle and the old town are situated towards the northern edge of Masyaf.

The castle
ⓘ *Wed-Mon 0900-1800 in summer, 0900-1500 in winter, S£75, students S£5.*
The origins of this castle are by no means clear. The Hellenistic, Roman and Byzantine architectural fragments that have been recycled in its existing fabric indicate that some sort of defensive structure existed here long before its rise to fame as an **Ismaili** stronghold in the 12th century. In 1103 it was captured by the Crusader Raymond St Gilles, and in 1127-1128 it was purchased by the Banu Munqid clan who had by then entered into a loose treaty of non-aggression with the Crusaders. By 1140 it had been taken over by the Ismaili Assassins (see box, page 154), for whom it became an important strategic centre and one of a number of castles in the Jebel Ansariye in which they took refuge from Sunni persecution. In 1176 the newly established Ayyubid ruler Salah ud-Din laid siege to Masyaf, in an attempt to put an end to the wave of assassinations they were carrying out against Sunni leaders, including himself. However, he broke off the campaign rather suddenly, having apparently finally succumbed to the threats of the Assassins and subsequently some sort of mutual agreement even appears to have been

established between them. It was only a century later that the Assassins were finally ousted from their stronghold by the Mamluk Sultan, Baibars, in 1270.

In its present form the fabric of the castle is essentially Ismaili, as can be seen from the typically small, irregular stonework employed in its construction. Traces of earlier Crusader construction can also be seen in places, distinguished by more regular stonework employing larger blocks, as well as the occasional recycled classical column section laid horizontally to reinforce the walls. Entry to the castle is from the south side through a vaulted passage; note the large arch just inside the door, resting on Byzantine-period Corinthian capitals. The outer defensive walls and towers enclose a central keep. Although fairly ruined inside, there are still numerous passages and rooms to explore, and great views out across the plains from the central keep. In all, it is probably worth devoting at least an hour to visiting the castle. Of particular interest are the huge underground cisterns and chambers along the eastern side of the outer defensive walls. At the time of writing these still had to be fully excavated in order to determine exactly when they date from.

Masyaf to Krak des Chevaliers

If you have your own transport, there is a particularly scenic route from Masyaf to Krak des Chevaliers. Pick up the road heading south out of Masyaf. After about 1 km you pass a right turn signposted for Wadi al-Ayoun, Dreikish and Tartus (this road takes you across the Jebel Ansariye to **Tartus** on the Mediterranean coast; see page 153 for details of this route in reverse). Continuing straight on along this road, you pass through several small villages, the road climbing steadily up onto a plateau, until you reach a T-junction, 22 km from Masyaf. Turn right here and then left soon after to continue south towards Krak (turning right and then continuing straight on this road takes you up to the hill resort of **Mashta al-Helu**; see page 171). Just under 6 km further on, bear right at a fork and keep following this road. After a further 7 km you arrive in the village of Nasra (signposted 'Nasira'). Shortly before, Krak begins to come into view intermittently, in the distance off to the right. Leaving the village, bear left at a fork. Shortly after, you pass a very sharp right turn (the road to St George's Monastery) followed a little over 1 km further on by the right turn up to **Krak des Chevaliers**, 4 km away (see page 162).

Qala'at Abu Qobeis → For listings, see pages 145-150.

Although in a fairly advanced state of ruin, the beautiful setting for this small castle on the eastern slopes of the Jebel Ansariye with its spectacular views down onto the plains below, along with the particularly scenic drive to get there, make it well worth visiting.

Ins and outs

Getting there and away Pick up the road heading north out of Masyaf and after 5 km take the right turn signposted for Deir Mama (going straight leads up over the Jebel Ansariye via Qadmus to Banyas on the Mediterranean coast; see page 178). This small road skirts along the edges of the mountains with views down onto the plains below. Note that the signposts for villages along this road appear several kilometres before the villages themselves; distances given here are to the approximate centre of each village. You pass first through the Alawi village of Deir Mama (5 km from the Masyaf–Qadmus–Banyas road) and then 3 km further on, entering the village of Al Laqbeh, turn right over a small bridge (going straight takes you into the centre of the village).

Continue along this road, passing through the village of Qrayiat (2 km further on) and then after a further 4.5 km, fork left in the centre of Deir Shmail (signposted for Abu Qobeis). Soon after, the road descends almost to the level of the plain. Six kilometres beyond the fork in Deir Shmail, you arrive at a crossroads in the village of Saqliyeh.

Turn left at the crossroads (signposted for 'Abo Kbais'). The road winds its way up through a beautiful wooded valley, passing several restaurants on the left, idyllically situated by the side of a stream (these are only open for the summer, closing down for the winter by around the end of October), before arriving in the village of Abu Qobeis, 5 km from the crossroads in Saqliyeh. A sharp left turn in the village leads up to the castle itself, 2 km away. From the road-head it is a short, steep climb up to the castle.

The castle

Along with Qadmus and Qala'at al-Kahf high up in the Jebel Ansariye to the west, this castle was purchased by the **Ismaili Assassins** from a local emir, Ibn Amrun of the Banu Munqid clan, in the mid-12th century. Previously it had been occupied for a time by the Crusaders (who knew it as *Bokebeis*), and even when it came under the control of the Ismailis, they continued to pay an annual tribute of 800 gold pieces as well as a quantity of wheat and barley to the Hospitallers of Qala'at Marqab. Most of what can be seen today dates from the period of Ismaili occupation, with the ruins bearing their distinctive hallmark of small, irregularly shaped stonework.

Roughly circular in shape, the castle consists of an outer defensive wall with five towers and a central inner keep. A quick circuit of the area between the walls and keep reveals the existence of several large underground storage chambers. Some scrambling is involved to get in to the inner keep, which covers a tiny area and consists of a jumbled maze of half-ruined rooms, walls and vaulted chambers, as well as a crumbling tower. Most of all, however, it is the stunning views out over the plains to the east, along with the picturesque setting amidst olive groves, which make the visit worthwhile.

Abu Qobeis to the coast

The road from Saqlieh up to the village of Abu Qobeis continues west, following a very beautiful narrow, wooded valley to climb up into the mountains, leading eventually to the Mediterranean coast just north of Banyas. At the village of **Ad Delieh**, 21 km from Abu Qobeis, you can bear left (ask directions as the turning is not obvious) to make a detour to the ruins of **Qala'at Maniqa** (or continue straight for the direct route to the coast). The ruins are above the village of Wadi al-Qalaa, 6 km beyond Ad Delieh. Just beyond the mosque in the village a set of concrete steps leads up the mountainside to the castle, a steep 15-minute climb.

Returning to the road and continuing west, just beyond the village of **Wadi al-Qalaa** you pass behind a waterfall gushing down from overhanging cliffs. The countryside around here is very beautiful, the steep, terraced valley given over to tobacco as well as olives and figs. Turn left at a T-junction 6 km further on to rejoin the main road between Abu Qobeis and the coast (this junction is 8 km from Ad Delieh by the main road, and the turning is signposted to Wadi al-Qala). Soon after, the road passes through the village of **Dweir Baabda**, which spreads over a considerable area. The final section of this route is rather confusing and it's easy to get lost. Basically, as long as you are going downhill, you cannot really fail to end up intersecting with the coastal motorway, or else with a smaller road which runs roughly parallel to it for a while; if in doubt, keep asking for directions to Banyas.

Qala'at Maniqa Dating originally from the early 11th century, the construction of this castle is generally attributed to a local family. In the course of its history it appears to have been passed back and forth between the Ismailis and the Crusaders (who knew it as *Malaicas*), an example of the close but ambiguous ties that developed between the two. Thus, soon after being acquired by Rashid ud-Din Sinan, the leader of the Ismailis, some time between 1160 and 1180, it came under the control of the prince of Antioch, Bohemond III, who subsequently entrusted it to the Hospitallers in 1186. However, before long it was back in Ismaili hands, and remained so until they were finally driven out by the Mamluk sultan, Baibars, in 1270-1273.

The castle is strung out along a ridge running northeast-southwest, although today all that really remains are the outer defensive walls which can be best appreciated from outside; with a little bit of scrambling, you can also complete a circuit along the top of the walls. Inside, most of the area has now been cultivated. Towards the northeast end are the most substantial remains. Most of the fortifications were concentrated here, including the keep and a watchtower, as this was the weakest point in the castle's defences, being easily approached via a connecting spur. Nearby, there are several large, vaulted underground chambers, two of which appear to have served as stables.

Qasr Ibn Warden → *For listings, see pages 145-150.*

The remarkable Byzantine ruin of Qasr Ibn Warden occupies a lonely spot out on the edge of the desolate desert steppe. The sombre, graceful buildings juxtaposed against a backdrop of endless stretching desert make this ruin wonderfully atmospheric. Scrambling to the top of the crumbling palace, with the dust-filled wind whipping around you, allows for excellent views over this ancient military outpost. Come for sunset when the stones here turn golden as the light slowly fades away.

Ins and outs

Getting there and away Head north from the centre of Hama along the Aleppo road and turn right into Ziqar Street (at the crossroads just north of Omar Ibn al-Khattab mosque). After passing under the Hama motorway bypass you are in open countryside. You pass first through the village of Maarshour (15 km) and then Bardoneh (28 km), where there is a right turn signposted for Salamiyeh, 29 km to the south. Continuing straight, the surrounding countryside gradually begins to give way to semi-desert. In the village of Al-Hamra (42 km), bear right where the road forks (signposted for Qasr Ibn Warden).

The next two villages, Twalid Dabaghein (50 km) and As Srouj (53 km), are interesting for their distinctive 'beehive' houses (see box, page 140). Fork left in As Srouj (right takes you southeast to As Sa'en, en route between Salamiyeh and Isriye, see page 141), and soon after the striking ruins of Qasr Ibn Warden loom up ahead.

Background

Along with sites such as Rasafeh and Halabiye/Zalabiye, Qasr Ibn Warden appears to have formed part of a network of fortified complexes built by the **Byzantines** in the sixth century to consolidate their control over Syria and to act as defensive positions against the Persians to the east. Inscriptions have dated the complex to the last years of St Justinian's rule (AD 561-65). What is most remarkable about the buildings is that they display an architectural style which is not seen anywhere else in Syria, but appears instead to have been imported wholesale from the Byzantine capital, Constantinople.

Even the building materials are not local, the basalt having been brought a considerable distance either from the north or south, while the marble columns and capitals are thought to have come from Apamea.

It has been suggested that as it was set back considerably from the front line of Byzantine defences against the Persians (along the Euphrates), Qasr Ibn Warden was built primarily as a base from which to consolidate control over the Bedouin tribes of the area. The elegance and opulence of the buildings was perhaps intended to inspire a sense of awe and respect for the Byzantine rulers. Thus as well as fulfilling a practical function as the headquarters of an important military commander, Qasr Ibn Warden was perhaps as much a statement in itself, a piece of the grandeur of Constantinople recreated in the wilderness of the Syrian steppe, rather in the same way that the Umayyads attempted to make their own mark on the desert with the eastern and western Qasr al-Heirs.

The complex

ⓘ *Wed-Mon 0900-1800 in summer, 0900-1600 in winter, S£75, students S£5. If you arrive here and the ruin is locked, ask across the road for the caretaker, Abdullah, who has the keys.*
The complex consists of a palace, church and army barracks. Extensive restoration work has been carried out in recent years to both the church and the palace. Of the army barracks (to your left as you arrive at the site), only ruined fragments remain.

The Palace This building consists of a 50 sq m building with a large central courtyard. The south façade of the building, by which you enter, consists of wide bands of large, square black basalt blocks alternating with narrow bands of thin clay brickwork, creating a striking overall effect. The entrance has a frame of carved floral decorations along with Greek inscriptions and a Byzantine cross. Inside, you find yourself in a large entrance hall, with rooms off to either side, and the central courtyard ahead. Note the stone-carved symbols in each room, thought to indicate the function which it served. The first room on the right of the entrance hall for example has a symbol of a wine jar, perhaps indicating that it was a store room of some sort; the significance of the stone slab carved with an eagle in the adjoining room is open to speculation. A set of steps lead up from the right-hand wing to the first floor, probably used for accommodation. The restoration here is incomplete, but the basic plan, in the shape of a cross, is evident.

Returning downstairs, in the room to the left of the entrance hall there is a symbol of a set of scales, perhaps indicating some sort of judicial function. This leads through to a set of rooms running down the west side of the courtyard, thought to have served as a school. In the first room there is a stone slab carved with images of a sheep and fish, both potent symbols in the early Christian church. To one side of this is a small room, perhaps the office or residence of the schoolmaster, while on the other side is the main school hall. By the door is a well and an underground passage leading to the northeast, presumably an emergency escape route, also said (more fancifully) to have once linked Qasr Ibn Warden to Anderin 25 km away. Note the central pillars in the shape of a cross. A set of stairs also leads up to the roof from here. The central courtyard is scattered with stone slabs, two of which can be identified as a sundial and calendar, while another was the door to a safe. The rooms along the north side of the courtyard (opposite the entrance hall and adjoining rooms) served as the stables, while along the east side was the baths complex, complete with a well, its 60 m depth protected by a metal cover.

Beehive houses

So called for their distinctive egg-domed shape, 'beehive' houses were once a feature typical across much of northern Syria and southern Turkey, though they are now becoming rarer with the inexorable spread of concrete construction. You are most likely to see them heading north from Hama along the motorway, and also on the route along the Euphrates from Aleppo.

The harsh extremes of heat and cold in the region gave rise to the unusual shape of these whitewashed, mud-built buildings, which are surprisingly cool inside during the searing heat of summer, and equally well insulated against freezing winter nights. Today, most are used only for storage, but in the villages of Twalid Dabaghein and As Srouj they hold their own as traditional dwellings. If you are visiting Qasr Ibn Warden with a guide from Hama, they will undoubtedly arrange for a stop at one of the houses for tea. An electric fan and a TV may supplement the traditionally simple furnishings of rugs, cushions and the all-important family chest, but these villages still provide glimpses of a way of life that goes back centuries.

The church Though smaller, the church is architecturally more interesting. The huge lintel above the main entrance in the south side carries a Greek inscription, along with various symbols. Internally it follows a square plan with a central nave and two side aisles; on the north and west sides an upper-floor gallery of rooms overlooking the central nave still survives; these were reserved for women and reached by a set of stairs in the northwest corner. The north wall gives a good idea of the towering height of the building, although to this you must add the central dome (now collapsed), which would have brought the total height to 20 m. The dome was raised up on a drum, with *pendentives* (triangular segments of a sphere) used to make the architecturally difficult transition from a square plan to a circular dome, a challenge which the Byzantines were only just starting to get to grips with at this stage.

Al-Andarin

The ruins of Al-Andarin, once a sizeable Byzantine settlement known in Latin as *Androna*, are 25 km beyond Qasr Ibn Warden. Thought to have been founded sometime in the second century AD; most of the ruins date from the mid-sixth century. The site is spread over an area of 3 sq km, and includes a large army barracks and a total of 10 churches. Very little remains to be seen today other than the jumbled ruins of the barracks and one church. Unless you have a special interest, it is perhaps not really worth the extra time involved in visiting. Traffic along this last stretch of road to Al-Andarin is all but non-existent, making it essential to have your own transport.

Hama to Qala'at Shmemis and Salamiyeh

From Hama a road heads southeast towards the town of Salamiyeh, passing close to the ruins of Qala'at Shmemis en route. For details of this route and the castle ruins, as well as the possibility of continuing on to join the main Homs–Palmyra road, see page 278. There are regular bus and microbus services between Hama and Salamiyeh.

Isriye From Salamiyeh a surfaced road heads northeast to the Roman temple of Isriye, 90 km away. This road continues all the way to Rasafeh (see page 289). Standing at the crossroads of the ancient caravan routes between Quinnesrin (ancient *Chalcis ad Belum*, to the southeast of Aleppo) and Palmyra, and between Homs and Resafeh, Isriye (ancient *Seriana*) was an important Roman staging post. Today all that remains to be seen is the small but impressive and well preserved *cella* of a third-century AD Roman temple. Built of limestone, it reflects very much the style of Baalbek, with which it is contemporary, particularly in the richly carved decorations around the main doorway and on the relieving arch above it. Inside, a set of stairs embedded in the wall to the right of the entrance gives access to the roof (now collapsed).

Much of the public transport running from Homs or Hama to Raqqa on the Euphrates River now uses this desert road, though you will probably be required to pay the full fare for Raqqa. Bear in mind also that the luxury coaches running along this route will not necessarily stop to pick up hitchers. On balance, this is a site for which you really need your own transport. Make sure you have plenty of water and some food with you, just in case you are stranded with a puncture or breakdown.

Hama to Aleppo
Heading north from Hama, the motorway leaves the Orontes River to the west and begins its journey across the Central Plains, where an annual rainfall of more than 500 mm makes rain-fed agriculture possible, and you will see crops of wheat, cotton and sugar beet.

Maarat al-Numan → *For listings, see pages 145-150.*

Today the town of Maarat al-Numan is a small, dusty market town which at first sight offers nothing of obvious interest. It is well worth a visit, however, for its excellent mosaics museum, housed in an Ottoman khan.

Ins and outs
Getting there and away There are regular microbuses to Maarat al-Numan from both Hama and Aleppo. All the Pullman buses between Hama and Aleppo go past Maarat al-Numan but as these will drop you off by the side of the motorway, rather than in town, it's best to go by microbus.

Background
Known to the Greeks as *Arra* and to the Crusaders as *Marre*, the town takes its present name from a combination of these forms with the name of its first Muslim governor, Al-Numan Ibn Bashir, a companion of the Prophet Muhammad who was appointed by the Umayyad Caliph Mu'awiya. As a small though relatively prosperous town it has been continually fought over throughout its history and controlled at different times by Damascus, Aleppo and Hama. The most famous (or infamous) episode in its history dates from the time of the First Crusade, when it was besieged by the forces of Raymond de Saint Gilles, Count of Toulouse and Bohemond, Prince of Antioch in 1099.

Maarat al-Numan also has a less gory claim to fame as the birthplace of the blind poet Abu al-Ala al-Maari (AD 973-1057). Educated at Aleppo, Al-Maari twice visited Baghdad where he came into contact with Hindus and adopted vegetarianism. He was recognized as a outspoken freethinker for his time, even daring to write an artistic imitation of the Koran, an act considered sacrilegious by Muslims (though unlike Salman Rushdie he

An unholy crusade of cannibals?

From the very beginning, the Crusaders gained themselves a reputation for their barbaric behaviour amongst the inhabitants of Syria, and much of that reputation would appear to have been founded on the horrific events which occured at Maarat al-Numan. Following the fall of Antioch, the Crusaders had been plagued by a shortage of food, their raids on the surrounding countryside in the lean winter months failing to bring in anything like sufficient supplies to feed their large numbers. By the time they laid siege to Maarat al-Numan, many were already dying from malnutrition and starvation. Despite assurances from Behemond that Maarat al-Numan's inhabitants would be spared, after breaching the walls of the town as many as 20,000 of its inhabitants are reported to have been massacred.

But if such events were common during those times, what happened next was certainly not. In desperation, the starving Crusaders appear to have resorted to cannibalism. In a letter to the Pope one of the Crusader commanders wrote: "A terrible famine racked the army in Ma'arra, and placed it in the cruel neccessity of feeding itself upon the bodies of the Saracens." Another Crusader chronicler, Radulph of Caen, wrote even more explicitly, "In Ma'aarra our troops boiled pagan adults alive in cooking-pots; they impaled children on spits and devoured them grilled." For centuries after, the image of the Crusaders as fanatical cannibals lived on in Arabic literature. Some Arab commentators have even suggested that the behaviour of the Crusaders was born not of necessity, but rather out of fanaticism, their religious fervour leading them to view the Muslims as lower than animals. Thus Amin Maalouf in his book *The Crusades through Arab Eyes*, points to the words of the Crusader chronicler, Albert of Aix, who wrote: "Not only did our troops not shrink from eating dead Turks and Saracens; they also ate dogs!".

appears to have avoided having a *fatwa* served on him). One of his most famous works provided the inspiration for Dante's *Divine Comedy*.

The museum

ⓘ *Wed-Mon 0900-1800 in summer, 0900-1400 in winter, S£150, students S£10, no photos inside.*
The museum is just to the southeast of the main square (ask around for the *mat-haf*; locals are used to pointing foreigners in the right direction). It is housed within a huge 16th century khan (the largest in Syria) built by the Ottoman governor Murad Pasha. The building is very impressive, and an ideal setting for the superb collection of mosaics displayed both in the central courtyard and also in the arcades and large vaulted halls surrounding it. The mosaics date from the **Byzantine** period (mostly fifth to sixth century) and come from various nearby 'Dead City' sites. Some of them have been restored, revealing their original, crisp colours.

At the far end of the first hall to the right of the entrance is a particularly noteworthy mosaic depicting the legend of Romulus and Remus, the founders of Rome, being suckled by a wolf. At the far end of the next hall (going anticlockwise) is an equally impressive mosaic of a lion killing a bull. In addition, there are some beautiful statuettes, figurines, children's toys, pieces of pottery, coins and glassware dating from the Greek through to Ottoman periods. Unfortunately, the labelling of these artefacts isn't great, although the Roman period is identified in some cases.

Around town

Nearby, there is an interesting **mosque**, notable for its minaret, rebuilt after an earthquake in 1170 by the architect Hassan Ben Mukri al-Sarman in the style of the Great Mosque of Aleppo. To get there, turn right out of the museum and head down the main street. At the fourth side-street on your right you will be able to see the distinctive square tower-minaret; weave your way through the souq to reach it. In the courtyard of the mosque, the large pool for washing is particularly unusual. The water cistern itself is octagonal in shape, with 10 column sections topped by Corinthian capitals (clearly of Roman or Byzantine origin) supporting a dome on a 10-sided drum. Also in the courtyard is a smaller domed structure and a deep well. Close to the mosque is the **Madrassa Abu al-Farawis**, built by the same architect in 1199.

If you head northwest out of Maarat al-Numan on the road to Ariha, around 2 km from the centre you will pass on your left the remains of the original **citadel**. Consisting of a circular settlement surrounded by a dry moat, you can still see sections of the older, larger stonework dating from the Crusader period, interspersed with smaller, later stonework.

Ebla

Ebla is one of those sites, alongside Ugarit and Mari (Tell Hariri), which has provided a vital key to our understanding of Syria's ancient history, revealing the existence of a major Bronze Age civilization that was all but completely lost from the historical record. Excavations here in the 1960s and 1970s have placed Ebla firmly on the map. Yet the site itself is one that relies mostly on imagination if it is to inspire. For those not so inclined, and with no specialist interest, there is simply very little to see. A visit first to the museum at **Idlib** (see page 246), as well as those at Aleppo and Damascus, does, however, give an excellent insight into Ebla's significance.

Background

Excavations began at Tell Mardikh in 1964, carried out by an Italian team under the leadership of Paolo Matthiae from the University of Rome. By 1968 evidence of a substantial settlement had been uncovered, as well as a statue dating from around 2000 BC with an **Akkadian** inscription mentioning the name of a king, Igrish-Khep, of Ebla. Then in 1975 came the remarkable discovery of the Royal Palace and the virtually intact archives containing around 17,000 clay tablets inscribed in cuneiform script. These archives were invaluable. They provided unprecedented insights into a major civilization whose existence had only been guessed at until then, and they established beyond doubt that this was indeed Ebla, a once powerful and independent Bronze Age urban civilization.

The earliest stages of settlement at Ebla can only be guessed at, but it is now clear that the development of urban civilizations in southern Mesopotamia in the late part of the fourth millennium BC was mirrored also in Syria. By the mid-third millennium BC Ebla was flourishing as an important and distinctive urban civilization with a firm agricultural base supporting a population of up to 30,000. Its fame as a source of wood, textiles and metals was the basis for its wealth, fuelling lucrative trade which extended into Anatolia, Mesopotamia, southern Syria and beyond. Indeed, fragments of Egyptian alabaster vessels were found in the Royal Palace, along with quantities of lapis lazuli and tin (for smelting with copper) from Afghanistan, although it is likely that these were traded with Ebla through intermediaries. Politically, Ebla also wielded considerable influence, negotiating on equal terms complex treaties with neighbouring powers and even receiving a substantial tribute payment of gold and silver from Mari.

Sometime around 2250 BC Ebla was attacked and largely destroyed by the first great Akkadian king, Sargon, or by his grandson, Naram-Sin. Nevertheless, it survived as an urban centre, now under Akkadian influence, and flourished once again on a more modest level from around 2150-2000 BC, later falling under the orbit of the local kingdom of Yamkhad, centred on Aleppo, before being finally destroyed in the wake of the Hittite invasions around 1600 BC.

By the time the Egyptian Pharaoh Thutmoses III marched through here around 1500 BC en route to the Euphrates, it was probably completely in ruins. During the ninth and eighth centuries BC there was a small fortified Aramaic settlement here, and the site was also occupied on an insignificant scale during the Persian through to Byzantine periods. The ancient city of Ebla, meanwhile, was gradually completely buried under centuries of accumulated debris and the land eventually given over to agriculture, its existence only revealed once again to the world by the excavations carried out in the 1960s.

Ebla Archives Despite having been stored on wooden shelves largely destroyed by fire during the Akkadian attack, the archives, although strewn across the floor in rooms below the Royal Palace, appear to have been in roughly the same order as they had been stacked before the burning shelving collapsed.

The majority of the Ebla tablets are written in the Sumerian cuneiform script. The term 'cuneiform' is taken from the Latin *cuneus*, meaning 'wedge', after the distinctive wedge-shaped impressions characteristic of this form of writing. However, the archaeologists' work was further complicated by the fact that while the Eblaites used written Sumerian, their spoken language (Eblaite) was fundamentally different; it was essentially Semitic in character, although its exact relationship to other Semitic languages such as Akkadian, Amorite and Hebrew is still a matter of conjecture. Around 80% of the words appearing on the tablets are straightforward Sumerian (although 'straightforward' is perhaps somewhat misleading, given that this language and script is still only partially understood by experts). Of the remainder, the scribes of Ebla appear to have adapted the Sumerian cuneiform script to express words in Eblaite. Given the intrinsic differences between the two languages, translating the tablets was an imperfect science to say the least (in much the same way as writing Arabic words in English is problematic), and it is in this respect that the tablets are particularly difficult to decipher. Moreover, the cuneiform script was progressively modified over time, with a set of conventions lasting for a certain period, though without ever becoming fully standardized or being clearly separated from those of another period. Add to this the fact that the scribes left no spaces or separating marks between the words and it starts to become clear just how problematic and open to interpretation the process of translating the texts really is. At least the Eblaites generally wrote the words in the order that they were meant to be read, something of an improvement on earlier Sumerian practice.

The vast majority of the texts are of an administrative nature: economic records of the production and trade in textiles, metals, agricultural goods, etc. The remainder consists of lexical texts listing the Sumerian words for various objects, in some (though by no means all) cases with the Eblaite equivalent alongside, a few political and geographical texts and some literary texts. The political and geographical texts have been the main source of controversial claims regarding links with the Old Testament, while the literary texts appear to consist of copies of older Sumerian texts as well as some purely Eblaite texts that have not as yet been translated.

The ruins

ⓘ *Wed-Mon 0900-1900 in summer, 0900-1700 in winter, S£150, students S£10. There is no shade so bring adequate protection from the sun and lots of water.*

Extending over an area of 56 ha, the site is dominated by a central mound or acropolis on which the Royal Palace stood, along with various religious and administrative buildings. Surrounding this was a large residential area, of which nothing survives, and surrounding the whole settlement was a stone perimeter wall with earth foundations 60 m thick. Parts of the lower acropolis, including stairs leading up past the famous archives to the Royal Palace have been reconstructed to give some idea of what the buildings would have looked like. Most impressive visually are the excavated foundations of a monumental gateway in the perimeter wall to the southwest of the acropolis.

◉ Orontes Valley listings

For Sleeping and Eating price codes and other relevant information, see Essentials pages 19-21.

◉ Sleeping

Deir Mar Musa *p117*

The monastery attracts plenty of pilgrims, as well as casual visitors, and all are welcome to stay overnight (or longer). Larger groups should make arrangements in advance. Deir Mar Mousa, T011-742 0403, www.deirmarmusa.org.

Homs *p118, map p119*

The budget accommodation here can all be found in the centre, in the streets running off Shoukri al-Kouwatli St. Unfortunately it's all pretty abysmal and if you are in this accommodation bracket, you are better off coming to Homs as a day trip from Hama.
LL Safir Homs, Ragheb al-Jamali St (to the southwest of the town centre), T031-211 2400, www.safirhotels.com. An excellently run hotel, far and away the best on offer in Homs. Luxurious rooms (a/c, satellite TV) are decked out with all the mod-cons you'd expect at this price and there's a whole bag of facilities: swimming pool, restaurants, shops, bars, etc.
AL Lord Suites, Abdul Monem Riad St, T031-247 4008, www.lordsuiteshotel.com. This large, friendly hotel is right in the centre of town. The huge rooms here are sparsely furnished but come with a/c, satellite TV and

fridge and there's a restaurant, bar and internet centre.
C Al-Minas, off Corniche St (west of the town centre, near the sports stadium), T031-222 0224. This good-value, friendly place is in a quiet residential location. The rooms are simple but all have a/c and satellite TV.
E Al-Naser al-Jadid, Shoukri al-Kouwatli St. If you can get past the fact that the shared baths are pretty diabolical, this hotel, in an atmospheric old building right in the centre, is good for a night. The staff here are friendly and the rooms (with fan) are decently sized.

Hama *p123, map p126*

Hama has excellent accommodation options for all levels and some of the most helpful hotel staff in Syria. The 2 budget hotels (the Cairo and Riad) are both excellent value.
AL-A Noria, Kouwatli St, T033-512 414, www.noria-hotel.com. The friendly Noria has comfortable, spotlessly clean rooms that all come with a/c and satellite TV. Ask for one of the newly renovated rooms which are better value. There are also some funky suites, decked out in plush, modern furnishings, which can sleep up to 4.
A Orient House, Al-Jalaa St, beside Abdulazeez Adi School, T033-225 599, www.orienthouse-sy.com. This beautifully restored 135-year-old house features intricate tiling detail and courtyards shaded by hanging vines. The rooms here are all individually decorated; some featuring

window-seats and colourful rugs and lamps (all have a/c and satellite TV), and there's an atmospheric restaurant on site. It's tucked down a quiet alleyway half way between the town centre and the main bus station.

B New Basman, Kouwatli St, T033-224 838, www.basman-hotel.com. The rooms here are rather austere for the price, but they're all clean and come with a/c, satellite TV and balcony.

D Sarah, Abu Al-Fida St, T033-515 941, www.sarahhotel.com. This hotel, in a quiet location amid Hama's old town, has simple, decent-sized rooms (a/c, fan and satellite TV) and helpful staff. The top-floor restaurant has excellent views over the old town.

E Cairo, Kouwatli St, T033-222 280, cairohot@ aloola.sy. Well run and friendly, the Cairo has comfortable, spotlessly clean rooms (a/c, fan, satellite TV) that are well above the standard of accommodation usually found in this price bracket. There's a dormitory for those on a budget and they're geared up for travellers with a whole host of tours and services. Recommended.

E Riad, Kouwatli St, T033-239 512, riadhotel@ scs-net.org. This very social hotel is great for meeting other travellers and is run by the helpful Abdullah, who's a wealth of information. The Riad has large clean, simple rooms with a/c and satellite TV (some have balconies), there's dormitory accommodation, and if you're really strapped for cash you can sleep on the roof. Like the Cairo, they also offer a realm of tours and services. Recommended.

Qasr Ibn Warden *p138*

Abdullah, the caretaker who lives beside the ruins, is an extremely friendly Bedouin sheikh who is quick to extend his hospitality to visitors. You will almost certainly be offered tea, and perhaps a full meal at his house. It may also be possible to stay there overnight.

⓭ Eating

Deir Mar Musa *p117*
Meals are held communally. There are no fixed charges as such, although guests are expected to take part in the day-to-day life of the monastery, and make a donation towards its upkeep.

Homs *p118, map p119*

Ⅲ Mamma Mia, Safir Homs Hotel, Ragheb al-Jamali St. Good-quality Italian food can be found here so if you've been missing your pizza and pasta this place can satisfy your craving. In the summer dining is outside.

Ⅱ City Café, Shoukri al-Kouwatli St. Great for snacks, this popular diner serves a mixture of Arabic and international cuisine (burgers, pizza, etc) plus a huge range of fruit cocktails.

Ⅱ Prince, Shoukri-al-Kouwatli St. Next door to the City Café, this little restaurant serves up a similar menu.

Cafés

Baete, Shoukri al-Kouwatli St. This sophisticated, stylish café is the place to see and be seen in Homs. Ring the bell for entry and then head up to the lovely upstairs terrace for a drink and some people-watching.

Rawda Siyaha, Shoukri al-Kouwatli St. This large open-air café is set amid shady gardens and is a pleasant place to relax. There's a separate seating area for women and families and solo females will feel completely comfortable here.

Hama *p123, map p126*

If you're after cheap eats, Kouwatli St and the surrounding alleys have a host of falafel and *shawarma* stands, as well as bakeries, juice stalls and little diners where you can get a meal of chicken and chips.

Ⅲ 4 Norias, Adnan al-Malki St. Occupying a prime location on the river at the eastern end of town, this somewhat cavernous place is popular with groups and local families and serves up the usual Arabic fare.

¶¶ Aspasia, beside Azem Palace. This wonderful restored building has a huge courtyard dining area and lots of other nooks and crannies for more private dining. The Arabic food here is decent and good value.

¶¶ Family Club, near the Roman Orthodox church. This friendly, pleasant place in the Christian quarter serves up a good selection of Arabic food. It's very relaxed, there's an outdoor terrace and alcohol is served.

¶¶ Orient House, Orient House Hotel, Al-Jalaa St. Come here as much for the ambience as for the food. The restaurant serves a huge range of continental and Arabic cuisine and you can choose whether to eat in the beautiful courtyard or on the roof terrace. Alcohol served.

Cafés

There are several pleasant riverside cafés in Hama along Abu al-Fideh St, just before the old town, where you can sit and admire the *norias* while having a coffee and *narghile*.
Le Jardin, by Al-Nuri Mosque. The riverside location, overlooking the *norias* make the outdoor tables here a great place to linger over a drink or *narghile*, or to catch up with your diary. Alcohol served.

Masyaf *p135*

On the Masyaf-Krak road, on the right just before the turning signposted for Wadi al-Ayoun, Dreikish and Tartus, there is a pleasant restaurant set in large shady gardens of eucalyptus and pine trees serving the usual range of Arabic food. There are a number of simple restaurants in the old part of Masyaf, close to the castle, where you can get falafel sandwiches, kebabs, etc, as well as a couple of cafés.

O Shopping

Hama *p123, map p126*

Luxurious bathrobes and towels made from mixed cotton and silk are a speciality of Hama, and this is one of the few places in

Syria where they are still hand-woven on traditional looms.
Al-Madani, just off Abu al-Fideh St, www.loomed-almadani.com. Looming since 1853, the Al-Madani family make luxurious cotton products: towels, bathrobes, table-cloths, etc that make wonderful gifts. As well as their workshop/shop they also have a stand outside the entrance to Azem Palace.
Ateliers des Peintures, beside Azem Palace. If you'd like to pick up some contemporary art, the prices here are very reasonable.
Oriental Batman, just off Abu al-Fideh St. Aimed very much at tourists, this curiously named shop offers an interesting range of jewellery, woven and painted fabrics, linen, traditional costumes and all kinds of antiques/bric-a-brac. The owner makes some of the jewellery himself.

▲ Activities and tours

Hama *p123, map p126*
Hammams

Alatoman, Old Town. Daily, men 0800-1200 and 1900-2400, women 1200-1800. Despite the official hours this hammam does have a habit of opening the doors only when they feel like it. When open though, you can get the full hammam works with steam bath.

Tours

Both the **Cairo** and **Riad** hotels organize a wide range of tours to the sights in the surrounding area. You can also hire a car privately from them if you don't feel like joining up with other travellers.

❂ Transport

Deir Mar Musa *p117*

From Abbasseen Garage in Damascus, microbuses regularly shuttle to **Nabak** (1 hr, S£30) and back (this is the nearest town to the monastery). From here you will have to negotiate a ride; be sure to make arrangements for the return trip in advance if you want to avoid a long, hot walk down. Around S£300 for a wait and return would be reasonable, or around S£200-250 one-way, although you may find you have to bargain hard. Everyone has to walk the last part, from the ravine to the monastery.

Homs *p118, map p119*
Bus
Homs is a major transport hub and there's no need to book bus tickets in advance. The Pullman bus station is north of the town centre on Hama St. A taxi from the centre to here shouldn't cost more than S£30. Al-Ahliah bus company have plenty of departures from here. To **Damascus** their buses depart every 30 mins (2 hrs, S£110), **Hama** every hour (30 mins, S£30), and **Aleppo** every hour (2 hrs, S£115), as well as 4 buses per day running to **Lattakia** (2½ hrs, S£125) via **Tartus** (1½ hrs, S£65), at 1015, 1300, 1445 and 1900.

Kadmous have similar services to all the towns mentioned but also have buses to **Deir ez-Zor** (5 hrs, S£265) via **Palmyra** (2½ hrs, S£105) at 0730, 1130, 1300, 1445, 1730 and 2000.

Microbus
Right next door to the Pullman bus station is the large and confusing microbus garage; particularly useful for transport to Krak des Chevaliers and Hama. Microbuses to **Krak des Chevaliers** (1 hr, S£50) depart regularly, when full, from the right-hand side of the car park. Ask for the bus going to 'Al-Hosn' and locals will point you in the right direction. Don't forget to bring along your passport as they're quite efficient at registering foreigners from this microbus station. There are also frequent departures to **Hama** (45 mins, S£50) from here.

Train
The train station is on Al-Korniche St, to the southwest of the city centre. Heading south along Al-Korniche St, just before you reach the large 'Homs Tourism Department'

building, a subway gives access to the east side of the railway tracks, from where you can reach the station, a massive, Soviet-style edifice that is difficult to miss. All the services between Damascus and Aleppo call in here. To **Damascus** (2¼ hrs, 1st class S£135, 2nd class S£110) there are 3 express services per day at 0840, 1210 and 1845, and to **Aleppo** (2 hrs, 1st class S£130, 2nd class S£100) at 0915, 1830 and 2230.

Hama *p123, map p126*
Bus
The Pullman bus station (Garaget Pullman) is right at the end of Al-Murabet St. All the usual companies operate buses out of here and you shouldn't need to pre-book tickets. A taxi from the centre costs about S£30 or you can walk (about 20 mins from Kouwatli St) straight up Al-Murabet until the end, when you reach the large T-junction with Nasser Bin Sayar St. The bus station is across the road. Kadmous run buses to **Damascus** (3 hrs, S£100) several times per day, at 0800, 0900, 1100, 1230, 1400, 1700, 1800 and 2000; to **Aleppo** (2 hrs, S£100) at 0830, 0900, 0930, 1145, 1230, 1315, 1445, 1530, 1545, 1700, 1730 and 1845; to **Deir ez-Zor** (5½ hrs, S£300), via **Palmyra** (3½ hrs, S£140) at 0645, 1030, 1130, 1400, 1915 and 2315; and **Tartus** (2 hrs, S£100) at 0545, 0630, 0730, 1300, 1915 and 2130. Buses to **Damascus** and **Deir ez-Zor** all stop in **Homs** on the way. Al-Ahliah operate very similar schedules but also service **Lattakia** (3 hrs, S£160) with departure times at 0600, 0930, 1215, 1400 and 1815.

From Hama to **Krak des Chevaliers** you need to get a bus or microbus to Homs first and change there.

There's also **international departures** to Jordan from here. Al-Majid have 2 buses daily at 1300 and 2300 to **Amman** (9 hrs, S£750).

Car hire
There is a Hertz/Chamcar desk at the *Apamee Cham Palace Hotel*, T033-525 335.

Microbus

On the left-hand side of Al-Murabet St (just before the intersection with Nasser Bin Sayar St), is the south microbus station. From here there are regular services to most of the surrounding towns including: **Homs** (45 mins, S£50), **As Qeilebiyeh** (for Apamea) (40 mins, S£30), **Masyaf** (40 mins, S£40) and **Salamiyeh** (S£20).

If you want to catch a microbus to **Al-Hamra** (for Qasr Ibn Warden) (S£25) or to **Maraat al-Numan** (S£25), head to the other microbus stand on Iraq St, northeast of the centre.

Train

The train station is way out on the eastern edge of town. The express trains en route to **Damascus** and to **Aleppo** stop here.

Apamea *p131*

Microbuses run from the south microbus station in Hama via Mahardeh (for Qala'at Sheizar) to the town of **As Qeilebiyeh** (40 mins S£30). Change here to pick up a 2nd microbus to **Qala'at Mudiq** (10 mins, S£10). Departures are fairly frequent for both legs of the journey, although you should make sure that you set off for the return journey well before nightfall, and bear in mind that services are much less frequent on Fri.

Masyaf *p135*

There are regular **microbuses** running between Hama and Masyaf (40 mins, S£40) from the south bus station, and less frequently between Masyaf and Apamea (you may need to change in As Qeilebiyeh for this journey). The microbus station has been relocated to a new site to the north of the castle, though most microbuses also pick up passengers at the southern edge of town, on the Masyaf–Krak road. Bear in mind that all services quickly dry up around nightfall. Services are also much reduced on Fri.

Qala'at Abu Qobeis *p136*

Microbuses run from Hama's south microbus station to Abu Qobeis fairly regularly throughout the day (S£50). As always in this region, don't set out for the return journey back to Hama too late as services tend to dry up late in the afternoon.

Qasr Ibn Warden *p138*

Getting to Qasr Ibn Warden by public transport is something of a hit-and-miss affair. **Buses** run on an irregular basis from the fruit and vegetable market in Iraq St in Hama as far as the village of Al-Hamra. From here you have to hitch or negotiate a ride (traffic is minimal along this last stretch, but anything which does come past will almost certainly stop for you if they have room). In the cooler months this offers lots of potential for a great day out, but in the full heat of summer you may be better off opting for an organized trip through the Cairo or Riad hotels, or hiring your own taxi.

Maarat al-Numan *p141*

Regular **microbuses** run to Maarat al-Numan from both Aleppo (from the microbus station off Bab Antakya) and Hama (from the south microbus stations). It is a good couple of kilometres from the motorway exits into the centre of Maarat al-Numan, so try to avoid catching a Hama-bound service from Aleppo, or vice versa, as these will drop you off by the side of the motorway.

Maarat al-Numan is very near to the Dead City sites of Serjilla and Bara and you can hire microbuses to drive you out to the sites from here (though you'll need to bargain hard).

❶ Directory

Homs *p118, map p119*
Banks Shoukri al-Kouwatli St has a branch of CBS which changes cash and by the clock tower there's a **Banque Bemo** which has an ATM. **Post** The post office is located on

Abdul Monem Riad St, Sat-Thu 0900-1730.
Visa extensions The Passport and
Immigration office, Sat-Thu 0800-1400,
is on the 3rd floor of a building just off Ibn
Khaldoun St; entry from the street is via a
covered arcade. Fairly chaotic and inefficient;
not the best place to extend your visa. There
are several photo studios on the ground floor
if you need passport photos.

Hama *p123, map p126*
Banks The main branch of CBS is east of the
roundabout and clock-tower on Kouwatli St,
Sat-Thu 0830-1230. There's an ATM and a
busy but efficient exchange desk here.
There's also a row of standalone ATMs that
take foreign cards on Kouwatli St, on the
western side of the clock tower and a branch
of **Banque Bemo** with an ATM on Sadir St.
Medical services The private **Markhaz
al-Tobi** (Health Centre) hospital is in the
eastern part of town, T033-515 801. Always
ask first at your hotel for help if you need
medical attention. **Post** The post office,
Sat-Thu 0800-1400, is on the first right-hand
turn off Said al-Aas St after crossing the
bridge. **Telephone** Easycomm card-
phones are scattered around town and you
can buy phonecards from various shops and
kiosks. **Visa extensions** The Passport and
Immigration office, Sat-Thu 0900-1400, is
located on Ziqar St. Extensions of up to 1
month are issued on the spot with a bit of
to-ing and fro-ing between offices. It costs
S£150 and you need 5 passport photos and
a letter from your hotel.

Contents

Footprint features

The coast & the Jebel Ansariye

It will be the castles that bring you here. The most famous, Krak des Chevaliers, Qala'at Salah ud-Din and Qala'at Marqab, still resonate with reminders of the Crusades and the legacy they left. But this region offers so much more than just castles. The forest-clad mountains of the Jebel Ansariye and fertile coastal plains are a breath of fresh air after Syria's semi-arid interior.

This region's Mediterranean coastline stretches for over 180 km and, although most of the beach resorts fall well short of sun and sand worshippers' expectations, it is where you'll find the two major towns. Lattakia is a vibrant, modern city that amazes travellers with its liberal party atmosphere, while Tartus is a relaxed holiday town that has a fascinating dilapidated old city. Both towns make excellent bases for further exploration of the region.

Running parallel to the coast is the Jebel Ansariye range; isolating the coastal plain from the rest of the country. This relatively narrow strip of mountains hosts a verdant landscape of undulating terraced hills of olive groves, tobacco and orchards, rising to steep and inaccessible peaks clad in thick forest. This is the least visited region of Syria and also the most beautiful. This is also where you'll find those Crusader castles, some in a near pristine state of preservation and others mere crumbling ruins, but all of which will leave you awe-struck at the sheer brilliance of their design.

Ins and outs

Getting there and away
Both Lattakia and Tartus are well connected by public bus from the main inland centres of Damascus, Aleppo and Homs. There are also some decent train services, with the Aleppo to Lattakia route being an excellent alternative to the bus.

Getting around
Travelling up and down the coast is easy and straightforward, but the mountains present more of a challenge. Tartus and Lattakia make good bases from which to explore the Jebel Ansariye; the major places of interest (Krak des Chevaliers, Safita, Qala'at Marqab and Qala'at Salah ud-Din) can all be reached fairly easily by public transport. Bus and minibus services also operate to more remote areas but tend to be pretty erratic. Having said that, if you have plenty of time and patience, it is certainly possible to get around the mountains using a combination of public transport, hitching and the odd bit of walking.

In order to explore this area in detail, however, you really need your own transport. Even then, the greatest challenge is actually finding your way around. An intricate web of tiny roads criss-cross the region and navigating them is made all the more difficult by the absence of any really accurate maps or consistent signposting. The best available map is in the Ministry of Tourism free handout entitled *The Coast*. This covers the whole coastal strip along with the Jebel Ansariye, extending as far east as the Al Ghab plains (thus including Masyaf, Apamea, Jisr al-Shughur, etc). Unfortunately, however, in places the sheer density of tiny roads makes it very difficult (and in some cases, impossible) to read. Even if you follow our route descriptions carefully, your chances of getting lost are quite high. On the other hand (as always in Syria), you can be sure of plenty of help if you need it.

Over the last few years, the quality of the roads in the mountains has improved dramatically, with many of them having been widened and resurfaced. Nevertheless, there are still plenty of extremely narrow and heavily pot-holed roads (or worse still, sudden changes from one to the other). Together with the steep gradients and endless sharp twists and turns (not to mention the hazards of playing children or wandering animals), this makes for some extremely demanding driving conditions in places.
▶▶ *For the route from Qala'at Abu Qobeis west across the mountains via Qala'at Maniqa to Banyas, see page 136.*

Background
The Jebel Ansariye has historically acted as a barrier, with the Homs Gap, to the south of Tartus, providing the only easy access between the coast and the interior. As a result, the coast is culturally very distinct from inland Syria, its development linked to events in the Mediterranean basin rather than the Fertile Crescent or desert to the east. The success of the **Phoenicians**, who established a string of important city-states along the coast during the second to first millennium BC, was based firmly on maritime trade throughout the Mediterranean and indeed, all along the coast, wherever its natural features allowed for even the smallest of harbours, settlements have existed since ancient times. It was along this coast that the **Crusaders** established their foothold in the region during the medieval period, building castles up in the mountains to protect the corridor formed by the coastal plain and so allowing them to move between present-day Turkey in the north and Jerusalem, their ultimate goal and reason for coming to the region, in the south.

The Assassins

From their secure fortresses in the Jebel Ansariye, this radical branch of the Nizari Ismaili sect caused chaos in 12th-century Syria, becoming major players in the political intrigues of the period. Operating independently from the nominal Fatimid rulers of the era, they were responsible for masterminding the murders of many key regional figures such as the king of Jerusalem, Marquis Conrad of Montferrat.

Abhorred by the Sunni orthodoxy, the Assassins were founded in what is now present-day Iran by Hasan-i Sabbah who turned his disciples into highly trained killers who operated with such a degree of discipline and obedience that they seemed to go willingly on suicide missions to carry out their attacks.

The origins of their name are shrouded in myth but the most common explanation is that it comes from the Arabic word 'Hashishiyyin' (literally hashish users) which would explain their fearless attitude in the face of death. One suggestion is that the Assassins smoked cannabis before their suicide missions making them oblivious to their own safety. Another is that while drugged the emissaries would be introduced into a secret 'garden of paradise' to convince them of the heavenly joys that awaited them after their martyrdom. The fame of their fearless exploits spread to the West with the tales of Marco Polo and the word 'assassin' soon came to be used in English to mean someone who is hired to carry out a killing.

As well as presenting a natural barrier separating the coastal strip from the interior of Syria, the mountains have also served as a place of refuge for religious minorities facing persecution. Indeed, they take their name from one such group, the **Alawis**, also known as the 'Nusayriya' or 'Ansariya'. Similarly, the **Ismaili Assassins** (see box, above) took refuge here during the 12th century, consolidating their military strength by building a series of castles in much the same ways as the Crusaders.

Tartus → For listings, see pages 195-203.

Laid-back little Tartus is beloved by Syrian families who flock here for their holidays. Once the famed Crusader stronghold of *Tortosa*, the Old City area is now a fascinating dilapidated gem, with concrete structures of resident's homes built on top of the crumbling Crusader remains. Offshore is tiny Arwad Island, today little more than a backwater but in ancient times an important island-state that flourished as part of the Mediterranean's trading network. With its easy-going holiday atmosphere, Tartus makes a good base for exploring the southern part of the coast.

Ins and outs

Getting there and away Tartus has good bus connections to Damascus, Lattakia and Homs, and the train network has been recently extended making train travel to and from here a viable option. You can also take service taxis to Lebanon, though there's no bus service from here. **Kadmous** and **Al-Ahliah** bus companies both service Tartus and operate separate bus stations in town. It's best to travel here with Kadmous as their bus station, on Jamal Abd al-Nasser St, is right in the centre and an easy 10-minute walk to most of the hotels. A taxis from here to most hotels will cost approximately S£20.

If walking from the Kadmous bus station, cross the road and head west down Jamal Abd al-Nasser St to the traffic roundabout. Turn left onto Ath Thawra Street, keeping the park on your left side. At the clock tower (and the end of the park), turn right into Al-Wahda Street. The boat jetty is at the end of this street and most of the accommodation is situated in this area.

The train station and microbus station are out of the centre, at the end of Al-Mahatta Street. A taxi to the town centre should cost S£25.

Getting around Tartus is small enough to explore on foot. Taxis are everywhere and some drivers do use their meter. A ride anywhere within town shouldn't cost more than S£25.

Tourist information Tourist office ① *6 Tishreen Av, T043-223 448, Sat-Thu 0800-1800.* Inconveniently located around 2 km to the south of the train station. They can provide you with a free Ministry of Tourism map/pamphlet, but are otherwise of very little help.

Background
Early history In a classic example of the tail wagging the dog, Tartus really owes its existence to the small island of **Arwad** (ancient Greek: *Aradous*), some 3 km offshore from the modern city. In fact the town's name reflects this subservient status, being derived from *anti-Aradous*, or opposite *Aradous*. (For details of the history of Arwad Island, see Sights, below.)

The town was established by the **Phoenicians** (and called *Antaradous*) to act as a kind of service base for the more secure Arwad Island. This situation continued following Alexander the Great's capture of both town and island for the Greeks in 330 BC, and the imposition of Roman rule in 64 BC. In fact, it was not until the **Byzantine** period (AD 324-638) that Tartus began to outstrip Arwad in importance.

The deciding factor in the change is said to be the Emperor Constantine's preference for the mainland Christian population over the pagan inhabitants of Arwad Island. Tartus subsequently became known as *Constantia*, though the name does not appear to have stuck. The association of Tartus with the cult of the Virgin Mary, revived during the Crusader period, is attributed to the town's early Christian population, and there is reason to suppose that the chapel built here before the fourth century is one of the first in the region dedicated to the Virgin Mary.

The collapse of the Byzantine Empire in the seventh century saw the town fall into **Arab** hands, though the town was briefly recaptured in AD 968 when Nicephorus Phocas attempted to revive the moribund Byzantine Empire. However, by the time the **Crusaders** arrived from Europe in 1099, the town had been taken over first by the Fatimids (from Egypt), and then had fallen under the control of the Emir of Tripoli.

The crusades Except for the town's recent development and transformation into Syria's second port, the most important era in Tartus' history was the medieval period. Tartus was of immense strategic value to the maritime Crusader forces and, though the port was lost to the Muslims almost as quickly as it had been gained in 1099, a concerted effort by Raymond, Count of Toulouse (at the head of the Genoese fleet) saw Tartus recaptured in 1102. He subsequently set about turning the town into a fortified stronghold, renamed *Tortosa*. In addition to the fortress, work also began on the construction of the Church of Our Lady of Tortosa.

However, divisions within the Crusader community allowed **Nur ud-Din**, the Muslim ruler of Aleppo, to capture the city briefly in 1152; an event which led Baldwin IV, king of Jerusalem, to hand over control of the city to the **Knights Templar**. Despite their formidable military reputation, the Templars did not appear to have learnt the lessons of their Frankish predecessors, and in 1188 Nur ud-Din's nephew, Salah ud-Din, was able to capture and sack most of the town. The Templar garrison survived by retreating into the *donjon* of the fortress, from where they managed to hold Salah ud-Din at bay. Following the withdrawal of the Arab army, the Templars set about refortifying not just

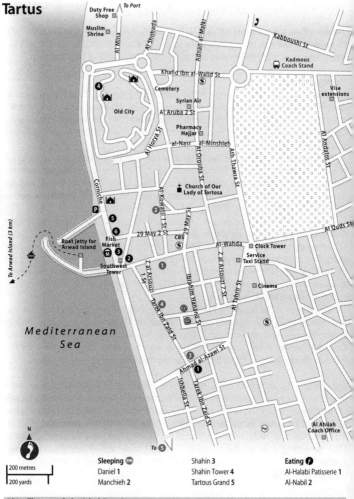

Tartus

Duty Free Shop
To Port
Muslim Shrine
Al Mina
Al Shohada
Adnan al-Malki
Kabboushi St
Kadmous Coach Stand
Khalid Ibn al-Walid St
Cemetery
Visa extensions
Syrian Air
Al Aruba 2 St
Old City
Pharmacy Hajjar
al-Nasr al-Minshieh
Al Hora St
Al Qrouba St
Ath Thawra St
Al Andalos St
Corniche
Church of Our Lady of Tortosa
Al Kowatli St
S.Abu Ali St
Fish Market
29 May 2 St
Boat jetty for Arwad Island
Southwest Tower
CBS
Al-Wahda
Clock Tower
Al Quds St
To Arwad Island (3 km)
Zal Arsouzi 1 St
Tarek Ibn Zaid St
Ibrahim Hanno St
Zal Arsouzi 7 St
Al Tahrir St
Service Taxi Stand
Cinema
Mediterranean Sea
Ahmad al-Azawi St
Tarek Ibn Zaid St
Isnbella St
Al Ahliah Coach Office
To S

200 metres
200 yards
N

Sleeping
Daniel 1
Manchieh 2

Shahin 3
Shahin Tower 4
Tartous Grand 5

Eating
Al-Halabi Patisserie 1
Al-Nabil 2

Tortosa but the surrounding countryside as well, building a network of castles that guarded the approach to their coastal stronghold. Tortosa withstood several prolonged assaults by the Mamluk sultan, Baibars in 1267 and 1270), though the fall of the Templars' stronghold of Acre (in modern-day Israel) in 1291 meant that the writing was on the wall for the Crusader presence in the Holy Land. The Templars rapidly withdrew to Arwad Island and though they maintained a garrison there for the next 12 years, they were hardly able to influence events on the mainland; by 1303 the last of the knights had withdrawn to Cyprus.

Al-Yamak **3**
Cave **4**
Sahara **5**

TicTac **6**

Few details are known about the town's subsequent history, though it appears that most of it may have been destroyed as early as the 14th century. Its revival began under the Ottomans (1516-1917), who used both Tartus and Arwad as a base, though the town's real expansion must be credited to the period of post-Syrian independence. Tartus is now Syria's second port (after Lattakia), with a growing industrial sector.

Old City

Tartus' principal attraction is the remains of the medieval city. Effectively, this actually means the Crusader fortress, an area covering little more than 500 m by 500 m. What makes it so interesting though is the way in which the local population has blended the old with the new, adapting Crusader walls and vaults into integral parts of their homes. This is no carefully landscaped museum piece but a living community, warts (well, rubbish and graffiti) and all. Tracing the lines of the original Crusader buildings is rather problematic given the number of later additions, and you will probably be quite content wandering the narrow alleyways, through the arches and vaults, and just seeing what turns up around the next bend. The open square in the centre is a great place to stop for a cup of tea, watch the comings and goings, and soak up the atmosphere. The most impressive remains identifiable today are those of the lower storey of the main **keep**, or *donjon*, facing the sea. This has now been restored and is used to host exhibitions and special events. When there is nothing on, you will just have to try your luck and see if you can find someone willing to show you around the huge vaulted halls inside. The former **chapel** is difficult to locate, it is hemmed in by contemporary dwellings, and in an advanced state of disrepair. When the fortress was constructed, the sea almost certainly extended right up to its walls. The *glacis* of the **southwest tower** of the outer city wall can be seen to the south of the fortress, where Al-Wahda Street meets the Corniche (it now has a model windmill on the top).

Church of Our Lady of Tortosa and museum
ⓘ *Al-Kowatly 1 St, Wed-Mon 0900-1800 in summer, 0900-1600 in winter, S£150, students S£10.*
Work began on this thoroughly imposing piece of Crusader architecture in 1123, though what you see today actually dates to the 13th century. The fortress-like appearance of the church, with its heavily buttressed walls, is no accident: it was meant as much as a defensive structure as a place of worship. Originally there was a square tower at each corner, though today only those at the eastern (rear) end of the church remain, complete with their narrow arrow slits. The entrance façade to the west features a central arched doorway, with twin-arched windows above, topped in turn by a third smaller one. To either side, arched windows mark the north and south aisles. In the northwest corner is a small octagonal minaret, added in the late 19th century, although there is no evidence that the church was ever actually converted into a mosque.

If possible, the interior is even more imposing than the exterior, austere yet beautiful with its massive pillars, soaring arches and barrel-vaulted ceiling towering above you. It follows the traditional triple-apse basilica plan, with a central nave flanked by side-aisles. The symmetry of the church is broken only by the cube-shaped base of one of the pillars dividing the north aisle from the nave. It is thought that this was the result of an attempt to incorporate an earlier chapel dating from the Byzantine period into the plan of the Crusader church.

In turn the church has served as a mosque and a barracks, but is now used as a **museum**. Although poorly labelled there are some interesting exhibits. On the left as you enter is a series of striking marble coffins dating from the Phoenician period (fifth to fourth century BC), carved in the shape of human figures with carefully sculpted faces, each with different features and remarkably realistic expressions of serenity. The left-hand side-aisle contains fragments of sacrificial statues from Amrit (also fifth to fourth century BC), various pieces of pottery and a case of Stone Age tools. In the side-apse at the end is a large terracotta urn with various smaller jars arranged around it. Occupying the central apse is a massive marble sarcophagus dating from the Roman period (late second to early third century AD), its proportions every bit as imposing as the church itself. Tomb robbers made a hole in the rear, understandably enough electing not to try and lift the lid. Dotted around the central nave are various ornately carved capitals, a headless marble statuette of Bacchus with the obligatory grapes in hand, and a couple of other headless statues. The right-hand side-apse contains three mosaics from Jableh, all unfortunately with large sections missing; that of Psoiden, goddess of the sea, is most striking in that her face and most of her body still survive. The right-hand side-aisle contains a mixture of artefacts spanning 13th-14th century BC Ugarit through to the Islamic period. Dotted around the church grounds are numerous architectural fragments, as well as some statues and sarcophagi.

Arwad Island

ⓘ *Boats leave regularly for Arwad from the jetty at the end of Al-Wahda St (last boat back is around sunset). The trip takes 20 mins. S£25 1-way. You need to show your passport on departure from the mainland. Note that the island gets particularly busy on Fri and public/religious holidays.*

The tiny island of Arwad, measuring just 800 m by 500 m, has had a significant impact on this section of the Syrian coast; so much so that Tartus itself, owes its very presence to the existence of this island. The short boat trip out here is fun, and while the island's general state of dilapidation (rubbish-strewn alleys and densely packed houses whose walls are covered in graffiti) is sorrowful, it's an intriguing and atmospheric place.

Background The island appears to have been first settled in the third millennium BC by the Canaanites, though it subsequently became a pawn in the battle for hegemony between Pharaonic Egypt and the Hittite Empire. Arwad subsequently passed through the hands of the Assyrians, Chaldeans and Persians, when it formed part of the coastal Phoenicia province. Faced with the Greek invasion around 330 BC, the Arwadi fleet joined the Persian navy, though Alexander the Great's forces were too strong and the island fell. Nevertheless, Arwad enjoyed a degree of autonomy until the Romans annexed it in 64 BC.

The island declined in importance during the Byzantine period largely as a result of the development of Tartus, though the Muslim armies saw Arwad's strategic significance and constructed two small fortresses during the Crusader/Ayyubid period. The Knights Templar briefly occupied Arwad following their retreat from the mainland. Turkish troops refurbished the fortresses as barracks during the Ottoman period, with the French Mandate authorities later using them as prisons for those fighting against colonial rule.

Visiting the island You can quite happily spend a couple of hours randomly exploring the island's narrow lanes, perhaps having lunch at one of the many quayside restaurants, as well as checking out the two forts on the island. The first, generally referred to as the **Ayyubid fort**, is on the east side of the island (close to the harbour and clearly visible as you arrive). It is at present closed to visitors. On either side of the main gateway are carved reliefs of lions tethered to palm trees.

The **central fort**, reached by following the narrow lanes inland (west) from the harbour, is worth a visit. The original wooden doors, clad in steel bands, are still in place. As with the Ayyubid fort, the gateway is flanked by reliefs of lions tethered to palm trees, though these are more worn and faded. Inside, there is a green and shady courtyard and garden with large date palms growing in it. The fort doubles as a **museum** ⓘ *Wed-Mon 0900-1800 in summer, 1000-1600 in winter, S£150, students S£10,* with the displays housed in the rooms surrounding the courtyard. The fort also incorporates a small mosque, with its square tower-minaret and the two white domes of the prayer hall rising up from the roof. The battlements, with their distinctive crenellations topped by small pyramid-shaped decorations, together with the small overall size of the fort, almost give it the feeling of a model.

At the northern edge of the island, huge weathered blocks of stone can be seen at the water's edge, remnants of a **Phoenician defensive wall**. Not far from here (heading left, back to the quay) is the boat-building yard where there are usually at least two or three boats in the process of being built.

Beaches

The amount of rubbish strewn across the beaches, plus the clear evidence of raw sewage being pumped into the sea, deters most foreign visitors from viewing Tartus as a beach resort. However this doesn't deter Syrian holidaymakers, who come here in large numbers for their Mediterranean experience. Fridays are particularly popular, with numerous charabancs parked up along the sea front, with picnics and barbecues on the go, and families enjoying the surf.

Syrian women bathe fully clothed, and any Western women brave enough to run the gauntlet of the rubbish and raw sewage in the water should know that bikinis are definitely not suitable. A swimming costume beneath a T-shirt and shorts is the absolute minimum you should wear.

Amrit

The site of Amrit, some 7 km to the south of Tartus, is a reminder of this stretch of coastline's early appeal to settlers. Several monuments remain from a number of different periods in the settlement's history, though it has to be said that unless you have a particular fascination with the archaeology and architecture of the periods concerned, Amrit is only of limited interest.

Ins and outs

Getting there and away Going by public transport, take an Al-Hamadiyyeh-bound microbus (15 minutes, S£10) from the microbus station on 6 Tishreen Avenue and get off at the signposted fork for Amrit. Follow this tree-lined road, passing the 'Biological Pest Control/Citrus Board' centre on the left after 400 m, and then the entrance to an army camp, also on the left, after a further 500 m. Having crossed a small bridge over a dried up stream (the Amrit/Maratos River), take the dirt track to the left where you see a sign on the right reading 'Rest Camp' (400 m beyond the army camp entrance). This track takes you to the caretaker's building, from where a path leads to the temple compound, stadium and *tell* (mound).

It is not possible to walk directly across to the *meghazils*, situated to the south (the area is fenced off). Instead you must continue south on the paved road. After passing a sign announcing 'Amrit Touristic Project Phase I', the road bends round to the left and then you arrive at a gate on the left (just over 1 km from the 'Rest Camp' sign). Just inside are a couple of modern buildings and a path leading to the *meghazils*. The caretaker here will probably try to lend you his torch, for which he will expect some payment when you return (there is no official entrance fee for either part of the site). To return to Tartus, if you continue along the paved road you will rejoin the main road after a further 1 km, from where you can flag down any passing minibus.

If you have your own transport, head south along Ath Thawra St, until you reach the right turn for Amrit, clearly signposted a little under 5 km from the centre of Tartus.

Background

The earliest remains here are located on the *tell* (mound) and date to the end of the third millennium BC. Some archaeologists suggest that the settlement here was founded by the Amorites as one of the many harbours that they established along the Syrian coast, whilst others contend that it was founded as a mainland religious centre by the Phoenicians of Arwad island.

Amrit reached its peak between the sixth and third centuries BC, with the religious buildings being heavily influenced in style by the Achaemenid Persians (who in turn borrowed freely from Egyptian and Mesopotamian architecture). Alexander the Great is believed to have rested here in 330 BC whilst his army marched on to Damascus, with the settlement taking the Greek name of *Marathos*. Amrit's subsequent history is not entirely clear. It has been suggested that it was wrestled from the control of the Arwadis in the second century BC, and that when they returned in 140 BC they destroyed it. Others suggest that Amrit gradually lost its importance with the expansion of *Antaradous* (Tartus) and was eventually abandoned.

The ruins

ⓘ *Admission free, the caretaker doesn't get many visitors, so he is keen to show guests around and share a cup of tea, a tip would be appropriate. Bring water and sun protection, and wear good walking shoes.*

The key attraction at the site is the **temple compound**, which dates from Amrit's era as a Phoenician religious centre. The temple compound comprises a 3-m-deep sacred basin (38 m by 48 m) that was dug to form an artificial lake sometime in the late fifth or early sixth century BC. It was fed by a network of canals that delivered water from a spring that was believed to have healing properties. The floor and sides of the basin are made of natural rock and are unlined. At the centre of the basin stands a 5.5 m high platform hewn from the bedrock, upon which stood the central altar. It is topped by an Egyptian-style cornice. The basin is surrounded by a wide pavement which originally had colonnaded arcades on the south, west and east sides. Part of the colonnade, consisting of monolithic rectangular slabs, has been reconstructed. Whilst the general design on the temple compound strongly reflects Egyptian and Mesopotamian influences, the remains of a number of sixth to fourth century BC statues found in the basin have strong Greek and Persian characteristics. So possibly the temple had a number of dedications; the god Melqart (later assimilated in the Greek period with Hercules); the Egyptian god of healing, Echmoun; or indeed one of the many gods derived from the Baal root.

To the north of the temple compound the outline of a small **stadium** (230 m by 30 m) can be seen. Lines of seating are visible on the north and south sides, whilst two paths on the east side suggest an entrance and an exit. The west side was used as a quarry. Dating the stadium has been problematic. It is generally believed to be Hellenistic, dating to the fourth century BC, though some sources have suggested that it may have been the venue for a sporting event hosted by the ancient Syrians in the 16th century BC that the Greeks later adapted and called the Olympic Games.

The **tell** of the original settlement is located just to the east of the temple compound, though it is generally pretty unremarkable. The same can be said of the **rock-cut house** to the southeast of the *tell*. A number of artefacts found at the site can be seen in the modern building occupied by the caretaker.

Much of the area to the south of the temple compound is part of the Phoenician cemetery. Of particular note here are two giant funerary monuments, known locally as **meghazils** (spindles). The first is 7 m high, cylindrical, and features four lions carved in the Persian style around its base (unfinished). The second is a little smaller at 4 m high, and formerly featured a five-sided pyramid at the top. Both have underground burial chambers below, with *loculi* cut into the walls. There is a third *meghazil* nearby, but it lies close to a military installation. The barrels of various heavy artillery pieces are visible sticking out from amongst the trees and undergrowth; be careful where you point your camera.

Krak des Chevaliers (Qala'at al-Hosn) → For listings, see pages 195-203.

TE Lawrence, who visited no fewer than 49 castles in a whirlwind tour of the region during a summer's vacation from Oxford, described it simply as "the finest castle in the world". Krak des Chevaliers ('Qala'at al-Hosn' in Arabic) is one of Syria's prime attractions and shouldn't be missed. It is certainly the best preserved and most impressive of the Crusader castles anywhere in the Middle East. The sheer scale and complexity of the fortifications and its near-perfect state of preservation will leave you speechless the first time you set eyes on it.

Krak des Chevaliers can be comfortably visited as a day trips from Homs or Hama, but if you can, stay here overnight so you can witness the castle at sunrise, often shrouded in mist, and at sunset, when the castle's stones turn golden in the light. In any case, it is well worth making the effort to arrive early; by late morning coach loads of organized group tours arrive from Damascus and you will find yourself sharing Krak's splendours with hordes of other tourists.

Ins and outs

Getting there and away There are a couple of interesting and extremely scenic routes to Krak: one from Masyaf and the other from Safita. Both are well worth trying if you have your own transport. → See pages 136 and 170, for further details.

Buses leave regularly for Al-Hosn village (just below the castle) from the microbus station in Homs. From Hama you need to take a bus or microbus to Homs and change there. Microbus drivers will drop you off at the castle entrance. If you're staying the night at Baibars Hotel, just beyond the castle, they may even drop you there if you ask nicely. The last microbus back to Homs generally leaves at around 1500-1600 in summer, and around 1400 in winter, but check this and err on the side of caution as services vary greatly according to demand. Be aware that on Friday services from Al-Hosn are much less frequent. A taxi from Homs will cost approximately S£900.

If you're driving, Krak des Chevaliers can be reached easily by taking the exit off the Homs-Tartus motorway (clearly signposted on overhead signboards for 'Hosn Citadel' and 'Marmarita') and heading north. The exit is 40 km from Homs (or 32 km from the exit off the Homs bypass for the Tartus/Lattakia motorway) and 55 km from Tartus (coming from Tartus, there is another exit 9 km earlier that is signposted less clearly for 'Qala'at Hosn' and 'Al-Hosn'; ignore this). After leaving the motorway it is a further 15 km to the castle; follow the road for 11 km (ignore the left turn after 4 km signposted 'Al Hosn Castle' and 'Ammar Tourist Resort'), passing through two villages, before taking a rather poorly signposted left turn to climb for 4 km up to the castle, passing through the village of Al-Hosn which nestles below it.

Background

The castle that you see today is primarily the work of the Hospitallers, who occupied it from 1144-1271. However, as with nearly all the Crusader castles in the Middle East, they occupied and expanded a pre-existing castle, in this case one originally built by the emir of Homs in 1031 and garrisoned by a colony of Kurds. The name 'Krak' is thought to have come from its original name *Hosn al-Akrad*, 'the Castle of the Kurds'. Following the Hospitallers' occupation of the castle, it became known as Krak des Chevaliers, Krak of the Knights. Its strategic value lay in its location overlooking the all-important Homs Gap, which gave access from the coast to the interior of Syria. Indeed, it has been suggested that the site may have been occupied by the Egyptians during their struggles against the Hittites, which culminated in the famous battle at Kadesh (Tell Nebi Mend) in the 13th century BC.

By the time the First Crusade entered Syria in 1097, the castle was largely deserted. However, with the Christians' imminent approach, preceded by horrific tales of the massacre at Maarat al-Numan, the population in the immediate vicinity took refuge inside. Attracted by the provisions that had been stored there, the Crusaders (led by Raymond de St Gilles) laid siege. The inhabitants meanwhile, convinced that they would suffer the same fate as the people of Maarat al-Numan, soon abandoned it after a half-hearted attempt at resistance, slipping out under the cover of night. The Crusaders quickly moved on, however, and the emir of Homs reoccupied it.

In 1110 it was retaken by Tancred, the regent of Antioch, and placed under the control of the County of Tripoli, forming its easternmost outpost. But throughout their time in the Middle East, the Crusaders faced a continuing problem of insufficient manpower,

Krak des Chevaliers

constantly having to spread themselves thinly over a large area, and in 1144 Raymond II, Count of Tripoli, elected to hand over control of the castle to the independent military order of the **Hospitallers**. Nur ud-Din (then the emir of Aleppo and nominally aligned to the Fatimids of Egypt) besieged it in 1163, but was eventually driven back by the combined forces of Tripoli and Antioch. In 1170 the Hospitallers, by now a hugely wealthy and successful outfit, undertook a massive project to enlarge and strengthen it. Over the next hundred years, they transformed what had previously been a strategically located but somewhat insubstantial castle into an impregnable stronghold. So much so that in 1188, when Salah ud-Din was returning from his victory over the Kingdom of Jerusalem at Hattin, he abandoned his siege of it after just one day, concentrating instead on other easier targets in the area, including Tartus, Lattakia and Qala'at Salah ud-Din.

It was not until 1271 that Krak des Chevaliers finally fell to the Mamluk sultan, **Baibars**, although his success appears to have stemmed as much from subterfuge as from military superiority. After a month of sustained assault, the Mamluks had breached the outer walls, although the inner castle still remained intact. Daunted by the sheer strength of these inner defences, Baibars gave up hope of penetrating them by force and, according to some accounts, instead tricked the Hospitallers inside into a treaty of surrender, supposedly forging a letter from the Hospitallers' Grand Master in Tripoli ordering them to surrender. Whatever the exact circumstances, Baibars agreed to allow them safe passage to Tripoli, provided that they left the Middle East for good, and on the basis of this agreement the Hospitallers duly relinquished their castle. By this time they numbered just a few hundred, as opposed to the castle's full complement of 2000 or so; and it is a tribute to Krak's formidable defences that despite such a paltry number of troops, they were still able to hold out for so long against Baibars, and in all probability could have continued to do so for much longer had they not agreed to surrender.

Under Mamluk control, further repairs and modifications were made to the castle, which they used as a military base. However, soon afterwards, with the Crusader threat receding, the castle declined in military importance. Instead, it was occupied by local peasants, who lived within the castle walls until they were finally relocated in 1934 by the French authorities to the present village of Al-Hosn just below. Other than some fairly minor restoration work carried out by the French in the course of clearing the village from within the castle walls, and later by the Syrian authorities, the castle is essentially unchanged from the 12th to 13th centuries, an impressive testament to its durability.

The castle

① Daily 0900-1800 summer, 0900-1600 winter, S£150, students S£10. Official guides are on hand at the entrance. There are toilet facilities just inside the castle, a short way up from the entrance. A torch is very useful for exploring the darker corners of the castle.

Outer defences Coming from the Homs–Tartus motorway (or else from Masyaf to the north), the final approach to Krak des Chevaliers is from the east, the road climbing up to it through the village of Al-Hosn. If you arrive via the route from Safita, however, the final approach is from the southwest. It is from here that you can get the best overview of Krak des Chevaliers (if you have arrived from the east, it is worth walking round to this point for an overall perspective on the castle before entering).

Built on a spur coming from a higher mountain to the southwest, the basic plan of the castle consists of two concentric defensive walls with bastions and towers encircling a central keep which is integrated with the inner walls. The ditch running between the outer and inner defensive walls could be filled with water, supplied by an **aqueduct** which flowed in from the south and in normal circumstances simply supplied the large reservoir between the walls at the southern end of the castle. The inner defensive walls were built raised up on a huge sloping base, or *glacis*, looming formidably above the outer walls, so that even if the outer walls were breached, the defenders would still occupy a commanding position above their attackers. Along the western side of the castle, the land falls away steeply into a 300-m-deep valley, making an attack from this side all but impossible. The outer wall on this side is particularly well preserved (it was in fact never subject to attack), with five identical round towers evenly spaced along its length. The blunt southern end of the castle is its most vulnerable point, because it can be easily approached from the higher ground to the southwest and, consequently, there are more defensive towers on this side.

Inner defences The main entrance to the castle is from the east side, through a **square tower**. Today a modern bridge replaces the original drawbridge which most probably once existed here. Although built by the Crusaders, the lengthy inscription on the face of this tower commemorates the restoration work carried out on the castle by Baibars in 1271. The large **rectangular tower** to the left of it, and also the next one along, are of Mamluk construction. Once through the entrance doorway (note the huge metal-clad door, also Mamluk), a gently sloping **passage** climbs to the left, its low, wide steps designed to allow horses to negotiate it. The vaulted roof provided protection from above, while the opening in it served both to allow light in and to provide the defenders with a vantage point from which to pour boiling oil (or anything else unpleasant they could lay their hands on) onto any attackers who managed to penetrate this far. The first room on the left is part of the Mamluk tower to the left of the main entrance. Today this houses some toilets, while steps lead up to the room above. Continuing up the passage, the long vaulted chamber immediately after is thought to have served as **stables** (you can also get to these from the upper room of the Mamluk tower). Further along the passage there is access to the ramparts above the stables. Both these ramparts and the accompanying arrow slits have been restored. The passage next goes through a sharp U-bend. Instead of following it, bear off through an opening in the bastion in front.

This takes you through into the area between the inner and outer walls. In front of you is a large, stagnant **reservoir** running along the length of the southern wall of the castle, while rising up from it is a steeply sloping **glacis** built up against the inner southern walls with their three massive towers. Usually such a glacis was meant to prevent attackers undermining the foundations of the walls and causing their collapse. However, since in the case of Krak these were built onto solid bedrock, it has been suggested that it was intended to reinforce the walls against the effects of earthquakes (one had caused extensive damage to the castle in 1170), or to prevent attackers from sheltering under the walls. With a thickness of some 25 m at its base, the *glacis* presents an imposing edifice; certainly its steep, precisely engineered stonework was enough to dissuade Baibar's troops (who dubbed it 'the mountain') from trying to scale it. The gateway from which you have emerged is set in an octagonal-shaped bastion. The two headless lions facing each other above the doorway (now partially obscured by grass and bushes growing from between the cracks in the stonework) appear at first glance to be Mamluk (the lion was Baibar's insignia). In fact they are Crusader in origin, this bastion having been built in the second half of the 13th century, towards the end of the Hospitallers' time here.

To your left is a complex which once served as **baths**. Dating from the Arab period of occupation, these are now in a fairly advanced state of ruin, the domed roofs of the various rooms all collapsed. Running along the inside of the castle's southern outer wall is a long vaulted chamber which probably served as the castle's **main stables**, while above is a square central tower, flanked on either side by circular towers. Before entering the stables, take a look inside the **eastern circular tower**. A single arched window gives impressive views out over the village of Al-Hosn and the plain to the east. This tower, like its counterpart flanking the square central tower on the other side, dates from the time of Baibars. Entering the main stables and walking half way through them, a set of stairs lead down on the left to a secret door (now sealed) in the base of the central square tower. At the far end of the stables, you can gain access via a short passage to the **western circular tower**. The room inside, on the same level as the stables, contains a massive central octagonal pillar bearing an Arabic inscription. Stairs lead up, either from the passage linking the stables and circular tower or from outside, to give access to the ramparts of the outer defensive wall and also to the roof of the stables, from where you can gain access to the **central square tower**. According to an inscription, this was built by the Sultan Qalaun (the successor of Baibars) in 1285, though it probably stands on the base of an earlier

Crusader tower. The main room is dominated by a massive central square pillar taking up much of the available space. A spiral staircase leads up onto the roof, from where you can get a good idea of the vulnerability of the southern end of the castle, as well as an impressive view of the *glacis* and towers of the southern inner wall behind.

Leaving the complex of towers and stables along the southern wall and following the ditch between the inner and outer walls around in a clockwise direction, the whole length of the western inner wall is also faced with a steep *glacis*. Meanwhile, to your left, you can see the arrangement along the inside of the outer western wall, with a protected gallery running below the upper ramparts. The square tower at the northern end of the inner western wall is known as the **tower of the king's daughter**. Three sets of relieving arches, one above the other, adorn the sheer face of this otherwise plain tower. The lowest of these was not entirely decorative, the arches concealing machicolations from which boiling oil or projectiles could be rained down on attackers. However, modifications carried out to this tower by the Crusaders resulted in it being raised to a higher level. The machicolations were filled in and two sets of blind arches built into the wall above, followed by new machicolations in a different style. Of the three towers in the northern end of the outer walls, the westernmost known popularly as the **tower of the windmill** ('Bourj al-Tauneh' in Arabic), once housed a windmill. The remaining two form a barbican protecting a small postern gate in between, from which the Crusaders could mount surprise attacks against the enemy. Continue all the way round to enter the inner castle via a set of steps. This brings you to the top of the sloping passage by which you first entered, and which you branched off of at the point where it made a U-turn.

Inner castle A set of steps leads up through a tall gateway into the courtyard of the inner castle. In front of you is a portico which leads through into the great hall, to your left is a large vaulted area supported by square pillars (often dubbed the 'pillared hall'), and to your right is the chapel.

The **portico** (or *loggia*) is striking in that it is by far the most 'artistic' feature of the castle. Dating from the second half of the 13th century, towards the end of the Hospitallers' occupation, it shows a particularly delicate application of the Gothic style, which had begun to develop in France a century earlier. The façade consists of two arched doorways and five arched windows separated by pilasters. The windows in particular, each with a central dividing *colonnette* and circular *tympanum*, are typically Gothic. An inscription carved in Latin on the extreme right-hand window reads: "*Grace, wisdom and beauty you may enjoy but beware pride which alone can tarnish all the rest.*" Inside, the delicate ribbed vaulting of the ceiling, divided into seven bays, is also typically Gothic. In the rear wall of the portico are two doorways which lead through into the **great hall** beyond. Dating from the 12th century, this gloomy, austere space is much more in keeping with the typical Crusader style, although it is still essentially Gothic. It would have served as a banqueting and meeting hall. Behind this is a long vaulted chamber, stretching for 120 m along the whole length of the western inner wall, and arcing round at its northern end to terminate at the chapel. Dubbed the **'long room'**, this area served a number of functions, principally as the kitchens and main storage area, but also as accommodation. To the south (left as you enter) there is an old oven, and on the other side of a partition just beyond is a well.

The **chapel** dates from the first phase of the Hospitallers' occupation, during 1142-1170. The interior is largely bare of decoration, except for the barrel vaulting, a plain cornice and shallow pilasters. Following the Mamluk occupation, the chapel was converted into a mosque, and you can see the *mihrab* which was built into the south wall. Originally the chapel was entered from the west, but this doorway was bricked up and an external staircase built against this wall, probably by the Hospitallers during their final years in the castle. Climbing this staircase takes you to the northern part of the upper courtyard. From here you can gain access to the **tower of the king's daughter**. A narrow spiral staircase leads up onto the roof of the tower, from where there are excellent views (on a clear day you can see Safita to the northwest).

Returning to the lower courtyard, the cavernous vaulted area supported by square pillars (the so-called **pillared hall**) probably served as a general area for cooking, eating, storage and accommodation. At the back (to the south) there are two **storage rooms** one behind the other, both containing huge olive oil storage jars with only their bases remaining, embedded in the ground rather like honeycombs or cocoons. The second room also contains a well. During the Crusader period, all the storage areas of the inner castle were said to contain sufficient provisions to last for five years.

A set of stairs climbing above the doorway by which you first entered the courtyard of the inner castle gives access to the roof of the pillared room. To your right parts of a circular stone structure, the purpose of which is unclear, still remain on the otherwise concreted-over terrace. In front of you is a slightly raised vaulted area, supported by square pillars. A set of stairs leads up to the roof of this, from where you can gain access to the three towers defending the inner southern wall of the castle. The central and left-hand (southeast) towers are the most imposing, their massive bulk designed to take the full brunt of any final assault on the castle. Basically rectangular in shape, the southern face of each is rounded in order to stand a better chance of deflecting missiles fired from the high ground to the south without sustaining serious damage. The right-hand (southwest) tower is circular in shape and much more delicately built. Although it also forms part of the inner southern defences, it is thought to have served primarily as the living quarters of the 'lord' of the castle. A spiral staircase gives access to a light and airy room with ribbed vaulting supported on *colonnettes* built into the walls and a frieze of rosettes running around the room. The roofs of the central and right-hand towers give the best views, both towards Safita to the northwest and the Homs Gap to the south.

Around Krak des Chevaliers For listings, see pages 195-203.

The beautiful valley to the northwest of Krak is known as *Wadi Nasara* ('Valley of the Christians'). On the winding roads between tiny villages with their old-stone houses and terraces draped with vines, the only traffic you're likely to encounter are slow chugging tractors coming back from the fields. Olive groves alternate between forest and farmland and in the spring the entire valley is alive with wildflowers.

This area has remained a centre of Greek Orthodox Christianity since the sixth century. Today 27 out of the 32 villages in the valley are Christian. Of the remaining five, four are Alawi while just one (Al-Hosn) is Sunni Muslim.

St George's Monastery
① *Daily 0600-2000, free.*
Visible from the ramparts and towers of Krak des Chevaliers, the Greek Orthodox monastery of St George originally dates back to the sixth century, and the reign of Justinian. The modern church, to your right as you enter the main courtyard, dates from 1857. The entrance passage to the church features a delicate triple arch, with the two

The coast & the Jebel Ansariye ● 167

central supporting columns clearly of Byzantine origin. Inside the church is a beautiful carved wooden *iconostasis*, the gold painted icons depicting various scenes from the life of Christ. The old chapel, probably dating from 13th century, is located beneath the main courtyard, reached by a set of stairs opposite the modern church which leads down to a lower level courtyard. It contains a smaller *iconostasis*, also very beautiful, and icons depicting scenes from the life of St George. The monastery's most important icon, a depiction of St George slaying the dragon, was at one stage stolen and appeared on the art market in London before being returned.

Also at this lower level, beyond an archway protected by a metal grille, is the entrance to what is believed to be the original sixth-century monastery, as well as various large earthenware *amphorae* which were used to store wine and olive oil. This oldest part of the monastery was only discovered seven years ago. The monastery is a popular place of pilgrimage amongst Christians, particularly around the time of the feast of St George, held each year on 6 May, and the feast of the elevation of the Holy Cross, on 14 September.

Getting there and away You need your own transport to access the monastery. You can hire a car and driver at Krak des Chevaliers. If you're driving to reach the monastery, return to the road leading north from the Homs–Tartus motorway, turning left to follow it north, and then bear left at a fork after just over 1 km. After a further 3 km you arrive at the monastery on the left.

Tartus to Safita

The road from Tartus up to Safita is perhaps not the best introduction to the Jebel Ansariye region; having been widened to near motorway proportions along the first stretch, it is now seemingly always busy with traffic, and lined with haphazard, half-finished concrete buildings for most of the way. Nevertheless, as you get closer to Safita and the road begins to climb from the coastal plain, you begin to get glimpses of the olive groves, orchards and vegetable farming that make these fertile mountains so prosperous. Safita's tall square Crusader tower, meanwhile, comes in and out of view with the twists and turns of the road long before you reach the town itself.

Qala'at Yahmur

Around 9 km after crossing over the motorway, a small unmarked right turn leads to the village and small fort of Qala'at Yahmur, only really worth a detour if you have plenty of time. Taking this turning, bear left where the road forks and then continue straight through the village to arrive at the fort, 2 km from the main road. First fortified by the Byzantines under the Emperor Nicephorus in the 10th century, it was subsequently occupied by the Crusaders and came under the control of the Hospitallers in 1177. They carried out substantial modifications to the fort, which they knew as Chastel Rouge. Salah ud-Din briefly captured it during his campaign of 1188, but the Crusaders soon regained control and held it until 1289, when it finally fell to the Mamluk sultan, Qalaun. The fort consists of a solid, squat watchtower surrounded by defensive walls, all basically intact though in a poor state of repair.

The town of Safita is spread across two hills, one dominated by the remains of the Crusader castle and the other boasting the somewhat less attractive *Safita Cham Palace* hotel. Although growing rapidly around its sprawling outskirts, the old part of town around the castle is still very picturesque, with lots of old buildings and narrow cobbled streets. The population is divided roughly equally between Alawi and Greek Orthodox, the latter having settled here early in the 18th century. Safita is popular as a summer resort, attracting lots of holidaymakers from the Gulf, and during the height of the season its small roads get heavily congested with traffic. However, the streets come alive with people in the early evening, as the younger generation of the Greek Orthodox population stroll around, women arm-in-arm and men watching, each side sizing up potential husbands and wives.

Ins and outs

Getting there and away You can get microbuses to Safita from Homs and Tartus. During summer Kadmous run two daily buses here from Damascus. The main microbus station is near the roundabout at the east end of town.

Background

The name Safita (shortened from Bourj Safita) is the Arabic translation of the name by which the Crusaders knew it: *Chastel Blanc* or 'White Castle'. Thought to have originally been built by the Crusaders in the first years of the 12th century in the course of the First Crusade and designed to form a forward defence for the port of Tartus, it was subsequently largely dismantled by Nur ud-Din, to whom it fell in 1167. After reoccupying it, the Crusaders handed over control to the Templars. (The damage wrought by Nur ud-Din, along with a severe earthquake in 1202, necessitated major rebuilding work.) The Templars remained in possession of it until 1271, when it was taken by the Mamluk sultan, Baibars, who shortly after took Krak des Chevaliers.

The White Tower

① *There are no fixed opening hours or entry fees, though a donation towards the upkeep of the church is expected. If the tower is locked, ask at the Al Bourj restaurant by the entrance for the keys.*

Today, just about all that remains of *Chastel Blanc* is the central tower, or *donjon*, although originally this was surrounded by two lines of defensive walls, in typical Crusader style. The ground floor of the tower was the Crusader's chapel, and, never having been deconsecrated or turned into a mosque, it continues to serve as a Greek Orthodox church today, dedicated to St Michael. The entrance leads directly into the church from the west. The semi-domed apse at the far end, together with the barrel-vaulted ceiling, bear evidence in the marked fissures running through them of the damage caused by the earthquake of 1202. The stone and wood *iconostasis* in front of the apse is modern, although many of the icons in the church are clearly very old. The only source of light is from narrow arrow slits framed in arched bays. These arrow slits reveal the thickness of the walls and serve as a reminder of the building's primarily defensive function.

In the corner to your right as you enter is a long, steep flight of stairs leading up to the first floor, which was probably used as accommodation. This consists of a long vaulted chamber with three massive central pillars, cruciform in shape. The ceiling has been plastered at some stage, although much of this has fallen away to reveal the stonework underneath.

Note the machicolation situated directly above the entrance to the church, allowing boiling oil to be poured on any would-be attackers. Note also the bell in the narrow arched window beside the machicolation. This arched window would appear to be a modified and widened arrow slit. A further flight of stairs takes you up onto the roof, from where there are superb views in all directions, with both Tartus and Krak des Chevaliers being visible on a clear day. On leaving, if you follow the cobbled street east, round past the rear of the tower, you pass through the remnants of the eastern outer gate and walls.

Safita to Krak des Chevaliers

This scenic route to Krak (around 34 km in all) is worth undertaking, providing you have the time and patience. In places the road is very narrow and heavily pot-holed, though sections of the route have been upgraded.

Bear right at the roundabout at the eastern end of Safita (signposted for Mashta al-Helu and Kafroun) and then bear left at the next roundabout (1500 m further on). Follow this road and take the second left turning you come to (a little over 6 km from the second roundabout). The first left turn, 1500 m earlier and directly opposite a petrol station, is the turning for Mashta al-Helu (see below); there is a route to Krak via this road, but it is far more complicated.

Just over 1 km after taking the left turn, bear right where the road forks and then keep going straight. You pass through a small village, and then through the village of **Burj al-Arab** (6 km beyond the left turn), literally 'Arab Tower', so named after the small, solitary medieval watchtower of black and white stone which still stands in the village, clearly visible from the road. Continue straight, passing through the village of Tell al-Hawash (4 km beyond Bourj al-Arab), soon after which there are good views on your left, down towards a large lake formed by a recently built dam. A little over 2 km past Tell al-Hawash, turn left onto a good new road signposted for 'Amar Tourist Resort'.

After 3 km you come to a crossroads. Turn left here, and then right 1 km further on. Bear right where the road forks soon after and then, in the village of **Jereina**, some 5 km after the last junction, turn left opposite an old church (signposted 'Amar Tourist Resort'). The road climbs very steeply from here, passing after a little over 1 km the **Amar Tourist Resort** on the left. A little further on there are wonderful views out over the valley to your left, with St George's Monastery visible on the far side. Continue straight, past the car park before arriving at Krak des Chevaliers. Approaching from this direction, your first views of the castle are from above, providing an excellent overall perspective.

Route to Mashta al-Helu via Krak des Chevaliers Bear right at the roundabout at the eastern end of Safita (signposted for Mashta al-Helu and Kafroun) and then bear left at the next roundabout (1500 m further on). Follow this road and take the first left turning you come to (5 km from the second roundabout, situated directly opposite a petrol station). After just under 4 km, where there is a right turn signposted for St George's, follow the road round to the left to keep going straight. Just under 3 km further on, after passing through a couple of small villages, there is another right turn signposted for St George's. Both these turnings offer beautiful routes to Krak des Chevaliers, but you really need a local guide to get you through the maze of tiny roads and villages. Keep going straight, to arrive eventually in Kafroun (10 km further on), from where it is a further 3 km up to Mashta al-Helu.

Mashta al-Helu and around

Essentially a hill resort, Mashta al-Helu is popular amongst Syrians as a summer retreat from the heat of the plains. The countryside here is beautiful and there are lots of opportunities for pretty walks in the surrounding area. Just outside of town is the extraordinary cave network of Al-Douaiyat and the Christian pilgrimage mountain of Jebel Saidi.

Ins and outs

Mashta al-Helu has regular microbus connections to and from Safita during the summer months. Outside of summer, services are much less frequent. The microbus stand is in the town main square.

Al-Douaiyat caves

① *0900-1300 and 1500-1900 daily, summer only, S£25, the caretaker will guide you around, armed with his torch.*

The Al-Douaiyat cave network, 2 km above Mashta, leads a couple of hundred metres into the mountainside. At first the caves appear to be nothing special, but a narrow passage brings you to the most impressive part, thick with stalactites, stalagmites and pillars, all lit by strategically placed lights. The café here is worth checking out. The shaded terrace has fantastic views out over the valleys below. To get to the caves, turn right at the fountain and clocktower which mark the main square in the centre of Mashta al-Helu (coming from the Mashta al-Helu Resort. After 600 m follow the road around to the right (by a church), and then turn sharp left 200 m further on, immediately after a metal arch spanning the road. Follow this road up past a new housing development, and fork right after 500 m (signposted for the caves).

Jebel Saidi

Mashta's other claim to fame is the nearby Jebel Saidi, an extinct volcano with a distinctive conical shape. A Roman structure, either a fortress or a temple, is believed to have stood on the flat-topped summit. Today, the only structure is the outline of a small chapel, also believed to be very old, its walls standing to a height of just 1 m or so, with various contemporary statues of Mary adorning the semicircular apse. As the statues suggest, the chapel is dedicated to the Virgin Mary. The mountain and chapel are a major focus for the Festival of the Virgin Mary, celebrated each year on 15 August. The festivities begin the evening before and carry on right through the night, with large crowds of pilgrims cramming onto the mountain top and celebrating to the accompaniment of fireworks and singing and dancing. To get there, take the turning on the right below the Mashta al-Helu Resort (heading down to Kafroun from the centre of Mashta), just after the twin metal arches over the road. Keep following this road (unsurfaced in places) as it winds its way to the top, just over 2 km from the main road.

Mashta al-Helu to Masyaf → *For listings, see pages 195-203.*

From Mashta al-Helu you can continue east to join up with the route running between Masyaf and Krak des Chevaliers. Coming from Kafroun and the *Mashta al-Helu Resort*, turn right in the main square and after 600 m bear right at the church. The road winds its way through the mountains, passing through the village of **Jweikhat** before starting to descend. After just over 7 km there is a right turn signposted for St George's; this is the road to Krak. A little further on is a left turn heading north towards Masyaf (see page 136 for details of the route between Masyaf and Krak des Chevaliers).

Tartus to Hosn Suleiman

This route takes you through the village Dreikish (which can also be easily reached from Safita), and then through increasingly rugged and beautiful mountain scenery to the imposing ancient ruins of Husn Suleiman.

Head north along the seafront from the Crusader fortress/'old city' of Tartus, and then bear right at the roundabout. Keep going straight, along Khaled Ibn al-Walid Street, then Jamal Abd al-Naser Street, and across the railway line. Follow the road through a one-way system as you leave Tartus and continue straight on over the coastal motorway (4 km from the centre of Tartus). Keep following this road, passing through the villages of **Bismaqa** and **Bamalkeh**, the latter with a couple of summer restaurants beside the road. Just under 29 km after crossing over the motorway, go straight across a large roundabout marking the start of **Dreikish**. Around 400 m further on, bear left at a mini-roundabout to head into the centre of Dreikish (bearing right at this mini-roundabout puts you on the road to Safita, around 14 km to the south).

Following the main road through Dreikish, around 12 km after leaving the village, bear right where the road forks in a small village (signposted 'Q Hosson Suleiman'). The road climbs steeply from here and the scenery becomes increasingly picturesque. Just under 5 km further on, take a very sharp right turn (in effect a switchback), again signposted 'Q Hosson Suleiman'. Around 500 m after taking this turning, bear left; the ruins of Husn Suleiman are visible from here less than 1 km down the narrow valley.

Hosn Suleiman

Seen from a distance, the ruins of Husn Suleiman look rather meagre, but close-up the sheer scale of the stone blocks used in the outer wall of the compound is truly awesome. It is reminiscent (although not in terms of its state of preservation) of the roughly contemporary Baalbek in Lebanon. That such a monument should have existed here is all the more remarkable when you consider its isolated location, high up in the mountains. It is as much this setting, as the site's ancient origins and monumental scale, that give it such a magical feel.

Ins and outs

Getting there and away There are very limited microbus services running between Safita and Hosn Suleiman. A more realistic option is to take a microbus from either Tartus or Safita to Dreikish and hire a taxi from there. See above for instructions if driving from Tartus.

Background

The name now given to the ruins (meaning literally Suleiman's Citadel) is entirely misleading: this was in fact a temple and it had nothing to do with Suleiman. Originally (during the late fourth to early third century BC) the site is thought to have been a Semitic/Canaanite centre of cult worship dedicated to the god Baal. Later, it probably came under the control of the Phoenicians, whose main base on the coast was the island city of *Aradous* (Arwad, just off the coast from Tartus). Baal subsequently became associated with the Greek god Zeus, and was worshipped here in his local form as Zeus Baetocecian, along with the god Astarte. Under the Romans, this tradition continued to flourish. The existing temple ruins date mostly from the second century AD, although construction probably first began a century earlier. Inscriptions found at the site confirm that it continued as an important centre for the worship of Zeus well into the fourth century, long after Christianity had been adopted as the official religion.

The temple
The temple consists of a large open rectangular compound measuring 134 m by 85 m and pierced by gateways in each wall, in the centre of which is a small *cella* (the temple's inner sanctuary). The main entrance is on the north side; a triple doorway interspersed by two niches. This doorway was once enclosed both inside and out by a *propylaeum* (monumental entrance). However, all that remains today are the fragments of collapsed columns along with their bases which once formed the *portico* to the *propylaeum*. Carved lions, very weathered and faint, can be seen at either corner of the north wall. The undersides of the massive monolithic lintels that crown each entrance to the temple compound are carved with an eagle, its wings outstretched. Those in the east and west gates are the best preserved, while that of the central doorway on the north side is just discernible. On the east and west gates there are in addition winged victories on either side of the lintels, supporting it. The central *cella* is today a jumbled mass of stones; it stood on a platform and the stairs leading up to it can still be seen. Fragments of the walls of the *cella* also survive, on which can be seen semicircular engaged columns.

Across the road from the main temple there is a small building known locally as *Ed Deir* ('The Monastery'), suggesting that during the Christian era it served this purpose. Originally it almost certainly served as a secondary temple, perhaps dedicated to the god Astarte. The *portico* is well preserved, with a clearly visible winged eagle above the lintel. This temple once stood within a larger compound, and to the north of it traces can be seen of what appears to have been a Christian basilica.

Tartus to Masyaf
This route traverses the breadth of the Jebel Ansariye to arrive at the town of Masyaf with its Ismaili castle overlooking the plains to the east.

Follow directions out of Tartus as for Husn Suleiman, except instead of crossing over the coastal motorway, turn left onto it to head north towards Lattakia. Around 8 km after joining the motorway, take the exit signposted to Sheikh Badr and Hussein Bahr (ignore the exit signposted for Sheikh Badr and Tartus soon after joining the motorway: the exit you want is opposite a large mound topped by a towering statue of Assad). Having passed a huge cement factory, the road climbs up into the hills, passing through the village of Hussein al-Bahr before arriving at a crossroads in the village of **As Soda**, 6 km from the motorway. There is an interesting church here, as well as several Ottoman period buildings. Go straight over the crossroads and continue straight on to **Sheikh Badr**, 12 km further on, from where you can make the interesting detour to **Qala'at al-Kahf**. Continuing straight along the main road, a road joins from the right at a mini-roundabout, follow the road round to the left to **Sheikh Badr**. It is a further 4 km on to Sheikh Badr from here.

Qala'at al-Kahf

This must surely be one of the most isolated and romantically located of all the castles to be found in the Jebel Ansariye. There may not be that much left to see of the castle itself, but its stunning location makes the considerable detour involved in reaching it well worth the extra effort.

Ins and outs

Getting there and away There is no public transport to the castle. If you're driving be aware that though the castle is actually just 16 km from Sheikh Badr, the road is winding, narrow, steep and very rough in places, and you should allow at least 45 minutes each way, plus time to explore once you get there.

Approaching Sheikh Badr from the coast, a theatrical statue of an Arab fighter holding his rifle aloft marks the start of the village. Exactly 1 km beyond the statue, bear left at a mini-roundabout, and then left again at a second mini-roundabout, 100 m further on. After 500 m, bear right at a third roundabout. Two kilometres further on, entering a small village, bear left where the road forks. The road begins to climb; after around 700 m, follow the road sharply round to the left and then fork right immediately after in a second village. The road descends steeply through an increasingly rugged and beautiful landscape of steep, thickly wooded hills and rocky outcrops, crosses a small bridge and seasonal stream and then climbs again to another village just under 2 km further on. Fork left in this village to descend, before climbing again to arrive at a T-junction just under 1 km further on. Turn left here; the road descends steadily down the side of a valley, crosses a bridge and then climbs again up the other side in a long 'V' before arriving at a large concrete school building on the left, and a left turn signposted to 'Q. AlKahaf' (just under 3 km from the last T-junction). Taking this left turn, the road climbs very steeply before arriving at another T-junction just over 1 km further on. Turn right here; after just under 1 km, follow the road sharply round to the right and keep going for another 3 km until you reach a sharp left turn signposted 'Qala'at a Kahf 3 km'. Travel 1 km down this track, then fork left to arrive at the foot of the castle, 1500 m further on.

Background

The strategic advantages of the site were first recognized by a local emir, Ibn Amrun of the Banu Munqid clan, who built a castle here some time during the 11th century. In 1134, Qala'at al-Kahf was acquired by the Assassins (see box, page 154), two years after their acquisition of Qadmus, as part of their policy of establishing themselves in the Jebel Ansariye. It became one of the headquarters used by the Syrian leader of the Assassins, Rashid ud-Din Sinan (The Old Man of the Mountain) from 1164-1193. In 1197 Count Henry of Champagne, recently appointed by Richard the Lionheart as Regent of Jerusalem, visited the castle, seeking to secure an alliance with Sinan's successor against the Sunni Muslim threat to the Crusaders. According to legend, the new leader of the Assassins sought to prove to Henry the unswerving loyalty of his followers by ordering two of them to hurl themselves from the ramparts, which they promptly did. Ironically, Henry died shortly afterwards when he fell from a window of his palace at Acre.

During the next century it was the turn of St Louis of Acre (King Louis IX of France and leader of the ill-fated Sixth Crusade of 1249) to negotiate with the Assassins. The Assassins apparently sent emissaries to St Louis, demanding that he pay them an annual tribute. Louis responded by sending back the emissaries laden with gifts. Later he sent one of his friars, Yves le Breton, to Qala'at al-Kahf and finally succeeded in securing an alliance.

That the castle only fell to the Mamluk sultan Baibars in 1273, two years after the fall of Krak des Chevaliers, is an indication of its near-impregnability. It continued to fulfil a military function well into the Ottoman era, but was finally destroyed in 1816. The English adventurer, Lady Hester Stanhope, had taken up the cause of a French captain who was being held captive in the castle and managed to persuade the Ottoman governor of Tripoli, Mustapha Barbar, to lead an expedition against it to free the captain and also to destroy it once and for all.

The castle

The ruins of the castle first come into view some way off, identifiable by the reinforcing stonework around the top of the high rocky outcrop on which it stands. From the end of the track, continue on foot along a narrow, overgrown path which leads around the right-hand side of the base of the outcrop. You pass first a gateway, its massive stone lintel now fallen, followed by a couple of vaulted underground chambers on the right. The path then passes through a small artificial cave cut into the rock, which formed the lower entrance to the castle (perhaps the source of its name, which translates literally as 'Castle of the Cave'). Note the Arabic inscription above the entrance to the cave. Further on, the path doubles back to climb up the side of the outcrop, giving access to the area inside the walls. Almost nothing remains here, the Ottoman governor of Tripoli apparently having carried out Lady Stanhope's wishes diligently. Here and there are the crumbling fragments of buildings half hidden amongst the undergrowth, some largely collapsed or earth-filled vaulted chambers and the circular openings of enormous water cisterns hewn into the rock. The views of the surrounding countryside, however, are stunning and this makes an excellent spot for a picnic.

Nearby is what is popularly believed to be the **tomb of Rashid ud-Din Sinan** himself. To reach it, take the right-hand fork as you make the final approach to the castle. This climbs to the summit of the ridge adjacent to the castle where, amongst the trees, there is a small whitewashed shrine said to contain his tomb. The views from here are also spectacular.

Sheikh Badr to Masyaf

Returning to Sheikh Badr and continuing east along the main road, it is a further 12 km on to Wadi al-Ayoun (Valley of the Springs), a picturesque village famous for its plentiful spring water and its mulberry groves. The village is another popular summer retreat amongst Syrians and there are a number of houses where you can rent rooms or apartments. Ask around in the village if you are interested in doing this. There are several simple restaurants along the main road through the village.

Leaving Wadi al-Ayoun, the road climbs through rugged limestone hills and pine forests before starting to descend. After around 10 km you come to what is in effect a T-junction. Turn left here (signposted 'Mosyaf'), and descend steadily with glimpses of Masyaf's castle and the plains beyond, before arriving after a further 10 km at another T-junction. This is the road running north-south between Masyaf and Krak des Chevaliers. Turn left here for the centre of Masyaf, around 1 km further on.

Tartus to Lattakia

The motorway from Homs to Tartus continues north along the coast all the way to Lattakia, passing en route the impressive Crusader castle of Qala'at Marqab, the small town of Banyas, and Jableh with its large, if ruinous, Roman theatre. It is a fast though often busy road, the journey direct from Tartus to Lattakia (around 90 km) taking no more than one hour.

Qala'at Marqab

Perched high up on a spur and dominating this stretch of the coastline where the coastal plain is reduced to a narrow corridor between sea and mountains, Qala'at Marqab is striking even from a distance for its huge size and sombre, brooding appearance. Built from black basalt rock, it is one of the most impressive Crusader castles after Krak des Chevaliers and Qala'at Salah ud-Din, and well worth a visit.

Ins and outs

Getting there and away By public transport, take a microbus from either Tartus or Lattakia to Banyas (the microbuses all arrive and depart from the main street). From here either catch a microbus to Zaoube or Marqab village. The microbuses to Zaoube run right past the castle but services are irregular. Microbuses to Marqab village (S£10) drop you around 2 km short of the castle. If you want to take a taxi from Banyas, you will have to negotiate a price according to how long you want to spend there. Around S£200-300 for the return trip with one or two hours for a visit would be reasonable.

If you are driving, probably the easiest way of getting to Qala'at Marqab is to leave the motorway at the Banyas/Qadmus exit and head into Banyas. When you reach the seafront, turn left and follow the road south through the town for just under 2 km until you reach a left turn signposted (not very clearly) for Qala'at Marqab. This road crosses over the motorway via a bridge and climbs up into the mountains. Some 4 km after crossing the motorway, take a very sharp right turn to double back and climb up to the castle, 1 km further on, or else keep going straight to wind your way around the eastern side before arriving at the entrance.

Alternatively, coming from Tartus along the motorway, take the exit signposted for 'Marqab Citadel' and then 'Zobeh' and 'Al Baydar'. Around 700 m after leaving the

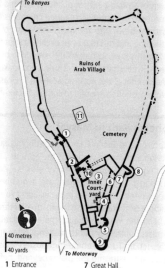

Qala'at Marqab (Margat)

To Banyas

Ruins of Arab Village

Cemetery

Inner Courtyard

To Motorway

40 metres
40 yards

1 Entrance
2 Barbican Gate
3 Well
4 Chapel
5 Main Keep
6 Storage/kitchens
7 Great Hall
8 East Tower
9 South Tower
10 Offices
11 Ottoman Khan

motorway, bear round to the left where the road forks to keep the castle directly in front of you. Around 1.5 km further on, take the small left turn signposted to 'Markab Castil' on a blue sign, after another 1 km turn right and then immediately left (both turnings are likewise indicated by blue 'Markab Castil' signs). The small road climbs very steeply, giving excellent views of the castle's hefty southern fortifications higher up. Finally, bear left to reach the entrance, just over 4 km from the motorway.

Background

Despite the obvious strategic significance of the site, commanding both the narrow coastal strip and the valley running east towards Qadmus and Masyaf (both of which were to become important Ismaili strongholds), a castle was only built here as late as 1062 by a local Muslim chieftain. Until then, it would appear that the far more ancient town of Banyas had fulfilled the function of controlling movement up and down the coast. When the Crusaders took Banyas in 1098 they made no attempt on the castle, and it was only in 1104 that it was occupied by the **Byzantines**. Sometime during the first half of that century it passed into Crusader hands, becoming part of the principality of Antioch. It was entrusted as a feudal endowment to the Mansoer family and then in 1186 sold to the Knights Hospitallers. It was known to the Crusaders as *Margat*, its Arabic name, Qala'at Marqab, translating literally as 'Castle of the Watchtower'.

The **Hospitallers** immediately started major construction work to strengthen its fortifications, particularly at its more vulnerable southern tip. Just two years later it must already have been a formidable stronghold since Salah ud-Din opted to bypass it as he swept up the coast after his victory over the Crusaders at Hattin. It subsequently withstood attacks by the Emir of Aleppo Malik al-Daher in 1204 and the Turkoman emir Saif ud-Din Balban in 1280.

However, the fall of Krak des Chevaliers in 1271 greatly strengthened the hand of the Mamluk sultan **Baibars**, and he was able to enforce an agreement whereby the revenues from its dependent lands were divided between the Hospitallers and the Mamluks. When Baibar's successor, Qalaun, besieged it in 1285, the dwindling manpower (and morale) of the Hospitallers made its capture relatively easy. Having successfully undermined the foundations of the huge south tower and so breached the castle's outer defences, the Mamluk forces began a sustained bombardment of the inner fortress. The Hospitallers soon decided that further resistance was futile and surrendered. Under the Mamluks, the castle was repaired and continued to serve as an important military stronghold until the Ottoman period, although its primary function appears to have been as a prison.

The castle

ⓘ *Wed-Mon 0900-1800 in summer, 0900-1600, in winter, S£150, students S£10. A torch is useful for exploring the darker corners of the castle. There are a couple of snack places outside.*

The castle conforms to a basic triangular plan defined by the ridge on which it is situated. Like Krak des Chevaliers, it has an outer and an inner line of defensive walls. On the north, east and west sides the mountain falls away in an almost sheer drop, providing a formidable natural defence. Only at the southern end (the sharp point of the triangle) is the ridge connected to the main body of the mountain. It is here that all the castle's most formidable fortifications have been concentrated, including the main keep. As you approach, there are good views of the southern defences. The bands of white marble in the rounded tower of the outer walls here date from the Sultan Qalaun's repairs after he had caused its collapse.

Entry to the castle is through a **square tower** in the western walls. To the north can be seen a series of rounded towers in the outer walls. A set of stairs leads up to the tower, where there is a ticket office. Turn right to exit the tower and head south between the outer and inner walls. After a short distance, on the left, is a **barbican gate** giving access via a flight of stairs to the inner courtyard and main area of interest. In the centre of the courtyard is a **well** with a huge water cistern below.

At the southern end of the courtyard is the **chapel**; its simple, austere architecture reminiscent of the Church of Our Lady of Tortosa in Tartus. Built towards the end of the 12th century, around the time that the castle was acquired by the Hospitallers, it represents an early example of the Gothic style, with traces of Romanesque. The main entrance is on the west side, with a smaller one on the north. On either side of the main apse at the eastern end of the church are two small **sacristies**. On the ceiling of the northeast sacristy (the one to the left of the apse as you face it) you can see fragments of original frescoes depicting the 12 apostles at the Last Supper.

To the south of the chapel are a number of rooms and vaulted halls forming a complex of buildings that probably served as the barracks and main reception area. These buildings surround the main **keep** or *donjon*, a massive three-storey tower, rounded on its southern and eastern sides, with walls up to 5 m thick in places. You can climb via a series of stairs right up to the roof, from where there are excellent views, particularly west towards Banyas and the Mediterranean.

Returning to the main courtyard, running along its eastern and northeastern side is a series of rooms which were most likely used as **storage chambers** and **kitchens**. The rooms on the eastern side lead through to a long hall facing onto the eastern outer defensive walls, which perhaps served as the **great hall**. From here you can gain access to a large **eastern tower** built into the outer defensive wall.

On the western side of the courtyard (adjacent to the point at which you first entered the inner courtyard), steps lead up to a series of rooms. These give access to a room above the barbican entrance which has been restored and is now used as the office of the curator of the castle. Postcards are on sale here and the curator is generally on hand to offer visitors coffee or tea.

The large northern area of the castle is of lesser interest. Access to it can be gained most easily by heading north from the western tower by which you first entered the castle. In the centre are the remains of large Ottoman-period **khan**, with a later upper storey added and now topped by two communications masts. Scattered to the north of this are the ruins of an **Arab village** which grew up here following the castle's fall to Qalaun, while the area to the southeast was used as a **cemetery**. Most of the inner wall, except on the western side, has been dismantled, its stones used in the construction of the village, but it is still possible to follow the line of the outer walls in places. However, the whole area is heavily overgrown, making it difficult to wander round.

Banyas to Masyaf via Qadmus

This road has been upgraded to a broad highway for much of the way, making it a fast, easy (and at the same time very beautiful) route between the coast and the Al-Ghab plains. From the centre of Banyas, head back up to the coastal motorway and cross directly over it (if coming from Tartus or Lattakia, the exit is signposted for Banyas and Qadmus). The road climbs steeply and follows the southern side of a wide, deep valley, with superb views across it. Around 22 km after crossing the motorway, a fork off to the right takes you into the centre of **Qadmus**, a distinctive village clustered around a pointed rocky outcrop.

Qadmus today is an important centre of tobacco production, and was once a major Ismaili stronghold. The rocky outcrop on which their castle stood is visible from a considerable distance, although all that remains today is the main gateway, and inside a few old buildings in amongst the more modern ones. Having been acquired by the Assassins from a local emir in 1132 (see Qala'at al-Kahf, above), control of the castle appears to have switched between the Crusaders and the Ismailis a number of times, although precise details of its history are surprisingly scarce. Finally, in the 19th century it was destroyed by Ibrahim Pasha, during his brief challenge to the might of the Ottoman Empire. There may not be much left to see of the castle, but there are lots of beautiful old Ottoman-period houses dotted around the village, and an interesting mosque with an octagonal minaret. With the main highway now bypassing the village, it is also pleasantly relaxing and traffic-free, and worth stopping off at for a wander round. There are a couple of simple takeaway places, offering falafel sandwiches, etc, along the main street.

Continuing east from Qadmus, the road climbs through rocky hills for a while, before beginning to descend. After a little under 18 km there is a left turn signposted to Deir Mama. This is the route to Qala'at Abu Qobeis (see page 136). Continue straight to arrive at Masyaf, 5 km further on (see page 135).

Jableh

The town of Jableh gained its importance from its small harbour and has, as a result, been occupied since Phoenician times. Today it is a small but busy market town, famous mostly for the ruins of the enormous roman theatre in the centre of town.

Ins and outs
Getting there and away There are frequent microbuses to here from Lattakia and Tartus.

Background
In Phoenician times the town was known as *Gabala* and formed part of the kingdom of Arwad. After the Roman conquest led by Pompey in 64 BC it appears to have enjoyed considerable prosperity, to judge by the large theatre that was built during this period. It maintained its importance during the Byzantine era, when it became the seat of a bishopric under the patriarchs of Antioch. In AD 638 it fell to the Muslims, and then during the Ayyubid period was taken once again by the Byzantines in AD 969, only to fall once more to the Muslims in 1051. It was taken by the Crusaders, led by Raymond St Gilles, in 1098. Salah ud-Din captured it during his campaign of 1188, but after his death the Crusaders regained control, subsequently handing it over to the Hospitallers in 1207. Finally in 1285 it was taken by the Mamluk sultan Qalaun, shortly after he had captured Banyas and Qala'at Marqab, and remained in Muslim hands thereafter.

Sights
Theres is a huge **Roman theatre** ① *Wed-Mon 0900-1700, S£75, students S£5*, in the centre of the town, to the south of the main microbus station. Though nowhere near as well preserved as the theatre in Bosra, it is comparable in size, with an estimated capacity of around 7000 people. Most impressive are the cavernous twin-vaults running underneath the semicircle of tiered seating, which together give some idea of its scale.

Nearby (between the microbus station and the theatre) is the **Mosque of Sidi Ibrahim Ben Adham**, named after a Muslim saint whose tomb it contains. Built following his death in AD 778, it stands on the site of an earlier church built by the Byzantine emperor Heraclius (AD 610-641). In the souqs and alleyways running between the town centre and the seafront there are various fragments of old buildings and tiny mosques in amongst the more modern buildings.

Lattakia → *For listings, see pages 195-203.*

Funky modern Lattakia is where Syrians come to play. This bustling port (Syria's busiest and most important sea outlet) is one of Syria's least conservative towns. The streets are lined with international fashion-brand outlets and modern coffee shops, and it's not unusual to see confident young women striding around town in tight T-shirts and body-hugging skinny jeans. In the evenings the pavements are a vibrant scene as groups of youths crowd onto the café terraces to gossip and eye each other up.

The town's less-traditional vibe is due, in part, to its long history of constant contact with the outside world. There may be few physical reminders of Lattakia's historical importance left to see but Lattakia remains today what it has always been throughout the centuries: a Syrian window opening onto the wider world.

There are few attractions in Lattakia that could be described as 'sights' but it's a friendly town in which to spend a couple of days and makes an excellent base for day trips to nearby attractions such as Ugarit (Ras Shamra), Kassab, Qala'at Salah ud-Din and the northern beaches.

Ins and outs

Getting there and away Lattakia has good connections to Damascus, Tartus and Homs from its Pullman bus station and there are also services from Antakya (in Turkey) to here. Its three different microbus stations are spread over town and connect many of the local villages on the north and eastern regions of the coast. If you're coming from Aleppo, it's best to come here by train.

Lattakia's airport is 25 km southeast of town. It is mainly used for flights to and from Damascus although there is also one flight per week to Cairo. A taxi from the airport to the centre of town will cost approximately S£400.

The Pullman bus station, the train station and the main microbus station (that services the eastern villages) are all located on Abdul Kader al-Housseiny Street, a few minutes' walk from each other. It's about a 30-minute walk into town from here and manageable if not too hot. A taxi from in front of the train station to the town centre costs S£30.

If you are coming from Kassab you will be dropped at the microbus station near Assad Sports Stadium, about a 20-minute walk from town. A taxi from here to the centre costs S£25.

Getting around Lattakia is mostly manageable on foot. If you don't want to walk, there are plenty of taxis about (some even have working meters) and a journey within town shouldn't cost more than S£30. Lattakia also has two city bus lines that visitors may find useful. Bus Route 1 regularly runs past the train station to the corniche and bus Route 3 runs all the way along the corniche to its southern end. City buses are green coloured and tickets cost S£10.

Tourist information The **tourist office** ① *14 Ramadan St, T041-416 926, Sat-Thu 0800-2000*, has friendly staff and can give you a free map of the town.

Lattakia

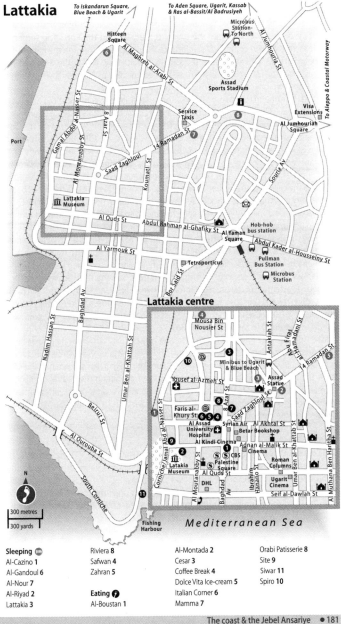

To Iskandarun Square,
Blue Beach & Ugarit

To Aden Square, Ugarit, Kassab
& Ras al-Bassit/Al Badrusiyeh

Microbus
Station-
To North

Hitteen
Square

Al Jumhouria St

Al Maghreb al-Arabi St

Assad
Sports Stadium

To Aleppo & Coastal Motorway

Service
Taxis

Visa
Extensions

Al Jumhouriah
Square

Gamal Abdul al-Nasser St

Al Moutanabby St

8 Azar St

Saad Zaghloul

Koumati

14 Ramadan St

Souria AV

Port

Lattakia
Museum

Al Quds St

Abdul Rahman al-Ghafiky St

Al Yaman
Square

Hob-hob
bus station

Abdul Kader al-Housseiny St

Al Yarmouk St

Bor Said St

Tetraporticus

Pullman
Bus Station

Microbus
Station

Nadim Hassan Av

Baghdad Av

Umar Ben al-Khattah St

Belrut St

Al Ourouba St

N

300 metres
300 yards

South Corniche

Fishing
Harbour

Lattakia centre

Mousa Bin
Nousier St

Antakiah St

Abu Firas

14 Hamadani St

14 Ramadan St

Minibus to Ugarit
& Blue Beach

Yousef al-Azmeh St

Assad
Statue

Saad Zaghloul

Faris al-
Khury St

Al Assad
University
Hospital

Syrian Air

Al Akhtal St

Betar Bookshop

Adnan al-Malik St
Cinema

Al Kindi Cinema

CBS

Palestine
Square

Roman
Columns

Latakia
Museum

Al Quds St

Ibrahim
Hanano Av

Corniche/Jamal Abd al-Nasser St

DHL

Baghdad Av

Al Moutanabby St

Umar ben al-Khattab St

Ugarit
Cinema

Al Muthana Ben Haritha St

Seif al-Dawlah St

Mediterranean Sea

Sleeping
Al-Cazino 1
Al-Gandoul 6
Al-Nour 7
Al-Riyad 2
Lattakia 3

Riviera 8
Safwan 4
Zahran 5

Eating
Al-Boustan 1

Al-Montada 2
Cesar 3
Coffee Break 4
Dolce Vita Ice-cream 5
Italian Corner 6
Mamma 7

Orabi Patisserie 8
Site 9
Siwar 11
Spiro 10

Background

Lattakia was almost certainly founded as a small Phoenician fishing village around 1000 BC, though it was not until the fourth century BC that the emerging settlement developed into a town of any real significance. Having passed through the hands of the Assyrians, Persians and Alexander the Great's Greek army, it was the **Seleucid** ruler Seleucus I Nicator (311-281 BC) who established Lattakia as a major town within his empire (the town taking its name from the emperor's mother).

Lattakia continued to prosper after Pompey's Levantine adventure at the head of the Roman army in 63 BC, taking the Roman name of *Laodicea ad Mare*. Having been made a free town with tax raising rights, *Laodicea's* port developed further with the town becoming renowned for its wine production and export. The Christian church appears to have gained an early toe-hold in *Laodicea*, and there are several mentions of the Christian community here in the New Testament (*Colossians 4: 13-16; Revelation 3: 14-22*). For a short period under the emperor Septimus Severus (AD 193-211), Laodicea served as the capital of the Roman *Provincia Syria*, though this role later reverted back to the rival city of Antioch. The city was also one of those taken by the extraordinary Queen Zenobia (see box, page 260) when she challenged the might of the Roman emperor Aurelian in the late third century AD.

During the **Byzantine and early Arab periods**, the town suffered badly at the hands of man and nature. It was devastated on several occasions not just by the battle for hegemony between the declining Byzantine Empire and the growing Persian and Arab powers, but also by a series of earthquakes. Hardly had the city recovered before it grabbed the attention of the Crusader forces. Between 1097 and 1287, control of it passed repeatedly between Crusader and Arab hands, before the Christians were finally expelled from the Holy Land. Even then, the successors to the Crusader legacy (the Cyprus-based Lusignans) returned to sack the city in 1367.

After much of the Levant fell under Ottoman Turk control, Lattakia went into decline as rival ports were preferred for development, and by the end of the 19th century Lattakia was once again little more than a fishing village. The town's revival began in the 1920s under the French Mandate authority, with Lattakia becoming the capital of the Alawi State administrative unit. The Alawi connection is also credited with Lattakia's recent rapid resurgence, the al-Assad family links to the town being instrumental in the decision to redevelop the harbour into Syria's premier port.

Lattakia Museum

ⓘ *Al-Corniche, Wed-Mon 0800-1800 in summer, 0800-1600 in winter, S£150, students S£10.*

Lattakia's small museum is housed in a former caravanserai dating from the Ottoman period. It features an eclectic collection of artefacts excavated from sites in the surrounding area. The upper storey was added to the caravanserai during the French Mandate period, when the building served as the residence of the governor of the Alawi State. The imposing vaulted arcades of the caravanserai, partially clad in climbing plants and surrounding a small area of lawn and trees, provides a cool and peaceful respite from the throng and traffic of the city; likewise the museum's large gardens, which are dotted with an impressive array of columns, capitals, architectural fragments, sarcophagi and olive presses. Of particular note are the three beautifully carved marble statues in front of the caravanserai, one of them (the only one still with its head intact), sporting a thoughtful, melancholy expression.

Entering the museum, the first room on the right contains artefacts from **Ugarit** (mostly pottery items and clay tablets with cuneiform inscriptions) dating from the 16th to the 13th centuries BC. The second room features objects from a number of sites – stone tools and weapons, pottery jars, amulets, cylinder seals, human and animal figurines and jewellery – spanning the Stone Age through to the Roman and Byzantine periods. In the centre of the room is a large rectangular stone block with a depression chiselled into it in the shape of an animal skin. Unearthed at Ibn Hani (just to the north of Lattakia, near Ugarit) in 1982, it is believed to date to the Iron Age (14th-13th century BC) and to have been used as a mould for bronze and copper bullion. The third room features artefacts from the Greek, Roman and Byzantine periods found at various sites along the Syrian coast. These include coins, pottery figurines, glassware and a collection of oil lamps, some of which are beautifully decorated with delicate carved reliefs of animals, birds and mythical scenes. In the centre of the room is a pottery coffin with a distinctive cylindrical shape dating from the first century BC. The fourth room houses pottery, ceramics, coins, glassware, jewellery, armour and a Qur'an spanning the whole of the Islamic period, from the Umayyads through to the Ottomans. The fifth (and last) room is given over to a collection of contemporary paintings and sculptures.

Roman remains
There are several reminders of Lattakia's Roman past scattered across the town, though none could be said to be particularly impressive. In fact, the two main standing remains now serve as little more than centrepieces to traffic islands. To the south of the city centre is the **tetraporticus**: a group of four standing columns that with a vivid imagination could be envisaged as a four-sided gateway that once marked the east end of the *decumanus* (main east-west transverse street of the Roman town). It probably dates to the late second century AD.

At the point where Al Quds Street becomes Abd al-Rahman al-Ghafiky Street (opposite the *Ugarit cinema*), there are some standing granite **columns** that once formed part of a portico lining one of the Roman town's streets. The four columns on the traffic island in the centre of Al Jumhouriah Square, three of them topped by Corinthian capitals and two of them supporting a section of architrave, may be part of the Roman town's **Temple of Adonis**. (Take care not to get run over when crossing to the traffic islands to view these remains!)

South Corniche
Occupying a small peninsula at the southernmost tip of Lattakia is a short stretch of coastline which is in many ways far more attractive than Blue Beach (see below). It may not offer the same opportunities in terms of swimming and watersports, but it is certainly more picturesque. The peninsula is marked by low cliffs leading down to a shoreline which is mostly rocky, but where there are a few patches of sand and shingle. The waters here are crystal clear, though the cliffs and shoreline are unfortunately predictably rubbish strewn. On the eastern side of the peninsula is a tiny fishing harbour. There are several restaurants along here and in summer numerous impromptu cafés with plastic tables and chairs occupying strategic positions along the cliffs. This peninsula appears to be Lattakia's new up-and-coming district, with numerous fancy-looking luxury apartment blocks springing up all over the place. The South Corniche is quite a walk from the centre of town (around 2-3 km). City bus No 3 shuttles back and forth along the entirety of the cornice. Ask for 'Corniche Janoubi'.

The coast north of Lattakia offers Syria's best beaches, from the popular holiday spot of Blue Beach, to quieter sandy shores that can be easily reached for a half-day trip. Females should be aware that Syrian women bathe fully clothed and bikinis are completely unacceptable here. Except on the private hotel beaches at Blue Beach, women should wear a T-shirt and shorts over the top of their swimming costume.

Blue Beach (Shaati al-Azraq)
Around 8 km to the northwest of Lattakia is the resort known as Blue Beach (Shaati al-Azraq in Arabic), which, during the summer, throngs with Syrian families on holiday. The area is alive with amusement arcades, stalls selling all kinds of tacky beach souvenirs, snack bars and simple restaurants. Nights are particularly lively, with all the stalls brightly lit and pumping out Arabic music, and couples and families out in their droves promenading. By contrast, in the low season everything closes down and the place is completely dead.

Getting there and away During the high season there are regular microbuses running between the centre of Lattakia (from the corner of Antakiah Street and Abdullah Ibn Masud Street) and Blue Beach (S£5).

If you are driving, head north from the centre of Lattakia on 8 Azar Street and then follow signs for the Sports City Complex and **Le Meridien** hotel. A little over 4 km from the centre of town, go straight over a roundabout (the flyover which crosses this roundabout gives access to the Sports City, a huge complex built in the late 1980s when Syria hosted the Mediterranean Games). Another 3.5 km brings you to a second roundabout. Some 200 m in front of you is the **Côte d'Azur de Cham** hotel. Bearing left brings you after 600 m to the **Le Meridien** hotel. The spit of land beyond the **Le Meridien** hotel is given over to private holiday apartments. Bearing right at the roundabout, you pass a campsite on the left after a little over 1 km, and then after another 3 km, a small road on the left leading up to entrance to the site of Ugarit (signposted).

The beaches of Birj Islam and Wadi Qandeel
Just north of Lattakia are two of Syria's nicest beaches. Pretty Birj Islam is a small cove of white sand, its bay dominated by a large rock that juts out of the sea just offshore. A bit further north is the black sand beach of Wadi Qandeel. The crystal-blue water at both beaches is clean, and fine for swimming, and the shores here have much less rubbish than others on the coast.

Getting there and away During summer regular microbuses run between Lattakia and both beaches, from the microbus station on Al-Jalaa St, next to Assad Stadium, in Lattakia (one hour, S£25). To return to Lattakia you have to wait for the microbus to fill up. Later in the afternoon, services become less frequent so plan on leaving the beach by mid-afternoon. During winter public transport is practically non-existent. A taxi from Lattakia to either beach costs approx S£300.

Ugarit

Known locally as Ras Shamra (literally 'Fennel Headland'), Ugarit is considered to be one of the most important Bronze Age sites in the Middle East, providing as it does one of the key 'touchstones' for archaeological and historical research into this period. Home to one of the world's first alphabets, Ugarit was discovered completely by accident in 1928, by a farmer ploughing his field. Excavations soon after began uncovering objects from Egypt, Greece and Mesopotamia, among others; evidence that Ugarit was Syria's first great trading city, its port linking Syria with the wider ancient Mediterranean world.

Ugarit

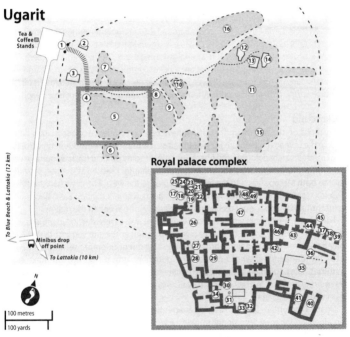

Ugarit
1 Entrance gate
2 Ticket office
3 Fortress walls
   & postern gate
4 Great Square
5 Royal palace complex
6 Small palace
7 Northern palace
8 Stone vessel building
9 Residential area
10 House of Rapanou

11 Acropolis
12 Temple of Baal
13 High Priest's house
14 Temple of Dagan
15 Southern block
16 Northeast block

Royal Palace Complex
17 Main entrance
18 Reception area
19 Square room
20 Passage

21 Secretary's office
22-23 Adjoining rooms
24 Main courtyard
25 Porch
26 Throne room
27 Banquet hall
28 Courtyard
29 Oven
30-31 Southern Archive
   room
32 Southwestern Archive
   room

32-33 Necropolis
33 Interior garden
34 Gardener's lodge
35-36 Eastern Archive
   rooms
37-38 Shops/store rooms
39 Workshop
40 Large hall
41 Small room
42 North entrance
43 Room
44 Courtyard II

There are substantial remains on view at Ugarit, particularly the royal palace complex, though they are nowhere near as grand as Syria's classical-era ruins. Unless you have a particular interest in the Bronze Age period, you may be disappointed. Important artefacts discovered at Ugarit can be seen in the National Museums in Damascus and Aleppo (and to a lesser extent in the Lattakia Museum), though many of the more important items are now in the Louvre Museum, Paris.

Ins and outs
Getting there and away Microbuses to Ugarit (S£10, 25 minutes) depart from the corner of Antakiah Street and Abdullah Ibn Masud Street in Lattakia, passing via Blue Beach and dropping passengers at the junction just 200 m from the site entrance. To return, just flag down any passing microbus.

If you are driving, head north from the centre of Lattakia on 8 Azar Street as if for Blue Beach. At Iskandarun Square (signposted around 2.5 km from the centre), turn right, and then left at the junction 400 m further on to join Ugarit Street heading north. Around 6 km from the centre of town, bear left at a large roundabout (signposted 'Meridien, Côte d'Azur, Ugarit'). Just over 2 km further on, fork left (signposted 'Raas Shamra'), and look out for the turning on the right just over 1 km further on, clearly signposted for Ugarit (the entrance is 200 m down this road). Alternatively, you can get there from Blue Beach.

Background
Excavations on the *tell* (mound) at Ugarit have revealed evidence of occupation dating back to the seventh millennium BC. Nevertheless, it is the Bronze Age (3300-1200 BC) that most interests archaeologists and historians here. At some point in the late fourth or early third millennium BC, a population of Mesopotamian origin settled at the site, providing links to both Mesopotamia to the east and Cyprus to the west. The city's harbour (Minet al-Beida, some 1.5 km northwest, but now off-limits within a military area) became the point through which copper technology was largely introduced to the region

For reasons that are as yet unclear, the city went into severe decline in around 2000 BC, though layers of ash in the lower levels of stratum at the site suggest that the city may have been captured and burnt. Among subsequent migrants settling at the site were the **Canaanites**, who remained the dominant group here for the next eight centuries. The beginning of the second millennium BC represents the dawn of the city's first golden age, and by the 18th century BC we have textual proof that the name Ugarit was in common usage.

Ugarit's potential quickly drew the attention of the **Egyptians**, though Ugarit remained an independent kingdom (with a locally drawn royal dynasty) sandwiched between the far greater powers of Egypt and Mesopotamia. Ugarit's kings must have been statesmen of some ability to avoid having their kingdom subsumed into the mass of one of the neighbouring empires and there is even considerable evidence that Ugarit maintained close links with other empires, notably the **Minoan** civilization on Crete. The city also developed a reputation for excellence in bronze-working, adding another string to the bow of the city's economic base.

By the beginning of the Late Bronze Age (c 1550 BC), Ugarit was drawn closer and closer into Egypt's orbit, though the growing power of the **Mitannite** Dynasty in Mesopotamia meant that Ugarit still had to continue to walk the narrow tightrope of international diplomacy. It is even possible that Ugarit played an intermediary role between the Egyptians and Mitannites. They had much to gain from stability, the peace

The Ugarit alphabet

It wasn't any bigger than a finger, but the tiny clay tablet unearthed at Ugarit's royal place was the most exciting find. Carved into the tablet were the 30 symbols that made up the Ugaritic alphabet. Based on a simple 'one-sound, one-sign' system, this alphabet presented a great leap forward in writing from earlier regional languages.

Texts and tablets unearthed from the Royal Palace's vast archives revealed the use of many other languages in Ugarit. Much of the diplomatic correspondence was in Babylonian (or Akkadian), the lingua franca of the region. Other texts

were found in Hourrian, Cypro-Minoan, Hittite cuneiform and Sumerian, plus inscriptions in hieroglyphic Hittite and Egyptian. These written languages relied on hundreds of complex symbols and signs to represent syllables or complete words, which is why the texts written in the simplified language of Ugaritic, was such a discovery.

It's thought that sea-faring Syrians from Ugarit took their new alphabet to Greece where the Greeks would eventually use it to establish their own alphabet, making Ugaritic one of the most ancient alphabets in the world.

that emerged greatly enhancing Ugarit's wealth-generating capacity and resulting in the city's golden age of the 14th and 13th centuries BC. Under King **Niqmadou II** (1360-1330), Ugarit traded with Egypt, Mesopotamia, Anatolia and the Aegean region, many of the transactions resulting from this great trade being recorded in the documents found at the site. Several of the buildings seen at the site today, including Niqmadou II's royal palace complex, date to this golden period.

The rise of the **Hittites** in the Anatolia region to the north posed a considerable threat to the independence of Ugarit, with the Ugarit kings going to great lengths to appease them (including requests to the Egyptian pharaohs to send gifts). However, correspondence discovered at the site here leaves no doubt that the Hittites considered Ugarit effectively part of their extended empire. Nevertheless, despite these pressures, the city continued to build links with the outside world, notably the Aegean region.

When Ugarit's end came it was remarkably swift, though not necessarily cataclysmic. The invasion of the region by the Sea Peoples (most famously the **Philistines**) around 1200 BC may have seen the city attacked, though there is reason to suggest that Ugarit's decline is equally attributable to the collapse of the palace-based economy brought about by changing technological needs that the subsequent Iron Age demanded. The site was later occupied during various periods, though Ugarit's golden past was never recreated, and the city lay largely forgotten until the chance find by a local farmer in 1928.

The ruins

① *0900-1800 summer, 0900-1600 winter, S£150, student S£10, toilets and café at the site entrance. Inside the site it is very overgrown in places and there is little shade; wear decent walking shoes, bring plenty of water and have adequate protection against the sun. In the full heat of summer, time your visit for the early morning or late afternoon. Helpful information signs and arrow signposts put up by the 'Louvre Museum Ras Shamra Archaeological Mission', help guide you around.*

The tour of the site begins at the main entrance gate. Before ascending the steps to the ticket office, it is worth examining the remains of the **fortress walls and postern gate** just to the right (south). The defensive wall was first built in the 15th century BC, though considerably strengthened during a later period. This involved levelling off the slope of the mound to an angle of 45° and covering it with stone, thus forming a difficult to climb *glacis*. The wall and *glacis* at this point was further fortified by a tower, probably built to defend the postern gate. It is generally believed that the gateway here was for royal usage, with the main gateway (along with most of the rest of the fortress walls) not having survived the ravages of time. Ascend the steps to the ticket office, then descend the other side towards the **great square** at the entrance to the royal palace complex.

Royal palace complex The palace complex dates to the city's golden age (14th-13th centuries BC), covering an impressive 10,000 sq m and featuring some 90 rooms, five large courtyards and an interior garden. It is worth bearing in mind that what you see today is merely the remains of the ground floor; the palace previously had an upper storey where most of the living quarters would have been (the remains of several staircases can still be seen).

The **main entrance** to the complex was through a large wooden gateway, whose stone pillar bases can still be seen. Inside the entrance is a small paved **reception area**. A doorway on the east side of the square leads into a **square room**, which in turn leads north through a passage into a **secretary's office**. The adjoining rooms are where the Western Archive was found (see box, page 187).

Returning to the square room, head south into the palace's **main courtyard**. The courtyard's paved floor is well preserved, as are the conduits used to channel water throughout the complex. The well in the southwest corner of the courtyard provided much of the palace's supply of water. Pass from the main courtyard into the porch and then into what has been dubbed the **throne room**. From here you can reach the **banquet hall** to the east. Head south into another large, impressive courtyard labelled the **reception hall**, at the centre of which stands a sunken pool with steps leading down into it from the east side. Remains of the channels that brought water from outside the palace walls can be clearly seen. Also of note here is the well on the west side of the courtyard and the cistern in the southeast corner. In the southwest corner a small **oven** was found. The purpose of this oven was to bake the tablets upon which the letters, treaties, inventories and texts were written. The treasure of important finds gathered here is known as the Tablets of the Oven. To the south of the courtyard lie the two rooms in which the **Southern Archive** was found. The room to the west revealed the **Southwestern Archive**.

Following the water channel east from the Reception Hall, you come to the palace's large **interior garden**. The small structure on the north side next to the well and bucket has been identified as the **gardener's lodge**. The three rooms to the north of here are where the **Eastern Archive** was found. The two large structures on the south side of the garden are thought to have been shops or store rooms. The building in the northwest corner of the garden appears to have been the **workshop** where the garden's ivory furniture was built (many fragments of ivory were excavated from the garden area). Just to the west of this you can walk through a large hall and small room to reach the **north entrance** of the palace, where you can still see the notches in the wall on which the wooden gate used to hang. Retrace your steps through the large hall and via another room to the west to reach a large courtyard, signposted **Courtyard II**. On the east side of this courtyard can be seen the bases of two stone pillars that once supported a porch, inside which is a well. In the main part of the courtyard, meanwhile, is a rectangular basin. Lying to the north of this large courtyard are a series of three sepulchral vaults dug beneath the rooms that served as the palace **necropolis** (signposted the 'Royal Tombs').

Small palace The 'Small palace' is south of the royal palace complex; you enter it from the west side. It is fairly ruinous inside and nothing is labelled. The principal feature is the central room containing a large underground burial chamber with steps leading down to it from the west side and an arched roof which is still largely intact. The room immediately to the southeast contains another smaller but better preserved burial chamber.

Northern palace and residential area Following the path east from the entrance to the royal palace complex along the outside of the north wall, you pass a fairly ruinous area on the left known as the Northern Palace. It is difficult to identify individual buildings here, though a section of the main sewer canal can be seen. Among the solid structures located in this area are the royal stables. Further on, you come to a sign for the **'Stone Vessel building'**, so-called because of the huge stone urn – completely intact – discovered inside. This marks the start of the **residential area**, comprising a fairly large concentration of spacious private houses, criss-crossed by a network of streets. Bearing off slightly to the left here, you come next to a sign for the **House of Rapanou**, a spacious 34-room villa, complete with its own excellently preserved underground mausoleum. It was here that the so-called Library of Rapanou was discovered.

Acropolis A little beyond the House of Rapanou, an arrow points you along a path towards the acropolis. Just before you get there you pass a deep trench. Dug by the archaeologists, this stratographic sounding covers the periods from the eighth to second millennium BC. A little further up, you come to the **Temple of Baal**, believed to have been the patron deity of Ugarit. Unfortunately, though it is signposted, it is now almost completely in ruins and there is little to see. Continuing along the path, you pass a deep water cistern, partially covered by a stone slab, and the indistinct ruins of the **High Priest's house**, where the Library of the High Priest was discovered. Further on is the **Temple of Dagan**, dedicated to the god of the underworld in the Ugarit pantheon. This temple, comprised of two rectangular courtyards surrounded by 4- to 5-m-thick walls, is slightly better preserved though there is still not much to see.

To the south side of the acropolis is what is referred to as the **southern block**, though there is little to see here and it is badly overgrown. Many of the structures discovered here are thought to have been homes and artisans' workshops. Two separate dwellings in the southern block revealed the Southern Block Library and the Library of the Magician Priest. Likewise, the **northeast block**, to the north of the acropolis, is badly neglected, though the mound of accumulated debris from the various excavations does provide a good vantage point from which to view the site.

Kassab → *For listings, see pages 195-203.*

Sprawling out over the hillside, the town of Kassab, with its concrete high-rise apartment blocks springing up all over the place, is no oil painting. Its situation, on the other hand, is. Set amongst the foothills of the Al-Aqra Mountains, right up against the defacto border with Turkey, this beautiful area is great for walkers. The predominantly Armenian population of the town is friendly and the place has a relaxed air about it. It is very popular as a summer retreat from the heat of the plains, particularly with Aleppines and visiting Gulf families, many of whom rent apartments for the whole of the summer. For around one week before and after the Feast of the Assumption on 15 August it gets particularly busy here and there is little chance of finding accommodation. In contrast, during low season (September-May) it gets very cold and wet, with heavy snow in the depths of winter, and the town more or less completely closes down.

Ins and outs

Getting there and away During the summer season there are regular services from the microbus station on Al-Jalaa Street, next to Assad Stadium, in Lattakia (1½ hours, S£25). Bear in mind that the last service back to Lattakia usually leaves well before nightfall. Out of season, services are much less frequent, drying up altogether in the dead of winter.

If you are driving, head north out of Lattakia as if for Ugarit and bear right at the large roundabout around 6 km from the centre of town (signposted for 'Turkey, Kassab, Al Bassit'). Keep going straight along this road surrounded by fertile plains given over to highly productive agricultural land. Further north the road begins to climb into the foothills of the Al-Aqra Mountains, passing through olive groves and thick pine forests. A few kilometres after passing a right turn (25 km from the roundabout) signposted for the village of Balloram, you pass on your right a particularly beautiful lake set amongst pine forests. Towards the north end of the lake there are a couple of restaurants overlooking it. Just over 5 km beyond the right turn for Balloram, there is a left turn signposted to '**Al-Bassit**' and '**Badroussieh**', the start of the road leading down to these resorts. Continuing straight, a little under 5 km further on you pass through the small village of Qastal Ma'af. After another 6 km you reach a right turn signposted to **Aleppo** (this road joins the highway between Lattakia and Aleppo). Continuing straight, after a further 7 km, fork left for **Kassab**. (If you carry on going straight, you reach the Turkish border.) From the fork it is around 4 km on to Kassab.

Ras al-Bassit and Al-Badrusiyeh → *For listings, see pages 195-203.*

Along the northernmost stretch of Syria's Mediterranean coast, are the beach resorts of Ras al-Bassit and Al-Badrusiyeh. The stretch of coastline here is unusual for its distinctive black-sand beaches, which are relatively clean compared with elsewhere along the coast, but are still beset by rubbish. However, the setting is quite beautiful, with mountains rising dramatically to the north and east. Al-Badrusiyeh consists of a long stretch of seafront lined with a variety of stalls, snack bars, billiards tents and shops selling seaside paraphernalia; Syria's answer to Blackpool perhaps? Ras al-Bassit is much the same, although it is rather more developed. During the summer it gets extremely busy here. By around mid-September the crowds start to leave and it is much quieter, only picking up again towards the end of April/beginning of May.

Ins and outs

Getting there and away During the summer season there are regular services from the microbus station on Al-Jalaa Street, next to Assad Stadium, in Lattakia (one hour, S£25). Public transport here dries up completely when summer ends.

If driving, follow the directions in the Kassab section (above). From the turning for Ras al-Bassit and Badrusiyeh it is 12 km down to the coast, the road descending steeply through the mountains. Approaching the coast, there is a signposted right turn for Badrusiyeh, while keeping straight takes you into Ras al-Bassit. There is another route to Ras al-Bassit and Al-Badrusiyeh directly from Kassab, along an extremely scenic and equally winding road. The turning is signposted from the main square in Kassab; keep following this road for around 16 km to arrive at the resorts.

Qala'at Salah ud-Din (Saône)

Known as Saône to the Crusaders, today Qala'at Salah ud-Din sits alone on a dramatic narrow ridge, surrounded by deep gorges of pine forest. Its wild and isolated setting makes it hard at first to understand why the Crusaders (or indeed the Byzantines and Phoenicians before them) should have chosen this lonely location for a castle. In ancient times though, the castle was supremely placed. A main route between Aleppo and Lattakia passed through the nearby village of Al-Haffeh, enabling the Crusaders to control movement along the road while the castle's high setting allowed them commanding views of the plains below. Despite all these advantages, in the end they were powerless to stop Salah ud-Din from capturing the castle in 1188.

Ins and outs

Getting there and away Regular microbuses run from the main microbus station, behind the Pullman bus station, in Lattakia to **Al-Haffeh** (30-45 minutes, S£20). From here you must either walk (around 6 km, see route description below) or take a taxi. There are plenty of taxis waiting at the microbus drop-off point in Al-Haffeh. The taxi journey shouldn't cost any more than S£50 one-way but you will have to bargain hard for this price since many of the vehicle owners in the village have cottoned on to the possibility of charging tourists exorbitant rates. There are no taxis waiting at the castle to take you back to Al-Haffeh, you either have to bargain a return fare with waiting time or walk. Take care to return to the village well before nightfall in order to be sure of picking up transport returning to Lattakia. Microbuses also run from Al-Haffeh on to the summer hill resort of **Slunfeh**. A taxi from Lattakia to Qala'at Salah ud-Din with one hour waiting time shouldn't cost any more than S£1000 return.

If walking from Al-Haffeh, from where the microbus drops you off, head straight up the street for about 20 m until the right-hand turn-off clearly signposted as 'Qala'at Salah ud-Din St'. Turn here and walk up the street. After about 1500 m you'll reach a signposted fork in the road. Turn left here and follow the road all the way up to the castle. It's a good 6-km walk, mostly up-hill and at times quite steep but there are beautiful views of the surrounding area along the way. Try to do it early in the morning before it gets too hot.

If you're driving, from Jumhouriah Square in Lattakia, head east along Aleppo Avenue, following signs for Damascus and Aleppo. Just after passing the **Tishreen University** grounds on the right, continue straight over a large roundabout (2 km from Jumhouriah

Qala'at Salah uh-Din (Saône)

1 Rock needle	5 Stables	9 Mosque	12 Byzantine citadel
2 Entrance tower	6 Water cistern	10 Palace & baths	13 Tea house
3 Tower	7 Main keep	complex	14 Byzantine chapel
4 Tower	8 Postern gate	11 Water cistern	15 Crusader church

50 metres
50 yards

Square). Keep going straight (past an exit for the Aleppo road) following signs for Tartus and Damascus now, to join the coastal motorway heading south. Take the exit signposted 'Slunfeh, Al-Haffeh, Salah ud-Din Citadel' (just over 14 km from Jumhouriah Square), turning left at a T-junction after 700 m to go under the motorway. A little over 1 km further on, turn right at what is effectively a crossroads (signposted). Keep following this road for around 20 km to arrive in the centre of Al-Haffeh. Drive through the village and take the clearly signposted right turn around 2 km further on. After 1500 m fork left (this is also signposted, but not clearly). After 500 m you'll pass, on your left, a restaurant with excellent views across a deep ravine to the castle, before descending steeply and then climbing to reach the castle, just over 2 km beyond the restaurant.

Background

Although known today as Qala'at Salah ud-Din, this name was only given to the castle in 1957, in commemoration of Salah ud-Din's capture of it in 1188. To the Crusaders it was known as *Saône*, a name corrupted in Arabic to *Sayhun*. In its present form the castle dates mostly from the 12th century, although its origins go back much further. Early in the first millennium BC, the site was fortified by the **Phoenicians** and they were still in possession of it when Alexander the Great passed through Syria in 333 BC, en route for Egypt. In the second half of the 10th century the **Byzantines**, led by the Emperor John Zimisces, advanced into northern Syria; re-establishing the duchy of Antioch and seizing the site from the Hamdamid Dynasty of Aleppo. The remains of the fortifications they built can still be seen in the old citadel which stands on a small hillock in the centre of the eastern half of the castle, and also in the traces of defensive walls, all now enclosed within the later and more substantial work of the Crusaders.

The **Crusaders** first gained possession of the castle early in the 12th century. By 1119 it had been entrusted as a feudal endowment to Robert of Saône (from whom it took its name), by Roger, Prince of Antioch. It was to remain in Crusader hands until its capture by Salah ud-Din in 1188. During this period, the Crusaders carried out major building works, largely rendering the Byzantine fortifications redundant and giving it the overall form you see today. As such, it represents an example of early Crusader castle architecture, unusual for this period in terms of its extravagant scale and execution.

Its fall to **Salah ud-Din** in 1188 is in many ways surprising. He had bypassed other major Crusader strongholds in the region (notably Krak des Chevaliers and Qala'at Marqab), concentrating his attention on smaller, more easily taken castles. However, having conquered Lattakia, he moved on to Saône and laid siege to it. Two days later, the walls of the lower court on the north side were breached and the Crusader forces, insufficient in number to defend such a large castle, soon surrendered.

After its fall, the castle remained in Muslim hands. It was controlled first by the family of a local emir loyal to the Ayyubids, the Nasr ud-Din Manguwiris, before being handed over to the Mamluk sultan Baibars in 1272, during his campaign to drive the Crusaders from the region. In 1280 it briefly fell into the hands of Sonqor al-Ashtar, a governor of Damascus who rebelled against the Mamluks, but was returned to Mamluk control under the sultan Qalaun (Baibar's successor) in 1287 after a brief siege. Subsequently its strategic importance appears to have declined and it fell into obscurity, housing a village for a time but later being abandoned.

The castle

① Wed-Mon 0900-1800 in summer, 0900-1600 in winter, S£150, students S£10. Toilets are located at the bottom of the steps leading up to the entrance.

Approaching the castle from the village of Al-Haffeh, it is worth stopping briefly before descending into the ravine for an overview of the castle. What you see from this side is the largely ruined western lower courtyard and the Byzantine citadel. Having dropped down to the bottom of the ravine, crossed a stream and then climbed again up the other side, you pass through a deep narrow canyon between two walls of sheer vertical rock. Incredible though it may seem, this is man-made, having been hewn out of the rock in order to separate the ridge on which the castle stands from the main body of the mountain to the east. Towards the northern end of the canyon is a free-standing needle of rock rising to a height of 28 m which was left when the surrounding rock was chiselled away in order to allow a drawbridge to be extended from the castle, providing an alternative entrance/exit. The eastern fortifications of the castle rise almost seamlessly from the natural rock, towering above you imposingly. The canyon is thought to have first been carved out by the Byzantines and then widened and deepened by the Crusaders.

Before entering the castle, follow the road as it climbs up the side of the ravine to the south. From this direction you get an even better view of the castle layout, in particular the concentration of Crusader fortifications along its more vulnerable eastern side; as well as the walls and towers along the southern side.

Eastern defences Entry to the castle is through the last of three solid rectangular towers in the southern walls. A long flight of concrete steps climbs up to the tower. Leaving the entrance hall (where the ticket office is located), more or less directly in front of you is the mosque (see below). Turn right to follow the line of the southern walls towards the **eastern fortifications**. The three rectangular towers along the southern walls each have a staircase which gives access to the first floor and roof. These are typical of the early Crusader style, both in terms of their shape and the prominently bossed and neatly jointed large square blocks used in their construction.

A doorway immediately to the left of the easternmost rectangular tower gives access to the **stables** and **water cistern**. Going through the doorway, on your right are steps leading down into the huge barrel-vaulted water cistern. On the left, meanwhile, a second doorway leads through into the stables, a large vaulted area, its low roof supported by large, squat pillars. Tucked away in the far southeast corner of the stables is a doorway giving access to a small room in the central semicircular tower of the eastern defences. Along with the other semicircular towers on the eastern defences, this was originally built by the Byzantines and substantially modified and strengthened by the Crusaders. The northernmost of this set of three towers can likewise be accessed from the stables, and also has a stairway beside it leading up to the ramparts, from where there are truly vertiginous views down into the rock-cut canyon below.

Immediately to the north of the stables is the main **keep** (*donjon*), a squat, solidly built two-storey square tower which formed the final defensive position of the castle. With walls over 5 m thick it would certainly have presented a formidable challenge to any would-be attacker. A plain doorway in the west wall leads into a single large room, with a massive central pillar supporting the vaulted ceiling. The interior is very poorly lit, the only natural light coming through the doorway and the narrow arrow slits in the walls. A set of stairs on your left as you enter leads up to the first floor, the room here being identical except that the ceiling is lower and windows in three of the walls make it much lighter. The stairs continue up to the roof of the keep, from where there are good all-round views.

To the north again of the keep is a series of rooms, their ceilings collapsed, followed by a large hall with its arched ceiling still intact. The latter once formed the **postern gate**, giving access to the castle via a drawbridge supported on the needle of rock rising from the floor of the artificial canyon. This complex of buildings to the north of the main keep and extending around the northeast corner of the castle are all of Byzantine origin, with only the postern gate showing signs of later modification by the Crusaders. Note also the crumbling inner line of walls running parallel to the eastern fortifications; these are likewise of Byzantine origin.

Mosque, palace and baths complex Doubling back the way you came, you can visit next the **mosque**, which dates from the Mamluk occupation, probably during the reign of the Sultan Qalaun (1280-1290). Steps lead up to an arched and vaulted porch which takes you in to the prayer hall. Note the mosque's distinctive square minaret. On the higher ground just to the northwest of the mosque is the **palace and baths complex**, which dates from the Ayyubid period (late 12th to early 13th century). The main entrance, leading first into the palace, is from the eastern side, through a restored doorway elaborately decorated in typical Ayyubid style with stalactites and geometric patterns of interlocking stonework. Inside is a vaulted reception hall with an opening in the centre of the ceiling to let light in, and arched *iwans* to the left and right. Straight ahead is another doorway preceded by an arched semi-dome which leads into the baths complex. The main room here (its roof no longer intact) contains a shallow circular pool in the centre of the floor, with channels leading into it. On the north side of the room is an arched *iwan* flanked by two tall, arched passageways which lead through into the bathing rooms. To the west of the palace and baths complex, perched on top of a small hillock, is the original **Byzantine citadel**, now in an advanced state of ruin, its surviving stonework noticeably inferior to that of the Crusader fortifications.

Rest of the castle A path leads north from the palace and baths complex taking you past the entrance to a huge **water cistern** set against the northern walls. The vast, echoing proportions of the interior, with its barrel-vaulted roof and steps leading down inside, is truly awesome. Next to it are two smaller and somewhat more ruinous cisterns. All of these were built by the Crusaders and, along with the first cistern in the southeast corner of the castle, provided a sufficient store of water to survive a lengthy siege.

From here you can follow a path westwards along the northern walls, passing the remains of the Byzantine citadel up on your left until you reach a Crusader-period building which today serves as a **teahouse** selling refreshments and postcards. From here you can look down over the lower (western) courtyard of the castle, separated from the upper (eastern) courtyard by a ditch. This western half of the castle is almost entirely ruined and heavily overgrown. Only the line of the walls and towers is still discernible, along with a tiny **Byzantine chapel**. In the distance an artificial lake can be seen and, on a clear day, the plains around Lattakia and the Mediterranean sea beyond. Although there's not much to see if you descend to this part of the castle, it's a beautiful lonely spot to wander round. There is a track that runs down to the lower courtyard from the right-hand side of the teahouse. Only descend if you are wearing good hiking shoes and your legs are well protected against the thick brambles.

Staying on the upper courtyard, from the teahouse continue along the footpath, which completes a circuit around the hillock and Byzantine citadel to arrive back at the entrance tower, passing en route the ruins of a **Crusader church** on the left, on the far side of which are the ruins of a much smaller **Byzantine chapel**.

Qardaha

Qardaha's chief (and indeed only) claim to fame is that it is the birthplace of the late Hafez al-Assad, president of Syria for nearly 30 years. When Assad rose to power, Qardaha was a tiny, remote Alawi village hidden away in the mountains. The development that has been somewhat gratuitously lavished on it neatly reflects the remarkable reversal in fortunes that the Alawi community experienced during Assad's rule. The result of all this spending is rather eerie; all wide boulevards and fancy villas but not enough people, making Qardaha feel like a posh ghost town.

Ins and outs

Getting there and away Microbuses from Lattakia leave from the microbus station beside the Pullman bus station (30 minutes, S£20).

If you're driving, the exit for Qardaha is clearly signposted off the coastal motorway 17 km to the south of Lattakia. From here you follow a broad four-lane highway which is completely out of proportion to the volume of traffic travelling along it.

Hafez al-Assad Mausoleum

Hafez al-Assad and his eldest son Basil (who was killed in a car accident in 1994) are buried in a vast echoing mausoleum just on the left as you come into town. Internally the mausoleum is simple in design and has an aura of solemnity. Hafez's tomb is in the centre of the room, while Basil's grave to the side.

⊙ The coast and the Jebel Ansariye listings

For Sleeping and Eating price codes and other relevant information, see Essentials pages 19-21.

⊜ Sleeping

Tartus *p154, map p156*
Most of Tartus' mid-range hotels are located on the corniche and are targeted at local tourists; they are often full of large groups of holidaying Syrians. For the cheapest of the cheap hotels, head away from the port on Al-Wahda St. There's a scattering of rock-bottom cheapies in the 2 blocks before the clock tower.
L Shahin Tower, Tarek ibn Zaid St, T043-329100, www.shahinhotels.com. Tartus' answer to a 4-star hotel has spotlessly clean rooms with a/c, satellite TV, balcony and large baths, helpful smiley staff, restaurant, bar and one massive empty lobby. It's shiny and modern but the decor is a bit cheap for the price being asked and a little on the bland side.

B Shahin, Tarek ibn Zaid St, T043-315001, www.shahinhotels.com. The Shahin Tower's older sister hotel down the road, has just been newly refurbished and is looking great. The room decor is nearly exactly the same as they've used in the Shahin Tower but you're paying less than half the price. Spotlessly clean rooms (a/c, satellite TV and balcony) come with sparkling new modern baths. The service is friendly and there's a restaurant and bar. Recommended.
C Tartous Grand, Al-Corniche, T043-355600. This giant cement-slab of a hotel sits right on the corniche looking a bit worse for wear. Inside it's all a bit retro; the funky, character-filled, pink rooms (a/c, satellite TV, fridge and balcony) are large and clean, if verging on a teensy bit shabby. Unfortunately it's a fair way from the rest of town.
E Daniel, Al-Wahda St, T043-312757. A wonderful family-run hotel right in the centre of the action. The bright, simple rooms all come with fan, crisp white linen

on the beds and decent-sized attached bath, and are kept spotlessly clean. It's welcoming, friendly and the best budget deal in town. Recommended.

E Manchieh (formerly known as the 'Raffoul'), Al-Kowatli St, T043-220616. Small quiet hotel with 10 simple but clean rooms (with fan). Most rooms have shared bath. The owner's main business is the grocery store on the corner below the hotel; enquire here if the hotel is locked.

Krak des Chevaliers *p162, map p163*

While all the hotels in this area claim to stay open all year, during the winter months (late Nov to Mar), it is very cold up here and, except in the more expensive places, you may well find them closed, or perhaps with just a token caretaker in residence.

Of the hotels listed below, only **Baibars** and **Round Table** are really practical without your own transport. If you do have your own transport, it is also worth considering the various hotels along the road to St George's (see Around Krak des Chevaliers, below).

B Francis, 4 km southwest of Krak, follow the road around to the west side of the castle and keep going; the resort is on your left and clearly signposted, T031-773 0949, www.francis-hotel.com. A lovely tranquil place with helpful staff. Clean and comfortable rooms all come with a/c, satellite TV and large modern baths. There are also good-value suites (with kitchenette and balcony) that can sleep 5. The swimming pool has a terrace with stunning views over the valley. Restaurant.

C Baibars, 1 km southwest of Krak, follow the road around to the west side of the castle, past **Al-Kala'a Restaurant** and the car park, and take the right turn (clearly signposted) soon after, T031-734 1201, akrmbibars@mail.sy. This friendly hotel is all about the view. Superbly situated, the clean simple rooms here (a/c, satellite TV) have huge windows which look directly across the valley to Krak des Chevaliers. Most rooms have balconies so you can sit and admire the

castle while enjoying a beer on your private terrace. Excellent value. Recommended.

E Round Table, Follow the road around to the west side of the castle, just before the car park take the left-hand turn and follow this road round until you come to a signposted gravel driveway on the left, T031-734 0280. This place is primarily a restaurant (see below) but has 4 very basic rooms with attached bath. Camping is also allowed in the grounds.

Around Krak des Chevaliers *p167*

All the sleeping options here are in the village of Al-Mishtala, next to the monastery. If you're looking for peace and serenity this is the place, but because of the lack of public transport it's only really practical for those with their own car.

AL Al-Wadi, Main Rd, Al-Mishtaia, T031-773 0456, www.alwadihotel.com. This luxury hotel has subtle, traditional decor in the common areas and spacious rooms with a/c and satellite TV. There's a restaurant, bar and swimming pool and the terrace has incredible views of Krak des Chevaliers in the distance.

D Al-Fahd, Main Rd, Al-Mishtaia, T031-773 0822. The rooms here (fan only) are definitely no-frills but they each have a balcony and tiny bath. There's a lovely shady garden and a swimming pool from where you can look out to the castle. Zoher the enthusiastic owner speaks English and French.

Safita *p169*

AL Safita Cham Palace, Safita Cham St, T043-531131, www.chamhotels.com/cham_safita. Rather more modest than the rest of the Cham's chain of hotels, and a little in need of refurbishment in places, but occupying a commanding position with great views out over the surrounding countryside. Rooms come with a/c, satellite TV, attached bath and balcony (all with views). Restaurant, bar, swimming pool and sun terrace. The cost of a double room falls hugely outside of summer.

C Safita Bourj, from roundabout at eastern end of town, bear right – signposted Mashta and Kafroun – and hotel is on left after around 1 km, T043-521932. This friendly little place has reasonable rooms with fan, attached bath and balcony. There's a little English spoken.

Mashta al-Helu *p171*
AL Mashta al-Helu Resort, on the hillside just before the town, T043-584000, www.mashtaresort.com. Comfortable rooms all with a/c, satellite TV and balcony. There are also suites which can sleep up to 6 people and come complete with kitchen and lounge. Outside of Jul-Aug there are excellent discounts. Restaurant, bar, swimming pool.

Lattakia *p180, map p181*
Lattakia's hotel scene is decidedly overpriced during the high-season of Jul and Aug (on which these prices are based). If you visit out of season you can get amazing discounts of up to 50%. For luxury hotels you need to head to Blue Beach.
A Al-Cazino, Al-Corniche, T041-461142, www.alcazino.com. The rather grand façade and old-style high-ceilinged lobby are wonderfully atmospheric but the entire place desperately needs refurbishment. Decent-sized rooms (with a/c, satellite TV and fridge) are bland and tired-looking but the staff are lovely and you can't beat the old-world ambience.
A Riviera, 14 Ramadan St, T041-211806, www.riviera-sy.com. Lattakia's top hotel, although the lobby is a bit of a car-crash of Oriental design, and it's a long way from the town centre. There are comfortable, clean, modern rooms all with a/c, satellite TV and decent-sized baths.
C Al-Gandoul, Jamal Abdul al-Nasser St, T041-477 680. Popular with holidaying Syrian families, the Al-Gandoul could do with a lick of paint and a bit of a scrub. The moderately clean maroon-themed rooms, with a/c, TV and fridge, are decent but it's a fair walk from the town.
C Al-Nour, 14 Ramadan St, T041-243980. Despite the grotty red and blue carpets that

are simply screaming to be ripped out, this hotel is the best deal in town in this category. The spacious rooms all have a/c, satellite TV, fridge and modern baths. Some rooms come with balcony (though there's not much of a view). The staff here are super-helpful and you get to ride up to your room in the slowest lift in the world.
D Al-Riyad, Opposite the Assad statue, 14 Ramadan St, T041-476315, www.alriad hotel.com. Right in the middle of the action, the friendly Al-Riyad has large cheerful rooms with a lime-green and blue colour scheme. Rooms come with fan and satellite TV, and some have balconies. It doesn't cost much more to upgrade to an a/c room. Good value.
E Lattakia, Shikh Daher, T041-479527. Right in the heart of town, the bright, spick-and-span rooms here come with or without bath (all have fan and TV, and some with a/c and balcony). The helpful owner, Muhammad, runs a tight ship and the place is spotlessly clean. There's free guest use of the kitchen and you can hang out on the sofas and play backgammon in the reception. Recommended.
E Safwan, Mousa bin Nousier St, T041-478602, safwanhotel@go.com. Some of the rooms here (a/c, satellite TV, some with attached bath) are verging on being dilapidated and desperately need a lick of paint (ask to see a few before choosing) but there's kitchenettes for guest use, a rooftop dormitory for those on a tight budget, stacks of books and magazines at reception, and the friendly manager, Muhammad (who's an obsessive Tin Tin fan), is a fount of knowledge on the local area and extremely helpful. Recommended.
E Zahran,14 Ramadan St, T041-245128, zahran-hotel@hotmail.com. Decent-sized rooms (some with balcony) with a/c and satellite TV. A bit noisy but a good fall-back if the Lattakia and Safwan are full.

Blue Beach (Shaati al-Azraq) *p184*
Lattakia's 2 premier beach resort hotels are located here. There is a dramatic variation

in prices between the high season (1 Jun-15 Sep), when both resorts are at their busiest, and the low season (the rest of the year), when they are very quiet (or completely deserted in winter) and you can pick up rooms at bargain prices. Sometimes there are also excellent deals on offer towards the end of the high season. The price categories below reflect standard charges for the high season.

LL Le Meridien, Shaati al-Azraq, T041-428736, www.lemeridien.com. Choice of seafront or garden rooms all with a/c satellite TV and minibar. Has all the bells and whistles you'd expect from an international luxury chain resort: restaurants, bar, swimming pool, private beach, shops, bank, etc, but the decor inside could do with a serious update – think circa 1970s.

AL-A Côte d'Azur de Cham, Shaati al-Azraq, T041-428700, www.chamhotels.com/azur. The massive lobby is a gaudy oriental-overload but the rooms (which come with a/c, satellite TV and balcony) are rather nice. There are all the same facilities as at the Meridien but the 600-m private beach here is definitely the better of the two.

Kassab *p189*
C Al-Rawda, on left as you head up the hill from the main square, on the back road to Ras al-Bassit, T041-711008. Clean simple rooms, all with attached bath. Closed Sep-May.
E Motel Vahe, just beyond the main square, T041-710224. All the clean basic rooms here have at least 3 beds but the manager is quite happy to just charge the double occupancy rate. Very friendly and good English spoken. Closed Sep-May.

Ras al-Bassit and Al-Badrusiyeh *p190*
Most of the accommodation here consists of chalets and apartments usually rented out for a period of weeks or months, although it may be possible to rent one on a nightly basis (around US$20-60 for 2 people depending on the facilities) subject to availability.

B Bassit Tourist, Ras al-Bassit, T041-429668. Plain rooms with a/c and attached bath. Expensive for what you get. Restaurant.

🍴 Eating

Tartus *p154, map p156*
Predictably enough, fish is popular here, though it is not cheap. If you wander past the fish market in front of the harbour, you can get an idea of what is available (and perhaps go for some self-catering). Prices vary significantly according to the type of fish, and the season. The cheapest period is from mid-Oct to mid-Nov, when it is excellent value. Most of the restaurants are strung out along the corniche. Around the clock tower there are quite a few cheap *shawarma* places and there are 2 excellent supermarkets on Al-Wahda St, just past the Daniel Hotel as you head towards the boat jetty.
🍴 Al-Yamak, 4th floor, Chamber of Commerce building (the entrance is on the east side, not on the Corniche itself). Reputedly one of the best fish restaurants in Syria and a favourite haunt amongst politicians, VIPs, etc. As well as fish there's also excellent-value, high-quality Arabic dishes. Alcohol served.
🍴 Cave, Al-Corniche. One of the oldest restaurants in Tartus, set in a wonderfully atmospheric vaulted chamber which forms part of the Old City. Seafood is the speciality here, and there's some good continental cuisine. They have an unfortunate penchant for playing Celine Dion CDs but apart from that, it's great.
🍴 Sahara, Al-Corniche. Comfy sofas inside and shaded terrace out front. One of the nicest and most popular places of the many restaurants along the corniche to sit and while away a few hours. The menu is, unsurprisingly, strong on seafood. Alcohol served.
🍴 TicTac, Al-Corniche, Modern a/c indoors eating or outdoor patio. Good for seafood and Arabic cuisine. Popular with local tourists in the evenings.

Al-Halabi Patisserie, Ahmed al-Azawl St. Great for quick snacks, this excellent bakery sells a wide-range of cheap savoury pastries and Syrian-style pizzas.

Al-Nabil, Al-Wahda St. Busy, basic canteen serving a wide range of Arabic and fish dishes. Make sure you know the price of your fish before ordering.

Bars and cafés

Most of the restaurants along the corniche double up as cafés and are happy for you to sit with a coffee and a *narghile* without eating. Nearly all of them serve alcohol as well. **Cave** has its own bar. There's a liquor store a couple of doors up from the Daniel Hotel.

Krak des Chevaliers *p162, map p163*

Enterprising locals have set up a few simple eateries in the gardens of their houses on the road down to the **Round Table** restaurant. In Al-Hosn village your options are limited to simple falafel places.

Al-Kala'a, follow the road around to the west side of the castle, it's the big 2-storey building opposite the car park, T031-734 0493. If you come for dinner don't let the big, empty dining hall put you off (most business comes from lunchtime tour groups). This restaurant does one of the best mezze spreads in Syria. Excellent-value meals of lots of different mezze plus chicken and chips. Say a big 'yes' to the delicious garlic sauce when they offer it. It's a good idea to ring ahead and let them know you're coming for dinner so they can get it prepared for you. Alcohol served.

Round Table, follow the road around to the west side of the castle, just before the car park take the left-hand turn and follow this road round until you come to a signposted gravel driveway on the left, T031-734 0280. Pleasant outdoor terrace and good Arabic buffet. Alcohol served.

Around Krak des Chevaliers *p167*

Al-Naeem, Main Rd, Al-Mishtala, take the left-hand turn 100 m out of the village,

T031-773 0822. Dine on a terrace surrounded by lemon trees and vines. This friendly family-run place cooks up wonderful Arabic dishes. There's no menu as such, just ask what they're cooking that day. The manager is slowly building some rooms as well so it's worthwhile checking to see if they have accommodation.

Safita *p169*

Al-Bourj, by the entrance to the tower. This restaurant has excellent views out over the surrounding countryside. They serve a standard selection of Arabic meals and snacks at slightly inflated tourist prices.

Al-Kanater, Ibrahim Hanano St (south of tower). Occupying the 1st floor of what was formerly a *madrassa* (Islamic school) and later used by the French as a 'club', the Al-Kanater has pleasant decor, friendly staff and good-quality Arabic food at reasonable prices. Alcohol served.

Lattakia *p180, map p181*

If you want a break from Arabic cuisine then Lattakia is your town. The town is awash with restaurants serving up Lattakia-versions of Western-style favourites such as burgers, steaks, pasta and pizza. Most of the restaurants are clustered between 8 Azar St, Al-Akhtal St, Al-Moutanabby St and Yousef al-Azmeh St and there's usually a 10% tax added to your bill. There are also a few lovely restaurants, with nice coastal views, along the South Corniche. For cheap *shawarma* and falafel head to the area around the Assad Statue on 14 Ramadan St, where you'll find a dozen joints churning out the usual fare.

Cesar, 8 Azar St. Cesar does everything from traditional Arabic cuisine (mezze kebab, *shish tawouk*) to the continental classics of steak and pizza. It's a friendly place and the manager speaks good English.

Italian Corner, Al-Moutanabby St. Huge portions of pasta and pizza are dished up here. Quiet at lunchtime but in the evening it's a popular hangout for young local hipsters, who sit on the terrace smoking *narghile* and people watching. Alcohol available.

Mamma, 8 Azar St. Cute little restaurant with a small but good menu of continental favourites (steak, lamb chops, escalope, pizza). It's popular so get here early before the locals. Alcohol available.

Siwar, sign in Arabic only, South Corniche. Popular with government bigwigs, this rather upmarket establishment serves up seafood dishes and Arabic cuisine. The terrace (lovely when the evening breeze begins) has nice sea views. Alcohol available.

Spiro, Al-Corniche. Its reputation for good Arabic food is well deserved. Choose to eat either inside the cavernous dining hall or under the shady grape vines on the terrace.

Dolce Vita Ice-cream, Al-Akhtal St. When it's hot and the going gets tough, the tough go for ice cream. Excellent ice cream parlour dishing up everyone's favourite way of cooling down.

Cafés

Coffee culture is alive and well in Lattakia and there's some excellent modern-style cafés as well as a couple of wonderfully traditional *ahwa* (Arabic coffee) joints.

Al-Boustan, 8 Azar St. The bustling sidewalk terrace is the place to watch the world go by. As well as *ahwa*, they have great fruit juice, *narghile* and ice cream.

Al-Montada, Adnan al-Malik St. Atmospheric, traditional place that's noisy with the sound of backgammon and chess pieces being slapped down in heated games. Frequented by Lattakia's older, more traditional generation.

Coffee Break, 8 Azar St. A decent cup of coffee as well as snacks and light meals can be found at this popular modern coffee shop that's right on a busy intersection. The terrace is perfect for people-watching.

Orabi Patisserie, opposite the car-park, 8 Azar St. Good pastries, cakes and coffee and if you've got a laptop, there's Wi-Fi access too. The outside terrace (in part of the car park across the road) isn't the nicest of settings but you can't knock the coffee.

Site, Adnan al-Malik St. The terrace seems to be where the local posers all hang out, so a drink here can be quite entertaining. Watch the Gucci sunglasses brigade checking each other out while you enjoy a coffee or a beer.

Blue Beach (Shaati al-Azraq) *p184*

The 2 luxury hotels offer a wide range of upmarket eating options with prices to match. For budget eating, try the numerous snack stalls in the vicinity of the **Côte d'Azur de Cham** hotel. As well as the usual *shawarmas* and *falafels*, *mannoushi* and Syrian-style pizzas are particularly popular. There are also a few simple restaurants serving the usual range of Arabic cuisine, but watch out for overcharging.

Kassab *p189*

There are several simple snack places along the main street.

Kilekia, just beyond the main square. Easily the nicest place to eat, with a lovely vine-shaded terrace and great views. They offer the usual range of Arabic fare plus fish dishes.

🜚 Bars and clubs

Lattakia *p180, map p181*
Most of the restaurants double up as bars, serving beer, wine and even cocktails, and it's fine to just have a drink and not order food. The outside terraces at **Italian Corner** and **Site** are particularly popular for drinking and are open till late.

⊛ Festivals and events

Lattakia *p180, map p181*
16-18 Sep Lattakia in Memory Festival. This annual 3-day festival of Lattakia's history features a Phoenician boat contest, Ugarit exhibitions and a rather un-historic windsurfing competition.

○ Shopping

Lattakia *p180, map p181*
From a Syrian point of view, Lattakia has great appeal as a shopping destination. Many international designer labels have outlets here and window shopping while out for an evening stroll is a favourite pastime. There's not much in the way of souvenirs though.

Bookshops
Betar, Jareer St, off Al-Akhtal St. Stocks UK newspapers and has an English-language section.

▲▲ Activities and tours

Blue Beach (Shaati al-Azraq) *p184*
Swimming
Full-day use (until 1900) of the private beach and swimming pool at the Côte d'Azur de Cham costs a whopping S£1000 per person for non-guests. The private beach here is surprisingly nice and single females will feel totally comfortable, but it's still exceedingly overpriced.

Bicycle hire
There are quite a few bike-hire places around the resorts (a nice way to get to Ugarit from here, if it's not too hot).

⊕ Transport

Tartus *p154, map p156*
Bus
The busy Kadmous bus garage on Jamal Abdel al-Nasser St is your best bet for bus services from Tartus. It's an easy 10-min walk from Al-Wahda St; turn left at the clock tower and walk to the traffic roundabout. Turn right and the Kadmous garage is just up the street a few metres, on your left.

Kadmous have frequent services to **Lattakia** (1 hr, S£60), **Homs** (1 hr, S£60) and **Damascus** (4 hrs, S£200), that leave approximately every hour. There is 1 daily

service to **Hama** at 0730 (1½ hrs, S£100), or jump on a bus to Homs and change there. For **Aleppo** change in Homs as well.

The Al-Ahliah bus station is on Ath Thawra St and services the same destinations but with less frequent departures.

Microbus
The microbus station is by the train station on 6 Tishreen Av. It costs S£25 to get here in a taxi.

Transport from here operates on a 'depart when full' basis and consists of a mixture of microbuses and old 'hob-hob' buses. There are regular departures for **Safita** (45 mins, S£20), **Dreikish** (45 mins, S£20), **Masyaf** (1 hr, S£30), **Homs** (1 hr, S£40) and **Al-Hamadiyyeh** (for **Amrit**) (15 mins, S£10).

Service taxis
International service taxis leave for **Tripoli** (S£350) and **Beirut** (S£700) in Lebanon, from near the clock tower on Al-Tahrir St. By mid-morning services begin to dry up and they stop altogether by about midday.

Train
Train services to and from Tartus have been improved and extended in recent years and it's now quite feasible to travel from Tartus by train. There is 1 daily service to **Damascus** at 1500 (1st class S£170, 2nd class S£140), and a daily departure to **Aleppo** at 1600 (1st class S£215, 2nd class S£180). To **Lattakia** there are 2 trains per day at 0625 and 2000 (1st class S£55, 2nd class S£45).

Safita *p169*
Microbus and bus
The main bus station is near the roundabout at the east end of town. Most services are in the form of microbuses, which run to **Tartus** (45 mins, S£20), **Homs** (1 hr, S£50), **Dreikish** (S£20), and **Mashta Helu** (S£20). There's also a very limited service to **Hosn Suleiman** (S£15). During summer **Kadmous** also run Pullman buses from their ticket office opposite the entrance to the Safita Cham Palace. There are 2 services daily to **Damascus** at 0700 and 1500 (S£100).

Taxi

There's a private taxi stand next door to the Kadmous ticket office.

Mashta al-Helu *p171*

Services to and from **Safita** leave when full from the microbus stand in the main square. You can also hire a microbus privately from here to explore the surrounding area but you'll have to bargain hard.

Lattakia *p180, map p181*

The main bus and microbus stations and the train station are all located within a 5-min walk of each other. It costs S£30 to get here from the centre in a taxi.

Air

Al-Basil International Airport is 25 km southeast of town. There's 2-3 flights to **Damascus** every day except Tue (1 hr, S£1244) and a service to **Cairo**, Egypt, once a week on Thu (S£10,950).

The Syrian Air office, T041-476100 (airport T041-833513), is on 8 Azar St. As well as buying tickets for flights from Lattakia, you can book and reconfirm international flights with Syrian Air from Damascus here. The best travel agency in town is **Julia Dumna**, on Baghdad St, T041-454577, who can help you book any onward flights.

Bus

All Pullman buses leave from the main bus station (Garagat Pullman) located behind the train station on Abdel Kader al-Houseiny St. From here there are regular departures to Damascus, Tartus, and Homs, as well as international services over the Turkish border to Antakya.

Kadmous have buses to **Tartus** every half hour (1 hr, S£60), to **Damascus** roughly every 2 hrs (4½ hrs, S£250), and to **Homs** every hour (4 hrs, S£125). **Al-Ahliah** buses ply some of the same routes and also go to **Hama** 5 times per day on a rather circuitous route via Tartus and Homs: 0645, 1230, 1415, 1600, 1700 and 1930 (3½ hrs, S£160).

If you're heading to Aleppo, it's best to take the train.

The old 'Hob-Hob' bus station is located between the main bus station and the train station on Abdel Kader al-Houseiny St. You can catch rickety old buses to **Damascus** and **Aleppo** from here that depart when full and stop en route on demand but as the Pullman buses are so cheap there's not much point in using them.

International departures

For **Antakya** in Turkey, **Al-Hassan Company** has a minibus that leaves from the main bus station at 0700 daily (4 hrs, S£500). To Lebanon, you can catch a service taxi to **Tripoli** (S£500) or **Beirut** (S£800), from the parking lot of the 'Hob-Hob' station.

Car

Budget have an office on Baghdad St, inside the Engineering Union Building, T041-454577.

Microbus

Lattakia has 3 different microbus stations that service different local towns. The locations of the stations have been changed a few times in recent years and there is talk of changing them yet again. Always check with your hotel for up-to-date information.

To **Blue Beach and Ugarit**: microbuses leave regularly from the corner of Antakiah St and Abdullah Ibn Masud St (Blue Beach: 10 mins, £S5. Ugarit: 20 mins, S£10).

To **Kassab and the northern beaches**: microbuses to the north all leave from the microbus station next to Assad Stadium on Al-Jalaa St. They leave quite regularly but you'll have to wait for them to fill up: **Kassab** (1½ hrs, S£25), **Ras al-Bassit** (1 hr, S£25), the beaches of **Birj Islam** and **Wadi Qandeel** (30 mins, £S20).

To **the eastern villages**: microbuses leave from the microbus station behind the Pullman bus station. From here there are quite frequent services to **Al-Haffeh** (for **Qala'at Salah uh-Din** (45 mins, S£20) and **Slunfeh** (1 hr, S£25), as well as many other destinations to the east.

Train

Lattakia Train Station, on Al-Yarman Sq, is useful for getting to Aleppo. The train journey there winds through the forested hills and cliffs of the Jebel Ansariye and quite picturesque farmland.

There are 6 daily trains to **Aleppo**: 2 fast services at 0625 and 1725 (2½ hrs, 1st class S£160, 2nd class S£135), and 4 slower trains at 0700, 1000, 1540 and 2100 (3½ hrs, 1st class S£70, 2nd class S£50). There's 1 train per day to **Damascus**, inconveniently leaving at 0200 (5 hrs, S£155), and to **Tartus** there's a daily service at 1515 (1 hr, S£40).

🟦 Directory

Tartus *p154, map p156*

Banks Banks are open Sat-Thu 0800-1200. The CBS branch on Al-Orouba St has an ATM. There is also a small CBS on Al-Wahda St that is just for foreign exchange. Banque Bemo has an ATM that should take all foreign cards on Ath Thawra St, east of the clock tower. **Internet** Log On Internet Café and Cybernet Café are opposite each other in an alleyway off Ibrahim Hanano St. Both charge S£50 per hour. You need to bring your passport to register. **Medical services** The New Medical Centre, just off 6 Tishreen Ave, to the south of the railway station, T043-317319, is a good private hospital. There is a pharmacy on nearly every street. **Post** The main post office (Sat-Thu 0800-2000, Fri 0800-1400) is on the corner of 6 Tishreen Ave and Jamal Abdul al-Nasser St. **Telephone** At the telephone office, on Ath Thawra St, you can buy phonecards and use the card-phones outside. **Visa extensions** Ministry of Interior, Dept of Immigration and Passports, off Andalos St, to the east of the large park, Thu-Sat 0800-1400. You need to bring your passport, 2 photos, and a letter from your hotel (this isn't always asked for), and then buy a form with an excise stamp on it (S£30) from the office on the 1st

floor. Take the form to the 2nd floor, fill in a couple of forms and your extension will be issued on the spot. This is one of the more efficient places at which to get your visa extended.

Lattakia *p180, map p181*

Banks The main branch of CBS is on Baghdad St, Sat-Thu 0830-1330. It has an ATM and you can change cash here. If your card is playing up in the CBS ATM you can try the ATMs at the Bank of Syria and Overseas, across the road from CBS, or Banque Bemo on Al Quds St. Both these banks' ATMs should take all foreign cards. **Internet** Centrenet Café and 24 Internet Café are both on Al-Moutanabby St and have fast connections. **Medical services** The Al-Assad University Hospital, 8 Azar St, T041-478782, is Lattakia's best hospital. There are pharmacies all over town. **Post** The main post office is in a small cul-de-sac off Souria Av (around 200 m northeast of the roundabout known as Al Yaman Sq), Sat-Thu 0800-1900. For stamps, poste restante, etc go to the 1st floor. DHL have an office on Seif al-Dawlah St, opposite the post office. **Telephone** The telephone office is on the corner of Al-Moutanabby and Seif al-Dawlah St, open daily 0800-2300. There are 4 card-phones inside. When the desk selling phonecards is closed there is always at least one tout offering them for a small mark-up. **Visa Extensions** The Passport and Immigration Office is just to the northeast of Al-Jumhouriah Sq. The sign on the building reads 'Brancne Des Passeportes in Lattakia'. Open Sat-Thu 0800-1400 (though the 'big chief' doesn't get there until 0900 at the earliest). You need a grand total of 6 passport photos and bring a letter from your hotel as it's sometimes asked for. You will be sent to-ing and fro-ing between the 2nd and 3rd floors in order to accumulate all the necessary paperwork. Otherwise, it's reasonably efficient and you should get your extension within an hour or so.

Contents

Footprint features

Aleppo isn't for the shy or squeamish. As brash and bawdy as Damascus is demure, this city is a total assault on your senses. From the labyrinthine souqs of the Old City, the pungent aromas of spices, cheese and blood from the butcher stalls' carcasses rise up in the afternoon heat. Shoppers jostle for space on the cobblestone alleyways, dodging bicycles, carts and diesel-spewing pickups piled precariously high with goods. The Old City is no dusty old relic, but a functioning commercial hub where past and present blend into one.

Sitting high and mighty above it all is Aleppo's citadel; a colossal structure that once provided the main defence of the city. Its elaborate throne room, hammams and palace remains, a reminder of the time when the military might of the Arabic Muslim empires were at their zenith.

When all the heat and noise get too much, head to the Jdaide Quarter; home to Aleppo's Armenian population. Here, the pace of life slows down considerably. Behind the high stone walls that frame the narrow lanes are lavishly decorated architectural gems of the Ottoman era, some of which have been restored to their former glory.

Outside the city, in the surrounding limestone hills, are the lonely tumbledown ruins of the Dead Cities – eerie, overgrown reminders of Byzantium's long hold over the region, now just forgotten rocks, among which shepherds graze their sheep.

Aleppo

Except for the museum (in the town centre) and the Citadel, Aleppo's main sights are all concentrated inside the ancient quarters of the Old City and the Jdaide Quarter. Most of the sights here have no admission charge as the khans and monuments within the city are not museum pieces, but buildings that are still fully utilized by merchants and businesses today.
▸▸ For listings, see pages 226-232.

Ins and outs

Getting there and away
Aleppo has frequent bus and decent train services to Damascus and the northern centres in Syria, as well as connections to Turkey and Lebanon. The various microbus stations, spread over the city, service the smaller towns in the surrounding area.

The airport is 10 km to the east of Aleppo, off the main highway to Raqqa and Deir ez-Zor. It mainly deals with domestic flights to Damascus but there are also direct international flights to a number of European and Middle Eastern cities. A taxi from the airport to the centre of town should cost around S£300.

In an effort to ease the city's congestion problems, all intercity buses now arrive and depart from the Al-Ramousah bus station, an inconvenient 8 km out of town. There are frequent services from here to Damascus and all major centres north of the capital, and there's usually no need to pre-book. A taxi from here to Aleppo centre is about S£100. There is talk of changing the location of this bus station yet again, so always ask your hotel for up-to-date information. The international (Karnak) bus station is in the town centre on Al-Maari Street. Buses and share taxis from Antakya (in Turkey) arrive here, as well as from Lebanon.

The train station (known as Baghdad Station) is situated at the end of Baghdad Street, one block after the park, about 2 km from Aleppo town centre. There are a few services a day from Lattakia and Damascus and daily services from the towns in the east: Deir ez-Zor, Hassakeh and Qameshli, as well as a twice-weekly service to Turkey. It has an extremely helpful information desk with English-speaking staff. To walk from the station to the centre of town, from the exit walk straight down Baghdad Street. After one block, cross the intersection with a park on your right-hand side. Walk straight ahead and turn right into Majd al-Din al-Jabri Street (keeping the park on your right-hand side at all times). After about 1km the park ends and you arrive at Kouwatly Square. A taxi from the train station to the centre will cost approximately S£40.

Getting around
Aleppo is reasonably compact and best explored on foot. Should you need them, there is no shortage of taxis prowling the streets of Aleppo. Fares should not exceed S£30 for journeys within the centre. Aleppo's chaotic extensive local bus system is best avoided. If you do decide to give it a go the main terminal for local buses is the City Bus Station off Bab Antakya Street.

Orientation
The citadel and the Great Mosque, at the heart of the Old City, are Aleppo's most important landmarks. Running east-west between the citadel and Bab Antakya Street are

the main souqs, with Bab Antakya Street and its accompanying line of Mamluk city walls marking the western limits of the old city.

To the northwest of this is the main 'downtown' area of the modern city, where you will find the museum, the tourist office, the post and telephone office, many cheap restaurants, and the majority of the cheaper hotels. Taking its name from the hotel, Baron Street, running north-south, is the main focus for travel agents and airline offices.

To the north of the citadel the northern limits of the old city are marked by the modern Al-Khandak Street (unlike Damascus, Aleppo's old city area is no longer clearly delineated; only along its western side do the city walls still survive). To the north of Al-Khandak Street is the Jdaide quarter, where most of Aleppo's Christian population lives and works.

Tourist information

Tourist office ① *opposite National Museum, Baron St, T021-222 1200, 0830-2400.* The friendly staff here can supply you with the usual free maps, but have little else in the way of useful information. The Tourist Police are based in the same building. **Note** If you have your own vehicle, you can park it in the parking area in front of the tourist office. This is where campervans often seem to end up staying.

Background

Earliest stages

Like Damascus, clues to the earliest stages of Aleppo's history come only from written records, the continuous layers of settlement since then having buried almost all archaeological evidence under a living city, which still thrives and grows. The earliest references to the city (then known as *Halab*) come from Hittite archives of the second millennium BC found at Mari and at sites on the Anatolian plateau. At that time Aleppo was the centre of the powerful Amorite kingdom of **Yamkhad**, which counted Ugarit and Ebla (both of which were by that time in decline) amongst its vassal states, although its exact relationship with the Amorite (or Babylonian) Empire of Hammurabi remains uncertain.

Hittites

Amorite rule in northern Syria gradually succumbed to pressure from the Hurrians and Mitannians from the northeast and east, and from the Hittites of the Anatolian plateau to the north. It was the **Hittites** who eventually held sway in northern Syria. Aleppo was probably made a vassal state during the 17th century BC under their ruler Hattusilis, and then in the early years of the 16th century BC his successor Mursilis I went on to overthrow Hammurabi's Empire. During the following centuries Aleppo was for a time controlled by the **Hurrians** and **Mitannians**, while also briefly coming under the control of the Egyptians following the campaigns of the Pharaoh Thutmosis III (1490-36 BC). Around 1370 BC the Hittites, under the leadership of Suppiluliuma, once again took control of the city.

Assyrians, Babylonians and Seleucids

Soon afterwards, around 1200 BC, the Hittite Empire crumbled in the face of the invasion of the so-called **Sea Peoples**. In the aftermath of the destruction they wrought, small fragmented centres of **neo-Hittite** (or Syro-Hittite) power re-emerged, one of them centred on Aleppo. The absence of any centralized power in Syria created a vacuum that was eventually filled in the ninth century BC by the rising **Assyrian** Empire to the east. Aleppo was at first able to maintain partial independence as a vassal state, but was later totally subjugated by the Assyrian king Tiglath Pileser III (744-727 BC). The Assyrians were overthrown by the **neo-Babylonians** in 612 BC, and they in turn by the **Achaemenid Persians** following the capture of Babylon in 539 BC. The Persians ruled until the defeat of their king Darius at the hands of **Alexander the Great** in the battle of Issus in 333 BC. Following Alexander's death in 323 BC, Aleppo became part of the **Seleucid** Empire of Seleucus Nicator. A new city, named *Beroia*, was founded here and enjoyed a certain degree of prosperity thanks to its proximity to the Seleucid capital, Antioch.

Romans and Byzantines

Following the Roman conquest of Syria in 64 BC, Aleppo remained under **Roman** and **Byzantine** rule for the next six centuries. This period was one of relative stability, and although Aleppo was somewhat eclipsed by the rise of new trade routes through Palmyra to the south and Cyrrhus to the north, it nevertheless thrived, most notably as a centre for the export of olive oil, the Romans having established highly productive olive groves in the limestone hills to the north and west. It also served as an important military outpost guarding Rome's northern borders. Aleppo's earliest surviving monument dates from this period, in the form of the fourth-century **Cathedral of St Helena**, subsequently converted into a *madrassa* (the Madrassa Halawiye).

Rise of Islam

With the decline of Byzantine power in the late sixth to early seventh century AD, Aleppo suffered heavily at the hands of the **Sassanid Persians** who sacked the city, though it was subsequently retaken by the Byzantines for a brief period before falling in AD 637 to the **Muslim** Arab forces of Khalid Ibn al-Walid. Located on the peripheries of the Islamic Empire, it was eclipsed somewhat by Damascus, which soon became the seat of the Umayyad Dynasty, and later by Baghdad, seat of the Abbasid Dynasty. Instead, the city established a certain measure of independence under its own local dynasties, breaking away from the Abbasids in the 10th century to became the centre of the **Hamdanid** Dynasty, founded by a tribe of Arab refugees from Iraq. Under the leadership of Saif ud-Daula (AD 944-967) the Hamdanids waged war energetically against the Byzantines, prompting them to retaliate and leading to the sacking of Aleppo in AD 962, and again in AD 969. In 1017 the **Fatimids** of Cairo briefly extended their influence north to include Aleppo, but by 1023 the city had once again achieved a certain degree of independence under the **Mirdasids**, a nomadic Arab tribe whose rule lasted until 1079 and depended on maintaining a delicate diplomatic balance between Fatimid and Byzantine interests.

Seljuk Turks and Crusaders

In the meantime, the **Seljuk Turks**, began to make their presence felt in northern Syria. They took control of Aleppo in 1070, leaving it at first to be ruled as a vassal state by the Mirdasids but later installing their own Seljuk rulers. The rise to power of the Seljuks and the threat they posed to the Byzantine Empire prompted the First Crusade. Having taken Antioch in 1098, the **Crusaders** went on to surround Aleppo, cutting it off from its agricultural land and severing its trade links with the Mediterranean, although they failed to take the city itself. It again came under attack in 1124 from the Crusader forces of Jocelyn of Edessa and was only saved when the Seljuk ruler of Mosul, Bursuqi, sent a relieving force in response to the entreaties of Ibn al-Khashab, the *qadi* of Aleppo. Bursuqi incorporated Aleppo into his realm and his son, Zengi, established the **Zengid** Dynasty; under his rule (1128-1146), and that of his son Nur ud-Din (1146-1174), Aleppo became a focus for resistance to the Crusaders.

After years of neglect the city also experienced something of a renaissance, with lots of new construction being undertaken, most notably in the form of *madrassas* (religious schools) which were established in an attempt to restore Sunni orthodoxy in the face of the various heresies which prevailed at the time, particularly the Assassins (see box, page 154) who had been welcomed in Aleppo by its former ruler Ridwan.

Salah ud-Din's success

Nur ud-Din's son Al Salih ruled the city until his death in 1183 and was succeeded by **Salah ud-Din** who had by that time overthrown the Fatimid Caliphate in Cairo and established the **Ayyubid** Dynasty which was at last able to fully unite the Muslim world against the Crusader threat. His son Al-Zaher Ghazi ruled the city from 1193-1215. During his reign, most of the Citadel's existing fortifications were built, while the city flourished, establishing an international trading reputation through the signing of a number of treaties with Venice which allowed Europeans direct access to Muslim markets without having to go through the Crusader states along the coast.

Mongols and Mamluks

However, Aleppo was not able to withstand the new threat which came from the north in the form of the **Mongols**, who sacked the city in 1260. Although the **Mamluks** quickly moved into Syria from their base at Cairo to drive back the Mongols, Aleppo remained largely forsaken at the northern extremities of their empire and it was not until the 14th century, when it became a base for Mamluk campaigns against the Armenians, that any attempts were made at repairing the destruction that the Mongols had caused. Even then, it was only in the 15th century, after the second Mongol invasion of 1400, that it began to regain its former wealth, with the trade routes which had been diverted to the north via the Black Sea and Cilicia once again being directed through Aleppo.

Ottoman rule and the French Mandate

In 1516 Aleppo became part of the **Ottoman** Empire and continued to flourish as a centre of trade. The souqs and khans for which the city is famous nearly all date from the late Mamluk and early Ottoman period, with the British, French and Dutch setting up office in the city alongside the Venetians under a series of 'capitulation' treaties. The European presence in the city also ensured a special position for the various local Christian communities, who became important intermediaries for the merchants in carrying out their trade, and under the capitulations enjoyed a protected status. By the 18th century, however, Aleppo's fortunes were beginning to decline in the face of continuing competition from the new sea route to China and India, as well as routes through the Persian Gulf, Red Sea and across Russia. Apart from a brief spell from 1831-1840 when it became part of Ibrahim Pasha's breakaway state, Aleppo remained under Ottoman rule until the collapse of their empire at the end of the First World War. Aleppo's Armenian community, which had been growing steadily in the last decade of the 19th century as a result of the brutal suppression of Armenian nationalism elsewhere in the Ottoman Empire, saw a massive influx when that repression degenerated into full-scale genocide during the First World War, and today the strong Armenian presence remains a distinctive feature of the city.

In the early years of French Mandate rule, Aleppo (like Damascus) was made the capital of an independent mini-state, although this arrangement only lasted for three years. By the time full independence came in 1945, the French had given much of the old Ottoman province of Aleppo to Turkey. This created great animosity between the two countries and resulted in a severing of the city's historically strong cultural and economic links with the Turks.

Modern Aleppo
Although now cut off from its traditional Mediterranean outlet of Antakya (ancient Antioch, now lying inside Turkey), Aleppo's historic function as a trading city still continues. Nowadays it is traders from the various states of the former Soviet Union who descend upon the city to buy up the textiles for which it is famous. These groups of traders are a prominent feature of Aleppo; frequently taking over whole hotels in the downtown area and stacking their lobbies full of huge packaged bales to be loaded onto buses and trucks for the journey home.

Walking the fine line between modernization and preserving the city's historical fabric has been Aleppo's biggest issue in recent years. Ongoing migration from rural areas in the past 50 years has seen the city's population explode. This migration led to many wealthier inhabitants abandoning the overcrowded Old City for the newly built suburbs outside; leaving their houses either empty or rented to poor tenants who couldn't afford to maintain them. Also, up to the 1970s the government's zeal to modernize led to haphazard demolition of parts of the city. Both these factors threatened to destroy Aleppo's rich cultural heritage.

Since then serious efforts have been made to preserve the area. In 1986 Aleppo's Old City was declared a UNESCO World Heritage Site and in 1994 a project to rehabilitate and develop the Old City was born. This project (still ongoing, see box, page 225) is slowly succeeding in revitalizing Aleppo's oldest areas and ensuring that the city's wealth of history is preserved for generations to come.

Aleppo Citadel
① Al-Qala'a St, T021-326 4010, Wed-Mon 0900-1800 summer, 0900-1600 winter, S£150, students S£10.
Dominating the centre of Aleppo is the citadel, its steep-sided, artificial-looking mound rising abruptly to a height of more than 50 m above the maze of surrounding souqs and streets. Unusually for Syria, although the sides have been shaped over the centuries to give them their uniform slope, this is not an artificial tell (or *mound*) formed from the accumulated debris of successive settlements, but is a natural feature.

Background
To date, the earliest evidence of settlement on the citadel mound comes in the form of two lions carved out of basalt rock dating from the neo-Hittite period (10th century BC), perhaps remnants of a temple. During the Seleucid period, the mound was used for defensive purposes and a citadel established here, along with the new town of *Beroia*. At the same time, a pre-existing temple to the local god Hadad was dedicated to the Greek equivalent, Zeus. Little is known about the site in subsequent centuries, although there is evidence of Byzantine occupation in the form of cisterns and a church, later incorporated into a mosque. It is also known that the Byzantine emperor Julian the Apostate came here to offer sacrifices to the god Zeus in the fourth century, suggesting that the temple still existed, despite the adoption of Christianity as the official religion. In the 10th century AD the Hamdanid ruler Saif ud-Daula built a royal palace on the mound and from then on it

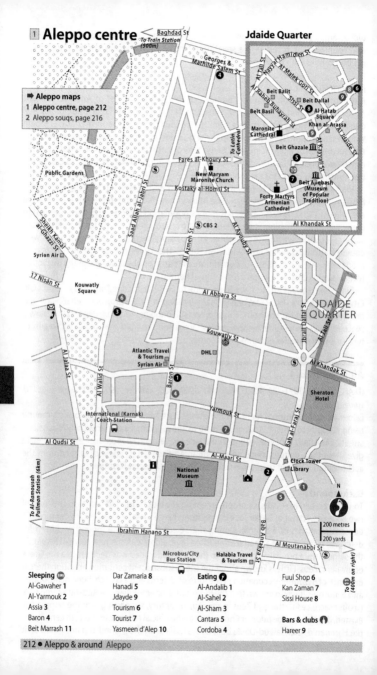

Baghdad St
To Train Station (500m)

Georges & Mathilde Salem St

➡ Aleppo maps
1 Aleppo centre, page 212
2 Aleppo souqs, page 216

Al Tall St
Nayya al-Hamidien St
Al Malek Gori St
Beit Balit
Beit Dallal
Al Raheb Bizhayran St
Sissi St
Beit Basil
Al Hatab Square
Khan al-Arassa
Maronite Cathedral
Al Kayyali St
Al Jdaide St
Beit Ghazale
Beit Ajiqbash (Museum of Popular Tradition)
Forty Martyrs Armenian Cathedral

Public Gardens

Fares al-Khoury St

To Latin Cathedral

New Maryam Maronite Church
Kostaky al-Homsi St

Al Khandak St

CBS 2
Al Azmeh St
Al Ayoubly St

Syrian Air

17 Nisan St

Sheikh Kamal al-Ghazzi St

Kouwatly Square

Al Abbara St

JDAIDE QUARTER

Kouwatly St

Atlantic Travel & Tourism
DHL
Syrian Air

Ibrail Daltal St
Al Tall St

Al Khandak St

Al Jalaa St

Al Walid St

Baron St

Sheraton Hotel

Yarmouk St

International (Karnak) Coach Station

Al Qudsi St

Al-Maari St

National Museum

Bab al-Faraj St
Bab Antakya
Clock Tower
Library

To Al-Ramouseh Pullman Station (6km)

Ibrahim Hanano St

N

200 metres
200 yards

Microbus/City Bus Station
Halabia Travel & Tourism

Al Moutanabbi St

To (400m on right)

Sleeping		Eating	
Al-Gawaher 1	Dar Zamaria 8	Al-Andalib 1	Fuul Shop 6
Al-Yarmouk 2	Hanadi 5	Al-Sahel 2	Kan Zaman 7
Assia 3	Jdayde 9	Al-Sham 3	Sissi House 8
Baron 4	Tourism 6	Cantara 5	
Beit Marrash 11	Tourist 7	Cordoba 4	Bars & clubs
	Yasmeen d'Alep 10		Hareer 9

was occupied continuously. The most striking features of the Citadel today – the encircling moat, stone *glacis* and imposing entrance bridge and monumental gateway – all date from the Ayyubid period, during the reign of Salah ud-Din's son, Al-Zaher Ghazi. Following the Mongol invasions of 1260 and 1400, the Citadel underwent extensive repairs. During the Mamluk period it ceased to fulfil such an important defensive function, and was used instead as the governor's residence and barracks for troops.

Outer defences

The Citadel is most imposing from the outside. The stone cladding of the steep-sided (48 °) *glacis* only survives in places, but coupled with the deep (22 m) encircling moat it gives a good idea of just how impregnable it would have appeared to any attacker. By far the most impressive feature overall is the sole entrance to the Citadel, consisting of an outer defensive tower followed by an entrance bridge leading up to a monumental gateway, the 20 m high **outer defensive tower** dates from 1211. After passing through this tower, the **entrance bridge** ascends up towards the monumental gateway, eight arches supporting it as it spans the moat.

The **monumental gateway** provides the crowning glory of this defensive ensemble, a solid and imposing rectangular tower of such massive proportions that it is practically a citadel in its own right. Either side of the tall and deeply recessed arched entrance is a series of box machicolations and above these an upper storey (representing the throne room, see below). The gateway which Al-Zaher Ghazi built originally consisted of two towers which rose to the level of the machicolations. Following the first Mongol attack of 1260, the Mamluk sultan Al-Ashraf Khalil carried out extensive repairs, commemorated in a long band of Arabic inscription just below the machicolations. The inscription praises the sultan in typically effusive terms as, "*lord of kings and sultans, champion of justice throughout the universe, the Alexander of his time, conqueror of capitals, he who put to flight the Frankish, Armenian and Mongol armies, and gave new strength to the glorious Abbasid Dynasty ...*"

In the early 16th century the gateway was further modified with the upper-storey throne room being added, so joining the two towers together. The gateway consists of a passage which passes through no less than five turnings and three doors before giving access to the inside of the citadel. The first door is placed on the right inside the recessed arched entrance to prevent would-be attackers from using battering rams on it. Above it are two twin-headed serpents, their bodies intertwined in knotted coils. The doors themselves are of solid iron, reinforced with heavy studs and decorated with horseshoe and arrow-head motifs. The next two doors have carved lions, one pair facing each other on the lintel above, the next pair facing to the front and flanking the door on either side. These were believed to be imbued with magical powers aiding the defence of the citadel. The successive right-angled turnings were of more practical use in slowing the momentum of any attacker. After the last of the turnings, a rising passage takes you past various rooms, probably used as barracks and stables.

The palace and baths From the monumental gateway, a street leads north across the top of the hill. On the right, immediately after you exit the monumental gateway, is a series of doors. The fourth doorway gives access to a chamber with a narrow passage at the end, and steps leading down to a large vaulted and pillared chamber, from where more steps (steep and uneven) lead down to another chamber. These chambers are thought to be of Byzantine origin, and to have been used as a prison and a storage room, and at a later date possibly also as a water cistern. Back on the street, a set of stairs on the right (immediately after the doorway leading to the underground chambers) doubles back and up towards the extensive remains of the **Ayyubid Palace**, built by the Ayyubid ruler Al Aziz in 1230, but destroyed by the Mongols 30 years later. The partially restored entrance to the palace consists of a striking doorway with beautiful honeycombing rising to a small conch shell semi-dome, and a surround of alternating bands of black and cream stone carved with geometric patterns. Built onto the palace (towards the rear) is a large Mamluk-period **baths complex** which has been extensively restored.

If you continue past the entrance to the Ayyubid Palace you can gain access, via a courtyard, to the Mamluk **throne room**, which occupies the upper floor of the monumental gateway by which you first entered the Citadel. The entrance to the throne room is particularly impressive, with a stalactited semi-dome and a surround of alternating bands of black and cream stone.

This provides a suitably grand introduction to the throne room itself, a huge square room which has been immaculately restored to its former glory. The lavishly and intricately carved and painted wooden ceiling is particularly impressive. Four pillars support a central square, which in turn supports an octagonal drum with three panels of stained glass in each face of the octagon. Hanging from the centre is a large inlaid wood chandelier, and on the floor below a small fountain. The entire floor is paved with marble in intricate geometric patterns, while the lower parts of the walls are adorned with wooden panels similarly carved with geometric designs. In the right-hand corner, stairs lead down to a series of vaulted chambers with more holes in the floors for pouring oil onto attackers, and access to arrow slits overlooking the approach to the monumental gateway. (You can descend all the way down to the passageway leading through the monumental gateway if you wish.)

Returning to the courtyard at the main entrance to the throne room, there is a set of stairs leading to the **upper battlements**. From here you can get an excellent overview of the layout of the citadel to the north. There is no railing on the inside edge, however, and it is a long drop down into the courtyard, making it a definite no-go for vertigo sufferers.

Along the citadel's main street

Returning to the main street and following it north, on the left is another **baths complex** which has been fully restored. Opposite the main entrance to these baths, a cobbled path with a channel running down the centre leads off to the right. This takes you to a large **amphitheatre**, an entirely modern concrete structure erected in the 1970s. Back on the main street, a little further up, on the left, is the small **Mosque of Abraham**, so called after the legend that this was the spot where Abraham used to milk his cow (see box, page 215). The mosque was built by Nur ud-Din in 1167 on the site of an earlier church, two columns of which are preserved inside the prayer hall, on the north wall. According to local legend, this church was also one of the many supposed resting places for John the Baptist's head (see also the Umayyad Mosque in Damascus, page 50).

A little further up past the Mosque of Abraham, to the right of the main street, is a deep area of ongoing **excavations** being carried out by a Syrian-German team. The excavations have uncovered the foundations of a temple dating back to the ninth century BC. There is not as yet that much to see of the temple itself, but the different types of stonework at various levels, from huge stone blocks towards the bottom to smaller ones higher up, are graphically displayed.

At the end of the main street, on the left, is the **Great Mosque of the Citadel**, built by the Ayyubid Sultan Al-Zaher Ghazi in 1214. Much of what you see today is a

A town called milk

At bus stations throughout the country you'll hear the touts shouting out 'Halab, Halab, Halab'. No, you haven't missed a major town on the map; they're actually announcing a bus going to Aleppo. Halab is the local name for Syria's second city and although its ancient origin is obscure, there's a local legend that may explain its source.

'Halab' is the Arabic word for 'milk' and it's said that Abraham (the prophet that Jews, Christians and Muslims all trace the roots of their faith too) once lived in what is now Aleppo and would give weary travellers passing through milk from his cow to sustain them on their trip.

Whether or not this is how Aleppo became known as Halab we'll never know, but at least you'll know where that bus is going next time the touts start shouting.

reconstruction, though in places you can still see patches of the original stonework. The mosque is in fact quite small, but beautifully proportioned and has a quietly understated simplicity about it which somehow adds to the overall effect. Inside is a courtyard with a tiny central fountain and three fir trees, and surrounding the courtyard on three sides is an arcade. The prayer hall occupies the fourth side, and aside from the *mihrab* is adorned only with a dome in the ceiling, supported on an octagonal drum with a window in each face. In the northeast corner of the mosque is a square minaret.

To the east of the mosque (to the right of the path where it ends, as you face to the north) is a long rectangular building which served as a **barracks**. This dates from 1839 and was built by Ibrahim Pasha, son of Muhammad Ali, both Ottoman commanders who between them briefly challenged the might of the Ottoman Empire, ruling over Syria for a time. The building today houses a **café** with a terrace which occupies a section of the ramparts of the citadel, offering great views out over Aleppo.

South of the citadel

There are a number of interesting monuments to the south of the Citadel which can be visited as a leisurely walking tour. None of them are dramatically spectacular, but they provide some interesting insights into Aleppo's medieval architecture, as well as offering the opportunity to get away from the main tourist trail.

Just to the south of the entrance to the citadel is the **Madrassa as-Sultaniye** (also known as the Madrassa Zahiriye), with a small green in front of it. Building work on this *madrassa* was started by Al-Zaher Ghazi and completed around 1225 by his son Al Aziz. A squat octagonal minaret rises directly above the entrance, while inside, in the centre of the courtyard, are four tall palm trees. The *mihrab* in the prayer hall is particularly fine, decorated with beautifully delicate inlaid marble patterns. A small side room contains the tombs of Al-Zaher Ghazi and other members of his family.

Behind (to the south of) the Khan ash-Shouna, meanwhile, is the **Khusuwiye Mosque**. Dating from 1537, this was the first Ottoman building to be erected in Aleppo, its distinctive rocket-shaped minaret typically Turkish in style. The man responsible for its construction was none other than Sinan Pasha, architect of the Tekkiyeh as-Suleimaniyeh Mosque in Damascus (see page 65) and, most famously, of the Suleimaniye Mosque in Istanbul.

The street leading east just to the south of the Madrassa as-Sultaniye brings you to the **Al-Utrush Mosque**. This 15th-century mosque was started in 1403 by the emir Aq Bogha al-Utrushi who, in a typically Mamluk tradition, intended it to act also as his mausoleum. It was completed by his successor Emir Damir Dash. The main entrance façade of the mosque in particular is lavishly decorated.

Taking the main road heading southwest from the Al-Utrush Mosque, go straight across a mini-roundabout, then past the 14th-century Al-Tawashi Mosque on the right, its windows flanked by slender colonettes, to arrive after around 500 m at the **Bab al-Maqam**. This southern gate of the Old City was first built by Al-Zaher Ghazi towards the end of the 12th century, and later rebuilt during the reign of the Mamluk sultan Qait Bey in 1493. Today this remnant of the old city stands rather isolated and forlorn-looking amidst the surrounding modern developments and roads.

Just under 1 km further to the southwest of Bab al-Maqam is the **Madrassa Faradis**, which manages to retain a wonderful overall atmosphere of antiquity and tranquillity, and is well worth the extra detour to reach it. Take the small road leading southwest from the square across the road from Bab al-Maqam (not the main road leading due south). Arriving at a fork, bear right along the road which passes through a cemetery on either side, then take the first left turn along a cobbled street and the *madrassa* is around 50 m down this street, on the right. The Madrassa Faradis (literally 'School of Paradise'), was built in 1234-1247 by the widow of Al-Zaher Ghazi, Daifa Khatun, who was also both the niece and daughter-in-law of Salah ud-Din. The simple honeycombed entrance leads through to the main courtyard with a central pool surrounded on three sides by an arcade supported on slender columns of classical origin. The prayer hall, on the south side of the

② Aleppo souqs

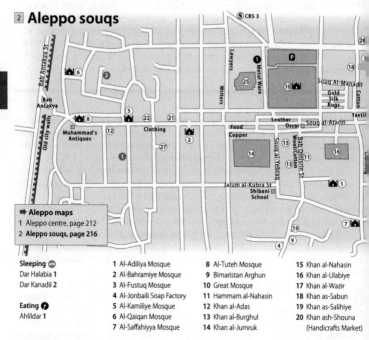

➡ **Aleppo maps**
1 Aleppo centre, page 212
2 **Aleppo souqs, page 216**

Sleeping 😊
Dar Halabia **1**
Dar Kanadil **2**

Eating 🍴
Ahlildar **1**

1 Al-Adiliya Mosque
2 Al-Bahramiye Mosque
3 Al-Fustuq Mosque
4 Al-Jonbaili Soap Factory
5 Al-Kamiliye Mosque
6 Al-Qaiqan Mosque
7 Al-Saffahiyya Mosque

8 Al-Tuteh Mosque
9 Bimaristan Arghun
10 Great Mosque
11 Hammam al-Nahasin
12 Khan al-Adas
13 Khan al-Burghul
14 Khan al-Jumruk

15 Khan al-Nahasin
16 Khan al-Ulabiye
17 Khan al-Wazir
18 Khan as-Sabun
19 Khan as-Salihiye
20 Khan ash-Shouna
(Handicrafts Market)

courtyard, has a triple-domed ceiling and boasts a particularly elegantly decorated *mihrab* with geometric designs of different coloured marble. At either end of the prayer hall are rooms containing the tombs of Muslim saints. On the opposite side of the courtyard to the prayer hall is a large arched *iwan*. Behind this is a vaulted hall (restored in recent years), which was the *madrassa's* original school room.

Souqs and khans of the Old City

When you explore Aleppo's souqs you are plunging into a world which lies at the heart of the city's very existence. The medieval maze of narrow alleyways, covered over with stone vaulting, are wonderfully atmospheric; the tiny shops trading in a bewildering array of traditional goods and wares, with only the occasional tourist-orientated handicrafts or antiques shop. With their stone vaulting, the souqs are blissfully cool and shaded in the fierce heat of summer, and protected to some extent against the rain and cold in winter. The variety of sights, sounds and smells, meanwhile, is fascinating, as is the sheer diversity of peoples – Arab, Turkish, Armenian, Kurdish, Iranian – all drawn to what is one of the great commercial crossroads of the Middle East.

While the rest of the week is hectic, on Fridays the souqs are closed and completely deserted, with metal roller-blinds pulled down over all the shops. An eerie silence replaces the usual bustle, broken only by occasional gangs of kids whizzing through on their bicycles.

21 Khan at-Tutun al-Kabir
22 Khan at-Tutun as Saghir
23 Khan Khayr Bey
24 Khusuwiye Mosque
25 Madrassa al-Halawiyya
26 Madrassa as-Sultaniye
27 Madrassa Muqaddamiye
28 Matbakh al-Ajami

Background

The main souq, known as **Souq al-Atarin** runs east-west between the Citadel and Bab Antakya, with smaller ones running parallel in places, and perpendicular branches to the north and south at regular intervals. This grid pattern of streets is believed to reflect the much earlier plan of the Hellenistic town established by the Seleucids in the fourth to third century BC, with Souq al-Atarin corresponding roughly with the later Roman *decumanus*. In their present form the earliest parts of the souqs date from the 13th century, although for the most part they were built by the Ottomans from the 16th century onwards. The great khans (or caravanserais) which are to be found amongst the souqs soon came to be occupied by the European traders who were drawn to the city. The Venetians were the first to arrive, in the 13th century, but within a few hundred years the English, French, Belgians and Dutch had all established themselves here.

Touring the souqs

① *If you would like to enter any of the mosques described in the tour below, dress modestly (long sleeves and long trousers/skirts) and women must wear a headscarf before entering.*

The main 'heart' of the souqs is to the south and east of the Great Mosque, and this is one place from where you can conveniently enter them, following the small alleys that lead south from Jamia al-Ayyoubi St on either side of the mosque. For the purposes of this description, however, the souqs are followed from east to west, heading from the Citadel towards Bab Antakya, with detours off to the north and south to visit important places of interest en route.

The northeast quarter Heading clockwise around the citadel from its entrance (back towards Jamia al-Ayyoubi Street), a small arched entrance on the left, signposted 'Al-Madina Souq' marks the point of entry into the souqs. This first section (known in fact as Souq al-Zarb) sells mainly materials for Bedouin tents, before giving way to shops selling all manner of fabrics and clothing. Taking the first available right turn brings you to the entrance to the **Khan Khayr Bey**, on the right. This khan, with its entrance gateway of black and white stone, dates from 1514, shortly before the Mamluks were swept from power by the Ottomans. It is now entirely given over to shops selling fabrics. The stretch of souq running past the entrance to the khan has been carefully restored to show off the domes in the roof to their full effect.

Returning to the main souq and continuing west, you soon arrive at a crossroads. Turning right here, you arrive at a dog-leg at a point where the covered vaulting of the souq ends. Here the elaborately decorated (though unfortunately largely obscured) entrance to the **Khan al-Sabun**, or 'soap khan' faces you. This building dates from the late 15th to early 16th century, and is an excellent example of Aleppo's Mamluk architecture. Inside, the khan today houses a variety of different businesses. Aside from the large rectangular building dominating the courtyard (a later addition), most of the architectural features of the khan are original, with some minor modifications here and there. The overall effect is actually quite picturesque, the courtyard still has its original cobblestones, and overhead vines provide some shade.

Back at the crossroads on the main souq, if you head south, just after the covered souq ends, on the right is the entrance to an attractively restored khan which today houses a couple of tourist-orientated antiques/handicrafts shops. This khan actually forms part of the Al-Adiliye Mosque (see below), bordering the east side of its courtyard; it is possible to enter the mosque via a passageway just to the south of the khan (take the next doorway on the right after the khan). Further on, on the right, is the **Al-Saffahiyya Mosque**. This mosque dates from 1425 and is decorated with alternating bands of black and white stone in typical Mamluk fashion, while the octagonal minaret is adorned with richly carved decoration.

Returning to the main souq and continuing west, the next right turn leads up to Jamia al-Ayyoubi Street along the east wall of the Great Mosque. This street is given over to silks and fabrics. Leading off it to the right at regular intervals is a series of tiny streets, the first couple selling carpets and rugs, while the next few form the heart of the brightly lit and affluent **gold souq**.

The southeast quarter Back on the main souq (now **Souq al-Atarin**, the 'Spices Souq'), the next left turn takes you down to Bab Qinisrin Street, passing several interesting monuments en route. A short distance down on the left is the **Hammam al-Nahasin**.

Directly opposite is the entrance to the **Khan al-Nahasin** (literally 'Khan of the Coppersmiths'). This was the warehouse and consul of the Venetians from 1539. The building on the south side of the courtyard is the **Old Consulate Residence** ① *open by appointment only, contact the Belgian consulate, T021-362 2666*, that was lived in by Adolphe Poche, who was born here in 1895 and served as the consul of Austria-Hungary, Austria, the Netherlands and Belgium in turn. Adolphe Poche was a keen historian and archaeologist who amassed an impressive collection of antiques and archaeological artefacts which are still preserved within the building.

Continuing south, a small alleyway off to the left brings you to the **Al-Adiliya Mosque**, built in the mid-16th century by the Ottoman governor of Aleppo, Muhammad Pasha. This is easily the most beautiful mosque in Aleppo, and it is also wonderfully tranquil, with its tree-lined courtyard far from the intruding noise of traffic. Two lines of columns and arches support a portico in front of the prayer hall, the inner arcade marked by a series of small domes. The main doorway to the mosque is particularly richly and finely executed, as are the blue and white glazed tiles in the arches above the windows, with their delicate foliate designs and Qur'anic calligraphy. Inside, a huge central dome dominates the prayer hall and the tile work is repeated, while above the *mihrab* is a panel of very beautiful stained glass.

Keep walking south along Qinisrin Streeet to the next intersection. Just to your right is the **Shibani School** ① *Jalum al-Kubra St, Wed-Mon 0900-1600, free*, which in the 19th century housed a Franciscan order school that educated some of Syria's most important literary and political figures. This grand old complex decayed due to neglect in the 20th century but has been fully restored as part of The Project for the Rehabilitation of The Old City of Aleppo (see box, page 225). It now houses a permanent exhibition on the project within the building. The friendly guide Mustafa is happy to show you around.

Walk the few metres back to the corner and continue south along Bab Qinisrin. After following the street through a dog-leg (here you pass the Ottoman-period **Khan as-Salihiye**), you arrive at the **Bimaristan Arghun** on the left. Originally a private house, this building was converted into a mental asylum in 1354 by the Mamluk governor Arghun al-Kamili and was still in use at the beginning of the 20th century. The impressive honeycombed entrance leads through to the main courtyard with a central pool and fountain, surrounded by tiny cells. From the main courtyard, a narrow passageway leads through to three smaller courtyards, again surrounded by cells. There is a display of scary old medical equipment in the cells of one. The atmosphere is one of tranquillity, rather as if this were a *madrassa* of some sort, although the bars on some of the cells and the rings for chaining up the patients hint at a less serene past. Opposite is the **Al-Joubaili Soap Factory**. Although recently fitted out with a new door, inside it remains distinctly un-renovated and is still used as a soap factory. Sacks and boxes of soap, and rusting, empty olive oil barrels are stacked up high in the gloomy vaulted chambers, which are pervaded by the faint aroma of olive oil soap. Continuing along the street, now running south-west, you arrive after 200 m or so at **Bab Qinisrin**, the best preserved of Aleppo's old city gates. Variously dated to the 10th-13th century according to which source you consult, it is known for sure to have been restored in 1501 by the Mamluk governor Qansawh al-Ghawri. Outside the gate, around 200 m to the west, two towers of the old city's defensive walls can be seen; like the gate, in their present form they date to the Mamluk period.

The southwest quarter Returning now to the main Souq al-Atarin and continuing west, you arrive next at the **Khan al-Jumruk** (literally 'Customs Khan', the place where customs duties were levied on goods arriving in Aleppo). This is the largest of Aleppo's khans. Completed in 1574, it accommodated the French, English and Dutch consuls, and also their financial offices. The impressive entrance gateway (on your left as you head west; the vaulting of the souq here is marked by a large dome) is decorated with alternating bands of black and white stone with a patterned surround and an inscription above. Inside, the khan, which covers an area of over 6000 sq m, is still in use, accommodating for the most part fabric wholesalers. Stairs in the passageway leading through to the main courtyard, and in the corners of the courtyard, give access to the balcony running around the first floor; from here you can get a good overview of the khan and look down on the otherwise largely obscured mosque in the centre of the courtyard.

Continuing west, after about 150 m you come to the **Al-Bahramiye Mosque** on the left. Built in 1583 by Ottoman governor of Aleppo, Bahram Pasha, it is particularly notable for its beautifully decorated *mihrab*. The second lane leading off to the left after passing the mosque brings you to the entrance of the **Madrassa Muqaddamiye** on the left. Like the Madrassa Halawiye, this was originally a church before being seized and turned into an Islamic theological school in retaliation for the atrocities carried out by the Crusaders in 1124. The beautifully decorated entry porch is the most striking feature today. The inscription above it is dated to 1168.

The northwest quarter Returning to the main souq, along this final stretch there are a few more khans to be seen, although they are not so interesting. Shortly before arriving at Bab Antakya, you pass the small **Al-Tuteh Mosque** (literally 'Mosque of the Mulberry Tree'). Although rather dilapidated today and not particularly noteworthy, it is believed to stand on the site of the first mosque to be built in Aleppo, in the seventh century. In its present form it is largely an Ayyubid construction, the Kufic inscription and surrounding decoration dating to the late 12th century. Some of the large stone blocks used in its construction are clearly of Roman origin, probably recycled from the Roman triumphal arch which stood on the site of the present Bab Antakya.

A few twists in the lane bring you finally to **Bab Antakya**, in its present form a 13th-century Ayyubid construction, partly utilizing blocks from the original Roman triumphal arch which stood here, and further modified in the 15th century. Rather than exiting it onto the busy thoroughfare of Bab Antakya Street, you can bear off to the right just before, ascending along a beautiful cobbled street which runs along the **Mamluk ramparts** of the old city walls, from where you can look down onto the general chaos below. After around 50 m you pass the small **Al-Qaiqan Mosque**, an early Ottoman period construction which incorporates two ancient basalt columns either side of the entrance. A stone block (now removed) bearing a Hittite inscription from the 14th century BC was found in the wall of this mosque. The higher ground off to the right as you follow the ramparts north is thought to represent the site of the ancient village which existed here and became incorporated into the new city of *Beroia* established by the Seleucids. At the north end of the ramparts you descend into a butchers' souq; turning left brings you out just south of the intersection of Bab Antakya Street with Mutannabi Street.

The Great Mosque

① *Entry from Jamia al-Ayyoubi St, admission free, modest dress is required for admission, non-muslim women must pay S£50 for hire of abeyya (cloak), everyone must remove footwear before entering.*

The Great Mosque of Aleppo (also known as the Umayyad Mosque or the Jami Zakariye) illustrates very well the city's multi-layered history. Founded in the early eighth century AD by the Umayyad caliph Al-Walid, it was built on the grounds of the sixth-century Cathedral of St Helen, itself situated on the site of the Roman and Hellenistic market-place. Towards the end of the 11th century the first Seljuk sultan, Tutush, built the square minaret which still survives today. The rest of the mosque was destroyed by fire in 1169 and subsequently rebuilt by Nur ud-Din, with further extensive modifications carried out by the Mamluks in the 15th century.

Overall, the mosque does not match the grandeur of the Umayyad mosque of Damascus. Nevertheless, the façade of the prayer hall is quite striking, with a series of large arches decorated with wooden lattice-work and an ornate central entrance. The patterning of the worn marble slabs of the courtyard is also quite effective, managing to achieve a certain understated elegance. Inside the prayer hall, the carved wooden *minbar*, dating from the Mamluk period, is particularly beautiful. Immediately to the left of the *mihrab*, in an arched recess protected by a metal grille, the head of Zachariah (the father of John the Baptist) is believed to be interned, hence one of the mosque's alternative names. The minaret rises to a height of 45 m. It represents the oldest part of the mosque and is considered to be amongst the earliest examples of the distinctive Syrian-Islamic architectural style which was later developed by the Ayyubids and Mamluks.

Around the Great Mosque

West of the mosque

Just to the west of the Great Mosque, and directly opposite its west entrance, is the entrance to the **Madrassa Halawiye**. This *madrassa* incorporates the remains of the Cathedral of St Helen. For a long time after the building of the Great Mosque in the grounds of the cathedral, the two institutions are believed to have co-existed harmoniously. However, at some stage after 1124 it was seized and converted into a *madrassa*, allegedly in retaliation for the atrocities committed by the Crusaders against the Muslims when they attacked the city.

Entering the *madrassa*, you find yourself in a rather unassuming courtyard surrounded on three sides by what were originally students' cells. The west wall (opposite you as you enter) has two large arches in it, the left one bricked up, while the right one has been glassed over. A doorway in the glassed-over arch leads into the original prayer hall, notable for its beautifully carved wooden *mihrab*, dating from 1245, during the reign of Nur ud-Din. This hall is generally kept locked, but the caretaker is usually on hand to open it up. A wide range of postcards, as well as some books and pamphlets, are displayed for sale on a table inside.

Returning to the courtyard, a doorway topped by a wooden porch in the left arch leads through into a large hall. The ceiling is dominated by a central dome resting on an octagonal drum. The two arches, which support the dome on the north and south sides, rest on columns topped by ornately carved Corinthian capitals. On the west side, a semi-dome is supported on six columns arranged in a semicircle, the capitals of two of them even more exuberantly carved than the others, with their acanthus leaves curling in different directions as if caught by the wind. This is all that remains of the Cathedral of St Helen, but the beautiful columns and capitals, along with the traces of decoration on the walls, give an inkling of its former splendour.

East of the mosque Heading east (towards the citadel) along Jamia al-Ayyoubi Street from the Great Mosque, after around 150 m you come to a small open square on the right, at the back of which is the **Al-Fustuq Mosque** (literally 'Mosque of the Pistachios'). Built in 1349, this small mosque has been restored in recent years and is now once again fully functional. On the east side of the small square in front of the Al-Fustuq Mosque is the main entrance to the large **Khan al-Wazir**. This dates from the 17th century and is considered to be amongst the most impressive of Aleppo's khans. It is the entrance doorway that is the most striking feature, with its alternating bands of black and white stone and elaborately decorated arched window above the doorway. Note also the two medallions with reliefs of chained lions. Inside, the khan is imposing for its sheer size, with its original and heavily worn cobblestone paving still intact in places. Some carpet sellers have set up shop here, draping the walls and balconies with a colourful selection of old and new rugs from around the Middle East, and beyond.

Jdaide quarter

This district, with its narrow cobbled streets, retains much of its distinctive historic charm and the Maronite and Armenian cathedrals, although relatively recent constructions, are nevertheless fascinating to visit. (Sunday is probably the best day to come, when there is a service in progress, or on one of the many religious festivals days.) In the evenings here, the streets throng with Christian families, bringing with them an ambience worlds away from the atmosphere of Muslim Aleppo. True to the entrepreneurial spirit that spawned this district, it is also here that you can find several excellent restaurants and luxury hotels, set in elegant and stylishly restored houses and palaces dating from the 17th and 18th centuries. Most of these have complexes of underground caves and passages beneath them, dug to provide refuges during times of persecution. According to local tradition, some of these passages once led all the way into the citadel.

Background
The Jdaide Quarter (literally 'New quarter') was developed during the late Mamluk period to accommodate the growing numbers of Christians, mostly Armenian and Maronite, who were drawn to Aleppo by the commercial opportunities it offered for the astute entrepreneur. By the 17th and 18th centuries it had grown into a wealthy district with many elegant houses belonging to prosperous local Christian families. One of these now houses the Museum of Popular Tradition, although it is the architecture of the building itself which is the main attraction.

Visiting the Jdaide Quarter
From the large intersection at the north end of Bab al-Faraj Street, cross Al-Khandak Sreet so that The Sheraton Hotel is opposite you. Follow the small lane that runs east parallel to Al-Khandak Street (the entrance to this lane is around 20 m to the east of the pedestrian street leading northeast from the main intersection). After 100 m or so, a small left turn

brings you to the **Forty Martyrs Armenian Cathedral**. A small church dating from the 15th century originally stood on the site. This was replaced in 1639 by a larger complex, which was in turn partially rebuilt in 1869, then extensively restored in 1950. The interior is well worth a look for the beautiful paintings and icons that adorn the walls. There is also a bookshop and museum in the grounds of the cathedral.

Following the street due east from the cathedral, on the left just before you reach an intersection is the entrance to the **Beit Ajiqbash**, which now houses the **Museum of Popular Tradition** ① *corner Al-Kayyali St, Wed-Mon 0800-1400, S£75, student S£10*. Built in 1757 by the wealthy Christian Ajiqbash family, this is one of the best examples of such houses in Jdaide. In traditional Arab style the building is centred around a large courtyard with a fountain and trees for shade, and a large arched *iwan* in one wall with a richly decorated roof and porch. Combined with the Mamluk-style bands of black and white stone around the doorways in the courtyard, and the exuberant carved stone decoration above the windows, the overall effect is both striking and pleasing. The rooms themselves have elaborately painted ceilings and cornices, and contain displays of old weaponry, inlaid wood furniture, intricately decorated copper pots and plates, jewellery, clothing and some wacky mannequins that lurk in the corners. The large room opposite the arched *iwan* is particularly lavishly decorated throughout. From the courtyard, stairs lead up to the roof, from where there is access to one room containing an eclectic collection of old sewing machines, spinning wheels, a mangle, a press for shaping felt hats, wooden printing blocks and other assorted items.

Turning left into Al-Kayyali Street, to head north at the intersection just to the east of the entrance to the Museum of Popular Tradition, after 40 m (soon after an alleyway leading to Yasmeen d'Alep Hotel) you come to the **Beit Ghazale**. Dating from the 17th century, and once a very grand complex complete with its own hammam, it has in recent years fallen into disrepair and at the time of writing it was closed for restoration as part of the Project for the Rehabilitation of the Old City of Aleppo. Once re-opened (hopefully at some stage in late 2010) it will become a museum.

On the south side of Al-Hatab Square is the **Khan al-Arassa**. Built in 1654, today the most interesting feature of this large khan or caravanserai is the entrance, with its heavy wooden doors and decorated band framing the main archway and the smaller inset arch. Inside, a barrel-vaulted passage leads through to the khan itself, which today houses a bakery.

Taking either of the left turns leading west from Al-Hatab Square, you come to the large and comparatively recent **Maronite Cathedral**, dating from 1873-1923. The entrance façade is particularly imposing, consisting of a triple gateway flanked by square towers topped by pyramid-shaped roofs. This leads through to a courtyard with a statue of St Elie, to whom the cathedral is dedicated. The main doorway of the cathedral itself is framed by bands of black and honey stone, with interlocking patterns in the arch, and intricate geometric decorations above that.

In the series of narrow pedestrian streets leading north from the northernmost of the two streets running between the Maronite Cathedral and Al-Hatab Square can be found a number of other elegant 17th- to 18th-century merchants' houses. Along Sissi Street, next door to **Sissi House** restaurant, there is **Beit Dallal**, while along Al Raheb Buhayrah Street are **Beit Balit** and **Beit Basil**. However, they are privately owned and occupied, and gaining entry to them can be difficult.

Aleppo National Museum

ⓘ *Baron St, T012-221 2400, Wed-Mon 0900-1800, S£150, student S£10, no photography allowed.*

Aleppo's museum is second only to the Damascus National Museum in terms of its remarkable collection of exhibits, and is well worth a visit. Unfortunately, the quality of the presentation does not always do justice to the subject matter, although efforts have been made to improve the labelling and interpretations. Dotted around the gardens of the museum are some beautiful statues, *stelae* and architectural fragments. The entrance to the museum is dominated by three huge basalt statues of gods standing atop equally massive animals. These were discovered at Tell Halaf (Guzana) in the Jezira region (in the far northeast of Syria) in 1912. They date from the ninth century BC and represent examples of the neo-Hittite (or Syro-Hittite) art which developed in Syria following the collapse of the Hittite Empire.

For a chronological perspective you should work your way round the museum in an anticlockwise direction. In the open area to your right as you enter is the **prehistoric** display including the near complete skeleton of a child from the middle Palaeolithic era that was unearthed at Dederiyeh. There are artefacts covering the Palaeolithic, Mesolithic and Neolithic periods: flint tools, figurines, a burial urn and various pottery items, including some beautiful painted pottery from the Halaf and Ubaid cultures.

First hall

The first hall begins with artefacts from the Jezira region, including examples of the famous alabaster figurines from the Eye Temple at Tell Brak (discovered by the archaeologist Max Mallowan, husband of Agatha Christie). This is followed by an extensive collection of Bronze Age finds from Mari (Tell Hariri), including distinctive statuettes of Mari priests, clay tablets inscribed with cuneiform text, cylinder seals, a larger statue of an Amorite spring goddess and a bronze lion from the Temple of Dagan. If you are planning on visiting Mari, it is here that you can get a real idea of the importance of the site in terms of the archaeological finds which were discovered there. Next there is a small section covering finds from Hama, including one of the huge basalt lions which guarded the Royal Palace on the citadel mound there. The rest of this hall is given over to finds from Ras Shamra (Ugarit), on the Mediterranean coast just to the north of Lattakia: bronze figurines, some inlaid with gold, dating from the second millenium BC, bronze tools and weapons, bronze and gold jewellery, ivory objects, stone friezes, painted pottery and alabaster figurines. Many of the pieces clearly show the strong Egyptian influence which resulted from the close trading contacts between Ugarit and the Pharaohs of Egypt during the 14th-13th centuries BC. Other pieces reflect Mycenaean and Lyprian styles, indicating the influence of trading links with the Aegean region.

Second hall

The second hall is divided into three sections. The first is dominated by numerous massive basalt statues, sphinxes and friezes of gods and god-kings from Tell Halaf (Guzana). All are executed in the same style, and date from the same period as the statues at the entrance to the museum. The second section is devoted to items from Tell Arslan and Tell Hadjib (also in the Jezira region), and dominated by more massive basalt statues, friezes and a pair of carved lions. These all date from the Assyrian period (ninth-seventh centuries BC). In sharp contrast to the massive proportions of the basalt pieces is the collection of small, delicately carved ivory panels displayed in wall cases. These were discovered in the

Preserving the past for the future

It may be a bit of a mouthful to say but the Project for the Rehabilitation of the Old City of Aleppo is doing a fine job of making sure that Aleppo's character remains intact. Partially funded by the Syrian authorities and by the German government (through the German Agency for Technical Cooperation, or GTZ), this wonderful scheme is endeavouring to preserve as well as revitalise the densely packed neighbourhoods of the city's most ancient quarter.

As well as restoring ancient monuments (which Aleppo has in abundance) the project is encouraging the district's social and economic regeneration to improve the lives of the Old City's 118,000 inhabitants. Restored buildings now host health centres and cultural foundations, residents are offered interest free micro-credits and free technical advice to help maintain their homes, proper sewer networks and water pipes have been established and measures to tackle garbage collection and traffic management are being established.

It's no mean feat and progress may be slow, but gradually the city of Aleppo is showing the world that it is possible to preserve the past and move forward into the future at the same time.

so-called Ivory House at Tell Arslan and date to the ninth century BC. Believed to have been used to decorate furnishings, the workmanship is generally recognized as Phoenician, with evidence of Egyptian, Aegean and Syrian influences. The last section contains artefacts from Tell Ahmar on the Euphrates (to the north of Lake Assad), where an Assyrian period royal palace was discovered within the walls of the citadel mound. There are several massive obelisks and friezes carved with figures in the Egyptian style from the palace on display here, but more interesting is the series of fragments of frescoes (reproductions of the originals) which adorned the walls of the palace. They are strikingly life-like and beautifully executed, and all the more remarkable when you consider that they date from the eighth and seventh centuries BC.

Third hall

The third hall is divided into two sections. The first contains a varied collection of artefacts from various different sites, including basalt friezes from Ain Dara (to the northwest of Aleppo) and alabaster figurines, pottery, jewellery, cylinder seals, etc from Tell Chuera (in the desert region between the Balikh and Kabour rivers, to the north of the Euphrates). The second section is given over to artefacts from Tell Mardikh (Ebla), including a selection of clay tablets inscribed with cuneiform script, and various fragments of wooden furniture dating from the Early Bronze Age (2400-2250 BC) inlaid with shells and carved with delicate human and animal figures. The central courtyard of the museum contains various basalt pieces, a large rectangular mosaic floor, and a reconstruction of an underground tomb.

Upstairs

Upstairs, the first hall contains exhibits from various sites along the Euphrates, most of which were 'rescue' excavations carried out prior to their inundation by the river as a result of the construction of the huge dam at Ath Thawra. There are separate displays by the Syrian, German, Dutch, Belgian, Italian, French, British, American and Japanese missions which carried out the excavations. The second hall contains artefacts from the classical era, including pottery, coins, statues, glassware, mosaics and lots of funerary *stelae* from Palmyra. Although there are some beautiful pieces, unfortunately the labelling is very poor. The third hall (closed for renovation at the time of writing) is dedicated to the Islamic era and includes a scale-model of Aleppo's citadel and surrounding areas. Finally the fourth hall houses contemporary Syrian art. For those interested, it is well worth a look.

⊙ Aleppo listings

For Sleeping and Eating price codes and other relevant information, see Essentials pages 19-21.

⊜ Sleeping

Aleppo *p207, maps p212 and p216*
There are a great many budget hotels, nearly all concentrated in a small area bounded by Baron St, Al Maari St, Al-Kouwatly St and Bab al-Faraj St. However, many are often booked out by groups of Eastern Europeans who come to Aleppo on trading visits, while some are extremely basic and best avoided. Bear in mind that this is also Aleppo's red-light district; lone females may feel slightly uncomfortable.

Most of the top-end accommodation is found in the quiet back streets of the Jdaide district, where some beautiful old Ottoman-era houses have been converted into luxury hotels.
LL-AL Yasmeen d'Alep, Al-Kayyali St, Jdaide, T021-212 6366, www.yasmeenalep.com. Charming, attentive service sets this place apart. Just 8 individually decorated rooms, featuring lots of original stonework, in a lovingly restored 17th-century house. All rooms boast luxuriously appointed modern baths, satellite TV, Wi-Fi and a/c, and open onto a grand old courtyard which is simply magical when lit up at night.
AL Beit Marrash, Al-Shabaniyyeh St, T021-333 3150, www.beitmarrash.com. This tranquil hotel is hidden away down a tiny alleyway off busy Al-Moutanabbi St. Stylishly furnished rooms (satellite TV, fridge, a/c, Wi-Fi) open out onto a huge courtyard decked out with lemon trees, vines, pretty flowers and a trickling fountain. A peaceful, secluded gem.

AL Dar Zamaria, Abdul Malek bin Marwin St, Jdaide, T021-363 6100, www.darzamaria.com. A sprawling, elegant conversion of 4 old houses, interconnected by narrow alleys. Huge rooms (with satellite TV and a/c) feature lots of old oriental inlaid furniture and ornate touches and open out onto majestic courtyards. Courtyard restaurant and underground bar.
AL Jdayde, Al-Hatab Sq, Jdaide, T021-212 1197, www.jdaydehotel.com. Spotlessly clean, quiet rooms with a/c and satellite TV; slightly let down by bland character-less furnishings. Some rooms have beautiful hand-painted wood-beam ceilings. Excellent rooftop restaurant (see eating) with unparalleled views over the city.
A Hotel Baron, Baron St, T021-211 0880, hotelbaron@mail.sy. Agatha Christie (Rm 203), TE Lawrence (Rm 202), and Ataturk (Rm 201) all once slept here and the common areas still ooze the atmosphere of a bygone era. Unfortunately the rooms in Aleppo's first and still most famous hotel have undergone a rather featureless makeover, but on the plus side, now include working a/c and decent bathroom plumbing. The quirky ground-floor bar (see bars and clubs) is not to be missed. Parking available.
B Dar al-Kanadil, signposted from Bab Antakya, up the stairs beside Al-Kamiliye Mosque on Souq al-Atarin, Old City, T021-332 4908, www.daralkanadil.com. Lovingly restored, Dar Kanadil has all the atmosphere of the Jdaide district hotels for half the price. Large airy rooms (with a/c, Wi-Fi) have wonderful original old tile floors and lots of individual touches, while attached baths are chic and modern. All rooms open

onto a large peaceful courtyard. Excellent value, recommended.

B Tourism, Corner Kouwatly St and Al-Walid St, T021-211 3602. Centrally located and very popular with Arab business travellers. Decent-sized clean rooms all with a/c, TV and fridge. Some rooms can be noisy.

C Dar Halabia, signposted from Bab Antakya, Lisan ad-Din al-Khatib St, Old City, T021-332 3344, www.dar-halabia.com. A quiet oasis, with bags of character, slap in the heart of the souq. The central courtyard is festooned with lamps and glorious old antiques. The simply furnished rooms (some with a/c) are brightened by lovely textiles and period furniture. Library, Wi-Fi, upstairs terrace to lounge in. Recommended.

D Al-Gawaher, Bab al-Faraj St, T021-223 9554, www.algawaher-hotel.webs.com. Very popular backpacker joint with helpful staff. Decent-sized clean rooms (a/c and TV) with tiny basic bathrooms. Funky rooftop terrace chill-out area. Good-value singles.

D Al-Yarmouk, Al-Maari St, T021-211 6154. Ride the creaky elevator up to the Al-Yarmouk, and prepare to journey back in time. The spacious rooms (a/c, TV, fridge) are decked out with circa-1950s furniture while the 'saloon', with its over-stuffed sofas and gaudy chandeliers, simply drips faded grandeur. The friendly staff are a bonus.

D Hanadi, Bab al-Faraj St, T021-223 8113. Hanadi's owner, Walid, is quietly turning this hotel into an Aleppo backpacker institution. Delightfully helpful staff and the screamingly pink decor can't help but put a smile on your face. All 12 rooms (a/c, fan, fridge, TV) open out onto a sunny communal area, great for meeting other travellers. The only letdown is the very basic attached baths with squat toilets. Recommended.

D Tourist Hotel, Al-Dala St, T021-211 6583. The homeliest little hotel in Aleppo. Potted plants abound at this well-run cheerful place. Spick-and-span airy rooms all have TV, fan, a/c, and share clean bathrooms (2 rooms have attached bath). Good value singles.

E Assia, Al-Maari St, T021-211 5214. On the 5th floor of this building, the Assia has clean, sparsely furnished basic rooms (fan, TV, attached bath) and friendly staff.

🍴 Eating

Aleppo *p207, maps p212 and p216*
The area bordered by Bab al-Faraj St, Al-Maari St, Baron St and Kouwatly St contains dozens of cheap and cheerful restaurants which can all turn out a meal for around S£150. Places to eat are scarce in the Old City souq area but there's dozens of bakeries and hole-in-the-wall falafel and sandwich joints to grab a snack. Aleppo's most atmospheric dining options are concentrated in the Jdaide Quarter and even in the poshest places here, you won't break the bank.

♥♥♥ Jdayde Rooftop, Jdayde Hotel, Al-Hatab Sq, Jdaide, T021-212 1197. Swish fine dining on a breezy rooftop with wonderful views over the city. Varied menu of Arabic specialties. Bar area with comfy sofas to lounge in while you enjoy a *narghile*. Alcohol served.

♥♥♥ Sissi House, Sissi St, T021-221 9411. Set in a beautifully restored 18th-century merchant's house, and offering a pleasant, atmospheric venue in which to dine out in style. Outdoor seating in summer in central courtyard, or indoors in lavishly ornate rooms. Downstairs is a bar in a hand-dug cave which, according to the owner, is believed to have once been connected by a network of tunnels to the Citadel. Menu is a mix of French and Arabic dishes. Order the cherry kebab, their house specialty. Alcohol served.

♥♥ Ahlildar, just off Jamia al-Ayyoubi St, beside the Great Mosque, Old City, T021-331 1320. A massive menu that covers Western and Arabic dishes, and does a good breakfast too. Come up here to watch the world pass by on the breezy upstairs terrace overlooking the mosque.

♥♥ Al-Andalib, Baron St. Very popular rooftop restaurant next door to the Baron Hotel. You don't get much choice (there's *mezze* plus 4 types of kebab), but it's good-value and service is swift. It can get lively later in the evening (once the *arak* starts to flow). Eat early for a less rowdy experience. Alcohol served.

¶ Cantara, off Al Kayyali St, T021-212 2010. Open 1200-1600 and 1900-late. Excellent little Italian place (pasta, pizza, etc), with attentive service. Pleasant courtyard, as well as upstairs terrace and seating inside. Alcohol served.

¶ Cordoba, Georges and Mathilde Salam St, T021-224 0868. This long-standing favourite has a wide-ranging menu that offers Armenian and Turkish dishes as well as Aleppine specialities. Try the *toshka* (spicy meat and cheese grilled on bread) and the *maajouk* (barbequed meat with cheese, pistachios, red peppers and pine nuts). Friendly staff will help you select your meal.

¶ Kan Zaman, off Haret al-Yasmin St, T021-363 0299. Set in a very elegantly restored house with an airy roof terrace that boasts great views out over Jdaide. Large menu of good quality Arabic cuisine, with lots of salads, mezze and kebabs on offer. The *yabrak* (stuffed vine leaves) is particularly good. Alcohol served.

¶ Fuul Shop, Beside Dar Zamaria hotel, Musa Bin Nusayr St, Jdaide district, open from 0700. If you like *fuul* (mashed fava beans), you simply have to try this place. The *fuul* served here is delicately spiced with garlic juice and chilli sauce, very different from the standard Syrian style. Get here early to get your share.

Cafés

On Yarmouk St, near Bab al-Faraj St, is a line of several excellent fresh juice stands. The 2 cafés opposite the entrance to the citadel are comparatively expensive, although the outside seating is very pleasant and you have prime views of the citadel from here. Most of the restaurants along Georges and Mathilde Salam St also double as rather upmarket cafés, where Aleppo's well-to-do come to enjoy a drink and a *narghile*. This is a fun place to sit back and people watch.

Al-Sahel, 1st floor, Al Sahel hotel, Al-Maari St. The large balcony here overlooking the clock tower and the chaotic junction, is a pleasant, atmospheric place to watch the world go by.

Al-Sham, Saad Allah al-Jabri St. Features chessboards stuck to the tables; there are usually a dozen or so games on the go every evening, so if you fancy a game of chess, this is the place to come.

🍸 Bars and clubs

Aleppo *p207, maps p212 and p216*
Aleppo isn't known for its nightlife and everything pretty much shuts down by midnight. As well as below, **Kan Zaman Restaurant**, **Sissi House** and the rooftop of the **Jdayde Hotel** are all good for a drink.

Baron Hotel, Baron St. The bar here is steeped in atmosphere with decor and furniture largely unchanged since Lawrence's time. Order a gin and tonic, sit back on one of the squishy old sofas and soak up this hotel's eccentric history.

Hareer, Musa Bin Nusayr St, Jdaide district, open 1900-late. A pleasant atmosphere, good variety of alcohol and nice views from the rooftop terrace.

🎉 Festivals and events

Aleppo *p207, maps p212 and p216*
Jul/Aug Jazz Lives In Syria Festival. 1 week of international jazz performances held at Aleppo citadel.
Sep Silk Road Festival. A program of cultural events celebrating this ancient trade route with events held in Damascus, Aleppo and Palmyra.

🛍 Shopping

Aleppo *p207, maps p212 and p216*
At first glance the souqs of the Old City don't have the same amount of handicrafts and

souvenir shops as Damascus, as they aren't specifically orientated towards tourism. Delve a little deeper below the surface though and you'll find fabulous silk and cotton textiles, gold, copper and brassware, Bedouin-style jewellery, Syrian lamps, carpets and cheap antiques. The famous Aleppine olive oil soap is everywhere and makes a great souvenir. For a rough idea of where different goods are grouped together, see the Aleppo Souqs map.

On Al-Hatab Sq in the Jdaide quarter there are a couple of excellent antique shops with a wide selection of goods. **Muhammad's Antiques**, opposite Al-Tuteh Mosque, Souq al-Atarin. A tiny dusty treasure trove where shelves sag under the weight of mountains of old silver, copper and brassware. Grab a feather duster from Muhammad, the friendly owner, and start hunting.

Oscar, Souq al-Atarin. Quirky, kooky and definitely entertaining; Majid, Alaadin and Muhammad stock a bewildering array of colourful silk and cotton textiles in their cheerful little store. The shop is a tiny haven right in the middle of the souq where you can sit back with a coffee and have a chat with the well-travelled owners while browsing their shelves.

Sebastian, Al-Qala'a St. For top-quality handmade local goods this place should be top of your list. Lamps, jewellery, glass and silverware all compete for space in this little shop. Upstairs there are also antique kilims and carpets galore. The friendly owner, Muhammad, can also pack and ship your goods home for you.

Souq Ash-Shouna, opposite the entrance to the citadel, Al-Qala'a St. For those that prefer a less crowded shopping experience than the Old City, this converted handicrafts market sells a wide range of souvenirs at fixed prices. It's a good place to get a feel for the cost of goods before diving back into the souqs to bargain.

Bookshops

Sheraton Hotel bookshop, Bab al-Faraj St. In the hotel foyer, this bookshop stocks a quite good range of English-language titles as well as books on Syria.

▲▲ Activities and tours

Aleppo *p207, maps p212 and p216*
Hammams

Hammam al-Nahasin, off Souq al-Atarin. Daily 1000-late, men only. Basic steam costs S£200. Full massage and scrub is S£500. This bathhouse dates originally from the 12th or 13th century, although most of its original architectural features have been obscured by renovation.

Hammam Yalbogha al-Nasri, to the right from the citadel entrance, Al Qala'a St, T021-362 3154. Daily 1000-0200, women only Mon, Thu, Sat 1000-1700. These baths (also known as Hammam Lababidiyeh) are the largest and most lavish in Syria. Thought by some to date originally from the seventh century, the present buildings are of 14th-century Mamluk origin. At the time of writing they were undergoing restoration work but it's hoped they will be back in full working order by 2011.

City tours

Nearly all the hotels can organize a guide for a half- or full-day city tour.
Ahmed Moudallal, T021-267 1719, amoudallal@hotmail.com. Constantly recommended for his city tours, the wonderfully eccentric Ahmed Moudallal will show you the nooks and crannies of the Old City that you'd otherwise miss. Tours are packed with history and Ahmed's own hilarious stories. Highly entertaining. (US$5 per person, per hour).

Tour operators

Most of the luxury hotels, and some of the mid-range ones, have tour operators attached to them. In addition, most of the budget hotels which deal with backpackers offer tours to St Simeon and the Dead Cities. If you can get a group together these can be reasonable value, and allow you to get round a greater number of sites more quickly than would be possible by public transport. **Halabia Travel and Tourism**, Bab Antakya St, T021-224 8497, www.halabia-tours.com. The manager, Abdel Hay Kaddour, has been involved with Syrian tourism for years and this very professional tour company have a host of services for tourists. They can organize country-wide or local tailor-made itineraries of any length, including pickup from border or airport and help with sorting out visas. They also run Euphrates excursions, including dinner and overnight stay with a Bedouin family (US$50 per person/minimum 2 people). Car hire is available (US$50-$70 per day including unlimited mileage and insurance), and they can also arrange a car with driver (US$60-$100 per day). For long-stay accommodation, they have houses for rent with full facilities in the Old City area (US$600-US$1000 per month).

● Transport

Aleppo p207, maps p212 and p216
Air
Aleppo airport is 10 km to the east of the city. A taxi out will cost approximately S£300. Syrian Air operate direct international flights from Aleppo to a number of European and Middle Eastern cities including **Athens**, **Beirut**, **Cairo**, **Dubai**, **Istanbul**, **Madrid**, **Munich** and **Rome**. They also have 2-5 domestic flights daily to **Damascus** (S£1750).

BMI, Egypt Air, Gulf Air, Royal Jordanian and Turkish Airlines all operate flights from here. International airport departure tax is S£1500. This tax is currently being phased out at Damascus airport and the same may happen in Aleppo. Ask at your hotel for up-to-date information.

Most of the airline offices are on Baron St including the following: **Atlantic Travel and Tourism**, T021-211 2978, a friendly English-speaking travel agency who can organize onward flights. **Syrian Air**, T021-212 5501, is based at the office next door.

Bus
Domestic departures are from the Al-Ramousah Pullman Station. From the centre of town a taxi there costs about S£100. There are about 30 companies located here, which between them offer regular departures to all the major cities in Syria. There is no need to pre-book as services are generally frequent enough.

Kadmous has 6 services per day to **Damascus** (4½ hrs, S£200), via **Hama** (1½ hrs, S£100), at 0030, 0700, 0900, 1200, 1600 and 1800. To **Tartus** (3½ hrs. S£200), via **Homs** (2 hrs, S£135), there are 9 departures daily; 0730, 0930, 1100, 1145, 1330, 1445, 1715, 1930 and 2130. A bus to **Raqqa** (2½ hrs, S£125) leaves twice daily at 0530 and 1330; and to **Deir ez-Zor** (4½ hrs, S£200) the bus departs at 1300 and 1530.

International departures are from the International (Karnak) Bus Station on the corner of Al-Maari St and Baron St in the centre of town. It's a 15- to 20-min walk from Bab Antakya or from the Jdaide Quarter. There are frequent departures by bus and share taxi, to **Antakya** in Turkey from here. Al-Joud run buses across the border to Antakya twice a day at 0530 and 1200 (4½ hrs, S£250). **Share taxis** leave at all times of the day from here and charge approx S£500 per person. By far the most comfortable way to travel to Antakya is with the HAS bus. They have 1 daily departure at 1400 in a 16-seater minibus (3½ hrs, S£350). The drivers are friendly and help with border formalities. This route is busy so booking at least 1 day in advance is recommended. To **Beirut**, services all seem to depart at 2400 (7 hrs, S£250). Services to **Amman** mostly seem to leave at 2300 (9 hrs, S£450).

Car hire
Halabia Travel and Tourism can arrange car hire (see above).
Europcar, T021-211 2238, www.europcar.sy, and Budget, T021-212 6885, www.budget-sy.com, are both based inside the **Sheraton Hotel**, Bab al-Faraj St.

There's an underground car park on Bab Antakya St (just before Bab Antakya gate) that charges S£100 per day for parking.

Microbus

There are several different microbus stations in Aleppo. The dusty parking lot just off Bab Antakya St (basically opposite Bab Antakya gate) is where you can get a microbus to **Daret Aazah** (S£35), from where it is a further 6 km or so of walking or hitching to **St Simeon (Qala'at Samaan)**. If you walk through this parking lot you'll find yourself in the large, bustling **Microbus/city bus station** from where you can get old hob-hob style buses and microbuses to towns south of Aleppo. From here there are fairly regular departures to **Ariha** (S£75) and **Maarat al-Numan** (S£75), which are both useful for getting to Bara and Serjilla. There are also services to **Idlib** (S£85), **Harim** and dozens of other destinations.

Microbuses to most destinations north of Aleppo leave from a microbus station far to the north of the city centre known as 'Garage Sahat Shahira Mol'. A taxi from the city centre to here costs about S£70. There are regular departures to **Afrine** (for **Ain Dara**) (S£95), **Azaz** (for **Cyrrhus**) (S£75) and **Nabul** (S£35) among many others.

To **Qala'a Najm** you need to go to the **East bus station** on the ring road east of the Old City. A taxi from the centre will cost about S£35. From here you can jump on a bus to **Ain al-Arab** and ask to be dropped off in Membij or at the turn-off to the castle.

Train

Baghdad Train Station handles services all over Syria and into Turkey. It shouldn't cost anymore than S£40 to get here from anywhere in town in a taxi or it's about a 25-min walk from the centre. There are 3 express services per day to **Damascus** (4¼ hrs, 1st class S£240, 2nd class S£120), via **Hama** (1¼ hrs, S£100) and **Homs** (2 hrs, S£130) at 0640, 1010 and 1645. There is also 2 slower overnight departures at 2400

(S£240) and 0350 (S£120). The 2400 departure also has 2-berth sleeper compartments (S£505).

The scenic train journey to **Lattakia** is very pretty. The route journeys through farmland before ascending through the spectacular Jebel Ansariye. There are 2 express services per day at 0600 and 1730 (2½ hrs, 1st class S£160, 2nd class S£135), and 3 normal services at 0445, 0648 and 1545 (3½ hrs, 1st class S£70, 2nd class S£50). To **Deir ez-Zor** (4 hrs, S£175), via **Raqqa** (2 hrs, S£120), there is 1 fast train daily at 1610. A daily, slow, overnight train leaves at 2315 to **Qamishle** (7 hrs, S£175) and goes via Raqqa and Deir ez-Zor. Be aware that the train stations in Qamishle, Raqqa and Deir ez-Zor are inconveniently placed and it's generally much easier to take a bus to these destinations.

To **Turkey**, an overnight seater-only train leaves at 2100 on Mon and Thu to **Adana** (7 hrs, S£1060) and **Mersin** (9 hrs, S£1245). Services to **Istanbul** are set to resume when track maintenance has been completed at some stage in 2010. When it does, the Aleppo–Istanbul Toros Express leaves Aleppo every Tue at 1105 reaching Istanbul Haydarpasa Station on Wed at 1755, though delays are common. The service does the same journey in reverse from Istanbul every Sun, leaving at 0855. Tickets can be purchased from the international ticket window at Aleppo Station (1-bed compartment S£5000, 2-bed compartment S£3450). There is no restaurant car on the train so make sure you bring food.

ⓘ Directory

Aleppo p207, maps p212 and p216
Banks Banks are generally open Sat-Thu 0830-1330. There are several ATMs in Aleppo that are linked to the international networks. The following branches of CBS all have ATMs attached and handle currency exchange. **CBS,**

Al-Azmeh St (the bank is on the 1st floor and entry is from the back of the shopping arcade); CBS, Corner Bab al-Faraj St and Kouwatly St; and CBS, Al-Moutanabbi St. Be aware that cards on the Maestro network sometimes do not work in CBS ATMs. The Sheraton Hotel on Bab al-Faraj St has an ATM which accepts all foreign cards and there's a Bank of Syria and Overseas on Saad Allah al-Jabri St (opposite the park) that has an ATM. Cultural centres British Council, Al-Sabeel Dabbagh Building, Franciscan St, T021-228 0302, www.britishcouncil.org/syria. French Cultural Centre, Rue Faycal, T021-227 4460. Internet Concord Internet, Kouwatly St. You need to bring your passport to register. Medical services There are plenty of pharmacies in the downtown. If you fall ill, the best step initially is to seek help from your hotel who will call a local doctor for you. The Aleppo University Hospital, T021-223 6120, is in the modern western district of Aleppo, opposite the Pullman al-Shahba hotel. It offers a generally high standard of facilities and treatment. Post The main post office is situated on the southwest corner of Kouwatly Sq in the downtown area and is open daily

0800-1700. The parcel post office is next door. DHL have an office just off Kouwatly St, open 0930-2300. Telephone There are Easycomm card-phones dotted around all over the city, with phonecards being sold from nearby shops, kiosks, etc. You can also buy them from the central telephone office, which shares the same building as the main post office on the southwest corner of Kouwatly Sq. Visa extensions Passport and Immigration Office, north of the citadel entrance, Sat-Thu 0800-1330. You need 4 passport photos, a letter from your hotel and must pay S£25. Get there early and you may be able to complete the process within less than an hour, When busy it can take most of the morning. It is possible to get extensions of up to 1 month here (some travellers report getting 2 months, although there seem to be no fixed rules on this). If you want an extension of more than the standard 2 weeks, be sure to make this very clear at every stage of the process, otherwise 2 weeks are all that you will be given. There are several shops across the road from the office where you can get passport photos on the spot.

Around Aleppo

In spring, the rugged limestone hills surrounding Aleppo are illuminated by dramatic gold shafts of sunlight, the blues, pinks and yellows of wild flowers speckle the fields, and the olive groves are in full blossom. Showers are frequent but afterwards the air is fresh and the sun lights up the landscape. Such is the setting for the numerous ruins of Christian settlements dating from the Byzantine era (the so-called Dead Cities). There are literally hundreds of sites but the most popular (and most substantial ruins) to visit are St Simeon (Qala'at Samaan) to the north and Bara and Serjilla in the south.

In addition to the Dead Cities there are a number of sites dating from other periods which can also be visited as day trips from Aleppo. These include the first millennium BC neo-Hittite temple of Ain Dara to the north of Qala'at Samaan, the 12th-century AD Arab castle of Qala'at Najm on the Euphrates River to the northeast of Aleppo (both covered in this section), the third millennium BC site of Ebla (covered as a diversion from the motorway between Hama and Aleppo, see page 143) and the town of Maarat al-Numan with its impressive mosaics museum (also en route between Hama and Aleppo, see page 141).

Exploring this region can be difficult due to inefficient public transport. To see the Dead Cities properly it makes more sense to hire a car/driver for the day. ▸▸ For listings, see page 253.

Background

To the west of the motorway en route between Hama and Aleppo there is an area of rugged limestone hills that starts a little to the north of Apamea and extends in a rough arc almost up to Cyrrhus, near the Turkish border northwest of Aleppo. Known in classical times as the *Belus Massif*, these hills consist of a broken series of ranges that can be divided into three distinct areas: the northern **Jebel Samaan**; the central **Jebel al-Ala** and **Jebel Barisha**; and the southern **Jebel Riha** (also known as the Jebel Zawiye).

On the face of it, this landscape appears harsh and inhospitable, dominated by jagged, broken limestone outcrops amongst which small, fragmented and barely productive pockets of land are painstakingly cleared and cultivated. And yet, during the Byzantine era the *Belus Massif* flourished, supporting an unprecedented density of towns and villages. Its fascination today is that such a large number of these settlements should have survived (in all, more than 750 have been documented), and in such a remarkable state of preservation. Certainly, the ravages of time have reduced many to barely discernible scatterings of ruins, but others remain eerily well preserved – almost as if abandoned only in recent times – although their distinctive architecture hints at far more ancient origins.

Today they are known popularly, though somewhat misleadingly, as the 'Dead Cities' (none would appear to have ever grown to more than the size of a small town). The reasons as to why such a high density of settlements should have flourished in this region have been the subject of much speculation. The key, it would appear, lay in the relative political and economic stability which followed the Roman conquest of Syria. This allowed rich landowners from the plains to contemplate such long-term projects as planting olive groves in the hills of the *Belus Massif* (it takes at least 10 years before an olive tree actually starts to yield fruit). It also allowed trade to flourish unhindered so that the settlements which began to develop were able to sell their lucrative crop in regional centres – particularly Antioch with its access to more distant Mediterranean markets but also Aleppo and Apamea – and buy the items of everyday life which they were unable to produce in their otherwise marginal environment.

The economics of this trade obviously worked in the olive growers' favour, generating significant surpluses, so that by the Byzantine era these settlements were growing steadily in size and number. Fuelled by this newfound prosperity they flourished from the fourth to seventh centuries AD, and in the remains left behind can be seen examples of all the major trends in the early development of **Byzantine** architecture, most notably in terms of the churches, but also in the other public buildings, such as baths and markets as well as the 'vernacular' architecture of common houses.

However, the **Persian invasions** of the seventh century brought instability to the region, and soon after, following the **Arab conquest**, the region became a frontier zone between the Byzantine and Arab worlds. Trade was disrupted and as a result these settlements found themselves cut off from their all-important markets. No longer able to support themselves through the trade in olives, they were gradually forced to abandon their settlements and return to the plains where subsistence agriculture was possible; by the 10th century the region had been almost completely depopulated. It was not until this century that it began to be settled again (particularly the northern parts, where olives are once again being cultivated and you get a sense of how the region would once have appeared, at least agriculturally).

It is due to this abandonment of the region for 10 centuries or more (and to the use of durable limestone as the primary building material) that we owe the remarkable state of preservation of the Dead Cities; elsewhere around the Mediterranean basin, most early Byzantine architecture was adapted or built over, but in this region only time, the elements and the occasional earthquake have taken their toll, leaving largely intact these atmospheric relics of a bygone era.

Many of the ruins still stand in splendid isolation, hidden away amidst the limestone hills. Sometimes, however, you will find small, rather ramshackle contemporary farming settlements amidst the ancient remains, with former Byzantine buildings pressed into service as cattle shelters and sheep pens, or repaired and lived in once again. Elsewhere, stones from the ruins have been recycled and you may see a beautifully carved limestone lintel amongst the concrete and breeze-block of a modern house. Some might be taken aback at such seemingly flagrant disregard for these monuments, but the truth is that there are simply far too many sites for the Department of Antiquities to have any hope of preserving them all. And anyway, there is something quite refreshing about this blending of ancient and modern; as with the souqs of Aleppo, what you see is living history, not some neatly packaged heritage theme park.

Northwest of Aleppo: Jebel Samaan

The Jebel Samaan is the setting for St Simeon (Qala'at Samaan); a tumbledown basilica that is a lasting monument to one of early Christianity's kookiest ascetics. It's also the easiest site to get to by public transport from Aleppo. Unless you have a lot of time and patience, the rest of the sites in this area are best visited by hiring a car/driver. If you have your own transport, you can combine a trip to St Simeon with a number of other sites in the area. The church of Mushabbak, directly en route to St Simeon is well worth visiting. The sites of Al-Qatora and Rozzita are of lesser interest, but only a short detour from the main route. Basofan, Burj Haidar and Kharrab Shams, sites at intervals along the road heading east from St Simeon, have beautiful locations worth seeing quite apart from the ruins themselves. This road also joins up with the main road between Aleppo and Afrine, making for a convenient round-trip back to Aleppo. Alternatively, you can continue north from St

Simeon to neo-Hittite Ain Dara, and from there continue on to Afrine. A detour to the north from the main Afrine–Aleppo road takes you to Cyrrhus, near the Turkish border.

Head west out of Aleppo on Ibrahim Hanano Street, which subsequently becomes Saif al-Dawla Street. After passing under the railway line, turn right at a large junction consisting of a roundabout complete with flyover and underpass, and then first left around 150 m further on, at a junction with traffic lights. Go straight across one crossroads and then straight on again at a large roundabout with a statue of a soldier on horseback in the centre (this roundabout marks the junction with the main ring road around Aleppo). This road, which leads directly to **Daret Aazah**, is frequently signposted for 'Samaan Castle' or 'Qala'at Samaan'. The road passes through Aleppo's rapidly expanding suburbs before reaching open countryside. After 25 km a turning (signposted 'Kasr al Mashabak') leads off to the left up a rough track to the ruins of **Mushabbak Church**, visible some 500 m away from the road on top of a small hill. Around 1 km before this turning there is a left turn signposted '**Camping Kaddour**' 10 km (see Sleeping, page 253).

Mushabbak Church

ⓘ *The caretaker is usually on duty here to collect an entrance fee of S£75, students S£5.*

This small but imposing monument is one of the best preserved Byzantine basilica churches in northern Syria, its basic structure still more or less completely intact. It probably dates from the late fifth century, around the same time that nearby St Simeon was developing into an important pilgrimage centre, and perhaps served as a stopping point on the pilgrimage route to St Simeon. It follows the standard *basilica* plan of a central nave and two side aisles, with two rows of five columns dividing the aisles from the nave. Note the variety of capitals atop the columns. The semi-domed apse at the eastern end is flanked by two side apses. The central nave has a *clerestory*, or upper stage, rising above the side aisles, with nine arched windows on either side. The clerestory and its windows would have added an overall sense of light and height to the church, probably an indication of the more advanced architectural influences coming from St Simeon.

Outside the church, on its west side, is a quarry where the stone used in its construction was presumably cut. A little further away, to the northwest, is an **underground tomb** with three arched bays and nearby a small circular opening to a large water cistern as well as various other rock-cut features. Around 100 m to the east of the church are the ruins of what appears to have been a **monastery complex**, parts of which are today occupied by local shepherds.

Al-Qatora and Rozzita

From the turning for Mushabbak, it is a little over 4 km further to the centre of the village of **Daret Aazah**. Follow the signposts through the village to pick up the road for St Simeon. After 3 km there is a signposted turning left along a metalled road for Al-Qatora (1 km) and Rozzita (4.5 km). Taking this turning, in the village of Al-Qatora there are various fragmented ruins, including one corner of a building – possibly a Roman villa. Continuing past the village, to the left of the road there are a number of **rock-cut tombs**, some with heavily weathered inscriptions and carvings of figures. These, like the ruins in the village itself, are of Roman origin, dating from the early second to mid-third century AD, when the settlements in the region were just beginning to achieve a certain level of prosperity. Further on, scattered amongst the village and surrounding fields of Rozzita (or Zarzita), are various fragments of what appears to have been a late fifth- to early sixth-century **monastic community**.

Al Qatora to St Simeon

Returning to the main road, 2 km after the turning for Al-Qatora and Rozzita, bear right at a fork to reach St Simeon (straight on for Deir Samaan and Ain Dara). A little further on, where the road again forks, bear left for St Simeon (right for Basofan, Burj Haidar and Kharrab Shams; see below).

St Simeon → *For listings, see page 253.*

The beautiful fifth-century church of St Simeon represents the largest and most important surviving Christian monument of the early Byzantine period. It is surpassed only by the later (sixth-century) Hagia Sophia in Constantinople (Istanbul) and was not matched in Europe until the 11th and 12th centuries. On a steep-sided ridge with sweeping views out across the Afrine River Valley to the northwest, and beyond to the Kurd Dag and Amanus mountains across the Turkish border, the ruins of the church of St Simeon are remarkably well preserved, and really give a sense of the true splendour of this pilgrimage site in its heyday. It is worth timing your visit so you can see the ruins either in the early morning or the late afternoon, when the stones are illuminated to a golden glow. If you do this, you will also avoid the main rush of tour groups, which start to arrive from mid-morning and have usually all left by mid-afternoon.

Ins and outs

Getting there and away Fairly regular microbuses run from the dusty parking lot just off Bab Antakya St in Aleppo as far as the village of Daret Aazeh (30 minutes, S£35), from where it is a further 6 km or so to the site. If you do not want to walk or hitch, it is usually possible to negotiate a ride for the last stretch privately, perhaps with the microbus you came on from Aleppo, although you may be charged as much as S£200 to go and come back. Be aware that microbuses back to Aleppo from Daret Aazeh tend to peter out by late afternoon.

Background

The construction of the church of St Simeon was an imperial project, undertaken on a huge scale and employing architects and skilled artisans from Constantinople and Antioch. The cult status achieved by St Simeon during his life (see box, page 238) had considerable political significance. The Eastern Church at that time was in a state of internal turmoil, brought about by obscure theological disputes as to the nature of Christ (most notably the Monophysite schism). This in effect pitted the church of Antioch against that of Constantinople, and to the imperial authorities in Constantinople the cult of St Simeon provided a welcome distraction from a dispute which was threatening their authority. After his death, by taking over responsibility for the construction of the church, they hoped to reinforce their power by associating themselves with this enormously popular saint.

In AD 526 and again in AD 528, only years after all the building work was completed, northern Syria was rocked by violent earthquakes, although the damage to the church appears to have been surprisingly minimal. In the seventh century the region fell to the **Muslim Arab** invaders. It was retaken by the **Byzantines** in the 10th century and subsequently the whole complex was fortified (it is probably from this time that its present name, Qala'at Samaan, meaning 'fortress of St Simeon' originates). The **Hamdanids** of Aleppo, led by Said ud-Daula, recaptured it in AD 985, then in 1017 it was sacked by **Fatimid** forces from Egypt. Nevertheless, it continued to exist as a pilgrimage centre late into the 12th century, after which it was abandoned and, thanks to the depopulation of the area, left largely untouched until now.

The ruins

ⓘ *0900-1800 in summer, 0900-1600 in winter, entry S£150 (students S£10). There are lots of postcards, as well as various booklets and souvenirs, on sale at the ticket office. The toilets are in the block to your left after you enter the site.*

The site consists of a huge church, the most important feature of the pilgrimage site, and various accompanying buildings, all on a long, narrow ridge which was artificially levelled. The church is centred on St Simeon's pillar; a large octagonal courtyard surrounds the pillar, and radiating from this are four large basilicas arranged in the shape of a cross. Immediately to the southeast is an L-shaped monastery complex and chapel, while further to the south is a second group of buildings, including a small baptistry and basilica.

From the ticket office a path leads up onto the top of the ridge; to your left (south) is the baptistry, while to your right (north) is the main **Church of St Simeon**. Turning to the right, you are in fact approaching along the last stretch of the processional route, or *Via Sacra*, which originally led up from Deir Samaan on the plain below, past the baptistery and so to the church. In front of you is the main triple-arched entrance, leading via a *narthex* (entrance hall) into the southern basilica. In its architecture, the overall design of the entrance is typically Roman although the rich and elaborate carved decoration shows distinctive local influences. For example, the acanthus leaves on the capitals of the pillars curve delicately almost as if they were blowing in the wind. Decorative features such as this are believed to be innovations first employed at St Simeon which later became typical designs of Byzantine architecture.

Passing through the southern basilica you come to the octagonal courtyard, at the centre of which is all that remains of St Simeon's famous pillar, reduced to a worn and insubstantial lump of stone by the countless pilgrims who over the centuries have chipped away pieces to take home as holy relics. It has been suggested that the courtyard was originally covered by a wooden roof and that when this collapsed during one of the earthquakes of the early sixth century it was subsequently left open to the sky. Tall, wide arches link the columns which stand at the points of the octagonal courtyard, with four of these leading through to each of the basilicas.

The eastern basilica is longer than the others and ends in a large apse flanked by two smaller ones. This was the only section of the building where services were actually conducted; the other basilicas were in effect assembly halls in which pilgrims could gather. The eastern basilica is also slightly out of line with the symmetry of the overall cross-shaped design of the complex. The reasons for this are not entirely clear. It has been suggested that the builders wished to orientate it towards true east. However, while the other three basilicas do not quite line up exactly with the cardinal points of the compass, neither does the eastern one, even with its adjusted alignment. Certainly, the architects were constrained to some extent by the local topography, and the need to centre the whole structure on the position of St Simeon's pillar. This can be seen at the far end of the western basilica, where an artificial terrace had to be built out from the steep slope of the ridge in order to support it. There are particularly good views from here out over the Afrine Valley to the mountains beyond.

Outside the northern basilica is an area of higher ground from where you can get a good overall perspective of the layout of the church. Just inside the outer enclosure wall (this was part of the fortification work carried out following the Byzantine reoccupation of

Pillars of wisdom

St Simeon Stylites (literally 'St Simeon of the Pillar') was born in AD 386, the son of a Cilician farmer. Drawn to a life of asceticism from a young age, he joined a monastery at 16. Wishing to detach himself further from the world he gained permission to withdraw from the main community and lead a life of solitude and meditation on the hill where the Church of St Simeon now stands. Unfortunately solitude and meditation went out the window when large numbers of pilgrims began to flock to the site, attracted by his reputation for extreme piety.

It was this that prompted St Simeon to find a rather severe way to maintain his

detachment. In AD 417 he had a 3-m-tall pillar constructed with a platform on top. From then onwards, until his death in AD 459, 42 years later, he lived his life on top of a series of pillars, each taller than the one before, culminating in one which was 17-20 m high. And as if living on top of a pillar, utterly exposed to the elements for years on end was not a sufficiently extreme act of asceticism in itself, he spent most of his time standing, with his arms raised to heaven in prayer, or else bowing repeatedly. It's known that once a week his disciples brought him food by means of a ladder, though unfortunately the records are silent about what arrangement he had for relieving himself.

the site in the 10th century) is a small funerary chapel. From here you can also work your way round to the outside of the triple apse at the end of the eastern basilica. Interestingly, the curve of the apses extends beyond the basic rectangular shape of the basilica, a design for which the only precedent was at Qalb Lozeh (see page 245) but which was later to become typical of Syrian Christian architecture.

In the area between the south and east basilicas, there are the ruins of a **chapel** and **monastery** complex, much of it now reduced to a tumbled mass of stones but with the odd section still standing. This would have housed the resident monks and more important visitors (most people would have stayed at Deir Samaan down below).

The **baptistery** stands 150 m or so to the south of the main church. Here, those who had made the pilgrimage to the church of St Simeon but were not Christian would be baptized before being allowed into the church itself. The neatly proportioned building is topped by an octagonal drum which would once have supported a domed or conical wooden roof. Inside, there is an octagonal room, on the east side of which is a semi-circular apse with a half-dome roof and steps leading down to what was in effect a walk-through baptismal font. In the bottom of the baptismal font a fragment of patterned mosaic floor still survives. Immediately to the south, attached to the baptistery, are the remains of a small **basilica**, now largely in ruins. To the right of the baptistery as you approach from the main church, there are the scant remains of what appear to have been a hostel and stables. Below this (to the southwest of the baptistery), two arches still survive of a triple-arched **monumental gateway**, with two imposing square towers immediately to the south. The gateway stood at the top of the *Via Sacra* from Deir Samaan, marking the main entrance to the complex. The towers, meanwhile, are part of the 10th-century fortifications added by the Byzantines. If you clamber up onto one of these towers, you can get a good overview of the ruins of Deir Samaan below. You can descend on foot by this route to the ruins of Deir Samaan, scattered amongst the field below. Alternatively, if you are heading north to Ain Dara by car, the main road passes through them.

Deir Samaan

This complex started life as a small agricultural community. Early in the fifth century a monastery was founded here, where for a short time St Simeon lived as part of the monastic community (hence Deir Samaan: 'Monastery of Simeon'). Following his death and the construction of the church of St Simeon, Deir Samaan flourished as the last stopping point for pilgrims before they made the final ascent up to the church. **Hostelries**, **bazaar stalls**, **monasteries** and a **church** were established here in the fifth and sixth centuries, in what must have been a thriving centre accommodating thousands of pilgrims at a time. A little way up the hill is a partly reconstructed **monumental arch** that marks the start of the *Via Sacra* leading up to the church of St Simeon. Most of the other surviving remains of Deir Samaan are in a fairly advanced state of ruin, although the basic outlines of the buildings and in places sections of walls, etc can be clearly discerned. The ruins are interesting to wander round, although they in no way match the splendour of the church of St Simeon itself.

East to Basofan, Burj Haidar and Kharrab Shams

The turning heading east from the road leading up to St Simeon traverses a rugged upland section of the Jebel Samaan, arriving after 23 km at the main road which runs between Aleppo and Afrine. After 5 km you reach the village of **Basofan**. To the right of the road, largely concealed amongst the fields and houses of the village, are various scattered ruins, including a column and arch attached to a contemporary house. A large church once existed here dedicated, according to an inscription, to St Phocas and dating from AD 491-492. However, little of it remains to be seen. Most of the ruins here are half-buried, the ground level having risen over the centuries, and other are now used as cattle shelters.

A further 3 km along the road, you come to the village of **Burj Haidar**, where there are more substantial ruins amongst the houses. Many of the modern buildings feature stones recycled from antiquity. The ancient settlement here dates back at least to the end of the third century AD. By the sixth century it had grown to become a thriving Christian community with several churches and a monastery. The ruins of a mid-fourth-century church lie in the centre of the village, inside a farmyard. Originally a three-aisled structure, only two rows of columns and arches which separated the aisles survive. To the north of it is a large tower built of huge roughly cut slabs of stone. On the west edge of the village are the ruins of a sixth-century monastery. To the left of the road as you head east out of the village there is a small well preserved chapel with a rectangular building attached to it.

Continuing east, after 5 km you arrive at the village of **Kharrab Shams**. Just before you reach the village, clearly visible off to the left of the road are the remains of a well preserved fourth-century church. The side aisles of the church are completely collapsed but the central arcaded nave with its five arches on either side is almost perfectly preserved, giving the building a striking, if slightly odd, appearance. The church bears a strong stylistic resemblance to the church at Mushabbak, which dates from the late fifth century, leading to suggestions that it was rebuilt around this time. Certainly, there is evidence of different phases of construction. Note, for example, how on the south side there are 10 windows in the upper *clerestory*, while on the north (older) side there are only five. There are numerous other ruins scattered around the church, including door frames, parts of walls, dwellings which have been built onto natural caves and rock-cut tombs. The first settlement here in fact goes back to the pre-Roman era. On top of the hill behind the church there are the ruins of a small chapel and, on the way up to it, what appears to have been a Roman villa, its well preserved walls built of massive slabs of stone. From the top of the hill, away to the northwest a cluster of ruins – the Dead City site of Barad – are clearly visible.

Returning to the road and continuing east, 10 km or so beyond Kharrab Shams you arrive at a T-junction. Going right (south) takes you back to Aleppo, 15 km away. Going left (north) you are on the main road to Afrine; a detour from this road takes you to the ruins of Cyrrhus near the Turkish border (the route described below heads north from St Simeon, passing Ain Dara, to join the Aleppo–Afrine road at Afrine).

North to Ain Dara and Cyrrhus

From the fork for St Simeon, the main road passes through the ruins of Deir Samaan, heading north across a fertile plain. It then follows the **Afrine River** as it winds its way through fields, orchards and gently rolling hills. Towards the northern end of the village of Basoutah, 15 km from the St Simeon turning, there is a petrol station. It is just under 4 km further on to the village of Ain Dara, where there is a clearly signposted left turn for the ancient mound and archaeological site of Ain Dara, 2 km away along a newly surfaced access road.

Ain Dara

The large mound at Ain Dara shows evidence of settlement from the first millennium BC through to the 16th century AD. The feature of greatest interest, however, is the neo-Hittite temple dating from the 10th-9th century BC. In 1980 a relief depicting a figure identified as Ishtar was discovered, which suggests that the temple was dedicated to this Semitic fertility goddess. Of Babylonian/Assyrian origin, Ishtar was equated with Astarte, the Phoenician goddess of fertility and love, who was in turn identified with the Egyptian goddess Isis and later with the Greek and Roman goddesses Aphrodite and Venus. Despite the archaeological importance of the site, some may find it somewhat disappointing to visit. The main temple is encircled by a band of concrete supported on pillars, the beginnings of a seemingly abandoned plan to erect a protective structure over the ruins.

Ins and outs

Getting there and away From St Simeon, you can continue hitching north, but be aware there is little traffic on this road. From Aleppo, microbuses run to the town of Afrine (one hour, S£95) from the north microbus station (known as 'Sahat Shahira Mol') which is a considerable distance from the city centre. From Afrine you have to walk or hitch the 7 km to the site or negotiate a return ride with a taxi.

The ruins

ⓘ *Open daily during daylight hours. S£75, students S£5. The caretaker lives in the archaeologists' buildings at the foot of the mound. From there it's a short walk to the top.*

The main temple occupies the northwest area of the mound. The steps leading up to the south entrance of the temple are flanked by two carved lions, and running around the outer walls are more friezes of lions and sphinxes. However, the elements have caused extensive damage to the carvings, the black basalt stone cracking and flaking so that many of the reliefs are barely discernible. Carved into the stone paving leading from the entrance to the inner temple are huge footprints, perhaps meant to convey the presence of the goddess Ishtar at the temple. To the southwest of the main temple there is a huge statue of a lion carved from basalt, its crude, massive proportions typical of the neo-Hittite style (as seen at the Aleppo Museum).

Ain Dara to Cyrrhus

Continuing north from the turning for Ain Dara, after a further 6 km you arrive at a T-junction with the main Aleppo–Afrine road. Turning left here takes you into the small, predominantly Kurdish town and district centre of **Afrine**, where there are a few simple restaurants, but no hotel. Turning right, the road leads first northwest, before bearing south towards Aleppo. After 11 km you arrive at a crossroads; the left turn here is clearly signposted for 'Nebi Huri' (the Arabic name for Cyrrhus). However, a recent dam-building project, and the associated creation of a large lake, has rendered this a rather complicated route by which to approach the site, involving a lengthy and confusing detour.

The more straightforward option is to go via the town of **Azaz**. Around 5 km further along the main road, take the clearly signposted left turn for Azaz. Go straight across the first roundabout you come to (just under 4 km from the main road; the microbus station is located here), and then go left 400 m further on at a second roundabout in the centre of the town (signposted 'Turkia as-Salama'). After a further 600 m, turn left again. This road is very scenic, taking you through the rolling limestone hills and olive groves.

After around 17 km you pass through the small village of Deir Sowan, and then some 2.5 km further on you come to the first of two steeply hump-backed **Roman bridges**. This first one consists of three arches spanning the upper reaches of the Afrine River, while the next one (1.5 km further on) consists of six arches spanning the Sabun Sayu River. Both date from the late second century AD. They show signs of having been repaired and strengthened in the Byzantine and Islamic periods, but, even so, the fact that they are still serviceable is no small tribute to the original engineering skills of the Romans, and clearly illustrates the importance they attached to road building. A little under 2 km further on, you come to a sharp right turn signposted to 'Al Nabi Houry' (just under 1 km away along a rough track), while a little further on, on the left, is a distinctive hexagonal Roman tower tomb.

Cyrrhus (Nebi Huri)

Following the conquest of Syria by Pompey in 64 BC, Cyrrhus became part of the Roman Empire. In the mid-first century AD it was made into an administrative centre and headquarters of a legion. Its interest to the Romans was both as a military base from which they could conduct their campaigns against the Armenians to the north, and as a commercial centre on the trade route between Antioch and the Euphrates River crossing at Zeugma (in Turkey, near Birecik). During the third century it suffered invasion and occupation at the hands of the Persians on a number of occasions, but began to recover as an important centre of Christianity in the fourth century. It was here that the remains of St Cosmas and St Damien were buried, making it a popular place of pilgrimage, known at that time as Hagiopolis. Theodoret, to whom we owe much of our knowledge of St Simeon, was bishop here from around AD 423-450. During the mid-sixth century the town was refortified and its garrison strengthened by the emperor Justinian in an attempt to make it into a bulwark against the Persian threat. Even after the Muslim conquest of AD 637 it continued as an important Christian centre. During the early 11th century it was taken by the Crusaders and placed under the control of the Count of Edessa. In 1150 it was recaptured by Nur ud-Din but subsequently appears to have lost its strategic significance, and was abandoned soon afterwards.

Ins and outs

Getting there and away By public transport Cyrrhus is difficult to get to. There are microbuses from the north microbus station 'Sahat Shahira Mol' in Aleppo to the town of Azaz (S£75), 23 km to the southeast of Cyrrhus. From there, the only viable option is to negotiate a return ride with a taxi, since traffic is very limited on the road to the site.

The ruins

Beside the road is a **Roman tower tomb** dating from the late second to early third century AD. The squat, solid hexagonal tower has a pyramid-shaped roof with a bulb of carved acanthus leaves at its apex. The lower floor now houses the tomb of a 14th-century Muslim saint and has been extended to accommodate a small mosque as well. Steps lead up inside the tower to the upper floor, where arched windows in each face look out onto the surrounding countryside.

The track leading from the road to the main ruins of Cyrrhus passes first through the heavily ruined remains of the **South Gate** of the city. From here it follows what was the north-south oriented *cardo maximus*, to arrive at the **theatre**, which dates from around the mid-second century AD, making it roughly contemporary with the theatre at Bosra. Measuring 115 m in diameter originally, it would have been even larger than the theatre at Bosra, though today, in its half-ruined state, this is difficult to imagine. The theatre formed the main focus of excavation and reconstruction work carried out here by French teams from the 1950s onwards. Its basic outline is still clearly discernible, while scattered all around are column sections, carved capitals and huge slabs of masonry. Around 500 m to the north of the theatre, further along the line of the *cardo maximus*, the outline of a very large rectangular building or compound can be seen. In the southwest corner of this you can see the remains of what appears to have been a tower with an arched gateway. Directly to the east of (and downhill from) the theatre, the apse and basic outline of a basilica **church** can be discerned, while further east and downhill again are traces of further buildings.

Sitting on top of the steep hill, directly behind the theatre is the city's **citadel**, now largely ruined but with parts of it surviving, including a bastion and arch. As you would expect from a fort, it has impressive panoramic views. Also up on the hill, traces of the **defensive walls** can still be seen following the contour of the hill, particularly to the northeast of the citadel. Both the citadel and defensive walls date from the refortifications carried out by Justinian, although they stand on the foundations of the Hellenistic/Roman defences, reusing much of the original stonework.

West of Aleppo: Jebel al-Ala

Extending north-south in a narrow ridge of hills, the Jebel al-Ala is perhaps the most rugged and isolated stretch of the Belus Massif, and yet somehow strangely beautiful. This is the setting for the beautifully preserved church of Qalb Lozeh, as well as a number of other sites. Scattered amongst the hills are also a number of small Druze communities which have been here since the 10th century.

Border crossing: Syria–Turkey

The **Bab al-Hawa** border is the main crossing between Syria and Turkey and all service taxis and buses from Damascus or Aleppo will use this one. It's an extremely busy border and if you're travelling on a large bus expect delays due to customs searches on the Turkish side. If you're in a service taxi or minibus you generally whizz through the border reasonably fast. From the border it is only 45 minutes to Antakya, from where buses leave for destinations all over Turkey.

Exit formalities here are straightforward. On the Syrian side you have to pay S£550 departure tax and then get stamped out of the country (don't forget to have your entry card with you to hand in to the border official). Your bus/taxi will then head to the Turkish side where you need to pay for your tourist visa.

Nearly all nationalities are granted three-month Turkish tourist visas on arrival. Some nationalities (including New Zealand and South Korea) are given free entry. Australian, US and most European nationalities pay US$20. Check beforehand.

The Turkish side of the border is quite spread out and in the past two years they have moved the office where you pay for your visa three times. Your bus/taxi driver will point out where you have to go. There are clean toilets, a good duty-free store, and a money exchange on the Turkish side. There are plenty of money-exchange places in Antakya which will also change your Syrian pounds into Turkish lira.

Aleppo to Qalb Lozeh

Head west out of Aleppo on Ibrahim Hanano Street to join the Damascus motorway. After around 6 km, take the exit signposted for Bab al-Hawa. The exit appears rather suddenly, but don't worry if you miss it as there is a second exit 800 m further on which joins up with the first. To begin with the road is a busy four-lane highway which passes through an area of fairly built-up linear settlement. Around 18 km after leaving the motorway, where the main road swings round to the right, there is a left turn signposted for Idlib (and also, slightly confusingly, to Jisr al-Shughur and Lattakia).

Just under 4 km further on there is a second left turn signposted to Idlib. Carrying straight on, after a little under 9 km, just as you enter the village of **Tal al-Karamah** and the main road bends round to the right, it crosses a particularly well preserved section of **Roman road**. The most impressive section branches off straight ahead from the right-hand bend. It is raised above the level of the surrounding countryside and built of large, carefully hewn stone blocks, heavily worn but surprisingly intact.

Just over 1 km further on there is a right turn signposted to St Simeon and Daret Aazah, and then, after a little under 4 km, you come to a large (and rather confusing) roundabout/junction. Go straight across, and then bear right immediately after, following signs for 'Harem' (Harim). The road passes through the small town of **Sarmada** before heading across open countryside characterized by dramatic and desolate hills of bare rock. Around 6 km from the roundabout/junction, the ruins of a couple of buildings (the remains of a sixth-century **Byzantine monastery complex**) are clearly visible off to the right, halfway up a rocky ridge. Soon after, you come to a crossroads; a path from here leads between drystone walls towards the ridge, from where you can reach the ruins. Of far greater interest, however, are the ruins of Baqerha and Khirbet Khateb.

Baqerha and Khirbet Khateb To reach this impressive Dead City site, turn right at the crossroads and follow the narrow winding road as it climbs steeply up onto the ridge and then through a small village, to arrive after 3 km at an extensive cluster of ruins on the right. Dating from the late fifth to early sixth century AD, this was clearly a substantial settlement. Amongst the ruins you can identify at least three **churches** and numerous **private houses**, as well as **civic buildings**, **towers** and deep **wells**. Continuing another 800 m or so up the road, you come to a small solitary **chapel** on the left, with the remains of what appears to be a **tower** next to it. The roof of the chapel is missing, but otherwise it is remarkably well preserved, and adorned with a distinctive style of wave-pattern decoration running around the ground floor and upper storey windows (a feature common to many of the ruins at this site). Higher up the hillside there are more ruins. Though it doesn't look like it, you can actually reach these ruins by following the road; turn left at a T-junction after 500 m and they are to the left of the road after a further 500 m. There is plenty to explore here, but the hightlight is the remains of a large triple-aisled basilica **church**. The most impressive feature is the elaborately decorated front façade, leaning precariously but still standing in all its glory right the way to the tip of its third-storey gable end. Another 200 m further up the road, marked by a gateway of heavy stone slabs beside the road on the left, are the remains of a second century AD **Roman temple** dedicated to Zeus Bombos (literally Zeus of the Altar). The gateway is just about all that remains of the temple's *temenos*, but the *cella* is quite well preserved, with the rear wall and parts of the side walls still standing. On a clear day there are excellent views from here out across the plains below.

Harim Another 1 km brings you back to the main road, a little over 3 km beyond the crossroads; turn right to continue west towards Harim. Very soon after, you pass through a small village. A little under 5 km further on there is a left turn signposted for 'Qalb Lawza' and 'Hattan', but the more interesting route is to go via the town of Harim. After just over 11 km you arrive at a roundabout in the centre of Harim. On a steep hillock near the centre of the town are the crumbling ruins of a **fortress**. Although a stronghold was first established here by the Byzantine emperor Nicephorus Phocas in 959, the existing ruins date largely from the construction work carried out by the Ayyubid ruler of Aleppo, Al Zaher Ghazi, in 1199. From 1097 when it was captured by the Crusaders prior to their siege of Antioch until the late 13th century when it was largely destroyed during the Mongol invasions, control of Harim passed back and forth repeatedly between the Crusaders and Muslims. Today little remains of the fortifications, although there are good views from the top, and a couple of pleasant **restaurants** down below.

Harim to Qalb Lozeh From the roundabout in Harim, take the signposted turning for Qalb Lozeh. After just under 2 km, fork right onto a rough old road (clearly signposted for 'Kalb Lawza', 'Bnabel' and 'Kafer Keela'). The road, narrow and poorly surfaced in places, climbs steeply up into the hills of the Jebel al-Ala, with excellent views back down onto the plains below. At the village of **Bnabel**, 4.5 km beyond the fork, the well preserved remains of a Roman villa are visible to the right of the road. After another 4 km, having passed various scattered ruins, you arrive at what is effectively a crossroads. Immediately before, a small road leads off to the left to the site of **Kirk Bizeh** (clearly visible from the road), where there are the ruins of a fourth-century church and assorted other buildings. Turn sharp right at the crossroads and it is less than 1 km to the village of Qalb Lozeh. The church of Qalb Lozeh is towards the far end of the village, close to the road.

Qalb Lozeh

The small village of Qalb Lozeh (literally 'Heart of the Almond'), predominantly Druze like most of the villages in this part of the Jebel al-Ala, is an unlikely setting for this unusual church. Thought to have been built as early as AD 450, it was (like the church at Mushabbak) perhaps conceived as a stopping place for pilgrims en route to visit Deir Samaan – already an important pilgrimage centre even before St Simeon's death. Thus it pre-dates the church of St Simeon, and in its layout represents the earliest example of a broad-aisled basilica church. Both its design and decoration provide an excellent early example of the Syrian style of Byzantine ecclesiastical architecture.

Ins and outs
Getting there and away Microbuses run from the city/microbus station (off Bab Antakya Street) in Aleppo to Idlib (S£85). From there you can get a microbus to Harim. From Harim, hitching is not really practical given the extremely limited amounts of traffic on the road to Qalb Lozeh, so you will have to negotiate a return ride with a taxi (or anyone you can find who is willing to take you).

The church
ⓘ *Open daily during daylight hours, S£75, students S£5. The church is kept locked and the current caretaker lives in the village of Bnabel, 5 km away, so if you arrive late in the day you may find that he has already gone home.*

Initially it is worth making a tour of the outside of the church. The *narthex* or entrance hall at the west end of the church is flanked by two towers which were originally joined by a broad arch (now collapsed). Beyond this, the lintel of the central doorway is topped by its own, much smaller arch. At the opposite end of the church, the apse, decorated with engaged colonnettes between the windows, extends beyond the basic rectangular plan. Known as a *chevet*, this extension of the apse represents a departure from earlier church designs where the apse was contained within the exterior rectangular plan. It is a feature repeated in the eastern basilica at St Simeon. The south side of the church has three richly decorated doorways, once protected by wooden porches, and a line of arched windows. The north side has two doorways, one of which you enter through. Inside, two rows of three broad arches supported on piers divide the central nave from the side aisles. The southern side aisle still retains parts of its roofing, consisting of long slabs of limestone laid horizontally. The central nave would originally have been covered with a wooden roof, the windows of the *clerestory* providing light to the interior, unobstructed by the flat-roofed side aisles. At the east end of the church, the half-domed semicircular apse, framed with elaborate decoration, is beautifully preserved.

South from Qalb Lozeh
Rather than returning the way you came, you can continue south from Qalb Lozeh, following the line of a high exposed ridge of the Jebel al-Ala, before descending to join the main road between Harim and Idlib. Around 2.5 km to the south of Qalb Lozeh is a rough track on the left which leads in 500 m or so to the site of Behyo.

Behyo The settlement here is thought only to have been established in the fifth century (quite late compared with other Dead City sites). Despite the particularly harsh and rugged environment in which it is set, it quickly grew to a substantial size and what remains to be seen today, although heavily ruined, extends over a wide area. Bathed in sunlight the ruins are very atmospheric, and the views from here quite spectacular. The partially standing remains of a sizeable church are clearly discernible; while all around amongst the scattered ruins are large masonry blocks bearing fragments of carved decoration and Byzantine crosses, as well as a number of olive presses.

Returning to the road and continuing south, you pass some insubstantial ruins and then through a couple of villages, before descending steeply down to a T-junction in the town of Kafr Takhariem (17 km from Qalb Lozeh). Turning left here leads south and then southwest to Idlib (35 km), while right leads back to Harim, 10 km to the north.

Idlib → For listings, see page 253.

Idlib is the chief town of the Mouhafazat (Governorate) of the same name. A series of roads radiate from the town, connecting it with the road leading to the Syrian/Turkish border crossing of Bab al-Hawa (see below, West to Qalb Lozeh), the main Aleppo–Damascus motorway and the road to Lattakia. It's not the most interesting town but it does have an excellent museum which is well worth a visit for its impressive collection from the excavations at Ebla (Tell Mardikh).

Ins and outs
Getting there and away From Aleppo's city/microbus station (off Bab Antakya Street) regular microbuses depart for Idlib (S£85).

Getting around Idlib's museum is on the east side of town, beside Ath Thawra Square (actually a large roundabout on the ring road).

Idlib museum
① Wed-Mon 0900-1800 in summer, 0900-1600 in winter, S£150, students S£10.
There are various pieces of mosaics, carved friezes, capitals and other architectural fragments in the gardens of the museum which are worth a look. Inside, on the ground floor, there are more mosaics (some of them very impressive), terracotta figurines, various items of pottery and ceramics, and an extensive collection of coins spanning the Roman through to the Ottoman periods. There are also some displays of costumes and fabrics (very much in the usual 'popular traditions' mould), and some contemporary paintings. The main focus of interest, however, is the 'Ebla Pavilion' on the first floor. The displays here are well presented and there is an impressive collection of the famous clay tablets inscribed in the Sumerian cuneiform script. Other artefacts include fragments of furniture covered in gold leaf, incredibly intricate terracotta figurines, gold and lapis lazuli jewellery, fragments of inlaid friezes and a relief of the Semitic fertility goddess Ishtar. All these artefacts, together with the various photos of the site at the time of the excavations, go a long way towards bringing Ebla to life. Also upstairs, at the opposite end to the 'Ebla Pavilion' are cases displaying a rich and impressive collection of artefacts from various other sites in the vicinity of Idlib.

Southwest of Aleppo: Jebel Riha (Jebel Zawiye)

The Jebel Riha, with its gently rolling landscape and pockets of rich, fertile agricultural land is less isolated than the Jebel al-Ala. You can reach the concentration of Dead City sites in the Jebel Riha either from the Lattakia highway or from Maarat al-Numan on the Damascus–Aleppo motorway. From Maarat al-Numan (see page 141), pick up the road heading due west towards Kafr Nubbul, passing through a more or less continuous string of villages along the way. Turn right at the mini-roundabout in the centre of Kafr Nubbul (12 km), and then after 1 km take the small right turn signposted for Bara, 7 km to the north, passing a number of other sites en route. From the Lattakia highway, take the turning leading south 6 km to the west of Ariha (see below, Aleppo to Lattakia). Follow this road, bearing left wherever it forks ambiguously, passing through the village of Ehesem before arriving at the village of Bara, 14 km away.

Bara

The modern village of Bara, strung out along the main road, is growing rapidly and is close to becoming a small town in size. The ruins are scattered over a large area, in amongst the dry-stone walls of fields, olive groves and orchards to the west of the modern village, with a number of narrow roads and tracks linking the most important ruins. Without your own transport, getting around the ruins involves quite a bit of walking; in hot weather be sure to bring plenty of water and adequate protection against the sun.

Ins and outs

Getting there and away Unusually, it is actually possible to get all the way to the modern village of Bara by public transport. Microbuses run fairly regularly from the city/microbus station (off Bab Antakya Street) in Aleppo to Ariha (S£75), from where there are less frequent microbuses on to Bara. Be sure to check what time the last microbus leaves Bara for the return journey. From Bara modern village though it is quite a hike around the ruins; negotiate with your microbus driver to take you the rest of the way.

The ruins

ⓘ *The only monument at Bara which is kept locked is the large pyramid tomb. If you want to inspect the sarcophagi inside in more detail, contact the site guardian, Hussein Aboud. His office is on the main street running through the modern village, with a sign announcing 'Directeur General D'Antiquities, Guardien de Al Bara'. He does not speak English, but the local teacher, Hassan Al Shaf, does. He can help find someone to guide you around the site if you wish, and possibly also arrange overnight accommodation; contact him in advance (preferably in the evening) on T023-450134.*

As you enter Bara from the north, there is a sharp right turn at the start of the village signposted for the 'Ruins of Bara'. Taking this turning, fork left after 500 m and follow the narrow road past various fragments of ruins to arrive in a further 600 m at a **pyramid tomb** on the left. This is the smaller and plainer of two such tombs to be found at Bara. Its pyramid-shaped roof is almost completely intact, while inside there are the broken remains of three sarcophagi. Next to the tomb are the remains of a large rectangular building, with one arch inside still standing. A little way away, across the road from the pyramid tomb and up on higher ground, the remains of a large church and monastery complex are clearly visible.

Back on the road, turn left immediately beyond the pyramid tomb and keep going for around 500 m, past various other fragments of ruins, to arrive at the **large pyramid tomb** on the right. Only about half of its pyramid roof survives, but, as if to make up for this, it is much more ornate. The lintel above the door is richly decorated, while running around the top of the square base on the outside of the building are two bands of carved decoration. In each corner is a carved pilaster, and in each face two small, arched windows. The entrance to the tomb is protected by a locked iron grille, but you can peer inside, where there are five sarcophagi, all still with their lids intact and with carved medallions containing Byzantine crosses.

A short walk across the fields more or less directly opposite the pyramid tomb brings you to the ruins of a large monastery complex, distinctive as you approach it from this side for the large rectangular window flanked by two smaller square ones, each with Byzantine crosses on the lintels. A little further on is a large complex of several buildings, though to the untrained eye it presents little more than a confusing jumble of walls, arches and tumbled-down ruins. Back on the road, just past the large pyramid tomb, a left turn leads back towards the modern village. Going straight on, you pass on the right an **underground tomb** with a triple-arched porch protecting a square portal which leads into the burial chamber, where arched bays have been carved into the walls to hold sarcophagi.

Further on you come to the monastery of **Deir Sorbat**, Bara's best preserved monument after the pyramid tombs. At the centre is a church with its walls still standing to a height of two storeys, pierced by windows and doorways decorated with Byzantine crosses. Various rooms have been built onto the church, while dotted around are the ruins of several other buildings. The remains of the various other **churches** are scattered around the area between the modern village and the road linking the two pyramid tombs; a path leads past one of them, but the others can only be reached by scrambling over a number of drystone walls. To the northeast of the main concentration of ruins are the remains of the Arab fort of **Qala'at Abu Safian**, today in an advanced state of ruin.

Serjilla

If you've only got time to visit one Dead City site, make it Serjilla. Once an extensive settlement that prospered from the cultivation of grapes and olives, the remains of Serjilla allow you to picture what this town was once like when still inhabited. The ruins sit in an enchanting spot, scattered across a depression in the hills. A visit here is made more rewarding by the excellent information posts that are dotted throughout the site.

Ins and outs

Getting there and away If you're driving from Bara, the signposted turn-off to Serjilla is 300 m south of Bara modern village. The ruins are just over 3.5 km down this road.

From Aleppo, on public transport, regular microbuses ply between Aleppo's city/microbus station (off Bab Antakya Street) and Maarat al-Numan (S£75) and Ariha (S£75). If you want to cover Serjilla and Bara in one trip it's probably best to go to Ariha and from there catch a microbus to Bara (see above). From Maarat al-Numan you can try to convince your microbus driver to take you the rest of the way (if there are a few of you this can be economical) or hitch.

If you're coming from Hama, you can catch regular microbuses to Maarat al-Numan from the Iraq Street microbus stand.

The ruins

ⓘ *Wed-Mon 0900-1800 in summer, 0900-1600 in winter, S£75, students S£5. There is a small restaurant beside the site. Toilets are inside the site to the left, ask the caretaker for the key.*

From the road-head, a path leads down past the well preserved remains of a **baths complex** on the left, and next to it an **andron**, or meeting hall. The baths, which have been dated to AD 473, are an indication of the wealth of this community and are unusual in that they date from the Christian rather than the Roman period. The American team from Princeton University who carried out excavations here discovered a large mosaic covering the floor of the main hall of the baths, but when they returned six years later it had been removed. Traces of murals (now destroyed) were also found on the walls.

Continuing along the path, also on the left, are the ruins of a **church**, of which little remains, with an underground burial chamber below it. On the hillside to the left above the church is a particularly large and well preserved **villa** with its two storeys still standing. Note how two of the rooms inside each contain an arch which would have supported the ceiling. This is a feature which can be seen amongst the ruins of many of the Dead Cities; here the good state of preservation makes its structural significance much clearer. Behind the house is a sunken building containing an olive press. Scattered across the hillside to the southeast are the ruins of numerous other houses.

South of Bara

There are a number of other ruins of lesser interest which can be visited as short diversions off the road heading south from Bara. Some 3 km to the south of Bara there is a turning west signposted for the ruins of **Bshala**, 1.5 km away. Also, 6 km to the south of Bara a turning east is signposted for the ruins of **Rabia** and **Shinshrah**, 3 km and 5 km away respectively. While these sites do not have anything particularly notable to offer amongst the scattered ruins, the isolated setting of the latter two, with their panoramic views of the the surrounding rolling hills and olive groves, is gently impressive.

Ruweiha and Jerada

The two Dead City sites of Ruweiha and Jerada are east of Bara. The best way to get to them is by turning south off the Lattakia highway into the the town of **Ariha** (see page 251, Aleppo to Lattakia). After turning off the highway, go straight on past a fork with a petrol station in the crook of the fork and then bear left at the roundabout soon after. The road climbs steeply into the Jebel Riha, passing a couple of summer restaurants with excellent views down onto Ariha and out over the plains around Idlib. Some 14 km after the Lattakia highway exit, where the road bends round to the right, there is a fork off to the left signposted for the 'Ruins of Roweiha and Gerada' (straight on leads to Maarat al-Numan).

You come first to the ruins of **Ruweiha**, to the left of the road after 4 km, set in a dramatic landscape of rolling hills on an open plateau. There are a couple of modern buildings, but elsewhere surviving buildings of the ancient settlement have simply been reoccupied. Some scrambling is necessary as many of the ruins are now enclosed within dry-stone walls. Close to the road there are the ruins of a **church**, with a series of columns and arches which once separated the nave from a side-aisle still standing. Many of the buildings here are of almost palatial proportions, an indication of the high degree of prosperity which the town must have achieved. Their excellent state of preservation, meanwhile, gives an idea of the quality of workmanship involved. Further away from the road to the northeast, after passing through the main body of the ruins, there is a second larger church, now used as a farm. This has been identified from an inscription as the **Church of Bissos**, dating from the sixth century. The domed structure on the south side of the church housed the tomb of Bissos, who was perhaps the local priest or bishop. At the eastern end of the vilage there is a small, perfectly intact **funerary monument** with even its roof still in place. It looks distinctly Roman in style, with two hefty columns supporting the triangular *pediment* of the porch. A little further to the east is what was clearly the burial area of the settlement. Close to the road there are a couple of **underground tombs** with decorated entrances. Various other underground burial chambers are dotted around, their entrances sealed by massive stone lids, though some of these have been jacked up on stones, allowing you to peer inside. There are also a couple of more elaborate above-ground mausoleums, one topped by a massive sarcophagus which, along with its lid, is still intact.

The ruins of **Jerada** are 3 km further on, interspersed with the buildings of a contemporary village. They include a couple of **watchtowers** dating from the fifth or sixth century, one of them still standing to its full height, along with the ruins of several buildings and a church. The presence of watchtowers perhaps indicates the greater vulnerability of settlements such as this, which were closer to the desert and so liable to attack from nomadic tribes.

Continuing east from Jerada, you arrive after a further 3 km at the sliproad leading from the Damascus–Aleppo motorway to the village of Babila. **Note** If you wish to reach Jerada and Ruweiha from the motorway, the turning is signposted for 'Babila, Grada', 70 km to the south of Aleppo and 14 km to the south of the turning for Ebla, or 6 km to the north of the turning for Maarat al-Numan.

Northeast of Aleppo

Heading northeast from Aleppo, the landscape is flat and featureless, with vast expanses of rain-fed arable land gradually giving way to arid semi-desert. By the time you reach Qala'at Najm, on the banks of the Euphrates, the land is parched and barren, despite the presence of this mighty river. Although certainly an impressive site (and all the more so for its setting), it is a long way to come, particularly as a round trip from Aleppo. If you have your own transport and are planning to visit the Jezira region, you could use this as an alternative route into the Jezira.

Aleppo to Qala'at Najm

To join the road leading northeast towards Qala'at Najm, follow directions as for the Euphrates highway (see page 285). After leaving the Euphrates highway, the first 31 km or so, up until you arrive at a roundabout and exits for Tadef and Al Bab, is along a broad four-lane highway. A further 45 km along a normal two-lane road brings you to a second roundabout, the left turning here signposted to 'Monbej', 2 km away.

Membij The town of Membij was a centre for the cult worship of the Mesopotamian goddess Atargatis and her consort Hadad during the Persian period. The town was Hellenized and renamed Hierapolis by Seleucus I Nicator in the third century BC. The worship of Atargatis, which involved various bloody ritualistic practices including the sacrifice of children, continued during Roman times and Membij became perhaps the most important religious centre in Syria, its fame spreading throughout the Roman Empire. Today, however, Membij is a dusty, uninspiring place with nothing to see and little to recommend it.

Some 17 km further on from the roundabout/exit for Membij there is a small left turn signposted to 'Qalaat Najem', 14 km away. Taking this turning, after passing through a couple of small villages, the Euphrates River appears, almost like a mirage, up ahead. Soon after, you arrive at the castle itself.

Qala'at Najm

Known as *Caeciliana* to the Romans, this site was an important crossing point on the Euphrates, from where Roman forces were able to launch offensives against the Parthians of Mesopotamia. The present castle was first built by Nur ud-Din in the 12th century but subsequently largely reconstructed by the Ayyubid ruler of Aleppo, Al-Zaher Ghazi (the son of Salah ud-Din), in the early 13th century. Al-Zaher Ghazi was also responsible for much of the fortification work carried out on Aleppo's citadel and the parallels between the two are obvious, particularly in terms of the stone glacis surrounding the castle. The Mongol invasions of the late 13th and early 14th century took their toll on the castle, however, and soon afterwards it was abandoned.

Ins and outs

Getting there and away Old hob-hob style buses and microbuses leave from Aleppo's East bus station (known as 'Garage Sharqi') heading to Ain al-Arab fairly regularly (S£65). All these buses run via Membij and the turn-off for Qala'at Najm. Make sure that someone understands where you are going so that you can be dropped off at the right place. From the turning it is still a further 14 km and there is little traffic along this road. It's better to be dropped in Membij rather than at the turn-off and from there you can negotiate a return fare with a taxi driver.

The castle

① Open daily during daylight hours, there is no official admission fee. The caretaker gives a guided tour so tip him for his efforts. A torch is useful for exploring the castle's darker corners.

The castle stands on a natural high point by the banks of the Euphrates, with inspiring views out over the river, which flows past here in a broad and majestic sweep, and the mud-brick village of Qala'at Najm nestled below. In recent years a joint Syrian-Spanish team has carried out extensive restoration work on the castle, to impressive effect. The stairway and neatly arched bridge leading up to the entrance is a modern reconstruction. The inscription above the tall arched entrance gate details the work carried out by Al Zaher Ghazi in the 13th century. This leads through into a large vaulted entrance hall. Bearing off to the left from here and ascending, you arrive at the castle's **palace**, built around a central courtyard with a basin and fountain in the centre and arched *iwans* around the sides. Steps lead down from here to the **dungeons**, where traces of a church dating from the early Byzantine period have been identified. A passage leads from the courtyard through to the palace's **hammam**, where traces of ceramic waterpipes can be seen. A number of large, cool rooms served as storage, with deep grain pits and water cisterns. Two flights of stairs take you up to the roof of the palace, from where there are excellent views. Returning to the entrance hall, if you go right and then left through a dog-leg, you find yourself in a long, vaulted passage which has been identified as the **souq** or market; note the remains of rings cut into the walls for tethering animals. From here you can gain access to the upper **ramparts** of the castle (once again with excellent views), and the **mosque**.

Aleppo to Lattakia

The route to Lattakia is varied and picturesque. Having crossed the plateau to the southwest of Aleppo, it traverses the northern reaches of the Jebel Riha, before descending to the fertile plains of the Orontes River (and crossing it at Jisr al-Shughur). Having crossed the Orontes, it climbs steeply, winding its way through the Jebel Ansariye mountains before descending to the broad coastal plain surrounding Lattakia.

Unfortunately, the road is also extremely busy with heavily laden trucks crawling along what is the only route connecting Lattakia with the main transport corridor between Aleppo and Damascus. A motorway is planned which will eventually connect Lattakia with Aleppo. The first stretch after leaving the Damascus–Aleppo motorway has already been upgraded to motorway dimensions, while west of Ariha a certain amount of widening work is in progress. For the most part, however, the road is narrow and, particularly through the Jebel Ansariye mountains, quite treacherous in places. You are strongly advised to avoid driving this route at night. If you are travelling between Aleppo and Lattakia by public transport, the train journey along this route is easily the most scenic in Syria and well worth considering as an alternative to going by road.

From the centre of Aleppo, head west along Ibrahim Hanano Streeet to join the Aleppo–Damascus motorway. Continue past the exit for the Syrian/Turkish border post at Bab al-Hawa (6 km; also signposted for Idlib and, slightly confusingly, Ariha, Jisr al-Shughur and Lattakia). Take the next major exit, just over 40 km further on, signposted for Ariha, Jisr al-Shughur and Lattakia (and also Saraqeb and Idlib). Following this road (effectively a motorway for this first stretch), you arrive after 22 km at an interchange (left for the town of Ariha and the road to the Dead City sites of Ruweiha and Jerada; right for the town of Idlib, see above). Continue straight, passing after another 6 km the left turn for Bara. Further on the road begins to descend from the hills of the Jebel Riha with views down onto a fertile, patchwork quilt landscape of fields extending over the Al-Ghab plains of the Orontes River. In the small village of Frikeh (or Ferayka), a little over 28 km from the Ariha/Idlib junction, there is a left turn signposted for amongst others 'Madiq Citadel'. This road runs due south along the Al Ghab plain to Apamea (Qala'at Mudiq), 34 km away (see page 134). After a further 7 km, you arrive in the centre of Jisr al-Shughur.

Jisr al-Shughur The town of Jisr al-Shughur has since ancient times been an important crossing point over the Orontes River. In the Seleucid period it was known as *Seleucia ad Bellum* and in Roman times as *Niaccuba*. The bridge across the Orontes here in fact dates back originally to Roman times, although it has been repaired and strengthened numerous times over the centuries (note the variety of stones from which the piers and arches are built). In its present form it is essentially a Mamluk construction of the 15th century. The town itself is busy with traffic passing through, but quite attractive in its way, with a number of old buildings from the Ottoman period still surviving. There are a number of cafés and simple restaurants along the main road.

Just over 1 km after leaving the town, where the road swings round sharply to the right, a road branches off to the left (ie straight ahead). This road runs south along the edges of the Al Ghab plain, with the mountains of the Jebel Ansariye rising immediately to the west, taking you past the ruins of Qala'at Burzey and the turning for Slunfeh (and also past Apamea, off to the east, and eventually all the way to Masyaf). Following the main road round to the right, you soon begin to climb steeply into the Jebel Ansariye. The road winds its way through picturesque hills dotted with cherry orchards, fields and small villages, with the Aleppo–Lattakia railway repeatedly crossing and recrossing it on high viaducts. There are numerous turnings off the main road, including (distances from Jisr al-Shughur); 32 km turn left for Salma and Slunfeh; 36 km turn right for Rabia and Kassab (see page 189); 41 km turn left for Salma and Slunfeh (alternative route); 46 km turn left for Haffe (or Al Haffeh, from where you can visit Qala'at Salah ud-Din; see page 191). Having descended from the Jebel Ansariye, the road runs across the coastal plain to arrive in Lattakia (see page 180), 75 km from Jisr al-Shughur and 180 km from Aleppo.

⊙ Around Aleppo listings

For Sleeping and Eating price codes and other relevant information, see Essentials pages 19-21.

⊙ Sleeping

St Simeon *p236*
E Camping Kaddour, on the main road, before St Simeons, right-hand turn-off signposted 'Camping', T021-332 3344, halabiatour@net.sy. Inside this large walled complex there are olive and fig trees dotted around providing a limited amount of shade. There is a simple but clean toilet/shower block with hot water, and a Bedouin tent-style café. This is a friendly, well run place, and something of a haven for overlanders who have just crossed into Syria via the Bab al-Hawa border. With your own transport, it also makes for a great base from which to explore the Dead City sites in the surrounding areas.

Idlib *p246*
AL Carlton, on the Ariha Rd (on the southern outskirts of town), T023-225500. This luxury hotel primarily caters for tour groups. There are comfortable though somewhat bland rooms with a/c and satellite TV and also some

bungalows arranged around a courtyard, with beehive-style domed ceilings and traditional hammam-style bathrooms. Restaurant, coffee shop, bar. Small outdoor swimming pool, as well as a large and very ornate hammam (Turkish baths) downstairs in the basement.

⊘ Eating

Idlib *p246*
There are several simple restaurants in the centre of town where you can get the usual kebabs, roast chicken, hummus, etc.

⊖ Transport

Idlib *p246*
The main bus/microbus station is on the east side of town, south of the museum and set back slightly to the east of the ring road, here known as Palestine St. There are fairly regular services from here to **Aleppo**, **Lattakia**, **Ariha** and **Maarat al-Numan**.

Contents

Footprint features

Palmyra & around

Without a doubt, Palmyra is Syria's number one attraction. After trundling through the desert plains for miles, the majestic remains of this ancient caravan town are suddenly stretched out before you, backed by the lush green palms of the oasis and the scruffy buildings of modern Tadmor.

Even as late as the 1920s the journey here was a long (five days or so) and arduous one, which required careful planning and usually an armed escort. Although the journey now involves no more than a comfortable cruise across the wide expanses of the Syrian desert in an air-conditioned coach, it is easy to understand why Palmyra, 'bride of the desert', still fires our imaginations.

Save your sightseeing for sunrise and sunset when the ruins are bathed in a golden light and the tour buses have disappeared for the day. Despite Palmyra's tourism boom, at these times it is still possible to be the only person wandering through the temples and remains of this once-mighty city. During the afternoon, when the heat descends over the desert like a blanket, and even the postcard hawkers slump asleep in the nearest shade, it's best to do as the locals do and take a siesta.

Ins and outs → *For listings, see pages 279-282.*

Getting there and away
Despite its desert setting, seemingly in the middle of nowhere, Palmyra ('Tadmor' in Arabic) is only 3½ hours from Damascus and there are regular bus services here from Damascus, Homs and Hama. All the buses heading to Deir ez-Zor will also stop here. If you're coming from the east (from Deir ez-Zor and Raqqa), nearly all the Damascus-bound buses also make a stop in Palmyra.

When coming by bus from Damascus be aware that some bus drivers on this route stop on the outskirts of Palmyra, just before town, and tell tourists that this is the bus stop. If this happens to you, sit tight; you have to drive through the town to get to the bus stop.

At the time of writing, a large new bus station (beside the current bus stop) was being built and all Pullman services are planned to depart and arrive from there. From the bus stop/station there are always loads of taxis and tuk-tuks waiting to drive you into town. It costs about S£30 from here to the centre of Tadmor.

For route information on driving to Palmyra from Damascus and Hama, see page 276.

Getting around
Everything a traveller could need in Tadmor is situated on Main Bazaar Street so once in town you'll have no need for a taxi. The main ruins of Palmyra are also easily walked to from Tadmor town. Unless you really enjoy long walks, you will need to hire a taxi to take you out to the tower tombs or to Qala'at Ibn Maan on the hill above town. There are usually a few taxis waiting around the museum entrance which are ready to take you to either. Most of the hotels can also arrange a driver.

The main ruins, enclosed within what is commonly referred to as Zenobia's wall, are spread over a large area. While this makes it relatively easy to avoid the organized groups touring the site, it also means that during the summer, when it gets ferociously hot during the day, only the early morning and evening are really suitable for walking around the ruins. Likewise, you will get the best results in terms of photography during these times. The Sanctuary of Bel, Qalat Ibn Maan (Arab castle), the museums and the most important of the temple tombs observe fixed opening times and charge an entrance fee.

Palmyra may be well connected by bus, but to explore deeper into this region (such as a trip to Qasr al-Heir al-Sharki) you are going to need to hire a car/driver. There are plenty of taxi drivers in Palmyra who you can hire for a day/half-day to take you out into the desert, and all the hotels also have recommended drivers you can use.

Tourist information
The **Tourist office** ① *opposite the museum, T031-591 0574, daily 0800-1400 and 1800-2400 (in theory at least; in practice there is rarely anyone in attendance after dark)*, has fairly helpful and informed staff who can provide you with a map and recommend guides for the ruins.

Background

Early accounts
Evidence of the earliest periods of settlement in Palmyra is fragmented. Archaeological finds have confirmed that the oasis and surrounding area was a focus for settlement as far back as the Palaeolithic and Neolithic eras, when the climate of the region would have been significantly wetter and milder.

The silk route that wasn't

Take a look at a map of the ancient trade routes that traversed the east and one thing becomes apparent – the spectacular desert caravan city of Palmyra wasn't a natural contender for a stopover along the way. The natural direction would be to follow the Euphrates north, but the skilled and wily Palmyrenes weren't going to be halted in their quest for commercial domination by a silly thing like geography. These consummate traders and merchants sent silver-tongued agents to the towns and ports further east to shape a new path that would have Palmyra as its headquarters. So the caravans of silks, spices and slaves, precious stones, perfume and prostitutes began heading across the vast plateau of the Syrian desert to arrive at Palmyra's gates, where a fair and regulated taxation system allowed the Palmyrenes to grow rich off the profits of trade. And this city, surrounded by the empty nothingness of the desert, became the commercial capital of its day.

The first written records concerning Palmyra date from the second millennium BC. **Cuneiform texts** found in the archives of Mari (see page 300) and Kultepe (in the Cappadocia region of present-day Turkey) dating from the beginning of the second millennium BC, as well as later **Assyrian texts** dating from the end of the second millennium BC, make reference to Aramaic-speaking nomads from around Palmyra. The **Second Book of Chronicles**, meanwhile, relates the legendary tale of the founding of Tadmor by King Solomon during the first millennium BC. This reference is now recognized as being an error, the chronicler having confused Tadmor (Palmyra) with Tamar in the desert near the Dead Sea in present-day Israel, but the mix-up in itself indicates that Palmyra was already a well-known town.

Seleucid struggles

Having been controlled for a time first by the Assyrians and then the Persians, Palmyra later became part of **Alexander the Great's** Macedonian Greek Empire. Following Alexander's death in 323 BC, the eastern part of the empire was divided between two of his generals, Ptolemy and Seleucus. Ptolemy controlled Egypt while Seleucus took control of Babylonia, soon extending his power to include Palmyra and most of Syria. Poor relations with Ptolemy's Empire, which likewise grew from its base in Egypt to encompass parts of southern Syria, including Damascus, meant that the Seleucids tended to favour the more northern (and therefore safer) trade route from their main capital Seleucia, along the Euphrates then across via Aleppo to Antioch. In time, however, the Seleucid Empire came under simultaneous pressure from the Parthians to the east and the emerging Roman Empire to the west. First the Parthians (successors to the Persians) took control of Babylonia, thus confining the Seleucids to Syria, and then in 64 BC the Romans annexed Antioch, establishing themselves along the Levantine coast and effectively bringing an end to the Seleucid Empire.

Profits from Parthians

This new power balance left Palmyra in a no man's land between the **Parthians** and **Romans**. As the two powers locked into a continuing but inconclusive cycle of invasion and counter-invasion, the Palmyrenes managed to establish a unique, if precarious, niche for themselves. Despite the conflict between the two powers, there was also a common interest to be had in the continuation of trade between east and west. The collapse of the Seleucid Empire had resulted in the decline of the northern trade route along the Euphrates, which became an area of uncertainty and instability, and this provided the opportunity for Palmyra to establish itself as the principal trading post on a more direct desert route between Dura Europos and Emesa (Homs). Thus the Palmyrene traders became middlemen in a mutually beneficial trade between two hostile powers. Pliny the Elder, writing in AD 77, even went so far as to suggest that Palmyra played a mediating role between the two: "*Enjoying certain privileges with the two Great Empires, that of the Romans and that of the Parthians, Palmyra is sought out whenever disputes occur.*"

Roman renewal

The history of Palmyra up to this point provides the key to understanding its distinctive culture and style of art and architecture. First it came under Hellenistic influence, and then the competing influences of the Parthians and Romans, whilst all the time maintaining a certain degree of independence from all three. The exact balance of opposing influences and autonomy is difficult to determine, although it is clear that as time progressed, in practical terms it was the Roman influence that grew while Palmyra flourished as the most important caravan city of Syria. Thus when Mark Antony sent horsemen to loot Palmyra in 41 BC, the inhabitants fled with all their belongings to the safety of Parthian-controlled areas beyond the Euphrates. However, by AD 19 statues of Germanicus, Tiberius and Druses were erected in the Temple of Bel by Fretensis, the Roman legate of the 10th Legion, and by around AD 60 the Roman Senate was instituted as the sole governing body of Palmyra. Thus Palmyra in effect became a tributary buffer state of the Romans against the Parthians.

Even more important than the earlier collapse of the Seleucid Empire for Palmyra was the Roman annexation of the Nabatean Empire and its capital **Petra** in AD 106. Previously Petra had rivalled and probably surpassed Palmyra as a trading city, but now a significant portion of that trade passed through Palmyra, with the rest going via Egypt. When **Hadrian** visited Palmyra in AD 128, he awarded it the status of a 'free city', allowing it to set and collect its own taxes. This, now dominant, trading city flourished in the relative stability achieved under Hadrian and his successors, and it is this period, during the second and early third centuries AD, that is considered the height of Palmyra's wealth and success.

The Severans

The next series of events to influence Palmyra's fate came with the marriage of Septimus Severus to Julia Domna, the daughter of the high priest of Emesa (Homs), an event which ensured greater direct Syrian influence in the affairs of Imperial Rome. Severus divided the administration of Syria in two, with Palmyra becoming part of *Syria Phoenicia* with its capital at Emesa. Under his successor Caracalla, Palmyra was raised in status to a *colonia* and granted *ius italicum*, or freedom from the burden of paying taxes to Rome. At the same time, Rome's constant campaigns against the Parthians fully engaged its armies, forcing Palmyra to strengthen its own defensive capabilities.

Under Alexander Severus (AD 222-235) Palmyra and the Syrian provinces successfully held out against the Sassanids, who rose to replace the Parthians as the great power in the east. But after his death, both internal Imperial power struggles and rebellions, together with invasions from outside, led to a period of decline in the empire which became a jungle of intrigue, blood and uncertainty. For Palmyra, this provided an

Queen Zenobia

Ambitious, gutsy and intelligent, the extraordinary Queen Zenobia of Palmyra challenged the might of the Roman Empire and nearly brought it to its knees. A woman of exceptional ability – fluent in Greek, Latin, Aramaic and Egyptian and a skilled military commander and talented leader – Zenobia claimed descendancy from that other ambitious woman of antiquity, Cleopatra. In the rigidly male-dominated world of that era she led her troops to victory over a huge chunk of Rome's eastern empire before finally being defeated and captured by Aurelian in AD 272.

"Those who say I have only conquered a woman do not know what that woman was," Aurelian wrote after her capture, setting the tone for the many historians who would later bestow Zenobia with the qualities of enduring beauty, noble character and chastity.

Not much is known about Zenobia's demise. Some say she committed suicide, others that she was led through the streets of Rome in shackles of gold, and some insist that she married a Roman governor and lived to a grand old age in a villa near Tivoli. Whatever the truth, the exploits of the desert queen of Palmyra continue to inspire and enthral visitors here today.

opportunity to exercise greater independence. **Odainat** (Septimius Odaenathus), a local noble, assumed the title of king. His position was enormously strengthened when in AD 260 he defeated the Sassanid king Shapur, who in the same year had himself defeated the Roman emperor Valerian. Odainat's success in defeating this trouble-maker was a major relief for the struggling Roman Empire, and earned him the honorary title of *corrector totius orientis*. Ever ambitious, however, he went one step further in naming himself 'king of kings', a title borrowed from the Sassanids he had just defeated. In subsequent campaigns he succeeded in reaching their capital Ctesiphon (on the Tigris River in modern-day Iraq) thus effectively neutralizing the Sassanian threat. In AD 268 he was murdered during a campaign against the Goths in Cappadocia, according to some sources on the instructions of his wife Zenobia.

Zenobia

Odainat had set the stage for the last great episode of Palmyra's history. Wahballat, his only surviving son was still a child, so his wife Zenobia took power as regent. An almost legendary figure even in her own time, Zenobia was certainly the most colourful and unusual personality to emerge from Palmyra, even if her over-reaching ambition was ultimately to lead to the decline of what had become a rich and powerful city-state (see box, above). Her assumption of power alarmed Rome and a force was sent to subdue her. But she easily defeated this force, and, perhaps seeking to outdo her husband's campaigning enthusiasm, she went on to seize control of the whole Province of Syria. Not content with this, she then besieged Bosra, the capital of the Province of Arabia, and shortly afterwards successfully invaded Egypt. **Aurelian**, the Roman emperor at the time, at first sought to appease her by 'granting' her son the various titles that Odainat had assumed, but when she declared Wahballat 'Augustus' (ie 'Emperor'), he was forced to confront this direct challenge to Rome's authority. After several clashes with the Palmyrene army, he took possession of Palmyra in AD 271. Zenobia was captured while trying to flee across the Euphrates and taken back to Rome as a captive of Aurelian.

Defeat and decline

Early in AD 272, Palmyra revolted against Roman occupation, but was once again taken by Aurelian and his troops who this time sacked the city, though they did not completely destroy it. Palmyra never recovered from this defeat, and although it continued to function as a city for a couple of centuries, it never regained its former wealth and importance. Roman garrisons were stationed there, and **Diocletian** (AD 284-305) built a defensive wall around the main monuments, turning it into a fortified garrison town. This wall, along with other building projects such as the complex now known as Diocletian's Camp, fundamentally altered the appearance of the city from that of its original 'classical' period.

Christianity first became established around the late third to early fourth century and later, during the reign of the Emperor **Justinian** (AD 527-565), the churches and fortifications of Palmyra were partially restored. Shortly after, however, the Eastern Roman (Byzantine) Empire collapsed. The next mention of Palmyra comes in AD 634, when the Arab Muslim general **Khalid Ibn al-Walid** captured the city after laying siege to it. From then on, it continued as a small and relatively insignificant settlement, fortified once more as a strategic desert outpost by the Arab general **Abdul Hassan Yussuf ibn Fairouz** in 1132-1133.

The 'rediscovery' of Petra

Notwithstanding the Arab's fortification of the temple of Bel in the 12th century, and possibly the building of the first castle on the hill overlooking the town at this time, Palmyra fell gradually from its former state of glory into disuse and then oblivion. Apart from the small village that established itself within the *temenos* of the temple of Bel, the monuments were left to the ravages of time and weather, becoming steadily more deeply buried in sand.

It was not until the second half of the 17th century that interest in the ruins began to be awakened amongst the European traders who had their headquarters in the khans of Aleppo's souqs. Intrigued by tales of these fabulous ruins, an English expedition, led by Dr Huntington, a British trader based in Aleppo, set out to visit them in 1678. They fared badly, reaching the ruins only to be robbed, even of their clothes, before fleeing back to Aleppo. They returned again in 1691, this time led by a Dr Halifax, better prepared with a letter of introduction from a local tribal sheikh and a substantial armed escort. This second visit resulted in *Relation of a Voyage to Tadmor*, published in 1895, and the first descriptions and drawings of the ruins. Particularly interesting was the discovery of Greek inscriptions alongside the then unknown Palmyrene script, and through these, the identification of Odainat as king of Palmyra and husband of the, until then, purely legendary Queen Zenobia. Dr Halifax relates how their interest in the inscriptions was interpreted: *"For this notion stickes in ye heads of all these people, that the Frankes goe to see old Ruines only because there they meet with Inscriptions which direct them to some hid treasure ..."*

In 1710 the Swede Cornelius Loos visited Palmyra on behalf of Charles XII of Sweden, making further drawings, but it was not until the detailed work of English architects Messrs Wood and Dawkins in 1751 that any systematic examination of the ruins was undertaken, and widespread interest began to be shown abroad. Subsequent visitors from the early 19th century onwards, amongst them in 1813 the eccentric Lady Hester Stanhope, came more as tourists and did very little to further existing knowledge about the ruins.

Finally, before the **First World War** the Germans, who were by that time closely allied with the Ottoman Turks, carried out a detailed inventory of the city and its monuments, the first proper archaeological survey of the ruins. When it was finally published in 1932, it formed the basis of subsequent exploration which began in earnest after the War. In 1929 the French archaeologists H Seyrig and R Amy arrived at the site. They found the compound of the temple of Bel occupied by a small Arab village, which they set about removing, giving rise to the present town of Tadmor, before beginning excavations on the temple. In 1939-1940 Seyrig excavated the Agora. Archaeological work intensified after the Second World War with a series of foreign archaeological expeditions, taken over after independence by the Syrian Directorate-General of Antiquities, and continuing to this day. Indeed, part of the magic of Palmyra lies not only in what there is to see, but in imagining what treasures remain hidden under the sands.

Note Today Tadmor is a dusty town with a frontier feel and depends on tourism for much of its economy. As such, you'll probably encounter more minor hassle here than anywhere else in Syria. Compared to much of Asia though, the hawkers/touts here are a friendly bunch and their pestering is only mildly annoying.

Sanctuary of Bel

① *At the eastern end of the ancient city centre, entrance is just off the main road. Daily 0900-1800 in summer, 0900-1600 in winter, S£150, students S£10. There are various books for sale at the entrance, toilets are located in the southeastern corner of the complex.*

This is by far the largest and best preserved of the temple sanctuaries at Palmyra. The sanctuary consists of a central **cella**, or temple, contained within a large **temenos** (sacred enclosure) marked by huge walls, in places leaning precariously, shored up with concrete footings and buttresses, or else completely destroyed and replaced by low makeshift structures. These walls originally date from the second to third century AD, although they suffered severe damage from earthquakes and were subsequently reinforced and modified for defensive purposes during Arab times. A walk around the outside reveals examples of the original Palmyrene and later Arab building work. The northwest corner provides the best example of the original walls, with the sequence of pilasters and framed windows topped by triangular pediments well preserved. The later rebuilding work is clearly visible along the eastern (rear) wall, where various architectural fragments have been incorporated at random, and many of the recycled stone blocks have been placed on their sides, revealing the original locating grooves.

According to an inscription above the low doorway in the recessed arch of the main tower, the monumental entrance, or **propylaeum**, to the enclosure was converted into a defensive citadel by the Arab general Abdul Hassan Yussuf Ibn Fairouz in 1132-1133. Originally it would have consisted of a broad flight of stairs leading up to a massive portico supported by eight pillars and finally a triple gateway some 35 m wide. But it seems that the portico section had collapsed by the time Fairouz arrived, leaving him with three sides of a future 'keep' to complete along with the present fourth wall. Once inside the sanctuary, you can see the heavily weathered triple gateway consisting of an enormous central portal, its lintel now fallen, and two side portals. The space between the triple entrance and the outside Arab wall is strewn with massive tumbled blocks of stone.

Today the courtyard of the *temenos* is striking for its size, a large open space littered with sections of fallen columns, in places neatly laid out in rows, with the *cella* in the centre. Originally, running around the inside perimeter there was a *peristyle*, or covered corridor, consisting of a double colonnade around the north, east and south sides and a single colonnade along the west side. The single line of columns along the west side are significantly taller, the *propylaeum* and outside wall forming the second line of support for the ceiling. To the left as you enter, seven of these columns are still standing, complete with their crowning *entablature*, although the decoration on this has been almost totally weathered away. A sunken passageway from outside leads under the columns by means of an arch; his passage was probably used to bring animals into the *temenos* to be sacrificed at the altar, the remains of which are in front and to the left of the central *cella*.

Approaching the *cella* from the monumental entrance, there is the sacrificial altar to the left, with only its base remaining. Its outline is partially obscured by the foundations of a later **banqueting house** (numerous clay tokens, distributed as invitations to the ritual banquets, were found here). On the right are the remains of a **sacred basin** where ritual ablutions presumably took place. Various **water channels** can still be seen leading to the basin.

The *cella* of the sanctuary of Bel is offset slightly to the east of the centre of the enclosure, creating a larger space between it and the monumental entrance. The present building can be firmly dated to AD 32 from a dedication inscribed on the pedestal of a statue found in the temple (now housed in the Palmyra Museum). However, this was also the site of an earlier temple of Bel, dating from the Hellenistic period and probably made from mud. The low mound, or *tell*, on which these temples were built has revealed evidence of worship dating back to between 1500 and 2200 BC. Surrounding the huge rectangular building was a broad *peristyle* supported by massive fluted columns; along the east (rear) side these columns, 18 m high, are still standing complete with their entablature and they provide a powerful sense of the colossal scale of the temple. The outer portal, which originally formed part of the peristyle, now stands alone, its massive lintel slightly slipped, but still in place following the restoration undertaken by the French in 1932. On the right as you pass through this portal there are two richly carved **stone beams** from the roof of the *peristyle*. The first depicts Aglibol, the moon god, hand in hand with Malakbel, here symbolizing fertility, while behind it the second depicts a camel carrying a tabernacle, attended by priests and worshippers. The swirling shapes of veiled women in the scene are well preserved and it is interesting to see that the use of the veil was a practice which long predated Islam. The **inner portal** has lost its lintel, but the walls either side are complete and the massive single-section stone slabs used to form the sides of the door frame are a good reminder of the awesome engineering feats involved.

Inside, the temple consists of a single chamber with an **adyton**, or large niche, at either end. Around the walls are various fragments of the original ceiling to the *cella*. At the southern end (to your right as you enter) is the smaller of the two *adytons*, possibly originally having contained a movable image of Bel which would have been paraded round the sanctuary on special occasions. However, the crowning glory is the **ceiling** inside: a massive single slab of richly carved, excellently preserved stone with a circular pattern of alternating acanthus and lotus leaves at its centre. This in turn is surrounded by a wide geometric border and enclosed within a square which is then surrounded by a broad border of octagonal shapes containing rosettes interspaced by a complex pattern of squares and triangles. The ceiling of the southern *adyton* was the inspiration for many decorated ceilings in country houses around Britain during the 18th-century Neo-Classical period. A later addition to the south *adyton* was the small *mihrab* dating from the 12th century, when the temple was converted into a mosque. On either side of the *adyton*, at ground level, are entrance ways that give access to stairs leading up to the roof, although these are now locked.

The north *adyton* is larger and would have formed the main focus of worship. Its façade is more complex and imposing, while the absence of steps was meant perhaps to emphasize its elevated position above the mass of worshippers. The ceiling of the north *adyton* also consists of a single slab of carved stone; at the centre is a *cupola* with the busts of the seven planetary divinities (Jupiter at the centre, surrounded by Helios, Selene, Ares, Hermes, Aphrodite and Cronos) and surrounding this is a thin band containing the 12 signs of the zodiac. The underside of the lintel over the entrance to the *adyton* bears a carving of an eagle (representing Jupiter/Bel) with wings outstretched across a star-studded sky. Concealed by the façade are two side chambers to the left and right of the *adyton*, the one to the left containing stairs (kept locked) which give access to the roof of the *cella*.

Civic Centre

The colonnaded street

Seen from the vantage point of the Arab castle, the colonnaded street clearly forms the backbone of the ancient city of Palmyra, its spidery line of columns stretching for over a kilometre. The street can be divided into three main sections, each with its own alignment. The first runs from the temple of Bel to the monumental arch, the second through the main civic centre from the monumental arch to the tetrapylon and the last from the tetrapylon to the partially restored funerary temple. The street was in fact built and developed from west to east, so in the following description, one should bear in mind the reverse chronology. The important temples and public buildings which are found along and off to either side of the street are described as they appear.

Between the *propylaeum* of the temple of Bel and the monumental arch, which today stands as the most prominent feature at the entrance to the civic centre of the ancient city, there was originally a section of colonnaded street, wider than the rest. From the temple of Bel a series of re-erected columns mark the left-hand side of this street, their line interrupted by some low buildings in front of the temple. Just across the modern road as you approach the monumental arch are four large re-erected columns, taller than the ones proceeding it. These formed the portico of an **exedra**, the paved area behind still visible. Further along the same side there are the foundations of what were probably shops and other buildings, including a small *nymphaeum* with a water tank at the rear.

The **Monumental Arch** towers impressively at the end of this section and combines great stylistic and decorative beauty with ingenious functional design. Essentially, due to the piecemeal development of Palmyra and resultant departures from what might otherwise have been a grand overall plan (see below), the monumental arch had to be carefully designed to link two sections of street which ran at a 30° angle to each other. In effect there are two monumental arches each aligned to their respective streets and joined together to form a V-shape. Approaching from the temple of Bel, the central arch of what was once a triple-arched arrangement is completely missing and only the side arches, themselves heavily weathered, remain. Seen from the opposite side, the triple arch is fully intact and the rich and varied decoration lavished on it has been well preserved, displaying a bewildering array of geometric and floral designs that are typically Syrian in their execution. Note also the decoration on the undersides (soffits) of the arches. Here, the side arches would have been located under the covered *porticos* which lined the narrower street on either side. Tellingly, this arch dates from the late second to early third century AD during the reign of Septimus Severus, when Palmyra was at the height of its prosperity.

Passing through the arch, you enter the area of the **main civic centre**. To the left, immediately after the monumental arch, are the remains of the **Temple of Nebo** (or Nabu). The temple originally consisted of a trapezoid-shaped *temenos* with the main temple or *cella* at the centre. Today only the podium of the temple remains, together with the lower courses of the outer wall and the column bases of the *peristyle* (some now re-erected) which ran around three sides of the courtyard. The *propylaeum*, or monumental entrance to the temple, was on the south side, so that what one sees from the colonnaded street is the rear of the temple compound, which also formed the back wall of the shops that lined the street. Between the *cella* and the *propylaeum* of the temple compound was an altar, today partially restored with concrete pillars. Nebo,

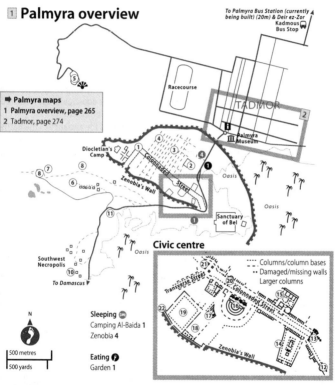

1 Palmyra overview

To Palmyra Bus Station (currently being built) (20m) & Deir ez-Zor
Kadmous Bus Stop

TADMOR

Racecourse

Palmyra Museum

➡ **Palmyra maps**
1 Palmyra overview, page 265
2 Tadmor, page 274

Diocletian's Camp

Colonnaded Street

Zenobia's Wall

Oasis

Oasis

Oasis

Sanctuary of Bel

Southwest Necropolis

To Damascus

N

500 metres
500 yards

Sleeping
Camping Al-Baida 1
Zenobia 4

Eating
Garden 1

Civic centre

······ Columns/column bases
·· Damaged/missing walls
Larger columns

Transverse Street

Colonnaded Street

Zenobia's Wall

Archaeological sites
1 Funerary temple
2 Temple of Baal Shamin
3 Christian basilica
4 Peristyle house
5 Qala'at Ibn Maan
6 Tower Tomb of Iamliku

7 Tower Tomb of Elabel
8 Tower Tomb of Atenatan
9 Tomb 36
10 Hypogeum of the Three Brothers
11 Afqa Spring

Civic Centre
12 Exedra
13 Monumental arch
14 Temple of Nebo
15 Baths of Diocletian
16 Theatre
17 Senate
18 Tariff Court

19 Agora
20 Nymphaeum
21 Tetrapylon
22 Banquet hall

identified with the Roman god Apollo, was particularly popular amongst the Palmyrenes. In the Babylonian pantheon he was the son of Mardok, Lord of Heaven. His role as scribe of the Table of Destinies gave him considerable influence over the fortunes of humans, a fact which the merchants of Palmyra, forever concerned with the uncertainties of trade in a continually changing world, must have kept at the front of their minds. Although the ruins are not much to look at today, this temple had a fundamental influence on the development of the layout of Palmyra. Were it not for the existence of the temple on this spot, it would have been possible for the colonnaded street to run in a straight line for its whole length from the funerary temple to the Temple of Bel. Rather than risk incurring his displeasure by relocating the temple, the Palmyrenes opted to alter the direction of the street at the Tetrapylon to avoid it, and again at the Monumental Arch to get back on course for the Sanctuary of Bel.

Returning to the colonnaded street, it is this next section between the monumental arch and the *tetrapylon*, dating from the mid to late second century AD (ie contemporary with the monumental arch), which is the best preserved. On one side, many of the columns that supported the covered *porticos* are still standing (or have been re-erected), complete with their characteristic protruding brackets which would have held statues of the civic notables who helped finance the building work, and crowning *entablature*. The porticos housed various shops, and many of the lintels from the doorways, now scattered on the ground, bear inscriptions identifying the trade and the proprietor.

On the right, a little further along from the temple of Nebo, is the entrance to the **Baths of Diocletian** (the sign reads 'Bathes of Zenobia'), marked by four monolithic columns standing forward from the main line of the portico and rising considerably higher. The columns are also distinctive for being of pink granite (brought from Egypt), in contrast to the locally quarried yellow limestone so characteristic of the rest of Palmyra. These columns once supported the portico to the entrance of the baths; they are also the only part of the complex actually dating from the time of Diocletian (AD 284-305), with the baths complex probably dating from around a century earlier, during the reign of Septimus Severus. The actual baths, which were excavated in 1959-1960, exist now for the most part only in outline. Most prominent is the large central basin, partially surrounded by a colonnade of Corinthian columns, which has been identified as the *frigidarium*.

A little further along the colonnaded street, the columns of the portico on the left are interrupted by a wide, beautifully decorated arch marking the start of a transverse street which curves around the rear of the theatre in a semi-circle to rejoin the main street. A colonnade runs along the outside edge of this street and is joined half-way round by a colonnaded street coming from a large gate in Zenobia's wall to the south.

The theatre, senate and agora

Until the 1950s the **theatre** ① *daily 0900-1800 in summer, 0900-1600 in winter, S£75, students S£5*, was, for the most part, buried under sand, giving no hint of its true scale. When it was first excavated, there were nine rows of seating rising up the *cavea*, divided into 11 sections. There are now 14 rows of seating, although it has been argued that in the original, above the twelfth row, only a wooden structure would have existed. The stage and elaborately decorated *scaenae frons* (stage façade) have been carefully restored.

To the southwest of the theatre there are the remains of a number of other civic buildings. Three-quarters of the way round the transverse street, after the turning towards the gate in Zenobia's wall, there are the remains of a small building which is generally recognized as the **Senate**, although its small size has led some to dispute this. A row of eight truncated columns marks the portico to the entrance. Inside was a small peristyled courtyard, of which only the column bases remain, with an apse-shaped chamber at the far end. This apse, with its tiers of seats arranged in a semi-circle, is what led the archaeologist Seyrig to identify the building as the Senate.

Immediately to the southwest of the Senate is a large walled courtyard area, today known as the **Tariff Court**, primarily due to the fact that the **Palmyra Tariff** was discovered here. This huge inscribed stone slab (1.75 m by 4.8 m) dates from AD 137 and sheds an insight into the commerce of the city. Written both in the Palmyrene dialect and Greek, it meticulously details the taxes due on goods – from perfumes to bronze statues – sold in or passing through the city. The tariff also outlines charges for use of the all-important spring water and even mentions a tax on prostitutes working in the city, as well as codifying various fiscal and other laws concerning the different traders based in the city. It is now housed in the Hermitage Museum in St Petersburg.

The main entrance to the Tariff court was from the southwest side, although the elaborate portico was largely destroyed during the building of 'Zenobia's' wall (in fact the building work on this section was carried out by Diocletian during the third century) which lies just beyond it. The portico led to a grand triple entrance, of which two of the portals still remain. The southeast wall of the courtyard is no longer standing, but drawings made in the 1790s by LF Cassas indicate that it was identical to its northwest counterpart, with windows framed by strongly moulded architraves, interspaced with pilasters. In the northwest wall there are three doorways which lead into the adjacent Agora, the central one of which was known as the Senators' Gate.

The **agora** was the public meeting place of the city, a focal point where news and views were exchanged, and a great deal of the commerce on which Palmyra's wealth depended was carried out. The large, walled courtyard contained a colonnaded portico running around its edges, of which the majority of the columns, or at least their lower sections, still survive. The walls follow the same pattern as those of the Tariff Court, with windows interspaced by pilasters, and in addition a total of 11 doors. The columns would all have had the characteristic brackets bearing statues of civic notables (over 200 in all, including additional statues along the walls themselves). The accompanying inscriptions have provided a wealth of information on the public life of the city. Each colonnade was reserved for different social groups: senators along the east colonnade, Roman and Palmyrene officials along the north, soldiers along the west and caravan leaders to the south. On the lintel above the Senators' Gate in the east wall was an inscription (no longer in place) to the family of Septimus Severus, who through his marriage to Julia Domna, the daughter of the high priest of Emesa (Homs), came to have such a strong influence on Palmyrene politics. In the southwest corner of the courtyard steps lead up through a doorway into a small separate banqueting hall, complete with benches for guests, as well as an altar and niche which once would have housed the presiding deity. A bold, well preserved band of geometric decoration based around a swastika motif runs around the walls (the swastika is an ancient symbol, thought to have originated in India, and was associated with the sun, peace and good luck). Building work on both the Agora and the Tariff Court started around the middle of the first century AD, with the earliest inscription in the Agora dating from AD 71, at the beginning of Hadrian's reign.

The nymphaeum and tetrapylon

Returning now along the last section of the semi-circular transverse street, you pass on the left a series of small cubicles, perhaps shops or ticket booths for the theatre. By the arch which leads back onto the main colonnaded street, there is a course of stone blocks with a hole bored through the centre which would once have carried a water pipe. This is part of an aqueduct dating from the Byzantine period, probably during the reign of Justinian (AD 527-565). Its presence suggests that the original Palmyrene water system must have failed by this time, while the fact that no attempt was made to conceal it below ground level is an indication of the relative decline in Palmyra's wealth.

Opposite the archway leading back onto the main colonnaded street, there are the remains of a small **nymphaeum** or water fountain, marked by four columns (three still standing) set forward from the main colonnade to form a portico, and behind it a semi-circular *exedra* where the fountain would have been located. Just to the left of the columns are two large stepped platforms which once held honorific columns marking the start of a street leading towards the temple of Baal Shamin. A little further along is the imposing tetrapylon. Before reaching it, the last series of eight columns on the left (counting from the arch) are of particular interest for their inscriptions. Below the bracket of the sixth column is an inscription to "Septimius Odainat, King of Kings and Corrector of all the East". The bracket of the next column, however, is missing, the partially defaced inscription being dedicated to his wife, Queen Zenobia. Both inscriptions date from AD 271, and it seems likely that after Aurelian's capture of the city in AD 272, the statue of Zenobia, who was considered a traitor by the Roman emperor, was destroyed and her inscription defaced. That of Odainat presumably survived, his loyalty to the Roman Empire being somewhat greater. (He had, after all, defeated the Sassanids and stopped short of his wife's Imperial ambitions.) Behind this series of columns there are the remains of a building with a peristyled courtyard of fluted columns.

The **tetrapylon** is an imposing structure which, like the monumental arch, conceals a change in the direction of the colonnaded street, as well as providing a suitably grand visual counterbalance to the Sanctuary of Bel. It consists of a large square platform set in an oval plaza with four huge pedestals standing at the corners of the platform, each originally bearing four massive granite columns (brought once again from Egypt) topped by an entablature. At the centre of each pedestal, amongst the columns, there would have been a statue. The monument was in ruins until the 1960s, with the columns all collapsed. When excavation work started, only the fragments of one of the granite columns were found. Much to the horror of purists, the monument was therefore reconstructed using coloured concrete for the other 15 columns. While the authenticity of the reconstruction can certainly be questioned, it undoubtedly enhances the overall effect of the ruins. Leading off at an angle to the left from the tetrapylon, a series of columns mark a second transverse street that runs down towards Zenobia's wall to the south.

In sharp contrast to the central section of the colonnaded street, the last section, from the tetrapylon to the funerary temple, has been subject to much less of the meticulous excavation and reconstruction lavished on the central stretch. The broken line of columns is matched by a confused jumble of fallen stonework scattered haphazardly along the street. Nevertheless, more than 60 columns have been re-erected along this stretch in recent years. The only clearly discernible feature is on the left, approximately 100 m from the *tetrapylon*, where there are the remains of an **exedra**, its semi-circular plan clearly visible, which was possibly another *nymphaeum*.

Approaching the end of the colonnaded street, there seems to be an even greater concentration of fallen masonry piled up in great heaps, while the bases of the last few columns on the right-hand side can be seen to rise in a stepped fashion. It has been suggested that there was a flight of steps here leading up to a large arch which would have framed the funerary temple beyond it in a dramatic fashion. The **funerary temple** itself is really more of an elaborate family tomb dating from the late second to early third century. The portico, with its six columns supporting the remains of a well proportioned pediment, stands today just as it was found, although the walls of the tomb itself have been reconstructed with the extensive use of concrete. A stairway behind the rear wall leads down into the crypt below, also extensively restored with concrete.

Diocletian's Camp and Temple of Allat

From in front of the funerary temple a wide transverse street dating from the second century leads southwest, its course marked by intermittent re-erected columns. This street led towards an oval piazza followed by a gate in the southern wall of the city, known as the Damascus Gate. Just a small part of the outline of the oval piazza is visible today, marked by a few standing columns, while the Damascus Gate is an indistinct pile of jumbled ruins. Before reaching this, an avenue, once framed by a huge portal, leads off to the right to the ruins of a complex known as **Diocletian's Camp**. The area is interesting in that, although it represents one of the earliest settled areas of the city, it was subsequently extensively overlain by the later buildings of Diocletian's camp. This 'camp', dating from the late third to early fourth century AD, was built by Sosianus Hierocles, Governor of Syria under the emperor Diocletian (AD 284-305) in the period following the defeat of Zenobia and neatly reflects Palmyra's change in status from a powerful and largely independent trading city to a military outpost of the Roman Empire.

Halfway down the avenue, another one intersects it, running at right angles; this junction was once marked by a large *tetrapylon*, of which only the pedestals and a couple of the columns remain. To the right of the *tetrapylon* is a series of distinctive fluted columns which, along with a heavily weathered doorway and the foundations of the inner *cella*, are all that remains of the **Temple of Allat**. These somewhat meagre remains date from the second century AD, although there was a temple compound on this site as early as the first century BC. At the end of the avenue are the foundations of a *propylaeum* which led through to what was once an enclosed square or miniature forum. In front of you, a broad flight of stairs, so heavily worn as to seem almost as if they have melted in the heat, leads up to what was the **Temple of the Standards**. At the top of the steps, four tall columns, one still standing, supported a portico which led directly through a triple doorway into the *cella* of the temple. This consisted of a large rectangular hall with an apse-shaped chamber opposite the entrance, parts of which still survive, where the various military insignia of the Roman army were housed. Strictly speaking, it is only this apsidal chamber which can be termed the Temple of the Standards; the exact function of the building as a whole is still unclear, and interpretation of the remains are further complicated by the fact that an earlier building was modified and extended in order to create it. It has been suggested that the whole area was previously Zenobia's Palace; the street plan and tetrapylon, which are known to predate Diocletian's occupation, certainly suggest a grand, monumental complex. Behind the Diocletian's camp is the low hill of Jebel Husseiniye, with a section of the northern fortifying wall running straight up its slope before swinging round and descending to run along the southern perimeter of the city. From the top of this hill there are good views out over the ruins.

Temple of Baal Shamin

The Temple of Baal Shamin is the most important of the ruins in the area to the northeast of the main colonnaded street. It can be reached either from the main *tetrapylon* on the colonnaded street, or from the main road via the *Zenobia* hotel. There are several stages of building work, the north courtyard being the oldest, followed by the *cella* and then the south courtyard. The main *cella*, restored in the 1950s by Swiss archaeologists, is today the only part of the temple compound still largely intact. Its construction in AD 131 was financed by Male Agrippa, a local merchant prince, who was so wealthy that when Hadrian came to visit the city in AD 129, he paid for all the expenses associated with his visit. The *cella* has a large portico supported by six pillars, the front four originally supporting a triangular *pediment* rather like that of the funerary temple. On the projecting bracket of one of the front pillars is an inscription telling us of Male Agrippa's funding of the temple, and of Hadrian's visit to Palmyra.

The inside of the *cella* consists of a central *adyton* fronted by a semicircular structure with fluted double columns on either side, and two side chambers. Although closed off and partially obscured by a tree growing inside, you can still peer in. During the fifth century it was converted into a church. In front of the entrance is an altar dating from AD 113. Parts of the north courtyard date from as early as AD 17, while the smaller south courtyard dates from AD 149. It is interesting to note the differing styles to be found in the capitals of the columns which formed the colonnaded peristyles of both courtyards; those of the north courtyard are mostly replacements dating from reconstruction work carried out by Odainat in AD 258 and show an apparently Egyptian influence, while those of the south courtyard are in the traditional Hellenistic Corinthian style.

Little else remains in this area to the northeast of the main colonnaded street, which once comprised Palmyra's more affluent residential area. There are the scant remains of a later Christian basilica about 150 m to the northwest, and another smaller one to the southwest of it. Elsewhere, only a couple of peristyles of Roman houses still survive.

Qala'at Ibn Maan

① *Open daily 0900-dusk, S£75, students S£5, you only have to pay if you enter the inside of the castle.*

Occupying a choice position on the high hilltop overlooking the ruins is the Arab castle of Qala'at Ibn Maan. If for no other reason, the castle is worth a visit to see the panoramic views of Palmyra, as well as north along the ridges of Jebel al-Tadmoria. Sunset is the best time, with the ruins illuminated to a golden colour by the fading light. Sunrise is also very beautiful, although the ruins are then in silhouette against the rising sun. A metalled road winds its way up to the castle, or else there is a good, though steep, path which zig-zags up the side. A bridge, replacing the original drawbridge, gives access over the moat to the castle gate. Inside, there are several levels and numerous rooms to explore, with the best views being from the highest terrace to the south.

The castle is popularly attributed to Fakhr ud-Din, a Lebanese Maanite Emir who challenged the Ottomans in the early 17th century, extending his power base east from Mount Lebanon, deep into the Syrian desert, before being captured and finally executed by the Ottomans in 1635. However, it has also been suggested that Fakhr ud-Din only in fact occupied and extended an earlier castle which stood on the site, perhaps dating from the 12th century, around the same time as the temple of Bel was fortified by the Arab general Abdul Hassan Yussuf ibn Fairouz.

Valley of the Tombs and Southwest Necropolis

ⓘ *To gain access to Elabel, the largest and best preserved of the tower tombs in the Valley of the Tombs, and to the impressive Hypogeum of the Three Brothers at the Southwest Necropolis, both of which are kept locked, you must buy a ticket at the Palmyra Museum (S£75, students S£10). Visits are at 0830, 1000, 1130 and 1600. On Tue there are only 2 visits, at 0900 and 1100. On Fri there is no 1130 visit, while in winter the last visit is brought forward to 1430. Times are subject to change so ask at the museum. There are plenty of other tombs but due to lack of staff, only the 2 above tombs are officially open at the moment. If you want to visit any others, check with the museum if you are able to access them.*

The Valley of the Tombs provides a fascinating insight into the burial practices of the Palmyrenes, and the great importance they clearly attached to honouring the dead. The oddly forlorn tower tombs found here are no match for the ruins of Palmyra itself, but their setting has an eerily unreal atmosphere (all the more so at twilight, or on a moonlit night). As well as the major tombs described below, the valley is scattered with numerous others in varying states of decay. At the time of writing only the tombs of Elabel and the Hypogeum of the Three Brothers were open to the public.

A newly surfaced road branches off from the main road around 100 m before the entrance gate of the **Palmyra Cham Palace** hotel and climbs up over a low saddle between the hills of Umm el Belquis to the right and Jebel Muntar to the left. At the point where the road bends to the left, one can follow a footpath leading off to the right to a series of tower tombs clustered in a row around the ridge of Umm el Belquis. The best preserved of these is the **Tower Tomb of Iamliku** which is unfortunately kept locked, and is not included in the standard museum tour. Dating from AD 83, this well preserved four-storey tower tomb has an impressive carved lintel above the door, and higher up an inscription identifying the family to which it belonged. Immediately above the inscription is a window decorated with a relief of two winged figures, their heads missing. The inside of the tomb consists of tiers of burial compartments, or *loculi*, built into the walls, stacked five high and interspaced by Corinthian pilasters; four sets on the right-hand wall and three on the left-hand wall with a stairway towards the rear where the fourth would otherwise be. The ceiling is elaborately decorated with a complex pattern of diamond and triangular designs. The other tower tombs in this group are less well preserved and have not been sealed. The next largest after that of Iamliku has a tunnel leading from the rear of the building directly into the hill behind, with burial compartments dug into the rock to either side. Stairs lead up as far as the third storey, although this has no floormaking access to the roof impossible.

Continuing along the main track, you arrive eventually at a small group of tower tombs set on level ground at a point where the valley has opened out. The excellently preserved **Tower Tomb of Elabel** dominates this group. This building dates from AD 103 and is named after one of the four founders, the other three being Shaqai, Moqimo and Maani. All were sons of the Wahaballat of Maani, who was closely involved in the building of the temple of Nebo. The doorway, with its impressive lintel, is in the south face of the tomb, while above it there is an inscription in Palmyrene and Greek and above that, an arched niche. Inside, the walls are arranged in the standard fashion, with tiers of compartments interspaced by Corinthian pilasters. Above the door there is a bust of the curator, Elabel's son and, as in the tomb of Iamliku, the ceiling is decorated with geometric designs and rosettes. Stairs lead up through three storeys, before arriving at the roof, from where there are excellent, if a little precarious, views out over the valley and across to the main ruins. At the rear of the tomb (outside) there are steps leading down to an underground burial chamber which is also kept locked. Although dank, smelly and strewn with rubbish, the presence of this underground chamber is interesting in that it shows the combination of a tower tomb with a *hypogeum* (underground tomb); generally tower tombs were of earlier origin and hypogea a later development, suggesting that this building represented a kind of transition stage. Amongst the same group is the **Tomb of Atenatan**, now kept locked and its tower disintegrated to a distinctive spire, and the minimal remains of the **Hypogeum of Yarhai** which has been dismantled and reconstructed in the Damascus museum.

From the tower tomb of Elabel it is possible to return to the main road via the course of the *wadi* (seasonal stream), which runs slightly to the north of the track you arrived by, keeping the ridge of Umm el Belquis and the Iamliku cluster of tower tombs to the right. This route takes you past numerous ruined tower tombs and temple tombs scattered across the floor of the *wadi*. Along this route there are the remains of what is simply labelled as '**Tomb 36**'. Only the base of the tower remains, with numerous fragments laid out within the foundation walls and in the immediate vicinity. Many of the fragments are beautifully decorated, with the added bonus that they can be inspected close-up, revealing the skill and precision with which the detailed carving work was executed.

To reach the **Hypogeum of the Three Brothers** at the Southwest Necropolis, follow the main road south past the entrance to the **Cham Palace** hotel for around 300 m before branching off to the right along a rough track. This remarkably well preserved underground tomb (recently restored) dates from AD 160-191 and was still in use by AD 259. Steps lead down to the entrance doorway, where the large lintel carries an inscription in Aramaic detailing how the hypogeum was founded by the three brothers Naamai, Male and Saadai, and how at a later stage certain areas of the tomb were sold off, perhaps suggesting that the family fell on hard times. Inside, the tomb follows a standard plan consisting of an inverted T-shape, with burial compartments built into the wall of each gallery. The main gallery, straight ahead of you as you enter, consists of plastered brickwork, the ceiling decorated with painted floral and geometric designs, the patterns still remarkably well preserved. A circular panel depicts the abduction of Ganymede, son of Troy, by Zeus (appearing as an eagle) who wanted him as his cup bearer. At the far end of the chamber is a scene from *Iliad* in which Achilles, disguised in women's clothes and concealed amongst the daughters of Lycomedes, king of Skyros, is discovered by Ulysses who has come to take him from the mortal world. Thus both frescoes emphasize man's mortality, while at the same time offering the promise of a role in the after-world. Another fresco depicts the three brothers, each framed in an oval medallion and held up by winged victories. In the right-hand side gallery there are three sarcophagi, with headless figures reclining on couches. In the left-hand side gallery there is a large sarcophagus of Male decorated with a frieze depicting him in Parthian dress reclining on a couch. Again, his head is missing but the detail of the decoration is impressive.

Southeast Necropolis

The Southeast Necropolis can be reached by continuing south along the main road from the **Cham Palace** hotel. Just over 2 km past the entrance to the **Cham Palace**, take the left turn immediately after the petrol station. Follow this road for a little over 3 km to arrive at the necropolis, just to the left of the road (at the time of writing it was not signposted and a small, squat building, partially built of ancient stones, was the only landmark). Returning, if you continue along the road, it will bring you out (after a few twists and turns) onto the eastward continuation of JA Al-Naser Street; turn left to head back into Tadmor's Main Bazaar.

All the tombs of the Southeast Necropolis are underground, so when you arrive here, there only appears to be desert. However, the lack of anything to see above ground is more than made up for by what is concealed below.

The underground tombs here were accidentally uncovered in the 1950s when the Iraq Petroleum Company was laying an oil pipeline in the area. Running across the stairs leading down to the **Arteban Tomb** is a section of this pipeline. The doors of the tomb consist of two massive stone slabs, decorated with demon-like griffins and both still swinging on their hinges. Inside, the cradle-vaulted tomb follows much the same inverted T-shaped plan as the Hypogeum of the Three Brothers, except that there are two additional side galleries half-way down the main gallery. Many of the burial *loculi* still have their original funerary busts in place. Just inside the doorway, to your right, is one glass-covered *loculi* containing a skeleton. At the far end of the main gallery, framed within an arch, is a frieze depicting Arteban attended by various figures. The tomb dates from the second half of the first century AD.

The nearby **Japanese Tomb** ① *at the time of writing this tomb was officially closed to the public but can be opened up at special request – ask at the museum*, first excavated in 1994. The tomb takes its name from the fact that the restoration work was carried out by Japanese archaeologists (although the completely unpronounceable names of the tomb's two patrons, 'Bwlh' and 'Bwrp' might have something to do with it. The immaculate crispness of the restoration work is not to everybody's taste, though it certainly gives you an excellent insight (perhaps even better than the reconstruction of the Hypogeum of Yarhai in the National Museum in Damascus) into what these tombs would have looked like originally. The entrance to the tomb consists of a massive single-slab stone door with carved panels and two small griffins. The lintel of the doorway is richly decorated, while above this is a carved satyr's head and an inscription dedicating the tomb, which dates from AD 128, to the two brothers Bwlh and Bwrp. Leading off on either side of the main gallery as you enter are two arched side-chambers (note the medusa faces carved into the keystones of the arches, designed to ward off evil spirits). In each side-chamber is a sarcophogus topped by a sculpture depicting a family banqueting scene. Both these side-chambers are comparatively simple; according to the inscription above the door they were given away in AD 220 and AD 222. Running around the main gallery is a particularly ornate frieze, while carved into the walls are the burial *loculi*, sealed by funerary busts. At the far end is a large frieze illustrating another family banqueting scene, presumably that of Bwlh and Bwrp.

Afqa Spring

The Afqa Spring, by the roadside in front of the **Palmyra Cham Palace**, was originally Palmyra's life source and raison d'être, providing the sole water supply to the oasis. The discovery of numerous incense altars in the vicinity, including two dedicated by the curator Bolanos in AD 162 to 'Zeus the Most High', and others to Yarhibol, as well as the references in the Palmyrene Tariff, indicate the importance of the spring to the Romans. The name itself, which is Aramaic for 'source' or 'issue', confirms its existence since earliest times. Today, the spring has unfortunately dried up, probably because of the extensive digging of tube-wells. Water from the spring was sulphurous and warm, and used to emerge at a steady 33°C. Steps lead down to a bathing area, while a locked doorway leads to an underground cavern beneath the hill of Jebel Muntar, through which the water once flowed. Channels lead from the spring to the nearby groves of date palms, olives, pomegranates, figs and apricots, although today these are irrigated from tube-wells.

Palmyra Museum

① *Wed-Mon 0800-1800 in summer, 0800-1600 in summer, S£150, students S£10.*

This great little museum, by the entrance to Tadmor town, contains an interesting selection of artefacts, dominated by numerous Palmyrene religious artefacts and funerary art objects, along with a variety of other pieces.

Going round in an anticlockwise direction, the first room contains a number of incense altars found around the Afqa Spring, and various large tablets and plinths for statues inscribed with dedications. These are written in the Palmyrene script, a dialect of Aramaic with a strong Arabic element, reflecting the large Arab population. Aramaic, and later Greek, were the *linguas francas* of the region before the Roman era, and the continued use of both in Palmyra emphasized its independence from Rome.

In the centre of the second room is an impressive scale-model of the Sanctuary of Bel as it would have looked in its heyday, and beside it a smaller scale-model of Diocletian's Camp. Around the edges of the room are various elaborately decorated architectural fragments, including a particularly striking triangular pediment framing a carved bust.

The third room contains various honorary statues and busts and a bas-relief of a Palmyrene standing by his ship, an indication of the importance of maritime trade for Palmyra, which through the ancient port of Spasinu Cherax on the Euphrates-Tigris estuary, had access to the trade routes to India.

Along the length of the rear of the museum is a gallery displaying a variety of artefacts: statues of various gods and goddesses, mosaics, glazed pottery, jewellery, coins, delicate Palmyrene and Byzantine glassware and carved reliefs. A particularly fine piece is the lintel taken from the Temple of Baal Shamin with a relief depicting the god Baal Shamin

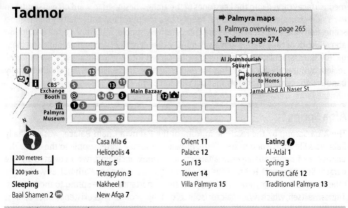

Tadmor

➡ **Palmyra maps**
1 Palmyra overview, page 265
2 Tadmor, page 274

200 metres
200 yards

Sleeping
Baal Shamen 2

Casa Mia 6
Heliopolis 4
Ishtar 5
Tetrapylon 3
Nakheel 1
New Afqa 7

Orient 11
Palace 12
Sun 13
Tower 14
Villa Palmyra 15

Eating
Al-Atlal 1
Spring 3
Tourist Café 12
Traditional Palmyra 13

(fertility) as an eagle with outspread wings sheltering Malakbel (a sun god) and Aglibol (the moon god). Two mosaics taken from the Patrician Houses behind the Sanctuary of Bel, one depicting scenes from the legend of Achilles and Odysseus, and the other of Centaur the hunting god, are displayed. The collection of coins includes some with the heads of Zenobia and her son Wahballat which were discovered in 1991, providing the first evidence that Zenobia went so far as to mint her own currency. At the far end of the hall is a partially restored statue of the goddess Allat-Athena with one arm raised, found in the Temple of Allat by a Polish team in 1975.

The last three rooms contain a selection of excellently preserved funerary busts, many of them with strikingly expressive features, as well as a number of sarcophagi with elaborately carved reliefs and various fragments of textiles and papyrus with Greek and Palmyrene lettering.

Around Palmyra

Talila Reserve
Some 24 km from Palmyra this biodiversity conservation reserve is a wonderful project that hosts two types of gazelle, various other animals and at least 20 different types of birdlife. To get there, take the signposted turn-off for the reserve about 12 km out of Palmyra on the road to Deir ez-Zor. A return taxi from Palmyra to the reserve, with waiting time would cost approximately US$30.

Qasr al-Heir al-Sharki
① *No official opening hours, if the site is locked you need to collect the key from the caretaker who lives in the house on the left side of the ruins. If you are collecting the key, beware of the dogs here; their impersonations of rabid, demented, flesh-starved creatures intent on tearing you limb for limb are extremely convincing, S£75, students S£5.*

Improbably set in the midst of the desert, without even an oasis in the immediate vicinity to justify its existence, is the desert palace known as Qasr al-Heir al-Sharki (literally 'eastern walled-palace'). Although it in no way matches the grandeur of Rasafeh to the north, it still makes an interesting day trip from Palmyra, perhaps as much for the drive through the desert to get there and the opportunity to visit one of the many Bedouin camps in the vicinity, as for the site itself.

Getting there and away Qasr al-Heir al-Sharki is 110 km northeast of Palmyra on the road to Deir ez-Zor and then around 30 km north of the main road. The easiest way to get there is to hire a vehicle and driver in Palmyra which will cost around S£2000 (good value if you get a microbus and go as a group). Make sure your driver is familiar with the route and bear in mind that after rains a 4WD is essential. Visiting the site is perfectly possible with your own transport, providing the conditions are suitable, although the main difficulty is in finding it. The road hasn't yet been completed and the various dirt tracks left by Bedouin pickups are numerous and confusing.

The easiest route is to take the signposted turning left after around 70 km towards the village of Al-Sukhneh. From Al-Sukhneh there are reasonably obvious tracks leading towards the village of Al-Taibeh 32 km away. This route leads you past a line of impressive fluted cliffs off to the left which fall away gradually before you reach Al-Taibeh, a sizeable village complete with its own petrol pumps, although these look completely derelict and abandoned. From here you must bear off to the east (right), past a small oasis on the edge of the village to arrive at the ruins some 15 km away. This last stretch is the least obvious, with numerous tracks branching out into the desert, so it might be advisable to try to find a local to show you the way. From a distance, the ruins have an odd appearance, with the sections of newly cut limestone used in the restoration standing out sharply against the older, weathered stonework.

Background Very little is known about this site, both in terms of its inception and purpose. One theory, given some of its architectural features, is that it dates originally from the Byzantine period, while others argue that it was entirely an Arab project that borrowed materials from Roman and Byzantine sites around Palmyra. As to its purpose, theories range from it being an extravagant hunting lodge and pleasure gardens to an intensive market-garden/agricultural community. The most generally accepted explanation is that the main complex was built by the Umayyad Caliph Hisham Ibn Abd al-Malik during AD 728-729 (he was also responsible for the Qasr al-Heir al-Gharbi to the west), perhaps on the site of an existing agricultural settlement and that it acted primarily as a khan, or caravanserai, on the route between Damascus and Mesopotamia, while also serving as a means of subduing the surrounding nomadic tribes.

The ruins The site consists of two walled compounds adjacent to each other, a larger one to the west and a smaller one to the east. The larger compound to the west has an entrance gate in each of the four walls, which have been extensively restored with newly cut limestone to give such an odd appearance from a distance (and close up for that matter). Semi-circular towers are placed along the walls at regular intervals. Inside, there existed in effect a completely self-sufficient community. Although excavations carried out in the 1960s and early 1970s established the basic plan, today little can be distinguished with any certainty. The large brick-lined cistern, surrounded by a courtyard in the centre of the compound is still discernible, along with various fragments of the buildings which were ranged around the sides. In the southeast corner are the remains of what were a mosque, royal palace and olive press.

The second, smaller compound is kept locked. The main gateway in the west wall is well preserved, with the semi-circular towers either side of the gate decorated with distinctive bands of brickwork in a characteristically Mesopotamian style. Inside, it follows the same basic plan as the larger compound, with a cistern surrounded by a courtyard in the centre. Around this was a colonnaded porch (a few of the columns are still standing) with rooms ranged around the walls. This compound probably acted as a khan for passing caravans, and perhaps also as barracks for the army.

Between the two compounds is a small square minaret with steps climbing part of the way up inside. Surrounding the two compounds was a wall, traces of which are still visible. The whole complex was watered by means of an aqueduct that led from a dam by the village of Kom (or Qawm), 30 km to the north. To the east of the two compounds was a walled garden measuring 3 km by 6 km, and surrounding the whole settlement was a further mud-brick wall, over 22 km in circumference, sections of it still traceable as you approach from the south, some 5 km before reaching the main complex.

Damascus to Palmyra

Leave Damascus on the Aleppo motorway, and after 24 km take the signposted exit for Palmyra. Having exited the motorway, turn left and then right soon after (it is well signposted). After a further 20 km, go straight ahead at a roundabout/fork as you enter the town of **Dumeir** (bear left to bypass the town). An old signpost by the roadside here indicates Baghdad, 800 km away.

There is an impressive **Roman temple**, in the centre of the town, which is well worth a visit. Both the enclosure and the temple are kept locked; ask around and the caretaker, who lives locally, will soon appear; from the roundabout/fork, follow the road towards the centre of town for just under 2 km, going straight over a second roundabout on the way, and then take the second right turn after a marked dip in the road as it crosses a wadi. The solid, imposing outline of the temple is visible at the end of the main street. Today it is set in a fenced-off enclosure, its foundations some 3 m below the level of the surrounding buildings. Although the existing structure, which has undergone extensive restoration, is of Roman origin, an altar to the Semitic god Baal Shamin dating from AD 94 found here suggests that it was originally a Nabatean temple. In AD 245 it was dedicated to the god Zeus Hypsistos, a local version of Zeus. At a crossroads on the east-west route between Homs and Palmyra and the north-south route between Damascus and Rasafeh, the building possibly started life as a staging post, which perhaps explains its square plan, unusual for a temple of this period. Some of the stone blocks in the walls bear Greek inscriptions. Inside, a small room to the right of the entrance contains a stone carved with figures on each face. During the Arab period the temple was used as a fortified tower which is why the large arched doorways at the front and rear have been bricked up, and the level of the walls raised above the pediments capping the arches.

Qasr al-Heir al-Gharbi

ⓘ *To reach the ruins turn left towards Homs and follow the road for around 35 km, at which point the ruins can be made out 2 km off to the right.*

On your way east to Palmyra, it is possible to make a short diversion from the tiny settlement of **Al Basiri** to visit the ruins of Qasr al-Heir al-Gharbi (literally 'western walled palace'). Although this palace must once have been impressive, all the major architectural features have been removed, including the massive central gateway which now adorns the entrance to the National Museum in Damascus. The remaining ruins are in a very advanced state of dilapidation and unless you have a special interest, the ruins of Qasr al-Heir al-Sharki ('eastern walled palace') to the northeast of Palmyra (see page 275) are far more rewarding to visit.

First occupied in the first century AD by settlers from Palmyra, and later the site of a Byzantine/Ghassanid monastery in the sixth century, the palace appears to have been built in the eighth century by the Umayyad Caliph Hisham Ibn Abd al-Malik, who is thought to have built Qasr al-Heir al-Sharki at around the same time. It is probable that the palace served primarily as a hunting lodge and desert retreat for the Umayyad rulers of Damascus, but, like its eastern neighbour, it perhaps also served as a means of maintaining close contacts with the desert tribes from which the Umayyads themselves had originated. It also appears to have supported gardens (watered by an aqueduct running from a dam built 15 km to the south by the Palmyrenes).

Hama to Palmyra via Qalat Shmemis

If you have your own transport, this is certainly the most beautiful route, combining both open desert and hilly steppes, as well as a chance to see some 'beehive' houses. Covering the journey in 196 km, this route follows a good modern road (not marked on older maps) before joining the main Homs–Palmyra road. From Hama, take the road southeast towards Salamiyeh (the exit for Salamiyeh off the ring-road which passes to the east of Hama is clearly signposted). Around 18 km beyond the Hama ring road, at about the same time as you spot the huge concrete silos of a grain-processing factory, Qalat Shmemis. Depending on the season, there may be various tracks leading up to the volcano from the main road, or more conveniently there is a small surfaced road running from the town of Salamiyeh, a further 10 km away; entering the town, turn left by the petrol station and then left again, and follow this road for a little over 3 km to the foot of the volcano, comes into view.

This ruined castle is perched strikingly on the top of an extinct volcano whose perfect conical outline, completely bare of vegetation, contrasts sharply in spring with the green hills and fields surrounding it. The castle dates from the 13th century and was built by the Ayyubid Governor of Hama, Assad ud-Din Shirkoh. The climb up to the rim of the volcano on a path from the end of the metalled road is steep but fairly straightforward; getting into the castle, however, is more difficult. You must first descend into the crater and then scramble up. Note that the large slit in the rock wall of the castle, which looks like an entrance, is in fact a cave. You can gain entry from a point just to the right of the cave, which involves a tricky climb up through the last part (though there is a slightly easier access from the opposite side of the castle). Today little remains of the castle except for the walls themselves; there are panoramic views of the surrounding countryside, but the most striking thing about this site is the view of it from a distance.

Salamiyeh

The town of Salamiyeh, 33 km from Hama, known in Hellenistic/Roman times as Salamias, was an important stopping place on the route to Rasafeh. It continued to flourish under the Byzantines, and during the Islamic era became an important **Ismaili** centre, being the birthplace of the first Fatimid Caliph Ubaydullah. Driven out by the Mongol invasion of 1401, many Ismailis left the refuge of the mountains during the 19th century and once again came to settle around Salamiyeh. Today, Salamiyeh is a small but lively market town used by farmers from the surrounding countryside. Recycled Byzantine architectural fragments can be seen in some of the older buildings, while in the centre is an Ismaili mosque, thought to date originally from the 11th century, and a beautiful old hammam.

Note A road leads northeast from Salamiyeh to the Roman temple of Isriye, 90 km away (see page 141) and extends all the way to Rasafeh.

Ask directions through the centre of town to pick up the road for Palmyra. Keep going straight through the villages of **Tal Atout** and **Bural Sharki** (the latter 16 km from Salamiyeh). The surrounding land becomes progressively less intensively cultivated, steadily giving way to scrubland and semi-desert. Around 26 km beyond Bural Sharki, bear right at the fork in the centre of the small town of **Aqeirbat** (80 km from Hama, petrol available), and then turn right at a crossroads just over 1 km further on. After heading across flat, stony scrubland, the road begins to climb, winding through low hills dotted with stunted pine trees, and then through dramatic desert scenery, desolate and bare. Around 75 km beyond Aqeirbat, you link up with the main Homs–Palmyra road. Turn left here and it is a further 45 km to Palmyra (see Homs to Palmyra, above).

Palmyra to Deir ez-Zor

The route from Palmyra to Deir ez-Zor, 210 km away, is on a good road heading northeast across the desert. Some 4 km out of town there is a petrol station on the main road, which is the last one for just over 175 km, until 30 km short of Deir ez-Zor. This road takes you through a barren, inhospitable landscape of open desert and low steppes stretching into the distance in all directions. During spring there is a thin covering of grass and numerous Bedouin camps spring up, grazing their sheep and cattle on the short-lived pasture.

◉ Palmyra listings

For Sleeping and Eating price codes and other relevant information, see Essentials pages 19-21.

⬤ Sleeping

Palmyra *p257, maps p265 and p274*
Palmyra experiences huge fluctuations in room prices between the high season, when hotels are often at capacity, and the low season, when the majority are empty. The official definition of 'high season' varies somewhat from hotel to hotel (and depends also very much on demand), but as a rough guide it generally runs from mid-Mar to the end of May, and from mid-Sep to mid-Nov, with some hotels counting an additional high season period over Christmas and New Year. Outside of these times it is often possible to negotiate significant discounts (up to 50% in some cases), although there are a few hotels which maintain fixed prices throughout the year. During the Palmyra Desert Festival, hotels are likely to be booked up well in advance and it can be difficult to find a room. Prices, meanwhile, go sky-high across the board, with many hotels charging as much as three times their normal high season rate. Many hotels include breakfast, though you should check this when enquiring after room prices. All the hotels listed here have heating, which is essential during winter; in the cheaper places you should check that it is actually working before taking a room. Be aware that some hotels change management yearly which means that a hotel that was great one year could be diabolical the next.

A Heliopolis, Tadmor, T031-591 3921, Heliopolis-palmyra@usa.net. There are great views over the ruins from this well-run, friendly hotel. The spacious rooms (a/c, satellite TV and fridge) are clean and comfortable and come with larger than average baths. There's a bar, restaurant and off-street parking.
A Zenobia, beside the ruins, T031-591 8123. There's no denying that the Zenobia has the best location in town, right beside the ruins. The rooms here are full of atmosphere with some nice artistic touches. Unfortunately the hotel was closed at the time of writing but was due to open up again soon.
B Casa Mia, Tadmor, T031-591 6222, casa-mia@live.com. This little place, on a quiet back street, is the closest Palmyra comes to a boutique hotel. The stone-walled rooms here are decked out with subtle, traditional touches and new modern baths. Rooms are set around a walled courtyard that doubles as a small restaurant (see below). Recommended.
B Tetrapylon, Tadmor, T031-591 7170. The lobby is worryingly space-age but the light-filled rooms here are fine. There's a/c, satellite TV and fridge as standard and some of the rooms have excellent views over to the ruins.
B Tower, Main Bazaar, Tadmor, T031-591 0116. The rooms at this welcoming hotel (a/c, satellite TV) vary hugely in size so have a look at a few. It's on the expensive side for what you get so see if you can bargain them down.
B Villa Palmyra, Main Bazaar, Tadmor, T031-591 0156, villapalmyra@mail.sy. The decent-sized, clean rooms here are

comfortably furnished (a/c, satellite TV) if a little bit bland. Some rooms are much larger than others so ask to see a few before deciding. There's a good restaurant and a basement cave bar with an excellent array of alcohol.

C Ishtar, Main Bazaar, Tadmor, T031-591 3073, www.ishtarhotel.net. This friendly, popular place, smack in the middle of town has spotlessly clean rooms (all with a/c, some with satellite TV) and helpful staff. There's also a good restaurant and their basement cave bar is the best place in town to meet other travellers. Recommended.

C Nakheel, Tadmor, T031-591 0744, mohamed1st2@yahoo.com. Colourful kilims cover the walls and floors of this character-filled little hotel. Large rooms (with tiny baths) come with a/c and there's a Bedouin-style restaurant as well.

C Orient, Tadmor, T031-591 0131, www.orient hotel.sy.com. Just like staying at grandmas. The chintzy rooms here all have a/c, satellite TV and frilly floral bedcovers with a homey feel. It's all topped off by welcoming staff.

D New Afqa, Tadmor, T031-591 0386, mahran_afqa@hotmail.com. The rooms here may be simple but they're spotlessly clean and come with a/c, satellite TV and fan.

D Palace, Tadmor, T031-591 1707. This cheerful hotel is a good option with small, clean, a/c rooms and friendly staff.

E Baal Shamen, Tadmor, T031-591 0453. This very basic but friendly hotel has cleanish rooms that all come with bath. There's also a dormitory for extra money-saving.

E Camping Al-Baida, just beyond the Sanctuary of Bel. This peaceful, shady campsite is well run and has clean facilities. It's a great little place to pitch a tent or park up your campervan. There's a pool and they can also do meals here.

E Sun, Tadmor, T031-591 1133, sunhotel-sy@ hotmail.com. By far the best of the cheapies, this cute little place has spick-and-span good-sized rooms with fan and bath, and friendly management. There's a dormitory for the budget-conscious and if you're really

scraping by you can sleep on the roof. They also can rustle up yummy home-cooked meals. Recommended.

❼ Eating

Palmyra *p257, maps p265 and p274*
Palmyra will never be known for its variety of cuisine but most of the restaurants here can do wholesome local specialities that are filling and tasty. Most of the hotels have restaurants as well. For really cheap meals, there's some good little *shawarma* and falafel stands further along main bazaar, as you head away from the tourist shops and hotels.

₮₮₮ Zenobia, right beside the ruins. Definitely Palmyra's fanciest dining option; the outdoor terrace here is a lovely place to have a meal. The dishes here are a step above the food elsewhere and there are some nice twists on Syrian specialities. Alcohol served.

₮₮ Casa Mia, Casa Mia hotel, Tadmor. Away from the hustle and bustle this tranquil courtyard is a lovely spot for a meal. There's no menu as such, just check the blackboard and order whatever tasty, rustic meal they're cooking that day.

₮₮ Garden, opp Zenobia hotel. Set amid the date palms of the oasis, this quiet restaurant serves up good grills and mezze and is a relaxing place to hang out for a few hours. There's a swimming pool as well.

₮₮ Spring, Main Bazaar, Tadmor. This restaurant has a quirky Bedouin-style eating area upstairs. They can rustle up all the usual Arabic staples and the mezze dishes here are excellent.

₮₮ Traditional Palmyra, Main Bazaar, Tadmor. Perennially popular, this little place spills out onto the surrounding pavement in the evening. There's some continental dishes on offer here as well as local fare. Their speciality is *mansaf* (chicken with yoghurt and nutty rice) and *kawag* (a kind of slow-cooked vegetable stew). There's also a separate menu with a wide variety of filling pancakes which are a meal within themselves. Alcohol served.

Cafés
Al-Atlal, opposite the museum, Tadmor. This cheerful café is a pleasant place to sit awhile and have a coffee and *narghile*.
Tourist, Main Bazaar, Tadmor. Always bustling with locals, seemingly intense with concentration on their backgammon games, this traditional café has good *narghile* and coffee.

🍸 Bars and clubs

Palmyra *p257, maps p265 and p274*
There's no independent bars as such, but the restaurant at the **Zenobia** hotel is great for a pre-dinner drink, with views out over the ruins and Corinthian capitals from the terrace. It's a lovely place at sunset. All the restaurants that serve alcohol don't mind you just coming for a drink either.

The **Ishtar** Hotel and **Villa Palmyra** Hotel both have basement cave bars and you don't have to stay there to make use of them. Both serve a whole range of alcohol and neither seems to have an official closing time.

🎉 Festivals and events

Palmyra *p257, maps p265 and p274*
Apr/May Palmyra Desert Festival. This popular 3- to 4-day annual festival attracts vast crowds of Syrians as well as foreign tourists. If you're hoping for a quiet, crowd-free visit to the ruins, this is probably not the best time to come. There are camel and horse-racing competitions, and various performances of folk dancing and music; with the main performances being held inside the roman theatre.

⛰ Activities and tours

Palmyra *p257, maps p265 and p274*
Most tour operators work out of the hotels and you'll have no problems finding a driver to take you out to the surrounding area or further. There are also various camel treks into the desert on offer varying from one day to longer, some with overnight stays in Bedouin encampments.

Guides
The **Tourist office** has a list of official guides for the ruins and there's always a few guides hanging about the entrance to The Sanctuary of Bel.
Salem Al-Kayem, T094-452 3095, is a highly recommended Palmyra guide whose tours are packed full of historical information and quirky facts about Palmyra.

Tour operators
Fuaz Asad, T094-422 6217, can organize private and small-group transport or tours to the surrounding area as well as all over Syria. He can arrange overnight desert stays with Bedouin families, camping trips and camel and horse trips as well. He's honest, friendly and speaks excellent English.

🚌 Transport

Palmyra *p257, maps p265 and p274*
Bus
For the moment most buses arrive and depart from near the **Sahara Cafe**, 2 km to the northeast of the centre. This is all about to change when they open the new bus station currently being built about 30 m further along the road. It's about S£30 from town to here in a taxi. There are at least 15 companies offering services all over the east and to Damascus, Aleppo and Homs in the west, from here. **Kadmous** have services to **Damascus** (3½ hrs, S£175), at 0900, 1230, 1330, 1630, 1700 and 1930; to **Homs** (2½ hrs, S£105), at 0930, 1330, 1530, 1700 and 1930; and **Deir ez-Zor** (2½ hrs, S£125) at 0930, 1030, 1245, and then 1 bus every hour from then on.

Microbus

At the eastern end of Main Bazaar, on Al-Joumhouriah Sq, you can catch old 'hob-hob' buses and microbuses to **Homs** (2½ hrs, S£75) every 30 mins until about 1600. They're rather squashy and uncomfortably hot but can be quite fun.

❶ Directory

Palmyra *p257, maps p265 and p274*
Banks At the moment there is still no ATM in Palmyra. Bring enough cash to see you through. There is a **CBS** exchange booth right by the museum which does foreign exchange, daily 0800-1300 and 1800-2030.
Internet Palmyra Traditional Restaurant has an internet café inside and there's also Wi-Fi here if you have your laptop. **Moonlight Internet**, opposite the museum, is another good place to check your email. **Post** The post office is by the roundabout at the western end of Tadmor, near the museum, Sat-Thu 0800-1400. **Telephone** There are 2 card-phones for national and international calls just outside the post office (accessible 24 hrs). You can buy phonecards inside the PO during opening hrs, but check first that one of the card-phones is actually working, as both are sometimes out of order.

Contents

Footprint features

Border crossings

Euphrates River & the Jezira

The journey here through the vast desert steppe is long and arduous with the monotony of the beige stony plains only broken by tiny, forlorn villages that somehow hang on in the heat and dust. Rising majestically out of the emptiness is the enormous walled city of Rasafeh, a lonely ruin where you're likely to be the only visitor. On reaching the Euphrates the landscape suddenly comes alive, as this ancient river nurtures the surrounding land and the river's banks erupt in a riot of greenery, with fields of cotton and corn. The blue waters of the Euphrates were historically an important medium for trade, a fact marked by the extensive ruins that can still be found beside it.

To the northeast is the Jezira (literally 'island' in Arabic) region; home to most of Syria's one million Kurds. This area encompasses ancient northern Mesopotamia, and outside its bustling dusty market towns lay the nondescript mounds and *tells* that have yielded so much information as to humanity's first steps towards civilization.

Ins and outs

Getting there and away
The main towns in the region all have decent bus services connecting each other and Damascus and Aleppo to the west. Most buses heading to/from Damascus stop in Palmyra on the way. The train network is improving slowly with a new express service now running from Aleppo to Deir ez-Zor via Raqqa, as well as the excruciatingly slow overnight service from Aleppo to Qamishle via the main regional towns. Both Deir ez-Zor and Qamishle have airports with regular flights to Damascus.

Getting around
Although all the main towns in the Jezira and Euphrates region can be quite easily reached by a mixture of Pullman bus and microbus journeys, getting to the surrounding sights can present some difficulty. With a lot of time (and patience) the major sights can be visited by a mixture of microbus and walking (and maybe some hitching) but those with less time would be better off hiring a car or driver. Even travellers with time up their sleeve would do well to consider this option during the summer months when the heat here is stifling and walking a few kilometres to a site becomes a gruelling chore. With a car, you could cover the main sights in this region (Dura Europos, Mari, Qala'at Jaber and Rasafeh) in two days with an overnight in Deir ez-Zor.

Background

The Jezira region is of enormous importance in archaeological terms, forming part of the **Fertile Crescent**, which played such a central role in the origins of settled agriculture. Extensive excavations at sites such as Tell Brak and Tell Halaf (ancient *Guzana*), archaeologists have found remains of some of the earliest settlements in the Near East and many more *tells* await excavation.

The incredible spawning of culture in this region is thanks to the Euphrates (*al-Furat* in Arabic) which rises in Turkey's eastern Anatolian plateau and flows southeast through Syria, dividing the desert from the rain-fed plains of the Jezira. This region gave birth to the ancient city-states of **Mesopotamia** ('the land between two rivers' – the Euphrates and the Tigris), most of which extends into present-day Iraq.

Aleppo to Raqqa

For the first 80 km or so out of Aleppo, the road passes through a rather monotonous landscape, cultivated in places but often barren, the Euphrates being a long way to the northeast. Even after the town of Meskene, when you are running parallel to this great river, irrigated farmland comes in small patches, with the desert never far away.

Euphrates Highway
To join the Euphrates Highway you have to head east out of Aleppo in the direction of the airport. However, Aleppo's often confusing one-way systems and chaotic traffic make this no mean feat. **One route out of the city:** From the junction at the north end of Bab al-Faraj Street, in the centre of Aleppo, head east along Al-Khandak Street. After a short distance, the one-way system forces you to turn right; go left at the next roundabout you come to (into Al-Sejn Street), then left again at the T-junction at the end of this street, and

The Kurdish question

While the plight of the Kurds in neighbouring Iraq and Turkey has led to long-running conflicts, a large number of Syria's one million Kurds have suffered a more silent fate. A 1962 census carried out by the government (ostensibly to eliminate illegal immigration) led to 100,000 Kurds being stripped of their Syrian citizenship. The number of stateless Kurds in Syria is now estimated to have grown to 200,000. Known as 'maktoum' (Arabic for 'nothing') they are considered non-entities in the country they live in; not allowed to own property, to marry Syrian citizens, to hold a driving licence, or to be employed in professional jobs, reduced to living on the very edge of society.

With the founding of Iraq's Kurdish region, some of these stateless Kurds have begun crossing the border to try to find a better life there. But with the Kurdish authority unable to issue passports or grant refugee status without the go-ahead from the central Iraqi authorities, they find themselves trapped in the same cycle.

In recent years the Syrian government has begun talking about resolving this tragedy. President Bashar al-Assad himself has spoken of wanting to rectify this issue and grant citizenship to the people affected. For the 200,000 stateless Kurds of Syria this solution cannot come quickly enough.

then right at the next T-Junction. You are now on Bab an-Nasr Street, the continuation of Al-Khandak Street. At the Bab an-Nasr roundabout, on the northeast corner of the old city, turn left and then follow Al-Abbassin Street north, up to the next major junction. Turn right here and follow signs for Aleppo Airport. Just over 9 km from the centre of Aleppo by this route, take the exit signposted for Raqqa and Membij to join the Euphrates Highway (at this stage a motorway) heading east. The exit immediately before (signposted for Hama and Damascus) puts you on the motorway in the opposite direction to bypass Aleppo and join the Aleppo–Damascus Highway.

There is an exit clearly signposted for **Membij** 6 km after joining the Euphrates Highway. This is the start of the route to Qala'at Najm, see page 251. At this point, the Euphrates Highway turns from a motorway into a normal two-lane highway. After a further 39 km, you pass through **Deir Haffer**, a half-built, rather miserable looking place, and then, in another 40 km, arrive at **Meskene**, also somewhat uninspiring, although there is an interesting monument nearby.

Meskene minaret

Around 5 km to the northeast of Meskene (as the crow flies), on the edges of Lake Assad, there is a solitary 13th-century Ayyubid brick-built octagonal minaret with stairs inside leading up to the top, from where there are panoramic views out onto the lake. A little beyond the minaret, on the shores of the lake, there are a few insubstantial ruins dating from the Byzantine period. This is all that remains of an ancient transit point on the Euphrates where caravans on the trade route between the Mediterranean and Mesopotamia switched between land and river transport.

The area of land between the modern town and the minaret is criss-crossed by irrigation channels, making it difficult to reach it directly. One route is as follows: 2 km beyond Meskene's police post (by the road on the right at the east edge of the town), turn left along a small road running along the east side of a large irrigation channel. After just over 4 km, turn left to cross over the channel on a bridge and follow a smaller irrigation channel running off the main one at right angles. After just under 2 km, turn right and cross over this channel on another bridge. The surfaced road now turns to a rough track running through a village. Around 500 m further on you come to a kind of T-junction, from where the tower is visible up ahead.

Raqqa → *For listings, see pages 309-314.*

The hot, dusty market town of Raqqa stands on a section of the Middle Euphrates, at its junction with the Balikh River (the classical *Balissus*). There is not a great deal to see and do in town, despite efforts to restore its historical remains, and you definitely couldn't call it pretty. Instead it is the town's function as a market centre for the surrounding countryside that gives Raqqa its greatest appeal. The bustling main street is crammed with gold and textile shops and, in the cool of the evening, the whole place thrums with window-shopping families. Bedouin come here from far and wide to shop and trade creating a colourful spectacle on market days. If you don't have your own transport, Raqqa is also a base from which to visit Rasafeh, Qala'at Jaber and the Euphrates Dam.

Ins and outs
Getting there and away Raqqa is well connected by road with Aleppo to the west and Deir ez-Zor to the southeast. There are also services connecting it with Damascus, either via Aleppo, or else the desert road via Salamiyeh. The main luxury coach/minibus station is just past Rashid Ramadan Square, a little to the south of the town centre. The microbus stand is across the road. It's an easy five-minute walk into the town centre from here and a taxi to the mid-range hotels costs about S£25. Raqqa's train station is inconveniently located way to the north of the centre. The services to Deir ez-Zor and Qamishle pass through here on their way from Aleppo. A taxi to the centre from the train station costs about S£30.

Getting around Raqqa is easily managed on foot, though there are taxis available everywhere should you want one and a journey within town shouldn't cost more than S£25.

Orientation The main road is Quneitra Street and the town centre is marked by the clock tower. This is where you'll find the cheap eateries and, just to the east on Kouwatly Street, the one decent budget hotel and Raqqa's museum. Further east are the remains of the old city. South of the clock tower are the bus stations while north, this road is a 3-km stretch of shops and a busy jam-packed commercial hub. The mid-range hotels are both in a slightly quieter area, west of the centre.

Background
The great historian-geographer Pliny suggests that the town here was first established by Alexander the Great, though the credit probably lies with his general Seleucus Nicator, who went on to establish the **Seleucid** Empire. The settlement's development is due to one of his successors, Seleucus II Callinicus (246-225 BC), who gave his name to the early town. The strategic importance of a town controlling much of the Middle Euphrates basin was further emphasized when the battle lines became drawn between the Byzantine Empire and the rising power of the Sassanid Persians. The town was close to this zone of contact and was the scene of a major battle in AD 531 in which the Christian army was resoundingly beaten.

The rise of **Arab** power across the region produced the town's golden period (and the settlement becoming known as 'Raqqa', or 'flat land' in Arabic). The Umayyad caliph Hisham (AD 724-743) is said to have built two palaces here, though it was the succeeding (and rival) **Abbasid** Dynasty who enhanced Raqqa's status as a major Euphrates town. The caliph Al-Mansur (AD 754-775) made the town the administrative capital of the province of Jezira, and laid the foundations of the stout defensive walls that can still be seen today. The later Abbasid caliph Harun al-Rashid (AD 786-809) substantially remodelled the town, and added a neighbouring twin settlement to serve as his summer capital.

Raqqa's subsequent history is not so glamorous. It may have enjoyed a brief period of fame as the centre of a noted glazed ceramic-ware industry, possibly introduced by Salah ud-Din, but following its sacking by the Mongols in 1258 the town went into terminal decline. Raqqa's recent revival is very recent indeed, dating just to the last four decades. It is once again the administrative capital of the province in which it stands, and is the main commercial market for the region.

Old city walls and gates
The partially restored **city walls** are credited to the Abbasid caliph Al-Mansur, who fortified Raqqa as his advance headquarters against the Byzantine threat. The distinctive horseshoe shape is said to be based on the original circular plan for the defence of Baghdad, though adapted here to take account of the Euphrates to the south (the walls

Raqqa

400 metres
400 yards

N

Sleeping	Eating	Al-Waha 4
Karnak 1	Al-Buston 1	
Lazaward 2	Al-Naeem 2	
Tourism 3	Al-Rashid 3	

on this south side, parallel to the river, have largely disappeared). The bases of many of the 100 or so round towers that punctuated the city walls at every 35 m or so can still be seen, though only one gate has survived to any great height. In fact, there is now reason to suppose that the substantial **Bab Baghdad** (Baghdad Gate) in the southeast corner is actually mid-12th century AD and not Abbasid.

Qasr al-Banat
Around 400 m north of Bab Baghdad are the remains of the ninth-century AD Qasr al-Banat, or 'Palace of the Maidens'. The palace features a fountain set in a courtyard at its centre, with a high-arched hall (or *iwan*) on each side, though for whom the palace was built is still not entirely clear. The palace has been partially restored, though it is now fenced off and the gate on the west side is usually locked.

Great mosque
The great Friday mosque complex occupies a whole city block more or less at the centre of the old walled city. Like the city walls it was originally built by the Abbasid caliph Al-Mansur (around AD 772), though much of what you see today dates to the restoration programme undertaken by Nur ud-Din (1165-1166). In its prime the complex would have been an impressive sight, surrounded by a 100 m by 100 m wall (up to 5 m high) complete with 11 towers, though the remains to be seen today can only hint at this former splendour. In the northeast corner stands a 25 m high tower, probably part of Nur ud-Din's efforts, whilst along the south side stand 11 remaining arches of his impressive colonnade (that bears the inscription detailing his restoration work). At the centre of the complex is a small green-domed shrine.

Raqqa museum
① *Wed-Mon 0900-1800 in summer, 0900-1600 in winter, S£150, students S£10.*
Raqqa's museum features a small collection of artefacts excavated from the numerous sites of different periods in this region. Some of the figurines and items of pottery dating back as far as the fourth millennium BC are quite impressive, but most of the more important finds are now housed in the national museums in Aleppo and Damascus, or else have gone abroad.

Rasafeh → For listings, see pages 309-314.

The dramatic, desolate ruins of the huge walled city of Rasafeh, on the fringes of the desert, is one of the Euphrates region's most impressive and intriguing sights. Inside the walls, scattered ruins rise up between a sea of slumping mounds that curve wave-like up to the walls; all that's left of the famed Byzantine pilgrimage centre of Sergiopolis. Eerily silent and devoid of tourists, Rasafeh's lonely location is half the allure. By midday the temperature here soars and the gypsum ruins glisten from under their crust of sand further heightening the remote and inhospitable terrain that this, once massive, city was built in.

Ins and outs
Getting there and away Microbuses run regularly between Raqqa and Mansura (25 minutes, S£20), but it's another 20 km from Mansura to Rasafeh. From here you either have to negotiate a ride (approx S£500 return) or hitch. Be aware that traffic from here along the road to Rasafeh is limited. Unless you are lucky, you really have no choice but to try to negotiate a ride.

Background

Rasafeh is thought to be the *Rezeph* of the Bible (2 Kings 19.12 and Isaiah 37:12) and it is also possible that it was referred to in certain Assyrian texts, although no firm archaeological evidence has as yet been discovered to confirm this. During the third century AD the Roman Emperor **Diocletian** established a fortified caravan town here, on what was an ancient trade route between Damascus and the Euphrates (via Dumeir and Palmyra; later named the *Via Diocletiana* in his honour). Following the fall of Dura Europos to the Sassanid Persians in AD 256, Rasafeh also marked the new boundary between Roman west and Sassanid east.

It rose to fame after the martyrdom in AD 305 of **Sergius**, a Roman soldier who converted to Christianity and was executed for refusing to perform sacrifices to Jupiter. With the official recognition of Christianity following the Edict of Milan in AD 313, Sergius soon came to be revered as a saint and his burial place here began to attract large numbers of pilgrims. By the late fourth to early fifth century his fame was such that the settlement was renamed *Sergiopolis* in his honour. New ramparts were constructed, along with a basilica and water cisterns to supply its growing population.

During the reign of **Justinian** (AD 527-565), it reached the height of its prosperity. As part of a chain of frontier defences against the continuing Sassanid threat (including also Halabiye and Zalabiye on the Euphrates, see page 294), Justinian stationed a large garrison here and completely rebuilt the defensive walls surrounding Rasafeh on a far grander scale, constructing them out of stone instead of mud-brick. At the same time he undertook an extensive programme of building works within the city (although Procopius ascribes the water cisterns to Justinian, they appear to have been started earlier and perhaps only enlarged during his reign).

Ultimately, however, Rasafeh was unable to withstand the repeated attacks of the **Sassanid Persians** and in AD 616 it was finally sacked by Chosroes II. Following the Arab Muslim conquest of Syria, the **Umayyad Caliph Hisham** restored much of the city and built a palace for himself here in the eighth century. However, Abu al-Abbas, the founder of the **Abbasid Dynasty** in AD 750, largely destroyed his palace, and is even said to have had Hisham's bones dug up and flogged, such was his hatred for this Umayyad leader. Despite a severe earthquake towards the end of the eighth century the city continued to be occupied, although in a much impoverished state. A small Christian community appears to have coexisted alongside the Muslim one until the 13th century, by which time its population had greatly dwindled. Following the **Mongol** invasions it was abandoned altogether. In the ensuing centuries the encroaching sands of the desert did much to protect what remained of the city from the ravages of time.

Rasafeh

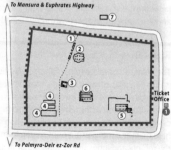

To Mansura & Euphrates Highway

To Palmyra-Deir ez-Zor Rd

N

200 metres (approx)
200 yards (approx)

Eating 🍴
Ticket Office Café

1 North Gate
2 Metropolitan Church
3 Khan
4 Water Cisterns
5 Basilica A (Church of St Sergius)
6 Basilica B
7 Ghassanid Palace

The ruins

ⓘ *Open daily during daylight hours, S£75, students S£10. Bring plenty of water and adequate protection against the sun; even in winter it can get extremely hot during the day, while in summer the heat is ferocious. Café/ticket office and toilet are outside the walls by the basilica entrance. It's perfectly acceptable to enter from the North Gate and buy your ticket when exiting via the basilica, after you've finished your tour.*

The walls Rasafeh's walls form a rough rectangle averaging 500 m by 400 m, with a variety of differently shaped towers at regular intervals and circular bastions on each corner. The main entrance is through the **North Gate**, off to the left of the approach road. Dating from Justinian's reconstruction of the city walls, its triple gateway is remarkably well preserved and represents a beautiful example of Byzantine architecture. Originally there was a single outer entrance (now missing) leading through to a courtyard and to the inner triple gateway, consisting of a large central portal flanked by two smaller side ones. The capitals of the six columns framing the portals, and the five arched friezes spanning them, are a riot of exuberant decoration, and a suitably grandiose introduction to this great caravan city.

Once through the gateway, you get a sense of Rasafeh's size (over 20 ha); a strange, almost lunar landscape spread out before you, the result of years of digging by the Bedouin in search of treasure. The north wall of the city in particular deserves closer inspection from the inside. You can see clearly the semi-circular vaulting of the arcades which allowed troops to move under protection between the towers. With a little care it is possible to climb up to the upper galleries for good views out over the city. The building material used here is a coarse crystalline stone known as gypsum, which would have been a brilliant white when first cut but has been dulled over the centuries by the elements.

South from the North Gate From the North Gate a path (excavated along the first stretch to reveal one of the city's main thoroughfares) is clearly discernible running south, though at a slightly south-westerly angle. Following it, on the left after around 100 m are the remains of what was probably Rasafeh's **metropolitan church**. Today the best preserved feature is the main apse, with part of its semi-dome surviving and a band of decoration above the three windows which pierce it. On either side is a square chapel, in typical Byzantine style. More unusual is the fact that the basic rectangular basilica plan was modified so that the walls curved outwards to give a circular effect, perhaps in order to accommodate a central domed roof. Dated to around AD 520, similar examples of this 'circle within a square' plan (at Bosra and Ezraa) also date from the first half of the sixth century.

Continuing southwards along the path, after around 100 m, the somewhat insubstantial remains of a **khan** can be seen on the left. After another 100 m or so, shortly before the south walls of the city, you come to a set of underground **water cisterns** on the right; two huge ones which are interconnected, with a set of very rough and uneven steps leading steeply down to them (to the left of the path), and two smaller ones. The sheer size of the two larger ones in particular is breathtaking; 13 m deep, 58 m long and with a combined capacity of over 15,000 cu m. Their near-perfect state of preservation after nearly 15 centuries is equally remarkable.

The basilicas Heading roughly east from the cisterns brings you to Rasafeh's two main basilica churches, imaginatively dubbed 'basilica A' and 'basilica B' by the German archaeologist Johannes Kollwitz who was responsible for their excavation. The first one you come to, **basilica B**, is poorly preserved, except for a completely intact semi-domed side apse, and tall tower built onto the central apse with a staircase leading up inside (do not climb up, as the upper part of the tower is very unstable). Its ground plan reveals it to have been almost as large as the second, much better preserved church. The second church, **basilica A** (often referred to as the Church of St Sergius, but in fact revealed by an inscription discovered in 1977 to have been dedicated as the Church of the Holy Cross), is the best preserved and most impressive of the ruins at Rasafeh, after the walls themselves. Completed in AD 559, this church is thought to have replaced the earlier basilica B as the main focal point for the ever-increasing numbers of pilgrims. Some restoration work has been carried out on it in recent years, giving a better idea of how it would have looked. Most striking are the two rows of three enormous arches which separate the central nave from the side aisles, in much the same style as the earlier church at Qalb Lozeh (see page 245). However, in this case the architects appear to have been somewhat over-ambitious and soon afterwards (perhaps due to an earthquake) it was necessary to insert an arrangement of two smaller arches and three columns within each of the main arches for additional support. The apse of the church is also well preserved, with two rectangular chapels flanking it.

Outside the walls Outside the city walls, to the northeast of the North Gate, are the ruins of a building closely resembling a church (and mistakenly identified as the burial spot of St Sergius until recently) which has now been identified as a **Ghassanid palace** or audience chamber. The Ghassanids were an Arab tribe who entered into an alliance with the Byzantines, patrolling the desert on their behalf and helping to control the other tribes of the region.

Southwest to Homs

As you approach the site there is a turning off to the left along a newly built road. This runs southwest across the desert, passing **Isriye**, see page 141, and Salamiyeh (on the route between Hama and Palmyra, see page 278), before arriving in Homs. Although this is a good-quality road, used by some of the luxury coaches running between Raqqa and Homs, Hama or Damascus, it is still an isolated desert route. If you intend to drive this way, make sure you have plenty of water and some food, just in case of a breakdown or puncture.

South to Palmyra

A surfaced road runs nearly for the entire distance across the desert between Rasafeh and the town of Sukhneh, just off the highway running between Deir ez-Zor and Palmyra. Work was on-going on the road to finish surfacing the entire length at the time of writing but was expected to be completed soon. The dirt-road portion has many different trails to choose from and is poorly signposted, which make it difficult to know which one to follow; therefore until the road is completely surfaced (check with locals before you begin) a local guide is strongly recommended.

Ath Thawra Dam, Lake Assad and Qala'at Jaber → *For listings, see pages 309-314.*

If you are travelling north from the desert, the sparkling blue waters of Lake Assad and the mammoth Ath Thawra Dam will be quite a shock. The contrast in landscape is sudden; the beige plains suddenly giving way to green fields of cotton and corn and pine-forested hillsides with the huge artificial lake stretching far into the distance. Past the dam, the shores of the lake are a popular holiday spot for locals who come here for picnics, rowdy music-filled boat trips and to paddle, fish and swim in the crystal-clear waters. One popular picnic spot is beside the shore of Qala'at Jaber; an impressive Arab castle that sits majestically on its own island on the lake and has impressive views of Lake Assad and the surrounding area.

Ins and outs

Getting there and away There are regular microbus services from Raqqa to Ath Thawra (45 minutes to one hour), and less regular bus services from Aleppo, though unfortunately there is no public transport from Ath Thawra to Qala'at Jaber itself. You have to either negotiate a ride with a taxi driver in Ath Thawra or try hitching (there is much more traffic on Friday, when many families head out there for a picnic). Bear in mind that services between Ath Thawra and Raqqa tail off towards nightfall. If you are planning to camp the night at the restaurant (see eating below), the owner will pick you up from Ath Thawra for free.

If you're driving, once you have crossed to the north side of the dam, follow the road for just under 3 km and take the left turn signposted for Qala'at Jaber. The castle is a further 14 km from the turning.

There is a police checkpoint on the road just before the dam where you will need to show your passport and, if driving, register your vehicle in their logbook.

Background

Began in 1963, Syria's massive Ath Thawra dam project took 10 years, and was the country's most ambitious construction project ever. The dam is a remarkable piece of engineering, stretching 4500 m in length and measuring 500 m wide at its base, with its construction creating the huge artificial Lake Assad.

The project's objective was to generate enough electricity through the dam to make Syria self-sufficient as well as to reclaim vast areas of desert for cultivation. However, although its successes have been considerable (especially in irrigating huge areas of desert), the building of several dams upstream in Turkey since its construction has severely diminished the dam's hydroelectric power-generating capacity.

Qala'at Jaber

① *Wed-Mon 0900-1800 in summer, 0900-1600 in winter, S£75, students S£5.*

Standing on a promontory now lapped by the waters of Lake Assad and reached by a narrow causeway, the first views of Qala'at Jaber as you approach are extremely impressive, though you could argue it's the vast expanse of Lake Assad stretching out into the distance that is the real attraction here. Some local fishermen supplement their income by taking tourists out on the lake, and there are numerous excellent picnic spots along its shores.

Before the creation of the lake, the castle guarded an important crossing point on the Euphrates. During the 11th century it was controlled by the local Beni Numeir tribe before falling to the Seljuk sultan, Malik Shah in 1087. Early in the 12th century it fell to the Crusaders and came under the control of the Count of Edessa. Zengi, the ruler of Aleppo, having occupied Edessa in 1144, was assassinated while laying siege to the castle in 1146. Three years later, however, it fell to his son Nur ud-Din, who later carried out extensive rebuilding work. It remained in Ayyubid hands until the Mongol invasions of the 13th century, after which it was abandoned, except for a brief period of occupation by the Mamluks.

The walls are perhaps the most impressive feature of the castle. They have been extensively restored, in places quite subtly, but elsewhere with somewhat incongruous modern bricks. Enough of the original brickwork (consisting of small red bricks, typically Mesopotamian in style) survives to give a good idea of how it would have looked originally. Entered via a long sloping ramp and monumental gateway, the inside of the castle is largely in ruins and little has been excavated. In the centre there is a large brick minaret (all that survives of the mosque) and the foundations of various buildings. The main attraction, though, is undoubtedly the spectacular views out over Lake Assad.

Halabiye and Zalabiye

Founded by Queen Zenobia, when Palmyra was at the height of its power, the lonely ruins of Halabiye and Zalabiye were built in a prime position to control commercial river traffic along the Euphrates. The remains you can see today date from the sixth century AD, when the emperor Justinian greatly expanded and again refortified the site as one of the frontier posts forming a line of defences against the Sassanid Persian threat. Like all the Byzantine positions along the eastern frontier, it did eventually fall to the Sassanids, and after the Arab conquest was largely abandoned.

Today the remains of these once strategic strongholds occupy a peaceful spot beside the winding river and are surrounded by crop fields.

Ins and outs

Getting there and away Any public transport running along the Euphrates Highway between Deir ez-Zor and Raqqa/Aleppo can drop you off at the turning in the tiny village of Shiha, but from there you have to be prepared to walk or hitch the remaining 9 km. There is a shop by the turning selling cold drinks; a sign on the wall reads 'Welcome You'.

If you're driving, the left turn (north) off the highway to reach these sites is clearly signposted (for 'Halapipe' and 'Zalapiye') in the tiny village of Shiha, 84 km from the Raqqa exit (if you arrive in Tibni you have gone too far). If you are coming from Deir ez-Zor, it is 44 km to Tibni and then a further 4 km to the village of Shiha and the turning. Once you've turned off the main highway, the narrow road joins the river and follows it, passing through a small village before arriving at the ruins of Halabiye on the left after 9 km.

To reach the site of Zalabiye, cross the river on the rickety wooden bridge to the north of Halabiye and follow the road that doubles back southwards and climbs up past Zalabiye railway station. Approximately 1 km beyond the station, branch right on a rough track and cross over the railway line to arrive at the ruins (in all just under 6 km from Halabiye).

The ruins

ⓘ *The entrances to both sites are not kept locked. There is an admission fee of S£75 for Halabiye (the caretaker will come find you if he's not in the ticket office). There is no admission fee to Zalabiye. Try to visit early in the day before the heat hits its peak. There are no toilet facilities at either site.*

The most impressive feature of **Halabiye** is the **walls**. Those facing the river have for the most part been eroded away, but to the north and south, rising up the hillside, are two lines of well preserved walls that meet in an apex at the top of the hill, where the main citadel is located. Built of the same crystalline gypsum as found at Rasafeh, the walls are marked by large bastions placed at regular intervals. Three-quarters of the way up the north wall, one of the bastions has been extended to accommodate a large building, the **praetorium** or imperial barracks. It is a steep climb up to the **citadel** at the top of the hill, but the views out over the Euphrates once you get there are well worth the effort. Of the town which existed within the walls, only the outlines of some of the buildings can be made out, including two churches and a forum occupying the central area.

On the opposite bank of the river, **Zalabiye** was the twin fortification of Halabiye. Very little remains to be seen here, due in part to its position on the outside edge of a bend in the river, which has over the centuries undercut the riverside walls and swept them away. The views out over the river as it sweeps past in a wide curve are nevertheless impressive.

Deir ez-Zor → *For listings, see pages 309-314.*

The thriving town of Deir ez-Zor is spread along the southern banks of the Euphrates and stands at an important crossroads. This is where the two major routes of this region meet: the Euphrates Highway running between Aleppo and the Iraqi border at Abu Kamal, and the desert route from Damascus through Palmyra and on to Hassakeh and Qamishle in the northeast. Although there is little to see here, it is a pleasant and convenient place to break a journey if coming from or heading to Palmyra, and the most practical base for visiting Dura Europos, Mari, Halabiye and Zalabiye.

Ins and outs

Getting there and away There are good transport links by road with the rest of the country. The Pullman bus station is situated 2 km to the south of the centre (a longish walk

Deir ez-Zor

Sleeping 😴
Al-Arabi al-Kabir 1
Al-Jamia al-Rabi 2
New Omayad 6

Ziad 8

Eating 🍴
Aseel 1

Mr Frishte 3
Nadi Mohandiseen 4

or short taxi ride). If you want to walk into town, turn right onto the main road and then first left after around 100 m. Keep following this road (8th Azar Street) into the centre of town. On the way, you pass the microbus station, which covers transport to the local destinations. A taxi ride from the Pullman bus station to the centre will cost approximately S£20. Deir ez-Zor Airport is about 7 km southeast of town and has services to Damascus. The train station is to the north of the town and has a couple of daily services from Aleppo.

Getting around Aside from the bus station and train station, everything in Deir ez-Zor is within easy reach on foot. Taxis are readily available should you want one.

Tourist information The tourist information office is down a small side street off Khalid Bin Walid Street (heading east, take the first right turn after the turning with the entrance to the **Al Jamia al-Arabia** hotel and it is less than 100 m down on the right). They have a photocopied map of the town in English and a few of the usual handouts. There is also an office at the bus station, though it is seemingly permanently closed.

Deir ez-Zor Musuem
① *Al-Imam Ali St, Wed-Mon 0900-1800 in summer, 0900-1600 in winter, S£150, students S£10.*
Opened in 1996 this excellent little museum is the result of extensive collaboration with, and funding from, Germany. Adopting a modern format that incorporates reconstructions and clear, informative explanations, the fascinating and often strikingly beautiful exhibits are truly brought to life.

There are four main sections to the museum, covering prehistory, ancient Syria, the classical periods and Arab-Islamic/popular traditions. It is the first two, and to a lesser extent the third sections, which are the most impressive. The Jezira has proved to be a treasure trove for archaeologists; and the region, which is littered with *tells* marking prehistoric and ancient settlements, is still very much a focus for archaeological research. The museum brings together some of the most fascinating (and most recent) finds from the region, and is successful in drawing together in a dynamic, coherent manner the historical phases and cultural developments at the various sites, as well as the way in which they relate to each other, and to the wider history of the region.

Holy Martyrs Armenian Church
① *If the church is closed, ring on the bell and someone will open it up for you.*
Built in 1990, this church has a quiet, understated beauty about it. Steps lead up from the street into a peaceful courtyard. Inside the main chapel, a central cross-topped pillar rises up from a lower ground level where the bones of those who died in the Armenian genocide are preserved around the base. Windows in the dome of the chapel allow the sunlight to play on the cross, contrasting with the semi-darkness below.

Euphrates River
On arriving in Deir ez-Zor, you may be forgiven for mistaking the small, disappointing branch channel which runs through the town for the Euphrates itself. A walk across the bridge from the central square brings you to the suspension footbridge which spans the actual river. More than 1 km wide at this point, it is altogether a far more impressive sight. In the late afternoon and early evening the bridge throngs with people out strolling and enjoying the views; at sunset the river is at its most beautiful. The gardens and café on the far side make for a nice spot from which to enjoy the river.

Deir ez Zor to Dura Europos

From Deir ez-Zor, the Euphrates Highway continues southeast down to the Iraqi border at Abu Kamal. After 44 km you come to a big roundabout and fork leading off to the left to the small town of **Mayadin** on the banks of the Euphrates, 2 km from the main road. There are two pleasant tea shops here, on the banks of the river which flows past, broad and powerful at this point.

Near the town, and clearly visible from the Euphrates Highway, are the ruins of **Qala'at al-Rabha**. From the fork for Mayadin, continue southeast along the main road for 1.5 km to a crossroads and turn right (signposted) towards the castle (left to Mayadin). After 1.5 km, turn left and follow this road for a further 1.5 km to reach the castle. The ruins stand on the edge of the desert plateau which stretches away to the southwest. What remains to be seen today dates largely from the reign of Nur ud-Din (1146-1174), who built a castle here on the foundations of an earlier Abbasid fortification as part of his attempts to unite Syria into a single cohesive Arab Muslim Empire. The castle is in an advanced state of dilapidation, although impressive from a distance and with plenty of underground chambers and passages to explore inside (for which a torch is essential).

The next stretch of the Euphrates Highway passes through farmland and an almost continual string of villages and settlements. The largest of these is Al-Ashara (23 km from the turning for Qala'at ar-Rabha), where there are shops and a couple of simple restaurants. After passing through the village of Tishreen (14 km further on), the road climbs up onto a desolate and forbidding plateau, from where there are occasional glimpses of the Euphrates. Off to the left of the road, the western walls of Dura Europos gradually come into view, and soon you come to a metalled access road leading to the site just over 1 km from the main road. The turning is 46 km from the Mayadin junction and 90 km from Deir ez-Zor.

Dura Europos (Tell Salihiye)

Rising startlingly out of the desert, the city's defensive walls looming out of the plains, the ancient city of Dura Europos occupies a section of plateau directly overlooking the Euphrates River to the east and bounded to the north and south by deep ravines. Most remarkable from an archaeological point of view are the frescoes discovered here, and the insight these have provided into Judaic and early Christian art. Some of those frescoes are now housed in the National Museum at Damascus (and all the most important treasures are now housed in museums around the world) and today you come here as much for the stunning location as for the site itself. Sitting on the eastern edge of the city, the ground drops away suddenly with sweeping views down over the Euphrates. It's a silent, lonely spot only made more dramatic by the merciless heat beating down and the howl of the dust-filled wind whipping around you.

Ins and outs
Getting there and away Frequent microbuses run from Deir ez-Zor down to Abu Kamal on the Iraqi border; just ask to be dropped off at the Dura Europos turning ('Tell Salihiye' in Arabic). The site is just over 1 km from the main road, a manageable walk except in summer when the temperature soars. It is usually fairly easy to pick up transport on to Mari or back to Deir ez-Zor from the turning, though be aware that on Fridays public transport here and back slows to a trickle. A taxi from Deir ez-Zor to Dura Europos return, with waiting time, will cost approximately US$30.

Getting around If it's unbearably hot when you arrive (or you're just feeling lazy) you can ask Shakr, the site guardian at the ticket office, if he'll give you a motorbike tour of the ruins. A tip of S£200 would be appropriate for this. He can also give you a lift on his motorbike back to the main road turn-off.

Background

Earliest history Although its history appears to go back even further (*Dura* is an Aramaic word meaning 'fortress'), the city as we know it is of Hellenistic origin, founded during the reign of **Seleucus I Nicator** by one of his generals named Nicanor around 300 BC (the *Europos* was added at this time, after the name of the birthplace of Seleucus in Macedonia). Once again, its role was to protect and control trade along the Euphrates, as well as forming part of a defensive chain of military/caravan towns strung out along the northern and eastern borders of the Seleucid Empire, including also Edessa (present-day Urfa in Turkey), Nisibin (present-day Nusaybin, just across the border from Qamishle) and Seleucea-on-the-Tigris (southern Iraq). Planned on an ambitious scale and containing within it a fully fledged city laid out in traditional Hellenistic grid pattern, its position soon became precarious with the steady westward advance of the Parthians.

Parthians and Romans Eventually, as the Seleucid Empire declined, whether by assault or accommodation, Dura Europos became in effect a **Parthian** city sometime around the first century BC and thus began to absorb many eastern influences. With the Roman conquest of Syria in 64 BC, the city found itself in a delicate position at the contact point between the Parthian and Roman empires. Given the importance of the Euphrates River as a trade route to both powers, an uneasy truce was maintained for the best part of two centuries and Dura Europos was able to flourish alongside Palmyra (though always to a certain extent eclipsed by it) as a trading city. In AD 115 the Roman emperor **Trajan** occupied Dura Europos, in his attempts to extend the Roman Empire beyond the Euphrates. Despite his initial successes, he was soon forced into retreat and died in Turkey on his way back to Europe. His successor, **Hadrian**, allowed Dura to return to Parthian control and reverted to a policy of non-interference.

In AD 164 Lucius Verus, the co-emperor alongside Marcus Aurelius, again occupied the city and by AD 211 it had been formally declared a Roman colony by **Septimius Severus** who established a permanent garrison there. The Romans built temples, baths and other public buildings while steadily increasing the size of the garrison in response to the growing threat from the newly emergent **Sassanid Persians** who were replacing the Parthians as the major power in the east. Despite its military importance to the Romans, and its continuing close ties with Palmyra, its

Dura Europos

Euphrates River

Palace of the Dux Ripae

Temple of Bel
Temple of Azzanathkona
Praetorium
Mithraeum

Main Citadel & Palace

Synagogue
Agora
Strategion Palace

Temple of Adonis
Temple of the Gaddé
Temple of Atargatis

Palmyra Gate
Baths Complex
Temple of Artemis

2nd Entrance
Christian Chapel
Theatron

Temple of Zeus Kyrios

To Highway

N

400 metres (approx)
400 yards (approx)

importance as a commercial city was by this time steadily declining because of the Sassanid threat. Finally, in AD 256 it fell to the Sassanid king **Shapur I**, who sacked the city. It was subsequently briefly occupied by the **Palmyrenes**, but during the Byzantine period was left abandoned in favour of other sites such as Rasafeh and Halabiye/Zalabiye.

Rediscovery The site was first 'rediscovered' in 1920, when a British expeditionary force took refuge there and uncovered a fresco in one of the ruined buildings. Systematic excavations were then carried out by the Americans and French in the 1920s and 1930s. Ironically, the final frantic attempts of the Roman garrison to defend Dura Europos against the Sassanids were directly responsible for preserving the frescoes for which it is so famous; in order to reinforce the western wall the Romans built a makeshift embankment against it from the inside, burying many of the buildings along its line in the process, including the synagogue, and so protecting its frescoes from the elements. A joint Syrian-French team has been carrying out restoration work on the site in recent years.

The ruins

ⓘ *Daily 0900-1800 in summer, 0900-1600 in winter, S£75, students S£5, if the site is locked when you arrive phone Shakr the site caretaker, T0999 242 072. There is no shade and no toilets or facilities on site so bring lots of water and adequate sun protection. If you get stuck for transport back to Deir ez-Zor, the caretaker can put you up for a night at his house, just ask.*

The walls The approach road brings you to the main **Palmyra Gate**. Set between two solid bastions linked by a passageway over the inner arch, the gateway is functional and imposing. It is thought to date from around 17 BC, when the Parthians began strengthening the original Seleucid walls. The **walls** represent a combination of the original Seleucid work consisting of stone surmounted by mud-brick, and the later Parthian work which is entirely in stone. In places they stand up to 9 m high, with the regularly spaced towers for the most part still surviving. This is the main entrance to the site. To the right is a subsidiary gate, just to the right of which is the **Christian chapel**. Converted from a private house around AD 240, it represents the earliest known example of a Christian place of worship in Syria. Murals depicting scenes of Adam and Eve, a shepherd tending his flock and various miracles were uncovered here and are now displayed in the Yale University Art Gallery. Further to the south was the **temple of Zeus Kyrios**. To the north of the Palmyra Gate, amongst a cluster of ruins close to the walls that included also the **temple of Adonis**, is the site of the **synagogue**.

Along the decumanus The main path running eastwards from the Palmyra Gate follows the line of the **decumanus**, or main east-west thoroughfare of the Seleucid city. You pass first a heavily ruined **baths complex** on the right. After about 300 m, on the left are the jumbled and indistinct remains of the Seleucid **agora**, covered in Parthian times with a more chaotic bazaar. A little further on, just to the right of the path, are the remains of the **temple of the Gaddé**. One block further to the south is the site of the **temple of Atargatis**, and next to it the **temple of Artemis**. Just to the southeast of this is a restored **theatron** (minature theatre), with nine tiers of seating arranged in an oval. Continuing along the main path, just after the temple of Gaddé, you pass through the remains of a **monumental gateway** before descending into a *wadi* (valley). Across the *wadi*, on the hillside to the right, are the remains of what is generally referred to as the **strategion palace**. Dating from the original Seleucid founding of the city, this is thought to have acted either as the residence of the *strategos* or chief magistrate, or else to have been the city's original citadel. Its façade has been rebuilt by French and Syrian architects using local stone and traditional stonecutting techniques. Beside the strategion palace is a reconstruction showing what a typical house at Dura Europos is thought to have looked like.

From the *wadi* you can ascend to the **main citadel and palace**, which occupies a long ridge of high ground directly overlooking the Euphrates. Dating from the later Seleucid period (early second century BC), only the western face still survives, the rest of it having been undercut and swept away by the Euphrates over the centuries. Although little remains, it is worth climbing up to for the views it gives out over the Euphrates.

The northern quarter In the northern section of the city there are further remains, mostly relating to the Roman military camp which was established in this area in the second century AD. All the ruins are discernible in outline only. To the northwest of the main citadel and palace, also overlooking the Euphrates, is the **palace of the Dux Ripae** (literally the 'palace of the commander of the river bank') which housed the Roman garrison commander and dates from the final period of Roman occupation in the third century.

Against the north wall of the city is the **praetorium** or main barracks, also occupying the site of the **temple of Azzanathkona**. In the far northwest corner where the north and west walls meet is the **temple of Bel** (or temple of the Palmyrene Gods). This was the building first uncovered by the British expeditionary force, revealing the wall paintings which inspired further excavation work at Dura Europos. To the south of it, against the west wall, is a temple, or **mithraeum**, dedicated to the worship of *Mithras*, a cult of Persian origin which became popular amongst the Roman military. Other remains in the area include assorted barracks, baths and a small amphitheatre.

Mari (Tell Hariri)

The low mound rising from the plain between the main road and the Euphrates looks unassuming enough as you approach it. Yet it was here in 1933 that the chance discovery by a Bedouin nomad of a fragment of statue led to the subsequent excavation of an archaeological site which, like Ebla and Ugarit, has proved to be of crucial importance to our understanding of the ancient history of Syria. However, despite its enormous archaeological significance, very little remains to be seen at Mari, and for most visitors it is not a place that fires the imagination. The Aleppo and Damascus museums (and also the Louvre in Paris) are where the most significant finds are now displayed. In addition, the excellent museum at Deir ez-Zor contains many beautiful artefacts from Mari as well as a reconstruction of part of the famous Zimri-Lim Palace.

Ins and outs
Getting there and away From the turning for Dura Europos, the Euphrates Highway continues southeast, descending from the plateau and passing through two small villages, before arriving at the left turn-off for Mari (signposted) 400 m from the main road. The turning is 28 km from the Dura turn-off and 118 km from Deir ez-Zor.

As for Dura Europos, frequent microbuses run from Deir ez-Zor down to Abu Kamal on the Iraqi border. Ask to be dropped at Tell Hariri.

Background

The earliest evidence of settlement so far discovered at Mari dates back as far as 4000 BC. However, it was during the **Early Syrian II** (or Early Dynastic) period (c 2900-2300 BC) that Mari rose to become a powerful independent city-state on the Euphrates. Its wealth depended both on the intensive cultivation of the surrounding land using irrigation water from the Euphrates, and widespread trading links. Excavations from this period have revealed large temples dedicated to the goddesses Ishtar, Ninni-Zaza, Ishtarat, Ninhursag and Dagan which were lavishly decorated and filled with statues, as well as a successively rebuilt palace/temple complex. Close relations existed with the city of Ebla, with which it was contemporary, their often conflicting interests being resolved through payments of gold and silver.

Following the rise to power of the **Akkadian** Empire founded by Sargon of Akkad around 2350 BC, Mari came for a while under its control and was somewhat eclipsed by it. With the break-up of the Akkadian Empire around 2200 BC, a period of unrest followed about which little is known. One local dynasty, the city of Ur in southern Mesopotamia, is known to have extended its control as far as Mari at one point. Sometime around 2000 BC, however, the arrival of the **Amorites** (a Semitic people who migrated from the south) saw a renewed period of prosperity and independence for Mari. An Amorite, Yaggid-Lim, founded the Lim Dynasty there and began work on the famous Zimri-Lim palace.

The Mari archive Undoubtedly the most significant find from the palace was an archive containing around 15,000 clay tablets inscribed in Akkadian (or Old Babylonian) cuneiform script. These have given us an unprecedented insight into the Lim Dynasty and the political, economic and social life of Mari under their reign. Agriculture was highly developed with complex irrigation systems which, as well as allowing intensive cultivation, appear also to have served as transport canals. The city raised revenues by taxing the long-distance trade which passed through it between southern Mesopotamia, Anatolia and southern and western Syria. It also engaged in its own trade, most importantly in the raw materials for the production of bronze (tin from northwestern Iran and copper from Cyprus), but also wood, oils, wines and semi-precious stones. An inscription found on the foundation stone of the Shamash temple which was built by Yakhdun-Lim (the son of Yaggid-Lim) details his exploits in this respect: "...*no other king residing in Mari had ever – since, in ancient days the gods built the city of Mari – reached the (Mediterranean) Sea, nor reached and felled timber in the great mountains, the Cedar Mountain and the Boxwood Mountain, he, Yakhdun-Lim, son of Yaggid-Lim, the powerful king, the wild bull among kings, did march to the shore of the sea, an unrivalled feat, and offered sacrifices to the Ocean as (befitting) his royal rank while his troops washed themselves in the Ocean...*" (translation by AL Oppenheim).

The period of Amorite rule was one of complex political relations. We know from the Mari archives that around 1800 BC Zimri-Lim (the grandson of Yaggid-Lim) was driven from Mari by Shamshi-Adad, another Amorite who was in effect the founder of the Assyrian Empire. Interestingly, Zimri-Lim took refuge in the kingdom of Yamkhad with its capital at Aleppo, indicating the importance of this power centre at the time. Following the death of Shamshi-Adad, Zimri-Lim was able to regain control of Mari around 1775 BC, allowing himself a brief but highly successful period of rule (it was during this period that he greatly extended the palace begun by his grandfather and richly decorated it, leading archaeologists to attribute it entirely to him initially). By around 1758 BC he was overthrown by Hammurabi, the ruler of Babylon, who was steadily expanding his empire across southern Mesopotamia and even into Assyria. Hammurabi largely destroyed Mari and afterwards it was abandoned, with the exception of brief periods of limited occupation centuries later in the Seleucid, Parthian and Sassanid periods.

The ruins

① *Daily 0900-1800 in summer, 0900-1600 in winter, S£75, students S£5. There is a small, friendly tea shop by the archaeologists' base at the entrance to the site, with postcards, etc on sale.*

From the tea shop and archaeologists' base, head northeast onto the *tell*, to arrive at the main covered area of excavations, representing the **Palace of Zimri-Lim**. Inside, you can wander around the complex (and confusing) network of rooms, corridors and courtyards which formed this huge palace (in all it consisted of 275 rooms spread across 2.5 ha). What you see is only the basic plan of the building (more like a reconstruction of First World War trench conditions according to one couple), with all the murals which adorned it having been removed, not to mention the numerous statues and treasures and the huge archive of clay tablets.

Outside, the other excavated remains of the city of Mari, covering an area of 60 ha, have largely been eroded away by the elements. To the east of the southeast corner of the covered excavations of the Palace of Zimri-Lim, a high terrace marks the site of what has been identified by some as a **ziggurat**, which would make it a forerunner of the later Mesopotamian ziggurat (stepped tower) tradition. Clustered around it are the temple of Dagan, the temple of Shamash and the temple of Ninni-Zaza, all of them only barely discernible. This was also the site of a palace dating from the mid-third millennium BC (partly built over by the later Zimri-Lim palace). To the west of the southwest corner of the covered excavations is the **temple of Ishtar**, dating from around 2500 BC.

Abu Kamal

It is a further 10 km to the small town of Abu Kamal (or Al-Bukamal). There are a few cafés and simple restaurants in the centre of town, and even a small, very basic hotel. However, other than engaging in predictable conversations as to the rights and wrongs of the occupation of Iraq with the many Iraqis living in the town, the only conceivable reason for coming here is to be able to boast that you have been to within 10 km or so of the Iraqi border.

Deir ez-Zor to Hassakeh

From the centre of Deir ez-Zor, head east along 6th Ayyar Street (following the branch channel of the Euphrates), and then turn left to cross over the Euphrates itself and join the main road to Hassakeh and Qamishle. After leaving behind the irrigated farmland of the Euphrates basin, the road heads northeast through desert before turning more northwards at the village of **Suar** (52 km from Deir ez-Zor, village centre off to the right from the main road, signposted for 'Tal Sheikh Hamad', amongst others).

Tell Sheikh Hamad Taking this turning, you can make a diversion to visit the archaeological site of Tell Sheikh Hamad, on the east bank of the Khabur River. After crossing the river, follow the road north for around 20 km to reach the site. The excavations carried out here have revealed it to be the ancient *Dur-Katlimmu*, a provincial capital of the **Middle Assyrian** Empire that emerged in the second half of the 14th century BC following the collapse of the Mittanian Empire. Administrative archives discovered here demonstrate that it exerted control over a sizeable area. A so-called 'Dark Age' followed the arrival of the

'Sea Peoples' around 1200 BC, but during the ninth century BC the **Assyrian** Empire (in this period usually termed neo-Assyrian) rose to prominence once again. By the late eighth century BC *Dur-Katlimmu* had tripled in size, with 4 km of walls enclosing a town of around 100 ha. The citadel stood at the southeast corner overlooking the river (corresponding with the existing tell), while the town extended north along the banks of the river (parts of it are revealed in a series of excavated plots complete with mud-brick walls, paved floors, sections of a drainage system, a well and bread-baking oven).

Marqadeh Continuing north from Suar along the main road, it follows the west bank of the Khabur River, passing through fertile agricultural land. At the village of **Al-Husein**, 22 km from the turning for Suar, you can see Tell Sheikh Hamad across the river, along with another smaller *tell* nearby. Entering the village of **Marqadeh** (88 km from Deir ez-Zor and 13 km from Al-Husein), there is a small Armenian chapel up on the hillside to the left of the road, dedicated to those massacred here during the genocide. Completed in 1996, it houses some of the bones of the dead. After another 43 km you pass a right turn for **Shahddadi**, and soon after the road swings north again (having curved northwest to follow the Khabur River), running parallel to the railway line between Deir ez-Zor and Hassakeh. Numerous *tells* can be seen dotted around the countryside. Finally you arrive in Hassakeh, 188 km from Deir ez-Zor and 100 km from Marqadeh.

Hassakeh to Qamishle → *For listings, see pages 309-314.*

The largest town in the Jezira region and the capital of the Mouhafazat (Governorate) of the same name, Hassakeh's main importance derives from its role as a market centre for agricultural produce from the surrounding countryside. There is nothing here of special interest to tourists, though a new museum is scheduled to open in 2011 that will display the many artefacts uncovered at archaeological sites in the surrounding countryside. If you need to spend the night, you'd be better off in nearby Qamishle, which has a better range of hotels.

Ins and outs

Getting there and away The main bus station (Garagat Intilaqkh) is in the northwest corner of town, around 2 km from the centre. There are fairly regular connections by Pullman bus from Aleppo, Damascus, Palmyra and Deir ez-Zor. A taxi from here to the centre will cost about S£25. There are also frequent services from Qamishle and the surrounding towns by microbus from here. The train station is around 1 km to the northwest of the centre, at the east end of Al-Mahatta St. The two daily trains from Aleppo to Qamishle and vice versa, stop here.

Getting around You'll have no problems finding a taxi if you want one but other than for getting to and from the bus stations, and the train station, Hassakeh is small enough to wander around on foot.

Orientation Abdul Nasser Street (which runs east off the Assad statue roundabout) is the town centre. To get to the **Al-Sanabel** hotel, carry on down this street until you reach the clock tower and then head south for two blocks, towards the river. To head to Deir ez-Zor from here, cross the river and continue on this road. For the bus station and the road to Qamishle, head north from the Assad statue roundabout onto Fares al-Khoury St.

The **tourist information office** ① *1st floor of a complex on Fares al-Khoury St, near the Assad statue roundabout, Sat-Thu 0900-1400,* has a helpful, English-speaking manager.

Hassakeh to Tell Brak

The route used by luxury coaches travelling between Hassakeh and Qamishle goes via Tell Mansour to join the highway linking Aleppo with the Jezira region. A quieter and somewhat more scenic route, however (and the one still used by buses and microbuses), goes via Tell Brak on the old Qamishle road. Head north out of Hassakeh and then fork right after 13 km (signposted for Tell Brak; straight on signposted for Amuda). It is a further 27 km to the village of Tell Brak. Turn right at the roundabout in the village and it's another 2 km to reach the tell itself, which is clearly visible from a distance.

Tell Brak

This large *tell* was first excavated in 1937-1939 by the British archaeologist Max Mallowan (Mallowan was married to Agatha Christie. She accompanied her husband on his research in the Jezira and wrote an entertaining account of their experiences together: *Come, Tell Us How You Live*). The site proved to be of pivotal importance in terms of the insight it gave into Bronze Age settlement in the area. Amongst the best known finds was the **Eye Temple**, dating from between 3100 and 2900 BC (late Ubaid/Uruk to early-Syrian I period), so called due to the discovery of large numbers of small, highly distinctive idols with oblong flat bodies and 'heads' consisting of a large pair of eyes and eyebrows. Some of these are displayed in the new museum at Deir ez-Zor, or you can see them in Aleppo's museum. More recently, a later **Akkadian** palace and fortress was also discovered, dating from 2400-2300 BC, and also a 15th- to 16th-century BC **Mitannian** palace. Aside from the numerous pottery shards scattered all over the site, there is little for the casual visitor to see. However, it does make a lovely picnic spot, with good views in all directions over the surrounding plains.

Tell Brak to Qamishle

Returning to the main road and continuing north, after 36 km you arrive at a roundabout. Go straight over this (right for Yarobia on the Iraqi border, left for Aleppo, 412 km) to arrive in the centre of Qamishle, 10 km further on.

Qamishle → *For listings, see pages 309-314.*

This dusty border town has nothing of special interest for the traveller, but for those arriving from or travelling on to eastern Turkey, it is the main gateway into the region. It is also a good base from which to visit Ain Diwar and Ras al-Ain. As well as having a large Kurdish population, the town is also home to a substantial number of Christians of various dominations and it's a friendly place, quick to welcome strangers. Despite this, be aware that Qamishle's recent past is mired by outbreaks of violence. In 2004 riots broke out here during a football match between a local Kurdish team and a team from Deir ez-Zor. The government crackdown that followed left 15 dead. Since then there have been sporadic outbreaks of conflict between government forces and the local Kurdish population. If you're planning on visiting, you are advised to check the situation beforehand.

Border crossing: Syria–Turkey

The Qamishle/Nusaybin border is little used by travellers but if you're heading directly to eastern Turkey it makes more sense to cross the border here than at the border posts to the west of the country. Cross early as delays aren't unheard of. The border is 1 km north of town, a taxi from the centre will cost S£50 or you can walk. On the Syrian side you need to pay S£500 departure tax and then you have to walk between the Syrian and Turkish sides of the border.

Nearly all nationalities are granted three-month Turkish tourist visas on arrival. Some nationalities (including New Zealand and South Korea) are given free entry. Australian, US and most European nationalities pay US$20. Check beforehand.

Once stamped through on the Turkish side, you have to walk another 500 m into the town of Nusaybin. From there you can catch a *dolmus* (microbus) to the town of Mardin (30 minutes) from where you catch buses to all over Turkey.

Ins and outs

Getting there and away The main bus station handles both the Pullman buses and most of the microbuses. It's around 2 km to the southeast of the town centre. There are a few Pullman bus services per day from Damascus and Aleppo from here. The train station is a further 1 km or so to the southeast and has a daily overnight service from Aleppo. A taxi from either of these stations should not cost more than S£20-25. The separate microbus station, to the southwest of the town centre, has frequent services from Hassakeh. The airport is 3 km south of the town on the main road to Hassakeh and has services from Damascus. If you are arriving from the border with Turkey, a taxi to the town centre will cost about S£50 or it's a 15-minute direct walk straight into town.

Getting around The only time you'll need a taxi in Qamishle is if coming or going to the transport stations or to the border. The compact town centre is easily manageable on foot and when it's not too hot, even the Turkish border and bus station are within walking distance.

Orientation The centre of town is Hafez al-Assad Street, between the Assad statue roundabout and the river. This is where you'll find all the accommodation and lots of small restaurants. The main bus and train stations are off Zakl al-Arsuzi Street, which is the last road before the river. The separate microbus station is just off Al-Kouwatli Street (which runs southwest from the Assad statue roundabout), beside the football pitch. Gabrielle Restaurant is across the road from here. The Turkish border crossing is to the north of town.

East of Qamishle → *For listings, see pages 309-314.*

The main attraction here are the sites of Tell Halaf and Tell Mozan; once ancient important cities. Today there is basically nothing left at either site and you'd have to have a serious interest in the sites to visit. Important discoveries from the sites are now in museums across the world and the Aleppo Museum has a wonderful collection of finds from Tell Halaf.

From Qamishle by public transport the easiest option is to get a bus or microbus to Derbassiyeh and then another one from there onto Ras al-Ain (for Tell Halaf). Alternatively, there are direct buses and microbuses from Hassakeh. In either case, check what time the last services leave in the afternoon for the return trip.

If driving from Qamishle to Ras al-Ain, head west along Hafez al-Assad Street. Go straight across the Assad roundabout and then bear right at the next roundabout. After 27 km you pass through the village of Amuda, the road from then on running closely parallel with the Turkish border. Tell Mozan is 8 km beyond Amuda. Around 28 km from Amuda you pass through the small town of Derbassiyeh, from where it is a further 60 km on to Ras al-Ain.

To reach the tell from Ras al-Ain, take the road leading west from the telegraph office (distinguished by its tall communications mast) in the centre of town. After 4 km, just after crossing a small bridge, the *tell* is on your right.

Tell Mozan

Around 8 km beyond Amuda you pass on the right a large *tell*. This is Tell Mozan, excavated by Giorgio Buccellati and Marilyn Kelly-Buccellati, and identified in 1995 as ancient *Urkesh*, the capital of the late third millennium BC **Hurrian Empire**, which arose in the wake of the collapse of the Akkadian Empire. In Hurrian mythology *Urkesh* was also a holy city, the seat of the 'father of the gods', *Kumarbi*. Hundreds of seals were found at the site, some of them inscribed with cuneiform script. These were used to label jars, baskets and other containers that were kept in the royal storehouse. Their style is highly distinctive and gives insights into the little understood Hurrian civilization.

Ras al-Ain

This town and Turkish border crossing point is famous mostly for the nearby archaeological site of Tell Halaf. There is very little for the casual visitor to see at the *tell*, but nearby there are various **sulphur springs** where you can swim. Along the ring road around the south side of the town the **Sirob** and **Riad** restaurants both have pleasant outdoor seating with tables set in shallow pools of flowing sulphur spring water, allowing you to cool your feet while eating during the summer.

Tell Halaf (Guzana)

The site was first discovered in 1899 by Baron Max von Oppenheim, an Arabist and diplomat, attached to the German diplomatic mission in Cairo who was sent to survey the route of the Berlin to Baghdad railway. He left the diplomatic service in 1911 in order to excavate the site, returning after the First World War to complete his work from 1927-1929.

The earliest evidence of settlement here (known as the 'Halaf culture' after the site) goes back to the first half of the fifth millennium BC and is noted for its distinctive style of painted pottery consisting of very fine, thin wares made by hand or turned on a slow wheel and decorated with rich polychrome designs in a luminous glaze-like paint. This style was common to a vast area extending over much of eastern Turkey and northern Iraq during this period.

The site then appears to have been abandoned until the beginning of the first millennium BC, when it became the seat of one of the easternmost **Aramaic** states that had established themselves across northern Syria following the collapse of the Hittite Empire. Referred to in Assyrian records as *Guzana*, it was the capital of a region called *Bit Bahiani*. In the ninth century BC it began to pay tribute to Assyria, becoming an Assyrian province during the eighth century BC. The most substantial finds date from the period

Putting together the archaeological jigsaw

When von Oppenheim opened the Tell Halaf Musuem in 1930 in Berlin, he thought he was preserving the incredible basalt statues of ancient Guzana for future generations of study. He didn't bank on the destruction that the Second World War would bring. On 22-24 November 1943 the museum was bombed by the British and the resulting fire tragically destroyed all of the smaller finds from the site. Even worse, the huge basalt statues and reliefs of Tell Halaf were cracked while fire-fighters put out the blaze; the extreme temperature change from flame to water split the ancient sculptures into 25,000 pieces. Reduced to rubble, the fragments were crated up and stored in the deep cellar of the Pergamon Museum where, until recently, they lay gathering dust.

In 2002, using pre-war photographs as a guide, and 80 m of wreckage from the fire laid out before them, one of the most complex reassembly jobs in archaeology began. Reconstructing the 30 statues and reliefs has been a painstaking task for the experts who have spent eight years examining and identifying the fragments to restore each sculpture to its former glory. In 2010 the result of this massive archaeological jigsaw puzzle will be exhibited at Berlin's Museum of the Ancient Near East, when the statues of Tell Halaf are displayed once again to the public, for the first time in over 60 years.

when it was the capital of an independent Aramaic state ruled by the *Kapara* Dynasty (probably ninth-eighth century BC, but possibly earlier). A sizeable walled citadel and palace/temple complex occupied the main mound at this time, and it was from the palace/temple that the huge, imposing statues which form the entrance façade to the Aleppo Museum were found but most of the statues found at the site were carted away to Germany to be displayed in the Tell Halaf Museum that von Oppenheim founded in Berlin (see box, above).

After many years of neglect, new excavations at Tell Halaf began again in 2006 with a joint mission by Syrian and German archaeologists. Since then they have unearthed a grave dating from the tenth century BC, along with jewellery and fragments of textiles from the same period, and buildings of a settlement from the sixth millennium BC.

Just past the *tell* there is a turning left off the main road which leads to the **Kapreet sulphur spring**. Follow the side road for 1.5 km and then turn left again to arrive at the springs after 2.5 km. There is a deep pool fed by the spring which makes for a pleasant and popular (though exclusively male) place to swim.

Ain Diwar

Note Due to the sensitive situation, tourists are officially required to register with the police in Malkiyeh before visiting Ain Diwar.

To pick up the road to Ain Diwar, head east out of Qamishle on Hafez al-Assad Street. The road passes through fertile agricultural land, with the Taurus mountains rising to the north, across the border with Turkey. Continue straight through **Qahtaniyeh** (29 km), **Jawadiyeh** (56 km) and the twin towns of **Roumelian** and **Mabada** (67 km). Several old-style 'nodding donkey' oil wells can be seen in the area, still functioning though their significance is now completely eclipsed by the vast new oilfields which have been opened up near Deir ez-Zor. After 82 km, where the road forks, keep straight (left), to arrive at **Malkiyeh**, 95 km from Qamishle. Turn left in the centre of town to pick up the road to **Ain Diwar**, 17 km further on.

The village of Ain Diwar is perched on the edge of a plateau overlooking the Tigris River (the *Dijlah* in Arabic). The river here winds lazily through its wide valley in a broad sweep, while across the border to the northeast, the mountains of southeast Turkey rise up majestically, capped with snow for most of the year. Beyond the village, down on the banks of the Tigris, are the ruins of a **Roman bridge** which once spanned the river (over time the course of the river has changed so that the ruins now stand on dry land). The bridge dates originally from the second century AD, although it was subsequently modified by the Seljuks and Arabs in the 11th-12th centuries, and partially reconstructed by the Turks more recently. A rough track winds its way down from the plateau and then snakes round a low ridge to reach the bridge (approximately 7 km). After rain this track can be impassable except by 4WDs as it fords a substantial stream and is often churned up into deep mud.

The Tigris at this point marks the border with Turkey, and unfortunately the bridge is officially off-limits to tourists (although unofficially the local Kurds are more than ready to take you down there). Relations here between Turkey and Syria occasionally boil over regarding the Kurdish question, with Turkey accusing Syria of harbouring PKK activists amongst its Kurdish population. Officials talk of regular incidents of Turkish soldiers firing across the border; around 10 people are said to die each year in this way. Although the bridge itself is officially off-limits (and is likely to remain so), a visit to Ain Diwar is still worthwhile for the superb views out over the Tigris River and the Taurus mountains beyond. Just past the village, right on the edge of the plateau, there is a restaurant with a shaded terrace where you can enjoy the views.

◉ Euphrates River and the Jezira listings

For Sleeping and Eating price codes and other relevant information, see Essentials pages 19-21.

● Sleeping

Raqqa *p287, map p288*
Raqqa doesn't get many tourists, which explains the dearth of decent accommodation.
B Karnak, Saqr Quraysh St, T022-281107. If you can get past the crazy coloured brickwork in the foyer, which looks as if the owner put a 5-year-old in charge of decoration, you get a not-too-bad deal. There are large, bright, clean rooms with a/c, satellite TV and balcony, and the staff are extremely friendly. Swimming pool, restaurant, on-site parking and a bustling garden coffee shop.
C Lazaward, Saqr Quraysh St, T022-216120. The decent-sized rooms here come with a/c and satellite TV but no one's bothered to clean in the corners and the attached baths are a little shabby. Still, it's a friendly place and there's a decent restaurant too.
E Tourism, Kouwatly St (sign says 'Sayaha Hotel'), T022-220725. The large, very basic rooms (with fan) all have small attached baths. It's clean enough, central and will do for a night.

Rasafeh *p289, map p290*
E Camping at Rasafeh, near the café, T0944-226217. If you get stuck without transport, friendly Hamid, who runs the site ticket office/café, can put you up for the night. He has a tent (or you can use your own), or you can sleep on a mattress at his house just beyond the ruins. He'll even cook you breakfast. The toilet block here is clean and there's a shower too.

Ath Thawra Dam, Lake Assad and Qala'at Jaber *p292*
E Restaurant of the Shore, 1 km before Qala'at Jaber (signposted from road), T0956-932 314. Beside the shady restaurant, friendly Abdullah provides camping right on

the lake shore. You can bring your own tent or Abdullah can provide you with a tent, mattress and blanket. There are very basic toilet facilities here as well. If you're staying here you can ring Abdullah and he'll pick you up from Ath Thawra and drop you back there when you leave. He can also rent you a boat to go out to a nearby island. See also Eating, below.

Deir ez-Zor *p295, map p295*
B Ziad, just off Abou Bakr as-Siddiq St, T051-214596, www.ziadhotel.com. This well-maintained and busy hotel has comfortable, spotlessly clean rooms that come with a/c and satellite TV. Some rooms have balcony. The owner speaks German and English. Popular with tour groups so booking is recommended.
C New Omayyad (door sign only in Arabic), Al-Imam Ali St, T051-221220. A welcome addition to the Deir ez-Zor accommodation scene. This new, friendly hotel, in an old building that has vines dripping down its façade, has decent-sized rooms (with a/c and satellite TV), that are all kept spotlessly clean. Recommended.
E Al-Arabi al-Kabir, Khalid Ibn al-Walid St, T051-362070. Up a set of slumping marble stairs, the Al-Arabi has spartan but bright rooms that surprisingly come with a/c and satellite TV. All share clean but definitely dilapidated baths.
E Al-Jamia al-Arabia, Khalid Ibn al-Walid St, T051-351371. This welcoming little place is as basic as they come with simple rooms that only have sink and fan, but the friendly owner speaks English, the shared bathrooms are clean and it's one of the cheapest places in town. Recommended.

Hassakeh *p303*
At the time of research a large new 3-star hotel was currently being built on Abdul Nasser St, right next to the Assad statue roundabout, which will be a welcome

addition to Hassakeh's current poor accommodation options. There's a couple of budget hotels around the clock tower, on the streets that run off Abdul Nasser St but they're a grotty bunch and some don't even come with a fan.

Most of the restaurants are concentrated along Fares al-Khoury St and around the Assad statue roundabout.
D Al-Sanabel, between the clock tower and the bridge, T052-314019. Don't expect the rooms to live up to the rather swanky lobby but it's still the only recommendable place in town. The austere rooms here are clean and large and come with a/c, satellite TV and fridge.

Qamishle p304
Qamishle has a decent number of budget hotels, most boasting a/c and satellite TV. At the time of writing a new mid-range hotel, the **Ani Palace** was about to be opened in the centre of town, near to the **Ebla Hotel**.
E Al-Soufaraa, Hafez al-Assad St, T052-432993, www.alsoufaraa-hotel.com. The excellent-value rooms here are a step above all the other hotels in town. They're bright, clean and comfortable and come with a/c, satellite TV and fridge.
E Ebla, just off Hafez al-Assad St, T052-423447. Apart from the scary stuffed eagle presiding over reception, this quirky place with its friendly English-speaking staff is a good choice. The rooms are spartanly furnished but have a/c and satellite TV.

● Eating

Raqqa p287, map p288
There's a bunch of cheap *shawarma* stalls around the clock tower and bakeries all along Quneitra St.
₩ Al-Bustan, Hisham Ibn Abdul al-Male St. Pleasant open-air rooftop restaurant offering the usual range of Arabic dishes, as well as unlimited supplies of *arak*.

₩ Al-Naeem, 8 March St. Another rooftop restaurant, busy with families so good for lone women. Decent range of Arabic food.
₩ Al-Rashid, King Faysal St to the west of clock tower (enter through arch, sign above just says 'restaurant'). Looks distinctly decrepit from the outside, but is not so bad once you're in, with seating in a large open garden. There's fish from the Euphrates as well as the usual range of Arabic food. Beware of the cats who will try to join you for your meal. Alcohol served.
₸ Al-Waha, Ath-Thawrah St. Spotlessly clean café with friendly staff and outside seating.

Ath Thawra Dam, Lake Assad and Qala'at Jaber p292
₩ Restaurant of the Shore, 1 km before Qala'at Jaber (signposted from road), T0956-932 314. Even if you're not going to stay, drop by for a meal; the food here is magnificent. A tasty, huge set menu of fish (caught straight from the lake) or chicken with salad and several mezze dishes costs £S400. Alcohol available. See also Sleeping, above.

Deir ez-Zor p295, map p295
Along Khalid Bin Walid St, to the east of the main square, there are several cheap eateries serving the usual roast chicken, kebabs, hummus, falafel, etc. Heading north towards the bridge along 8th Azar St, there are couple of good falafel, hummus and *fuul* places.

A nice place to enjoy a cup of tea or cold drink is in the large café/garden on the north bank of the Euphrates (cross the suspension footbridge and turn left). On the south side of the Euphrates are a couple of restaurants with lovely locations overlooking the river. Unfortunately they charge inflated tourist prices for distinctly mediocre Arabic food.
₩ Aseel, Abou Bakr as-Siddiq St. Overlooking the branch channel of the Euphrates, the Aseel has the usual Arabic fare with a nice outdoor seating setting. Alcohol available.
₩ Nadi Mohandiseen, on the north side of the Euphrates, more or less directly opposite the **Tourist Blue Beach Restaurant** (cross by

the suspension footbridge and turn right just past the sports stadium and mini-funfair). This place does a good meal of Arabic food with seating in the large hall or out on a pleasant garden terrace overlooking the river. Alcohol available.

Mr Frishte (sign only in Arabic) Al-Imam Ali St. You can't miss the red plastic and glass façade of this fast-food place which is Deir ez-Zor's answer to McDonalds. Excellent sandwiches and burgers (the Mexican sandwich isn't very Mexican but is delicious all the same), plus larger meals. The menu is only in Arabic so ask the friendly cashier at the entrance to help you choose.

Hassakeh p303

Al-Hamra, signposted in Arabic only, right beside the Assad statue roundabout. This clean and well-run restaurant has a menu in English listing a range of mezze dishes and the usual kebabs. Highly recommended is the roast chicken, which is juicy and tasty, and comes with a delicious garlic and lemon sauce. They also serve *fuul* in the morning, and falafel and *shawarma* sandwiches during the evening.

Pizza Rami, just north of the Assad statue roundabout, Fares al-Khoury St. This little place serves up surprisingly good pizzas.

Qamishle p304

There are several simple kebab and falafel places along Hafez al-Assad St.

Gabrielle, opposite the microbus station. This cavernous place to the southwest of the town centre is probably Qamishle's most upmarket establishment. The menu has the usual range of Arabic cuisine and alcohol is served.

Simar, 3rd and 4th floor, large building 1 block west of **Ebla Hotel**, just off Hafez al-Assad St. The roof terrace here is a nice breezy place to come for dinner. There's no actual menu but they do all the normal grills and mezze. The *kofte* here is particularly good. Alcohol served.

O Shopping

Raqqa *p287, map p288*
Gold is cheap here and there are dozens of gold shops along Quneitra St north of the clock tower though the jewellery here is tailored towards the local market and won't be to some people's taste. Raqqa is also famous for the tailoring of *galabiyyas* (the full-length dress/robe worn by both men and women) and many of the *galabiyyas* sold in Aleppo and Damascus are originally made here.

Al-Faisal Fashion, Al-Frehat Building, Tal Abyd St. If you're looking for a traditional female *galabiyya* this huge store with hundreds of different designs, should be top of your list. Robes sold here cost half the price as in Aleppo.

O Transport

Raqqa *p287, map p288*
Bus
The Pullman bus station is to the south of the large statue of Assad on Rashid Ramadan Sq, close to the centre of town. There are at least 15 private companies here that operate services to Deir ez-Zor once an hour all day and night. **Kadmous** have departures for **Damascus** at 0630, 1000, 1200, 1630, 1930 and 2330 (6 hrs, S£275), via **Homs** (4½ hrs, S£190); **Deir ez-Zor** at 1615 and 2015 (2½ hrs, S£100); and 1 departure daily to **Aleppo** at 2130 (3 hrs, S£125).

Microbus
Across the road is the microbus stand. Among the many departures, there are regular services (departing when full) to **Mansura** (for **Rasafah**) (25 mins, S£20), and **Ath Thawra** (for Lake Assad) (30 mins, S£25).

Train
The train station is inconveniently located around 2 km to the north of town; keep following Quneitra St northwards to reach it.

A taxi here from the town centre will cost about S£30. There is a daily fast train to **Deir ez-Zor** at 1810 (2 hrs, 1st class S£55, 2nd class S£45) and an overnight service to **Qamishle** (4 hrs, S£100) via **Deir ez-Zor** (2 hrs, S£35) and **Hassakeh** (3 hrs, S£75) at 0200. The daily express service to **Aleppo** leaves at 0846 (2 hrs, 1st class S£120, 2nd class S£100), and the normal overnight service leaves at 0250 (3 hrs, 1st class S£75, 2nd class S£50).

Deir ez-Zor *p295, map p295*
Air
The Syrian Air office, T051-225552, is on a small side street to the north of the bank. The airport is 7 km to the southeast of the town centre, on the road to the Iraqi border. There are 2 flights per week to Damascus (1¼ hrs, S£2244).

Bus
All Pullman buses depart and arrive from the Pullman bus station, right at the end of 8th Azar St, to the south of the town centre. There are at least 15 different companies here, with buses (some VIP services) departing for Raqqa, Palmyra and Qamishle every hour throughout the day and night. Kadmous have hourly departures to **Damascus** from 0630 to 1930 (7 hrs, S£300); to **Homs** at 0800, 1300, 1700, 2300 and 0030 (6 hrs, S£265); and **Aleppo** at 0815, 1515, 1930 and 2400 (5 hrs, S£200). All these buses stop at **Palmyra** (2 hrs, S£125).

Microbus
Buses from the microbus station (1 km from the centre on 8th Azar St) depart when full. There are services to **Raqqa** (S£60), **Mayadin** (S£25) and **Abou Kamal** (for **Dura Europos** and **Mari**) (S£50), among others from here.

Train
The train station is a little under 3 km to the northeast of town and best reached by taxi. To walk there, cross the suspension footbridge, and then turn right when you reach a T-junction. The daily service to

Hassakeh (S£30) and **Qamishle** (S£55) passes through at 0400.

Hassakeh *p303*
Bus
To get to the main bus station from the centre of town, walk north along Fares al-Khoury St from the Assad statue and turn left at the large roundabout; it is by the next roundabout you come to (around 2 km). A taxi from the centre costs about S£25. Although all the Pullman buses depart from here, most of the companies have additional ticket offices in the centre of town. Kadmous operate services from here but more frequent connections are offered by **Al-Rafedain** who have a ticket office on Abdul Nasser St, close to Banque Bemo and opposite the mosque. To **Damascus** there are 4 VIP services a day at 0915, 1230, 1415 and 2345 (8 hrs, S£650), and 3 normal services at 0930, 2145 and 2330 (8 hrs, S£450). Buses to Damascus also stop in **Deir ez-Zor** (S£140) and **Palmyra** (S£275). There are also 4 buses daily to **Aleppo** at 0630, 1115, 1430 and 2000 (5 hrs, S£275).

Microbus
There are regular microbus services from the main bus station to all the surrounding towns and villages, including **Qamishle** (S£70) and **Deir ez-Zor** (S£100).

Train
To get to the train station from the centre of town, walk north along Fares al-Khoury St and turn left into Al-Mahatta St; the station is at the end of this street. The overnight service bound for **Aleppo** passes through at 2320 (6½ hrs, 1st class S£150, 2nd class S£100). The train to **Qamishle** is at 0400 and takes 2 hrs.

Qamishle *p304*
Air
Qamishle's tiny airport is 3 km south of town. A taxi here will cost about S£75. Syrian Air operate 1 flight per day (except Tue) to **Damascus** (1½ hrs, S£2244). They have an office right in the centre of town,

on Hafez al-Assad St (T052-420714) and at the airport (T-052-440330).

Bus

To get to the main bus station from the centre of town, head south along Zaki al-Arzusi St, take the second available left turn and keep straight along this road for around 1.5 km. The bus station is on the right, shortly after a crossroads. There are a dozen or so private companies operating out of here with morning and evening departures to Aleppo and Damascus. The Damascus buses mostly go via Palmyra. Kadmous has 3 buses at 0930, 2230 and 2330 to **Damascus** (10 hrs, S£350), that go via **Palmyra** (6 hrs, S£330). They have 1 daily bus to **Aleppo** at 2200 (7 hrs, S£175).

Microbus

At the main bus station you can get microbuses to **Malkiyeh** (for **Ain Diwar**) (S£70), **Derbassiyeh** (for **Ras al-Ain**) (S£80), **Tell Maruf** (S£35), **Tell Hamis** (S£40) and **Tell Brak** (S£35). There's another microbus station opposite the **Gabrielle Restaurant** to the southwest of town. From here there are frequent microbuses to **Hassakeh** (S£70) and **Amuda** (S£15). Microbuses depart when full.

Train

To get to the railway station, head south along Zaki al-Arzusi St for 1 km to the large roundabout and turn left there; it is on the right after 2 km. There is 1 daily departure at 2150 to **Aleppo** (8 hrs, 1st class S£175, 2nd class S£115) via **Hassakeh** (1½ hrs, 1st class S£75, 2nd class S£50), **Deir ez-Zor** (2½ hrs, 1st class S£110, 2nd class S£75), and **Raqqa** (5 hrs, 1st class S£150, 2nd class S£100).

East of Qamishle *p305*

Microbuses Run regularly from Qamishle to Malkiyeh, but not to Ain Diwar. To hire a taxi for the last stretch (17 km) is relatively expensive, costing S£200-300; it is also possible to negotiate a ride there by motorcycle for around S£100. If you want

to hitch, Fri is a good day to try as lots of families go there for picnics; otherwise there is usually next to no traffic on the road between Malkiyeh and Ain Diwar. **Note** Due to the sensitive situation, tourists are officially required to register with the police in Malkiyeh before visiting Ain Diwar.

❶ Directory

Raqqa *p287, map p288*
Banks There is a CBS branch on Kouwatly St that does foreign exchange. If you are stuck for cash out of bank hours, ask (subtly) at the gold shops along Quneitra St north of the clock tower. Most of them unofficially change money and give an excellent rate. **Medical services** The town's hospital is on Saqr Quraysh St, just to the north of the Karnak hotel. There are loads of pharmacies on Quneitra St. **Post** The main post office is on the southeast corner of the clock tower square. **Visa extensions** Visas can be obtained from the **Department of Immigration and Passports**, in the police station on Al-Baladiyyah St (enter through alleyway around the back, where you pay for the stamp in the kiosk).

Deir ez-Zor *p295, map p295*
Banks A branch of CBS is on Al-Imam Ali St, Sat-Thu 0800-1400. You can change money here and there is an ATM. **Medical services** The best hospital in Deir ez-Zor is the private **Badri Abboud**, on Abou Bakr as-Siddiq St, T051-221341. The Shell and Elf oil companies have a special contract with the hospital for their expatriate workers and so there are a couple of doctors here who speak good English. In an emergency they will also admit patients to their intensive care unit, which includes an operating theatre. **Post** The main post office is on Al-Imam Ali St. **Visa extensions** The Passport and Immigration Office is on Malik Bin Dinar St, Sat-Thu 0800-1400.

Hassakeh *p303*

Banks The main branch of the CBS is on Abdul Nasser St, west of the clock tower, Sat-Thu 0800-1230, they change cash with a minimum of fuss. Across the road is a Banque Bemo branch with an ATM that accepts foreign cards. **Medical services** The modern private Dr Baghdy hospital is on Al-Khabour St, T052-320940. **Post** The post office is on Abdul Nasser St, east of the clock tower, Sat-Thu 0800-1400. **Telephone** The telephone office shares the same building as the post office. Phonecards can be purchased here and there are card-phones outside.

Visa extensions The Passport and Immigration Office is on the street running west just north of the bridge over the Khabur river, Sat-Thu 0800-1430.

Qamishle *p304*

Banks CBS and Banque Bemo both have branches on Hafez al-Assad St, Sat-Thu 0800-1230. CBS change cash and Bankque Bemo have an ATM that takes foreign cards. **Medical services** The Al Razi Hospital, T052-427 303, is by the Assad roundabout and statue, and has some English-speaking doctors. **Post** The post office is open Sat-Thu 0900-1400.

Contents

Footprint features

Background

History

Though Syria only came into existence as a nation during the 20th century, the region it occupies has a history dating right back to the dawn of civilization, and indeed beyond. Traces of human activity here stretch back as far as the Old Stone Age or Palaeolithic era (as much as one million years ago). Moreover, this region has witnessed the evolution of the three great monotheistic religions – Judaism, Christianity and Islam – as well as playing a central role in the birth of civilization in terms of the development of settled agriculture, cities and writing.

The prehistoric era

Around 700,000 years ago, during the **Palaeolithic** period, *Neanderthal* man in the Middle East was engaged in primitive forms of hunting and gathering, utilizing simple stone tools to hunt large mammals such as elephants and hippopotami. This is the earliest evidence of 'human' activity to be recorded in the area.

During the **Epipaleolithic** or **Mesolithic** period (17,000-8500 BC), following the end to the last Ice Age some 15,000 years ago, *Homo sapiens* first made their appearance. The predominance of smaller, faster animals such as gazelles and wild goats necessitated the development of more sophisticated hunting skills, and correspondingly more specialized tools such as flint arrow-heads, spear-heads and knives have been uncovered from this period. Simultaneously, the gathering of wild plants began to take on a greater importance.

Early settlement

All around the peripheries of the Middle East, the Fertile Crescent provided the ideal conditions for the development of settled agriculture. This occurred towards the end of the Mesolithic period and during the early stages of the **Pre-Pottery Neolithic** period (8500-6000 BC). Wheat and barley appear to have been first cultivated around 10,000 years ago, while 8000 to 9000 years ago sheep and goats began to be fully domesticated. Hunting and gathering still played an important role, while the domestication of sheep and goats still required a semi-nomadic lifestyle in order to find suitable grazing. Gradually, however, small permanent settlements became more widely established.

During the **Pottery Neolithic** period (6000-4500 BC), baked clay (ceramic) wares made their first appearance. This period witnessed a marked reduction in levels of rainfall, and settlement tended to shift to riverside and coastal sites. In northern Mesopotamia and Syria, centred around the Kabur Triangle, the Halaf Culture developed (named after pottery finds dating from this period at Tell Halaf), overlapping with the Samarra culture of southern Mesopotamia. At sites such as Ras Shamra (Ugarit) on the Mediterranean coast, small settlements were being established.

The **Chalcolithic** period (4500-3300 BC) heralded the appearance of copper (first used in eastern Anatolia and central Iran). Village settlements based on agriculture spread throughout the whole of the region. Agriculture and animal husbandry both became more sophisticated. Wheat and barley began to be complemented by pulses, olives and flax, while further south, dates and grapes were being cultivated. As well as sheep and goats, cattle and pigs were kept, and the remains of dogs, donkeys, gazelle and foxes have also been found. Styles of pottery became more varied, while basalt was also being used for many utensils. By now there was a thriving trade in obsidian with Anatolia.

The first cities and empires

Out of these early settlements the first cities and city-states developed during the **Early Bronze Age** (3300-2250 BC). Initially, this took place in southern Mesopotamia, where the **Sumerian** civilization began to evolve from the fifth millennium BC. Here, an economy based on animal husbandry and large-scale irrigation of the river valleys between the Tigris and Euphrates rivers produced substantial surpluses. This in turn allowed powerful city-states to emerge with their specialized divisions of labour and complex social hierarchies and administrations. The most important was **Uruk** in southern Mesopotamia, from which the term 'Late Uruk culture' is derived. The most significant feature of the Sumerian civilization was the development of a form of writing based on the cuneiform script.

At the same time, from around 2900-2300 BC (a period in Syria generally referred to as the Early Syrian II period and in Egypt as the Early Dynastic period), the settlements at **Mari** (Tell Hariri) on the Euphrates and **Ebla** (Tell Mardikh) on the Central Plains to the south of Aleppo were also evolving into powerful city-states in their own right. Both developed their own systems of writing based on the cuneiform script of the Sumerians. The comparative developmental histories of southern Mesopotamia, Mari, Ebla and the Khabur plains have been described by one historian as a "research frontier looming on the horizon". Certainly the relationships between the various city-states and their embryonic empires were complex, and the discovery (made only in the 1960s) of a thriving Bronze Age city-state of the mid-third millennium BC at Ebla has forced historians to revise the emphasis previously given to the city-states of southern Mesopotamia in the early development of empires.

It would appear that while the growth of the southern Mesopotamian cities was fuelled by intensive irrigation-based agriculture, the extensive rain-fed plains of the Jezira and northwest Syria were also fuelling a similar growth in powerful city-states. Moreover, there appears to have been a steady shift in the centre of power, first from the southernmost portion of the Tigris-Euphrates alluvium to the dry farming plains of the Jezira, and then to the plains of northwest Syria around Aleppo. It has been suggested that the decline of the southern Mesopotamian centres of power was due to water-logging and salinization brought about by the intensive irrigation on which these city-states depended, a problem not encountered in the extensive rain-fed, grain producing regions of the Jezira and northwest Syria.

The development of these city-states was interrupted (or at least modified) in around 2350 BC by the invasion of the **Akkadians**, the first territorial empire to emerge in the ancient Middle East. This empire was founded by Sargon (2334-2271 BC), who initiated its expansion from its base in Mesopotamia, while his grandson Naram-Sin continued the process, extending the empire eastwards towards the Persian Gulf and westwards towards the Mediterranean.

The **Middle Bronze Age** (2250-1550 BC) brought with it major upheavals. Towards the end of the third millennium BC, the region was overrun by the **Amorites**, a Semitic people who emerged from the deserts to the south and east. After an initial period of disruption, city-states such as Mari absorbed these new peoples and began to flourish once again. Ebla, meanwhile, became part of the newly emergent Amorite kingdom of Yamkhad, based in present day Aleppo. By the 18th century BC, Mari had been destroyed by the **Babylonian** king Hammurabi, also of Amorite origin, who was extending his own empire from its base in southern Mesopotamia. **Ugarit**, however, was now entering its first golden age as a great trading city and continued to flourish by maintaining a delicate balancing act with the more powerful civilizations of Mesopotamia and Egypt.

Ancient 'super-power' rivalries

The **Late Bronze Age** (1550-1200 BC) saw further upheavals in the region. The expulsion of the Hyskos from Egypt by the pharaohs of New Kingdom Egypt in around 1550 BC was soon followed by a far greater **Egyptian** involvement in the region, particularly along the Mediterranean coast in centres such as Ugarit. Around the same time, a new people of Indo-European origin, the **Hittites**, were advancing into the region from the northwest. These were complemented by the **Hurrians** and later the **Mittanites** who arrived from the northeast. The latter two blended into a federation known as the **Mittani** kingdom. For a time, the Egyptian, Hittite and Mittani Empires formed a triangle of 'super-powers' fighting for control of the region. Eventually the Mittani kingdom was absorbed into that of the Hittites, the struggle for supremacy becoming a straight battle between the Egyptians and Hittites. The armies of the two powers finally met head on at Kadesh, though the outcome of the battle was inconclusive, with both sides claiming victory.

Despite these upheavals, it was during the Late Bronze Age that the first **alphabets** were developed, offering a massive improvement on the hugely complex cuneiform system first developed by the Sumerians, and the equally complex hieroglyphic system of the Egyptians. This momentous development occurred initially at Ugarit during the 14th century BC, and later at Byblos (in present-day Lebanon) towards the end of the 13th century BC, the latter being considered by many experts to represent the forerunner of our own alphabet. It was also probably towards the very end of the Late Bronze Age that the famous **Exodus** took place, when Moses led the **Israelites** out of slavery in Egypt and back to the 'Promised Land', his successor Joshua leading the 12 tribes across the Jordan River into Palestine.

Iron Age (1200-539 BC)

The start of the Iron Age saw two major migrations, which brought with them fundamental changes to the region. The first was the violent invasion of the **Sea Peoples**, about which remarkably little is known. As JD Muhly points out: "While the Egyptian texts refer to massed invasions by land and by sea of various groups collectively known as the 'Peoples of the Sea', it has been notoriously difficult to find any trace of such people in the archaeological record. Only the **Phillistines**, who gave their name to what was thereafter known as Palestine, subsequent to their settlement in the area as Egyptian garrison troops, can be identified in the archaeological context by their distinctive painted pottery" (JD Muhly in *Ebla to Damascus*). What is known, however, is that these Sea Peoples overthrew the Hittite Empire and largely destroyed Ugarit.

In the wake of the Sea Peoples came the **Aramaeans**, a semi-nomadic Semitic people who arrived from the deserts of Arabia and settled in central and northern Syria, blending with the small **neo-Hittite** kingdoms which had arisen in the wake of the destruction of the Hittite Empire. The Aramaeans also established themselves in Damascus, where they checked the expansion of the kingdoms of Judah and Israel to the south.

From the ninth century BC a new empire, that of the **Assyrians**, arose in northern Mesopotamia and gradually extended its control over most of the region. The Assyrians were in turn overthrown by the **Chaldeans**, who captured their capital, Nineveh, in 612 BC.

Persian period (539-333 BC)

Chaldean dominance of the region was short lived, with the **Achaemenid Persians**, led by Cyrus, capturing their capital Babylon in 539 BC, taking over control of their empire and

Chronology of archaeological and historic periods

Lower Palaeolithic	1,500,000-100,000 BC
Middle Paleolithic	100,000-40,000 BC
Upper Paleolithic	40,000-17,000 BC
Epipaleolithic (Mesolithic)	17,000-8500 BC
Pre Pottery Neolithic	8500-6000 BC
Pottery Neolithic	6000-4500 BC
Chalcolithic	4500-3300 BC
Early Bronze Age	3300-2250 BC
Middle Bronze Age	2250-1550 BC
Late Bronze Age	1550-1200 BC
Iron Age	1200-539 BC
Persian Period	539-333 BC
Hellenistic Period	333-64 BC
Roman/Nabatean Period	64 BC-AD 395
Byzantine Period	AD 395-636
Early Islamic Period	
Arab Conquest	AD 632-661
Umayyad Period	AD 661-750
Abbasid Period	AD 750-969
Fatimid Period	AD 969-1171
Crusader Period	AD 1097-1291
Late Islamic Period	
Zengid and Ayyubid Periods	AD 128-1260
Mamluk Period	AD 1260-1516
Ottoman Period	AD 1516-1918
Modern Period	AD 1918-present

extending it to include all of the Middle East, Egypt and Asia Minor. Persian rule was on the whole very well organized, with an excellent network of roads encouraging trade and communications within the empire. The coastal cities of the Phoenicians in particular flourished and Sidon (in present-day Lebanon), was made the capital of the fifth satrapy, encompassing both Syria-Palestine and Cyprus. The Sidonian fleet aided the Persians in their defeat of the Egyptians in 525 BC, and played a crucial role in their wars with the Greeks. Ultimately, however, the Sidonians overstepped the mark by establishing close trading relations with the Athenians and leading a coalition of Phoenician city-states in a rebellion against Persian rule, prompting the Persian king Ataxerxes III Ochus to lead a massive army against them in 350 BC.

Hellenistic period (333-64 BC)
Although the Persians were at first successful in their battles with the **Greeks**, ultimately it was the latter who triumphed, Alexander the Great of Macedon defeating the forces of Darius III at the battle of Issus in 333 BC. When he died at Babylon in 323 BC, Alexander was only 33 years old, but in the space of just 10 years he had succeeded in creating an empire larger even than that of the Persians.

After his death, Alexander's Empire was partitioned between his generals. Ptolemy I Soter gained control of Egypt, southern Lebanon and southern Syria (including Damascus), founding what became known as the **Ptolemid** Empire. Seleucus I Nicator, meanwhile, gained control of Mesopotamia, Asia Minor and northern Syria, establishing what became known as the **Seleucid** Empire. Over the next century, the Seleucids extended their control southwards, driving the Ptolemids back into Egypt, though at the same time they lost Asia Minor to the **Romans** and Mesopotamia to the **Parthians** (who arose from the ashes of the Persian Empire). Thus much of present-day Syria came to be controlled by the Seleucids.

The **Seleucids** continued the process, begun under Alexander, of Hellenization, 'founding' new cities such as Antioch (now called Antakya and in present-day Turkey), Apamea and Dura Europos. In addition the Seleucids made their mark on the great cities of the region, including Aleppo, Damascus, and many others. They laid out a distinctive grid pattern of streets and erected civic buildings and monuments, bringing with them Greek political and legal institutions, and indeed the Greek language. All the same, many of these cities were able to establish a high degree of autonomy within the empire, often amounting to near independence. The Seleucids, being relatively small in number, had no choice but to let them run their own affairs, albeit in a Hellenistic way. In the countryside, they made little or no impression.

By the second century BC, the Seleucid Empire was beginning to crumble. At the same time, the **Nabateans**, who had already established themselves as a powerful, semi-independent trading state in Petra, began to push northwards. Under King Aretas III (84-56 BC), they briefly succeed in extending their empire to include Bosra and Damascus. Similarly, the **Itureans**, a local tribal dynasty from the Bekaa Valley, began making raids on the coastal cities and inland centres. In the northern part of the empire, the Seleucids faced more serious threats from the Romans to the west, the **Armenians** to the north and the **Parthians** to the east.

Roman period (64 BC-395 AD)

The final fall of the Seleucid Empire came with the conquest of Antioch by the Roman general **Pompey** in 64 BC. The Romans created the province of Syria in their newly acquired territory and adopted Antioch as its capital. Initially, the Romans were much more concerned with their own internal power struggles, and at one stage the Parthians even succeeded in occupying much of Syria. Rome's bloody intrigues finally drew to an end with the abolition of the Roman Republic and the appointment of **Octavian** (Augustus Caesar) as the first Roman emperor in 29 BC.

Thus at first the Romans were only able to exercise loose political control, declaring the former city-states of the Seleucid Empire 'free cities'. In the south, the Nabatean kingdom continued to exist as an independent entity, keeping Damascus until as late as AD 54. After that it was pushed back into its former confines of Petra, though in AD 70 it pushed northwards again and briefly made Bosra the capital of its empire

Octavian's rise to the position of emperor in 29 BC heralded a gradual improvement in the overall state of affairs in the province of Syria. Though there were many areas over which they still had only nominal control, Roman rule brought with it peace and an orderly, efficient administration – the so called *Pax Romana* – which allowed the region to flourish economically. The loose federation known as the **Decapolis**, or 'Ten Cities', emerged, straddling the borders of present-day southern Syria and northern Jordan, with cities such as Bosra and Jerash (in present-day Jordan) benefiting from the north-south trade between Damascus and the Red Sea. In Damascus, the former temple of Haddad was gradually expanded and converted into a temple dedicated to the Roman god Jupiter, and the principal *Via Recta* (the Straight Street of the Bible) was widened and colonnaded. In the Syrian desert, Palmyra began to emerge as a major trading post on the route between Dura Europos and Emesa (Homs). Ironically, in the case of Palmyra, it was actually its position in the no man's land between Parthian and Roman power that helped it to flourish.

The Romans also developed their new province agriculturally and the area around Bosra became a major grain producing region, the 'bread basket' of the Roman Empire), while in the rocky limestone hills around Aleppo, richer landowners were able to embark on the long-term project of developing olive groves. Throughout Syria, it is the monuments of the Roman era which have survived, the ubiquitous building projects of the Romans having overlain those of the Greeks whom they replaced. Socially and culturally, however, the region's Hellenistic influences continued to be felt long afterwards. Greek remained the official language, and the Romans relied heavily on pre-existing Hellenistic administrative structures.

In AD 106, during the reign of Trajan, the empire was substantially reorganized. The Nabatean kingdom of Petra was incorporated into the empire and a new **province of Arabia** created alongside that of Syria, with Bosra as its capital. As a result of this, Palmyra entered its golden age, surpassing Petra in significance as a centre of trade.

The marriage in AD 187 of **Septimus Severus** to the daughter of the High Priest of Homs, Julia Domna, heralded a 'Syrian' line of Roman emperors, ensuring a greater direct Syrian influence in the affairs of Imperial Rome. However, during the rule of Caracalla (AD 211-217) and his successor Elagabalus (AD 217-222), the empire began to descend into degeneracy. The reigns of Alexander Severus (AD 222-235) and **Philip the Arab** (AD 244-249) provided brief respites, but by that time Rome's Empire in the Middle East was under serious threat.

Since the late second century, the advances of the Parthians from the east had become a major preoccupation. In the early part of the third century the Parthians were replaced by the **Sassanid Persians**, who posed an even more pressing threat. In 256 Dura Europos fell to the Sassanids. Four years later, the emperor Valerian was captured by the Sassanids and disaster was only averted when the king of Palmyra, Odainat, defeated them the same year. This set the stage for the legendary **Queen Zenobia** to establish Palmyra as an independent kingdom until the emperor Aurelian captured it in 271.

Diocletian's rule (AD 284-305) saw relative stability, but his death brought with it 20 years of civil war between the newly created eastern and western administrations of the Roman Empire. These only came to an end when Constantine managed to establish himself as sole emperor in AD 324, founding Constantinople as a second imperial capital in AD 330.

Byzantine period (AD 395-636)

In AD 312 Constantine had converted to **Christianity**, which was already spreading throughout the empire, despite the attempts of Diocletian to suppress it. A year later, the Edict of Milan officially gave Christians the right to practise their religion and by AD 380, Christianity had been adopted as the official religion of the Roman Empire. Although the Byzantine period can be said to have effectively started earlier (according to some interpretations, with the rise of Constantine to the position of sole emperor in AD 324), most historians date the Byzantine period from the official division of the Roman Empire into East and West in AD 395, with the Eastern Roman Empire becoming known as the Byzantine Empire.

Many of the former pagan temples of the Romans were converted into great churches during this era, for example at Damascus. In addition, numerous Christian communities flourished, particularly in the so called 'Dead City' region around Aleppo (and most famously at the pilgrimage site of St Simeon), but also throughout the rest of the empire. The Byzantine period in the Middle East spawned many fundamentally important innovations in religious architecture, the influence of which can still be seen today.

Under the reign of Theodosius II (AD 408-450), the '100 Year Peace' was established with the Sassanids, and the region was able to prosper as it had done under the Romans. During the reign of Justinian (AD 527-565), the Byzantine Empire again came under repeated attacks from the Sassanids, who on several occasions made deep incursions into Byzantine territory. Nevertheless, Justinian's rule was also marked by a flowering of Byzantine culture and architecture.

In AD 602, under the leadership of Chosroes II, the Sassanids launched a massive invasion. By AD 614 they had reached right down into the southern part of the empire and captured Jerusalem. In addition, Antioch, Aleppo, Damascus and Jerash were all occupied. In AD 616 they simultaneously conquered most of Egypt and Asia Minor, laying siege even to Constantinople. In AD 622 the Byzantine emperor Heraclius led a counter attack. His six-year campaign against the Sassanids drove them from most of the empire, but his success was short lived. The Byzantine Empire was on its knees, and in no position to resist the onslaught of the new power emerging from the deserts of Arabia, that of the Muslim Arabs.

The beginning of the Islamic Era

After the death in AD 632 of the founder of Islam, the **Prophet Muhammad**, the Arab tribes he had welded together into such a formidable force set about conquering the fertile lands to the north and west. Led by the military commander **Khalid Ibn al-Walid**, the Muslim Arab army captured Damascus in AD 635 and then withdrew to defeat the forces of Byzantium at the Battle of Yarmouk in AD 636, effectively marking the end of Byzantine rule in the region. They again occupied Damascus the same year, and then proceeded to sweep through the land of present day Syria, meeting little resistance from the local peoples. By AD 656 the whole of Persia had also been conquered.

These conquests took place under the rule of Muhammad's first three successors, the caliphs Abu Bakr (AD 632-634), Omar (AD 634-644), and Uthman (AD 644-656), who all maintained Medina as their capital. The fourth caliph, Ali (AD 656-661), whose assumption of the title of caliph was opposed both by the kin of Uthman (who had been assassinated) and by others in Medina, moved the Arab Muslim capital to Kufa in southern Iraq. However, the governor of Syria, Mu'awiya, was a close kinsman of Uthman, and he rose up in revolt. After Ali was murdered by disaffected members of his own camp (see Religion, page 339), Mu'awiya assumed the title of caliph, thus founding the Umayyad Dynasty.

The Umayyads (AD 661-750)

Mu'awiya promptly made Damascus the seat of the caliphate and capital of the empire, heralding the start of one of the most glorious periods in the city's history, and that of the region as a whole. Under the Umayyads, the empire grew to its greatest extent and by the end of the seventh century it stretched from Spain in the west to the Indus River in the east.

Though their origins were nomadic, the Umayyads were quick to adopt many aspects of the civilizations that had previously existed in the lands they now ruled. As Albert

Hourani comments: "Gradually, from being Arab chieftains, they formed a way of life patterned on that traditional among rulers of the Near East, receiving their guests or subjects in accordance with the ceremonial usages of Byzantine emperor or Iranian King." (Albert Hourani, *A History of the Arab Peoples*.) The synthesis of different influences – Graeco-Roman, Byzantine, Persian, Mesopotamian and indigenous – which occurred under the Umayyads is most graphically displayed in their architecture, and in particular their religious architecture. The famous **Umayyad Mosque** in Damascus, built during the reign of the sixth Umayyad caliph Khalid ibn al-Walid (AD 705-715), is the most spectacular example of this. But the Umayyads were also responsible for many other monuments, including Qasr al-Heir al-Sharki near Palmyra.

In retrospect, the Umayyads were seen as lax and corrupt by future Islamic Dynasties. Certainly, they did not place a major emphasis on religion, concentrating instead on developing their empire economically and politically. But, eventually, they did indeed fall into degeneracy. The last truly great Umayyad caliph, Hisham (AD 724-743) was followed in quick succession by a series of incompetent and debauched caliphs. The last of these, Marwan II, was overthrown following an uprising led by Abu al-Abbas, who went on to found the Abbasid Dynasty. One grandson of Hisham did manage to flee to Spain, maintaining the Umayyad lineage there for another 500 years.

The Abbasids (AD 750-1258)

The Abbasids sought to bring Islamic rule back to the more rigorous and theocratic interpretations they felt it deserved. They transferred the seat of the caliphate to Iraq, first to Kufa and then Baghdad. In doing so, they abandoned the blending of Eastern and Western influences which characterized Umayyad rule and brought to the empire a distinctively Mesopotamian and Persian emphasis. Syria, previously at the political heart of the empire, became a relatively insignificant backwater.

Initially, the Abbasids managed successfully to administer an empire which included the whole of the former Umayyad Empire except Spain and Morocco. By the mid-ninth century, however, their power was beginning to fragment, with numerous local dynasties appearing in Syria. The **Tulunid** and **Ikhshidid** Dynasties of Egypt in turn controlled parts of southern Syria from AD 868 to AD 969. The latter were ousted by the **Fatimids**, who went on to make Cairo their capital in AD 973 and later extended their power into Syria. The Fatimids represented the Ismaili branch of Shi'ite Islam, and as such were a direct threat to the power of the Sunni Abbasids, having set up their own rival caliphate. In the north, meanwhile, the **Hamdanid** and **Mirdasid** Dynasties ruled in turn in Aleppo from AD 944-1070. Both, however, were only nominal rulers, being at one time or another subject to either the Fatimids to the south or the Byzantines to the north (the Byzantines were making the most of the chaos and trying to regain territory in their former empire).

While all this was happening, the **Seljuk Turks**, originally chiefs of the Oghuz tribes of Transoxania, had conquered Persia and established a kingdom there with Isfahan as their capital. Being Sunni Muslims, they came to the aid of the Abbasids, who were experiencing their own domestic problems in Baghdad. In return the Seljuk ruler forced the Abbasid caliph to recognize him as 'Sultan' (literally 'Sovereign') of the Universal State of Islam. Thus the Abbasids became in effect helpless puppets of the Seljuks. The Seljuks occupied Aleppo in 1070 and defeated the Byzantines at Manzikert in eastern Anatolia in 1071. By 1076 they had extended their control over most of Syria, including Damascus, and largely ousted the Fatimids, though they were never strong enough to completely expel them from the region. After 1095 two Seljuk rulers emerged in Syria with Aleppo and Damascus as their capitals. These rulers set up what were in effect their own rival dynasties, both only nominally subservient to the Seljuk sultan in Isfahan.

Though the Abbasid caliphate continued to exist, nominally at least, until it was conclusively destroyed by the Mongols in 1258, in practice it faded into total insignificance.

The First Crusade

During the first part of the 11th century, the Fatimid caliph Al-Hakim had ordered the destruction of 30,000 churches in Egypt, Palestine and Syria (including the Church of the Holy Sepulchre in Jerusalem). This, along with the pleas of the Byzantine emperor, who was becoming increasingly alarmed at the Seljuk threat, prompted Pope Urban II to call for a crusade to restore the Holy Lands to Christian control.

Thus the **First Crusade** set off from Europe, arriving in Syria in 1097. To their surprise, instead of a formidable enemy in the form of the Seljuk Turks, what they found was a region deeply divided and fragmented into numerous petty principalities. While the Crusaders were united by their religious mission of a 'Holy War', the Muslim peoples against whom they were marching were thoroughly embroiled in their own domestic conflicts. After a nine-month siege they took Antioch, massacring many of its inhabitants, including its Greek Orthodox community. They then continued southwards along the Orontes River. Despite meeting little resistance, they were by this time in a sorry state, riven by disease and famine. The shortage of food in particular was reaching crisis point, prompting the infamous massacre at Maarat al-Numan. Continuing south, they swung inland through the Homs Gap, briefly occupying the castle which was later to become Krak des Chevaliers. After unsuccessfully besieging Aqra (near Tripoli), they headed straight down the Mediterranean coast, turning inland again near Jaffa to arrive at Jerusalem. After just over a month, on 15 July 1099, the Holy City fell to the Crusaders, its inhabitants, like those of Antioch, being subjected to an indiscriminate massacre.

After capturing Jerusalem, the great majority of the soldiers of the First Crusade returned home. Though the Crusaders were to remain in the region for another 200 years or so, their numbers were always dangerously few. In the absence of manpower they resorted instead to building formidable castles which could be easily defended with the minimum of soldiers. Today, numerous examples of these remarkable pieces of military architecture can be seen throughout Syria. Many of them (most famously Krak des Chevaliers, but also others such as Qalat Marqab and Qalat Salah ud-Din) are still in an excellent state of preservation.

The Zengids and Ayyubids (1128-1260)

A concerted response to the Crusaders came from the **Zengids**, nominally subservient to the Seljuks. The Zengid Dynasty was founded by Zengi, who in 1124 had helped lead a Seljuk force in the relief of Aleppo from a Crusader siege. In 1128 he became the ruler of Aleppo. Under his rule, and that of his son Nur ud-Din (1146-1174), Aleppo became a centre of resistance against the Crusaders.

In 1144 the County of Edessa (present-day Urfa in Turkey) fell to Nur ud-Din, prompting the **Second Crusade**. Their attempts to besiege Damascus failed and the whole expedition ended in something of a fiasco. By 1154 the Zengids had themselves gained control of Damascus, uniting the Muslim opposition to the Crusaders in Syria. In 1169 Nur ud-Din sent a huge force against the Fatimids in Egypt. Led by **Salah ud-Din** (known to European historians as Saladin), the Zengid forces over threw the Fatimids in 1171, restoring Sunni orthodoxy there and, nominally at least, the authority of the Abbasid caliph. After Nur ud-Din's death, Salah ud-Din returned to Syria and by 1186 had succeeded in uniting all the Muslim lands from Cairo to Baghdad under the **Ayyubid Dynasty** (named after his father Ayyub). In 1187, having defeated the Crusaders at the Battle of Hattin, he recaptured Jerusalem and also regained Acre, Sidon, Beirut and Byblos. The following year he conducted a whirlwind campaign which saw no less than 50 Crusader positions fall, although he avoided their most important and impregnable strongholds: Krak des Chevaliers, Qalat Marqab and Antioch.

The fall of Jerusalem prompted the **Third Crusade**, which by 1191 had recaptured Acre. The King of England, Richard I (Richard the Lionheart) is perhaps the best known figure of this Crusade, but despite twice coming to within sight of Jerusalem, he failed to take it. Instead, he signed a peace treaty in 1192 which guaranteed pilgrims free right of passage. After Salah ud-Din's death the following year, his successors failed to capitalize on the gains he had made and the Crusaders were able to recapture much of their former territory along the coast. The Ayyubid line continued until 1260, ruling from the twin capitals of Cairo and Damascus. It came to rely increasingly on Turkish slaves to man its armies and administer its empire. These slaves grew in power, giving rise to what became known as the Mamluk Dynasty (meaning 'owned').

The Mamluks (1260-1516)

The Ayyubid line in Damascus was brought to an abrupt end in 1260 by the invasion of the **Mongols**, who swept across Syria leaving a trail of destruction in their wake. Already in Cairo the **Mamluks** had risen to power in a coup in 1250, and they were able to defeat decisively the Mongols at the Battle of Ain Jalud in Palestine. One of the Mamluk generals at this battle was a man named **Baibars** who subsequently made himself sultan and took over from the vanquished Ayyubids. Baibars (1260-1277) proved himself to be a formidable adversary, unleashing the full force of his military genius on the Crusaders. By the end of his rule he had driven them from Antioch, Krak des Chevaliers and Safita. The offensive was continued by Qalaun (1280-1290) who dislodged the Crusaders from Qalat Marqab, Lattakia and Tripoli, and by his successor Khalil who took Acre and Tartus in 1291. The Crusaders continued to cling to a tiny foothold on the coast, occupying the island of Arwad until 1302, but already they had been reduced to little more than an anachronism.

The Mamluk genius was not purely military. During the 14th century they also presided over a remarkable programme of building works, the legacy of which is still very much in evidence in Damascus (their second capital after Cairo), and Aleppo. However, towards the end of the 14th century they were riven by internal power struggles which left their empire in Syria increasingly vulnerable to renewed attacks by the Mongols. The most devastating of these, led by Tamerlane, came in 1400, bringing devastation to much of their empire. Under the sultan Qait Bey (1468-1495), the Mamluks recovered somewhat, but they never achieved their former greatness, and in the first quarter of the 16th century they were overthrown by the Ottomans.

The Ottomans (1516-1918)

The Ottoman Turks, who had already established themselves in Asia Minor during the middle of the 15th century and made Constantinople their capital, met little resistance when they swept into Syria in 1516, led by the sultan Selim I (1512-1520). Under his rule, the Ottomans extended their empire into Egypt, capturing the last Mamluk sultan, and even into Arabia, taking the Islamic holy cities of Mecca and Medina. His successor, Suleiman the Magnificent (1520-1566), further extended the empire to include Serbia,

Hungary, Mesopotamia and all of North Africa except Morocco. Thus present-day Syria formed just a small part of a vast empire.

Nevertheless, the region benefited considerably from its incorporation into this new empire. An efficient administrative system was put in place, new trading links were established and ambitious building projects undertaken. It was during Suleiman's reign that the great Tekkiyeh as-Suleimaniyeh complex in Damascus was built. One of the first things Selim I had done on capturing Cairo was to proclaim himself caliph (since the final collapse of the Abbasid caliphate in 1258, the title had been held by a puppet of the Mamluks). The Ottomans took great care also to ensure that the great pilgrimage route to Mecca, which they now controlled almost in its entirety, was managed properly. As a result, they soon succeeded in legitimizing their assumption of the caliphate and establishing themselves as Protectors of the Faith. Damascus flourished in its role as the last great staging post on the *Hajj* to Mecca. Aleppo, meanwhile, was opened up to European traders by 'capitulation' treaties with the European powers and prospered even more vigorously, its souqs and khans thronging with commercial activity.

Inevitably for such a vast empire, Ottoman rule was rarely directly applied, with *pashas* or local governors holding office in the major cities and exercising control over large administrative districts. As long as taxes were collected and paid on time, and peace maintained, the sultans in Constantinople were happy not to interfere. At times, the local governors, or even their subordinate tax collectors, were able to carve out what amounted in effect to more or less fully independent kingdoms for themselves.

The 18th century saw a period of stagnation in the Ottoman Empire, which was followed in the 19th century by a more serious revolt. The viceroy of Egypt, Muhammad Ali (1805-1849) succeeded in establishing his own independent power base there, shaking off the authority of the Ottomans. His son, **Ibrahim Pasha**, carried the uprising into Syria and Lebanon in 1831, ousting the Ottoman forces from the region and carrying out wide ranging modernizing reforms. At one stage it seemed that the Ottoman Empire would collapse, but in 1840 the European powers chose to intervene on the side of the Ottomans, alarmed at this upset to the balance of power in the region and the threat that it posed to their interests.

The immediate result of greater European involvement was to open Syria up to greater European influence. Christian educational/missionary schools were established in Damascus and Aleppo and the latter began to flourish as a point of commercial and cultural contact with Europe. At the heart of Ottoman political power in Constantinople, meanwhile, the Ottoman sultan was deposed in 1909 by the revolutionary movement known as the 'Young Turks', who established the *Committee of Union and Progress (CUP)*. This brought with it an upsurge of Turkish nationalism which served to awaken amongst the Arab peoples a sense of their own Arab identity.

First World War and the Arab revolt The modern political geography of the Middle East was largely shaped during the decade from 1914 to 1924. The onset of the First World War was of enormous significance to the region, which suddenly became a focus of international concern. The decision of the Ottoman Turks to ally themselves with the Central Powers (Germany and Austria-Hungary) placed them in direct opposition to the Allies. The harsh indifference of the Turks to local Arab peoples, along with a breakdown of civic administration as the Turks focused their attentions on the war, brought widespread famine and epidemics. Arab feelings against the Turks increased, culminating in the Arab Revolt, with the Sharif of Mecca, Hussein Ibn Ali, as the figurehead.

As the concept of Arab nationalism began to develop at the turn of the century, notably amongst the urban middle classes of Syria, it soon became clear that the only source of leadership to which they could turn was provided by the emirate of Mecca – an Arab Dynasty of great Islamic standing that was directly descended from the Prophet. Among those who had recognized this were the British, who in 1882 had established themselves across the Red Sea in Egypt. The contacts that the British had established early on with the various sharifian factions paid dividends when the Ottomans entered the First World War on the side of the Central Powers.

When the CUP's puppet caliph Muhammad V declared the expected *jihad* against the Allies on behalf of the Islamic world, the impact on the Muslim populations in the Arab world and India was in fact negligible. The Ottoman-German advance into Aden did, however, mean that the Central Powers could threaten Allied shipping in the Red Sea and Suez Canal area (particularly now that the Germans had U-boats). Furthermore, their armies could be resupplied and reinforced by way of the Hejaz railway. Thus, for the Allies (and British in particular) a revolt in the Hejaz and Syria against the Ottomans would not only disrupt the Central Powers resupply lines to Aden, it might actually cut off the whole of the Ottoman-German forces in southern Arabia. Henceforth efforts were made by the British staff at the Arab Bureau in Cairo to increase contacts with Sharif Hussein and his sons.

The subsequent call to armed revolt against the Ottoman Empire that Sharif Hussein made in 1916 – the **Arab Revolt** – has been the subject of much reinterpretation over the years. How much the revolt was British inspired and how much it was the result of an indigenous bid for Arab independence is a moot point. Certainly, the Arab Revolt was of minor significance in the wider scheme of things. However, it was important in that by harassing vital Turkish lines of communications, most notably the Hejaz railway line which TE Lawrence and his band spent so much time blowing up, it forced the Turks to tie up large bodies of troops defending strategically unimportant corners of the Arabian peninsula (Medina included), allowing the British to consolidate their military position in Palestine, Egypt and the Red Sea.

End of the First World War and broken promises

The triumphant entry of the Allies and the Arab nationalist forces into Damascus on 1 October 1918 signalled the final collapse of the Ottoman Empire and defeat of the Central Powers. The end of the First World War saw Sharif Hussein's third son, **Feisal**, established in Damascus as the head of an Arab government that recognized the suzerainty of his father, the ruler of the Hejaz. Feisal, however, only controlled one of three Occupied Enemy Territory Administrations (this consisted of present-day Jordan, Syria and the inland areas of Lebanon, while the British controlled Palestine and the French the coastal areas as far north as present-day Turkey). Each of these OETAs was under the overall control of the British commander General Allenby who, while recognizing Feisal's government, described it as 'purely provisional'.

Feisal attended the Paris Peace Conference of 1919 and secured the promise of an International Commission of Inquiry to look into the question of Syrian unity. The **King-Crane Commission**, as it became known, recommended that, "the unity of Syria be preserved, in accordance with the earnest petition of the great majority of the Syrian people". However, in response to increasing French pressure, Britain agreed in September 1919 to withdraw its troops from Syria and Lebanon. In January 1920 Feisal managed to negotiate an agreement with the French Premier, Georges Clemenceau, which allowed a temporary French military presence along the coast in return for French acknowledgement of Syrian unity and Feisal's rule over the interior. The end of Clemenceau's term in office saw the agreement repudiated and in response the General Syrian Congress proclaimed Feisal king of all Syria. A month later, however, at the **San Remo Conference** in April 1920, Britain and France formally divided historic Syria between them, the French Mandate covering present-day Syria and Lebanon, while the British Mandate covered Palestine, Transjordan and Iraq. On 24 July 1920 Fesial was forced out of Damascus by the French, and later installed instead as the king of Iraq by the British.

The San Remo Conference had put into effect the **Sykes-Picot Agreement** of 1916. Despite this secret wartime agreement to carve the region up between the British and French, the British had also entered into the so called '**Hussein-McMahon Correspondence**' that had appeared (albeit vaguely) to commit Britain to assist the Arabs in attaining independence. In addition, in 1917, in a letter addressed to Lord Rothschild (and subsequently known as the **Balfour Declaration**), the British government appeared to commit herself to the establishment of a 'nation home for the Jewish people in Palestine'. Thus the Arabs were denied their own government, the region was divided along artificial lines, and the seeds of the bitter dispute over 'Palestine', still so fundamental to Middle Eastern politics today, were sown.

The French Mandate and the road to independence

The French Mandate was for Syria a period of traumatic dismemberment. First the French carved out *Grand Liban* in August 1920, adding Tyre, Sidon, Beirut, Tripoli, the Akkar region, the Bekaa Valley and the south to the protected Maronite enclave of Mount Lebanon to create the basis for the modern state of Lebanon. Then parts of the old Ottoman province of Aleppo were given to Turkey. Internally, meanwhile, the French dissected the country, creating two mini-states centred on Aleppo and Damascus while establishing separate Alawi and Druze 'enclaves' (in the mountains around Lattakia and the Hauran region to the south of Damascus respectively) and maintaining direct French rule in the northeast. By the time of the French withdrawal in 1946, Syria comprised an area of a little over 185,000 sq km, compared with the former Ottoman province of Syria which ran to around 300,000 sq km.

Within Syria, the desire for an united 'Greater Syria' was matched by the strength of feeling against the French administration and their policy of 'divide and rule'. In 1925 a revolt broke out amongst the Druze of the Hauran region, initially over local disagreements with the French, though it soon spread to Damascus and other parts of the country. The French response, which included the bombing of Damascus, was uncompromising and by 1927 the revolt had been suppressed.

In an effort to appease opposition to their rule, they allowed elections to take place in 1928 to a Constituent Assembly which was charged with drafting a constitution. The draft constitution declared that, "the Syrian territories detached from the Ottoman Empire constitute an indivisible political unity. The divisions that have emerged between the end of the war and the present day do not diminish this unity." This was unacceptable to the French and, after attempts to negotiate a compromise failed, they dissolved the Assembly in 1930 and unilaterally issued a new constitution less hostile to their rule.

New elections were held in 1932 and negotiations started on a Franco-Syrian treaty, but these also broke down and the Assembly was again dissolved in 1934. By 1936 growing opposition and disturbances which threatened to escalate into a full scale revolt prompted the French to send a Syrian delegation to Paris to discuss their demands.

The new French Popular Front government was more sympathetic and in September 1936 a Franco-Syrian Treaty was signed recognizing the principal of Syrian independence after a three-year 'handover' period. In 1938, however, with tensions growing in the wider region, the French announced that the treaty would not be ratified. The following year, in an effort to ensure Turkish neutrality in the Second World War, the enclaves of Antioch (Antakya) and Alexandretta (Iskanderun) were formally ceded to the Turkish (the source of a continuing territorial dispute between Syria and Turkey).

After the surrender of France to Germany in 1940, Syria came under the control of the Vichy government. In 1941, against a background of rioting in Syria, Free French and British troops soon succeeded in overthrowing the Vichy government and in September 1941 Syrian independence was formally recognized, in theory at least. In practice, however, the French held on to power, refusing to restore constitutional rule while the war still raged. In 1943 elections were finally held and a nationalist government formed with Shukri al-Kuwatli becoming the President of the Syrian Republic in August of that year. The handover of power was gradual and acrimonious. The Syrians refused to give in to French demands for a new Franco-Syrian Treaty as a condition for the final transfer of administrative and military services, leading to fresh disturbances in 1945 (and again the French bombing of Damascus). These were only quelled following British military intervention and the final departure of all French troops and administrative personnel. The departure of British troops in April 1946 at last heralded full independence for Syria.

Modern Syria

Early years of instability (1946-1958)
The early years of the Syrian Republic were marked by chronic instability and bitter disappointment. Having already been in existence as a separate entity for a generation, the appeal of restoring 'Greater Syria' (expressed in various proposals of union with Iraq) was tempered by a new sense of Syrian nationalism and a fear of being absorbed within such a union. Indeed, the parallel ambitions of Jordan's King Abdullah to lead a united 'Greater Syria' were viewed with outright hostility and politically Syria was more closely aligned with Egypt and Saudi Arabia than with either Iraq or Jordan.

The defeat of the Arab countries by the newly formed State of Israel in the **1947-1949 war** shook Syrian confidence and created much resentment within the country. In 1949 there were no less than three military coups. In 1950 a new constitution was put in place and Hashim al-Atasi, a widely respected politician, installed as president.

In 1951 there was another coup, engineered by Adib al-Shishakli (the leader of the final coup of 1949), who by 1953 had installed himself as president. The following year he, in turn, was ousted after popular demonstrations in Aleppo and Damascus. The 1950 constitution was restored, Atasi reinstated as president and new elections held.

On the international scene, Syria's position was full of paradox. The reappointment of Shukri al-Kuwatli as president in 1955 signalled increasingly close relations with Egypt. Syria was at the same time becoming much more anti-Western and pro-Soviet, protesting strongly against the formation of the Baghdad Pact (a defensive alliance aimed at curbing Soviet communist designs in the Middle East, which included Turkey, Iraq, Iran, Pakistan and Britain). The **Suez Crisis** and subsequent invasion of Sinai by Israel in 1956 with help from Britain and France only served to bolster anti-Western sentiments. Syria blew up the oil pipelines from Saudi Arabia and Iraq which passed through her territory en route to the Mediterranean and refused to repair them until Sinai was fully restored to Egypt. When America's **Eisenhower Doctrine** of 1957 was warmly received by King Hussein of Jordan and the Christian president of Lebanon Camille Chamoun, Syria found herself at loggerheads, politically at least, with every one of her immediate neighbours. Only Egypt appeared to share a similar outlook.

The UAR (1958-1961)

The pan-Arab nationalism being espoused by Gamal Abdul Nasser of Egypt had massive popular support throughout the region. Swept along in the tide of popular sentiment, in February 1958 Syria formally united with Egypt to form the **United Arab Republic (UAR)**, with Nasser as its president. Though popular in the beginning, the relationship soon soured, with the inevitable Egyptian political domination of Syria, as well as the economic cost, causing resentment. Despite the formation of a single UAR cabinet in August 1961, by September a military coup had put an end to what most now regarded as Egyptian imperialism and Syria announced her withdrawal from the UAR, leaving it defunct.

The Ba'ath rise to power

The **Ba'ath** ('Renaissance') party was founded by a Christian Arab academic, Michel Aflaq in 1947. It espoused a combination of socialism, secularism and pan-Arabism and grew steadily in influence in Syria, spreading also to Lebanon, Jordan, Iraq and Egypt. It was the Ba'ath party which was one of the driving forces behind Syria's short-lived union with Egypt, though within Ba'ath there were divisions between the pro-Egyptian, pro-Iraqi and nationalist camps. Following the collapse of the UAR, Syria experienced a couple more years of uncertain rule which saw the president ousted and then reinstated. In March 1963 a coup was staged by a Ba'athist military junta calling itself the National Council of the Revolutionary Command. The Ba'athist regime which followed purged the remaining pro-Nasserists from power, foiling a coup instigated by them, and set about implementing its socialist agenda, nationalizing banks, initiating land reform, etc. This disaffected the influential land-owning and merchant sections of society. In addition, by relying heavily on the military, which was dominated by religious minority groups and in particular the Alawis, the Ba'ath failed to win the support of the Sunni Muslim *ulema*. Politically the country was becoming polarized between conservative/traditional elements and modernizing socialist elements. In April 1964 these tensions erupted into civil disturbances in Hama which were swiftly suppressed.

At the same time, there were growing tensions within the Ba'ath party itself, between the moderate and long-standing civilian politicians, and the more extreme left-wing elements (including many radical young officers from the military). These tensions finally came to a head in February 1966, with the radical elements seizing power. Many of the moderate Ba'ath politicians, including the founder of the Ba'ath Michel Aflaq and the head of state General Amin Hafiz, were placed under arrest.

It was against this background of radicalism that the build up to the **Six Day War** of 1967 with Israel took place. In November 1966 Syria entered into a defence pact with Egypt, soon to be followed by Jordan. Throughout 1966 and early 1967 Syria increasingly became the focus for cross border attacks on Israel, while Egypt's actions in Sinai and the Gulf of Aqaba finally resulted in the outbreak of war on 5 June 1967. The war proved to be a disaster for Syria, with Israeli troops gaining control over the strategically vital Golan Heights and pushing forwards as far as the town of Quneitra (just 67 km from Damascus) before a UN-brokered ceasefire was implemented on 10 June.

Assad assumes power

The Six Day War of 1967 was another bitter disappointment for Syria and once again a serious blow to her self-confidence. The credibility of the 'progressive' Ba'athist regime which had come to power in 1966 was seriously undermined. In particular it began to be criticized for its heavy reliance on the USSR, and for its overriding emphasis on the importance of developing a neo-Marxist economy. The level of Soviet involvement in Syria was seen by many as bordering on imperialism, while the debacle of the Six Day War was seen as evidence that the regime was more interested in neo-Marxist ideology than the struggle against Israel.

A 'nationalist' camp within Ba'ath began to gain ground, one which recognized the need for a pragmatic approach to the economy and emphasized the importance of developing stronger ties with Syria's Arab neighbours and overthrowing Israel. The 'nationalist' camp was led by **Hafez al-Assad**, who gained control of the all-important Ministry of Defence. Initially Assad was constrained by Soviet threats to withdraw all aid, which would have left Syria greatly weakened militarily and economically. However, improved relations with China strengthened his hand. The power struggle came to a head over the question of Syria's support for the Palestinian guerrilla groups in Jordan, whose might was being challenged by King Hussein in a showdown which became known as Black September. Assad disapproved of direct Syrian military intervention on the side of the Palestinians, fearing that it would damage pan-Arab unity, and that the Palestinian guerrilla groups were about to trigger another confrontation with Israel at a time when Syria's military forces were too weak to have any chance of success.

In November 1970 Hafez al-Assad seized power, assuming the position of prime minister. By March 1971 he had made himself president, with a referendum confirming his position for a seven-year term. A legislative body, the People's Assembly, was formed, with the Ba'ath party being guaranteed 87 of its 173 seats to give it an overall majority (the Assembly was later enlarged to 200 seats). In order to broaden his power base, Assad went on to form the National Progressive Front, a coalition of parties headed by the Ba'ath. In March 1973 a new constitution was put into effect.

October War of Liberation (Yom Kippur War) 1973

On 6 October 1973 Syria and Egypt launched simultaneous attacks on Israel in an attempt to regain territory lost during the 1967 war. The attacks were timed to coincide with the Jewish Day of Atonement, Yom Kippur, the holiest day in the Jewish calendar, hence the popular name the **Yom Kippur War**, although in Syria the encounter is known officially as the **October War of Liberation**. Having taken Israeli forces by surprise, Syria and Egypt were able to make dramatic advances, Syria reclaiming a substantial portion of the Golan Heights. The subsequent Israeli counter-offensive saw both the Egyptians and the Syrians pushed back, in the case of the Syrians to within 32 km of Damascus. Egypt signed a disengagement agreement on 18 January 1974, but the Golan fighting dragged on, with an agreement not being signed until 30 May of that year. The outcome of this conflict was at best inconclusive, but it did at least allow Syria to claim some degree of victory and went a long way to restoring Syrian self-confidence, as well as strengthening Assad's position.

Assad's close co-operation with Egypt during the October War reflected the improved relations he had effected in that direction. Ties with the Soviet Union were likewise restored, and Syria began to receive substantial amounts of military and economic aid once again. In June 1974 diplomatic relations with America were also restored. The **Rabat Conference** of October 1974 resulted in a declaration that recognized the PLO as the 'sole legitimate representative of the Palestinian people'. From Assad's point of view this was highly significant in that it meant that Jordan had implicitly relinquished its claim to the West Bank and signalled that the Arab world was at last united in its approach to the Palestinian question.

Economic boom
The new found stability of Assad's regime, along with its relatively enlightened approach to economic development brought with it a veritable flow of foreign aid into Syria from Arab oil producing countries, the UN, World Bank, Europe and even the US. Before the October War foreign aid had averaged just US$50 million annually; after 1974 it jumped to US$600 million. At the same time, the sharp rise in world oil prices saw Syria's oil exports rocket in value from US$70 million in 1973 to US$700 million in 1974. Remittances from Syrians working in the Arab oil producing countries likewise shot up. In short, after faltering along without any real direction from one unstable regime to another, Syria suddenly started to experience a sustained period of solid economic development which brought with it tangible benefits to ordinary people.

The Alawis in particular benefited from the economic boom, but also other minority groups and previously neglected sections of society. Perhaps inevitably, however, the socialism of the Ba'ath regime gradually started to give way to more selfish opportunism. By 1976 there were around 3500 millionaires (in S£s), as compared with just 55 in 1963, the majority beneficiaries of the commissions, kickbacks and outright corruption which accompanied the government's close involvement in economic affairs. Muhammad Haydar, the vice-premier of Economic Affairs, was notorious for the personal wealth he amassed and became known as 'Mister Five Percent'. Assad's youngest brother Rif'at, unassailable in his position as commander of the elite Defence Companies which acted as a kind of praetorian guard for Assad's regime, indulged himself in a luxurious international jet-set lifestyle and enjoyed access to unlimited government funds.

Such gross iniquities began to breed resentment towards the Alawis. At the same time, the nouveau riche started to outstrip traditional merchants and landowners, whose political influence had already been weakened by the Ba'ath rise to power. Venerable religious families and the Sunni Muslim *ulema*, meanwhile, found themselves undermined by the rising tide of secularism. The seeds of a backlash against Assad, the Ba'ath and the ruling Alawi elite were being sown.

War in Lebanon
When Lebanon erupted into civil war in April 1975, Syria, understandably enough, took a keen interest and followed events closely. A destabilized Lebanon might open the door to an Israeli occupation of all or part of the country (or at least result in the emergence of pro-Israeli government in Lebanon). It also threatened the stability of Syria itself. Direct Syrian military intervention was therefore perhaps inevitable, and indeed came the following year. By the end of May 1976 there were an estimated 40,000 Syrian-controlled troops in Lebanon, and the following month Syria launched a full-scale invasion. Initially Syria's stated aim had been to protect the Palestinians, and subsequently to control their activities in Beirut. However, it soon became clear to Assad that his best hope lay in restoring stability to Lebanon by crushing the PLO and ensuring that a pro-Syrian government held power. Following the appeal of the Maronite president Suleiman Franjieh for help, Syria switched sides.

Thus Assad found himself attacking the PLO and their allies and defending the Maronite Christians, much to the dismay of the rest of the Arab world. (During the 15 years of civil war, Syria found itself aligned with practically every Lebanese faction at one time or another). By October the Arab League had 'regularized' the Syrian presence in Lebanon by giving authority to an Arab Deterrent Force (ADF) to maintain peace. The ADF was, however, dominated by Syrian troops and the Arab League in no position to dictate policy to Assad in what he regarded as his own backyard.

Syria's military involvement in Lebanon's civil war was a bitter, costly and long, drawn-out affair. On two occasions, following the 1978 and 1982 Israeli invasions of Lebanon, it very nearly resulted in another full scale war between Syria and Israel, and in the latter case did result in military humiliation for Syria.

Insurrection at home, disunity and war abroad

Syria's intervention in Lebanon in 1976 coincided with an upsurge in discontent at home. The economic boom was running out of steam, with many Gulf states withdrawing their aid in protest at Assad's assault on the Palestinians in Beirut. Social inequality was growing, and opposition to the regime was finding a further focus in the form of extremist Sunni Muslim groups which resented minority Alawi rule and the Ba'ath promotion of secularism. The most prominent of these groups was the **Muslim Brotherhood**, which originated in Egypt during the 1920s. Its original aim had been to bring about an end to British rule in Egypt and to establish an Islamic state in its place. In the context of Ba'athist Syria, its Islamist ideology quickly became a banner behind which all the disaffected sections of Syrian society could unite. Acts of terrorism against prominent Alawi figures became ever more frequent, the most prominent being the massacre of at least 32 Alawi officer cadets at Aleppo Artillery School in June 1979. Almost exactly a year later, assassination attempt was made on Assad himself.

This growing internal threat to the stability of the country was occurring in the context of serious setbacks for Assad abroad. The **Camp David** accords of 1978 led the following year to a full peace treaty between Egypt and Israel, seriously weakening the pan-Arab unity against Israel which Assad so cherished. On the Lebanese front, by 1981 the stand-off between Syria and Israel over the positioning of SAM missiles in the Bekaa Valley was threatening to escalate into a full scale confrontation, while at the same time Syrian troops found themselves fighting the Christian Phalangists they had previously been sent to protect. Israel, meanwhile, formally annexed the Golan Heights. To the east, the outbreak of the **Iran-Iraq War** in 1980 further added to the regional tension. Syria gave its support to Iran, reflecting the long-standing hostility which existed between the Syrian and Iraqi branches of the Ba'ath party. With Jordan offering its support to Iraq, Syria and Jordan found themselves once again at loggerheads and tensions between the two countries nearly escalated into open hostilities on several occasions.

At home things finally came to a head in February 1982 with a full-scale uprising against Assad's regime in the conservative town of Hama. It took three weeks before the uprising was finally quelled, and in the process much of Hama was devastated. Though Assad survived this challenge to his authority, the Israeli invasion of Lebanon in June of that year presented him with an even more serious problem. Many of Syria's fighter aircraft in the Bekaa Valley were destroyed, along with most of its SAM missiles. The Syrian presence in Lebanon was rendered all but impotent in the face of the sheer might of the Israeli military. By 1983 Syrian forces in Lebanon were under attack not only from the Israelis but also from Sunni Muslims in Tripoli, Maronite Christians in the centre of the country, and guerrillas loyal to Yasser Arafat in the Bekaa Valley (Assad had backed extremist elements within the PLO which were attempting to overthrow Arafat).

In November 1983 Assad suffered what was widely believed to be a heart attack and for several weeks disappeared completely from the public eye while convalescing. A power struggle ensued, with Assad's younger brother Rifa'at spearheading the challenge to Assad's supremacy. By March 1984 a showdown seemed certain. Eventually, following a dramatic face to face meeting between the two brothers, Rifa'at lost his nerve and Assad was able to reassert his authority. That year Rifa'at went into effective exile, along with others who had played a part in the confrontation.

In 1985 Assad was elected to a third seven-year term as president and his position at home appeared once more secure. On the international scene, however, Assad was isolated from the rest of the Arab world, both due to his support for Iran in the Iran-Iraq war, and his attempts to oust Arafat from the PLO. Suspicion in the West that Syria was involved in international terrorist attacks led to the US and most members of the EU imposing sanctions in 1986. Britain broke off diplomatic relations entirely. The Soviet Union, Syria's chief sponsor since 1980, became Assad's only firm ally, with economic and military aid from this quarter growing massively throughout the 1980s.

Gulf War

The Iraqi invasion of Kuwait in August 1990 gave Assad a chance to mend his bridges with the West. Having restored diplomatic relations with Egypt (severed since 1977 in protest at Sadat's peace overtures towards Israel), Syria agreed to send troops to Saudi Arabia as part of a pan-Arab deterrent force. Despite strong support for Saddam Hussein amongst Syria's Palestinians, Assad supported calls for an unconditional Iraqi withdrawal from Kuwait. By December it was estimated that Syria had more than 20,000 troops in Saudi Arabia. Officially, Assad maintained that they were only there to help defend Saudi Arabia from a possible Iraqi invasion, and they did not directly participate in the massive Desert Storm offensive against Iraq in early 1991. However, the very fact that Assad had aligned himself with the US-led anti-Iraq coalition represented a major turning point in Syria's international standing, both in the Arab world and in the West.

Assad's efforts to secure the release of Western hostages held in Lebanon helped to further improve relations with the US and Europe. Britain restored diplomatic relations and, at a time when the break-up of the Soviet Union heralded the end of its economic and military support, Syria began to receive substantial amounts of aid from Europe, Japan and the Gulf states. In Lebanon, Syria gained almost complete freedom to pursue its own ends. In October 1990 Syria suppressed the revolt led by General Michel Aoun and by May 1991 Syria had signed a formal Treaty of Brotherhood, Cooperation and Coordination with Lebanon, followed later that year by a Pact of Defence and Security. Although Syria was implicitly obliged as a result to recognize Lebanon as a sovereign state, it at the same time gave Syria complete control over Lebanon's economy and foreign policy.

Peace process

Perhaps the most important consequence of Syria's stance in the Gulf War was that America began to acknowledge Syria's key role in any future Arab-Israeli peace deal. Following the end of the Gulf War, America intensified diplomatic efforts to initiate negotiations between Israel, the Arab states and Palestinian representatives. In July 1991 Assad agreed to participate in direct negotiations with Israel at a regional peace conference. Although the historic **Madrid conference** of October 1991 was largely symbolic, a series of bilateral negotiations between Syria and Israel followed. From the Syrian point of view, the primary aim of these talks was to secure an unconditional Israeli withdrawal from the Golan Heights (occupied since the 1967 Six Day War) in return for peace. At the same time, however, Assad made it clear that any agreement with Israel would have to form part of a comprehensive settlement in the Middle East. Assad was well aware that Israel hoped to reach separate agreements with each of its neighbours, as it had already done with Egypt, so weakening the collective bargaining power of the Arab world, something which he wished to avoid at all costs.

Assad's decision in 1992 to allow Syrian Jews to leave the country if they wished was seen as a conciliatory signal towards Israel. Though a breakthrough on the issue of the Golan Heights at times seemed imminent, the various rounds of bilateral talks dragged on without any real progress. The signing of the Declaration of Principles (DOP, better known as the **Oslo Accords**) between Israel and the PLO in September 1993 represented a serious setback to Assad's attempts to maintain an united Arab front. Nevertheless, after a meeting between President Clinton and Assad in Geneva on 20 January 1994, Syria indicated its willingness to establish, 'normal, peaceful relations' with Israel. Progress continued until late 1994, when Assad suspended negotiations, ostensibly in protest at Israeli demands for a mutual reduction in the military presence around the Golan, but no doubt also in protest at the signing of a formal peace treaty between Israel and Jordan in October 1994.

Talks resumed in March 1995 and by May a 'framework of understanding on security arrangements' was announced. Syria maintained that any agreement on the Golan Heights would have to be linked to an Israeli withdrawal from southern Lebanon. Eventually the US-brokered plan collapsed after Syria objected to Israeli demands for early warning stations on the Golan. The assassination of Yitzhak Rabin in November 1995 threw the Peace Process into renewed uncertainty. Negotiations resumed with the new Israeli Prime Minister Shimon Peres. Initially, there were promising signs of progress, with Peres advancing a new 10-point plan. However, Hezbollah attacks on Israel from southern Lebanon continued, prompting Peres to retaliate with 'Operation Grapes of Wrath' in April 1996. Apart from the renewed carnage and bloodshed, this resulted in the negotiations stalling once again. In May 1996 the right-wing Likud leader Benjamin Netanyahu was elected prime minister. Netinyahu's uncompromising stance, refusing to cede an inch of the Golan to Syria (not to mention his policy of promoting Jewish settlements in the West Bank and East Jerusalem, and insisting on an extremely narrow interpretation of the Oslo II accords), effectively brought the Peace Process to a complete halt.

Many perceived the result of the 1999 elections in Israel and the victory of Ehud Barak's Labour party as a vote in favour of the Peace Process. However, early optimism that Barak would be able to reach a final agreement with the Palestinians, and even Syria, was soon replaced by a more realistic outlook. Initially, negotiations between Israel and Syria looked promising, but by January 2000 they had been broken off. In March 2000, the US President Bill Clinton and President Assad of Syria met in Geneva in an attempt to restart the talks, but without success.

Under intense pressure at home, Barak continued to press ahead regardless with his plans for a unilateral withdrawal from southern Lebanon. Though he had originally pledged that the withdrawal would be completed by July, events for once moved faster than predicted, and by the end of May 2000 the Israeli army had completely withdrawn from their infamous 'security' zone in southern Lebanon, ending 18 years of occupation.

The death of Hafez al-Assad

Less than three weeks later, on 10 June 2000, the death of President Hafez al-Assad of Syria was announced. The news reverberated around the world, with words such as 'crisis', 'turmoil', 'power struggle' and 'power vacuum' dominating the headlines. For years observers had speculated on the question of what would happen after Assad's death. Many argued that after so many years of dictatorial rule, Syria had none of the political structures necessary to cope with a smooth transition of power. In the event, however, the transition of power proved to be almost completely without problems. Nearly 30 years of relative stability and economic growth had created an increasingly affluent society with a sizeable middle class. The vast majority of Syrians, whether they privately detested Assad's regime or not, had no wish to see the country plunged into the chaos and uncertainty which marked its early years of independence. Nor were they keen to see an Islamic revolution along the lines of Iran.

Bashar al-Assad

Until his death in a car crash in January 1994, the charismatic Basil al-Assad, Hafez al-Assad's eldest son, had clearly been the *heir apparent*, his poster appearing widely alongside that of his father. Instead, his quieter and more retiring younger brother, Bashar al-Assad was recalled from his studies in London, where he was training to be an eye specialist, and sent to a military academy, quickly rising to the position of colonel. He was given responsibility for certain foreign policy issues, including one of the most important: Lebanon. In the months before his father's death, he had been involved in an anti-corruption drive which targeted high-ranking officials in what was seen by many as an attempt to sweep away some of the old guard and establish his own power base in the regime. The military training, foreign policy responsibilities and anti-corruption drive were all clearly part of the grooming process, but when his father died, Bashar was just 34 years old and had held no official position in the state or party hierarchy other than president of the country's computer society.

The first thing the Syrian parliament did in the hours following the death of Hafez al-Assad was to hurriedly amend the constitutions, lowering the minimum age of the president from 40 to 34, before nominating Bashar for the post. Equally urgently, it promoted him to the position of Commander in Chief of the armed forces, thereby giving him absolute power over the military. A week later he was elected general secretary of the Ba'ath party. By July 2000 he had been sworn in as president following a referendum in which 97% of voters, predictably enough, had endorsed his candidacy. On New Year's Day 2001, Bashar married 25-year-old Asma Akhras, a British-born computer science graduate from a prominent London-based Syrian family. Significantly, Akhras is a Sunni Muslim, thus providing something of a bridge between the minority Alawi background of the Assad family and Syria's predominantly Sunni population (see box, page 338).

Recent developments

Bashar's first months in office began with real hope of reform and political freedom. Media restrictions were eased and private publications were allowed to be distributed for the first time in nearly 40 years. The new president also ordered the release of 600 political prisoners. It was said that Bashar was keen to initiate a programme of reforms and modernization similar to that undertaken by King Abdullah II in Jordan. Behind the scenes though, the more conservative elements of the formidable military and secret police as well as the Ba'ath party were alarmed at the progress of modernization and after a brief period of openness Bashar moved more slowly and cautiously in an effort to consolidate his power and not antagonize the more conservative elements of his government. The granting of real political freedom in Syria has yet to be realized.

Since assuming office, regional events have provided a huge test to the young president. Spiralling violence in Israel and The Palestinian Territories led to the eruption of the second intifada and the official suspension of the Peace Process after an emergency summit in Sharm el-Sheikh between Arafat and Barak failed to reach any agreement. The resounding victory of hardliner Ariel Sharon in the Israeli elections of February 2001 hammered a final nail in the coffin for further peace talks between Syria and Israel.

The 9/11 attacks and George Bush's 'war on terror' significantly altered US-Syrian relations. Despite the Ba'ath government's history of dealing heavy-handedly with religious fanaticism on its own turf and the overall peaceful co-existence of religious minorities within Syria, the Syrian government's refusal to expel Palestinian organizations from the country led to the Bush Administration labelling Syria as 'an outpost of Tyranny' and adding Syria to a list of nations in an extended 'axis of evil'. The US-led invasion of neighbouring Iraq on 20 March 2003 and the on-going war there turned relations between Syria and the US even frostier when Syria was accused of failing to prevent, and even helping, foreign fighters slip over their 450-mile border with Iraq to join the insurgency against the coalition troops. In May 2004 the US government imposed economic sanctions against Syria and increasingly Syria found itself out in the cold.

The assassination of Lebanon's popular ex-prime minister, Rafiq Hariri (a vocal opponent of Syrian involvement in Lebanon) in Beirut on 14 February 2005 added to Syria's diplomatic woes. The bombing in downtown Beirut which killed twenty and wounded more than 100 led to massive protests in Lebanon against Syria's continued military presence within the country, and eventually the toppling of Lebanon's pro-Syrian government. It was widely believed within Lebanon that Syria had masterminded the assassination and despite Bashar al-Assad's strong rebuttal the international condemnation that followed resulted in Syria withdrawing its troops from Lebanon in April 2005 for the first time in 29 years. A UN report published in October 2005 implicated Syria and pro-Syrian elements within Lebanon in the assassination though Syria has continued to this day to proclaim its innocence.

The Hariri assassination left Syria further isolated from the west as Europe as well as the US turned their backs on the nation. With few other alternatives Syria began to look towards alliances with other so-called 'rogue states', establishing close ties with Iran and to a lesser level, North Korea. The nation's defiant dialogue with these traditionally anti-Western players led to September 2007's Israeli aerial raid on a military site in northern Syria. A few months later the US would accuse North Korea of trying to help Syria build a nuclear reactor at the bombed site. This strange episode has yet to be explained properly by either side.

As the US continued to appeal for the Syrian border to be tightened so that militants could not enter Iraq, Syria was desperately trying to cope with a massive influx of refugees coming the other way. By July 2007 the number of Iraqi refugees in Syria was estimated at close to 1.5 million, putting a severe strain on the country's public health and education services (which the refugees can access for free) as well as causing the cost of rent, particularly in Damascus where the majority of refugees have taken shelter, to more than double. As the war in Iraq continues to drag on, Syria has repeatedly called for help from the International Community to deal with the refugee burden placed on Iraq's neighbouring states.

Asma al-Assad – more than just the president's wife

She's not the typical spouse of a dictator. Voted French *Elle* magazine's most stylish political first lady in 2008 (beating France's own Carla Bruni to the title), Asma al-Assad (wife of President Bashar al-Assad), is an enigmatic figure in Syria's political landscape. Hailing from a prominent Syrian family, Asma was born and educated in the London suburb of Acton, and went on to gain a BSc with first-class honours at King's College, London. A high-flying investment banking career followed, working for JP Morgan in London, Paris and New York, before her marriage, in 2001, to the newly appointed President of Syria, Bashar al-Assad (who she had first met in London).

As First Lady of Syria, Asma has taken on a prominent public role as a passionate patron of the arts and a champion of development issues, particularly regarding education and the role of women in Syrian society. In a time when Syria is finding its way back onto the world stage this gutsy, intelligent and thoroughly modern woman could be President Assad's best asset in finding a way to bridge his nation's historic arguments with the West.

During the 2006 Israeli war against Hezbollah in Lebanon it was widely noted that Syria managed to keep out of the conflict although Israel's bombardment of the country was thoroughly condemned by President Assad and Hezbollah were roundly supported within Syria. During the conflict an approximate 200,000 Lebanese flocked into Syria seeking temporary shelter putting a further strain on the country's economy. In the aftermath of the war the European Union, and in particular France, have endeavoured to bring Syria back into the fold of the world community. A succession of visits to Damascus by European officials in 2007 signalled a significant thawing of attitudes towards the nation. The July 2008 meeting in Paris of President Assad, French President Nicolas Sarkozy, and the newly elected Lebanese Prime Minister Michel Suleiman ultimately led to diplomatic relations between Syria and Lebanon being established for the first time since both countries achieved independence.

In 2008, for the first time in eight years, Syria and Israel announced that they were resuming peace talks. The indirect talks, mediated by Turkey, were the first ever not to be sponsored by the US and were heralded as a new start by some commentators. Despite the suspension of talks in December 2008 due to the formation of a new Israeli parliament, both sides in recent months have made overtures that they are again ready to go back to the negotiation table.

At home President Bashar al-Assad has begun tentative progress towards reform and liberalization of the state-controlled economy with the opening of the Syrian stock exchange in 2009 and the gradual openings for foreign investment within the country. After nearly 10 years in the job it looks like Bashar al-Assad may finally be stepping out of the long shadow cast by his father.

Religion

Islam

The word Islam translates roughly as 'submission to God'. The religion's two central tenets are embodied in the creed, 'There is no god but Allah and Muhammad is his Prophet' (*Lah Illaha illa 'llah Muhammad Rasulu'llah*), which affirms the belief in the oneness of God and recognizes Muhammad as his divinely appointed messenger.

The *Qur'an* (generally referred to as the Koran in English) is Islam's holiest book. The word translates literally as 'recitation' and unlike the Bible, the Qur'an is considered to be the uncreated (ie direct) word of God, as revealed to Muhammad through *Jibril* (the angel Gabriel). The text consists of 114 *suras* (chapters). Each *sura* is classified as Meccan or Medinan, according to whether it was revealed to Muhammad in Mecca or Medina. Most of the text is written in a kind of rhymed prose known as *saj*, and is considered by Muslims to be inimitable. Each chapter of the Qur'an begins with the words *Bismillah al-Rahman al-Rahim* ('In the name of Allah, the Merciful, the Compassionate'), an invocation which is also heard in numerous everyday situations.

In addition to the Qur'an, there is the *Hadith* body of literature, a record of the sayings and doings of Muhammad and his followers, which forms the basis of Islamic laws (*Shariat*), and precepts. Unlike the Qur'an, the Hadiths are recognized to have been written by men, and are therefore potentially flawed and open to interpretation. Thus they are commonly classified into four major categories according to their trustworthiness: *Sahih* (sound, true, authentic), *Hasan* (fair, good); *Da'if* (weak); and *Saqim* (infirm). The two most revered compilations of Hadiths are those by *al-Bukhari* and *Muslim*. It is in the interpretation of the Hadiths that most of the controversy surrounding certain Islamic laws and their application originates.

While Muhammad is recognized as the founder of the Islamic faith and the principal messenger of God, Muslims also regard him as having been the last in a long line of Prophets, starting with Adam and including both Moses and Jesus. They do not, however, accept Jesus as the son of God, but simply another of God's Prophets. Both Jews and Christians are considered *Ahl-e-Kitab* ('People of the Book'), the Torah and the Gospels being seen as forerunners of the Qur'an in Islamic belief.

Nearly all Muslims accept six basic articles of the Islamic faith: belief in one God; in his angels; in his revealed books; in his Apostles; in the Resurrection and Day of Judgement; and in his predestination of good and evil. Heaven is portrayed in Muslim belief as a paradise filled with sensuous delights and pleasures. Hell, on the other hand, is portrayed as a place of eternal terror and torture, and is seen as the certain fate of all who deny the unity of God.

Islam has no ordained priesthood or clergy. The authority of religious scholars, learned men, imams, judges, etc (referred to collectively as the *Ulema*), derives from their authority to interpret the scriptures, rather than from any defined status within the Islamic community. Many Muslims complain that their growing influence interferes with the direct, personal relationship between man and God which Muhammad originally espoused.

Sunnis and Shi'ites

Following Muhammad's death, Islam divided into two major sects. Muhammad left no sons and therefore no obvious heir, and gave no instructions as to who should succeed him. There were two main contenders: **Abu Bakr**, the father of Aisha (one of Muhammad's wives); and **Ali**, the husband of Muhammad's daughter Fatima and his cousin. In the event Abu Bakr assumed the title of *caliph* (or vice-regent, from *Khalifat rasul-Allah*, 'Successor to the Apostle of God'). He died two years later in AD 634 and was succeeded by **Umar** who was killed in AD 644. **Uthman**, a member of the powerful **Umayyad** family, was chosen to succeed him but proved to be a weak leader and was murdered in AD 656.

At this point the aggrieved Ali managed to assume the title of caliph, thus ousting the Umayyads. However, **Mu'awiya**, the governor of Syria and a member of the Umayyad family, soon rose up in revolt. The two sides met in battle at Siffin on the upper Euphrates, but both eventually agreed to arbitration by delegates from each side. Some members of Ali's camp resented this, seeing such a move as submitting the Will of God to human judgement. Eventually, Ali was murdered by one of his own supporters in AD 661 and Mu'awiya proclaimed himself caliph. Ali's eldest son **Hassan** set up a rival caliphate in Iraq, but was soon persuaded to abdicate. All the same, the seeds of the schism in Islam had already been sown: between the Sunnis (those who accepted the legitimacy of the first three caliphs) and the Shi'ites (those who recognized only Ali as the first legitimate caliph). Later, when Mu'awiya died in AD 680, Ali's second son **Hussein** attempted to revolt against the Umayyads, but was defeated and killed in AD 681 at **Karbala**, providing the Shi'ites with their greatest martyr.

Followers of the **Sunni** sect, generally termed 'Orthodox', account for around 74% of the population in Syria. They base their *Sunna* (path, or practice) on the 'Six Books' of traditions. They are organized into four orthodox schools or rites named after their founders, each having equal standing. The *Hanafi* is the most common in Syria, and the most moderate. The others are the *Shafii*, *Maliki* and *Hanbali*, the latter being the strictest. Many Muslims today prefer to avoid identification with a particular school, preferring to call themselves simply Sunni.

Followers of the **Shi'ite** (or Shia) sect account for only a tiny minority of the population in Syria. Aside from the dispute over the succession of Muhammad, Sunnis and Shi'ites do not generally differ on fundamental issues since they draw from the same ultimate sources. However, there are important differences of interpretation which partly derive from the practice of *ijtihad* (the exercise of independent judgement) amongst Shi'ites, as opposed to *taqlid* (the following of ancient models) as adhered to by Sunnis. Thus Shi'ites divest far more power in their *imams*, accepting their role as an intermediary between God and man and basing their law and practice on the teachings of the Imams.

The majority of Shi'ites are known as *Ithna asharis* or 'Twelvers', since they recognize a succession of 12 imams. They believe that the last imam, who disappeared in AD 878, is still alive and will reappear soon before the Day of Judgement as the *Mahdi* (one who is rightly guided), who will rule by divine right.

Ismailis

The Ismailis are an offshoot of mainstream Shi'ite Islam. Following the death of the Sixth Shi'ite Imam Ja'far al-Sadiq in AD 765, there was a dispute as to the rightful heir to the title of Imam, with his eldest son Ismail being passed over by the majority of Shi'ites in favour of his younger son Musa al-Kazim. The Ismailis, however, recognized Ismail as the rightful imam. They are also known as *Sab'iya* or 'Seveners' since, unlike the Twelver Shi'ites, they recognize only seven principal imams after the death of the Prophet Muhammad. The philosophy of the Ismailis is a largely esoteric one, and a further name for them is the *Batiniyya* because of their emphasis on an esoteric (*batin*) interpretation of the Qur'an.

The Five Pillars of Islam

There are five practices or *Akran*, known as the Five Pillars of Islam, which are generally accepted as obligatory duties for Muslims.

Shahada: the profession of faith ('There is no god but Allah...'), which also forms the basis of the call to prayer made by the *muezzin* of the mosque.

Salat: the ritual of prayers, carried out five times a day at prescribed times; in the early morning before the sun has risen above the horizon, in the early afternoon when the sun has passed its zenith, later when the sun is halfway towards setting, immediately after sunset, and in the evening before retiring to bed. Prayers can be carried out anywhere, and simply involve facing towards the *Ka'ba* in Mecca and prostrating before God while reciting verses of the Qur'an.

Sawm: the 30 days of fasting during the month of Ramadan, the ninth month of the Muslim lunar calendar. It is observed as a fast from sunrise to sunset each day by all Muslims, although there are provisions for special circumstances.

Zakat: the compulsory payment of alms. In early times this was collected by officials of the Islamic state, and was devoted to the relief of the poor, aid to travellers and other charitable purposes. In many Muslim communities, the fulfilment of this religious obligation is nowadays left to the conscience of the individual.

Hajj: the pilgrimage to Mecca. Every Muslim, circumstances permitting, is obliged to perform this pilgrimage at least once in his lifetime and having accomplished it, may assume the title of *Hajji*.

Their theology is based on a cyclical theory of history centred around the number seven, which is considered to be of enormous significance. They are less restrictive in their customs and practice, allowing much greater freedom to women. Likewise, prayers are not linked to a specific formula. The mosque is replaced by a *jamat khana* which also serves as a community centre. Their spiritual head is the Agha Khan, who is considered a direct descendant of the Prophet Muhammad through his daughter Fatima.

First founded in the eighth century, they only really began to make their presence felt in North Africa from the beginning of the 10th century, going on to conquer Egypt in AD 969 and establish the powerful Fatimid Dynasty (named after the Prophet's daughter, Fatima) which flourished for the next two centuries, extending at the height of its power to include Egypt, Syria, North Africa, Sicily, the Red Sea coast of Africa, Yemen and the Hejaz region of Arabia (including the holy cities of Mecca and Medina).

However, under the Fatimids, the radical doctrines of the Ismailis (the source of their initial appeal) were gradually replaced by a more conservative outlook better suited to the responsibilities of such a powerful dynasty. This led to ideological conflicts which culminated in a major internal schism amongst the Ismailis. After the death of the eighth Fatimid caliph Al-Mustansir in 1094, there was a dispute over his succession. The conservative elements within the court, led by the Commander of the Armies who had risen to a position of great personal power, installed Al-Mustansir's younger and therefore more easily influenced son Al-Mustali as caliph, disinheriting his older son Nizar, who was subsequently killed after attempting to revolt.

The followers of Al-Mustali became known as *Mustalians* and the followers of Nizar as *Nizaris*. The Fatimid Dynasty, although it continued to rule in Egypt until 1171, was in terminal decline, finally being formally abolished by Salah-ud Din who restored Sunni orthodoxy and went on to establish the Ayyubid Dynasty. After the schism of 1094, the Mustalians (many of whom disowned the declining Fatimid Dynasty) established themselves on the outer peripheries of the Islamic world (notably in Yemen and India, where they are known today as *Boharis*). The Nizaris, meanwhile, began a period of intense political and doctrinal development in Persia, one outcome of which was the formation of the much feared **Assassins** who established themselves in Syria from the beginning of the 12th century. Small numbers of Nizari Ismailis are still found in Syria, in Masyaf, to the west of Hama, and in Salamiyeh, to the southeast.

Alawis

Like the Ismailis, the Alawis are an offshoot of mainstream Shi'ite Islam, although very little is known about their origins, beliefs or practices. According to their own traditions they originated from the Arabian Peninsula, moving to the Jebel Sinjar, a mountainous region between the Tigris and Euphrates, before arriving in Syria. The founder of their religion, Muhammad Ibn Nusayr, is thought to have developed its basic tenets in the ninth century, preaching that the One God was inexpressible and unknowable, but that a hierarchy of divine beings emanated from him, with Ali representing the highest of these. The term 'Alawi' (or 'Alawite') dates from the French Mandate period, meaning literally 'Followers of Ali'. Previously they were known as *Ansaris* or *Nusayris* after Muhammad Ibn Nusayr, and both names are used to describe Syria's coastal mountains (Jebel Ansariye or Jebel Nusayri), where they settled when they came to Syria.

Their doctrines are said to contain elements of Phoenician paganism, Manichaeism, Zoroastrianism and Christian Gnosticism. The Christian element, for example the belief in the symbolic significance of bread and wine and their observance of many Christian festivals, is strongly emphasized by many commentators. Inevitably for such an esoteric religion, where even amongst themselves only a few are full initiates, the numerous stories surrounding their beliefs and practices all to a greater or lesser extent combine elements of truth and fabrication. Those emanating from their orthodox Sunni critics have tended to be the most fantastic and far-fetched, encompassing all manner of sexual perversions and secretive ritual practices.

The Islamic doctrine of *Taqiya* (concealing or disguising one's religion, especially in times of persecution or danger) provided the key to their survival and perhaps goes a long way to explaining the supposed syncretic nature of their beliefs. In the eyes of the Sunni orthodoxy of the Medieval period, they were nothing short of heretical, and as such their religion was widely condemned as an abomination to Islam.

Certainly their history is one of constant persecution. From the time of the First Crusade (1098), their mountain strongholds were seized by the Crusaders, while early in the 12th century they faced similar encroachment from the Ismailis. Salah ud-Din, when he swept through the mountains in his campaign of 1188 forced them to pay him a hefty annual tribute. The Mamluk sultans inflicted heavy losses on them, according to the Muslim chronicler Ibn Battuta, massacring 20,000, and tried forcibly to convert them to Sunni Islam, making them build mosques in their villages, to which they supposedly responded by using them as cattle sheds. The oppression continued, more or less unabated, throughout the Ottoman period, mostly through the imposition of punitive taxes.

Remarkably, however, from a position as late as the 1920s of almost total social exclusion, a poor, largely uneducated rural community discriminated against and isolated in a harsh mountainous environment, the Alawis underwent a dramatic transformation. The French courted them as potential allies, giving them a separate 'enclave' in the mountains around Lattakia where they were concentrated, For the first time after centuries of relentless oppression they were presented with a unique opportunity, and it was one of which they made every use. In a total reversal of fortunes, today the Alawi totally dominate political and military hierarchy in the modern state of Syria (President Bashar al-Assad is himself an Alawi). The Alawi number around one million in Syria, representing nearly 12% of the total population. Over three-quarters of these live in the province of Lattakia where they form a two-thirds majority.

Druze

The Druze represent an offshoot of the Ismailis. Their religion developed in the 11th century AD, during the reign of the Cairo-based Fatimid caliph Al-Hakim (AD 996-1021). Al-Hakim allowed himself to be declared a divine representation of God and substituted his own name for that of Allah in mosque services. This blasphemous act, together with heretical decrees such as banning people from fasting during Ramadan or undertaking the pilgrimage to Mecca, earned him the condemnation of mainstream Ismailis of the Fatimid court. Indeed his disappearance in 1021, taken by his followers as an act of divine *ghayba* (concealment) pending his eventual return, was probably the result of a discreet assassination.

In the meantime one of his closest disciples, Muhammad Ibn Ismail al-Darazi, had left Egypt and began spreading the new faith in Syria, where he found a more receptive audience amongst a people who had already been exposed to various heterodox interpretations of Islam. The term 'Druze' is in fact an Anglicized form of the Arabic word *durzi*, which was in turn derived from this missionary's name. As with the Alawis, very little is known about Druze beliefs or practices. Indeed, even the Druze themselves are divided between the *juhhal* (ignorant) and the *uqqal* (intelligent), with only the latter being fully initiated into the doctrines of the faith. The Druze form an extremely tight-knit community, only ever marrying amongst themselves, and are said to have ceased accepting new members into their religion 20 years after the death of Al-Hakim. Mainstream Islam tends to regard the Druze either as a heretical offshoot or else as having nothing whatsoever to do with the Islamic faith.

Historically, the Druze were concentrated in the Lebanon mountains, particularly the Chouf and Metn. However, following the 1860 massacre of as many as 10,000 Maronites at the hands of the Druze and the subsequent French intervention, many of them migrated to Syria, settling primarily in the Hauran. Today in Syria they number around 430,000 but make up just 3% of the population.

Sufis

Sufism is the mystical aspect of Islam, often described as the 'science of the heart'. The word *Sufi* is most probably derived from the Arabic word *suf* meaning 'wool', a reference to the woollen garments worn by the early Sufis. The Sufis do not represent a separate sect of Islam; rather they aspire to transcend sects, emphasizing the importance of personal spiritual development, to be found only through the Qur'an.

Nevertheless, various different Sufi orders did emerge, the most famous of them being the *Mawlawiyya* or **Whirling Dervishes**. This Sufi order originated in Turkey, inspired by the 13th-century mystical poet Jalal ud-Din Rumi, and is best known for the whirling dance which forms part of their worship. The dance is performed to music and involves the chanting of the *dhikr*, a kind of litany in which the name of God is repeated over and over again. The Sufis had considerable influence in Syria. The famous Sufi mystic, Mohi ud-Din Ibn al-Arabi, is buried in Damascus and his tomb remains an important pilgrimage site for Sufis.

Christianity

Christian theology has its roots in Judaism, with its belief in one God, the eternal creator of the universe. Jesus, whom Christians believe was the Messiah or 'Christ' (literally 'Anointed One') and the son of God, was born in the village of Bethlehem, some 20 km south of Jerusalem. Very little is known about his early life except that he was brought up in a devout Jewish family. At the age of 30, he gathered a small group of followers and began to preach in the region between the Dead Sea and the Sea of Galilee. Two years later he was crucified in Jerusalem on the charge that his claim to be the son of God was blasphemous.

The New Testament of the Bible, which, together with the Old Testament, is the text to which Christians refer to as the ultimate scriptural authority, consists of four 'Gospels' (literally 'Good News'), and a series of letters by early Christians outlining the nature of Christian life.

Much of the early development of the Christian church took place within present-day Syria. At first, Christians faced persecution within the Roman Empire, but gradually, as the faith spread, it became more widely accepted. In AD 313 the emperor Constantine issued the Edict of Milan, which formerly recognized the right of Christians to practice their faith, and in AD 380 the emperor Theodosius declared it the official religion of the Roman Empire.

Soon afterwards, the Roman Empire was formally divided into East and West, with Constantinople (formerly Byzantium and today Istanbul) becoming the capital of the Eastern Roman Empire, better known as the Byzantine Empire. Under Byzantine rule, Christianity in the Middle East divided into numerous different churches. These different branches of the church arose out of somewhat obscure theological disputes over the nature of Christ, but also reflected the power struggles going on within the empire. Other regional centres of Christianity also developed their own theological doctrines and separate churches.

The orthodox **(Dyophysite)** view was that Christ was of two natures, divine and human, while the alternative view, that of the **Monophysites**, was that he was of one nature – purely divine. This latter interpretation was condemned as a heresy by the Council of Chalcedon in AD 451. The **Monothelite** doctrine, that Christ had two natures but one will, was seen as something of a compromise, and adopted by the Byzantine emperor Heraclius (AD 610-641) as a means of providing a solution to the Dyophysite versus Monophysite schism which was threatening to tear the church apart. In AD 680 the Sixth Ecumenical Council in turn condemned the Monothelite doctrine as heresy.

In the East, those who adhered to the orthodox (Dyophysite) view became known as **Melkites** (or Melchites), meaning literally 'King's Men', in reference to the fact that they maintained their allegiance to the Byzantine emperor in Constantinople. The Byzantine emperors, meanwhile, regarded themselves as defenders of the **Orthodox** Church. Followers of the Monophysite, Monothelite and other 'heterodox' (as opposed to orthodox) theologies founded their own churches, including: the Antioch based **Syrian** or **Jacobite** church, named after Jacobus Bardaeus, a sixth-century monk responsible for organizing the Monophysites of Syria into a church; the Egyptian **Coptic** church based at Alexandria; the **Armenian (Gregorian)** church; the **Nestorian (Chaldean)** church, founded by Nestorius of Cilicia in the fifth century; and the **Maronite** church which emerged in the seventh century.

To begin with, the Eastern Church of Constantinople and the Catholic (Latin) Church of Rome existed in broad, if at times uneasy, agreement, but over the centuries doctrinal differences intensified, culminating in the great schism of 1054, with the Eastern Church refusing to accept the supremacy of the Pope and recognizing instead the Patriarch of Constantinople as its head. Later, many of the independent churches in the east renounced the doctrines regarded as heretical by the Roman Catholic Church and acknowledged the supremacy of the Pope. They became known as **Uniate** Churches, but were allowed to retain their respective languages, rites and canon law in accordance with the terms of their union. At the same time, the independent churches continued to exist in parallel, with the exception of the Maronite church, which became fully united with the Roman Catholic Church. Thus today, there is in the Middle East the **Greek Orthodox** and **Greek Catholic** church, the **Syrian Orthodox** and **Syrian Catholic** church, and the **Armenian Orthodox** and **Armenian Catholic** church. In addition, the **Roman Catholic** church is itself represented. Later arrivals on the scene were the **Protestant** and **Anglican** churches, which began preaching in the Middle East during the 19th century.

In Syria, Christians account for around 10% of the population. The Greek Orthodox and Greek Catholic churches are the most important, although the Armenian Catholic church forms an important and tightly knit community, particularly in the city of Aleppo. There are also small communities of Armenian Orthodox, Syrian Orthodox/Catholics, Maronites, Roman Catholics, Protestants and Anglicans.

People

Arabs

The vast majority of the people of Syria can be termed Arab, though the term is an extremely broad one, encompassing many different religious and ethnic groups. It is helpful, therefore, to look first at exactly what is meant by the term 'Arab', and how its meaning has evolved over time.

The earliest known use of the word comes from an inscription of the Assyrian king Shamaneser III, which refers to the *Arabi*. Thereafter it appears frequently, either as *Arabi* or *Arabu*, in Assyrian and Babylonian inscriptions. 'Arab' first appears in the Bible (2 Chronicles 17:11), although it has been suggested that the 'mixed multitude' referred to in Exodus 12:38 as having accompanied the Israelites into the wilderness could equally be translated as 'Arabs' (in Hebrew, the word for each is *erev* and *arav* respectively, but in their written forms the vowels do not appear). More commonly, however, the Bible makes reference to the Ishmaelites. In Islamic and Hebrew tradition, the Arabs and the Hebrews are both descendants of the prophet Abraham, the Arabs through his son Ishmael and the Hebrews through his son Isaac. The birth of Isaac to Abraham's elderly wife Sarah meant that Ishmael (born to Abraham's concubine Hagar) was superseded as Abraham's natural heir, whose descendants would inherit the Promised Land. Ishmael instead went out into the desert (Genesis 21).

The traditional definition of an Arab, as reflected in the biblical interpretation, was a nomadic inhabitant of the deserts of northern and central Arabia. Indeed, the word 'Arab' is thought to have been derived from a Semitic root related to nomadism, perhaps the word *abhar* (literally 'to move' or 'to pass'), from which the word 'Hebrew' is also probably derived. The settled inhabitants of the rain-fed uplands of present-day Yemen could also be termed Arabs, and over the centuries many of the nomadic peoples traditionally recognized as Arabs themselves adopted a settled life based on agriculture and animal husbandry, but the broad definition of an Arab was at this stage fairly clear.

The definition of an Arab became more complicated with the arrival of Islam. The Islamic faith as revealed by the Prophet Muhammad was clearly intended, initially at least, specifically for the nomadic tribes of the Arabian Peninsula: ie the Arabs. However, the conquests of the seventh century resulted in the creation of a vast Arab Empire based on the precepts of Islam. Thus, Arab and Muslim identities became very closely intertwined, though the two were never synonymous.

Although Muslim and Arab identities came to be very closely identified with each other (at least by the Sunni Muslim majority in the region), there existed sizable minorities of Arab Christians (and indeed Jews), who had everything in common with their Muslim counterparts in terms of history, culture and language, but little in terms of religion. Ironically, the Christian Arabs were the first to articulate the concept of Arab nationalism, because they avoided the trap of confusing Arab and Muslim identities.

Thus the traditional definition of an Arab, as a nomadic inhabitant of the deserts of northern and central Arabia, was rendered inadequate by the 'arabization' of a far larger area, and much of what we today recognize as Arab culture and society has little in common with that of the nomadic desert tribes. Likewise, the tendency of mainstream Sunni Muslims to identify 'Arab' with 'Muslim' is flawed even within the Arab world, given the existence of non-Muslim Arab minorities, and completely untenable when you take into consideration the spread of Islam far beyond the bounds of the Arab world. Today, perhaps the nearest you can get to a definition of 'Arab' is a native speaker of the Arabic language, though this remains a very loose definition, Arabic being the native tongue of around 120 million people across the Middle East and North Africa. As the language of Islam, it is also known to millions more Muslims outside the Arab world.

Ethnic minorities

There are several different ethnic minorities within Syria that are specifically non-Arab, though, as pointed out above, there are various ethnic groups which can also be defined as 'Arab'.

Armenians

Syria's Armenian population is for the most part descended from the refugees who fled the Armenian genocide in Ottoman Turkey during the First World War. Between one and a half and two million Armenians are thought to have perished as a result of the genocide. In Aleppo many found a safe haven, and today whole quarters of Aleppo are dominated by Armenians who, as in the past, trade in textiles and fabrics, the distinctive Armenian script gracing their shop signs. There are also considerable numbers of Armenians in Deir ez-Zor and Hassakeh (the Jezira region witnessed the massacre of many Armenians at the hands of the Turks). The majority of Armenians in Syria are Christian (Armenian Orthodox or Armenian Catholic).

Kurds

The Kurdish people represent the single largest minority group in Syria, accounting for around 9% of the total population. They are concentrated to the north of Aleppo and in the north-eastern Jezira region bordering Turkey and Iran. The Kurdish people as a whole form an ethnic group straddling Syria, Turkey, Iraq and Iran. After the First World War, they were denied their promised homeland of Kurdistan and today continue to exist as a 'people without a country'. In Iraq and Turkey they have faced continual persecution as a result of their ongoing struggle for autonomy. In Syria the Kurds have fared somewhat better, although any possibility of freedom of political expression is out of the question.

Palestinians

In Syria, there are estimated to be more than 378,000 Palestinians, the majority of whom are concentrated in and around Damascus. They began arriving after the 1947-1949 Arab-Israeli War and then in greater numbers during the late 1960s and early 1970s. The majority are Sunni Muslim.

Other

Syria is also home to small numbers of **Circassians** (non-Arab Muslim refugees from the Russian Caucasus who came to Syria in the 19th and 20th centuries) and **Turks**. In addition, there is still a tiny community of **Jews**, numbering less than 100 and concentrated mostly in Damascus, with a few in Aleppo and Qamishle. Before 1948 there were around 30,000 Jews living in Syria, but the majority fled when the state of Israel was created. In 1992 those that remained (around 3500) were given permission to leave the country if they wished, an offer which the majority took up.

Books

There is a wealth of books on all aspects of the Middle East, in fact probably enough to fill a few libraries and keep you going for a lifetime. The following is a small selection. Many contain more detailed bibliographies for those who wish to explore further.

History and politics

Robert Fisk *The Great War for Civilization: The Conquest of the Middle East*, Harper Collins, 2006. Highly readable history of the Middle East since the First World War combined with Fisk's stories from the frontline as a reporter.
Robert Fisk *Pity the Nation: Lebanon at War*, OUP, 1997. Moving account based on Fisk's reporting of Lebanon's civil war, internationally acclaimed and compelling reading.
Albert Hourani *A History of the Arab Peoples*, Faber and Faber, 1991. Comprehensive and highly regarded work which focuses as much on the social as the political history of the Arabs.

Bernard Lewis *From Babel to Dragomans: Interpreting the Middle East*, OUP, 2004. Selection of the author's writings on the Middle East; covering politics, history and religion in the region.
Amin Maalouf *The Crusades Through Arab Eyes*, Al Saqi, 1984. Original account of the Crusades from the Arab perspective.
Peter Mansfield *The Arabs*, Penguin, 1992. Thorough overview of the history of the region.

Literature

Ulfat Idilbi *Sabriya: Damascus Bitter Sweet*, Quartet Books, 1995. Novel set in 1920s French Mandate Syria.
Ammar Abdulhamid *Menstruation*, Saqi, 2001. Explores sexuality themes and clashes within a strict religious framework.
Rafik Schami *The Dark Side of Love*, Arabia Books, 2009. Love saga of interwoven characters set in Damascus.

Religion

The Koran, Penguin, 1993. Well regarded translation of the Qur'an.

Karen Armstrong *Muhammad: A biography of the Prophet*, Phoenix Press, 2001. Highly readable biography of the founder of Islam.

Karen Armstrong *Islam: A Short History*, Weidenfield and Nicolson, 2005. Concise and accessible examination of Islam.

Bernard Lewis *The Assassins*, Al Saqi, 1985. Detailed and scholarly work examining the origins and history of the Assassins.

Edward Said *Covering Islam* Vintage, 1997. Examines the basis of Western stereotypes of Islam.

Travel

Gertrude Bell *The Desert and the Sown* (various imprints). Bell's classic account of her journey through the Middle East at the turn of the century.

Agatha Christie *Come, tell me how you live: An Archaeological Memoir* (various imprints). Entertaining account of Christie's time on an archaeological dig with her husband.

William Dalrymple *From the Holy Mountain: A Journey in the Shadow of Byzantium*, Flamingo, 1998, Highly readable account of a journey through the Christian world of the Middle East.

Marius Kociejowski *The Street Philosopher and the Holy Fool: A Syrian Journey*, Stroud, 2005. Evocative account of the author's journeys to Syria.

TE Lawrence *Seven Pillars of Wisdom* (various imprints). Lawrence's own account of the Arab Revolt and his part in it. Despite his somewhat impenetrable style, the book is a compelling one.

Colin Thubron *Mirror to Damascus*, Arrow Books, 1990. A poetic biography of this ancient city.

Contents

Arabic words and phrases

Learning just a few basic words and phrases of Arabic is not at all difficult and will make an enormous difference to your travelling experience. Being able to greet people and respond to greetings, point at something in the souqs, ask 'how much?' and understand the reply – such simple things are rewarding, enjoyable and of practical benefit. The greatest hurdle most people face is with pronunciation. Arabic employs sounds which simply do not occur in English, so your tongue and mouth have to learn to form new, unfamiliar sounds. With a little patience, though, you can soon pick up the correct pronunciation of most words (or at least good enough to make yourself understood). The following is just a very brief introduction and the Arabic transliterations are simplistic: the bottom line is that there is no substitute for listening to and practicing with a native speaker. Once you are in the Middle East you will have plenty of opportunities to do this. But before you go, language books and tapes can get you started.

Greetings and pleasantries

hello (informal 'hi')	*marhaba*	fine, good, well	*qwayees*
hello ('welcome')	*ahlan wa sahlan* (or just *ahlan*)	please	*min fadlak/fadlik (m/f)*
hello ('peace be upon you')	*asalaam alaikum*	thank you	*shukran*
		thank you very much	*shukran jazeelan*
hello (response)	*wa alaikum as-salaam*	you're welcome	*afwan*
		sorry	*aassif*
goodbye	*ma'a salaama*	no problem	*ma fesh mushkilay*
good morning	*subah al-khair*	Congratulations!	*mabrouk!*
good morning (response)	*subah an-noor*	Thank God!	*il hamdullilah!*
good evening	*musa al-khair*	What is your name?	*shoo ismak/ismik? (m/f)*
good evening (response)	*musa an-noor*		
good night	*tusba allah khair*	My name is...	*ismi...*
good night (response)	*wa inta min ahalu*	Where are you from?	*min wain inta/inti? (m/f)*
How are you?	*kif halak/halik?* or *kifak/kifik (m/f)*	I am a tourist	*ana siyaha*

Useful expressions

If God wills it	*inshallah*	expensive	*ghaali*
yes	*naam/aiwa*	cheap	*rakhees*
no	*laa*	enough, stop	*hallas*
Where is .....?	*wain...?*	let's go	*yallah*
How far?	*kam kilometre?*	good	*qwayees*
Is there/do you have...?	*fi....?*	bad	*mish qwayees/ wahish*
There is	*fi*		
There is not, there's none	*ma fi*	I understand	*ana afham*
How much?	*bikam/adesh?*	I don't understand	*mish afham*

Getting around

airport	*al matar*	straight ahead	*ala tuul*
bus	*al bas/autobas*	tourist office	*makhtab siyaha*
bus station	*mahattat al bas/ garagat*	map	*khareeta*
		city centre/old city	*medina*
taxi	*taxi*	hotel	*funduq*
service taxi	*servees*	restaurant	*mataam/restauran*
train station	*mahattat al atr*	museum	*matthaaf*
car	*sayara*	bank	*masraf/banque*
left	*shimal*	chemist	*agzakhana*
right	*yameen*		

Documents

passport office	*makhtab al jawazaat*	name	*ism*
passport	*jawas as safar*	date of birth	*tarikha al mulid*
visa	*sima*	place of birth	*makan al mulid*
permit	*tasrih*	nationality	*jensiya*

Glossary

A

ablaq alternating courses of contrasting stone, typical of Mameluke and Ottoman architecture (Arabic)

acanthus a conventionalized representation of a leaf, used especially to decorate Corinthian columns

acropolis fortified part of upper city, usually containing a political, administrative, or religious complex

adyton inner sancturay of the *cella* of a temple

agora open meeting place or market

amphora Greek or Roman vessel with a narrow neck and two handles, tapering at the base, used for transporting wine or oil

architrave lowest division of an *entablature* or decorated moulding round arch or window

apodyterium changing rooms of a Roman baths complex

apse semi-circular niche; in a Byzantine *basilica* this is always at the eastern end and contains the altar

atrium courtyard of a Roman house or forecourt of a Byzantine church

B

bab gate (Arabic)

barbican an outer defence, usually in the form of a tower, at the entrance to a castle

barrel vault a vault in the shape of a half-cylinder

basilica a Roman building/Byzantine church of rectangular plan with a central *nave* flanked by two side aisles and usually with an *apse* at one end

bastion strongpoint or fortified tower in fortifcations

beit house (Arabic)

bimaristan hospital, medical school (Arabic)

bir well (Arabic)

birkat pool or reservoir

burj tower (Arabic)

C

caldarium hot room in Roman baths complex

capital crowning feature of a column or pier

caravanserai see *khan* (Arabic)

cardo maximus main street of a Roman city, usually running north-south and lined with colonnades

castrum fortified Roman camp

cavea semi-circular seating in auditorium of Roman theatre

cella the inner sanctuary of a temple

chancel raised area around altar in a church

clerestory upper row of windows providing light to the nave of a church

colonette small, slender *column*

colonnade row of *columns* carrying *entablature*, or arches

column upright member, circular in plan and usually slightly tapering

crenellations battlements

cruciform cross-shaped

cuneiform script consisting of wedge-shaped indentations, usually made into a clay tablet, first developed by the Sumerians

cupola dome

D

decumanus major east-west cross-street in Roman city, intersecting with the *cardo maximus*

deir monastery (Arabic)

donjon (or keep) main fortified tower and last refuge of a castle

diwan see *iwan*

E

entablature horizontal stone element in Greek/Roman architecture connecting a series of columns, usually decorated with a cornice, frieze and architrave

exedra a recess in a wall or line of columns, usually semi-circular and traditionally lined with benches

F

forum open meeting place or market

fosse ditch or trench outside fortifications

frieze central section of *entablature* in classical architecture, or more generally any carved relief

frigidarium cold room in Roman baths complex

G

glacis (or *talus*) smooth sloping surface forming defensive fortification wall

groin vault two intersecting *barrel vaults* forming ceiling over square chamber, also called a cross vault

H

hammam bath house (Arabic)

haremlek private/family quarters of an Ottoman house (Arabic)

hypogeum underground burial chamber

I

iconostasis screen decorated with icons separating the *nave* and *chancel* of a Byzantine or Orthodox rite church

iwan (or *diwan/liwan*) open reception area off courtyard with high arched opening (Arabic)

J

Jami' Masjid Friday congregational mosque (Arabic)

jebel (or *jabal*) hill, mountain (Arabic)

K

kalybe open-fronted shrine with niches for statuary

keep see *donjon*

khan hostel and warehouse for caravans and traders consisting of walled compound with accommodation, stables/ storage arranged around a central courtyard (Arabic)

kufic early angular form of Arabic script (named after Kufa in southern Iraq)

L

lintel horizontal beam above doorway supporting surmounting masonry

liwan see *iwan*

loculus (plural *loculi*) shelf-like niche in wall of burial chamber for sarcophogus/ corpse

M

madrassa Islamic religious school (Arabic)

Mar Saint (Arabic)

maristan see *bimaristan*

masjid mosque (Arabic)

medina old city (Arabic)

mihrab niche, usually semi-circular and vaulted with a semi-dome, indicating

direction of prayer (towards Mecca) (Arabic)
minaret tower of mosque
minbar pulpit in mosque for preaching, to right of *mihrab*
muezzin man who recites the call to prayer (Arabic)

N

narthex entrance hall to *nave* of church
nave the central rectangular hall of basilica/church, usually lined with colonnades to separate it from the side-aisles
necropolis ancient burial ground
noria waterwheel (Arabic)
nymphaeum Roman monumental structure surrounding a fountain (dedicated to nymphs), usually with niches for statue

O

odeon small theatre or concert hall
orchestra paved semi-circular area between stage and *cavea* of Roman theatre

P

pediment triangular, gabled end to a classical building
peristyle colonnaded corridor running around the edges of a courtyard
pier vertical roof support
pilaster engaged pier or column projecting slightly from wall
portico colonnaded porch over outer section of doorway
praetorium Roman governor's residence or barracks
propylaeum monumental entrance to a temple

Q

qadi Muslim judge (Arabic)
qalat castle, fortress (Arabic)
qibla marking direction of prayer, indicated in a mosque by the *mihrab* (Arabic)
qubba dome (Arabic)

R

revetment facing or retaining wall in fortification

ribat Muslim pigrim hostel or hospice

S

sacristy small room in a church for storing sacred vestments, vessels, etc
salemlek area of Ottoman house for receiving guests
sanjak subdivision of an Ottoman *vilayet*
scaenae frons decorated stone façade behind the stage area of Roman theatre
seraya (or *serai*) palace (Arabic)
soffit the underside of a lintel
souq market (Arabic)
stela (plural *stelae*) narrow upright slab of stone, usually inscribed

T

talus see *glacis*
tariq road
tell artificial mound
temenos sacred walled temple enclosure surrounding *cella*
tepidarium warm room of a Roman baths complex
tessera (plural *tesserae*) small square pieces of stone used to form mosaic
tetrapylon arrangement of columns (usually four groups of four) marking major street intersections (eg between *cardo maximus* and *decumanus*) in Roman city
transept transverse section between nave and apse of church, giving a cruciform (cross) shape instead of basic rectangular shape
triclinium dining room of Roman house
tympanum the space enclosed in a *pediment*, or between a lintel and the arch above

V

via sacra sacred way used by pilgrims to approach shrine, etc
vilayet Ottoman adminsistrative province
vomitorium (plural *vomitoria*) entrance/exit to the seating area, or *cavea*, of a Roman theatre

W

wadi valley or watercourse with seasonal stream (Arabic)

Arabic cuisine → *For food and drink, see page 21.*

Bread

Known in Arabic as *khubz* or *eish* (literally 'life'), bread is the mainstay of the Arabic diet. It is baked unleavened (without yeast) in flat round discs and accompanies just about every meal or snack. Often it serves as an eating implement, or is rolled up with a filling inside to make a 'sandwich' snack. When it is fresh it is delicious although, surprisingly for a region where so much of it is consumed, it has often been standing about for the best part of a day by the time it reaches your plate.

Mezze dishes

Perhaps the most attractive feature of Arabic cuisine is the *mezze*. When done properly, this consists of a spread of numerous small dips, salads and nibbles of fresh raw vegetables, olive, etc, which are served as an extended starter course and, if the company is not teetotal, usually washed down with plenty of beer or arak. To fully appreciate a proper *mezze* spread you really need to be in a group of several people or you'll never get around the array of dishes; it also works out very reasonably when divided amongst several people. For smaller numbers you can just ask for a selection. If you do not want a full meal, you can always do away with the main courses and just concentrate on the *mezze*. Many of the items listed below are also served individually as a side dish in snack places and simple restaurants, or indeed as snacks in themselves. A selection of the more popular *mezze* dishes is given here.

baba ganoush (*moutabbal*) chargrilled eggplant (aubergine), tahini, olive oil, lemon juice and garlic blended into a smooth paste and served as a dip

falafel small deep-fried balls of ground, spiced chickpeas. Very popular, both as part of a *mezze*, and as the basis of one of Syria most ubiquitous snacks (see below)

fattoush salad of toasted croutons, cucumbers, tomatoes, onion and mint

hummus purée of chickpeas, tahini, lemon and garlic, served as a dip with bread

kibbeh ground lamb and bulghur (cracked wheat) meatballs stuffed with olives and pine nuts and fried or baked

kibbeh nayeh raw kibbeh, eaten like steak tartare

loubieh (*fasulya*) cooked French beans with tomatoes onion and garlic, served hot as a stew or cold as a kind of salad

mouhammara mixture of ground nuts, olive oil, cumin and chillis, eaten with bread

rocca rocket salad

tabouleh finely chopped salad of burghul wheat, tomatoes, onions, mint and parsley

taratour thick mayonnaise of puréed pine nuts, garlic and lemon, used as a dip

warak enab (*warak dawali*) vine leaves stuffed with rice and vegetables

'Main' meat dishes

So-called 'main' courses are more limited and consist primarily of meat dishes (usually lamb or chicken). Note that many listed below are also often served as snacks.

bamia baby okra and lamb in a tomato stew

bukhari rice lamb and rice stir-fried with onion, lemon, carrot and tomato

farouj roast chicken. Everywhere you go throughout Syria you will find simple restaurants, snack places and shops with roasting ovens outside containing several spits of roasting chickens. The standard portion is a half chicken (*nuss farouj*), sometimes served with a small portion of garlic dip and a few pickled vegetables and chips

kebab in Syria, if you ask for 'kebab', you will most likely be offered *kofte kebab*, though strictly speaking *kebab* is just chunks of meat char-grilled on a skewer

kofte kebab minced meat and finely chopped onions, herbs and spices pressed onto a skewer and chargrilled. You often order by weight

kouzi whole lamb baked over rice so that it soaks up the juice of the meat

mensaf a traditional Bedouin dish, consisting of lamb cooked with herbs in a yoghurt sauce and served on a bed of rice with pine nuts. You are most likely to come across this dish at Palmyra

saleek lamb and rice dish cooked in milk

shish taouk fillets of chicken breast chargrilled on a skewer. Extremely popular and on offer in practically every restaurant

Fish

The price of fish tends to be expensive, though from mid-October to mid-November supplies are more plentiful and prices fall correspondingly. It is most commonly either grilled or fried and served with lemon, salad and chips.

gambari prawns

hamour Red Sea fish of the grouper family

najil saddle-back grouper

samak nahri trout

sayyadiya delicately spiced fish (usually red mullet or bass) served with rice

shaour Red Sea fish of the emperor family

Sultan Ibrahim red mullet (literally 'King Abraham', ie the king of fishes)

Snacks

Traditional snack bars (and indeed many restaurants) serve a wide range of snacks. If you are on a tight budget, or are a vegetarian, many of these will become staples.

ejje omelette, usually with chopped onion and herbs

falafel the *falafel* sandwich must be the most ubiquitous snack throughout Syria; you will find snack bars serving this (and often only this) everywhere you go. Several *falafel* balls (see under *mezze* dishes) are crushed on an open piece of Arabic bread, garnished with salad and pickled vegetables (usually tomatoes, beetroot, onion and lettuce), topped by a yoghurt and *tahini* sauce and then rolled up into a 'sandwich'. They are very cheap and filling, though if you are on a tight budget and relying on them as a staple, they can get pretty monotonous. The freshness of the bread, as well as the filling, is what makes or breaks them

fatayer triangular pastry pockets filled with spinach, meat or cheese. These make great snacks and are usually sold from bakeries

fatteh an excellent, very filling snack consisting of *fuul* and *laban* mixed together with small pieces of bread and topped with pine nuts and melted butter. Also sometimes served with fried minced meat mixed in

fuul slow-cooked mash of fava beans and red lentils, dressed with lemon, olive oil and cumin, and sometimes a little yoghurt and *tahini* sauce. An excellent, filling and nutritious snack, traditionally a breakfast dish, though available any time of day

kushary staple of pasta, rice and lentils mixed with onions, chilli and tomato paste. More common in Egypt, but found also in Syria

mannoushi thin, crusty 'pizzas' topped with a thin layer of meat (*Lahmeh*), cheese (*Jebneh*) or *Zaatar*, a seasoning with thyme and *sumac*

'sandweech' both *falafels* and *shawarmas* are commonly referred to simply as 'sandweech'. In addition, there are numerous other fillings available in many snack bars

shawarma this is essentially a meat version of a *falafel* sandwich, and an equally ubiquitous snack bar favourite. Layers of lamb or chicken roasted on a vertical spit are sliced off into small flat breads and rolled up with salad, pickled vegetables and a garlic sauce into a sandwich which is then steeped in extra fat as a special favour. Again they are cheap and filling, and if you are on a tight budget and not a vegetarian you will no doubt be eating plenty of them

Dairy products
Some of these make an appearance in other dishes listed here, or else are popular as drinks in their own right.

ayran salty yoghurt drink, good refreshing rehydration material

halab milk

jebneh (*Jibni*) fairly hard and stringy white cheese

laban slightly sour yoghurt drink, also widely used in cooking as a milk substitute

labneh thick creamy cheese, often spiced and used as a dip, for example *Labneh Maa Toum*, with garlic and olive oil

Sweets
The range of sweets, pastries, biscuits and puddings on offer is enormous, but they all share one thing in common: copious amounts of sugar in one form or another. Most are served at restaurants, but to see the full range of what's on offer you should go to a patisserie, where you will be confronted by a bewildering selection. Many patisseries also have an area where you can sit and eat, and some also serve tea, coffee and soft drinks.

asabeeh rolled filo pastry filled with pistachios, pine nuts and cashews and honey

atait small pancakes stuffed with nuts or cheese and doused with syrup

baklawa layered pastry filled with nuts and steeped in honey and lemon syrup. Probably the most common and best known Arabic sweet

barazak crisp, light biscuits sprinkled with sesame seeds

basboosa semolina tart soaked in syrup

booza ice cream

borma crushed pine nuts or pistachios wrapped in shredded pastry and sliced into segments

halawat al-jebneh soft thick pastry stuffed with *labneh* cheese and steeped in syrup and ice cream

halwa a sweet made from sesame paste, usually studded with fruit and nuts and made in a slab

kamar ed-dine apricot nectar, often served as a break of fast during Ramadan

kunafi pastry stuffed with sweet white cheese, nuts and syrup

ma'amul biscuits stuffed with date, pistachio or walnut paste

muhalabiyyeh fine, smooth textured semolina and milk pudding, sometimes with pistachios, pine nuts and almonds, served cold

sanioura dry, crumbly macaroon-like biscuit

um ali literally 'Ali's mother', a pastry pudding with raisin and coconut, steeped in milk

um ali literally 'Ali's mother', a pastry pudding with raisin and coconut, steeped in milk

Drinks

ahwa (or *Kahweh*) coffee The Arab attitude to coffee is basically the stronger the better. The coffee is boiled up in tiny pots and served very strong in equally tiny cups, complete with a thick sludge of coffee grounds at the bottom. It is served without sugar (*sadah*), with medium sugar (*wassad*), or with lots of sugar (*helweh*). Cardamom is sometimes added to give a delicate aromatic flavour. Instant coffee is referred to everywhere as 'Nescafe' and is available on request in most places

arak Arabic equivalent of the Greek *oozo* or Turkish *raki*, a potent liqueur made from grapes (in fact the leftovers of wine pressing) and flavoured with aniseed. It is very popular and is usually drunk with ice and/or cold water which make the otherwise clear alcohol go a cloudy white

shay tea Generally drunk strong and black, and with copious amounts of sugar. Mint tea and green tea are also available, though not so popular.

narghile (or *shisha*) not exactly an item of 'cuisine', the narghile nevertheless goes hand in hand with eating and drinking. It consists of a large water-pipe, known also as a *shish*, through which tobacco, often flavoured with apple or strawberry, is smoked. *Narghiles* are enjoyed at great length in cafés throughout Syria alongside tea and coffee and endless games of cards and backgammon, or else after a meal

Index → *Entries in bold refer to maps.*

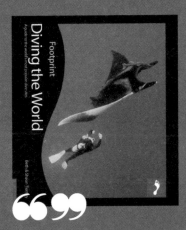

Credits

Footprint credits

Project editor: Felicity Laughton
Layout and production: Emma Bryers
Picture editors: Kassia Gawronski, Rob Lunn
Maps: Kevin Feeney
Series design: Mytton Williams
Proofreader: Jen Haddington

Managing Director: Andy Riddle
Commercial Director: Patrick Dawson
Publisher: Alan Murphy
Publishing Managers: Jo Williams,
Felicity Laughton
Digital Editor: Alice Jell
Design: Rob Lunn
Picture research: Kassia Gawronski

Marketing: Liz Harper, Hannah Bonnell
Sales: Jeremy Parr
Advertising: Renu Sibal
Finance and administration:
Elizabeth Taylor

Photography credits

Front cover: Thiele Klaus/4 corners
Back cover: RCH/Shutterstock

Printed in India by Aegean Offset Printers,
New Delhi

Footprint feedback

We try as hard as we can to make each
Footprint guide as up to date as possible
but, of course, things always change. If you
want to let us know about your experiences –
good, bad or ugly – then don't delay, go to
www.footprintbooks.com and send in
your comments.

Publishing information

Footprint Syria
1st edition
© Footprint Handbooks Ltd
February 2010

ISBN: 978 1 907263 03 3
CIP DATA: A catalogue record for this book
is available from the British Library

® Footprint Handbooks and the Footprint
mark are a registered trademark of Footprint
Handbooks Ltd

Published by Footprint
6 Riverside Court
Lower Bristol Road
Bath BA2 3DZ, UK
T +44 (0)1225 469141
F +44 (0)1225 469461
www.footprintbooks.com

Distributed in the USA by Globe Pequot Press,
Guilford, Connecticut